THE ANGLO-SAXON POETIC RECORDS

A COLLECTIVE EDITION

IV

BEOWULF AND JUDITH

BEOWULF
AND
JUDITH

EDITED BY

ELLIOTT VAN KIRK DOBBIE

PROFESSOR OF ENGLISH IN COLUMBIA UNIVERSITY

NEW YORK
COLUMBIA UNIVERSITY PRESS

PREFACE

The plan of the present volume follows as closely as possible that of the earlier volumes of this series. In a few respects, however, some modifications have been necessary. The enormous mass of the published scholarship on BEOWULF, particularly of the last fifty years, has made it impossible, within the limits of a collective edition of this kind, to pay adequate attention to all the historical and literary problems which might appropriately find a place in a separate edition of the poem. No systematic treatment is given to Germanic heroic legend in its comparative aspects, to monsters and critics, to folklore analogues from other literatures, or to problems of style and narrative technique. These matters are rarely of prime importance for the establishment of the text, and a precedent for my neglect of them here may be found in the treatment of WIDSITH and DEOR in Volume III of this series. Since, however, an editor's handling of an epic poem may depend to a large extent on his understanding of the historical background, I have included (in addition to the usual discussion of content, structure, date, and possible authorship) a statement of Scandinavian history of the late fifth and early sixth centuries as, according to my understanding, it is reflected in the poem. Furthermore, since no index of proper names is provided for in the plan of this edition, I have included a brief discussion of the Germanic peoples other than the Geats, Swedes, and Danes who are mentioned in the poem. The Finnsburh and Ingeld episodes, which require more detailed treatment than could be given them in the Notes, are also the subject of a separate section of the Introduction.

The treatment of JUDITH, on the other hand, is more exhaustive, since this poem presents comparatively few problems of general literary interest, and selection was therefore less necessary.

The Bibliography, in so far as it is concerned with BEOWULF, also reflects the limitations stated above. Part VI, which corresponds to the part labeled "Critical Discussions" in the other volumes of the series, is here called "Textual Criticism," a title which reflects its content more accurately. The very brief Part V, entitled "General Works," is not designed to include all comprehensive treatises on BEOWULF but only those which have proved of value in the preparation of this book and which would seem out of place among the briefer items in Part VI. The Bibliography is intended to include, subject to these limitations, all relevant items published through the end of June, 1952.

The Texts and Notes follow in general the pattern of the earlier volumes. In the text of BEOWULF I have included, within square brackets, conjectural restorations of matter now missing or illegible in the manuscript and not reported by the Thorkelin transcripts. I now regret the practice adopted in Volumes III and VI of this series, of not putting such conjectural restorations into the text. In the text of JUDITH, no square brackets have been necessary. The Notes are, necessarily, highly selective, but I have tried to include all suggestions for the interpretation or emendation of the text which seem to be still of value.

The edition of JUDITH by Dr. B. J. Timmer and Professor C. L. Wrenn's edition of BEOWULF appeared after the present volume was sent to press and therefore could not be used.

It is a pleasure to express my gratitude, for help and encouragement of various kinds, to Professors Frederick Klaeber and Ferdinand Holthausen, to Professors John Collins Pope and Howard Meroney, and especially to Professor Kemp Malone, who, in addition to other kindnesses, facilitated my use of photostats of the Thorkelin transcripts belonging to the library of the Johns Hopkins University at a time when no other reproductions of these transcripts were available. I also wish to express my gratitude to the John Simon Guggenheim Memorial Foundation for a fellowship which permitted me to enjoy a full year of respite from university duties during the academic year 1948–1949.

It is now twenty-four years since I first began work on *The Anglo-Saxon Poetic Records*, as research assistant to Professor George Philip Krapp, and it is high time that the project were brought to a close. No doubt this volume would be a better book if I had spent a year or two more on it, but as G. P. K. used to tell me, one must always leave something for the reviewers to say.

E. V. K. D.

CONTENTS

INTRODUCTION

I

THE MANUSCRIPT

MS. Cotton Vitellius A.xv of the British Museum, which contains the two poems edited in this volume, is composed of two originally separate manuscripts, which in all probability were not joined together until they became part of the great collection assembled by Sir Robert Cotton during the late sixteenth and early seventeenth centuries. The first of these two manuscripts is written in two hands of the twelfth century; the second, of which BEOWULF and JUDITH together form the larger part, was written, also by two scribes, at about the end of the tenth century.[1]

The combined manuscript was one of those damaged by the fire which swept the Cottonian collection in October, 1731, but fortunately the injury done to it was relatively slight,[2] consisting principally in a scorching of the upper and outer edges of the parchment. But for more than a hundred years after the fire the scorched edges of the folios were exposed to crumbling. It was not until some time after the middle of the nineteenth century— probably between 1860 and 1870, according to Förster[3]—that the separate folios were mounted in frames of heavy paper and a new binding provided for the entire volume, further loss by crumbling

---

[1] The definitive description of the manuscript is contained in Max Förster's *Die Beowulf-Handschrift* (Leipzig, 1919). The information presented below is based principally on Förster's statements, but I have also drawn freely from other printed sources, as well as from my own notes on the manuscript, made in 1931.

[2] Much less, for example, than was done to MS. Cotton Otho A.vi, containing the Alfredian version of Boethius, which is described in Volume V of this series, or to MS. Cotton Otho B.xi, which contained the Alfredian translation of Bede's Ecclesiastical History and the Anglo-Saxon Chronicle, as well as the SEASONS FOR FASTING, edited from a transcript in Volume VI of this series.

[3] *Die Beowulf-Handschrift*, p. 11.

thus being prevented. A further account of the damage done to the manuscript will be given below.

Before proceeding to a complete description of MS. Cotton Vitellius A.xv, it will be necessary to give some account of the three separate foliations which have been noted on the manuscript at various times and which have been a source of much confusion to editors.[4] The extant part of the twelfth-century manuscript comprises ninety folios; of the tenth-century manuscript which contains BEOWULF and JUDITH, 116 folios now remain. So far as we can tell, neither of these manuscripts was more complete at the time when they were added to the Cottonian collection. When they were combined into one volume, three parchment leaves were added at the beginning, thus making a total of 209 parchment folios. Two of the three added leaves still remain, but the first of them was removed in January, 1913, and inserted in the Latin psalter, Royal MS. 13.D.i*, to which it originally belonged. At the present time, therefore, the manuscript contains 208 parchment leaves.

The three foliations of the manuscript are as follows:
(1) The so-called "old foliation," written in ink at the upper right-hand corners of the parchment leaves at some time after the fire of 1731.[5] This foliation does not include the extra leaves added at the beginning and therefore runs from fol. 1 (the first leaf of the twelfth-century manuscript) to fol. 206 (the last leaf of the tenth-century manuscript). The text of BEOWULF begins on fol. 129a, that of JUDITH on fol. 199a. When the separate folios were mounted in paper frames and the entire book rebound, the "old foliation" was repeated in pencil on the upper right-hand corners of the paper frames. This is the foliation used by Zupitza in his facsimile edition of BEOWULF, as well as by nearly all later editors of that poem and by Cook in his edition of JUDITH.

---

[4] This account of the foliations is based on Hoops, *Englische Studien* LXIII, 1–11, who in several important particulars corrects the statement of Förster, *Die Beowulf-Handschrift*, pp. 4–10.

[5] The fact that these numbers are still preserved indicates that they must have been written after the greater part of the crumbling along the edges of the parchment had taken place. On most of the folios the number is written between the first and second lines of the text. A still earlier foliation, of the late sixteenth or early seventeenth century, appears on about thirty folios of the twelfth-century manuscript.

(2) A second foliation, added after the nineteenth-century rebind-ing of the manuscript and written in pencil in the lower right-hand corners of the paper frames. This foliation includes not only the parchment leaves added at the beginning (of which there were three at the time) but also two paper leaves which had been in-serted after fol. 56 and fol. 90 of the "old foliation." This second foliation, then, runs from fol. 1 to fol. 211. The first leaf of the twelfth-century manuscript is fol. 4, and the first leaf of the tenth-century manuscript is fol. 96; the text of BEOWULF begins on fol. 134a, that of JUDITH on fol. 204a. This is the foliation used by Förster in his description of the manuscript; he regarded it (but wrongly, as Hoops pointed out) as the latest of the three foliations. (3) The present official foliation, which was added in June, 1884.[6] The numbers are written in pencil in the upper right-hand corners of the paper frames, beneath the numbers belonging to the "old foliation." This official foliation includes the three parchment leaves then present at the beginning of the manuscript, but not the two paper leaves, and consequently runs from fol. 1 to fol. 209. The first leaf of the twelfth-century manuscript is fol. 4, and the first leaf of the tenth-century manuscript is fol. 94; the text of BEOWULF begins on fol. 132a, that of JUDITH on fol. 202a.

Of the three foliations described above, the latest and official one has been adopted in this volume, following the precedent of the texts edited from Cotton manuscripts in Volume V and Volume VI of this edition. Hoops has argued in favor of the "old folia-tion,"[7] principally on the grounds that it includes only the leaves of the manuscript which contain Anglo-Saxon texts and none of the extra parchment and paper leaves, and that it is the foliation used by Zupitza and by nearly all later editors. The second of these considerations is of slight merit, since the editors have used the "old foliation" merely because Zupitza used it, and Zupitza used it because the official foliation of 1884 had not yet come into existence at the time when he made his facsimile edition.[8]

---

[6] This date is indicated by a note on the paper flyleaf at the end of the manuscript.

[7] *Englische Studien* LXIII, 8–11.

[8] Wülker, who used the "old foliation" in his diplomatic and critical texts of BEOWULF, published in 1881 and 1883, adopted the new official foliation in his text of JUDITH, published in 1894. The official foliation has also been used by

To facilitate comparison with earlier editions, the "old foliation" has been noted in parentheses in the list of the contents of the manuscript, immediately below, and in Table I, at the end of this Introduction.

The contents of the manuscript are as follows:

PRELIMINARY LEAVES

fol. 2a (not in the "old foliation"). A list of the contents of the manuscript, written in the hand of Richard James, who was librarian of the Cottonian collection from about 1625 until his death in 1638. (Fol. 2b–3a are blank.)

fol. 3b (not in the "old foliation"). Some notes in English and French, in a sixteenth-century hand.

THE TWELFTH-CENTURY MANUSCRIPT

fol. 4a–59b (1a–56b). The Alfredian translation of the Soliloquies of St. Augustine.[9]

fol. 60a–86b (57a–83b). The Anglo-Saxon translation of the gospel of Nicodemus.[10]

fol. 86b–93b (83b–90b). The Anglo-Saxon prose dialogue of Solomon and Saturn.[11]

fol. 93b (90b). A short fragment of an Anglo-Saxon prose translation of the passion of St. Quintinus.[12]

THE TENTH-CENTURY MANUSCRIPT

fol. 94a–98a (91a–95a). A fragment of an Anglo-Saxon prose translation of the legend of St. Christopher.[13]

Sisam, *Modern Language Review* XI, 335–337, and by Rypins in his *Three Old English Prose Texts*. See also the remarks by Marjorie Daunt in *Year's Work in English Studies* IX (1928), 74–75.

[9] Most recently edited by W. Endter, *König Alfreds des Grossen Bearbeitung der Soliloquien des Augustinus* (Hamburg, 1922).

[10] Edited from this manuscript and from MS. Ii.ii.11 of the Cambridge University Library by W. H. Hulme, *PMLA* XIII (1898), 457–542.

[11] Edited by J. M. Kemble, *The Dialogue of Salomon and Saturnus* (London, 1848), pp. 178–197.

[12] Edited by G. Herzfeld, *Englische Studien* XIII (1889), 145; see also M. Förster, *Archiv* CVI (1901), 258–261.

[13] This and the two following texts have been most recently edited by S. I. Rypins, *Three Old English Prose Texts in MS. Cotton Vitellius A xv* (London, 1924).

fol. 98*b*–106*b* (95*b*–103*b*). *The Wonders of the East*, an Anglo-Saxon prose text also found in MS. Cotton Tiberius B.v. This text is illustrated with colored drawings.

fol. 107*a*–131*b* (104*a*–128*b*). An Anglo-Saxon prose translation of the Latin *Epistola Alexandri ad Aristotelem*.

fol. 132*a*–201*b* (129*a*–198*b*). BEOWULF.

fol. 202*a*–209*b* (199*a*–206*b*). JUDITH.

It is unnecessary to give a further account of the twelfth-century manuscript, since its connection with fol. 94*a*–209*b* is late and apparently quite fortuitous.[14] In the remainder of this Introduction the word "manuscript," when used without qualification, will refer only to the tenth-century manuscript which begins at fol. 94.

As has already been stated, the tenth-century manuscript now consists of 116 folios. The original length of this manuscript cannot be determined, since one or more texts may have preceded the legend of St. Christopher. We can, however, be certain of the loss of approximately thirty-five folios, at three places in the manuscript: (1) the beginning of the legend of St. Christopher, estimated by Förster at ten folios,[15] has been lost before fol. 94; (2) the beginning of JUDITH, estimated by Förster at three gatherings containing twenty-four folios,[16] has been lost before fol. 202; (3) the leaf which contained the last six lines of JUDITH (from *in swegles*, l. 344, to the end of the poem) has been lost after fol. 209. The missing lines at the end of JUDITH have, however, been copied in an early modern hand at the foot of fol. 209*b*. It is certain that this last leaf of JUDITH was lost prior to the fire of 1731, since the copy of its contents on fol. 209*b* has shared in the damage which resulted from that event.[17] That the losses before fol. 94 and fol.

---

[14] For the earlier history of this twelfth-century manuscript, which about the year 1300 belonged to St. Mary's abbey at Southwick in Hampshire, see Förster, *Die Beowulf-Handschrift*, pp. 53–55.

[15] *Die Beowulf-Handschrift*, pp. 76–77.

[16] *Ibid.*, p. 88. This estimate is based on the number of lines assumed to have been lost from JUDITH; see p. lxi, below.

[17] It is likely that this was a single folio attached to the last gathering of the manuscript. If we assume that it was the first folio of a complete gathering, it is difficult to conjecture when such a gathering could have been lost, since at least the ending of JUDITH must have survived into modern times, in

202 also took place before the fire is highly probable but cannot be proved.

The damage done to the edges of the parchment and the loss of the old binding have destroyed all direct evidence for the original size of the folios, as well as for the number and arrangement of the gatherings. On both points, however, estimates are possible. The area covered by the writing on the folios varies considerably from one part of the manuscript to another but is, on the average, about 18 by 11.5 centimeters, that is, about 7.1 by 4.5 inches. Assuming the usual proportion between the space covered by the writing and the total size of the folios, we may conclude that the manuscript in its original state can hardly have been smaller than 23 by 15 centimeters, or about 9 by 6 inches.

From the evidence of past and present displacements of folios in the manuscript, it is possible to conjecture the number and arrangement of the original gatherings.[18] For example, we have evidence of the earlier displacement of two single leaves in the text of BEOWULF. The present fol. 149 was numbered 131 in the "old foliation" and at that time must have stood between fol. 133 and fol. 134 (which were then numbered 130 and 132); similarly, fol. 192 was numbered 197 in the "old foliation" and must then have stood between fol. 200 and fol. 201 (then numbered 196 and 198). Since there are no losses of a folio in length from the text of BEOWULF, fol. 149 and fol. 192 must always have been single leaves with no cognate leaves attached. In the new binding both of these folios were restored to their proper places in the text, but another displacement, of an entire gathering of eight folios, was left uncorrected in the text of the letter of Alexander to Aristotle, where fol. 110–117 (107–114 in the "old foliation") should follow fol. 118–125 (115–122 in the "old foliation"). Information is also available concerning the first gathering of the manuscript. From

order to be copied at the foot of fol. 209b. The assumption that the lost leaf was the last one in a gathering of eight folios, which began at fol. 203, fails to account for the preservation of fol. 202.

[18] So far as can now be ascertained, no signatures, either letters or numbers, were ever provided in the tenth-century manuscript. But traces of signatures are preserved in the twelfth-century manuscript; see Förster, *Die Beowulf-Handschrift*, pp. 11–13.

the evidence of the "old foliation," we know that the first twelve folios of the manuscript once stood in the following order: 96, 97, 94, 95, 100, 101, 102, 103, 98, 99, 104, 105.[19] In the new binding, however, they were put in their proper relationship to each other. As Förster has shown,[20] the old arrangement of these folios is most convincingly accounted for by the assumption that fol. 94–103 constituted a gathering of ten folios which were placed in the wrong order by the early binder of the manuscript. Since the two groups of eight folios each (fol. 110–117 and fol. 118–125) which are still in incorrect order were in all probability two complete gatherings, we are left with the intermediate fol. 104–109, which must once have constituted a gathering of six folios.

With these facts and inferences at hand, it is possible to draw up a list of the probable gatherings of the manuscript, as follows:[21]

[I] a single gathering, probably of ten folios, lost before fol. 94

[II] fol. 94–103 (ten folios)

[III] fol. 104–109 (six folios)

[IV] fol. 110–117 (eight folios)

[V] fol. 118–125 (eight folios)

[VI] fol. 126–133 (eight folios)

[VII] fol. 134–141 (eight folios)

[VIII] fol. 142–150 (nine folios, including the single leaf now numbered 149)

[IX] fol. 151–160 (ten folios)

[X] fol. 161–168 (eight folios)

[XI] fol. 169–176 (eight folios)

[XII] fol. 177–184 (eight folios)

[XIII] fol. 185–193 (nine folios, including the single leaf now numbered 192)

[XIV] fol. 194–201 (eight folios)

[XV–XVII] three gatherings, probably totaling twenty-four folios, lost before fol. 202

[XVIII] fol. 202–209 (eight folios, to which was probably attached the single leaf, containing the end of JUDITH, which is missing after fol. 209)

---

[19] See the table in Rypins, *Three Old English Prose Texts*, p. xi. His second column must be translated into the present official foliation in order to give the numbers cited above.

[20] *Die Beowulf-Handschrift*, pp. 7–8.

[21] This list of the gatherings differs in some respects from that given by Förster, *Die Beowulf-Handschrift*, pp. 22–23; the principal point of difference is that it assumes that fol. 94–103 constituted a gathering of ten folios and fol. 104–109 a gathering of six folios, while Förster assumes two gatherings (fol. 94–101 and fol. 102–109) of eight folios each. In this respect Förster's list of the gatherings is inconsistent with his explanation of the old and inaccurate arrangement of fol. 94–103.

The number of lines for which the pages of the manuscript were ruled varies from nineteen to twenty-two. Only one of the pages, fol. 111*b*, appears to have been prepared for nineteen lines; in three other cases where less than twenty lines appear on a page (fol. 98*a*, 106*b*, 131*b*), the page has been left short at the end of a text. In the part of BEOWULF written by the first scribe each section number normally occupies a line of its own, and in such cases the number of lines actually written on the page is of course less by one than the number of lines for which the page was ruled. Similarly, at the beginning of BEOWULF (fol. 132*a*) the line of large capitals takes up the space which would ordinarily be devoted to two lines of text, and consequently there are only nineteen lines on this page instead of the twenty for which the page was ruled. The grouping of the pages according to the number of lines (including section numbers) written on them is as follows:[22]

fol. 94*a*–97*b*	20 lines	fol. 132*b*–165*b*	20 lines
fol. 98*a*	17 lines (incomplete)	fol. 166*a*–173*b*	22 lines
fol. 98*b*–106*a*	20 lines	fol. 174*a*–177*a*	20 lines
fol. 106*b*	19 lines (incomplete)	fol. 177*b*–179*a*	21 lines
fol. 107*a*–111*a*	20 lines	fol. 179*b*–181*b*	20 lines
fol. 111*b*	19 lines	fol. 182*a*–201*a*	21 lines
fol. 112*a*–125*a*	20 lines	fol. 201*b*	22 lines[24]
fol. 125*b*	21 lines	fol. 202*a*–208*b*	20 lines
fol. 126*a*–131*a*	20 lines	fol. 209*a*	21 lines[25]
fol. 131*b*	7 lines (incomplete)	fol. 209*b*	20 lines
fol. 132*a*	19 lines[23]		

The manuscript was written by two hands. The first of these extends from the beginning (fol. 94*a*) as far as the word *scyran*,

[22] It will be noted that on four folios (fol. 111, 125, 177, 179) a different number of lines was planned for each of the two sides. This is unusual (since the ruling was ordinarily done by scoring with a knife, producing a mark which would serve for both sides of the folio) but is paralleled by fol. 11 and fol. 111 of the Vercelli Book.

[23] Originally ruled for twenty lines, but two lines are occupied by the single line of capitals at the beginning of BEOWULF.

[24] Originally ruled for twenty-one lines, but -*geornost*, at the end of BEOWULF, is written at the beginning of an extra line.

[25] Originally ruled for twenty lines, but *wæron*, JUD. 322, is written at the beginning of an extra line.

BEOW. 1939, in the third line of fol. 175b; the second extends from *moste*, BEOW. 1939, to the end of JUDITH.[26] The first scribe, then, wrote approximately 70 percent of the extant manuscript. Although the two hands are necessarily of the same or approximately the same date, they differ markedly in appearance. The hand of the first scribe is small (though not unusually small for an Anglo-Saxon scribal hand), irregular in spacing and in the shape of the letters, and without heavy shading; the hand of the second scribe is much larger and more regular, with heavy shading of the vertical strokes, and, as Keller remarks,[27] seems to belong to an older school of insular writing than its companion hand. The two hands are ascribed by Keller[28] to "the last decades of the tenth century," but a date shortly after the beginning of the eleventh century is not impossible; Förster's dating of the hands at about the year 1000 (with a margin of error of one or two decades before or after that year)[29] seems most consistent with the evidence. The date of writing of BEOWULF and JUDITH is, then, about the same as the date of the Junius Manuscript and somewhat later than that of the Vercelli Book and the Exeter Book.

The most striking difference between the work of the two scribes is the great number of *io*-spellings (corresponding to normal West Saxon *ĕo, ēo, eō* of whatever origin) in the part of BEOWULF written by the second scribe. From *moste*, l. 1939, to the end of BEOWULF there are no less than 115 *io*-spellings, as compared with only eleven in the earlier part of the poem. The ratio of *io*-spellings to *eo*-spellings in the work of the second scribe is approximately

---

[26] Although Eduard Sievers noticed in 1871 that the hand of the three prose texts is the same as the first hand of BEOWULF (see Förster, *Die Beowulf-Handschrift*, p. 35, note 1), he did not publish this observation, and it was not until 1916 that the identity of the hands was pointed out in print, by Sisam, *Modern Language Review* XI, 335ff. Sedgefield, in his edition of BEOWULF (1st ed., 1910, p. 2, note; 2d ed., 1913, p. xiv, note), had identified the first hand of BEOWULF with the hand of the text immediately preceding, the letter of Alexander to Aristotle, but had said nothing about the other two prose texts. That the second scribe of BEOWULF also wrote JUDITH was apparently first pointed out in 1872 by Sievers, *Zeitschrift für deutsches Altertum* XV, 457.

[27] *Angelsächsische Palaeographie* (Berlin, 1906), p. 36.

[28] *Ibid.*, p. 37.

[29] *Die Beowulf-Handschrift*, p. 43. The whole of Förster's discussion of the dating, pp. 36–46, will amply repay study.

4 to 17; in the work of the first scribe the ratio is approximately 1 to 73.[30] The significance of these figures was first pointed out by Bernhard ten Brink in 1888.[31] Since there are no *io*-spellings at all in the text of JUDITH, also written by the second scribe, we cannot attribute to this scribe the *io*-spellings in BEOWULF. We must therefore assume that the *io*-spellings were due to an earlier scribe of BEOWULF and were a characteristic of the copy from which the two scribes of the present manuscript worked. These spellings were, in all but eleven cases, altered by the first scribe to the *eo*-spellings which were normal for him, but were retained in much greater number by the second scribe, who must therefore be considered the more careful copyist of the two.[32] The presence of the *io*-spellings in the earlier manuscript of BEOWULF is usually ascribed, following ten Brink, to a Kentish phase in the transmission of the text.

Throughout the manuscript the spacing between words and between the parts of compound words is irregular, not to say capricious. Not only are parts of single words often written separately (a practice which is not infrequent in other manuscripts of the period), but separate words are frequently joined together, with no spacing between them. In the part of BEOWULF written by the first scribe we find, for example, such spacings as *ingear dagum*, BEOW. 1, *nege leafnes word*, BEOW. 245, *þawit onsund reon*,

[30] My own count of the *io*-spellings agrees with the figures given by Rypins, *PMLA* XXXVI, 174, and by Klaeber, *Beowulf* (3d ed.), p. xc, note 4. But my count of the *eo*-spellings is slightly different from that given by Rypins; I found 807 *eo*-spellings in the work of the first scribe and 492 in the work of the second scribe.

[31] *Beowulf*, pp. 238–239.

[32] Rypins, *PMLA* XXXVI, 167–185 (reprinted with slight changes in *Three Old English Prose Texts*, pp. xiv–xxix), has taken violent exception to ten Brink's conclusions; he holds that the first scribe was more accurate than the second. But Rypins defines an "accurate" scribe not in the usual way, as one who preserves to a high degree the orthography of his original, but as one who is consistent in his spelling (on p. 180 he suggests that "scribal accuracy is manifested by a consistent use of one spelling"), and this confusion of terminology renders his conclusions invalid. The sum of Rypins's arguments, that the first scribe was a more consistent normalizer than the second, really bears out ten Brink's views. For criticisms of Rypins, see W. Keller, *Beiblatt zur Anglia* XXXIV (1923), 3, note 1, and J. Hoops, *Englische Studien* LXI (1927), 438–439.

BEOW. 539, *lade nelet ton*, BEOW. 569, *þhim selic homa*, BEOW. 812, and *begongge sacan ne tealde*, BEOW. 1773. In the hand of the second scribe such irregular spacings, though somewhat less common, are by no means rare; for example, *ingum stole*, BEOW. 1952, *syððan hemod sefan*, BEOW. 2012, *Swagio mor mod*, BEOW. 2267, *mere wio ingasmilts*, BEOW. 2921, *huse stið moda*, JUD. 25, *tohisbed reste*, JUD. 36, and *welge wealdan*, JUD. 103. The spacing of the manuscript is therefore of little value as a guide to the proper word division in such ambiguous sequences as *mægen hreð manna*, BEOW. 445, *on sæl meoto*, BEOW. 489, *medo stig ge mæt*, BEOW. 924, and *wigge weorþad*, BEOW. 1783.

For the place of origin of the manuscript and its early history there is no evidence whatever. The words "Laurence Nouell a.1563," written in a sixteenth-century hand at the head of fol. 94*a*, indicate that before it came to the Cotton collection the manuscript was in the library of Lawrence Nowell, the dean of Lichfield and well-known antiquary, but of its earlier owners nothing is known.

The extent of the damage done by the fire of 1731 varies considerably from page to page. In general, however, it may be said that fol. 94–131, which contain the three prose texts, and fol. 202–209, which contain JUDITH, are much better preserved than any part of the text of BEOWULF. In BEOWULF itself, the first thousand lines are in relatively better condition than the remainder; the worst damage of all has been done to fol. 170–184, which contain the text of ll. 1685–2339, and to fol. 201, the last folio of the poem. Three pages, fol. 182*a*, fol. 182*b*, and fol. 201*b*, are in particularly bad shape and show more damage than can reasonably be explained as a result of the fire. On these pages not only have the usual losses resulted from the crumbling of the edges of the parchment, but many words, even far from the edges of the leaf, have faded or otherwise become illegible. The damage to fol. 201 may perhaps be accounted for by the assumption that at some time prior to the seventeenth century BEOWULF and JUDITH became separated from each other (at which time, also, the beginning of JUDITH may have been lost), and that during this period fol. 201 was on the outside of the manuscript with no binding to protect it; this would also account for the difference between the very bad condition of fol. 201*b* and the relatively good state of fol. 202*a*. No such explanation, however, can be found for the damage to fol. 182, which in all probability was not even the outside leaf of a gathering.

Although some of the matter which has been lost from the manuscript can now be restored only by conjecture, we are fortunate in the possession of three modern transcripts which together supply a large proportion of the missing parts of the text and which will be described in the next section of this Introduction. For fol. 182, also, we have the results of an inspection of the manuscript under ultraviolet light, made by Dr. Robin Flower and utilized by Sedgefield in the text of his third edition of BEOWULF, while for fol. 201*b* we have photographs made under ultraviolet light and published, together with a diplomatic text of that page, by A. H. Smith.[33] All of these supplementary sources for the text have been put to account in the present edition; the textual details involved will be discussed in the Notes.

II

THE TRANSCRIPTS

The lost or damaged passages in the text of BEOWULF can be supplied in part from the two transcripts used by the first editor of the poem, the Icelander Grímur Jónsson Thorkelin. These transcripts, now preserved in the Great Royal Library at Copenhagen and recently reproduced in facsimile, were made during Thorkelin's visit to England in 1786–1787, one of them (known as "A") being the work of an unidentified copyist, the other (known as "B") the work of Thorkelin himself.

Transcript A, ninety pages in length, is written in a small and neat hand closely imitative of Anglo-Saxon script. That the copyist was unfamiliar with the language is evident from the mechanical way in which he worked; he seems to have copied the text letter by letter as best he could, reproducing the difficult ligatures (such as *cg* and *ec*) as exactly as possible, with no attempt to analyze them into separate letters. He left abbreviations unex-

---

[33] *London Mediæval Studies*, I, Part 2 (1938), 202–205.

panded and in general preserved the word division of the manuscript. He reproduced the capital letters of the manuscript, both
large and small, and, with some exceptions, the acute accent
marks. The errors which he made are those to be expected in a
mechanical copy, most of them involving the omission of one or
more letters or the confusion of letters of similar shape. Such
errors, common at the beginning of the transcript, become relatively less frequent in the later pages, written after he had become
more familiar with his task. Where he found the manuscript illegible, he left a space in his copy, sometimes a much larger space
than the extent of the lost matter would justify. In the course of
a later collation with the manuscript, he filled in many of these
gaps and corrected a number of his more obvious errors. Transcript
A also contains a few corrections and additions in Thorkelin's
hand, probably made at a later date.

Transcript B, Thorkelin's own work, is quite different from A.
It is arranged in accordance with the pages and lines of the Cotton
manuscript and is therefore 140 pages long, or as long as the Cotton
text. It is written in Thorkelin's own cursive hand, with no attempt to reproduce the forms of the Anglo-Saxon letters. Thorkelin did not observe the capitalization of the Cotton manuscript
but introduced capital letters at the beginnings of proper names,
where he recognized them as such. He expanded the abbreviations, not always correctly, and ignored the accent marks of the
manuscript. That Thorkelin's knowledge of Anglo-Saxon was insufficient for the task he set for himself, we know from his edition;
but he knew enough to avoid most of the mechanical mistakes of
the copyist of A, and his transcript, therefore, while displaying
its share of errors, makes a more favorable impression than A
upon the modern student. Like the copyist of A, Thorkelin made
a careful collation of his transcript with the original, adding words
and letters which he had omitted as indecipherable and making
many alterations, most of them for the better. Here and there
in B we find corrections in a similar but rather shaky hand, identified by Kemp Malone[1] as the hand of Thorkelin's later years,
when he was working on his edition.

[1] *PMLA* LXIV (1949), 1190.

The Thorkelin transcripts have been so thoroughly studied and described by Kemp Malone[2] that it is unnecessary to give a more complete account of them here. It may, however, be pointed out that in spite of the generally more accurate work done by Thorkelin himself, transcript A is of greater value than B, representing as it does a completely objective report of what the copyist saw in the manuscript. In dealing with B, one cannot dismiss the possibility that Thorkelin sometimes anticipated his later editorial work by introducing emendations or normalizations into his copy.[3] It is of interest to note that Thorkelin himself seems to have had considerable confidence in A, since in his edition he frequently used it as the basis of the text in preference to his own transcript.[4] In the description given below of the small capitals and accent marks in the manuscript, transcript A is used as a supplementary authority.[5]

A similar aid to the establishment of the text of JUDITH is to be found in MS. Junius 105 of the Bodleian Library, a transcript made by Franciscus Junius and used by Edward Thwaites as the basis of his edition of the poem, published in 1698.[6] Dating from at least eighty years before the fire of 1731,[7] Junius's transcript

[2] Especially in *Studia Neophilologica* XIV (1941–1942), 25–30; *PMLA* LXIV (1949), 1190–1218; and in the Introduction to the new facsimile edition of the transcripts.

[3] For example, B's reading ðæt a (with the letters -æt underlined) for the MS. ða, l. 980, and his reading *wealh* for the MS. *fealh*, l. 1200, are possibly intentional emendations of the text; see Malone, *Studia Neophilologica* XIV, 27.

[4] Examples of this preference, from the earlier lines of the poem, are: l. 11, *Goban* ed., goban A, gomban B; l. 19, *Scede landum* ed., scede landum A, sceðe landum B; l. 115, *Geweat* ed., Geweat A, Gewat B; l. 138, *eapfynþe* ed., eaðfynðe A, eað fynde B; l. 157, *ne þær witena* ed., ne þær witena A, ne þær nænig witena B.

[5] See the comments at the head of Tables III and IV, at the end of this Introduction.

[6] This paper manuscript is only twelve pages long and contains no other texts. The heading on the first page is: "Fragmentum historiæ Judith, descriptum ex Cottonianæ bibliothecæ MSto codice, qui inscribitur VITELLIVS. A.15. paginâ 199."

[7] Junius's first stay in England lasted from 1621 to 1651. He returned to England in 1674, at the age of eighty-five, to remain there until his death in 1677. The handwriting of MS. Junius 105, which is indistinguishable from that of the Boethius transcript in MS. Junius 12 (see *Records V, The Paris Psalter and the Meters of Boethius*, pp. xli–xliv), seems too vigorous and well

shows the text of the poem in its undamaged state (except for the loss of folios at the beginning), and in spite of occasional errors it impresses us as a careful and on the whole dependable copy.

Like Junius's other transcripts of Anglo-Saxon texts, MS. Junius 105 is written in a small hand imitative of Anglo-Saxon script. Junius supplied capital letters at the beginnings of the major divisions of the text and often at the beginnings of sentences, as well as in most proper names; he also added a rather inconsistent punctuation, not in the modern manner but roughly imitative of the pointing in the Cædmonian poems of MS. Junius 11. He frequently wrote ð for a þ in the manuscript, more frequently þ for an ð. He retained the abbreviations 7 and þ̄ but regularly expanded all the others.[8] He occasionally replaced the spelling of the manuscript by an equivalent form, as in ðær (MS. ðar), l. 2; ðæm (MS. ðam), l. 7; wille (MS. wylle), l. 84; drihten (MS. dryhten), l. 92; siððan (MS. syððan), l. 168; Assirium (MS. assyrium), l. 218; is (MS. ys), ll. 285, 286; þrymfull (MS. -ful), l. 74; weallgate (MS. weal-), l. 141; snellra (MS. snelra), l. 199; Juditðe (MS. iudithðe), l. 40; hand (MS. hond), l. 130; burhleoda (MS. burg-), l. 187, and Ebreisce (MS. ebrisce), ll. 241, 305. He adopted the uncorrected readings baldor, l. 32, gebrohten, l. 54, and forlæten, l. 150, although the corrected readings aldor, gebrohton, and forlæton are presumably to be taken as reflecting the final intent of the scribe. Four of his alterations of the manuscript reading seem to have been intentional emendations, ðeodnes for the MS. þeoðnes, l. 165, starian for the MS. stariað, l. 179 (both of which are adopted by modern editors), weras 7 wif for the MS. weras wif, l. 163, and the omission of þ̄ in l. 182 (where he also, by error, wrote syðor for the MS. swyðor). Alterations of the manuscript reading which were presumably unintentional are winessa (MS. wine swa), l. 67; weard (MS. wearð), l. 155; hluin mon (MS. hlummon), l. 205; elðeodriga (MS. elðeodigra), l. 215; bringan (MS. þringan), l. 249; fyrd (MS. fynd), l. 319; wundenloce (MS.

---

formed to be the work of a man of eighty-five, and it may therefore be inferred that the transcript was made before 1651.

[8] The only exceptions to this statement are þ̄, l. 151, which is written þæt, and -weriḡ, l. 229, sceaðū, l. 230, and fagū, l. 301, in which the abbreviations are retained.

wundenlocc), l. 325, and *sylfne* (MS. *sylfre*), l. 335. In l. 297 he copied only *lind*, though there was certainly at least one letter after *d* in the manuscript.

In a text of nearly 350 lines, the errors just enumerated do not bulk very large, and the Junius transcript may therefore be regarded as a dependable source for the missing letters in the text of JUDITH—a more dependable authority, in view of its early date and its generally greater accuracy, than either of the Thorkelin transcripts of BEOWULF.

III

SECTIONAL DIVISIONS IN THE POEMS

Like other long Anglo-Saxon poems, BEOWULF and JUDITH are divided into sections. There are 43 of these sections in BEOWULF, ranging in length from 43 to 142 lines, and averaging 74 lines. All of them are indicated, as in other poetical manuscripts, by a large, usually unornamented, capital at the beginning, which in some cases is followed by one or more small capitals. Most, but not all, of the sections are numbered. The first section, ll. 1–52, which was perhaps regarded as an introduction to the poem proper, is unnumbered but begins with a full line of small capitals in addition to the large initial *H*. The second section, ll. 53–114, bears the number I, and from that point the numbering is regular and consistent up to l. 1816, the end of section XXV.[1] The three following sections, ll. 1817–1887, 1888–1962, and 1963–2038, were originally numbered XXVII, XXVIII, and XXVIIII, but in each case the final *I* was later erased, making the numbers XXVI, XXVII, and XXVIII and bringing these sections into conformity with the preceding ones. The next section, ll. 2039–2143, which we would expect to be XXVIIII, is unnumbered; the next, ll. 2144–2220, is numbered XXXI. From this point to the end of BEOWULF the numbering of the sections is regular and consistent, except that at the beginning of section [XXXVIIII] the roman numerals have been omitted and that section XL was originally numbered XLI, the *I* having later been erased.

---

[1] According to Zupitza, the section number *XXIIII*, before l. 1651, may have been altered from *XXV*; this is, however, not certain, although the two *I*'s are undoubtedly blurred.

As we have seen, the most serious discrepancy in the section numbering is at ll. 2039–2143, where only one section is indicated by the capitalization but where there is a gap of two in the numbering. It is probable that this confusion goes back to the beginning of section XXVI, at l. 1817, where the scribe at first wrote *XXVII* but later corrected his error. There is no likelihood whatever that a section is missing from the text at this point. But it may reasonably be conjectured that the scribe of an earlier manuscript of Beowulf made a mistake in the numbering of section XXVI and continued to write incorrect numbers (greater by one than the correct number, in each case) to the end of the poem. The first scribe of the present manuscript then copied the incorrect numbers *XXVII* and *XXVIII* (for sections XXVI and XXVII, at l. 1817 and l. 1888 respectively), but later, observing that these numbers were wrong, corrected them. The second scribe, who began his work at l. 1939, at first copied the incorrect number *XXVIIII* at l. 1963 but then, noticing the discrepancy, altered it to *XXVIII*; he then omitted the number before l. 2039, intending to investigate further the problem of the section numbering,[2] but later, forgetting his good intentions, copied without alteration the incorrect numbers from *XXXI* (before l. 2144) to the end of the poem. This is, of course, no more than a hypothesis, but it gives a plausible explanation of the discrepancy in the numbering.[3]

For the most part, the sections in Beowulf begin where we would expect them to begin, that is, at a definite break in the narrative, where we are disposed to indicate a new paragraph. Twice, however, at l. 1740 and l. 2039, a new section begins in the middle of a sentence; it may or may not be significant that in both these places the first word of the new section is *Oðþæt (Oððæt)*.[4] At four other places in the poem, at ll. 559, 2144, 2460, and 2946,

[2] He forgot, however, to leave a space for the number to be supplied.

[3] Klaeber, *Beowulf* (3d ed.), p. c, note 7, suggests a somewhat simpler explanation, that the present unnumbered section (ll. 2039–2143) was originally divided into two sections, XXVIII and XXX, section XXX beginning at l. 2093. The discrepancy in the present manuscript would then be due to the omission by the second scribe of two section numbers and his failure to provide the proper capitalization at l. 2093.

[4] See the note on l. 1740. At Genesis 1248, in the Junius Manuscript, a new section begins with the word *Oðþæt*.

a new section begins in the middle of a speech but at a point of natural pause in the discourse.

The extant part of JUDITH comprises three full sections and the end of a fourth. Lines 1–14 of this poem are the closing lines of a section, the beginning of which, together with the earlier sections, is no longer preserved. The three sections which remain in their entirety are numbered X (ll. 15–121), XI (ll. 122–235), and XII (ll. 236–349). Each of them begins with a large unornamented capital, with no small capitals following. If we may judge b the three which remain, the sections in JUDITH were longer than those in BEOWULF, averaging about a hundred and ten lines in length.

A record of the sectional divisions in the two poems is given in Table II, at the end of this introduction.

IV

SMALL CAPITALS IN THE POEMS

In the more than thirty-five hundred lines of BEOWULF and JUDITH there are only sixty-eight small capitals.[1] This is a remarkably low number, reflecting a frequency of small capitals only about one-third as great as in the Junius Manuscript and very much less than in either the Exeter Book or the poetical portions of the Vercelli Book. Of the two scribes of the manuscript, the first was more inclined to use small capitals than his successor, fifty-three of the sixty-eight small capitals being in the part of BEOWULF written by him, as against only twelve in the rest of BEOWULF and three in JUDITH. In the prose texts written by the first scribe, the frequency of small capitals is considerably greater than in the part of BEOWULF which he wrote.

In BEOWULF, all but eight of the small capitals occur at the beginning of a new sentence or of an important syntactical division of a sentence. The eight exceptions are in *Swylce*, l. 830, *Hæþene*, l. 852, *Syþðan*, l. 886, *Swa*, l. 1048, *Syþðan*, l. 1077 (which is,

---

[1] This figure includes three which are doubtful but were probably intended to be small capitals, as well as five which are now missing from the manuscript but which are listed on the authority of Thorkelin A. See the note at the head of Table III, at the end of this Introduction.

however, doubtful), *Seleð*, l. 1730, *Ic*, l. 1829, and *Siðode*, l. 2119, all of which are preceded by a comma in the modern punctuation of the text.[2] In JUDITH, two of the three small capitals are at the beginning of a new sentence, the capital in *Swa*, l. 143, being the exception. The frequent capitalization of initial *i* which is so striking a feature of the Exeter Book and the Vercelli Book is not a characteristic of the present manuscript. Here the only word with initial *i* which is capitalized is *ic*, and it appears with a capital only seven times (three times in the hand of the first scribe and four times in the hand of the second scribe) out of a total of nearly two hundred occurrences. The names *Wealhðeo*, l. 1215, *Hroðgar*, l. 1840, and *Biowulf*, l. 1999, have initial small capitals, but undoubtedly because they begin new sentences rather than because they are proper names. It is of particular interest that the name *Iudith* and its inflectional forms are never capitalized; in the Exeter Book, on the other hand, *Iuliana* and its inflectional forms are invariably capitalized, presumably because of the initial *i*.

Because of the infrequency of the small capitals in BEOWULF and JUDITH, it is impossible to trace any clear structural intention in their use. But as a part of the record of the manuscript, the small capitals in these texts are listed in Table III, at the end of this Introduction.

V

ABBREVIATIONS IN THE POEMS

Except on the last page of BEOWULF, where the scribe was apparently pressed for space, the abbreviations used by the two scribes of this manuscript are of the types regularly found in other Anglo-Saxon poetical texts.

The tilde or macron is used by both scribes, but much more frequently by the second scribe. As in other manuscripts, it occurs most often in the dative ending *-um*, written *-ū*. In other positions the tilde is avoided by the first scribe, but it is frequent

---

[2] Some editors and commentators put a comma before *Swa*, l. 1142, taking this word as a subordinating conjunction rather than as an adverb; see the note on ll. 1142–1145. It is apparent from the eight words cited above that the small capital at the beginning of *Swa* is of little significance for textual criticism.

in the remainder of the manuscript. Examples are *hī* for *him*, used by the first scribe only twice (BEOW. 67, 671) but by the second scribe sixty-two times in BEOWULF and eighteen times in JUDITH; *þā*, *ðā* for *þam*, *ðam*, used by the first scribe only three times (BEOW. 425, 1073, 1421)[1] but by the second scribe thirty-three times in BEOWULF and seventeen times in JUDITH; *sū*, *sūne* for *sum*, *sumne*, used eight times by the second scribe (six times in BEOWULF and twice in JUDITH) but not at all by the first scribe. Other examples of the use of the tilde for *m* are *hā* for *ham*, BEOW. 374, 717, 2992; *frā* for *fram*, BEOW. 581, 2366, 2565, and *frō* for *from*, BEOW. 2556; *frōlice* for *fromlice*, JUD. 220, 301; *rū* for *rum*, BEOW. 2461, 2690, *gū* for *gum-*, BEOW. 1486, 1723, 2469, 2543, 2765; *grī* for *grim*, BEOW. 2860, and *grīme* for *grimme*, BEOW. 3012, 3085; *sȳle* for *symle*, BEOW. 2497 (reported by Thorkelin A), JUD. 15; *frȳða* for *frymða*, JUD. 5, 83, 189; *bear̃* for *bearm*, BEOW. 896. If A. H. Smith is right in reporting *hȳðo* in BEOW. 3155, this is one of the very few instances in Anglo-Saxon poetical manuscripts of a tilde used to indicate the omission of *n*.

The word *þonne*, *ðonne*, as adverb and as conjunction, is spelled out twenty-three times by the first scribe and abbreviated as *þōn*, *ðōn* twenty-three times. By the second scribe it is abbreviated twenty-one times and spelled out only five times. The word occurs only once in JUDITH, at l. 329, where it is abbreviated.

The abbreviation 7 for *and*, *ond* is regular throughout the manuscript, the word being spelled out only three times in BEOWULF (ll. 600, 1148, 2040), each time as *ond*, and not at all in JUDITH. As a prefix, *and-*, *ond-* is spelled out in BEOWULF about as often as it is abbreviated; it is spelled *and-* six times (ll. 340, 689, 1059, 1287, 1796, 2695) and *ond-* only once (l. 2938). To these examples must be added the four occurrences in BEOWULF of initial *h-* added to the prefix, *handlean*, l. 1541, *hondlean*, l. 2094, and *hondslyht*, ll. 2929, 2972.[2] The prefix *and-*, *ond-* does not occur in JUDITH. In the present edition the abbreviation, standing either for the conjunction or for the prefix, is everywhere resolved as *ond*.

---

[1] He also wrote *þǣ*, for *þæm*, in BEOW. 1191.

[2] Since these spellings are found in the work of both scribes, they probably go back to an earlier copy.

The word *þæt*, as pronoun or conjunction, is regularly written as *þ̄*, being spelled out only twenty-six times in Beowulf (twenty times by the first scribe) and not at all in Judith. The equivalent form of the conjunction, *þætte*, is abbreviated as *þ̄ te* three times in Beowulf (ll. 1256, 1942, 2924) and spelled out twice (ll. 151, 858); it does not occur in Judith. The conjunction *oþþæt, oðþæt* is everywhere abbreviated as *oþþ̄, oðþ̄* (once, in Beow. 66, as *oðð þ̄*).[3]

The only other abbreviation used by the first scribe (except for roman numerals) is the rune ☒, which is written for *eðel* in Beow. 520, 913, 1702. The second scribe, however, used a number of abbreviations besides those mentioned above: *æf̄t* for *æfter*, Beow. 2060, 2176, 2531, 2753, Jud. 18, 65; *dryh̄t* for (-)*dryhten*, Beow. 2722 (reported by Thorkelin A), Jud. 21, 274, 299; *ḡ* for *ge*, both finally and as a prefix, ten times in Beowulf and twenty-two times in Judith. On the last page of Beowulf (fol. 201*b*), where he apparently wished to avoid running over to another page, the second scribe also wrote *of̄* for *ofer* (ll. 3132, 3145), *m̄* for *men* (ll. 3162, 3165), *ḡnum̄* for *genumen* (l. 3165), and *dryh* for -*dryhten* (l. 3175). In Judith the name Holofernus is twice abbreviated as *holofern'* (ll. 7, 46).

In the prose texts written by the first scribe, abbreviations are used more sparingly than in the part of Beowulf which he wrote. In these texts 7 and *þ̄* are used regularly; the tilde is frequently used to indicate the omission of *m*, but the abbreviation *þ̄on*, for *þonne*, occurs only once (fol. 130*a*, l. 7). Except for these, the only abbreviations, except roman numerals, in the prose texts are *m̄* (for *men*, fol. 103*a*, l. 10) and *leō* (for *leon* or *leones*,[4] apparently a measure of distance, fol. 103*b*, l. 8); both of these less usual abbreviations are in the *Wonders of the East*.

---

[3] The spellings *ðæt* and *oþðæt, oððæt* are, as in other manuscripts, never abbreviated.

[4] The form *leones* occurs at fol. 98*b*, l. 6, and fol. 104*b*, l. 7, the form *leon* at fol. 98*b*, l. 20.

VI

PUNCTUATION AND ACCENT MARKS

Except at the ends of certain of the sectional divisions, the only mark of punctuation which we find in the two poems of the manuscript is the point.[1] The frequency of points is unusually low in both texts, and particularly so in JUDITH; the total number is somewhat less than seven hundred, of which JUDITH contains only seventeen.[2] The average frequency of points in BEOWULF is about the same in the part written by the first scribe as in that written by the second, approximately one point to every five verse lines. The corresponding figure for JUDITH is one point to every twenty verse lines. These figures are, however, of little significance, since the frequency of the points varies greatly from one part of the manuscript to another. The points are most frequent in the early part of the work of the second scribe, from l. 1963 to about l. 2500 of BEOWULF, while they are least frequent at the end of the work of the second scribe, in the closing passages of BEOWULF and in JUDITH.

As in other Anglo-Saxon manuscripts, the purpose of these points is by no means clear, since it is difficult to find any structural significance in them. Less than half the points coincide with important syntactical breaks in the text, where a modern editor would put a period or a semicolon, and at many places where we would expect punctuation (as at the ends of ll. 31b, 36a, 46b, 58b, and 63b of BEOWULF, to cite only a few examples), points are lacking. The beginning of a speech is one place where, if anywhere, we might expect punctuation in the manuscript, but of the forty-five speeches in BEOWULF and four in JUDITH, only sixteen are introduced by points. Nearly nine-tenths of the points occur at

---

[1] At two places in the text of BEOWULF, after *hafelan*, l. 1372, and *gemunde*, l. 2488, we find what appear to be colons, and they are so interpreted in Zupitza's transcription. But the use of a colon (a mark which is rare enough in Anglo-Saxon manuscripts) is so inconsistent with scribal practice elsewhere in the manuscript that it seems more probable that in each case the upper point is accidental.

[2] It is impossible to be certain of the number of points in BEOWULF, because of the generally poor condition of this part of the manuscript.

the end of a verse line, and most of the others at the end of the first half of a verse line. In the two poems together, only thirteen points occur elsewhere than at the end of a half-line. But in view of the infrequency of the points throughout the manuscript, it seems impossible that they could have had any metrical significance.

The punctuation at the ends of sections is less elaborate than in either the Vercelli Book or the Exeter Book. In the part of BEOWULF written by the first scribe (which ends in the middle of section XXVII), the usual punctuation at the end of a section is a single point. At the ends of sections VIII and VIIII, where in each case the last word of the section is carried over to the end of the following line, there are no points. After *twæm*, l. 1191, at the end of section XVII, and after *astod*, l. 1556, at the end of section XXII, the points are no longer preserved in the manuscript but are reported by Thorkelin A. In the remainder of the manuscript, written by the second scribe, the point is still the most frequent punctuation at the ends of sections, but in seven places the more elaborate punctuation :〜 occurs, at the ends of sections XXVII, XXXII, XXXV, XXXVII, XLI, and XLII of BEOWULF and section XI of JUDITH.

ACCENT MARKS IN THE MANUSCRIPT

The determination of the accent marks in the text of BEOWULF is not an easy task, not only because of the poor condition of this part of the manuscript but also because of the varying form and heaviness of the accents. In the part of the manuscript written by the first scribe, the accents are usually curved and broader at the upper end; in a few cases, however, they are straight. In the part written by the second scribe, the accents are formed by a straight and very thin slanting line, with or without a tag at the top. Sometimes only the tag or broader upper end of the accent is easily visible, sometimes only the curved or slanting line. It is therefore not always possible to tell whether a mark above a vowel in the manuscript is a genuine accent mark or an accidental stroke of the pen. Fortunately, in addition to the record of the manuscript text of BEOWULF provided by Zupitza's facsimile and transcription, we have at our disposal Thorkelin's transcript A, as well as the lists of accents prepared by Chambers and Sedgefield on the basis of their own careful examinations of the manuscript and appended to their editions.[3] A comparative study of these authorities gives us the 153 accent marks in the text of BEOWULF, varying considerably in degree of probability, which are listed in Table IV at the end of this Introduction. In the case of JUDITH, the problem is less difficult, since the manuscript is in much better condition from fol. 202 to the end than in most parts of BEOWULF, and there are consequently no doubtful accents in this poem. The thirty accents which are clearly visible in JUDITH, together with the 153 certain or possible accents in BEOWULF, give us a total of 183 accents in the poetical parts of the manuscript, or, in terms of percentage, .052 accents per verse line. This is a somewhat lower frequency than in the Exeter Book, where we have .072 accents per line, and much lower than in either the Vercelli Book, which has .161 accents per line, or the Junius Manuscript, where the corresponding figure is no less than .622 accents per line. In the text of BEOWULF, 79 of the 153 accents are in the part of the poem written by the first scribe, an average of .041 accents per line, and 74 in the part written by the second scribe, an average of .06 accents per line. In JUDITH, the corresponding figure is .086 accents per line. The second scribe, then, used accents somewhat more freely than his predecessor, but the figures do not differ so widely as to be of significance.

All of the 183 certain or possible accent marks in BEOWULF and JUDITH stand on long vowels or diphthongs. Ninety-four of these, or approximately one-half, occur in monosyllabic words, while of the remainder all but twenty-seven are on the stressed vowels of words of more than one syllable. Among the unstressed or partially stressed syllables which bear accent marks are three verbal prefixes, in *ábeag*, BEOW. 775, *áris*, BEOW. 1390, and *á cwæð*, JUD. 82, nearly all of the others being second elements of noun or adjective compounds, as in *un hár*, BEOW. 357, *deaþ wíc*, BEOW. 1275, [*orleg*] *hwíl*, BEOW. 2002, etc.

---

[3] R. W. Chambers, *Beowulf with the Finnsburg Fragment* (Cambridge, 1914), pp. xxxvii–xxxviii; W. J. Sedgefield, *Beowulf* (3d ed., Manchester, 1935), p. 155. The reports of the accents given by Wülker (in a table at the end of his first volume) and by Holder (as a part of his diplomatic text of the poem) are less dependable.

As in other Anglo-Saxon manuscripts, the purpose of these accent marks is by no means clear, but it may at least be pointed out that the restriction of the accents in BEOWULF and JUDITH to long vowels is in striking contrast to the other poetical miscellanies edited in this series, particularly the Junius Manuscript.

In the prose texts written by the first scribe, the frequency of accent marks is considerably greater than in the part of BEOWULF which he wrote; there are 111 accents in the 38 folios occupied by the prose texts, while in the first 38 folios of BEOWULF there are only 68 accents.[4] A further difference is that in the prose texts there are ten words in which an accent mark appears over a short vowel.[5] These differences are undoubtedly due to variations of scribal practice in the manuscripts from which he copied.

VII

BEOWULF

1. CONTENT AND HISTORICAL BACKGROUND

The story of BEOWULF is so well known that it is needless to summarize it in detail; it will suffice at this point to indicate the principal divisions of the narrative. These divisions are four in number: (1) the account of Scyld Scefing and his immediate descendants, ll. 1–85; (2) Beowulf's defence of the Danes against Grendel and his mother, ll. 86–1887; (3) his return to his own people, ll. 1888–2199; (4) his glorious reign, his fight with the dragon, his death and burial, ll. 2200–3182. The structural unity of the poem is provided by the life story of the hero, which is placed against a background of Scandinavian history of the sixth century. Nothing is known of this Beowulf, the hero of the Geats, except what is told us in the present text; his name does not appear in Scandinavian history, nor do we find him elsewhere in Old Germanic literature. His namesake Beowulf the king of the Danes, mentioned in l. 18 and l. 53 of the poem, is also not found in the Scandinavian tradition, but he appears in the West Saxon gene-

---

[4] The count of accent marks in the prose texts, like the other statistics for these texts which have been presented above, is based on Rypins's edition.

[5] These ten words are: *mid* (three times), *úp, úpheah, úngemellicu, óngean, gewrit, méc,* and *þé* used as a relative pronoun.

alogies as Beaw, Beo, or Beowius, the son of Scyld, Scyldwa, Sceldwea, or Sceldius. Whether or not the form *Beowulf*, which we find in our poem as the name of the son of Scyld, was originally *Beow*, as has been suggested,[1] there can be no doubt that the historical existence of such a king was accepted by the Anglo-Saxon chroniclers. But no such evidence is available for Beowulf the Geat, and there is no reason for believing that he was anything more than a fictitious hero invented by the poet. His name does not alliterate with that of his father Ecgtheow, or with any of the names of the Geatish princes, which alliterate in *H*- (Hrethel, Herebeald, Hæthcyn, Hygelac, Heardred), or with those of Weohstan and Wiglaf, the princes of the Wægmundings, to whom, as we are told in ll. 2813f., he was related. He cannot, then, be connected historically with the Geatish or with any of the other Scandinavian royal families.

But if Beowulf the Geat was a fictitious creation, the narrative of his martial achievements, first among the Danes and later among his own people, gave occasion for the insertion of a great variety of historical information concerning the early history of the Scandinavian kingdoms which seems, for the most part at least, to rest upon an authentic oral tradition. Some of this historical material agrees with the accounts preserved in Scandinavian sources, but more of it does not. Since in many places an editor's handling of his text may depend on his interpretation of the two historical traditions, the English and the Scandinavian, or upon the relative weight which he assigns to each, it is necessary to pay some attention to them here.

The three Scandinavian peoples with which BEOWULF is primarily concerned are the Geats, the Swedes, and the Danes. It is now generally accepted that the Geats are to be identified with the Gautar (Modern Swedish *Götar*) in what is now southern Sweden,[2]

---

[1] See the note on l. 53.

[2] The alternative theory, that the Geats are the Jutes, was first presented by Pontus Fahlbeck, *Antiqvarisk Tidskrift för Sverige* VIII, No. 2 (1884), 1–88, and has since been supported by other scholars, notably by Gudmund Schütte, *Journal of English and Germanic Philology* XI (1912), 574–602. But the identification of the Geats with the Gautar has been established beyond reasonable doubt by Henrik Schück, *Folknamnet Geatas i den fornengelska dikten Beowulf* (Uppsala, 1907), and by Kemp Malone, *Acta Philologica Scandi-*

who were conquered by the Swedes not long after the time of the action of the poem. Less is known about the Geats than about either the Danes or the Swedes, because of their early disappearance as an independent nation and the consequent blurring of their identity in the minds of later Scandinavian writers. But one event of Geatish history, Hygelac's ill-fated raid against the Franks reported in BEOWULF 1202–1214a, 2354b–2359a, 2913b–2921, is independently attested by a Frankish source. According to the *Historia Francorum* of Gregory of Tours, written in the latter part of the sixth century, the Danes under their king Chlochilaicus[3] undertook a naval expedition against Frankish territory during the reign of Theodoric, that is, between 511 and 534.[4] The attack was beaten off, and Chlochilaicus was killed. As was first pointed out by Grundtvig,[5] the Chlochilaicus of the Frankish chronicle is identical with the Hygelac of BEOWULF, and we are therefore able to assign approximate dates for the historical events alluded to in the poem.[6]

As might be expected, the Scandinavian sources for the early

---

navica IV (1929), 84–90. The name of the Gautar survives in that of Götaland, the southernmost of the three major territorial divisions of the modern kingdom of Sweden, as well as in the provincial names Östergötland and Västergötland.

[3] More probably Chochilaicus, the form found in the *Liber historiae Francorum*, written as late as 727 but based on Gregory.

[4] A more precise dating of this expedition (between 516 and 531, probably after 520) is offered by R. W. Chambers, *Beowulf: an Introduction* (2d ed., Cambridge, 1932), pp. 381–387.

[5] At first tentatively in *Nyeste Skilderie af Kjøbenhavn*, 1815, col. 1030, more fully two years later in his own periodical *Danne-Virke* II (1817), 285. See also his *Bjowulfs Drape* (Copenhagen, 1820), pp. lxi–lxii.

[6] Another continental text, the *Liber monstrorum de diversis generibus*, probably of the eighth century, mentions a "rex . . . qui imperavit Getis," whose name appears in one of the two manuscripts as Huiglaucus, in the other as Huncglacus (Moritz Haupt, *Opuscula* II [Leipzig, 1876], 223), but who can easily be identified with Hygelac (see Haupt, *Zeitschrift für deutsches Altertum* V [1845], 10). This text was long regarded as Frankish evidence that Chlochilaicus-Hygelac was a Geat and not a Dane, as he is described by Gregory. It is now, however, suspected that the *Liber monstrorum* was written in England. See the recent discussion in D. Whitelock, *The Audience of Beowulf* (Oxford, 1951), pp. 46ff.

history of the Danes and Swedes are extensive, but they are much later than BEOWULF and seem to derive from a widely different tradition. In the *Gesta Danorum* of Saxo Grammaticus,[7] finished in the early years of the thirteenth century, we find mention of Haldanus and his sons Roe and Helgo, of Hiarwarthus, Rolvo Krake, and Roricus; these names apparently correspond to those of Healfdene, Hrothgar, Halga, Heoroweard, Hrothulf, and Hrethric in BEOWULF. But in Saxo, Hiarwarthus is a Swede, the husband of Rolvo's sister Sculda, and Roricus, second after Rolvo Krake in the succession of Danish kings, is far away from Roe in the genealogical line. In *Hrólfs saga Kraka*,[8] which in its present form dates from the end of the fourteenth century, and in the Latin epitome of the lost *Skjöldunga saga* made by the Icelander Arngrímur Jónsson in 1596–1597,[9] we find Halfdan (Halfdanus) and his sons Hroar (Roas or Roë) and Helgi (Helgo), as well as Helgi's son Hrolf Kraki (Rolpho Krag). But Hjörvarth (Hiorvardus) is no more closely related to the stock of Halfdan than is Hiarwarthus in Saxo. There is no name in *Hrólfs saga* which corresponds to Hrethric in BEOWULF or to Roricus in Saxo, but in Arngrímur we find one Rærecus, who, however, is the son not of Roas but of Halfdanus' brother Ingialldus. Nor are there any names in the Scandinavian tradition which correspond to those of Heorogar and Hrothmund in the English poem. The incestuous union of Helgo (Helgi) and his daughter Ursa (Yrsa) from which Rolvo Krake (Hrolf Kraki, Rolpho Krag) was born, which is so conspicuous a feature of the Scandinavian accounts, apparently had no counterpart in the English tradition.

With the Scandinavian accounts of Swedish history the correspondences are no greater. In the enumeration of early Swedish kings contained in the *Ynglinga saga* (the first part of the *Heimskringla*, written by Snorri Sturluson in the first half of the thirteenth century),[10] Egil, Ottar Vendilkraka, and Athils, who are represented

---

[7] Most recently edited by C. Knabe and P. Herrmann (Copenhagen, 1931–date, still in process of publication). There is an English translation of the first nine books by Oliver Elton (London, 1894).

[8] Edited by Finnur Jónsson (Copenhagen, 1904); there is an English translation by Stella M. Mills (Oxford, 1933).

[9] Edited by Axel Olrik in *Aarbøger for Nordisk Oldkyndighed og Historie*, 2d Series, IX (1894), 83–164.

[10] Edited by Finnur Jónsson (Copenhagen, 1893–1901).

as ruling in succession over the Swedes, seem to correspond to Ongentheow, Ohthere, and Eadgils in BEOWULF. But in the *Ynglinga saga* no brother of Ottar is mentioned; the name Ali (*hinn Upplenzki*), usually equated with that of Onela, is borne by a Norwegian king. The name of Eanmund is probably reflected in that of Aun,[11] who, however, precedes Egil in the succession of kings reported in the *Ynglinga saga*. That the English tradition as a whole had Ongentheow as the name of Ohthere's predecessor, rather than a name corresponding to the Scandinavian name Egil, is indicated by the mention of Ongentheow as king of the Swedes in WIDSITH 31.

A more detailed account of the Scandinavian documents, which differ widely from each other in many details of the narrative, is impossible here;[12] but it is clear that their value as a guide to the interpretation of BEOWULF is extremely problematical. Statements of fact concerning Scandinavian history found in early texts other than BEOWULF, and conjectures based on these statements, are of service to the critic of BEOWULF only in so far as he can be certain that the poet and his audience were familiar with the same facts or had made the same conjectures; and such certainty is, in the nature of things, impossible. That the account of Danish and Swedish history found in the English poem is more accurate than that which we find in the Scandinavian documents cannot be proved, but it is unquestionable that BEOWULF represents an earlier and less romanticized tradition. If we limit ourselves to the information which can be derived from BEOWULF and WIDSITH and the other English texts, we may not obtain a complete story, but we will have one which, so far as it is preserved, is reasonably consistent—certainly far more consistent than a mingling of the English and Scandinavian traditions could ever be. It is our

[11] According to the brilliant conjecture by Kemp Malone, *The Literary History of Hamlet* I (Heidelberg, 1923), 67ff., who suggests that the person of Aun, who according to the *Ynglinga saga* ruled more than two hundred years, represents a confusion of two separate historical figures of the same name, the second of whom (the great-grandson of the first) corresponds to the Beowulfian Eanmund.

[12] The most complete survey of these materials in English is given by M. G. Clarke, *Sidelights on Teutonic History* (Cambridge, 1911). This book derives its value from the fullness of the data presented rather than from the soundness of the author's conclusions.

misfortune that the cultural continuity between the Anglo-Saxon poet and the modern reader has been broken, so that many of the allusions intended for the poet's audience and readily understood by them can now be interpreted only indirectly, if at all. But this misfortune is not alleviated by an attempt to bring into the picture narrative elements which may not have been known to the poet and his audience. The interpretation of BEOWULF is therefore best served by reliance upon the text itself, bringing narrative materials from other literatures into consideration only when they may serve to reinforce a conclusion already suggested by the text.

A survey of the principal events of Scandinavian history alluded to in BEOWULF, as they may be ascertained or inferred from the text of the poem and from other English sources, without recourse to the Scandinavian tradition, will be found in the next section of this Introduction.

Certain incidents of the poem, such as Beowulf's fights with Grendel and his mother and with the dragon, are traditionally classified as "fabulous," in contrast with the "historical" materials such as have been discussed above. But it is at least doubtful that such a classification was present in the mind of either the poet or his audience. We are inclined to classify the swimming match with Breca (ll. 506–589) as fabulous, and mythological interpretations of Breca and his people the Brondings have been attempted; but Breca's name appears in the "weold" catalogue in WIDSITH (*Breoca [weold] Brondingum*, l. 25) in close proximity to so indubitably historical a personage as Theodoric king of the Franks. Similarly, to our way of thinking the dragon is a fabulous element in the narrative, but the presence of flying dragons in Northumbria in the year 793 is attested by the sober pages of the Peterborough Chronicle. Hrothgar and Hygelac, Sigemund and Heremod, Grendel and his mother represent to us three separate levels of credibility, but there is no evidence that the poet of BEOWULF, in his ignorance of modern historical criticism, would share our convictions on that point. And all of these different elements of the narrative—the "fabulous" and the "historical," together with much that cannot be classified under either head—are inextricably combined. Beowulf's fights with Grendel and his mother do not take place in a vaguely defined Fairyland, where to us they would seem more at home, but at the court of Hrothgar, a Danish king of the early sixth century; the second of the two superhuman feats of swimming which are ascribed to him by the poet was an incident of Hygelac's raid against the Franks, the historicity of which is attested by Gregory of Tours. Such a mixture of the historical and the fanciful is a common feature of early narrative literature and requires no explanation in this particular case.[13]

2. THE GEATS, SWEDES, AND DANES

In this section an attempt will be made to outline the history of the three Scandinavian peoples, the Geats (*Geatas* or *Wederas*), the Swedes (*Sweon* or *Scylfingas*), and the Danes (*Dene, Scyldingas*, or *Ingwine*), as it is told in the poem and as it was apparently intended to be understood by the poet's audience. Since the affairs of the Geats and the Swedes were intimately connected, it will be convenient to consider these two kingdoms together.

The earliest of the Geatish kings mentioned in the poem is Hrethel, the father of Hygelac and Beowulf's grandfather on his mother's side (ll. 373–375*a*). We learn that Herebeald, the eldest son of Hrethel, was accidentally killed by his brother Hæthcyn (ll. 2435–2443) and that the king died of sorrow over the death of his heir (ll. 2462*b*–2471).

During the reign of Hæthcyn began the first of the two Swedish wars (ll. 2472–2489, 2922–2998). Whether hostilities were begun by Hæthcyn or by Ongentheow, who then ruled over the Swedes, it is difficult to decide, since ll. 2476*b*–2478, in which a hostile intent is attributed to the Swedes, seem inconsistent with ll. 2926–2927. But we are probably to understand that the first invasion was made by the Swedes, who attacked the Geats at Hreosnabeorh in Geatland (ll. 2472–2478), and that shortly thereafter Hæthcyn initiated a war of retaliation and invaded Sweden (ll. 2479–2489). The first results of the campaign were favorable to the Geats, who captured the Swedish queen. But Ongentheow, in a counterattack at Hrefnawudu, liberated his queen (ll. 2930*b*–2932) and killed Hæthcyn (ll. 2482*b*–2483, 2924–2925). The leaderless Geats were faced with extermination, but Hygelac, Hæthcyn's younger brother

---

[13] See D. Whitelock, *The Audience of Beowulf*, pp. 71ff., which appeared after the above had been written.

and successor, brought reinforcements and attacked the Swedes (ll. 2933–2960). Ongentheow was killed by the two brothers Wulf and Eofor (ll. 2961–2981), and the victory rested with the Geats.

Of the two sons of Ongentheow, Ohthere and Onela, we are not told which was the elder; but the narrative makes sense only if we assume that Ohthere was the older son and his father's successor.[1] How long he ruled we are not told, but it was apparently during his reign, while the Geats and Swedes were at peace, that Hygelac was killed in his unsuccessful expedition against the Franks.

After the death of Ohthere, his brother Onela usurped the Swedish throne to the exclusion of Eanmund, Ohthere's elder son and the rightful heir. Eanmund and his brother Eadgils, after an unsuccessful revolt, fled the kingdom and took refuge among the Geats (ll. 2379b–2384a). Onela, pursuing them, invaded the land of the Geats and killed Heardred, Hygelac's son and successor; he then withdrew to his own country, allowing Beowulf to succeed Heardred as king of the Geats (ll. 2202–2206, 2384b–2390).[2] In this campaign Eanmund was killed by Weohstan, Wiglaf's father (ll. 2611–2616a), who was in the service of Onela. At a later time Beowulf supported the destitute Eadgils, now the rightful heir to the Swedish throne, invaded Sweden, and killed Onela (ll. 2391–2396). This is the last of the hostile encounters between Geats and Swedes which are referred to in the poem as past events; but after the death of the childless Beowulf, Wiglaf predicts a renewal of hostilities (ll. 2999–3007a).[3]

A difficult problem is the relationship of Beowulf to the Wægmunding princes Weohstan and Wiglaf. It is to Beowulf that Wiglaf owes the *wicstede weligne Wægmundinga* (l. 2607) which his father formerly possessed; Beowulf, a Geat, speaks to Wiglaf of

[1] See Malone, *Philological Quarterly* VIII (1929), 406–407.

[2] It is not clear whether we are to understand from ll. 2389–2390a that Beowulf became a puppet king under the overlordship of Onela, or merely that Onela withdrew entirely, permitting the Geats their own choice of Heardred's successor. Beowulf's freedom to initiate the later campaign which resulted in the death of Onela supports the latter alternative.

[3] This prediction evidently refers to the war which, as we know, resulted in the extinction of Geatish independence and the absorption of the Geats into the Swedish kingdom.

"our race, the Wægmundings" (ll. 2813–2814a), and yet Wiglaf is elsewhere referred to as a Swedish prince (l. 2603). It is possible that Ecgtheow was a Swede[4] and that his connection with the Geats rested solely on his marriage to the daughter of Hrethel; more probably he is to be thought of as a Geat (though not one of the royal line) who was connected with the Wægmundings by a marriage, perhaps of his mother. In either case, Beowulf would be rather far from the direct Wægmunding line, and the *wicstede weligne* could hardly have been his to dispose of. But we are told (ll. 2611–2619) that Weohstan had been a partisan of Onela in the Swedish dynastic war and had killed Eanmund. The apparent paradox that Wiglaf was indebted to Beowulf for his own father's land may then be resolved by the assumption that after the victory of Eadgils and his accession to the Swedish throne, Weohstan's property had been declared forfeit but had been restored to Wiglaf through Beowulf's intercession.[5] It is of course also possible that the family relationships were never clearly outlined in the mind of the poet.

Danish history as presented in BEOWULF begins with Scyld Scefing, the founder of the Scylding dynasty, and his son Beowulf the Dane. Healfdene, Beowulf's son, left behind him three sons, Heorogar, Hrothgar, and Halga, and a daughter who (according to the accepted emendation of l. 62b) was the wife of the Swedish king Onela. Heorogar, Healfdene's successor, died young. His son Heoroweard was passed over in the succession, undoubtedly because of his youth,[6] and Hrothgar became king. At the time of the action of the poem Hrothgar's two sons, Hrethric and Hroth-

[4] As was suggested by E. E. Wardale, *Modern Language Review* XXIV (1929), 322.

[5] Lines 2620–2625a, which seem to imply that Weohstan lived among the Geats until his death, do not require us to assume that the *wicstede weligne* was in the land of the Geats rather than in Sweden. Weohstan would naturally have been unwelcome in the kingdom of Eanmund's brother. But see W. F. Bryan, *Modern Philology* XXXIV (1936), 113–118, who argues that the Wægmundings were a Geatish family and that Weohstan was "a Geat who was attached to the Swedish king [Onela] as a personal retainer."

[6] The only reference to Heoroweard is in ll. 2155–2162a, where it is stated that Heorogar gave his arms and armor to Hrothgar rather than to his own son. That Heoroweard had fallen into disfavor with his father, as has been suggested, seems to be disproved by the words *þeah he him hold wære*, l. 2161b.

mund, are still young (ll. 1188–1191), but the king's nephew Hrothulf enjoys a position of especial favor near the throne (ll. 1014*b*–1017*a*, 1162*b*–1165*a*) and is apparently regarded as a likely regent in case of Hrothgar's early death (ll. 1180*b*–1187). The close bond between Hrothgar and Hrothulf is also indicated in WIDSITH 45–49. From the fact that Hrothulf is not mentioned in connection with Heoroweard in BEOWULF 2155–2162*a*, we may infer that he was the son not of Heorogar but of Halga.[7] Of Halga's death, which apparently preceded the time of the action of the poem, we are given no information.

At the time of Beowulf's visit to Heorot, relations between Hrothgar and Hrothulf are described as most cordial; but the poet seems to protest too much on this point (ll. 1017*b*–1019, 1164*b*–1165*a*, 1228–1231), and we are evidently to understand that after Hrothgar's death Hrothulf failed in his duty to the young princes and usurped the royal power. From the passage in which Wealhtheow bespeaks Beowulf's favor for her sons (ll. 1216–1227), as well as from Beowulf's promise of a warm welcome to Hrethric at the Geatish court (ll. 1836–1839), we may surmise that at a later time Beowulf espoused Hrethric's cause against Hrothulf, much as he was to assist the Swedish prince Eadgils; but of all this the poet tells us nothing definite.

Heremod, whose disastrous career and unhappy death are referred to in ll. 901–915, 1709*b*–1722*a*, is identified in the poem only as a Danish prince, but in several of the West Saxon genealogies his name precedes those of Scyldwa (Sceldwea) and of Beaw. We may, then, assume that it was Heremod's death which plunged the Danes, now without a leader, into the period of misery from which they were rescued by the coming of Scyld (ll. 14*b*–16*a*). From the fact that the names of Heremod and Sigemund are so closely linked together in ll. 898–902*a*, we may perhaps infer that the poet believed Sigemund to have been a Dane also.[8]

---

[7] That he was Halga's son is definitely indicated only in the Scandinavian documents.

[8] The Sigemund legend is generally believed to have been of German (Frankish?) origin, but it is not impossible that it reached the English poet through Scandinavian channels. Fitela, Sigemund's companion in his adventures, corresponds to the Sinfjötli of the Sigmund-Signy section of the *Völsunga saga*.

The tragedy of Hnæf and Hengest at Finnsburh (ll. 1063–1159a), as well as the conflict between Danes and Heathobards which forms the subject of the so-called "Ingeld episode" (ll. 2024b–2069a), will be discussed in a later section of this Introduction.

3. OTHER GERMANIC PEOPLES MENTIONED IN THE POEM

Besides the Geats, Swedes, and Danes, several other Scandinavian peoples are mentioned in BEOWULF; in this category apparently belong the Heathoreams (l. 519), the Brondings (l. 521), and the Wendels (l. 348), all of whom are alluded to in WIDSITH, and probably also the Finns (l. 580). The country of the Heathoreams, where Breca came ashore after his swimming match with Beowulf, has been identified with the *Raumaríki* of the Scandinavian documents (the present-day Romerike, north and east of Oslo), or alternatively with *Haðaland* (the present-day Hadeland, which adjoins Romerike on the west).[1] The Brondings, Breca's own people, cannot be identified, and a mythological interpretation of both the Brondings and Breca was once popular;[2] but the occurrence of both names in WIDSITH 25 strongly suggests that to the author of that poem, at least, they were historical realities. It is not necessary to conclude from BEOWULF 520–521 that the Brondings were neighbors of the Heathoreams, since Breca, coming ashore in one place and having his home in another, would naturally go home, no matter how long a trip might be required. It is, therefore, not absolutely certain that the Brondings are to be thought of as a Scandinavian people. The Wendels (who are presumably the same as the *Wenlas* of WIDSITH 59) have been most often identified as inhabitants of the present-day Vendsyssel, in northern Jutland,[3] or, alternatively and with less probability, as the people

---

[1] See Kemp Malone, *Widsith* (London, 1936), p. 158, and the references given there.

[2] See, for example, Karl Müllenhoff, *Zeitschrift für deutsches Altertum* VII (1849), 420–421; T. Krüger, *Archiv* LXXI (1884), 136; K. Müllenhoff, *Beovulf* (Berlin, 1889), pp. 1–2.

[3] This identification is as old as the beginning of BEOWULF studies; it was made by Thorkelin in his edition, p. 268.

of Vendel in Uppland, Sweden,[4] or as the East Germanic Vandals.[5]

The Finns of l. 580, among whom Beowulf came to land after the swimming match, are usually identified with the North Baltic people still known by that name. But it would be surprising if Beowulf, swimming northward[6] from the land of the Geats and into the Skagerrack, should find himself in the North Baltic. An alternative possibility,[7] that these Finns were the inhabitants of Finnmarken at the extreme northern tip of Norway, is also geographically improbable. It seems best, therefore, to accept Henrik Schück's identification[8] of the Finns with the inhabitants of the district of Finnheden in southern Sweden.[9]

The West Germanic peoples mentioned in the poem whose identity is reasonably certain are the Jutes, the Franks, and the Frisians. The Jutes appear in two connections, first as the people among whom Heremod, while in exile, was treacherously killed (l. 902), and later as the allies of Finn in the so-called "Finnsburh episode" (ll. 1063–1159a), on whom the blame for the tragedy seems to have rested. The Franks, against whom Hygelac led the expedition in which he lost his life, are also referred to as *Hugas* (ll. 2502, 2914) and as *Hetware* (ll. 2363, 2916); these names, properly referring to originally separate tribes which had come under the domination of the Franks,[10] are apparently used inter-

---

[4] Knut Stjerna, *Arkiv för nordisk filologi* XXI (1904), 74–75, reprinted in English in K. Stjerna, *Essays on Questions Connected with the Old English Poem of Beowulf* (Coventry, 1912), pp. 55–56.

[5] Müllenhoff, *Beovulf*, pp. 89–90.

[6] That he was swimming northward may be inferred from ll. 547b–548a, *ond norþanwind heaðogrim ondhwearf.*

[7] Müllenhoff, *Beovulf*, p. 89.

[8] *Folknamnet Geatas*, pp. 28–29. This identification had previously been rejected by Bugge, *Beiträge* XII (1887), 53–54.

[9] On the other hand, the Finns mentioned in WIDSITH 20, 76 were probably the North Baltic people of that name; the Scride-Finns of WIDSITH 79 were undoubtedly the Lapps. See R. W. Chambers, *Widsith* (Cambridge, 1912), p. 213.

[10] The Hugas and the Hetware correspond to the *Chauci* and the *Chatuari(i)* of the Greek and Roman geographers; see M. Schönfeld, *Wörterbuch der altgermanischen Personen- und Völkernamen* (Heidelberg, 1911), pp. 131–132. The Hetware are also mentioned in WIDSITH 33.

changeably with *Francan*. According to the now usual interpretation, the name *Merewioingas*, l. 2921, is a genitive singular form, referring to a king of the Franks. The name of Frisians seems to be applied in BEOWULF to two separate groups of people. The Frisians under King Finn (ll. 1070, 1093, 1104, 1126), in whose land the action of the "Finnsburh episode" takes place, are evidently to be located in the old Frisian homeland east of the Zuider Zee, while the Frisians mentioned in connection with Hygelac's attack upon the Franks (ll. 1207, 2357, 2912ff.), whom we may judge to have been allies or political dependents of the Franks, were probably the West Frisians living on the other side of the Zuider Zee in what is now North and South Holland.[11] The Angles are not mentioned by name in BEOWULF, but Offa and his marriage to Thryth form the subject matter of one of the principal episodes of the poem (ll. 1931b–1962).[12]

The Heathobards, also mentioned in WIDSITH 49, appear to have been closely related to the Langobards or Lombards and perhaps represented a part of the common Bardish nation which remained behind when the Langobards migrated to the south.[13] The Wylfings (ll. 461, 471) or Helmings (l. 620), Wealhtheow's people,[14] are also probably to be thought of as living on the south shore of the Baltic. We are told (ll. 459–472) that Ecgtheow, Beowulf's father, having become involved in a feud among the Wylfings and being disowned by his own people for fear of involvement, sought Hrothgar as a mediator of the feud. It was un-

---

[11] According to R. Much in *Reallexikon der germanischen Altertumskunde* II (Strassburg, 1913ff.), 100, the West Frisians lost their independence to the Franks at the end of the seventh century. The poet may have been thinking of the conditions which prevailed in his own time, rather than those of the early sixth century.

[12] This Offa is presumably the fourth-century king of the continental Angles, who is mentioned several times in WIDSITH, but the episode finds its closest literary analogue in the story of his descendant Offa II, king of the Mercians from 757 to 796, and his wife Drida (or Quendrida), which is told in the Latin *Vitae Duorum Offarum* of about the year 1200. See especially Edith Rickert, *Modern Philology* II (1904–1905), 29–76, 321–376, and Chambers, *Beowulf: an Introduction*, pp. 31–40, 217–243.

[13] See Malone's extensive discussion, *Widsith*, pp. 155–158.

[14] The identification of the Wylfings and the Helmings is made possible by WIDSITH 29, *Helm [weold] Wulfingum*.

doubtedly because of his relationship by marriage with the Wylfings that Hrothgar was able to settle the affair satisfactorily.

The only East Germanic people alluded to in the poem are the Gepidae (*Gifðas*, l. 2494), who also appear in WIDSITH 60. From the fact that in BEOWULF they are mentioned together with the Danes and the Swedes, it is apparent that the poet thought of them as still living near the mouth of the Vistula rather than in their later home to the south.[15] The Goths are not mentioned by name in the poem, but the name of Eormanric, the famous king of the East Goths, appears in the allusion to Hama and the *Brosinga mene* (ll. 1198b–1201).[16]

4. THE FINNSBURH AND INGELD EPISODES

Two of the historical episodes in the poem, the story of Finnsburh (ll. 1063–1159a) and the so-called "Ingeld episode" (ll. 2024b–2069a), present unusually complicated problems of interpretation and require separate treatment.

The first of these episodes, the account of Hnæf's death in Frisia and the revenge later taken by his followers, is recited as part of the festivities at Heorot after the death of Grendel. The only other extant version of this story is the BATTLE OF FINNSBURH (or, more briefly, the "Fragment"), printed in Volume VI of this edition, which is apparently part of a heroic lay of several hundred lines covering more or less the same story as we find in the Finnsburh episode in BEOWULF.[1] Unfortunately the Fragment is very short and covers only a part of the fight in which Hnæf fell, while the episode in BEOWULF begins with the situation on the morning

---

[15] Malone, *Widsith*, p. 148. Only the dative plural form of the name is attested in Anglo-Saxon, and perhaps we should assume a weak noun *Gifðan*, as Malone does, rather than a strong *Gifðas*.

[16] Hama, mentioned in WIDSITH 124, 130, is the Heimir of the Scandinavian documents and the Heime of Middle High German story. The closest analogue to the passage in BEOWULF is the statement in the *Thidreks saga* (edited by H. Bertelsen, Copenhagen, 1905–1911), ch. 430 (429), that Heimir, after many years as an outlaw, entered a monastery, bringing with him, besides his horse, armor, and weapons, precious things to the value of ten pounds. See especially Chambers, *Widsith*, pp. 48–57.

[1] See *Records VI, The Anglo-Saxon Minor Poems*, pp. xiii–xix, for a discussion of this poem.

after this fight and carries the story on to the end. The value of the Fragment as a clue to the interpretation of the episode is therefore very slight, except in aiding us to establish the situation at the beginning of the episode and in supplying independent confirmation of some of the names which appear in the episode.[2]

The text of ll. 1063–1159a in the present edition is based on the following reconstruction of the Finnsburh story. Hnæf, a prince of the Scyldings, is the brother of Hildeburh, the queen of King Finn of the Frisians.[3] From the statement in l. 1074 that Hildeburh lost a son in the hostilities which immediately preceded the opening of the episode, we may infer that she had been married to Finn for many years. During a visit made to Finn's court by Hnæf and a body of his retainers (sixty men, according to the Fragment), a fight broke out between Danes and Frisians, in which Hnæf was killed. This fight is the one described in the Fragment. The immediate cause of the hostilities is not clear, but in ll. 1071–1072a a hint is given that the *Eotan* (usually identified as Jutes) bore a heavy responsibility for the trouble. The result of the fighting was a stalemate; Hnæf's men, leaderless in a foreign country and without resources, were in the utmost peril, while Finn's forces had been so depleted that he was unable to bring about a decisive victory. Finn therefore concluded a truce with Hengest, now leader of the surviving Danes, the terms of which are stated in ll. 1085b–1106. This truce was clearly nothing more than a temporary expedient, intended to serve until the winter was over and the Danes could return home. It is therefore not difficult to explain the fact, often commented on, that all the conditions of the truce as outlined in the poem represent concessions by Finn to the Danes, and that we are told of no counter-concessions by Hengest. Finn could afford to be generous, since his sole desire was to pacify his now unwilling guests until he could be rid of them.

The truce lasted, apparently without incident, through the re-

---

[2] The names of Hnæf, Hengest, and Guthlaf occur in both texts. Oslaf, mentioned together with Guthlaf in BEOWULF 1148, is probably the same person as the Ordlaf whose name occurs with Guthlaf's in l. 16 of the Fragment. The name Finnsburh appears only in the Fragment.

[3] This relationship is established by the reference to Hildeburh as *Hoces dohtor* in l. 1076, together with the statement in WIDSITH 29 that *Hnæf [weold] Hocingum*. In WIDSITH 27 Finn is described as ruler of the Frisians.

mainder of the winter; but with the coming of spring Hengest's
mind, until then preoccupied with the desire to return to his own
land, turned to the possibility of revenge for his lord's death and
for the injuries (unspecified in the text) which had been done to
the Danes. Receiving a clear reminder of his duty in the form of
a sword presented by one of his followers, and goaded by the
reproaches of Guthlaf and Oslaf, Hengest attacked Finn in his
own hall, in spite of the truce to which he had consented, and
killed him amid his warriors. The Danes carried away the Frisian
queen to her own people, together with Finn's royal treasure.[4]

Stated in these terms, the episode is a tragedy of three people—
of Hildeburh, deprived first of her brother and son and later of her
husband; of Finn, involved in a deadly feud which may not have
been of his own making; and particularly of Hengest, torn between
a sincere desire to observe the truce with Finn and the duty of
revenge to his fallen lord. Hengest was seemingly intended to be
the central figure of the story as told in BEOWULF, and the use of
the phrase *Hengest sylf* in l. 17 of the Fragment may be taken as
indicating that in that poem also, if the whole were preserved,
Hengest would play the leading role. The Finnsburh story, then,
would in its essence be "the tragedy of Hengest"—a phrase first
applied by Ayres.

In recent years, however, it has been maintained by some commentators, and particularly by Malone[5] and Girvan,[6] that Hengest
was not involved in the final victory of the Danes over Finn. According to Malone, Hengest drops out of the action after l. 1145,
and we are told nothing more about him;[7] the final onslaught of
the Danes against Finn was entirely in the hands of Guthlaf and
Oslaf, who had made a journey to Denmark (the *sæsið* of l. 1149)

[4] This reconstruction follows in general H. M. Ayres, *Journal of English
and Germanic Philology* XVI (1917), 282–295; Chambers, *Beowulf: an Introduction*, pp. 245–287; and W. W. Lawrence, *Beowulf and Epic Tradition* (Cambridge, Mass., 1928), pp. 107–128.

[5] *The Literary History of Hamlet* I (Heidelberg, 1923), 20–23; *Journal of
English and Germanic Philology* XXV (1926), 168–171; *ELH* X (1943), 283–284.

[6] *Proceedings of the British Academy* XXVI (1940), 350.

[7] In Malone's view the sword of l. 1143 has no connection with what follows
but was a gift made by Hnæf to Hengest at some earlier time. See the note
on *woroldrædenne*, l. 1142.

for the purpose of bringing reinforcements. Girvan believes that Hengest is no longer alive in the closing lines of the episode, that he and his followers were put to death by Finn as punishment for the breach of the peace involved in Hengest's acceptance of the sword at ll. 1142ff., and that Guthlaf and Oslaf, who had not been members of Hnæf's party, later came from Denmark to exact vengeance for the death of their kinsmen.[8] Both these interpretations absolve Hengest of the responsibility for Finn's death and thereby avoid the question which has bulked so large in the traditional interpretation of the episode: Why, if this recitation was made for a Danish audience, should it tell a story which imputes bad faith to a Danish leader? On the other hand it must be pointed out, in defence of the traditional interpretation, that if Hengest had no part in the final victory of the Danes—that is, if there was no "tragedy of Hengest"—then we are deprived of the tragic dilemma which, to the modern reader at least, is the chief attraction of the episode. The fact that Hengest is not mentioned by name in ll. 1146–1159a can be explained otherwise than by the assumption that he did not take part in these events.

In closing this brief discussion of the Finnsburh episode, it is necessary to add a few words about the tribes who take part in the action. Concerning the Frisians, Finn's people, there is little that need be said, but the identity of the *Eotan* and their relationship to the Frisians has been disputed. Although the name *Eotan* (or *Eotenas*) is used interchangeably with *Frysan* (*Fresan*) throughout the episode, it properly belongs to Jutes rather than to Frisians and may be understood to refer to Jutish allies or dependents of Finn who were staying at Finnsburh at the time of Hnæf's visit.[9] As has already been pointed out, it may reasonably be conjectured from ll. 1071–1072a that they, rather than Finn and his Frisians, were responsible for the original outbreak of hostilities at Finnsburh. The older identification of the *Eotan* with Hnæf's men, usually attached to the name of Hermann Möller[10] and most

[8] He accounts for the presence of Ordlaf (= Oslaf) and Guthlaf in the Fragment by assuming that in that poem the two fights, in which Hnæf and Finn were killed, are telescoped into one.

[9] See Chambers' discussion of this point, *Beowulf: an Introduction*, pp. 268–270.

[10] *Das altenglische Volksepos* I (Kiel, 1883), 94–95.

recently espoused by Girvan,[11] hardly requires refutation at this late date; except that it facilitates the improbable identification of the Hengest of the Finnsburh story with the Jutish Hengest who came to Britain with Horsa in 449 or thereabouts, there is little to commend it.

The "Half-Danes," Hnæf's tribe or family, also require comment. If *Healfdena*, l. 1069a (apparently genitive of a tribal name *Healfdene*, nowhere else recorded in Anglo-Saxon), is a genuine form, it is difficult to explain its meaning or to account for the implied distinction between Danes and Half-Danes. There is no mention of Hnæf or of his father Hoc in any of the Scandinavian accounts of Danish history; only in WIDSITH 29 do we elsewhere find a reference to Hnæf as ruler of the Hocings, immediately following the mention of the Sea-Danes. And yet three times in the episode (ll. 1069, 1108, 1154) we find Hnæf and his men described as Scyldings. The older explanation of the Half-Danes, which follows Bugge,[12] is that although related in some way to the Danes, they were not Danes in the full sense of the word; the chief merit of this view is that it is too vaguely conceived to be easily refuted. Malone[13] has explained *Healfdene* as the older dynastic name of the Scyldings, derived from the name of Healfdene, Hrothgar's father, whom he believes to have been the true founder of the Scylding dynasty.[14] This hypothesis has much in its favor, though we should perhaps expect such a form as *Healfdeningas* rather than *Healfdene*. Even more attractive is Edward Schröder's suggestion[15] that the tribal name *Healfdene* was the invention of an Anglo-Saxon poet on the basis of the personal name *Healfdene*, for if Schröder is right, no historical explanation of the Half-Danes is

[11] *Proceedings of the British Academy* XXVI, 352–353.

[12] *Beiträge* XII (1887), 29. A more specific formulation, stated by W. W. Lawrence, *PMLA* XXX (1915), 430f., is that the Half-Danes were "one of the allied clans making up the Danish people." Chambers, p. 171 of his edition, explains the Half-Danes as "a tribe akin to the Danes, but independent, or half independent of the central Danish power at Leire (Heorot)."

[13] *Arkiv för nordisk filologi* XLII (1926), 234–240. See also his later note in *Englische Studien* LXX (1935), 74–76.

[14] He would also explain the manuscript reading *við Halfdana* in the Icelandic *Grottasöngr*, stanza 22 (23), as meaning "against the Half-Danes," thus providing a putative Scandinavian parallel to the Anglo-Saxon form.

[15] *Anglia* LVIII (1934), 350.

necessary. It is of course also possible that *Healfdena* in l. 1069*a* is a scribal error for *Hringdena* or *Hocinga* or some other name.

The so-called "Ingeld episode" is part of Beowulf's report to Hygelac concerning the doings at the Danish court. Beowulf explains that Hrothgar, hoping to settle a bloody feud between Heathobards and Danes, has betrothed his daughter Freawaru to Ingeld, the young king of the Heathobards. The poem gives us no information as to the immediate historical background of this event, but from the evidence of the Scandinavian texts (particularly the first four chapters of *Hrólfs saga Kraka*) we may conjecture that Froda, Ingeld's father, has killed Healfdene in battle and that in revenge for this deed Healfdene's sons have burned Froda in his own hall.[16] Beowulf, who has little confidence in the proposed marriage as a device for settling the feud, suggests its probable result. Ingeld and his followers, he says, may well be vexed at the wedding feast by the appearance of Danish warriors bearing arms and armor taken from fallen Heathobards; an old Heathobard may incite a younger one to accomplish revenge for the death of his father, and the feud may break out afresh. That these future events suggested by Beowulf actually took place may be inferred from WIDSITH 45–49, where we are told of the defeat of Ingeld's warriors in a battle at Heorot.

The story of the relations between Danes and Heathobards presented in BEOWULF and WIDSITH is incomplete and highly allusive and offers abundant opportunity for conjectural restoration. The two principal problems presented are the relationship in time between Beowulf's visit to Heorot and the marriage of Freawaru, and the country in which the marriage took place. The traditional opinion on the first of these points, as expressed, for example, by Chambers[17] and Lawrence,[18] is that in this passage Beowulf is uttering a prophecy of coming events. Axel Olrik, however, in-

---

[16] There is nothing in the *Hrólfs saga Kraka* which corresponds to the Ingeld episode in *Beowulf*. The closest Scandinavian parallel to the episode is in Book VI of Saxo's *Gesta Danorum*, where, however, there are some differences: Ingellus, the son of Frotho, is a Dane, while his bride is the daughter of a king of the Saxons; also, the slaying is performed by Ingellus himself, rather than by an unnamed follower.

[17] *Beowulf: an Introduction*, p. 21.

[18] *Beowulf and Epic Tradition*, pp. 80f.

terpreting the present-tense forms in the passage as historical presents, believed that Beowulf is referring to events which have already happened.[19] Kemp Malone, likewise rejecting the interpretation of these lines as a prophecy, has argued that from l. 2032 to l. 2058a Beowulf is narrating events which are actually happening at Heorot at the time, and that not until the words oð ðæt sæl cymeð, l. 2058b, are the present-tense forms to be understood as having future meaning.[20] That is, the vexation of the Heathobards and the old warrior's incitation of the young warrior are continuing day by day, until, Beowulf thinks, the feud will break out again.

But neither the interpretation of Beowulf's speech as a prophecy, nor the alternative interpretations offered by Olrik and Malone, does justice to the words Mæg þonne, l. 2032, which, as in l. 1484, are most naturally taken as introducing a hypothetical situation in future time.[21] Beowulf can hardly be giving an unqualified prediction of what will happen (since we have no information that he possessed the second sight), nor, apparently, is he telling what has happened or is happening. Skeptical of the efficacy of royal marriages of convenience, he is suggesting what may happen if Hrothgar persists in his plan for the marriage.

With regard to the place of the contemplated marriage between Ingeld and Freawaru, it has generally been held that, in accordance with the usual rule governing the marriage of a king,[22] it was to take place at the court of the Heathobards, among the people over

[19] *Danmarks Heltedigtning* II (Copenhagen, 1910), 38, note. Olrik's assumption of the historical present tense in this passage has been challenged by Lawrence, *PMLA* XXX, 380, note 11; by Chambers, *Beowulf: an Introduction*, p. 21, note 3; and, at greater length, by J. M. Steadman, *Modern Language Notes* XLV (1930), 522–525.

[20] *Journal of English and Germanic Philology* XXXIX (1940), 77ff. The present-tense forms as far as l. 2058a he describes as consuetudinal presents. In l. 2032 he translates *Mæg . . . ofþyncan* as the equivalent of a simple present, "displeases."

[21] Compare also the similar use of *þonne* in *gif*-clauses, ll. 1104, 1822, 1836.

[22] R. Girvan, *Modern Language Review* XXVIII (1933), 246, cites the journey of Æthelberg, the daughter of King Æthelberht of Kent, to Northumbria to be married to Edwin. He suggests that the phrase *comes copulae carnalis* in Bede's account (*Historia ecclesiastica*, Book II, chapter 9, ed. C. Plummer I, 98, 20f.), applied to Paulinus, is the equivalent of *se fæmnan þegn* in BEOWULF 2059.

whom the bride was to be queen. But E. A. Kock[23] and Kemp
Malone[24] have preferred to locate the action of the episode at
Heorot. Malone's argument that if the slaying of the *fæmnan
þegn* had taken place in the land of the Heathobards, the Heathobard slayer would not have needed to flee, can however hardly be
sustained, since the lives of diplomatic envoys were as inviolate
then as in later times, and it would have been Ingeld's duty to
pursue him. The phrase *con him land geare*, l. 2062*b*, is of little
help in this connection, since it permits alternative arguments, that
if the slayer knew the country well he must have been in his own
homeland, or that if he was in his own homeland there would be
little point in the poet's saying that he knew the country well.
In all the argument that has been presented up to now, I can see
no reason for departing from the traditional view that the action
of the episode is to be placed at the Heathobard court.[25]

5. COMPOSITION AND DATE

At the present time most scholars are agreed that the text of
BEOWULF, as it has come down to us, is the work of a single author.
The older "patchwork" theories,[1] according to which the poem
grew into its present form through a series of accretions and
interpolations at the hands of several poets, are now no longer
relied upon to explain the occasional repetitions and incongruities
in the text which have troubled commentators since the early

[23] *Anglia* XLVI (1922), 173f.

[24] *Anglia* LVII (1933), 219f.; *Anglia* LXIII (1939), 111f.; *Journal of English
and Germanic Philology* XXXIX, 89f.

[25] In Book VI of Saxo's *Gesta Danorum*, the corresponding action is said
to have taken place in Denmark, but this proves nothing, since Saxo represents Ingellus as a Dane. If we may infer from Saxo's narrative that the
action of the episode in BEOWULF took place at Ingeld's court, then we must
locate it in the country of the Heathobards.

[1] The classic example of this approach to the poem is Karl Müllenhoff's
"Die innere Geschichte des Beovulfs," *Zeitschrift für deutsches Altertum* XIV
(1869), 193–244, later reprinted in his *Beovulf*, pp. 110–160. Other studies of
the same kind are to be found in Bernhard ten Brink, *Beowulf* (Strassburg,
1888), pp. 1–165, and R. C. Boer, *Die altenglische Heldendichtung I* (Halle,
1912), pp. 25–131. A recent attempt to dissect the poem, written long after
the principles on which it is based had been generally rejected, is W. A. Berend-
sohn's *Zur Vorgeschichte des "Beowulf"* (Copenhagen, 1935).

days of BEOWULF scholarship. There can be no doubt that the author derived his subject matter from many and varied sources, and the lack of consistency and stylistic smoothness in his handling of them is no more than we might expect to find in a literary tradition so new to the England of his day as the full-length epic poem.

It is also generally agreed that the author of the poem was a Christian and that the so-called "Christian" elements in the poem are not (as was once believed) later interpolations in an originally heathen composition.[2] Attempts to separate heathen and Christian strata in BEOWULF have been almost uniformly unsuccessful. Klaeber, in his thoroughgoing study of the Christian elements in the poem, has shown the extent to which these elements were an integral part of the poet's thought,[3] and one is forced to the conclusion stated by Brandl,[4] that he who wishes to eliminate entirely the nonheathen elements in BEOWULF must rewrite the poem.

But if the Christian spirit is an inseparable part of the fabric of BEOWULF, it is a simple and relatively undogmatic form of Christianity which we find. Klaeber's collections include references to the Creation, to God and the devil, to heaven and hell, to sin and the Last Judgment, and to the character of the pious man; but there are no allusions to Christ and the cross, to saints and angels, or to the more complicated doctrinal concepts such as we find abundantly in the poems of Cynewulf and his contemporaries.[5] The only biblical allusions are to the Creation (ll. 90b–98), to Cain and Abel (ll. 106–110, 1261b–1265a), and to Noah's flood

[2] The most recent restatement of the older position is by H. M. Chadwick, *The Heroic Age* (Cambridge, 1912), pp. 47–56, who believes that "the great bulk of the poem must have been in existence . . . an appreciable time before the middle of the seventh century," that is, at a time when the Christianization of northern England had hardly begun.

[3] *Anglia* XXXV (1911), 111–136, 249–270, 453–482; XXXVI (1912), 169–199; see especially *Anglia* XXXV, 471–482. A short but very informative discussion of this subject is given by C. W. Kennedy, *The Earliest English Poetry* (New York, 1943), pp. 87–91.

[4] In Paul's *Grundriss der germanischen Philologie* (2d ed.), II, 1, 1003.

[5] See Klaeber, *Anglia* XXXV, 480–482; Chadwick, *The Heroic Age*, pp. 47–48.

(ll. 1689b–1693); there are no references to events or personages of the New Testament, and apparently no dependence on a specifically Christian body of doctrine as contrasted with the more general Judeo-Christian tradition which is always the first to be assimilated in a newly converted society.[6]

In spite of the obvious influence of the new religion, the dominant tone of the poem is courtly rather than clerical and suggests that it was composed for a lay audience.   If the author was a cleric, as many have supposed, he could hardly have been a monk, but he may well have been a chaplain in a royal or noble household. Certain it is that he was a man of keen antiquarian interests and one who possessed a wide acquaintance with Germanic heroic legend.   If he was not a cleric, he must have enjoyed a very good education according to the standards for laymen of his time, possibly but not necessarily including some knowledge of the *Æneid*.[7]   If, as many scholars have assumed, Beowulf was unique in its genre, the influence of classical epic can hardly be doubted, since neither the Cædmonian poetry nor the heroic lays brought from the Continent could have afforded a sufficient model; but if, as seems likely, it was only one among a number of Anglo-Saxon epics dealing with themes from Germanic heroic legend, the spontaneous development of an epic genre among the Anglo-Saxons, with little or no influence from classical literature, is well within the bounds of probability.[8]

Estimates of the date of composition of Beowulf have ranged from the middle of the seventh century to the beginning of the tenth.   In the absence of any dependable external evidence (in particular, the lack of other long poems of the same type, with which it might be compared), opinions as to date must be based

[6] For a dissenting opinion on this point, see D. Whitelock, *The Audience of Beowulf*, pp. 6–8.

[7] See Klaeber, *Archiv* CXXVI (1911), 40–48, 339–359, and T. B. Haber, *A Comparative Study of the Beowulf and the Æneid* (Princeton, 1931). The parallel passages adduced in these works cannot, of course, do more than suggest a probable influence of Virgil on the Anglo-Saxon poet. The Homeric parallels suggested by A. S. Cook, *Philological Quarterly* V (1926), 226–234, and elsewhere, are perhaps merely coincidental.

[8] See the recent observations by J. R. Hulbert, *PMLA* LXVI (1951), 1171–1174.

either on general considerations of cultural history or on grammatical investigations of the text itself. Among studies of the latter type may be mentioned the investigations of the use of the definite article and the weak adjective,[9] and metrical tests designed to show whether or not certain Anglo-Saxon sound changes preceded the composition of the poem.[10] Of these studies it may be said that the results are often mutually contradictory and that in so far as metrical criteria are involved, present-day opinion tends to reject the assumption of metrical rigidity on which the tests were founded. Comparison with other poems based on verbal and phrasal parallels,[11] necessarily involving the assumption that the extant Anglo-Saxon poems are all that ever existed, has also failed to provide incontestable results. Even the double occurrence of the well-known line *enge anpaðas, uncuð gelad*, at BEOWULF 1410 and EXODUS 58, is susceptible of two explanations, either that it was borrowed from EXODUS by the BEOWULF poet or that it was borrowed from BEOWULF by the author of EXODUS[12]—if indeed it

---

[9] A. Lichtenheld, *Zeitschrift für deutsches Altertum* XVI (1873), 325–393; A. J. Barnouw, *Textkritische Untersuchungen nach dem Gebrauch des bestimmten Artikels und des schwachen Adjektivs in der altenglischen Poesie* (Leiden, 1902).

[10] L. Morsbach, "Zur Datierung des Beowulfepos," in *Nachrichten von der k. Gesellschaft der Wissenschaften zu Göttingen*, Philol.-Hist. Klasse, 1906, pp. 251–277, uses as criteria the loss of final *-u* after long root syllables and the loss of postconsonantal *-h-* before a vowel; his conclusion, which has been widely accepted, is that the poem could not have been written before 700. Morsbach's method was later extended to the study of the chronology of other poems by C. Richter, *Chronologische Studien zur ags. Literatur auf Grund sprachlich-metrischer Kriterien* (Halle, 1910).

[11] Klaeber, *Englische Studien* XLII (1910), 321–338 (on GENESIS A and BEOWULF); Klaeber, *Modern Language Notes* XXXIII (1918), 218–224 (on EXODUS and BEOWULF); P. G. Thomas, *Modern Language Review* VIII (1913), 537–539 (on DANIEL and BEOWULF).

[12] L. L. Schücking, *Untersuchungen zur Bedeutungslehre der angelsächsischen Dichtersprache* (Heidelberg, 1915), pp. 40–41, identifying this line as a literal translation of Exodus xiii. 18, 20 (*circumduxit per viam deserti . . . in extremis finibus solitudinis*), considered it good evidence that EXODUS preceded BEOWULF. But R. Imelmann, *Forschungen zur altenglischen Poesie* (Berlin, 1920), pp. 418–420, would find the source in Æneid XI, 524f. (*tenuis quo semita ducit, Angustaeque ferunt fauces aditusque maligni*), in which case the line would probably have been used first in BEOWULF. See also Klaeber, *Modern Language Notes* XXXIII (1918), 218–224; Klaeber, *Anglia* L (1926), 202–203; Schücking, in *Studies in English Philology* (Klaeber Misc., Minneapolis, 1929), pp. 213–216; Klaeber, *Archiv* CLXXXVII (1950), 71–72.

was not borrowed by one or both of these poets from a still earlier poem, now lost.

The "objective" tests for the date of BEOWULF have, then, failed to provide dependable results. Considerations based on the general cultural history of the Anglo-Saxons have, on the whole, produced greater agreement if not greater certainty. Schücking's attempt[13] to place the composition of the poem at the end of the ninth century or later, in a mixed English and Scandinavian culture, has been rightly rejected,[14] and most present-day authorities are inclined to accept a date in the first half of the eighth century. But Ritchie Girvan has suggested reasons for believing that the poem was written as early as the last quarter of the seventh century,[15] and more recently Miss Whitelock has argued that the later eighth century is well within the possible limits of date.[16] The evidence in the text for an original Anglian dialect has been usually interpreted as pointing to a Northumbrian origin, but the possibility of Mercian provenience cannot be wholly excluded on linguistic grounds. The problems of the date and place of writing of BEOWULF are, therefore, still unsettled, in spite of the erudition which has been brought to bear upon them during the past half-century.

Whether the poet derived any of his knowledge of Scandinavian history from written sources, we shall probably never know, but there is no reason to believe that all of his information on these matters could not have come to him through oral tradition. Of particular note is his knowledge of and interest in the Geats, whose kingdom had by his time been extinct for more than a century. A possible explanation of this interest, which has often been

---

[13] *Beiträge* XLII (1917), 347–410; see also his further remarks in *Beiträge* XLVII (1923), 293–311.

[14] Since immediate Scandinavian influence on the poem is ruled out by the forms of personal names, which must have resulted from regular Anglo-Saxon sound changes and which therefore must have been in the language at an early date. On this point, see especially Brandl, in Paul's *Grundriss der germanischen Philologie* (2d ed.), II, 1, 1000–1001; Erik Björkman, *Studien über die Eigennamen im Beowulf* (Halle, 1920), pp. 72–73, 76–77; Chambers, *Beowulf: an Introduction*, p. 323.

[15] *Beowulf and the Seventh Century* (London, 1935).

[16] *The Audience of Beowulf*, pp. 26–33.

suggested,[17] is that after the downfall of the Geatish kingdom a number of the Geats made their way to England and there preserved the memory of former glories. This can be no more than a supposition, but it is a tempting one, for certainly Wiglaf's prophecy (ll. 2999–3007a) would have more point if written for an audience of Geatish, or partly Geatish, extraction.

In conclusion, it should be said that the alleged influence of BEOWULF upon later Anglo-Saxon literature, as outlined, for example, by Brandl,[18] is unsubstantiated, and it is likely that if a larger body of Anglo-Saxon poetry had been preserved, no such influence would have been asserted. The author of ANDREAS, which is much closer to BEOWULF in style and spirit than any other of the Anglo-Saxon saints' lives in verse, may have used BEOWULF as a model, but on the other hand the phrasal resemblances between the two poems may be quite coincidental.[19] As for other Anglo-Saxon poems, such parallels prove nothing beyond the existence of a common stylistic reservoir from which all poets could draw. The presence in Anglo-Saxon charters and other documents of topographical names embodying elements which also occur as personal names in BEOWULF (such as *Beowan ham*, *Grendeles mere*, *Grindeles pytt*, and *Scyldes treow*)[20] proves nothing beyond the existence in England of such name elements, from some of which (such as *Grendel*) the poet may have drawn in naming the non-historical characters of his poem. That BEOWULF was the great epic of the Anglo-Saxons, from which later periods of Anglo-Saxon culture drew inspiration, is a proposition which cannot be refuted but which is repugnant to common sense.

[17] Most recently by F. W. Moorman, *Essays and Studies* V (1914), 76–89' Erik Björkman, *Finsk Tidskrift* LXXXIV (1918), 263–264; D. Strömholm' *Edda* XXV (1926), 233–249, and R. Girvan, *Beowulf and the Seventh Century*' p. 80. Moorman's evidence from place names of the North Riding is, however, not borne out by the North Riding volume of the English Place-Name Society's publications.

[18] In Paul's *Grundriss der germanischen Philologie* (2d ed.), I, 1, 1009–1011.

[19] See the recent article by L. J. Peters, *PMLA* LXVI (1951), 844–863.

[20] Such names are treated most systematically by G. Binz, *Beiträge* XX (1895), 141–186; on the name Grendel, see also Chambers, *Beowulf: an Introduction*, pp. 304–308.

VIII

JUDITH

As has already been pointed out,[1] the 349 lines of JUDITH which are still preserved are no more than a fragment of what was once a much longer work. The original length of the poem may be estimated from two bodies of evidence: (1) the relation of the extant text to the poet's source, and (2) the section numbers in the manuscript.

It has long been recognized that the source of our poem was the Latin Vulgate text of the apocryphal book of Judith.[2] The poet, however, did not follow the Latin text closely but omitted many nonessential features of the narrative and introduced a number of expansions and transpositions designed to increase the dramatic effect of the whole. Because of this freedom with which he handled his original, it is not easy to determine the exact passage in the Latin text which corresponds to the beginning of the Anglo-Saxon fragment. It is, however, probable that ll. 1–7*a* of the poem are the conclusion of some observations by the poet on the heroine's prayer in Judith xii.8 of the Latin text. The only earlier passage of the Latin which seems to have been used in the extant part of the poem is Judith x.19, which corresponds to ll. 46*b*–54*a* of the poem; the *fleohnet* described in these lines is the same thing as the *conopeum* of Judith x.19, which is not referred to in the twelfth chapter of the Latin text. To all intents and purposes, the poem closes with the end of chapter xv of the Latin, when the defeat of the Assyrians has been accomplished; no reference is made to Judith's later life, and her long hymn of praise (Judith xvi.2–21 in the Latin text) is omitted, only a brief reference being made to it (ll. 341*b*-345*a*) before the poet closes his work with some moralizing remarks of his own.

[1] See above, p. xiii.

[2] The Vulgate text of Judith is not only shorter than the Greek Septuagint text but varies from it in many details and apparently represents a new recension by St. Jerome himself, who says, "multorum codicum varietatem vitiosissimam amputavi." The English Bible (either the King James version or the Revised Version of 1881–1895, in both of which the translation of Judith is based on the Septuagint) is therefore an even less satisfactory basis of comparison than in the case of other Anglo-Saxon biblical poetry.

The most striking modification of the narrative in the hands of the Anglo-Saxon poet is the reduction of the number of principal characters to three—Holofernes, Judith, and Judith's unnamed attendant. The other persons in the Latin text, the Jews Ozias and Joacim, Achior the Moabite, and Vagao, Holofernes's lieutenant (who in the Latin text discovers the headless corpse of his leader), do not appear at all. Though King Nebuchadnezzar is likewise not mentioned, it is not improbable that some allusion was made to him in the part of the poem now lost. It is to be noted, however, that Holofernes is referred to as ðeoden (ll. 11, 66, 91, 268), hlaford (l. 251), eorla dryhten (l. 21), sinces brytta (l. 30), winedryhten (l. 274), and by other terms ordinarily reserved for kings and princes, and it may be that the poet intended to represent him as king of the Assyrians as well as their general.

Besides simplifying the cast of characters, the poet has achieved greater economy in the narrative by reducing the numerous speeches of the Latin original to four, three of which are spoken by Judith herself. These four speeches are: ll. 83–94a, Judith's prayer, uttered before she kills Holofernes; ll. 152b–158, her announcement to the people of her return to Bethulia; ll. 177–198, her speech while showing Holofernes's head to her people; and ll. 285–289a, the announcement to the Assyrians, by one of their leaders (Vagao in the Latin text), of the death of their general. All of these four speeches which remain are much expanded from their originals and achieve a dramatic effect which is wholly lacking in the Latin text.

Among the more striking additions made by the poet are the extended explanation of the fleohnet and its uses (ll. 46b–54a), the prediction of the fate which awaits Holofernes in hell (ll. 112b–121), and the long description of the battle (ll. 199–246a, continued in ll. 261b–267a, 301–323a). The second of these passages has ample precedent in the work of earlier poets (as in ELENE 762b–771, JULIANA 678b–688a, and elsewhere); the battle scenes are in the best Germanic tradition and lose nothing by comparison with similar scenes elsewhere in Anglo-Saxon poetry.

Returning now to the problem of the original length of the poem, we may apply the evidence of the Latin original in the following way. The extant fragment of the poem, corresponding to the Latin

text from the middle of the twelfth chapter to the end of the fif-
teenth, embraces approximately 30 percent of the entire story.[3]   If
the proportion between the length of the Latin text and the length
of the Anglo-Saxon was constant throughout, we would have, as
the original length of the poem, somewhat less than twelve hundred
lines.   But in view of the freedom with which the poet handled
his source in the part of his work which is still preserved, such an
estimate is inconclusive, and corroborative evidence must be obtained from the section numbers in the manuscript.   As has already been shown,[4] the three full sections of the poem which still
remain average about a hundred and ten lines in length; if all the
sections were as long as these, the entire poem of twelve sections
would have run to about 1320 lines, more or less, or about the
same length as ELENE.   This is the figure adopted by Förster,[5]
and it is on the basis of it that he assumes the loss of three full
gatherings, or twenty-four folios, from the manuscript before fol.
202.[6]   The difference between 1200 lines, indicated by the evidence
of the Latin source, and 1320 lines, determined from the evidence
of the sectional divisions, is not great, and the two figures may be
reconciled by one of two assumptions: (1) that the poet was relatively fuller in his treatment of the early part of the story, perhaps
supplying an introductory exposition similar to the one in DANIEL,
or (2) that the sections were of relatively shorter length toward the
beginning of the poem.

We may, then, conclude with some confidence that in its complete
form JUDITH was a poem of twelve or thirteen hundred lines.   In
marked contrast to this estimate is the statement by Cook that
"the poem seems virtually complete as it now is."[7]   Pointing to
the double occurrence of the verb *tweode*, in l. 1*b* and l. 345*b*, as well

---

[3] In the Vulgate text of Judith, as far as the end of chapter xv, there are
315 verses, of which the part from xii.10 to the end of chapter xv contains
ninety-five.

[4] See above, p. xxvi.

[5] *Die Beowulf-Handschrift*, pp. 88f.

[6] See above, p. xiii. Since the 8 extant folios of the poem contain 343 lines
and the first word of another, 32 folios would contain between 1350 and 1400
lines.   This number is close enough to the 1320 lines assumed on the basis of
the sectional divisions.

[7] *Judith* (1904), p. 21.

as to the repetition of ll. 6*b*–7*a* in ll. 344*b*–345*a*, Cook adds that "the lines which here [in the extant text] stand first are echoed so significantly at the end that it is difficult to believe that more than a very few lines are missing." But this judgment, which seems unduly subjective, is hardly sufficient to outweigh the conclusions reached above.

On the question of the date of the poem there has been little agreement. The older scholars, even including ten Brink,[8] Wülker,[9] and Ebert,[10] grouped it with the Cædmonian poetry, not only because of the Old Testament subject matter but also because of the undoubted similarities in spirit and treatment to Exodus. Resemblances to the Cynewulfian poems have also been noted, particularly in vocabulary and style, and Sarrazin[11] went so far as to ascribe Judith to Cynewulf. Neumann,[12] on the basis of a much more thorough study of the poem than Sarrazin had made, also considered Cynewulf the probable author. But tests based on meter and grammatical forms all point to a much later date than either Cædmon or Cynewulf.

Metrically the most striking feature of the poem is the high frequency of expanded (three-stress) lines. There are no less than sixty-six regular expanded lines (ll. 2–12, 16–21, 30–34, 54–61, 63–68, 88–95, 97–99, 132, 272–273, 287–290, 337–348), besides two lines (ll. 96, 349) which have a normal first half-line but a second half-line which conforms to the expanded rather than to the normal pattern, and one line (l. 62) which appears to have been an expanded line but the second half of which has been lost.[13] The

---

[8] *Geschichte der englischen Litteratur* I (Berlin, 1877), 59f. But in the second edition, revised by Alois Brandl (Strassburg, 1899), Judith is grouped with Genesis B and other later poems.

[9] *Grundriss zur Geschichte der angelsächsischen Litteratur* (Leipzig, 1885), pp. 140–142.

[10] *Allgemeine Geschichte der Literatur des Mittelalters im Abendlande* III (Leipzig, 1887), 24–26.

[11] *Beowulf-Studien* (Berlin, 1888), pp. 160–165.

[12] *Über das altenglische Gedicht von Judith* (Kiel, 1892).

[13] Although these figures are different from those given by Pope, *The Rhythm of Beowulf*, p. 100, his identification of the expanded lines does not differ materially from mine. His count of 136 verses (i.e., "half-lines" in the terminology of this edition) includes both halves of each of the 66 expanded lines mentioned above, or a total of 132, plus ll. 62*a*, 96*b*, 349*a* (for which he suggests the emendation [*sæs*] *ond swegles dreamas*), and 349*b*.

expanded lines in JUDITH are thus nearly 20 percent of the entire number, a much higher proportion than we find in any other Anglo-Saxon poems except the DREAM OF THE ROOD and MAXIMS I.[14]

Frequent attention has also been called to the relatively large number of end-rimes in the poem. We find seven cases in which the first half of a line rimes with the second half (*grunde:funde*, l. 2; *sīne:wīne*, l. 29; *nēosan:forlēosan*, l. 63; *nǣs:wǣs*, l. 113; *bewunden:gebunden*, l. 115; *gūðe:ūðe*, l. 123; *scǣron:wǣron*, l. 304) and one case in which the second half of one line rimes with the first half of the next (*strēamas:drēamas*, ll. 348f.). In addition there are a number of imperfect rimes, *bedreste:gehlǣste*, l. 36, and *hyrde:gestȳrde*, l. 60, where the vowels are not identical; *rondwiggende:wēnde*, l. 20, *gecoste:eornoste*, l. 231, *þoligende:ende*, l. 272, and *gedyrsod:god*, l. 299, where a stressed syllable rimes with an unstressed syllable.[15]

Although the high frequency of expanded (three-stress) lines in JUDITH seems not to provide any certain evidence as to date, the end-rimes are of greater significance. Many years ago Friedrich Kluge, in a study of rime in Old Germanic verse,[16] showed that while end-rime appears sporadically in the earliest Anglo-Saxon poetry,[17] its frequency increases in the later periods, and that rime may, within limits, be used as a criterion of date. If we disregard the RIMING POEM (which is a *tour de force* and not to be reckoned as in the same tradition as the other extant Anglo-Saxon alliterative poetry), we find that JUDITH far surpasses all the other extant poems, even the BATTLE OF MALDON, in the frequency of its end-rimes. Kluge would therefore assign JUDITH to the tenth century.

---

[14] The DREAM OF THE ROOD has 31 expanded lines (plus two half-lines of the expanded type) in a total of 156, or approximately the same percentage as JUDITH; MAXIMS I has 69 expanded lines (plus a few half-lines) in a total of 204, or nearly 35 percent. Following Pope, I exclude GENESIS B from consideration here, since it is a translation from Old Saxon.

[15] In this account of the end-rimes I ignore suffix rimes, such as *dēman : brogan*, l. 4, *þinre : þearfendre*, l. 85, etc. Foster, in his account of the rimes (*Judith*, pp. 28–33), treats these on an equal basis with the others.

[16] *Beiträge* IX (1884), 422–450.

[17] In BEOWULF, for example, we find *yrremōd : stōd*, l. 726; *wēn : gēn*, l. 734; *gefǣgon : gepǣgon*, l. 1014; *herepād : gebād*, l. 2258, and *wrecan : sprecan*, l. 3172, besides a number of other rimes which go beyond the limits of a single line.

Luick,[18] on linguistic evidence derived from his metrical study of the poem, also considers it a late work, though he does not suggest a definite period. Furthermore, in addition to the evidence which has already been presented, we find in JUDITH certain metrical irregularities which point to a late date. For example, in l. 279, *his goldgifan gæstes gesne*, we have four alliterating syllables; in l. 149, *of ðære ginnan byrig hyre togeanes gan*, we have two alliterating syllables in the second half-line and only one in the first; and in l. 55 we have the very unusual alliteration of *sn* with *st*. If these lines are not corrupt, they are evidence of a weakening of metrical standards which may be paralleled in the BATTLE OF MALDON but is still foreign to the BATTLE OF BRUNANBURH. So far as the metrical evidence goes, then, it favors dating JUDITH in the tenth century, and in the middle or late rather than the early part of that century. If we assume an earlier date for the poem, we are faced by the paradox of a poet who was so familiar with the older poetry that he could produce a work in the heroic style which falls little short of his models but was at the same time not always able to imitate, or not always desirous of imitating, the older and more rigid alliterative patterns. Such poets existed late in the tenth century (as witness the author of MALDON) but, so far as we know, not at any earlier period.[19]

The question of the original dialect of JUDITH also requires consideration. Foster[20] called attention to the Anglian (or Kentish) form *þēgon* (West Saxon *þǣgon*), l. 19, as well as to several unsyncopated verb forms, *sēceð*, l. 96, *hafað*, l. 197, and the past participle *ārēted*, l. 167, which is required by the meter, inferring from these words that the original dialect of the poem was Anglian. His

---

[18] *Beiträge* XI (1886), 490f.

[19] Brandl, in Paul's *Grundriss der germanischen Philologie* (2d ed.), II, 1, 1091, dates the poem in the tenth century, and C. W. Kennedy, *The Earliest English Poetry*, p. 282, more precisely in the first half of that century. On the other hand, Kemp Malone, in *A Literary History of England*, edited by A. C. Baugh (New York, 1948), p. 68, assigns it to the ninth century, though he admits the possibility of a later date. G. K. Anderson, *The Literature of the Anglo-Saxons* (Princeton, 1949), p. 133, suggests the latter half of the ninth century. R. Imelmann, *Beiblatt zur Anglia* XIX (1908), 6, would date the poem as early as 850.

[20] *Judith*, pp. 49–53.

conclusions are accepted by Cook.[21]   If, then, the poet wrote in
the Anglian dialect, he must have been a Mercian, since the existence of a poet of such powers in Northumbria in the late tenth
century is very unlikely.   But there is no need whatever to assume
an Anglian origin for the poem.   As Tupper has pointed out,[22]
unsyncopated verb forms are by no means rare in West Saxon
poetry; in the Meters of Boethius, for example, besides the more
usual syncopated forms we find not only *sēceð*, Met. 19, 8; 19, 45;
22, 15, and *hafað*, Met. 8, 46; 9, 63, but also unsyncopated forms
of many other verbs, such as *scrīfeð*, Met. 10, 29, *wealdeð*, Met.
21, 33, and *weorðeð*, Met. 13, 56; 18, 9; 28, 76.   Nor does *þēgon*
necessarily point to Anglian origin, since, like *āgēted*, BRUNANBURH
18, and *bestēmed*, BRUSSELS CROSS 2, it may be the result of close
imitation of the older poetic formulas.   Tupper's conclusion, that
"there seems to be no good grounds for regarding the JUDITH as
anything else than a West Saxon poem," is amply justified by the
available evidence.

Of the author of JUDITH and the circumstances of composition
we know nothing at all, but some ingenious suggestions have been
made.   Cook in 1888 presented at some length the hypothesis that
the poem was "composed, in or about the year 856, in gratitude
for the deliverance of Wessex from the fury of the heathen North-
men" and that it was dedicated to Judith, the second wife of King
Æthelwulf.[23]   Foster, accepting Cook's theory that the poem was
written in honor of an Anglo-Saxon noblewoman but placing its
origin in Anglian territory rather than in Wessex, argued that it
was composed in commemoration of Æthelflæd, the "lady of the
Mercians," the heroic daughter of King Alfred who, after the death
in 910 of her husband the alderman Æthelred, conducted with
vigor the resistance of Mercia against the Danes.[24]   Both of these

---

[21] *Judith* (1904), p. viii.   Cook also regarded *hēhsta*, ll. 4, 94, and *nēhsta*, l. 73,
as indications of a northern origin; but as Foster (*Judith*, p. 50) had already
noted, such forms are not uncommon in late West Saxon.

[22] *Journal of English and Germanic Philology* XI (1912), 82–89.   See also
Imelmann's arguments to the same effect, *Beiblatt zur Anglia* XIX, 2–3.

[23] *Judith* (1888), pp. xxiv–xxxiv.   Cook's further conjecture that the author
was Swithhun, bishop of Winchester, is of no merit and need be mentioned only
in passing.

[24] *Judith*, pp. 89–90.

theories appeal to the historical imagination, but neither is supported by any concrete evidence. Cook's hypothesis puts too much weight on the identity of names and involves dating the poem much earlier than most present-day scholars are inclined to date it; Foster's is preferable on chronological grounds but still fails to inspire conviction. There is, after all, no need to assume that the poet had any contemporary figure in mind. He was not the first poet, or the last, to be attracted by the story of the Jewish heroine.[25]

IX

TABLE I

CONTENTS OF THE FOLIOS OF THE MANUSCRIPT

In the following table, the folio numbers are given first according to the official foliation, and then (in parentheses) according to the "old foliation" of the eighteenth century.

BEOWULF

Folio	Line	to	Line
132a (129a)	1 Hwæt		21 fæder
132b (129b)	21 [bea]rme		46 umborwe-
133a (130a)	46 -sende		68 wolde
133b (130b)	69 medoærn		91 reccan
134a (132a)	92 cwæð		113 gi-
134b (132b)	113 -gantas		134 lengra
135a (133a)	134 fyrst		158 folmum
135b (133b)	159 [ac se] æglæca		181 god
136a (134a)	182a ne		203 logon
136b (134b)	203 þeah		228 wurdon
137a (135a)	229 Þa		252 fyr
137b (135b)	252 heonan		273 soþlice
138a (136a)	273 secgan		297 lagustrea-
138b (136b)	297 -mas		319 wið
139a (137a)	319 wrað		339 hige-
139b (137b)	339 -þrymmum		360 maðelode
140a (138a)	360 to		379 XXX-

[25] Ælfric's semi-rhythmical life of Judith, edited by B. Assmann, *Angelsächsische Homilien und Heiligenleben* (Kassel, 1889), pp. 102–116, seems to have no relation to the poem and need not be discussed here.

Folio	Line	to	Line
140*b* (138*b*)	379 -tiges		401 se
141*a* (139*a*)	401 hearda		423 wræc
141*b* (139*b*)	423 Wedera		444 he
142*a* (140*a*)	444 oft		464 Ar-
142*b* (140*b*)	464 -scyldinga		486 eal
143*a* (141*a*)	486 bencþelu		504 æfre
143*b* (141*b*)	504 mærða		523 beagas
144*a* (142*a*)	523 Beot		544 æt-
144*b* (142*b*)	544 -somne		565 mecum
145*a* (143*a*)	565 wunde		588 in
145*b* (143*b*)	588 helle		608 gelyfde
146*a* (144*a*)	609 brego		629 wiga
146*b* (144*b*)	629 æt		654 winærnes
147*a* (145*a*)	654 geweald		676 Beowulf
147*b* (145*b*)	676 Geata		697 gewiofu
148*a* (146*a*)	697 Wedera		718 ær
148*b* (146*b*)	718 ne		740 ge-
149*a* (131*a*)	740 -feng		762 mæra
149*b* (131*b*)	762 [þ]ær		782 sweg
150*a* (147*a*)	782 up		804 sigewæpnum
150*b* (147*b*)	804 forsworen		827 wið
151*a* (148*a*)	827 niðe		849 heolfre
151*b* (148*b*)	849 heorodreore		872 snyttrum
152*a* (149*a*)	872 styrian		895 dome
152*b* (149*b*)	895 sæbat		918 scynded
153*a* (150*a*)	918 Eode		938 beweredon
153*b* (150*b*)	939 scuccum		963 hrædlice
154*a* (151*a*)	963 heardan		986 hilde[1]
154*b* (151*b*)	986 hilderinces		1009 healle
155*a* (152*a*)	1009 gang		1032 fela
155*b* (152*b*)	1032 laf		1053 yr-
156*a* (153*a*)	1053 -felafe		1075 gare
156*b* (153*b*)	1075 wunde		1097 aðum
157*a* (154*a*)	1097 benemde		1119 wand
157*b* (154*b*)	1119 to		1139 swiðor
158*a* (155*a*)	1139 þohte		1159 læddon
158*b* (155*b*)	1159 to		1175 þæt
159*a* (156*a*)	1175 þu		1195 hrin-
159*b* (156*b*)	1195 -gas		1217 hæle
160*a* (157*a*)	1217 ond		1241 ge-
160*b* (157*b*)	1241 -beag		1264 gemearcod

[1] The letters *hilde*, at the end of fol. 154*a*, are repeated at the beginning of fol. 154*b*.

Folio	Line	to	Line
206a (203a)	154 murnan		176 æðele
206b (203b)	176 to		198 mine
207a (204a)	198 hand		221 scuras
207b (204b)	222 hildenædran		247 hæleð
208a (205a)	247 slæpe		272 ende
208b (205b)	273 eades		296 to
209a (206a)	296 frofre		322 wæron
209b (206b)	323 cwicera		344 sigorlean

X

TABLE II

SECTIONAL DIVISIONS IN THE POEMS

BEOWULF

[ ] Beow.	1–52	XXII Beow.	1473–1556
I Beow.	53–114	XXIII Beow.	1557–1650
II Beow.	115–188	XXIIII Beow.	1651–1739
III Beow.	189–257	XXV Beow.	1740–1816
IIII Beow.	258–319	XXVI[1] Beow.	1817–1887
V Beow.	320–370	XXVII[2] Beow.	1888–1962
VI Beow.	371–455	XXVIII[3] Beow.	1963–2038
VII Beow.	456–498	[ ] Beow.	2039–2143
VIII Beow.	499–558	XXXI Beow.	2144–2220
VIIII Beow.	559–661	XXXII Beow.	2221–2311
X Beow.	662–709	XXXIII Beow.	2312–2390
XI Beow.	710–790	XXXIIII Beow.	2391–2459
XII Beow.	791–836	XXXV Beow.	2460–2601
XIII Beow.	837–924	XXXVI Beow.	2602–2693
XIIII Beow.	925–990	XXXVII Beow.	2694–2751
XV Beow.	991–1049	XXXVIII Beow.	2752–2820
XVI Beow.	1050–1124	[XXXVIIII] Beow.	2821–2891
XVII Beow.	1125–1191	XL[4] Beow.	2892–2945
XVIII Beow.	1192–1250	XLI Beow.	2496–3057
XVIIII Beow.	1251–1320	XLII Beow.	3058–3136
XX Beow.	1321–1382	XLIII Beow.	3137–3182
XXI Beow.	1383–1472		

JUDITH

[IX] Jud.	1–14	XI Jud.	122–235
X Jud.	15–121	XII Jud.	236–349

[1] Originally written *XXVII*, but the last *I* erased.
[2] Originally written *XXVIII*, but the last *I* erased.
[3] Originally written *XXVIIII*, but the last *I* erased.
[4] Originally written *XLI*, but the *I* erased.

XI

TABLE III

SMALL CAPITALS IN THE POEMS

In the three words which are followed by question marks within parentheses, the initial letter is larger than ordinary, but is of the shape of a small letter rather than of a capital; it is uncertain in these cases whether the scribe intended a small capital, but it is probable that he did.

In five cases, small capitals have been lost at the edges of the parchment and are given here on the authority of Thorkelin A; they are marked "(A)."

BEOWULF

20 Swa	907 Swylce	1694 Swa
38 Ne	1035 Heht	1711 Ne (A)
43 Nalæs	1048 Swa	1730 Seleð
80 He	1077 Syþðan (A)[1]	1777 Ic
99 Swa	1142 Swa	1807 Heht
109 Ne	1168 Spræc	1814 Eode (A)
118 Fand (?)	1215 Wealhðeo	1822 Gif
144 Swa	1232 Eode	1829 Ic
175 Hwilum	1392 Ic	1840 Hroðgar
234 Gewat	1455 Næs	1999 Biowulf
452 Onsend	1482 Swylce	2093 To
473 Sorh	1497 Sona	2119 Siðode
480 Ful (?)	1518 Ongeat	2267 Swa
642 Þa (?)	1537 Gefeng	2794 Ic
655 Næfre	1545 Ofsæt	2877 Ic
723 Onbræd	1550 Hæfde	2880 Symle
830 Swylce	1573 Hwearf	2922 Ne
852 Hæþene (A)	1591 Sona	2928 Sona
864 Hwilum	1618 Sona	2971 Ne
883 Hæfdon	1623 Com	3087 Ic
886 Syþðan	1626 Eodon (A)	3101 Uton
898 Se	1659 Ne	

JUDITH

28 Swa	83 Ic	143 Swa

[1] This small capital is at least doubtful, but it is considered probable by Malone, *PMLA* LXIV, 1200.

XII

TABLE IV

ACCENT MARKS IN THE POEMS

In compiling the list of accent marks in BEOWULF, I have put more dependence on the statements of Chambers and Sedgefield than on Zupitza's transcription of the manuscript. Entries which are marked "(C)" are not clear in Zupitza's facsimile and are not reported by Sedgefield but are given on the authority of Chambers. Entries marked "(?)" are recorded by Zupitza but not by Sedgefield and are considered doubtful or are not recorded at all by Chambers. The twelve entries marked "(A)" are based on Thorkelin's transcript A. In one of these words, *sǽ geatas*, l. 1850, the *ǽ* is now lost from the manuscript; in the other eleven words an accent mark seems possible on the evidence of the facsimile but has not been recorded by any of the recent students of the manuscript.

The list of accent marks in JUDITH is based on photostats, which are much clearer than Zupitza's facsimile of BEOWULF, and on my own notes on this part of the manuscript.

BEOWULF

33 út fus	564 sǽ | grunde	1147 hám (A)
100 án (C)	579 sǽ	1149 sǽ siðe
123 gewát	603 mót	1162 wín (?)
128 wóp	660 gád	1163 gán (?)
210 gewát	681 nát	1167 mód
211 bát	690 sǽ rinc	1168 ár fæst (?)
264 gebád	742 bát (?)	1177 brúc
300 hál	759 astód	1187 ǽr
301 bád	775 ábeag	1201 rǽd
336 ár	780 bán fag	1223 sǽ
357 un hár	821 wíc	1233 wín
386 hát	895 sǽ bat	1274 ge wát
gán	911 on fón	1275 deaþ wíc
442 mót (C)	975 sár	1297 hád
449 ángenga	1038 fáh	1307 hár (C)
507 sǽ	1116 bán fatu (A)	1313 bád
537 gársecg	dón	1325 rún wita
544 sǽ (C)	1121 blód (A)	1331 wát

BEOWULF

1371 ǽr (C)	2086 síd (C)	2631 wig láf
1388 ǽr	2090 gedón	2641 gár | wigend
1390 áris	2103 cóm	2655 fáne
1394 gá	2109 sarlíc	2661 wæl réc[5]
1407 hám	2147 dóm (C)	2666 dóm (?)
1445 bán cofan	2155 hroðgár	2674 gár wigan (?)
1491 dóm	2166 dón (A)[1]	2679 stód
1516 fǽr gripe (A)	2196 brego stól (C)	2681 geswác (?)
1528 dóm (C)	2210 án[2]	2689 fýr draca
1546 brún ecg	2230 fǽr[3]	2701 fýr
1562 gód	2258 here pád	2716 wís hycgende (C)
1587 ǽr	gebád	2736 bád
1626 tó geanes (A)	2263 gód (?)	2743 líf
1652 sǽlac (A)	2270 hrán (?)	2751 líf
1685 sǽm (A)	2280 án (C)	2769 stód
1720 ge bád	2287 onwóc (C)	2820 dóm
1850 sǽ geatas (A)	2302 on bád (C)	2858 dóm
1863 lác	2308 fór	2898 ge rád
wát (?)	2342 ær gód	2944 cóm
1870 gód	2346 wíd flogan	2964 dóm (?)
1882 sǽ genga	2376 cyne dóm (C)	2992 becóm
1883 rád	2468 sár	3010 ád fære
1895 scír hame	2514 mán sceaða	3025 fús
1896 sǽ geap	2543 gód (A)[4]	3063 ellen róf
1924 sǽ wealle	2553 hárne	3076 wig láf
1960 wóc (?)	stán	3116 gebád
1962 gár | mundes	2558 hilde swát	3119 fús
1965 scán	2559 on swáf	3123 inwit hróf (?)
1966 fús	2568 bád	3138 ád
2002 [orleg] | hwíl	2577 gewác	3144 wud[u] réc
2043 gár cwealm (A)	2584 ge swác	3147 bán
2080 líc	2586 ærgód	hús (?)
2084 róf	2607 wíc | stede	3164 ǽr (A)

---

[1] Thorkelin A has *dōn*, but the tilde is evidently an error for the accent mark which Thorkelin's copyist saw (or thought he saw) in the manuscript.

[2] So originally, according to Zupitza, but now *ón*.

[3] So originally, according to Zupitza, but now *fǽs*.

[4] Thorkelin A has *gōd*, but the tilde is evidently an error for an accent mark in the manuscript.

[5] With *réc* altered from *rǽc* by erasure.

JUDITH

BIBLIOGRAPHY

I. MANUSCRIPT AND TRANSCRIPTS

1705 Wanley, Humphrey. Antiquæ literaturæ Septentrionalis Liber Alter. Seu . . . Librorum Vett. Septentrionalium, qui in Angliæ Bibliothecis extant, nec non multorum Vett. Codd. Septentrionalium alibi extantium Catalogus Historico-Criticus. Oxford, 1705. [Description of the MS., pp. 218f.]

1826 Conybeare, John J. See under III, below. [Collation of Thorkelin's edition of Beowulf with the MS., pp. 137–155.]

1872 Sievers, Eduard. Collationen angelsächsischer Gedichte. *Zeitschrift für deutsches Altertum* XV, 456–467. [Collation of Judith, pp. 461–462.]

1876 Kölbing, Eugen. Zur Beovulf-Handschrift. *Archiv* LVI, 91–118. [See also Kölbing's comments in *Englische Studien* V (1881), 241.]

1881 Holder, Alfred. Beowulf. I. Abdruck der Handschrift. Freiburg i.B., 1881 (2d ed., 1882; 3d ed., 1895).

1882 Zupitza, Julius. Beowulf. Autotypes of the Unique Cotton MS. Vitellius A xv in the British Museum. London, 1882.

1883 Wülker, Richard P. See under II, 1, below. [Diplomatic text of Beowulf, Vol. I, pp. 18–148.]

1890 Davidson, Charles. Differences between the Scribes of Beowulf. *Modern Language Notes* V, 85–89. [See also C. F. McClumpha, *ibid.*, pp. 245–246; C. Davidson, *ibid.*, pp. 378–379.]

1916 Sisam, Kenneth. The Beowulf Manuscript. *Modern Language Review* XI, 335–337.

1919 Förster, Max. Die Beowulf-Handschrift. (Berichte über die Verhandlungen der sächsischen Akademie der Wissenschaften, Vol. LXXI, No. 4.) Leipzig, 1919.

1920 Rypins, Stanley I. The Beowulf Codex. *Modern Philology* XVII, 541–547.

1921 Rypins, Stanley I. A Contribution to the Study of the Beowulf Codex. *PMLA* XXXVI, 167–185.

1923 Keller, Wolfgang. [Review of Förster, Die Beowulf-Handschrift.] *Anglia*, Beiblatt XXXIV, 1–5.

1924 Rypins, Stanley I. Three Old English Prose Texts in MS. Cotton Vitellius A xv. London, 1924. [Description of the MS., pp. vii–xxix.]

1928 Hoops, Johannes. Die Foliierung der Beowulf-Handschrift. *Englische Studien* LXIII, 1–11.

1928 Hulbert, James R. The Accuracy of the B-Scribe of Beowulf. *PMLA* XLIII, 1196–1199.

1929 Prokosch, Eduard. Two Types of Scribal Errors in the Beowulf MS. *In* Studies in English Philology . . . in Honor of Frederick Klaeber (Minneapolis, 1929), pp. 196–207.

1932 Rypins, Stanley I. The Beowulf Codex. *Colophon*, Part 10, [second item, not paged].

1938 Smith, A. H. The Photography of Manuscripts. *London Mediæval Studies*, Vol. I, Part 2, pp. 179–207.

1941– Malone, Kemp. Thorkelin's Transcripts of Beowulf. *Studia*
1942 *Neophilologica* XIV, 25–30.

1949 Malone, Kemp. The Text of Beowulf. *Proceedings of the American Philosophical Society* XCIII, 239–243.

1949 Malone, Kemp. Readings from the Thorkelin Transcripts of Beowulf. *PMLA* LXIV, 1190–1218.

1951 Malone, Kemp. The Thorkelin Transcripts of Beowulf in Facsimile. Copenhagen, London, and Baltimore, 1951.

II. COMPLETE TEXTS

1. Beowulf[1]

1815 Thorkelin, Grim. Johnson. De Danorum rebus gestis secul. III & IV. poëma danicum dialecto anglosaxonica. Copenhagen, 1815.

1833– Kemble, John M. The Anglo-Saxon Poems of Beowulf, the
1837 Traveller's Song, and the Battle of Finnesburh. Vol. I, London, 1833 (2d ed., 1835); Vol. II, London, 1837.

1847 Schaldemose, Frederik. Beo-Wulf og Scopes Widsið, to angelsaxiske Digte. Copenhagen, 1847 (2d ed., 1851).

1855 Thorpe, Benjamin. The Anglo-Saxon Poems of Beowulf, the Scop or Gleeman's Tale, and the Fight at Finnesburg. Oxford, 1855 (2d ed., 1875).

---

[1] To the editions of Beowulf here listed should be added the unpublished edition made by Eduard Sievers according to the principles of "Schallanalyse" and preserved in the library of the University of Leipzig. Citations from this edition in the Notes are based on Holthausen's 8th edition of the poem or on his statements in *Literaturblatt* LIX, 163ff.

1857   Grein, Christian W. M.   Bibliothek der angelsächsischen Poesie. Vol. I.   Göttingen, 1857.   [Beowulf, pp. 255–341.]

1861   Grundtvig, N. F. S.   Beowulfes Beorh eller Bjovulfs-Drapen. Copenhagen, 1861.

1863   Heyne, Moritz.   Beowulf.   Paderborn, 1863 (2d ed., 1868; 3d ed., 1873; 4th ed., 1879; 5th ed., revised by Adolf Socin, 1888; 6th ed., 1898; 7th ed., 1903; 8th ed., revised by Levin L. Schücking, 1908; 9th ed., 1910; 10th ed., 1913; 11th–12th ed., 1918; 13th ed., 1929; 14th ed., 1931; 15th ed., revised by Else von Schaubert, 1940).

1867   Grein, Christian W. M.   Beovulf nebst den Fragmenten Finnsburg und Valdere.   Cassel and Göttingen, 1867.

1875   Ettmüller, Ludwig.   Carmen de Beovulfi Gautarum regis rebus praeclare gestis atque interitu, quale fuerit ante quam in manus interpolatoris, monachi Vestsaxonici, inciderat.   Zürich, 1875. [Reduced to 2896 lines by the omission of the "Christian" passages.]

1876   Arnold, Thomas.   Beowulf, a Heroic Poem of the Eighth Century.   London, 1876.

1883   Harrison, James A., and Robert Sharp.   Beowulf, an Anglo-Saxon Poem; The Fight at Finnsburh, a Fragment.   Boston, 1883 (4th ed., 1894).

1883   Wülker, Richard P.   Bibliothek der angelsächsischen Poesie. Vol. I.   Kassel, 1883.   [Critical text of Beowulf, pp. 149–277.]

1884   Holder, Alfred.   Beowulf.   IIa. Berichtigter Text.   Freiburg i.B., 1884 (2d ed., 1899).

1888   Socin, Adolf.   See under Moritz Heyne, above.

1894   Wyatt, Alfred J.   Beowulf.   Cambridge, 1894 (2d ed., 1898).

1904   Trautmann, Moritz.   Das Beowulflied.   Als Anhang das Finn-Bruchstück und die Waldhere-Bruchstücke.   (Bonner Beitrage, Vol. XVI.)   Bonn, 1904.

1905–   Holthausen, Ferdinand.   Beowulf nebst dem Finnsburg-Bruch-
1906   stück.   Part 1, Heidelberg, 1905 (2d ed., 1908; 3d ed., 1912; 4th ed., 1914; 5th ed., 1921; 6th ed., 1929; 7th ed., 1938; 8th ed., 1948; addenda and errata to 8th ed. in *Archiv* CLXXXVII [1950], 125–126). Part 2, Heidelberg, 1906 (2d ed., 1909; 3d ed., 1913; 4th ed., 1919; 5th ed., 1929).

1908   Schücking, Levin L.   See under Moritz Heyne, above.

1910   Sedgefield, W. J.   Beowulf.   Manchester, 1910 (2d ed., 1913; 3d ed., 1935).

1914   Chambers, R. W.   Beowulf with the Finnsburg Fragment. Cambridge, 1914 (2d ed., 1920).   [Nominally a revision of Wyatt's edition, but actually an entirely new work.]

1922 Klaeber, Fr. Beowulf and the Fight at Finnsburg. Boston,
      1922 (2d ed., with supplement, 1928; 3d ed., 1936; supplement,
      1941; second supplement, 1950).
1940 Schaubert, Else von. See under Moritz Heyne, above.

2. *Judith*

1698 Thwaites, Edward. Heptateuchus, Liber Job, et Evangelium
      Nicodemi; Anglo-Saxonice. Historiæ Judith Fragmentum;
      Dano-Saxonice. Oxford, 1698.
1834 Thorpe, Benjamin. Analecta Anglo-Saxonica. London, 1834
      (2d ed., 1846).
1838 Leo, Heinrich. See under III, below.
1850 Ettmüller, Ludwig. See under III, below.
1857 Grein, Christian W. M. See under II, 1 above. [Judith, pp.
      120–129.]
1858 Nilsson, Lars G. Judith, Fragment af ett fornengelskt Qväde.
      Copenhagen, 1858.
1861 Rieger, Max. See under III, below.
1876 Sweet, Henry. See under III, below.
1880 Körner, Karl. Einleitung in das Studium des Angelsächsischen.
      Part 2. Heilbronn, 1880.
1888 Cook, Albert S. Judith, an Old English Epic Fragment. Bos-
      ton, 1888 (2d ed., 1889).
1888 Kluge, Friedrich. Angelsächsisches Lesebuch. Halle, 1888 (2d
      ed., 1897; 3d ed., 1902; 4th ed., 1915).
1894 Wülker, Richard P. Bibliothek der angelsächsischen Poesie.
      Vol. II. Leipzig, 1894. [Judith, pp. 294–314.]
1904 Cook, Albert S. Judith, an Old English Epic Fragment. Boston
      and London, 1904.
1923 Craigie, William A. Specimens of Anglo-Saxon Poetry. I. Bib-
      lical and Classical Themes. Edinburgh, 1923.

III. Partial Texts

1826 Conybeare, John J. Illustrations of Anglo-Saxon Poetry. Lon-
      don, 1826. [About 800 lines of Beowulf.]
1838 Leo, Heinrich. Altsächsische und angelsächsische Sprachproben.
      Halle, 1838. [Beowulf 1063–1162a, Judith.]
1847 Ebeling, Friedrich W. Angelsæchsisches Lesebuch. Leipzig,
      1847. [Beowulf 1063–1124.]
1849 Klipstein, Louis F. Analecta Anglo-Saxonica. Vol. II. New
      York, 1849. [Beowulf 1–114, 320–370, 499–661, 710–790, 1321–
      1382, 2694–2751, 3137–3182, Judith 15–349.]

1850 Ettmüller, Ludwig. Engla and Seaxna Scopas and Boceras. Quedlinburg and Leipzig, 1850. [Beowul 210–498, 607–661, 710–836, 991–1650, 2516–2820, 3110–3182, Judith.]

1861 Rieger, Max. Alt- und angelsächsisches Lesebuch. Giessen, 1861. [Beowulf 867–915, 1008–1250, 2417–2541, 2724–2820, 2845–2891, Judith.]

1870 March, Francis A. Introduction to Anglo-Saxon. New York, 1870. [Beowulf 1–11, 26–52, 64–82a, 99–129a, 144–152a, 194–269, 286–292, 301–319, 611–646a, 651b–653, 1455–1464, 1512b–1536, 1557–1564, 1687–1698a, 1789b–1803a.]

1876 Sweet, Henry. An Anglo-Saxon Reader. Oxford, 1876 (4th ed., 1884; 7th ed., 1894; 9th ed., revised by C. T. Onions, 1922; 10th ed., 1946). [Beowulf 1251–1650, Judith.]

1893 MacLean, G. E. An Old and Middle English Reader. New York, 1893. [Judith 122–235.]

1896 Smith, C. Alphonso. An Old English Grammar and Exercise Book. Boston, 1896 (2d ed., 1898). [Beowulf 611–661, 739–836, 2711b–2751, 2792b–2820.]

1915 Zupitza, J., and J. Schipper. Alt- und mitte'englisches Übungsbuch. 11th ed., Vienna and Leipzig, 1915. This first appeared as J. Zupitza, Altenglisches Übungsbuch, Vienna, 1874. [Judith 122–235.]

1919 Schücking, Levin L. Kleines angelsächsisches Dichterbuch. Texte und Textproben, mit kurzer Einleitung und ausführlichem Wörterbuch. Cöthen, 1919. [Beowulf 1063–1160a, 1888–2199.]

1919 Wyatt, Alfred J. An Anglo-Saxon Reader. Cambridge, 1919. [Beowulf 1–52, 499–606, 1251–1309, 1572b–1676, 1866–1919, 2270b–2344, Judith 15–121, 246b–291a.]

1922 Sedgefield, W. J. An Anglo-Saxon Verse Book. Manchester, 1922. [About 1160 lines of Beowulf.]

1927 Turk, Milton H. An Anglo-Saxon Reader. New York, 1927. [Beowulf 1–52, 194–331a, 702b–836.]

1929 Krapp, George P., and Arthur G. Kennedy. An Anglo-Saxon Reader. New York, 1929. [Beowulf 64–158, 710–836, 2550–2835.]

1931 Craigie, William A. Specimens of Anglo-Saxon Poetry. III. Germanic Legend and Anglo-Saxon History and Life. Edinburgh, 1931. [Beowulf 1–85, 456–469, 871b–915, 1063–1159a, 1197–1214a, 1706b–1722a, 1931b–1962, 2020–2069a, 2354b–2396, 2425–2508a, 2602–2625a, 2900–3007a.]

1931 Naumann, Hans. Frühgermanisches Dichterbuch. Berlin, 1931. [Beowulf 867b–897, 1063–1159a, 3137–3182.]

1935 Anderson, Marjorie, and Blanche Colton Williams. Old English
      Handbook. Boston, 1935. [Beowulf 491–661, 1345–1376,
      2669–2711.]
1939 Lehnert, Martin. Beowulf: eine Auswahl. Berlin, 1939. [Some
      1044 lines of Beowulf.]
1945 Mossé, Fernand. Manuel de l'anglais du moyen âge des origines
      au XIVe siècle. I. Vieil-anglais. Paris, 1945. [Beowulf 499–
      603a, 710–836, 1345–1376a, 2711b–2820, Judith 159–235,
      291b–349.]

IV. TRANSLATIONS[1]

1. Beowulf

1815 Thorkelin, Grim. Johnson. See under II, 1, above. [Latin.]
1820 Grundtvig, N. F. S. Bjowulfs Drape. Copenhagen, 1820.
      [Danish, in ballad meter.]
1837 Kemble, John M. See under II, 1, above. [English prose.]
1840 Ettmüller, Ludwig. Beowulf, Heldengedicht des achten Jahr-
      hunderts. Zürich, 1840. [German verse.]
1847 Schaldemose, Frederik. See under II, 1 above. [Danish.]
1849 Wackerbarth, A. D. Beowulf, Translated into English Verse.
      London, 1849.
1855 Thorpe, Benjamin. See under II, 1, above. [English, literal.]
1857 Grein, Christian W. M. Dichtungen der Angelsachsen stabrei-
      mend übersetzt. Vol. I. Göttingen, 1857. [German verse.]
1859 Simrock, Karl. Beowulf. Stuttgart and Augsburg, 1859. [Ger-
      man verse.]
1863 Heyne, Moritz. Beowulf, angelsächsisches Heldengedicht. Pa-
      derborn, 1863 (2d ed., 1898; 3d ed., 1915). [German verse.]
1872 Von Wohlzogen, Hans. Beovulf aus dem Angelsächsischen.
      Leipzig, 1872. [German verse.]
1876 Arnold, Thomas. See under II, 1, above. [English prose.]
1877 Botkine, L. Beowulf, épopée anglo-saxonne. Havre, 1877.
      [French prose.]
1881 Lumsden, H. W. Beowulf ... Translated into Modern Rhymes.
      London, 1881.
1882 Garnett, James M. Beowulf; an Anglo-Saxon Poem and The
      Fight at Finnsburg. Boston, 1882 (2d ed., 1885; 4th ed., 1900).
      [English verse.]

---

[1] Paraphrases of *Beowulf* and free translations intended for children or for
schools are not included here. No account has been taken of partial translations
of either poem.

1883 Grion, Giusto. Beovulf, poema epico anglosassone del VII secolo. Lucca, 1883. [Italian.]

1889 Wickberg, Rudolf. Beovulf, en fornengelsk hjältedikt. Westervik, 1889. [Swedish verse.]

1892 Earle, John. The Deeds of Beowulf. Oxford, 1892. [English prose.]

1892 Hall, John Lesslie. Beowulf, an Anglo-Saxon Epic Poem. Boston, 1892. [English verse.]

1893 Hoffmann, P. Beowulf ... aus dem Angelsächsischen übertragen. Züllichau, 1893. [German verse.]

1895 Morris, William, and A. J. Wyatt. The Tale of Beowulf, Sometime King of the Folk of the Weder Geats. Hammersmith, 1895 (2d ed., London, 1898). [English verse.]

1896 Simons, L. Beowulf, angelsaksisch Volksepos, vertaald in stafrijm. Ghent, 1896. [Dutch verse.]

1898 Steineck, H. Altenglische Dichtungen ... in wortgetreuer Übersetzung. Leipzig, 1898. [German, literal.]

1901 Hall, John R. Clark. Beowulf and the Fight at Finnsburg. London, 1901 (2d ed., under the title "Beowulf and the Finnsburg Fragment," 1911; new ed., revised by C. L. Wrenn and J. R. R. Tolkien, 1940; new ed., revised by C. L. Wrenn and J. R. R. Tolkien, 1950). [English prose.]

1902 Tinker, Chauncey B. Beowulf. New York, 1902 (2d ed., 1910). [English prose.]

1904 Child, Clarence G. Beowulf and the Finnesburh Fragment. Boston, 1904. [English prose.]

1904 Trautmann, Moritz. See under II, 1, above. [German, literal.]

1905 Vogt, Paul. Beowulf, altenglisches Heldengedicht. Halle, 1905. [German verse.]

1906 Gering, Hugo. Beowulf nebst dem Finnsburg-Bruchstück. Heidelberg, 1906 (2d ed., 1914). [German verse.]

1907 Huyshe, Wentworth. Beowulf, an Old English Epic. London and New York, 1907. [English prose.]

1909 Gummere, Francis B. The Oldest English Epic: Beowulf, Finnsburg, Waldere, Deor, Widsith, and the German Hildebrand. New York, 1909. [English verse.]

1910 Hansen, Adolf. Bjovulf [edited after the translator's death by Viggo Julius von Holstein Rathlou]. Copenhagen and Christiania, 1910. [Danish verse.]

1912 Pierquin, Hubert. Le poème anglo-saxon de Beowulf. Paris, 1912. [French prose; based on Kemble's text, reprinted on the opposite pages.]

1913   Kirtlan, Ernest J. B. The Story of Beowulf. London, 1913.
       [English prose.]

1914   Hall, John R. Clark. Beowulf, a Metrical Translation into Mod-
       ern English. Cambridge, 1914.

1916   Benedetti, A. La canzone di Beowulf, poema epico anglo-sassone
       del VI secolo. Palermo, 1916. [Italian.]

1919   Thomas, W. Beowulf et les premiers fragments épiques anglo-
       saxons. Paris, 1919. [French prose.]

1921   Rytter, Henrik. Beowulf og Striden um Finnsborg. Oslo, 1921.
       [Norwegian landsmaal.]

1921   Scott Moncrieff, Charles K. Beowulf Translated. London, 1921.
       [English verse.]

1923   Gordon, R. K. The Song of Beowulf. London and New York,
       1923. [English prose.]

1923   Leonard, William Ellery. Beowulf, a New Verse Translation.
       New York and London, 1923.

1925   Strong, Archibald. Beowulf Translated into Modern English
       Rhyming Verse. London, 1925.

1926   Crawford, D. H. Beowulf Translated into English Verse. Lon-
       don, 1926.

1926   Gordon, Robert K. Anglo-Saxon Poetry. London and Toronto,
       1926. [English prose.]

1934   Olivero, Federico. Beowulf. Turin, 1934. [Italian; based on
       Chambers's text, reprinted on the opposite pages.]

1935   Green, A. Wigfall. Beowulf, Literally Translated. Boston,
       1935.

1940   Kennedy, Charles W. Beowulf, the Oldest English Epic, Trans-
       lated into Alliterative Verse. New York and London, 1940.

1945   Bone, Gavin. Beowulf, in Modern Verse. Oxford, 1945.

1949   Waterhouse, Mary E. Beowulf in Modern English: a Transla-
       tion in Blank Verse. Cambridge, 1949.

2. Judith

1857   Grein, Christian W. M. See under IV, 1, above. [German
       verse.]

1858   Nilsson, Lars G. See under II, 2, above. [Swedish.]

1880   Körner, Karl. See under II, 2, above. [German, literal.]

1888   Cook, Albert S. See under II, 2, above.

1888   Morley, Henry. English Writers. II. From Cædmon to the
       Conquest. London, 1888. [English verse; later reprinted in
       A. S. Cook and C. B. Tinker, Select Translations from Old
       English Poetry (Boston, 1902).]

1889 Garnett, James M. Elene; Judith; Athelstan, or the Fight at Brunanburh; and Byrhtnoth, or the Fight at Maldon. Anglo-Saxon Poems. Boston, 1889. [English verse.]

1902 Hall, John Lesslie. Judith, Phoenix and Other Anglo-Saxon Poems. New York, 1902. [English verse.]

1926 Gordon, Robert K. See under IV, 1, above. [English prose.]

V. GENERAL WORKS

1839 Leo, Heinrich. Beowulf, dasz älteste deutsche, in angelsächsischer Mundart erhaltene, Heldengedicht nach seinem Inhalte, und nach seinen historischen und mythologischen Beziehungen betrachtet. Halle, 1839.

1883 Möller, Hermann. Das altenglische Volksepos in der ursprünglichen strophischen Form. Kiel, 1883.

1888 Sarrazin, Gregor. Beowulf-Studien. Berlin, 1888.

1888 ten Brink, Bernhard. Beowulf: Untersuchungen. Strassburg, 1888.

1889 Müllenhoff, Karl. Beovulf: Untersuchung über das angelsächsische Epos und die älteste Geschichte der germanischen Seevölker. Berlin, 1889.

1892 Foster, T. G. Judith: Studies in Metre, Language and Style, with a View to Determining the Date of the Oldenglish Fragment and the Home of Its Author. Strassburg, 1892.

1921 Chambers, R. W. Beowulf: an Introduction to the Study of the Poem with a Discussion of the Stories of Offa and Finn. Cambridge, 1921 (2d ed., 1932).

1928 Lawrence, W. W. Beowulf and Epic Tradition. Cambridge, Mass., 1928.

1935 Girvan, Ritchie. Beowulf and the Seventh Century. London, 1935.

1936 Malone, Kemp. Widsith. London, 1936.

1951 Whitelock, Dorothy. The Audience of Beowulf. Oxford, 1951.

VI. TEXTUAL CRITICISM

1854 Bouterwek, K. W. Cædmon's des Angelsachsen biblische Dichtungen I (Gütersloh, 1854), pp. c–cxviii. [Beowulf 15, 21.]

1856 Bouterwek, K. W. Zur Kritik des Beowulfliedes. *Zeitschrift für deutsches Altertum* XI, 59–113.

1859 Dietrich, Franz. Rettungen. *Zeitschrift für deutsches Altertum* XI, 409–448.

1862 Grein, Christian W. M. Die historischen Verhältnisse des Beo-
      wulfliedes. *Jahrbuch für romanische und englische Literatur* IV,
      260–285.

1863 Holtzmann, Adolf. Zu Beowulf. *Germania* VIII, 489–497.

1864 Rieger, Max. Bemerkungen zum Hildebrandsliede. *Germania*
      IX, 295–320. [Beowulf 525.]

1865 Grein, Christian W. M. Zur Textkritik der angelsächsischen
      Dichter. *Germania* X, 416–429. [Notes on Judith, p. 419.]

1868– Bugge, Sophus. Spredte iagttagelser vedkommende de olden-
1869 gelske digte om Beowulf og Waldere. *Tidskrift for Philologi og
      Pædagogik* VIII, 40–78, 287–307.

1869 Müllenhoff, Karl. Die innere Geschichte des Beovulfs. *Zeit-
      schrift für deutsches Altertum* XIV, 193–244.

1869 Scherer, Wilhelm. [Review of Heyne, Beowulf, 2d ed.] *Zeit-
      schrift für die österreichischen Gymnasien* XX, 89–112.

1871 Rieger, Max. Zum Beowulf. *Zeitschrift für deutsche Philologie*
      III, 381–416.

1872 Vetter, Ferdinand. Zum Muspilli und zur germanischen Alli-
      terationspoesie. Vienna, 1872. [Judith 90.]

1873 Bugge, Sophus. Zum Beowulf. *Zeitschrift für deutsche Philo-
      logie* IV, 192–224.

1876 Rieger, Max. Die alt- und angelsächsische Verskunst. *Zeit-
      schrift für deutsche Philologie* VII, 1–64.

1877 Cosijn, P. J. Beovulf 1695. *Taalkundige Bijdragen* I, 286.

1877 Kern, H. Angelsaksische Kleinigheden. *Taalkundige Bijdragen*
      I, 193–203. [Beowulf 2766.]

1877 Kern, H. Een Paar bedorven Plaatsen. *Taalkundige Bijdragen*
      I, 210–214. [Judith 263.]

1877 Schönbach, A. [Review of Ettmüller, Carmen de Beovulfi.] *An-
      zeiger für deutsches Altertum* III, 36–46.

1877 Suchier, Hermann. Ueber die Sage von Offa und Þryðo. *Bei-
      träge* IV, 500–521.

1878 Wülker, R. P. [Review of Arnold, Beowulf.] *Anglia* I, 177–186.

1879 Körner, Karl. [Review of Botkine's translation of Beowulf.]
      Englische Studien II, 248–251. [Lines 168 ff., 287, 489 f.]

1880 Kölbing, Eugen. Kleine Beiträge zur Erklärung und Textkritik
      englischer Dichter. I. *Englische Studien* III, 92–105. [Beo-
      wulf 168f.]

1881 Cosijn, P. J. Anglosaxonica. *Tijdschrift voor Nederlandsche
      Taal- en Letterkunde* I, 143–150. [Judith 312.]

1881 Gering, Hugo. [Review of Heyne, Beowulf, 4th ed.] *Zeitschrift
      für deutsche Philologie* XII, 122–125.

1882 Cosijn, P. J. Zum Beowulf. *Beiträge* VIII, 568–574.

1882 Kluge, Friedrich. Sprachhistorische Miscellen. *Beiträge* VIII, 506–539. [Beowulf 63, 1026, 1234, 1266.]

1884 Kluge, Friedrich. Zum Beowulf. *Beiträge* IX, 187–192.

1884 Krüger, Th. Zum Beowulf. *Beiträge* IX, 571–578.

1884 Sievers, Eduard. Zum Beowulf. *Beiträge* IX, 135–144, 370.

1885 Sievers, Eduard. Zur Rhythmik des germanischen Alliterationsverses. I, II. *Beiträge* X, 209–314, 451–545.

1886 Luick, Karl. Über den Versbau des angelsächsischen Gedichtes Judith. *Beiträge* XI, 470–492.

1887 Bugge, Sophus. Studien über das Beowulfepos. *Beiträge* XII, 1–112, 360–375. [Textual notes, pp. 79–112, 366–375.]

1887 Sievers, Eduard. Altnordisches im Beowulf? *Beiträge* XII, 168–200.

1887 Sievers, Eduard. Zur Rhythmik des germanischen Alliterationsverses. III. *Beiträge* XII, 454–482.

1887 Singer, S. Miscellen. *Beiträge* XII, 211–215. [Beowulf 1107.]

1888 Corson, H. A Passage of Beowulf. *Modern Language Notes* III, 193–194. [Line 2724.]

1889 Bright, J. W. [Review of Cook, Judith (1888).] *Modern Language Notes* IV, 240–244.

1889 Heinzel, R. [Review of Socin, Beowulf, 5th ed.] *Anzeiger für deutsches Altertum* XV, 189–194.

1889 Holthausen, Ferdinand. [Review of Kluge, Angelsächsisches Lesebuch, 1st ed.] *Literaturblatt* X, 445–449. [Notes on Judith.]

1889 Miller, Thomas. The Position of Grendel's Arm in Heorot. *Anglia* XII, 396–400. [Beowulf 834ff., 925ff., 982ff.]

1889 Sievers, Eduard. [Review of Socin, Beowulf, 5th ed.] *Zeitschrift für deutsche Philologie* XXI, 354–365.

1890 Joseph, Eugen. Zwei Versversetzungen im Beowulf. *Zeitschrift für deutsche Philologie* XXII, 385–397. [Lines 901–915, 1404–1407.]

1890 Zupitza, Julius. Zu Beowulf 850. *Archiv* LXXXIV, 124–125.

1891 Schröer, A. Zur Texterklärung des Beowulf. *Anglia* XIII, 333–348.

1892 Cosijn, P. J. Aanteekeningen op den Beowulf. Leiden, 1892.

1892 Holthausen, Ferdinand. Zur Textkritik altenglischer Dichtungen. *Beiträge* XVI, 549–552. [Beowulf 1117.]

1892 Neumann, Max. Über das altenglische Gedicht von Judith. Kiel, 1892.

1892 Pearce, J. W. Anglo-Saxon *scur-heard*. *Modern Language Notes* VII, 385–387, 506–507. [See also the comments by Albert S. Cook, J. M. Hart, and A. H. Palmer in *Mod. Lang. Notes* VII (1892), 505–506, VIII (1893), 121–122.]

1892 Sievers, Eduard. Zur Texterklärung des Beowulf. *Anglia* XIV, 133–146.

1893 Child, C. G. Stapol = patronus. (Sp. padron, Port. padrão.) *Modern Language Notes* VIII, 504–506. [Beowulf 926.]

1893 Koeppel, E. Zu Judith V. 62. *Archiv* XC, 140–141.

1893 Lübke, H. [Review of Cosijn, Aanteekeningen op den Beowulf.] *Anzeiger für deutsches Altertum* XIX, 341–342.

1894 Cosijn, P. J. Anglosaxonica. *Beiträge* XIX, 441–461.

1894 Holthausen, Ferdinand. Beiträge zur Erklärung und Textkritik altenglischer Dichter. *Indogermanische Forschungen* IV, 379–388. [Beowulf 2706.]

1894 Kaluza, Max. Die Metrik des Beowulfliedes. (Studien zum germanischen Alliterationsvers, Vol. II.) Berlin, 1894.

1894 Pogatscher, A. Zu Beowulf 168. *Beiträge* XIX, 544–545.

1894 Sievers, Eduard. Zum Beowulf. *Beiträge* XVIII, 406–407.

1895 Bright, J. W. Notes on the Beowulf. *Modern Language Notes* X, 85–88.

1895 Holthausen, Ferdinand. [Review of Cosijn, Aanteekeningen op den Beowulf.] *Literaturblatt* XVI, 82.

1895 Kaluza, Max. Die Schwellverse in der altenglischen Dichtung. *Englische Studien* XXI, 337–384.

1895 Martin, E. [Review of Kaluza, Der altenglische Vers.] *Englische Studien* XX, 293–296. [Beowulf 1514, 3027.]

1895 Sievers, Eduard. Beowulf und Saxo. *Berichte über die Verhandlungen der kgl. sächsischen Gesellschaft der Wissenschaften zu Leipzig*, Philol.-hist. Classe, XLVII, 175–192.

1896 Cosijn, P. J. Anglosaxonica. III. *Beiträge* XXI, 8–26. [Beowulf 1141, 1284.]

1896 Kluge, Friedrich. Der Beowulf und die Hrolfs Saga Kraka. *Englische Studien* XXII, 144–145.

1896 Kölbing, Eugen. Zum Beowulf. *Englische Studien* XXII, 325. [Lines 1027ff.]

1897 Konrath, W. Zu Beowulf 445b–446a. *Archiv* XCIX, 417–418.

1899 Holthausen, Ferdinand. Zu alt- und mittelenglischen Dichtungen. IX. *Anglia* XXI, 366–370. [Beowulf 2299, 2488.]

1899 Schröder, Edward. Steigerung und Häufung der Allitteration in der westgermanischen Dichtung. *Zeitschrift für deutsches Altertum* XLIII, 361–385.

1899   Trautmann, Moritz. Berichtigungen, Vermutungen und Erklär-
       ungen zum Beowulf. Erste Hälfte. *Bonner Beiträge* II, 121–
       192.

1900   Holthausen, Ferdinand. Zum Beowulf. *Archiv* CV, 366–367.
       [Lines 497f., 565ff.]

1900   Holthausen, Ferdinand. [Review of Bonner Beiträge, Vol. II.]
       Literaturblatt XXI, 62–64.

1900   Holthausen, Ferdinand. [Review of Holder, Beowulf, 2d ed.]
       Literaturblatt XXI, 60–62.

1900   Holthausen, Ferdinand. [Review of Socin, Beowulf, 6th ed.]
       Anglia, Beiblatt X, 265–274.

1900   Klaeber, Fr. Aus Anlass von Beowulf 2724f. *Archiv* CIV, 287–
       292.

1900   Sarrazin, Gregor. [Review of Socin, Beowulf, 6th ed.] *Englische
       Studien* XXVIII, 408–410.

1901   Holthausen, Ferdinand. Zu Beowulf v. 3157. *Anglia*, Beiblatt
       XII, 146.

1901   Holthausen, Ferdinand. Zum Beowulf. *Anglia* XXIV, 267–
       268. [Line 719.]

1901   Klaeber, Fr. A Few Beowulf Notes. *Modern Language Notes*
       XVI, 28–35.

1902   Barnouw, A. J. Textkritische Untersuchungen nach dem Ge-
       brauch des bestimmten Artikels und des schwachen Adjectivs
       in der altenglischen Poesie. Leiden, 1902.

1902   Boer, R. C. Eene Episode uit den Beowulf. *In* Handelingen
       van het 3de Nederlandsche Philologen-Congres (Groningen,
       1902), pp. 84–94. [Line 1934.]

1902   Holthausen, Ferdinand. Zu Beowulf v. 2577. *Anglia*, Beiblatt
       XIII, 78–79.

1902   Holthausen, Ferdinand. Zu Beowulf v. 665. *Anglia*, Beiblatt
       XIII, 204–205.

1902   Holthausen, Ferdinand. Zum Beowulf. *Anglia*, Beiblatt XIII,
       363–364. [Lines 1107, 1745ff.]

1902   Klaeber, Fr. Zum Beowulf. *Archiv* CVIII, 368–370. [Lines 497f.,
       1745ff.]

1902   Sievers, Eduard. Lückenbüsser. *Beiträge* XXVII, 572. [Beo-
       wulf 33.]

1902   Wright, Elizabeth M. Beowulf l. 1363. *Englische Studien*
       XXX, 341–343.

1903   Binz, Gustav. [Review of Trautmann, Berichtigungen.] *Ang-
       lia*, Beiblatt XIV, 358–360.

1903 Cook, Albert S. Notes on Judith. *Journal of English and Germanic Philology* V, 153–158.

1903 Hart, J. M. Allotria III. *Modern Language Notes* XVIII, 117–118. [Beowulf 1931.]

1903 Holthausen, Ferdinand. Zum Beowulf (v. 33). *Anglia*, Beiblatt XIV, 82–83.

1903 Holthausen, Ferdinand. Wægbora. *Anglia*, Beiblatt XIV, 49. [Beowulf 1440.]

1903 Krackow, Otto. Zu Beowulf v. 1225 und 2222. *Archiv* CXI, 171–172.

1903 Sievers, Eduard. Zum Beowulf. *Beiträge* XXVIII, 271–272. [Lines 48f.]

1903 Trautmann, Moritz. Finn und Hildebrand. (Bonner Beiträge, Vol. VII.) Bonn, 1903.

1904 Abbott, Wilbur C. Hrothulf. *Modern Language Notes* XIX, 122–125.

1904 Boer, R. C. Finnsage und Nibelungensage. *Zeitschrift für deutsches Altertum* XLVII, 125–160. [Textual notes on the Episode, pp. 133–139.]

1904 Bryant, Frank E. Beowulf, 62. *Modern Language Notes* XIX, 121–122. [See also his further remarks in *Mod. Lang. Notes* XXI (1906), 143–145, XXII (1907), 96.]

1904 Grienberger, T. von. Zu Beowulf. *Anglia* XXVII, 331–332. [Lines 1107ff.]

1904 Kock, Ernst A. Interpretations and Emendations of Early English Texts. III. *Anglia* XXVII, 218–237.

1904 Krapp, George P. *Scurheard*, Beowulf 1033, Andreas 1133. *Modern Language Notes* XIX, 234.

1904 Schücking, Levin L. Die Grundzüge der Satzverknüpfung im Beowulf. Part 1. Halle, 1904.

1904 Sievers, Eduard. Zum Beowulf. *Beiträge* XXIX, 305–331.

1904 Sievers, Eduard. Zum Beowulf. *Beiträge* XXIX, 560–576. [Line 6.]

1905 Binz, Gustav. [Review of Cook, Judith (1904).] *Englische Studien* XXXVI, 130. [Line 312.]

1905 Grienberger, T. von. [Review of Socin, Beowulf, 7th ed.] *Zeitschrift für die österreichischen Gymnasien* LVI, 744–761.

1905 Holthausen, Ferdinand. Beiträge zur Erklärung des altenglischen Epos. *Zeitschrift für deutsche Philologie* XXXVII, 113–125.

1905 Klaeber, Fr. Bemerkungen zum Beowulf. *Archiv* CXV, 178–182.

1905 Klaeber, Fr. Zum Beowulf. *Anglia* XXVIII, 448–456.
1905 Klaeber, Fr. Hrothulf. *Modern Language Notes* XX, 9–11. [See also his further remarks in *Mod. Lang. Notes* XXI (1906), 255–256, XXII (1907), 160.]
1905 Klaeber, Fr. Notizen zur Texterklärung des Beowulf. *Anglia* XXVIII, 439–447.
1905– Klaeber, Fr. Studies in the Textual Interpretation of Beowulf.
1906 *Modern Philology* III, 235–265, 445–465.
1905 Krapp, George P. Notes on the Andreas. *Modern Philology* II, 403–410. [Beowulf 28, 1916, 2334.]
1905 Scheinert, Moritz. Die Adjectiva im Beowulfepos als Darstellungsmittel. *Beiträge* XXX, 345–430.
1905 Smyth, Mary W. The Numbers in the Manuscript of the Old English Judith. *Modern Language Notes* XX, 197–199.
1905 Trautmann, Moritz. Auch zum Beowulf: ein Gruss an Herrn Eduard Sievers. *Bonner Beiträge* XVII, 143–174.
1906 Child, C. G. Beowulf 30, 53, 1323, 2957. *Modern Language Notes* XXI, 175–177, 198–200.
1906 Horn, Wilhelm. Textkritische Bemerkungen. *Anglia* XXIX, 129–132. [Beowulf 69ff.]
1906 Klaeber, Fr. Notizen zum Beowulf. *Anglia* XXIX, 378–382.
1907 Holthausen, Ferdinand. Zur altenglischen Literatur. III. *Anglia*, Beiblatt XVIII, 77–78. [Beowulf 719.]
1907 Holthausen, Ferdinand. Zur Textkritik altenglischer Dichtungen. *Englische Studien* XXXVII, 198–211. [Judith 9, 349.]
1907 Klaeber, Fr. Cynewulf's Elene 1262f. *Journal of English and Germanic Philology* VI, 197. [Beowulf 2261.]
1907 Klaeber, Fr. Minor Notes on the Beowulf. *Journal of English and Germanic Philology* VI, 190–196.
1908 Holthausen, Ferdinand. Zur altenglischen Literatur. VII. *Anglia*, Beiblatt XIX, 248–249. [Judith 273f.]
1908 Imelmann, Rudolf. [Review of Cook, Judith (1904).] *Anglia*, Beiblatt XIX, 1–8.
1908 Klaeber, Fr. Zum Beowulf. *Englische Studien* XXXIX, 463–467.
1908 Klaeber, Fr. [Review of Schücking, Beowulf, 8th ed.] *Englische Studien* XXXIX, 425–433.
1908 Schücking, Levin L. [Review of Holthausen, Beowulf, 1st ed.] *Englische Studien* XXXIX, 94–111.
1908 Tinker, Chauncey B. Notes on Beowulf. *Modern Language Notes* XXIII, 239–240.

1909 Imelmann, Rudolf. [Review of Schücking, Beowulf, 8th ed.] *Deutsche Literaturzeitung* XXX, 995–1000.

1909 Klaeber, Fr. [Review of Holthausen, Beowulf, 1st ed.] *Modern Language Notes* XXIV, 94–95.

1909 Klaeber, Fr. Textual Notes on the Beowulf. *Journal of English and Germanic Philology* VIII, 254–259.

1910 Grienberger, T. von. Bemerkungen zum Beowulf. *Beiträge* XXXVI, 77–101.

1910 Hall, John R. Clark. A Note on Beowulf 1142–1145. *Modern Language Notes* XXV, 113–114.

1910 Holthausen, Ferdinand. Zur altenglischen Literatur. XII. *Anglia*, Beiblatt XXI, 300–301. [Beowulf 1440.]

1910 Holthausen, Ferdinand. Beiträge zur Textkritik altenglischer Dichtungen. *Die Neueren Sprachen*, 1910, Ergänzungsband, pp. 127–128. [Beowulf 224, 2251.]

1910 Klaeber, Fr. Die ältere Genesis und der Beowulf. *Englische Studien* XLII, 321–338.

1910 Lawrence, W. W. [Review of Schücking, Beowulf, 8th ed.] *Modern Language Notes* XXV, 155–157.

1910 Schmitz, Theodor. Die Sechstakter in der altenglischen Dichtung. *Anglia* XXXIII, 1–76, 172–218.

1910 Schücking, Levin L. [Review of Holthausen, Beowulf, 2d ed.] *Englische Studien* XLII, 108–111.

1910 Sedgefield, W. J. Notes on Beowulf. *Modern Language Review* V, 286–288.

1910 Sievers, Eduard. Gegenbemerkungen zum Beowulf. *Beiträge* XXXVI, 397–434.

1911 Klaeber, Fr. Zur Texterklärung des Beowulf. *Anglia*, Beiblatt XXII, 372–374. [Beowulf 769, 1129f.]

1911 Lawrence, W. W. [Review of Sedgefield, Beowulf, 1st ed.] *Journal of English and Germanic Philology* X, 633–640.

1911 Schücking, Levin L. Altengl. *scepen* und die sogen. idg. Vokativreste im Altengl. *Englische Studien* XLIV, 155–157. [Beowulf 106.]

1911 Schücking, Levin L. Beowulf 1174. *Englische Studien* XLIV, 157.

1911 Thomas, P. G. [Review of Sedgefield, Beowulf, 1st ed.] *Modern Language Review* VI, 266–268.

1912 Blackburn, F. A. Note on Beowulf 1591–1617. *Modern Philology* IX, 555–566. [Assumes a misplaced folio; refuted by R. W. Chambers, *Mod. Lang. Review* X (1915), 37–41.]

1912 Bright, J. W. An Idiom of the Comparative in Anglo-Saxon. *Modern Language Notes* XXVII, 181–183. [Beowulf 69f.]

1912 Hart, J. M. Beowulf 168–9. *Modern Language Notes* XXVII, 198.

1912 Sievers, Eduard. Ags. *scepen*. *Englische Studien* XLIV, 295–296.

1912 Sievers, Eduard. Beowulf 1174. *Englische Studien* XLIV, 296–297.

1912 Stefanović, Svet. Ein Beitrag zur angelsächsischen Offa-Sage. *Anglia* XXXV, 483–525.

1912 Tupper, Frederick, Jr. Notes on Old English Poems. *Journal of English and Germanic Philology* XI, 82–103. ["The Home of the Judith," pp. 82ff.]

1913 Klaeber, Fr. Notes on Old English Poems. *Journal of English and Germanic Philology* XII, 252–261. [Judith 287ff.]

1913 Klaeber, Fr. [Review of Schücking, Beowulf, 10th ed.] *Anglia*, Beiblatt XXIV, 289–291.

1915 Klaeber, Fr. Observations on the Finn Episode. *Journal of English and Germanic Philology* XIV, 544–549.

1915 Lawrence, W. W. Beowulf and the Tragedy of Finnsburg. *PMLA* XXX, 372–431.

1915 Schücking, Levin L. Untersuchungen zur Bedeutungslehre der angelsächsischen Dichtersprache. Heidelberg, 1915.

1916 Bright, J. W. Anglo-Saxon *umbor* and *seld-guma*. *Modern Language Notes* XXXI, 82–84.

1916 Bright, J. W. Beowulf 489–490. *Modern Language Notes* XXXI, 217–223.

1916 Green, Alexander. The Opening of the Episode of Finn in Beowulf. *PMLA* XXXI, 759–797.

1916 Monroe, B. S. Notes on the Anglo-Saxon Andreas. *Modern Language Notes* XXXI, 374–377. [Judith 158, 329.]

1917 Ayres, H. M. The Tragedy of Hengest in Beowulf. *Journal of English and Germanic Philology* XVI, 282–295.

1917 Green, Alexander. An Episode in Ongenþeow's Fall. (Beowulf, ll. 2957–60.) *Modern Language Review* XII, 340–343.

1917 Hollander, Lee M. Beowulf 33. *Modern Language Notes* XXXII, 246–247.

1917 Holthausen, Ferdinand. Zu altenglischen Denkmälern. *Englische Studien* LI, 180–188. [Beowulf 1140f.]

1918 Hubbard, Frank G. Beowulf 1598, 1996, 2026: Uses of the Impersonal Verb *geweorþan*. *Journal of English and Germanic Philology* XVII, 119–124.

1918 Kock, Ernst A. Interpretations and Emendations of Early English Texts. IV. *Anglia* XLII, 99–124.

1918 Kock, Ernst A. Jubilee Jaunts and Jottings. 250 Contributions to the Interpretation and Prosody of Old West Teutonic Alliterative Poetry. *Lunds Universitets Årsskrift*, N.F., Avd. 1, Bd. 14, Nr. 26.

1918 Lawrence, W. W. The Dragon and His Lair in Beowulf. *PMLA* XXXIII, 547–583.

1919 Björkman, Erik. [Review of Schücking, Beowulf, 11th–12th ed.] *Anglia*, Beiblatt XXX, 121–122, 180–181.

1919 Brett, Cyril. Notes on Passages of Old and Middle English. *Modern Language Review* XIV, 1–9.

1919 Brown, Carleton. Beowulf 1080–1106. *Modern Language Notes* XXXIV, 181–183.

1919 Klaeber, Fr. Textual Notes on Beowulf. *Modern Language Notes* XXXIV, 129–134.

1919 Kock, Ernst A. Interpretations and Emendations of Early English Texts. V. *Anglia* XLIII, 298–312.

1919 Moore, Samuel. Beowulf Notes. *Journal of English and Germanic Philology* XVIII, 205–216.

1920 Bryan, W. F. Beowulf Notes. *Journal of English and Germanic Philology* XIX, 84–85.

1920 Holthausen, Ferdinand. [Review of Schücking, Beowulf, 10th ed.] *Zeitschrift für deutsche Philologie* XLVIII, 127–131.

1920 Hoops, Johannes. Das Verhüllen des Haupts bei Toten, ein angelsächsisch-nordischer Brauch. *Englische Studien* LIV, 19–23. [Beowulf 446.]

1920 Hubbard, Frank G. The Plundering of the Hoard in Beowulf. *University of Wisconsin Studies in Language and Literature*, No. 11, pp. 5–20.

1920 Imelmann, Rudolf. Forschungen zur altenglischen Poesie. Berlin, 1920. [Beowulf 1931.]

1920 Kock, Ernst A. Interpretations and Emendations of Early English Texts. VI, VII. *Anglia* XLIV, 97–114, 245–260.

1920 Schücking, Levin L. Wiðergyld (Beowulf 2051). *Englische Studien* LIII, 468–470.

1921 Bush, J. D. A Note on Beowulf 1600–1605. *Modern Language Notes* XXXVI, 251.

1921 Kock, Ernst A. Interpretations and Emendations of Early English Texts. VIII. *Anglia* XLV, 105–131.

1921 Schücking, Levin L. [Review of Chambers's edition of Beowulf.] *Englische Studien* LV, 88–100.

1922 Heusler, Andreas. [Review of Imelmann, Forschungen zur altenglischen Poesie.] *Anzeiger für deutsches Altertum* XLI, 27–35.

1922 Kock, Ernst A. Interpretations and Emendations of Early English Texts. IX, X. *Anglia* XLVI, 63–96, 173–190.

1922 Patzig, H. Zur Episode von Þryð im Beowulf. *Anglia* XLVI, 282–285.

1922 Thomas, P. G. Beowulf, ll. 1604–5, 2085–91. *Modern Language Review* XVII, 63–64.

1923 Holthausen, Ferdinand. Zu altenglischen Dichtungen. *Anglia, Beiblatt* XXXIV, 89–91. [Beowulf 769.]

1923 Kock, Ernst A. [Review of Klaeber, Beowulf, 1st ed.] *Arkiv för nordisk Filologi* XXXIX, 185–189.

1923 Laborde, E. D. Grendel's Glove and His Immunity from Weapons. *Modern Language Review* XVIII, 202–204.

1923 Malone, Kemp. The Literary History of Hamlet. I. The Early Tradition. Heidelberg, 1923.

1923 Patzig, H. Zum Beowulf-Text. *Anglia* XLVII, 97–104.

1923 Sedgefield, W. J. Old English Notes. *Modern Language Review* XVIII, 471–472. [Beowulf 223f.]

1924 Lawrence, W. W. [Review of Klaeber, Beowulf, 1st ed.] *Journal of English and Germanic Philology* XXIII, 294–300.

1924 Sewell, W. A. P. A Reading in Beowulf. [London] *Times Literary Supplement*, September 11, 1924, p. 556. [Line 6.]

1924 Williams, R. A. The Finn Episode in Beowulf. Cambridge, 1924.

1925 Cook, Albert S. Beowulf 159–163. *Modern Language Notes* XL, 352–354.

1925 Dunstan, A. C. Beowulf, ll. 223–4. *Modern Language Review* XX, 317–318.

1926 Crawford, A. J. "Ealu-scerwen." *Modern Language Review* XXI, 302–303.

1926 Klaeber, Fr. Beowulfiana. *Anglia* L, 107–122, 195–244.

1926 Mackie, W. S. Notes on Old English Poetry. *Modern Language Review* XXI, 300–301. [Beowulf 223f.]

1926 Malone, Kemp. The Finn Episode in Beowulf. *Journal of English and Germanic Philology* XXV, 157–172.

1926 Malone, Kemp. A Note on Beowulf 1231. *Modern Language Notes* XLI, 466–467.

1926 Malone, Kemp. [Review of Williams, The Finn Episode in Beowulf.] *Journal of English and Germanic Philology* XXV, 114–117.

1927 Addy, S. O. The *stapol* in Beowulf: Hall and Chamber. *Notes &* *Queries* CLII, 363–365. [Beowulf 926.]

1927 Thomas, P. G. Further Notes on Beowulf. *Modern Language* *Review* XXII, 70–73.

1927 Williams, R. A. Beowulf, ll. 1086–1088. *Modern Language Review* XXII, 310–313.

1928 Crawford, S. J. Beowulf, ll. 168–9. *Modern Language Review* XXIII, 336.

1928 Crawford, S. J. Grendel's Descent from Cain. *Modern Language Review* XXIII, 207–208. [Beowulf 1691.]

1928 Malone, Kemp. Hunlafing. *Modern Language Notes* XLIII, 300–304.

1928 Malone, Kemp. The Kenning in Beowulf 2220. *Journal of English and Germanic Philology* XXVII, 318–324.

1929 Holthausen, Ferdinand. Zu Beowulf V. 489f. und V. 3114f. *Anglia*, Beiblatt XL, 90–91.

1929 Hoops, Johannes. Altenglisch *geap, horngeap, sægeap*. *Englische Studien* LXIV, 201–211.

1929 Hoops, Johannes. War Beowulf König von Dänemark? *In* Britannica, Max Förster zum 60. Geburtstage (Leipzig, 1929), pp. 26–30.

1929 Jiriczek, O. L. Die Bedeutung von ae. *stede-heard* (Judith 223). *Englische Studien* LXIV, 212–218.

1929 Klaeber, Fr. Altenglische wortkundliche Randglossen. *Anglia*, Beiblatt XL, 21–32. [Beowulf 107f., 600, 769.]

1929 Klaeber, Fr. Jottings on Old English Poems. *Anglia* LIII, 225–234. [Judith 9, 125ff.]

1929 Malone, Kemp. The Daughter of Healfdene. *In* Studies in English Philology . . . in Honor of Frederick Klaeber (Minneapolis, 1929), pp. 135–158.

1929 Malone, Kemp. A Note on Beowulf, l. 2034. *Modern Language Review* XXIV, 322–323.

1929 Malone, Kemp. Notes on Beowulf. I. *Anglia* LIII, 335–336, 439.

1929 Moore, Samuel. Notes on Beowulf. *In* Studies in English Philology . . . in Honor of Frederick Klaeber (Minneapolis, 1929), pp. 208–212.

1929 Schücking, Levin L. Sona im Beowulf. *In* Britannica, Max Förster zum 60. Geburtstage (Leipzig, 1929), pp. 85–88.

1929 Wardale, E. E. Beowulf, ll. 848ff. *Modern Language Review* XXIV, 62–63.

1930 Ashdown, Margaret. Beowulf, ll. 1543ff. *Modern Language Review* XXV, 78.

1930 Bryan, W. F. *Ærgod* in Beowulf, and Other Old English Compounds of *ær*. *Modern Philology* XXVIII, 157–161.

1930 Lotspeich, H. G. Beowulf 1363, *hrinde bearwas*. *Journal of English and Germanic Philology* XXIX, 367–369.

1930 Malone, Kemp. Ingeld. *Modern Philology* XXVII, 257–276.

1930 Malone, Kemp. A Note on Beowulf, l. 1379. *Modern Language Review* XXV, 191.

1930 Malone, Kemp. Notes on Beowulf. II–V. *Anglia* LIV, 1–7, 97–98.

1930 Malone, Kemp. Old English (*Ge*)*hydan* "Heed." *In* A Grammatical Miscellany Offered to Otto Jespersen (Copenhagen and London, 1930), pp. 45–54.

1930 Malone, Kemp. Three Notes on Beowulf. *Journal of English and Germanic Philology* XXIX, 233–236. [Lines 304, 646f., 1056.]

1930 Steadman, J. M. The Ingeld Episode in Beowulf: History or Prophecy? *Modern Language Notes* XLV, 522–525.

1931 Crawford, S. J. Beowulfiana. *Review of English Studies* VII, 448–450.

1931 Ericson, E. E. Old English *swa* in Worn-Down Correlative Clauses. *Englische Studien* LXV, 343–350.

1931 Furuhjelm, Åke. Note on a Passage in Beowulf. *Neuphilologische Mitteilungen* XXXII, 107–109. [Lines 3066–3075.]

1931 Henel, Heinrich. *Stanboga* im Beowulf. *Anglia* LV, 273–281.

1931 Holthausen, Ferdinand. *Onsæl meoto*. *Anglia*, Beiblatt XLII, 249–250. [Beowulf 489.]

1931 Hoops, Johannes. Altenglisch *ealuscerwen, meoduscerwen*. *Englische Studien* LXV, 177–180.

1931 Imelmann, Rudolf. Beowulf 489f. *Englische Studien* LXV, 190–196.

1931 Klaeber, Fr., and Johannes Hoops. Altenglisch *ealuscerwen* und kein Ende. *Englische Studien* LXVI, 1–5.

1931 Lyons, Clifford P. A Note on Beowulf 760. *Modern Language Notes* XLVI, 443–444.

1931 Malone, Kemp. Ealhhild. *Anglia* LV, 266–272.

1931 Sievers, Eduard. Beowulf 3066ff. *Beiträge* LV, 376.

1931 Weber, Edmund. Seelenmörder oder Unholdtöter? *Neuphilologische Monatsschrift* II, 293–295. [Beowulf 171–179.]

1932 Holthausen, Ferdinand. Zu Beowulf V. 3074f. *Anglia*, Beiblatt XLIII, 157.

1932 Holthausen, Ferdinand. [Review of Hoops, Beowulfstudien.]
     Anglia, Beiblatt XLIII, 357–358.

1932 Hoops, Johannes. Beowulfstudien. Heidelberg, 1932.

1932 Hoops, Johannes. Kommentar zum Beowulf. Heidelberg, 1932.

1932 Imelmann, Rudolf. Beowulf 489f., 600, 769. *Englische Studien*
     LXVI, 321–345.

1932 Klaeber, Fr. Beowulf 769. *Englische Studien* LXVII, 24–26.

1932 Klaeber, Fr. Eine kleine Nachlese zum Beowulf. *Anglia* LVI,
     421–431.

1932 Krogmann, Willy. Ae. *isig*. *Anglia* LVI, 438–439. [Beo-
     wulf 33.]

1932 Krogmann, Willy. Ae. *orcneas*. *Anglia* LVI, 40–42.

1932 Krogmann, Willy. Ae. **scerwan*. *Englische Studien* LXVI, 346.

1932 Krogmann, Willy. Ealuscerwen und meoduscerwen. *Englische
     Studien* LXVII, 15–23.

1932 Malone, Kemp. Notes on Beowulf. VI. *Anglia* LVI, 436–437.

1932 Sedgefield, W. J. Emendations of the Beowulf Text. *Modern
     Language Review* XXVII, 448–451.

1933 Furuhjelm, Åke. Beowulfiana. *Anglia* LVII, 317–320. [Lines
     224, 305f., 3074f.]

1933 Girvan, Ritchie. [Review of Hoops, Beowulfstudien.] *Modern
     Language Review* XXVIII, 244–246.

1933 Holthausen, Ferdinand. [Review of Hoops, Kommentar.] *Ang-
     lia*, Beiblatt XLIV, 225–227.

1933 Imelmann, Rudolf. Beowulf 303ff. und 3074f. *Englische Studien*
     LXVII, 325–339.

1933 Imelmann, Rudolf. Beowulf 3074f.: Nachprüfung. *Englische
     Studien* LXVIII, 1–5.

1933 Klaeber, Fr. [Review of Hoops, Beowulfstudien.] *Englische
     Studien* LXVII, 399–402.

1933 Klaeber, Fr. [Review of Hoops, Kommentar.] *Englische Studien*
     LXVIII, 112–115.

1933 Krogmann, Willy. Ae. *gang*. *Anglia* LVII, 216–217.

1933 Krogmann, Willy. Bemerkungen zum Beowulf. *Englische Stu-
     dien* LXVIII, 317–319. [Lines 84, 850.]

1933 Malone, Kemp. Beowulfiana. *Medium Ævum* II, 58–64.

1933 Malone, Kemp. Notes on Beowulf. VII. VIII. *Anglia* LVII,
     218–220, 313–316.

1933 Malone, Kemp. [Review of Hoops, Beowulfstudien.] *English
     Studies* XV, 94–96.

1933 Malone, Kemp. [Review of Hoops, Kommentar.] *English
     Studies* XV, 149–151.

1933 Sedgefield, W. J. Further Emendations of the Beowulf Text. *Modern Language Review* XXVIII, 226–230.

1934 Clarke, D. E. Martin. Beowulfiana. *Modern Language Review* XXIX, 320–321.

1934 Hintz, H. W. The "Hama" Reference in Beowulf: 1197–1201. *Journal of English and Germanic Philology* XXXIII, 98–102.

1934 Krogmann, Willy. Ae. *eolet* (Beowulf 224). *Anglia* LVIII, 351–357. [See also his note in *Eng. Studien* LXX (1935), 323–324.]

1934 Stefanović, Svet. Zur Offa-Thryðo-Episode im Beowulf. *Englische Studien* LXIX, 15–31.

1935 Bouman, A. C. The Heroes of the Fight at Finnsburh. *Acta Philologica Scandinavica* X, 130–144.

1935 Cassidy, F. G. Suggested Repunctuation of a Passage in Beowulf. *Modern Language Notes* L, 88–89. [Lines 745ff.]

1935 Du Bois, Arthur E. Beowulf, 489–490. *Modern Language Notes* L, 89–90.

1935 Eliason, Norman E. Wulfhlið (Beowulf, l. 1358). *Journal of English and Germanic Philology* XXXIV, 20–23.

1935 Holthausen, Ferdinand. Zum Beowulf. *Englische Studien* LXIX, 433–434.

1935 Hoops, Johannes. Beowulf 457f.: For werefyhtum and for arstafum. *Englische Studien* LXX, 77–80.

1935 Hübener, G. [Review of Hoops, Beowulfstudien, and Hoops, Kommentar zum Beowulf.] *Literaturblatt* LVI, 241–243.

1935 Traver, Hope. Beowulf 648–649 Once More. *Archiv* CLXVII, 253–256.

1936 Malone, Kemp. [Review of Sedgefield, Beowulf, 3d ed.] *English Studies* XVIII, 257–258.

1936 Marquardt, Hertha. Fürsten- und Kriegerkenning im Beowulf. *Anglia* LX, 390–395.

1936 Schaubert, Else von. [Review of Hoops, Beowulfstudien.] *Literaturblatt* LVII, 26–31.

1936 Sedgefield, W. J. The Scenery in Beowulf. *Journal of English and Germanic Philology* XXXV, 161–169.

1937 Colgrave, B. "Scurheard." *Modern Language Review* XXXII, 281. [Line 1033.]

1937 Malone, Kemp. The Burning of Heorot. *Review of English Studies* XIII, 462–463.

1938 Brown, Carleton. Beowulf and the Blickling Homilies, and Some Textual Notes. *PMLA* LIII, 905–916.

1938 Holthausen, Ferdinand. [Review of Sedgefield, Beowulf, 3d ed.] *Literaturblatt* LIX, 163–167.

1938 Mackie, W. S. The Demons' Home in Beowulf. *Journal of English and Germanic Philology* XXXVII, 455–461.

1938 Sanderlin, George. A Note on Beowulf 1142. *Modern Language Notes* LIII, 501–503.

1938 Schaubert, Else von. Zur Gestaltung und Erklärung des Beowulf-Textes. *Anglia* LXII, 173–189.

1939 Andrew, S. O. Three Textual Cruxes in Beowulf. *Medium Ævum* VIII, 205–207. [Lines 648ff., 1379, 3074f.]

1939 Huppé, Bernard F. A Reconsideration of the Ingeld Passage in Beowulf. *Journal of English and Germanic Philology* XXXVIII, 217–225.

1939 Klaeber, Fr. Beowulfiana minora. *Anglia* LXIII, 400–425.

1939 Klaeber, Fr. Beowulf 769 und Andreas 1526ff. *Englische Studien* LXXIII, 185–189.

1939 Klaeber, Fr. A Few Beowulf Jottings. *Anglia*, Beiblatt L, 330–332.

1939 Klaeber, Fr. A Notelet on the Ingeld Episode in Beowulf. *Anglia*, Beiblatt L, 223–224.

1939 Krogmann, Willy. Altenglisches. *Anglia* LXIII, 398–399. [Beowulf 3114f.]

1939 Mackie, W. S. Notes upon the Text and the Interpretation of Beowulf. *Modern Language Review* XXXIV, 515–524.

1939 Malone, Kemp. Hygelac. *English Studies* XXI, 108–119.

1939 Malone, Kemp. Notes on Beowulf. IX–XI. *Anglia* LXIII, 103–112.

1939 Malone, Kemp. Swerting. *Germanic Review* XIV, 235–257.

1939 Whitelock, Dorothy. Beowulf 2444–2471. *Medium Ævum* VIII, 198–204.

1940 Brown, Calvin S., Jr. Beowulf's Arm-Lock. *PMLA* LV, 621–627.

1940 Crosby, H. Lamar, Jr. Two Notes on Beowulf. *Modern Language Notes* LV, 605–606. [Lines 212, 216.]

1940 Girvan, Ritchie. Finnsburuh. *Proceedings of the British Academy* XXVI, 327–360.

1940 Klaeber, Fr. Beowulf 2041: *beah*. *Anglia*, Beiblatt LI, 206–207.

1940 Magoun, F. P. Zu *Etzeln burc*, *Finns buruh* und *Brunan burh*. *Zeitschrift für deutsches Altertum* LXXVII, 65–66.

1940 Malone, Kemp. Ecgtheow. *Modern Language Quarterly* I, 37–44.

1940 Malone, Kemp. Freawaru. *ELH* VII, 39–44.

1940 Malone, Kemp. Time and Place in the Ingeld Episode of Beowulf. *Journal of English and Germanic Philology* XXXIX,
76–92.

1941 Holthausen, Ferdinand. Zu altenglischen Dichtungen. *Englische Studien* LXXIV, 324–328. [Beowulf 1107f.]

1941 Klaeber, Fr. A Few Recent Additions to Beowulf Bibliography
and Notes. *Anglia*, Beiblatt LII, 135–137.

1941 Lotspeich, C. M. Old English Etymologies. *Journal of English
and Germanic Philology* XL, 1–4. [Beowulf 224.]

1941 Mackie, W. S. Notes upon the Text and Interpretation of Beowulf. II. *Modern Language Review* XXXVI, 95–98.

1941 Malone, Kemp. Hygd. *Modern Language Notes* LVI, 356–358.

1941 Malone, Kemp. Notes on Beowulf. XII. *Anglia* LXV, 227–229.

1941 Malone, Kemp. Old English *beagas*. *Anglia*, Beiblatt LII,
179–180.

1942 Holthausen, Ferdinand. Zur altenglischen Wortkunde. *Anglia*,
Beiblatt LIII, 272–274. [Beowulf 1537.]

1942 Holthausen, Ferdinand. Zur Textkritik des Beowulf. *Studia
Neophilologica* XIV, 160. [Lines 460ff., 3168.]

1942 Meroney, Howard. Old English ðær "if." *Journal of English
and Germanic Philology* XLI, 201–209. [Beowulf 2570ff.]

1942 Pope, John C. The Rhythm of Beowulf. New Haven, 1942.

1942 Whitbread, L. Beowulfiana. *Modern Language Review*
XXXVII, 480–484.

1943 Brodeur, A. G. The Climax of the Finn Episode. *University
of California Publications in English*, Vol. III, No. 8, pp. 285–
362.

1943 Brodeur, A. G. Design and Motive in the Finn Episode. *In*
Essays and Studies (*University of California Publications in
English*, Vol. XIV), pp. 1–42.

1943 Holthausen, Ferdinand. Zum Beowulf. *Anglia*, Beiblatt LIV/
LV, 27–30.

1943 Kuhn, Sherman M. The Sword of Healfdene. *Journal of English and Germanic Philology* XLII, 82–95. [Beowulf 1020.]

1943 Malone, Kemp. Hildeburg and Hengest. *ELH* X, 257–284.

1943 Woolf, H. B. Subject-Verb Agreement in Beowulf. *Modern
Language Quarterly* IV, 49–55.

1944 Estrich, Robert M. The Throne of Hrothgar—Beowulf, ll. 168–
169. *Journal of English and Germanic Philology* XLIII,
384–389.

1944 Klaeber, Fr. Some Further Additions to Beowulf Bibliography
and Notes. *Anglia*, Beiblatt LIV/LV, 274–280.

1944 Klaeber, Fr. Zur Texterklärung altenglischer Dichtungen. *Anglia*, Beiblatt LIV/LV, 170–176.

1944 Mezger, Fritz. On *fæder feorme*, Beowulf, Line 21. *Modern Language Notes* LIX, 113–114.

1945 Malone, Kemp. Finn's Stronghold. *Modern Philology* XLIII, 83–85. [Beowulf 1125–1127a.]

1948 Andrew, S. O. Postscript on Beowulf. Cambridge, 1948.

1948 Splitter, H. W. Note on a Beowulf Passage. *Modern Language Notes* LXIII, 118–121. [Line 749.]

1949 Einarsson, Stefán. Beowulf 249: *Wlite* = Icelandic *Litr*. *Modern Language Notes* LXIV, 347.

1949 Lumiansky, R. M. The Contexts of O.E. "ealuscerwen" and "meoduscerwen." *Journal of English and Germanic Philology* XLVIII, 116–126.

1949 Whitbread, L. The Hand of Æschere: a Note on Beowulf 1343. *Review of English Studies* XXV, 339–342.

1950 Klaeber, Fr. Randglossen zur Texterklärung des Beowulf. *Beiträge* LXXII, 120–126.

1951 Malone, Kemp. A Note on Beowulf 2466. *Journal of English and Germanic Philology* L, 19–21.

1951 Mezger, Fritz. OE Hamweorðung, Beowulf 2998. *Journal of English and Germanic Philology* L, 243–245.

1951 Mezger, Fritz. Two Notes on Beowulf. *Modern Language Notes* LXVI, 36–38. [Lines 253, 446.]

1952 Dobbie, Elliott V. K. "Mwatide," Beowulf 2226. *Modern Language Notes* LXVII, 242–245.

1952 Eliason, Norman E. The "Improvised Lay" in Beowulf. *Philological Quarterly* XXXI, 171–179.

1952 Splitter, H. W. The Relation of Germanic Folk Custom and Ritual to Ealuscerwen (Beowulf 769). *Modern Language Notes* LXVII, 255–258.

TEXTS

NOTE ON THE TEXTS

In the text of BEOWULF, words and letters which (1) are now visible in the manuscript or were visible to Zupitza in 1880, or (2) are confirmed by the agreement of the original readings of the two Thorkelin transcripts, or (3) are reported by Sedgefield (3d ed.) on fol. 182, or by A. H. Smith on fol. 201b, are printed in roman type. Emendations of the manuscript reading are also in roman type, as in the other volumes of this series. Letters printed in italic type are reported by one of the two Thorkelin transcripts but not by the other, or, in a few cases, are reported by Wanley (in ll. 1–19, 53–73) or by Conybeare in his collation of Thorkelin's text. All letters placed within square brackets are conjectural. The term "original readings" as used above in connection with the Thorkelin transcripts refers to those parts of the text which were copied by scribe A or by Thorkelin in his role of scribe B but does not include later additions made by Thorkelin in either transcript. In distinguishing the original readings, I have followed Kemp Malone's article in *PMLA* LXIV (1949), 1190–1218.

In the text of JUDITH, words and letters now visible in the manuscript, as well as emendations of the manuscript reading, are printed in roman type. Letters printed in italic type are supplied from the Junius transcript.

BEOWULF

Hwæt! We Gardena   in geardagum,
þeodcyninga,   þrym gefrunon,
hu ða æþelingas   ellen fremedon.
   Oft Scyld Scefing   sceaþena þreatum,
5 monegum mægþum,   meodosetla ofteah,
egsode eorlas.   Syððan ærest wearð
feasceaft funden,   he þæs frofre gebad,
weox under wolcnum,   weorðmyndum þah,
oðþæt him æghwylc   þara ymbsittendra
10 ofer hronrade   hyran scolde,
gomban gyldan.   Þæt wæs god cyning!
Ðæm eafera wæs   æfter cenned,
geong in geardum,   þone god sende
folce to frofre;   fyrenðearfe ongeat
15 þe hie ær drugon   aldor[le]ase
lange hwile.   Him þæs liffrea,
wuldres wealdend,   woroldare forgeaf;
Beowulf wæs breme   (blæd wide sprang),
Scyldes eafera   Scedelandum in.
20 Swa sceal [geong g]uma   gode gewyrcean,
fromum feohgiftum   on fæder [bea]rme,
þæt hine on ylde   eft gewunigen
wilgesiþas,   þonne wig cume,
leode gelæsten;   lofdædum sceal
25 in mægþa gehwære   man geþeon.
   Him ða Scyld gewat   to gescæphwile
felahror feran   on frean wære.
   Hi hyne þa ætbæron   to brimes faroðe,
swæse gesiþas,   swa he selfa bæd,

---

4 sceaþena] sceaþen *AB*, sceaþena *Wanley*   6 eorlas] eorl   wearð]
wearð *A*, weard *B*, wearð *Wanley*   10 hronrade] *A letter erased between*
hron *and* rade   15 þe] ꝥ   21 bearme] rine (*altered from* rme) *A*, . . .þine
(*altered from* . . .rine) *B*, . . .rme *Conybeare*

30 þenden wordum weold　wine Scyldinga;
　　leof landfruma　lange ahte.
　　Þær æt hyðe stod　hringedstefna,
　　isig ond utfus,　æþelinges fær.
　　Aledon þa　leofne þeoden,
35 beaga bryttan,　on bearm scipes,
　　mærne be mæste.　Þær wæs madma fela
　　of feorwegum,　frætwa, gelæded;
　　ne hyrde ic cymlicor　ceol gegyrwan
　　hildewæpnum　ond heaðowædum,
40 billum ond byrnum;　him on bearme læg
　　madma mænigo,　þa him mid scoldon
　　on flodes æht　feor gewitan.
　　Nalæs hi hine læssan　lacum teodan,
　　þeodgestreonum,　þon þa dydon
45 þe hine æt frumsceafte　forð onsendon
　　ænne ofer yðe　umborwesende.
　　Þa gyt hie him asetton　segen ge[l]denne
　　heah ofer heafod,　leton holm beran,
　　geafon on garsecg;　him wæs geomor sefa,
50 murnende mod.　Men ne cunnon
　　secgan to soðe,　selerædende,
　　hæleð under heofenum,　hwa þæm hlæste onfeng.
　　　Ða wæs on burgum　Beowulf Scyldinga,
　　leof leodcyning,　longe þrage
55 folcum gefræge　(fæder ellor hwearf,
　　aldor of earde),　oþþæt him eft onwoc
　　heah Healfdene;　heold þenden lifde,
　　gamol ond guðreouw,　glæde Scyldingas.
　　Ðæm feower bearn　forð gerimed
60 in worold wocun,　weoroda ræswan,
　　Heorogar ond Hroðgar　ond Halga til;
　　hyrde ic þæt　*　*　*　wæs Onelan cwen,
　　Heaðoscilfingas　healsgebedda.
　　　Þa wæs Hroðgare　heresped gyfen,

48 beran] beran A, bera B　51 selerædende] sele rædenne　60 ræswan]
ræswa　62 wæs Onelan] elan　63 Heaðoscilfingas] With heaðo written
on an erasure?

65 wiges weorðmynd, þæt him his winemagas
   georne hyrdon, oðð þæt seo geogoð geweox,
   magodriht micel, Him on mod bearn
   þæt healreced hatan wolde,
   *medo*ærn micel, men gewyrcean
70 þonne yldo bearn æfre gefrunon,
   ond þær on innan eall gedælan
   geongum ond ealdum, swylc him god sealde,
   buton folcscare ond feorum gumena.
   Ða ic wide gefrægn weorc gebannan
75 manigre mægþe geond þisne middangeard,
   folcstede frætwan. Him on fyrste gelomp,
   ædre mid yldum, þæt hit wearð ealgearo,
   healærna mæst; scop him Heort naman
   se þe his wordes geweald wide hæfde.
80 He beot ne aleh, beagas dælde,
   sinc æt symle. Sele hlifade,
   heah ond horngeap, heaðowylma bad,
   laðan liges; ne wæs hit lenge þa gen
   þæt se ecghete aþumsweorum
85 æfter wælniðe wæcnan scolde.
       Ða se ellengæst earfoðlice
   þrage geþolode, se þe in þystrum bad,
   þæt he dogora gehwam dream gehyrde
   hludne in healle; þær wæs hearpan sweg,
90 swutol sang scopes. Sægde se þe cuþe
   frumsceaft fira feorran reccan,
   cwæð þæt se ælmihtiga eorðan worh[te],
   wlitebeorhtne wang, swa wæter bebugeð,
   gesette sigehreþig sunnan ond monan
95 leoman to leohte landbuendum
   ond gefrætwade foldan sceatas
   leomum ond leafum, lif eac gesceop
   cynna gehwylcum þara ðe cwice hwyrfaþ.

69 medoærn] ærn (*added later*) A, medo ærn (*with* medo *added later*) B, medo
ærn *Wanley*   70 þonne] þone   84 ecghete] secg hete   aþumsweorum]
aþum swerian   90 Sægde] *With the* g *inserted between* æ *and* d *by the same
hand*

Swa ða drihtguman   dreamum lifdon
100 eadiglice,   oððæt an ongan
fyrene fre[m]man   feond on helle.
Wæs se grimma gæst   Grendel haten,
mære mearcstapa,   se þe moras heold,
fen ond fæsten;   fifelcynnes eard
105 wonsæli wer   weardode hwile,
siþðan him scyppend   forscrifen hæfde
in Caines cynne.   Þone cwealm gewræc
ece drihten,   þæs þe he Abel slog;
ne gefeah he þære fæhðe,   ac he hine feor forwræc,
110 metod for þy mane,   mancynne fram.
Þanon untydras   ealle onwocon,
eotenas ond ylfe   ond orcneas,
swylce gi[ga]ntas,   þa wið gode wunnon
lange þrage;   he him ðæs lean forgeald.
115   Gewat ða neosian,   syþðan niht becom,
hean huses,   hu hit Hringdene
æfter beorþege   gebun hæfdon.
Fand þa ðær inne   æþelinga gedriht
swefan æfter symble;   sorge ne cuðon,
120 wonsceaft wera.   Wiht unhælo,
grim ond grædig,   gearo sona wæs,
reoc ond reþe,   ond on ræste genam
þritig þegna,   þanon eft gewat
huðe hremig   to ham faran,
125 mid þære wælfylle   wica neosan.
    Ða wæs on uhtan   mid ærdæge
Grendles guðcræft   gumum undyrne;
þa wæs æfter wiste   wop up ahafen,
micel morgensweg.   Mære þeoden,
130 æþeling ærgod,   unbliðe sæt,
þolode ðryðswyð,   þegnsorge dreah,
syðþan hie þæs laðan   last sceawedon,

---

106 scyppend] *With the* d *added by a different hand*   107 Caines] *With* in
altered from m *by erasure*   113 gigantas] gio ntas (*later altered by Thorkelin to* gigantas) *A*, gi ntas (*with* ga *later inserted by Thorkelin*) *B; see Note*

wergan gastes; wæs þæt gewin to strang,
laðond longsum. Næs hit lengra fyrst,
135 ac ymb ane niht eft gefremede
morðbeala mare ond no mearn fore,
fæhðe ond fyrene; wæs to fæst on þam.
Þa wæs eaðfynde þe him elles hwær
gerumlicor ræste sohte,
140 bed æfter burum, ða him gebeacnod wæs,
gesægd soðlice sweotolan tacne
healðegnes hete; heold hyne syðþan
fyr ond fæstor se þæm feonde ætwand.
Swa rixode ond wið rihte wan,
145 ana wið eallum, oðþæt idel stod
husa selest. Wæs seo hwil micel;
XII wintra tid torn geþolode
wine Scyldinga, weana gehwelcne,
sidra sorga. Forðam secgum wearð,
150 ylda bearnum, undyrne cuð,
gyddum geomore, þætte Grendel wan
hwile wið Hroþgar, heteniðas wæg,
fyrene ond fæhðe fela missera,
singale sæce, sibbe ne wolde
155 wið manna hwone mægenes Deniga,
feorhbealo feorran, fea þingian,
ne þær nænig witena wenan þorfte
beorhtre bote to banan folmum,
[ac se] æglæca ehtende wæs,
160 deorc deaþscua, duguþe ond geogoþe,
seomade ond syrede, sinnihte heold
mistige moras; men ne cunnon
hwyder helrunan hwyrftum scriþað.
Swa fela fyrena feond mancynnes,
165 atol angengea, oft gefremede,
heardra hynða. Heorot eardode,

  sincfage sel sweartum nihtum;
  no he þone gifstol gretan moste,
  maþðum for metode, ne his myne wisse.
170 Þæt wæs wræc micel wine Scyldinga,
  modes brecða. Monig oft gesæt
  rice to rune; ræd eahtedon
  hwæt swiðferhðum selest wære
  wið færgryrum to gefremmanne.
175 Hwilum hie geheton æt hærgtrafum
  wigweorþunga, wordum bædon
  þæt him gastbona geoce gefremede
  wið þeodþreaum. Swylc wæs þeaw hyra,
  hæþenra hyht; helle gemundon
180 in modsefan, metod hie ne cuþon,
  dæda demend, ne wiston hie drihten god,
  ne hie huru heofena helm herian ne cuþon,
  wuldres waldend. Wa bið þæm ðe sceal
  þurh sliðne nið sawle bescufan
185 in fyres fæþm, frofre ne wenan,
  wihte gewendan; wel bið þæm þe mot
  æfter deaðdæge drihten secean
  ond to fæder fæþmum freoðo wilnian.
   Swa ða mælceare maga Healfdenes
190 singala seað, ne mihte snotor hæleð
  wean onwendan; wæs þæt gewin to swyð,
  laþ ond longsum, þe on ða leode becom,
  nydwracu niþgrim, nihtbealwa mæst.
   Þæt fram ham gefrægn Higelaces þegn,
195 god mid Geatum, Grendles dæda;
  se wæs moncynnes mægenes strengest
  on þæm dæge þysses lifes,
  æþele ond eacen. Het him yðlidan
  godne gegyrwan, cwæð, he guðcyning
200 ofer swanrade secean wolde,

---

175 hærgtrafum] hrærg trafum 186 gewendan] *Originally* ge wenan, *but
an altered to* da *and* n *added by the same hand* 189 Healfdenes] *Originally*
healfdes, *but* s *altered to* n *and* es *added by the same hand*

mærne þeoden,   þa him wæs manna þearf.
Ðone siðfæt him   snotere ceorlas
lythwon logon,   þeah he him leof wære;
hwetton hige[r]oƒne,   hæl sceawedon.
205 Hæfde se goda   Geata leoda
cempan gecorone   þara þe he cenoste
findan mihte;   XVna sum
sundwudu sohte;   secg wisade,
lagucræftig mon,   landgemyrcu.
210 Fyrst forð gewat.   Flota wæs on yðum,
bat under beorge.   Beornas gearwe
on stefn stigon;   streamas wundon,
sund wið sande;   secgas bæron
on bearm nacan   beorhte frætwe,
215 guðsearo geatolic;   guman ut scufon,
weras on wilsið,   wudu bundenne.
Gewat þa ofer wægholm,   winde gefysed,
flota famiheals   fugle gelicost,
oðþæt ymb antid   oþres dogores
220 wundenstefna   gewaden hæfde
þæt ða liðende   land gesawon,
brimclifu blican,   beorgas steape,
side sænæssas;   þa wæs sund liden,
eoletes æt ende.   þanon up hraðe
225 Wedera leode   on wang stigon,
sæwudu sældon   (syrcan hrysedon,
guðgewædo),   gode þancedon
þæs þe him yþlade   eaðe wurdon.
    þa of wealle geseah   weard Scildinga,
230 se þe holmclifu   healdan scolde,
beran ofer bolcan   beorhte randas,
fyrdsearu fuslicu;   hine fyrwyt bræc
modgehygdum,   hwæt þa men wæron.
    Gewat him þa to waroðe   wicge ridan
235 þegn Hroðgares,   þrymmum cwehte

201 þearf] *With the* a *altered from* r *by the same hand*   204 -rofne] pofne
(*or* þofne?) *A,* forne *B*   207 XVna] .xv. *with the letters* na *written above* v
by the same hand

    mægenwudu mundum, meþelwordum frægn:
    "Hwæt syndon ge searohæbbendra,
    byrnum werede, þe þus brontne ceol
    ofer lagustræte lædan cwomon,
240 hider ofer holmas? * * * le wæs
    endesæta, ægwearde heold,
    þe on land Dena laðra nænig
    mid scipherge sceðþan ne meahte.
    No her cuðlicor cuman ongunnon
245 lindhæbbende; ne ge leafnesword
    guðfremmendra gearwe ne wisson,
    maga gemedu. Næfre ic maran geseah
    eorla ofer eorþan ðonne is eower sum,
    secg on searwum; nis þæt seldguma,
250 wæpnum geweorðad, næfne him his wlite leoge,
    ænlic ansyn. Nu ic eower sceal
    frumcyn witan, ær ge fyr heonan,
    leassceaweras, on land Dena
    furþur feran. Nu ge feorbuend,
255 mereliðende, minne gehyrað
    anfealdne geþoht: Ofost is selest
    to gecyðanne hwanan eowre cyme syndon."
      Him se yldesta ondswarode,
    werodes wisa, wordhord onleac:
260 "We synt gumcynnes Geata leode
    ond Higelaces heorðgeneatas.
    Wæs min fæder folcum gecyþed,
    æþele ordfruma, Ecgþeow haten.
    Gebad wintra worn, ær he on weg hwurfe,
265 gamol of geardum; hine gearwe geman
    witena welhwylc wide geond eorþan.
    We þurh holdne hige hlaford þinne,
    sunu Healfdenes, secean cwomon,
    leodgebyrgean; wes þu us larena god.
270 Habbað we to þæm mæran micel ærende,

---

250 næfne] næfre   255 minne] mine   263 Ecgþeow] *With the* g *inserted*
by the same hand   267 hige] *With the* g *altered from* n *by the same hand*
hlaford] *Written twice, but the second* hlaford *crossed out*

Deniga frean,　ne sceal þær dyrne sum
wesan, þæs ic wene.　Þu wast (gif hit is
swa we soþlice　secgan hyrdon)
þæt mid Scyldingum　scea*ð*o*na* ic nat hwylc,
275 deogol dædhata,　deorcum nihtum
eaweð þurh egsan　uncuðne nið,
hynðu ond hrafyl.　Ic þæs Hroðgar mæg
þurh rumne sefan　ræd gelæran,
hu he frod ond god　feond oferswyðeþ,
280 gyf him edwendan　æfre scolde
bealuwa bisigu,　bot eft cuman,
ond þa cearwylmas　colran wurðaþ;
oððe a syþðan　earfoðþrage,
þreanyd þolað,　þenden þær wunað
285 on heahstede　husa selest."
　　Weard maþelode,　ðær on wicge sæt,
ombeht unforht:　"Æghwæþres sceal
scearp scyldwiga　gescad witan,
worda ond worca,　se þe wel þenceð.
290 Ic þæt gehyre,　þæt þis is hold weorod
frean Scyldinga.　Gewitaþ forð beran
wæpen ond gewædu;　ic eow wisige.
Swylce ic maguþegnas　mine hate
wið feonda gehwone　flotan eowerne,
295 niwtyrwydne　nacan on sande
arum healdan,　oþðæt eft byreð
ofer lagustreamas　leofne mannan
wudu wundenhals　to Wedermearce,
godfremmendra　swylcum gifeþe bið
300 þæt þone hilderæs　hal gedigeð."
　　Gewiton him þa feran.　Flota stille bad,
seomode on sale　sidfæþmed scip,
on ancre fæst.　Eoforlic scionon
ofer hleorberan　gehroden golde,
305 fah ond fyrheard;　ferhwearde heold
guþmod grimmon.　Guman onetton,

274 sceaðona] sceaðona *A*, sceaðo *B*　302 sale] sole　303 fæst] *With*
the s *altered from* f *by erasure*　306 grimmon] grummon

sigon ætsomne,   oþþæt hy sæl timbred,
geatolic ond goldfah,   ongyton mihton;
þæt wæs foremærost   foldbuendum
310 receda under roderum,   on þæm se rica bad;
lixte se leoma   ofer landa fela.
Him þa hildedeor   hof modigra
torht getæhte,   þæt hie him to mihton
gegnum gangan;   guðbeorna sum
315 wicg gewende,   word æfter cwæð:
"Mæl is me to feran;   fæder alwalda
mid arstafum   eowic gehealde
siða gesunde.   Ic to sæ wille
wið wrað werod   wearde healdan."
320 Stræt wæs stanfah,   stig wisode
gumum ætgædere.   Guðbyrne scan
heard hondlocen,   hringiren scir
song in searwum,   þa hie to sele furðum
in hyra gryregeatwum   gangan cwomon.
325 Setton sæmeþe   side scyldas,
rondas regnhearde,   wið þæs recedes weal,
bugon þa to bence.   Byrnan hringdon,
guðsearo gumena;   garas stodon,
sæmanna searo,   samod ætgædere,
330 æscholt ufan græg;   wæs se irenþreat
wæpnum gewurþad.   þa ðær wlonc hæleð
oretmecgas   æfter æþelum frægn:
"Hwanon ferigeað ge   fætte scyldas,
græge syrcan   ond grimhelmas,
335 heresceafta heap?   Ic eom Hroðgares
ar ond ombiht.   Ne seah ic elþeodige
þus manige men   modiglicran.
Wen ic þæt ge for wlenco,   nalles for wræcsiðum,
ac for higeþrymmum   Hroðgar sohton."
340   Him þa ellenrof   andswarode,
wlanc Wedera leod,   word æfter spræc,

---

307 sæl timbred] æltimbred   312 hof] of   331 wlonc] *With the letters*
nc *written on an erasure*   332 æþelum] hæle þum   339 -þrymmum]
þrymmum *A*, ym mun (*later altered by Thorkelin to* þrymmum) *B*

heard under helme: "We synt Higelaces
beodgeneatas; Beowulf is min nama.
Wille ic asecgan   sunu Healfdenes,
345 mærum þeodne,   min ærende,
aldre þinum,   gif he us geunnan wile
þæt we hine swa godne   gretan moton."
　　Wulfgar maþelode   (þæt wæs Wendla leod;
wæs his modsefa   manegum gecyðed,
350 wig ond wisdom):   "Ic þæs wine Deniga,
frean Scildinga,   frinan wille,
beaga bryttan,   swa þu bena eart,
þeoden mærne,   ymb þinne sið,
ond þe þa ondsware   ædre gecyðan
355 ðe me se goda   agifan þenceð."
　　Hwearf þa hrædlice   þær Hroðgar sæt
eald ond anhar   mid his eorla gedriht;
eode ellenrof,   þæt he for eaxlum gestod
Deniga frean;   cuþe he duguðe þeaw.
360 Wulfgar maðelode   to his winedrihtne:
"Her syndon geferede,   feorran cumene
ofer geofenes begang   Geata leode;
þone yldestan   oretmecgas
Beowulf nemnað.   Hy benan synt
365 þæt hie, þeoden min,   wið þe moton
wordum wrixlan.   No ðu him wearne geteoh
ðinra gegncwida,   glædman Hroðgar.
Hy on wiggetawum   wyrðe þinceað
eorla geæhtlan;   huru se aldor deah,
370 se þæm heaðorincum   hider wisade."
　　Hroðgar maþelode,   helm Scyldinga:
"Ic hine cuðe   cnihtwesende.
Wæs his ealdfæder   Ecgþeo haten,
ðæm to ham forgeaf   Hreþel Geata
375 angan dohtor;   is his eafora nu
heard her cumen,   sohte holdne wine.

357 anhar] un hár   360 to his] thois A, to his B   375 his] With the
h altered from þ by erasure   eafora] eaforan   376 holdne] With the n
altered from r by erasure

Ðonne sægdon þæt sæliþende,
þa ðe gifsceattas Geata fyredon
þyder to þance, þæt he XXXtiges
380 manna mægencræft on his mundgripe
heaþorof hæbbe. Hine halig god
for arstafum us onsende,
to Westdenum, þæs ic wen hæbbe,
wið Grendles gryre. Ic þæm godan sceal
385 for his modþræce madmas beodan.
Beo ðu on ofeste, hat in gan
seon sibbegedriht samod ætgædere;
gesaga him eac wordum þæt hie sint wilcuman
Deniga leodum."
                    *   *   *
390   word inne abead:
"Eow het secgan sigedrihten min,
aldor Eastdena, þæt he eower æþelu can,
ond ge him syndon ofer sæwylmas
heardhicgende hider wilcuman.
395 Nu ge moton gangan in eowrum guðgeatawum
under heregriman Hroðgar geseon;
lætað hildebord her onbidan,
wudu, wælsceaftas, worda geþinges."
Aras þa se rica, ymb hine rinc manig,
400 þryðlic þegna heap; sume þær bidon,
heaðoreaf heoldon, swa him se hearda bebead.
Snyredon ætsomne, þa secg wisode,
under Heorotes hrof *   *   *
he*ard* under helme, þæt he on heoðe gestod.
405 Beowulf maðelode (on him byrne scan,
searonet seowed smiþes orþancum):
"Wæs þu, Hroðgar, hal! Ic eom Higelaces
mæg ond magoðegn; hæbbe ic mærða fela

384 þæm] þæim AB (in A, þæim is in Thorkelin's hand)   397 onbidan]
Originally on bidman, but m partly erased   401 heaðoreaf] heaðo rof
with an e added above the line after r by a different hand and the second o
altered to a   404 heard] heard B, not in A   406 searonet] seawo net A,
searo net B   407 Wæs] A letter erased after this word   Hroðgar] hroð
gar A, hrod gar B

ongunnen on geogoþe. Me wearð Grendles þing
410 on minre eþeltyrf   undyrne cuð;
secgað sæliðend   þæt þæs sele stande,
reced selesta,   rinca gehwylcum
idel ond unnyt,   siððan æfenleoht
under heofenes hador   beholen weorþeð.
415 Þa me þæt gelærdon   leode mine
þa selestan,   snotere ceorlas,
þeoden Hroðgar,   þæt ic þe sohte,
forþan hie mægenes cræft   minne cuþon,
selfe ofersawon,   ða ic of searwum cwom,
420 fah from feondum;   þær ic fife geband,
yðde eotena cyn   ond on yðum slog
niceras nihtes,   nearoþearfe dreah,
wræc Wedera nið   (wean ahsodon),
forgrand gramum,   ond nu wið Grendel sceal,
425 wið þam aglæcan,   ana gehegan
ðing wið þyrse.   Ic þe nu ða,
brego Beorhtdena,   biddan wille,
eodor Scyldinga,   anre bene,
þæt ðu me ne forwyrne,   wigendra hleo,
430 freowine folca,   nu ic þus feorran com,
þæt ic mote ana   ond minra eorla gedryht,
þes hearda heap,   Heorot fælsian.
Hæbbe ic eac geahsod   þæt se æglæca
for his wonhydum   wæpna ne recceð.
435 Ic þæt þonne forhicge   (swa me Higelac sie,
min mondrihten,   modes bliðe),
þæt ic sweord bere   oþðe sidne scyld,
geolorand to guþe,   ac ic mid grape sceal
fon wið feonde   ond ymb feorh sacan,
440 lað wið laþum;   ðær gelyfan sceal
dryhtnes dome   se þe hine deað nimeð.
Wen ic þæt he wille,   gif he wealdan mot,
in þæm guðsele   Geotena leode
etan unforhte,   swa he oft dyde,

445 mægen Hreðmanna. Na þu minne þearft
hafalan hydan, ac he me habban wile
dreore fahne, gif mec deað nimeð.
Byreð blodig wæl, byrgean þenceð,
eteð angenga unmurnlice,
450 mearcað morhopu; no ðu ymb mines ne þearft
lices feorme leng sorgian.
Onsend Higelace, gif mec hild nime,
beaduscruda betst, þæt mine breost wereð,
hrægla selest; þæt is Hrædlan laf,
455 Welandes geweorc. Gæð a wyrd swa hio scel."
Hroðgar maþelode, helm Scyldinga:
"For gewyrhtum þu, wine min Beowulf,
ond for arstafum usic sohtest.
Gesloh þin fæder fæhðe mæste;
460 wearþ he Heaþolafe to handbonan
mid Wilfingum; ða hine Wedera cyn
for herebrogan habban ne mihte.
Þanon he gesohte Suðdena folc
ofer yða gewealc, Arscyldinga.
465 Ða ic furþum weold folce Deniga
ond on geogoðe heold ginne rice,
hordburh hæleþa; ða wæs Heregar dead,
min yldra mæg unlifigende,
bearn Healfdenes; se wæs betera ðonne ic.
470 Siððan þa fæhðe feo þingode;
sende ic Wylfingum ofer wæteres hrycg
ealde madmas; he me aþas swor.
Sorh is me to secganne on sefan minum
gumena ængum hwæt me Grendel hafað
475 hynðo on Heorote mid his heteþancum,
færniða gefremed. Is min fletwerod,
wigheap gewanod; hie wyrd forsweop
on Grendles gryre. God eaþe mæg
þone dolsceaðan dæda getwæfan.

447 dreore] deore   457 For gewyrhtum] fere fyhtum   461 Wedera]
gara   465 Deniga] de ninga   466 ginne] gim me   479 dolsceaðan]
With the e *added above the line by another hand*

480 Ful oft gebeotedon beore druncne ·
ofer ealowæge oretmecgas
þæt hie in beorsele bidan woldon
Grendles guþe mid gryrum ecga.
Ðonne wæs þeos medoheal on morgentid,
485 drihtsele dreorfah, þonne dæg lixte,
eal bencþelu blode bestymed,
heall heorudreore; ahte ic holdra þy læs,
deorre duguðe, þe þa deað fornam.
Site nu to symle ond onsæl meoto,
490 sigehreð secgum, swa þin sefa hwette.''
Þa wæs Geatmæcgum geador ætsomne
on beorsele benc gerymed;
þær swiðferhþe sittan eodon,
þryðum dealle. Þegn nytte beheold,
495 se þe on handa bær hroden ealowæge,
scencte scir wered. Scop hwilum sang
hador on Heorote. Þær wæs hæleða dream,
duguð unlytel Dena ond Wedera.
Unferð maþelode, Ecglafes bearn,
500 þe æt fotum sæt frean Scyldinga,
onband beadurune (wæs him Beowulfes sið,
modges merefaran, micel æfþunca,
forþon þe he ne uþe þæt ænig oðer man
æfre mærða þon ma middangeardes
505 gehedde under heofenum þonne he sylfa):
''Eart þu se Beowulf, se þe wið Brecan wunne,
on sidne sæ ymb sund flite,
ðær git for wlence wada cunnedon
ond for dolgilpe on deop wæter
510 aldrum neþdon? Ne inc ænig mon,
ne leof ne lað, belean mihte
sorhfullne sið, þa git on sund reon.
Þær git eagorstream earmum þehton,

---

484 medoheal] *About three letters erased between* medo *and* heal 487
heoru-] heoru *B*, heorn *or* heora (*the* n *or* a *later changed, apparently by
Thorkelin, to* u) *A* 499 Unferð] HvN ferð 503 man] *Four or five
letters erased after this word*

mæton merestræta,   mundum brugdon,
515 glidon ofer garsecg;   geofon yþum weol,
wintrys wylmum.   Git on wæteres æht
seofon niht swuncon;   he þe æt sunde oferflat,
hæfde mare mægen.   þa hine on morgentid
on Heaþoræmas   holm up ætbær;
520 ðonon he gesohte   swæsne ⋆,
leof his leodum,   lond Brondinga,
freoðoburh fægere,   þær he folc ahte,
burh ond beagas.   Beot eal wið þe
sunu Beanstanes   soðe gelæste.
525 Ðonne wene ic to þe   wyrsan geþingea,
ðeah þu heaðoræsa   gehwær dohte,
grimre guðe,   gif þu Grendles dearst
nihtlongne fyrst   nean bidan."
      Beowulf maþelode,   bearn Ecgþeowes:
530 "Hwæt! þu worn fela,   wine min Unferð,
beore druncen   ymb Brecan spræce,
sægdest from his siðe.   Soð ic talige,
þæt ic merestrengo   maran ahte,
earfeþo on yþum,   ðonne ænig oþer man.
535 Wit þæt gecwædon   cnihtwesende
ond gebeotedon   (wæron begen þa git
on geogoðfeore)   þæt wit on garsecg ut
aldrum neðdon,   ond þæt geæfndon swa.
Hæfdon swurd nacod,   þa wit on sund reon,
540 heard on handa;   wit unc wið hronfixas
werian þohton.   No he wiht fram me
flodyþum feor   fleotan meahte,
hraþor on holme;   no ic fram him wolde.
Ða wit ætsomne   on sæ wæron
545 fif nihta fyrst,   oþþæt unc flod todraf,
wado weallende,   wedera cealdost,
nipende niht,   ond norþanwind
heaðogrim ondhwearf;   hreo wæron yþa.

516 wylmum] wylm   519 Heaþoræmas] hea þo ræmes   524 soðe] sode
A, soðe B   530 Unferð] hun fer[.] MS., hun ferð A, Hunferd B   537a
on] With the n added above the line by a different hand

Wæs merefixa   mod onhrered;
550 þær me wið laðum   licsyrce min,
heard, hondlocen,   helpe gefremede,
beadohrægl broden   on breostum læg
golde gegyrwed.   Me to grunde teah
fah feondscaða,   fæste hæfde
555 grim on grape;   hwæþre me gyfeþe wearð
þæt ic aglæcan   orde geræhte,
hildebille;   heaþoræs fornam
mihtig meredeor   þurh mine hand.
Swa mec gelome   laðgeteonan
560 þreatedon þearle.   Ic him þenode
deoran sweorde,   swa hit gedefe wæs.
Næs hie ðære fylle   gefean hæfdon,
manfordædlan,   þæt hie me þegon,
symbel ymbsæton   sægrunde neah;
565 ac on mergenne   mecum wunde
be yðlafe   uppe lægon,
sweo[r]dum aswefede,   þæt syðþan na
ymb brontne ford   brimliðende
lade ne letton.   Leoht eastan com,
570 beorht beacen godes;   brimu swaþredon,
þæt ic sænæssas   geseon mihte,
windige weallas.   Wyrd oft nereð
unfægne eorl,   þonne his ellen deah.
Hwæþere me gesælde   þæt ic mid sweorde ofsloh
575 niceras nigene.   No ic on niht gefrægn
under heofones hwealf   heardran feohtan,
ne on egstreamum   earmran mannon;
hwaþere ic fara feng   feore gedigde,
siþes werig.   Ða mec sæ oþbær,
580 flod æfter faroðe   on Finna land,
wadu weallendu.   No ic wiht fram þe
swylcra searoniða   secgan hyrde,
billa brogan.   Breca næfre git
æt heaðolace,   ne gehwæþer incer,

555 grape] *About seven letters* (hwæþere?) *erased after this word, at the end
of a line*   567 sweordum] sweoðū *A,* swe.. *B*   581 wadu] wudu

585 swa deorlice　dæd gefremede
　　 fagum sweordum　(no ic þæs fela gylpe),
　　 þeah ðu þinum broðrum　to banan wurde,
　　 heafodmægum;　þæs þu in helle scealt
　　 werhðo dreogan,　þeah þin *wit d*uge.
590 Secge ic þe to soðe,　sunu Ecg*lafes*,
　　 þæt næfre Grendel swa fela　gryra gefremede,
　　 atol æglæca,　ealdre þinum,
　　 hynðo on Heorote,　gif þin hige wære,
　　 sefa swa searogrim,　swa þu self talast.
595 Ac he hafað onfunden　þæt he þa fæhðe ne þearf,
　　 atole ecgþræce　eower leode
　　 swiðe onsittan,　Sigescyldinga;
　　 nymeð nydbade,　nænegum arað
　　 leode Deniga,　ac he lust wigeð,
600 swefeð ond sendeþ,　secce ne weneþ
　　 to Gardenum.　Ac ic him Geata sceal
　　 eafoð ond ellen　ungeara nu,
　　 guþe gebeodan.　Gæþ eft se þe mot
　　 to medo modig,　siþþan morgenleoht
605 ofer ylda bearn　oþres dogores,
　　 sunne sweglwered　suþan scineð."
　　　　 Þa wæs on salum　sinces brytta,
　　 gamolfeax ond guðrof;　geoce gelyfde
　　 brego Beorhtdena,　gehyrde on Beowulfe
610 folces hyrde　fæstrædne geþoht.
　　　　 Ðær wæs hæleþa hleahto*r*,　hlyn swynsode,
　　 word wæron wynsume.　Eode Wealhþeow forð,
　　 cwen Hroðgares,　cynna gemyndig,
　　 grette goldhroden　guman on healle,
615 ond þa freolic wif　ful gesealde
　　 ærest Eastdena　eþelwearde,

---

586 fela] *Not in MS.*　　589 wit duge] wit dug *followed by an erasure A,*
...nigt. *B; in the MS. the* e *of* duge *is altered from some other letter* (u?)
590 Ecglafes] ecg lafes *A*, Ecg þeoves *B*　　591 Grendel] gre del　　603 eft]
With the t *added above the line by the same hand*　　611 hleahtor] heleahtar
A, hleahtan *B*, Hleahtor *Conybeare*　　612 Wealhþeow] *With the final* w
added above the line by the same hand

bæd hine bliðne æt þære beorþege,
leodum leofne. He on lust geþeah
symbel ond seleful, sigerof kyning.
620 Ymbeode þa ides Helminga
duguþe ond geogoþe dæl æghwylcne,
sincfato sealde, oþþæt sæl alamp
þæt hio Beowulfe, beaghroden cwen
mode geþungen, medoful ætbær;
625 grette Geata leod, gode þancode
wisfæst wordum þæs ðe hire se willa gelamp
þæt heo on ænigne eorl gelyfde
fyrena frofre. He þæt ful geþeah,
wælreow wiga, æt Wealhþeon,
630 ond þa gyddode guþe gefysed;
Beowulf maþelode, bearn Ecgþeowes:
"Ic þæt hogode, þa ic on holm gestah,
sæbat gesæt mid minra secga gedriht,
þæt ic anunga eowra leoda
635 willan geworhte oþðe on wæl crunge,
feondgrapum fæst. Ic gefremman sceal
eorlic ellen, oþðe endedæg
on þisse meoduhealle minne gebidan."
Ðam wife þa word wel licodon,
640 gilpcwide Geates; eode goldhroden
freolicu folccwen to hire *fr*ean sittan.
þa wæs eft swa ær inne on healle
þryðword sprecen, ðeod on sælum,
sigefolca sweg, oþþæt semninga
645 sunu Healfdenes secean wolde
æfenræste; wiste þæm ahlæcan
to þæm heahsele hilde geþinged,
siððan hie sunnan leoht geseon ne meahton,
oþðe nipende niht ofer ealle,
650 scaduhelma gesceapu scriðan cwoman,
wan under wolcnum. Werod eall aras.
Gegrette þa guma oþerne,

641 frean] ean *preceded by a space A*, frean *B*   648 ne] *Not in MS.*   652
Gegrette] gret te

Hroðgar Beowulf,   ond him hæl abead,
winærnes geweald,   ond þæt word acwæð:
655 "Næfre ic ænegum men   ær alyfde,
siþðan ic hond ond rond   hebban mihte,
ðryþærn Dena   buton þe nu ða.
Hafa nu ond geheald   husa selest,
gemyne mærþo,   mægenellen cyð,
660 waca wið wraþum.   Ne bið þe wilna gad,
gif þu þæt ellenweorc   aldre gedigest."
      Ða him Hroþgar gewat   mid his hæleþa gedryht,
eodur Scyldinga,   ut of healle;
wolde wigfruma   Wealhþeo secan,
665 cwen to gebeddan.   Hæfde kyningwuldor
Grendle togeanes,   swa guman gefrungon,
seleweard aseted;   sundornytte beheold
ymb aldor Dena,   eotonweard abead.
Huru Geata leod   georne truwode
670 modgan mægnes,   metodes hyldo.
      Ða he him of dyde   isernbyrnan,
helm of hafelan,   sealde his hyrsted sweord,
irena cyst,   ombihtþegne,
ond gehealdan het   hildegeatwe.
675 Gespræc þa se goda   gylpworda sum,
Beowulf Geata,   ær he on bed stige:
"No ic me an herewæsmun   hnagran talige,
guþgeweorca,   þonne Grendel hine;
forþan ic hine sweorde   swebban nelle,
680 aldre beneotan,   þeah ic eal mæge.
Nat he þara goda   þæt he me ongean slea,
rand geheawe,   þeah ðe he rof sie
niþgeweorca;   ac wit on niht sculon
secge ofersittan,   gif he gesecean dear
685 wig ofer wæpen,   ond siþðan witig god
on swa hwæþere hond,   halig dryhten,
mærðo deme,   swa him gemet þince."
      Hylde hine þa heaþodeor,   hleorbolster onfeng

684 he] het

eorles andwlitan, ond hine ymb monig
690 snellic særinc selereste gebeah.
Nænig heora þohte þæt he þanon scolde
eft eardlufan æfre gesecean,
folc oþ́ðe freoburh, þær he afeded wæs;
ac hie hæfdon gefrunen þæt hie ær to fela micles
695 in þæm winsele wældeað fornam,
Denigea leode. Ac him dryhten forgeaf
wigspeda gewiofu, Wedera leodum,
frofor ond ful*tum*, *þæt hie* feond heora
ðurh anes cræft ealle ofercomon,
700 selfes mihtum. Soð is gecyþed
þæt mihtig god manna cynnes
weold [w]ideferhð. Com on wanre niht
scriðan sceadugenga. Sceotend swæfon,
þa þæt hornreced healdan scoldon,
705 ealle buton anum. Þæt wæs yldum cuþ
þæt hie ne moste, þa metod nolde,
se scynscaþa under sceadu bregdan;
ac he wæccende wraþum on andan
bad bolgenmod beadwa geþinges.
710 Ða com of more under misthleoþum
Grendel gongan, godes yrre bær;
mynte se manscaða manna cynnes
sumne besyrwan in sele þam hean.
Wod under wolcnum to þæs þe he winreced,
715 goldsele gumena, gearwost wisse,
fættum fahne. Ne wæs þæt forma sið
þæt he Hroþgares ham gesohte;
næfre he on aldordagum ær *ne* siþðan

---

698 fultum] ful tum *A*, fultum (*with* um *added later by Thorkelin*) *B* þæt
hie] þ̄ hie *A*, that hie (*added later by Thorkelin*) *B* 702 wide-] ride *A*, ride
(*added later by Thorkelin*) *B*, side *Conybeare* 707 scynscaþa] syn scaþa
713 besyrwan] be syrwan *A*, be syrvan (*with the* e *added later by Thorkelin
and then marked for deletion*) *B* 714 wolcnum] wole num *A*, wolc num *B*
718 ær ne siþðan] ær nes iþðan *A*, ær *followed by a space at the end of a page
and* siþðan *at the beginning of the next page B*

heardran hæle,   healðegnas fand.
720 Com þa to recede   rinc siðian,
dreamum bedæled.   Duru sona onarn,
fyrbendum fæst,   syþðan he hire folmum [æthr]an;
onbræd þa bealohydig,   ða *he* [ge]bolgen wæs,
recedes muþan.   Raþe æfter þon
725 on fagne flor   feond treddode,
eode yrremod;   him of eagum stod
ligge gelicost   leoht unfæger.
Geseah he in recede   rinca manige,
swefan sibbegedriht   samod ætgædere,
730 magorinca heap.   þa his mod ahlog;
mynte þæt he gedælde,   ærþon dæg cwome,
atol aglæca,   anra gehwylces
lif wið lice,   þa him alumpen wæs
wistfylle wen.   Ne wæs *þæt* wyrd þa gen
735 þæt he ma moste   manna cynnes
ðicgean ofer þa niht.   þryðswyð beheold
mæg Higelaces,   hu se manscaða
under færgripum   gefaran wolde.
Ne þæt se aglæca   yldan þohte,
740 ac he gefeng hraðe   forman siðe
slæpendne rinc,   slat unwearnum,
bat banlocan,   blod edrum dranc,
synsnædum swealh;   sona hæfde
unlyfigendes   eal gefeormod,
745 fet ond folma.   Forð near ætstop,
nam þa mid handa   higeþihtigne
rinc on ræste,   ræhte ongean
feond mid folme;   he onfeng hraþe
inwitþancum   ond wið earm gesæt.
750   Sona þæt onfunde   fyrena hyrde
þæt he ne mette   middangeardes,

---

721 onarn] *With the* o *altered from* s   722 æthran] *The final* n *altered from*
m?   723 he gebolgen] ....bolgen *A*, ...bolgen *B*, he *Conybeare*
734 wæs þæt wyrd] wes ꝥ wypd *A*, wæs wyrð *B*   747 ræste] *An erasure of*
about five letters after this word, at the end of a line; the first of the erased letters
seems to have been h

eorþan sceata,　on elran men
mundgripe maran.　He on mode wearð
forht on ferhðe;　no þy ær fram meahte.
755 Hyge wæs him hinfus,　wolde on heolster fleon,
secan deofla gedræg;　ne wæs his drohtoð þær
swylce he on ealderdagum　ær gemette.
Gemunde þa se goda,　mæg Higelaces,
æfenspræce,　uplang astod
760 ond him fæste wiðfeng;　fingras burston.
Eoten wæs utweard;　eorl furþur stop.
Mynte se mæra,　[þ]ær he meahte swa,
widre gewindan　ond on weg þanon
fleon on fenhopu;　wiste *h*is fingra geweald
765 on grames grapum.　Þæt wæs geocor sið
þæt se hearmscaþa　to Heorute ateah.
Dryhtsele dynede;　Denum eallum wearð,
ceasterbuendum,　cenra gehwylcum,
eorlum ealuscerwen.　Yrre wæron begen,
770 reþe renweardas.　Reced hlynsode.
Þa wæs wundor micel　þæt se winsele
wiðhæfde heaþodeorum,　þæt he on hrusan ne feol,
fæger foldbold;　ac he þæs fæste wæs
innan ond utan　irenbendum
775 searoþoncum besmiþod.　Þær fram sylle abeag
medubenc monig,　mine gefræge,
golde geregnad,　þær þa graman wunnon.
Þæs ne wendon ær　witan Scyldinga
þæt hit a mid gemete　manna ænig,
780 betlic ond banfag,　tobrecan meahte,
listum tolucan,　nymþe liges fæþm
swulge on swaþule.　Sweg up astag
niwe geneahhe;　Norðdenum stod

---

752 sceata] sceat *at the end of a line, followed by* ta *at the beginning of the
next line*　756 his] *With the* s *altered from* m　762 þær] ....ær *A*, ær
with the letters hw *added later before* æ *and then crossed out in pencil B*　764
his] his *B, not in A*　765 þæt] ræt *A*, þæt *B*　wæs] he wæs　775
besmiþod] *With the* d *altered from some other letter* (t?)　780 betlic] hetlic

atelic egesa,   anra gehwylcum
785 þara þe of wealle   wop gehyrdon,
     gryreleoð galan   godes ondsacan,
     sigeleasne sang,   sar wanigean
     helle hæfton.   Heold hine fæste
     se þe manna wæs   mægene strengest
790 on þæm dæge   þysses lifes.
      Nolde eorla hleo   ænige þinga
     þone cwealmcuman   cwicne forlætan,
     ne his lifdagas   leoda ænigum
     nytte tealde.   þær genehost brægd
795 eorl Beowulfes   ealde lafe,
     wolde freadrihtnes   feorh ealgian,
     mæres þeodnes,   ðær hie meahton swa.
     Hie þæt ne wiston,   þa hie gewin drugon,
     heardhicgende   hildemecgas,
800 ond on healfa gehwone   heawan þohton,
     sawle secan,   þone synscaðan
     ænig ofer eorþan   irenna cyst,
     guðbilla nan,   gretan nolde,
     ac he sigewæpnum   forsworen hæfde,
805 ecga gehwylcre.   Scolde his aldorgedal
     on ðæm dæge   þysses lifes
     earmlic wurðan,   ond se ellorgast
     on feonda geweald   feor siðian.
      Ða þæt onfunde   se þe fela æror
810 modes myrðe   manna cynne,
     fyrene gefremede   (he wæs fag wið god),
     þæt him se lichoma   læstan nolde,
     ac hine se modega   mæg Hygelaces
     hæfde be honda;   wæs gehwæþer oðrum
815 lifigende lað.   Licsar gebad
     atol æglæca; · him on eaxle wearð
     syndolh sweotol,   seonowe onsprungon,

---

793 ænigum] *With the* i *added above the line by the same hand*   796 feorh]
About five letters (feorh?) *erased after this word*   805 gehwylcre] *With the* c
added above the line by the same hand   811 wæs] *Not in MS.*   812 nolde]
nolde *A*, wolde *B*

burston banlocan. Beowulfe wearð
guðhreð gyfeþe; scolde Grendel þonan
820 feorhseoc fleon under fenhleoðu,
secean wynleas wic; wiste þe geornor
þæt his aldres wæs ende gegongen,
dogera dægrim. Denum eallum wearð
æfter þam wælræse willa gelumpen.
825 Hæfde þa gefælsod se þe ær feorran com,
snotor ond swyðferhð, sele Hroðgares,
genered wið niðe; nihtweorce gefeh,
ellenmærþum. Hæfde Eastdenum
Geatmecga leod gilp gelæsted,
830 swylce oncyþðe ealle gebette,
inwidsorge, þe hie ær drugon
ond for þreanydum þolian scoldon,
torn unlytel. Þæt wæs tacen sweotol,
syþðan hildedeor hond alegde,
835 earm ond eaxle (þær wæs eal geador
Grendles grape) under geapne hr[of].
Ða wæs on morgen mine gefræge
ymb þa gifhealle guðrinc monig;
ferdon folctogan feorran ond nean
840 geond widwegas wundor sceawian,
laþes lastas. No his lifgedal
sarlic þuhte secga ænegum
þara þe tirleases trode sceawode,
hu he werigmod on weg þanon,
845 niða ofercumen, on nicera mere
fæge ond geflymed feorhlastas bær.
Ðær wæs on blode brim weallende,
atol yða geswing eal gemenged
haton heolfre, heorodreore weol.
850 Deaðfæge deog, siððan dreama leas
in fenfreoðo feorh alegde,
hæþene sawle; þær him hel onfeng.
Þanon eft gewiton ealdgesiðas,

828 -mærþum] mær þum A, mær.. B   836 geapne hrof] gearne...... A,
geapne hr.. B   852 hæþene] Hæþene A, hawene B

swylce geong manig   of gomenwaþe
855 fram mere modge   mearum ridan,
beornas on blancum.   Ðær wæs Beowulfes
mærðo mæned;   monig oft gecwæð
þætte suð ne norð   be sæm tweonum
ofer eormengrund   oþer nænig
860 under swegles begong   selra nære
rondhæbbendra,   rices wyrðra.
Ne hie huru winedrihten   wiht ne logon,
glædne Hroðgar,   ac þæt wæs god cyning.
Hwilum heaþorofe   hleapan leton,
865 on geflit faran   fealwe mearas
ðær him foldwegas   fægere þuhton,
cystum cuðe.   Hwilum cyninges þegn,
guma gilphlæden,   gidda gemyndig,
se ðe ealfela   ealdgesegena
870 worn gemunde,   word oþer fand
soðe gebunden;   secg eft ongan
sið Beowulfes   snyttrum styrian
ond on sped wrecan   spel gerade,
wordum wrixlan.   Welhwylc gecwæð
875 þæt he fram Sigemundes   secgan hyrde
ellendædum,   uncuþes fela,
Wælsinges gewin,   wide siðas,
þara þe gumena bearn   gearwe ne wiston,
fæhðe ond fyrena,   buton Fitela mid hine,
880 þonne he swulces hwæt   secgan wolde,
eam his nefan,   swa hie a wæron
æt niða gehwam   nydgesteallan;
hæfdon ealfela   eotena cynnes
sweordum gesæged.   Sigemunde gesprong
885 æfter deaðdæge   dom unlytel,
syþðan wiges heard   wyrm acwealde,
hordes hyrde.   He under harne stan,
æþelinges bearn,   ana geneðde

---

867 cuðe] cuð e *with* r *erased between* ð *and* e   875 Sigemundes] sige munde
879 fyrena] fyrene *with* a *written above the final* e *by the same hand*

frecne dæde, ne wæs him Fitela mid.
890 Hwæþre him gesælde ðæt þæt swurd þurhwod
wrætlicne wyrm, þæt hit on wealle ætstod,
dryhtlic iren; draca morðre swealt.
Hæfde aglæca elne gegongen
þæt he beahhordes brucan moste
895 selfes dome; sæbat gehleod,
bær on bearm scipes beorhte frætwa,
Wælses eafera. Wyrm hat gemealt.
Se wæs wreccena wide mærost
ofer werþeode, wigendra hleo,
900 ellendædum (he þæs ær onðah),
siððan Heremodes hild sweðrode,
eafoð ond ellen. He mid Eotenum wearð
on feonda geweald forð forlacen,
snude forsended. Hine sorhwylmas
905 lemede to lange; he his leodum wearð,
eallum æþellingum to aldorceare;
swylce oft bemearn ærran mælum
swiðferhþes sið snotor ceorl monig,
se þe him bealwa to bote gelyfde,
910 þæt þæt ðeodnes bearn geþeon scolde,
fæderæþelum onfon, folc gehealdan,
hord ond hleoburh, hæleþa rice,
ᛉ Scyldinga. He þær eallum wearð,
mæg Higelaces, manna cynne,
915 freondum gefægra; hine fyren onwod.
Hwilum flitende fealwe stræte
mearum mæton. Ða wæs morgenleoht
scofen ond scynded. Eode scealc monig
swiðhicgende to sele þam hean
920 searowundor seon; swylce self cyning
of brydbure, beahhorda weard,
tryddode tirfæst getrume micle,
cystum gecyþed, ond his cwen mid him
medostigge mæt mægþa hose.

---

894 moste] *An erasure of about six letters after this word*   902 eafoð] earfoð

925 Hroðgar maþelode   (he to healle geong,
     stod on stapole,   geseah steapne hrof,
     golde fahne,   ond Grendles hond):
     "Ðisse ansyne   alwealdan þanc
     lungre gelimpe!   Fela ic laþes gebad,
930 grynna æt Grendle;   a mæg god wyrcan
     wunder æfter wundre,   wuldres hyrde.
     Ðæt wæs ungeara   þæt ic ænigra me
     weana ne wende   to widan feore
     bote gebidan,   þonne blode fah
935 husa selest   heorodreorig stod,
     wea widscofen   witena gehwylcum
     ðara þe ne wendon   þæt hie wideferhð
     leoda landgeweorc   laþum beweredon
     scuccum ond scinnum.   Nu scealc hafað
940 þurh drihtnes miht   dæd gefremede
     ðe we ealle   ær ne meahton
     snyttrum besyrwan.   Hwæt, þæt secgan mæg
     efne swa hwylc mægþa   swa ðone magan cende
     æfter gumcynnum,   gyf heo gyt lyfað,
945 þæt hyre ealdmetod   este wære
     bearngebyrdo.   Nu ic, Beowulf, þec,
     secg betsta,   me for sunu wylle
     freogan on ferhþe;   heald forð tela
     niwe sibbe.   Ne bið þe nænigra gad
950 worolde wilna,   þe ic geweald hæbbe.
     Ful oft ic for læssan   lean teohhode,
     hordweorþunge   hnahran rince,
     sæmran æt sæcce.   Þu þe self hafast
     dædum gefremed   þæt þin dom lyfað
955 awa to aldre.   Alwalda þec
     gode forgylde,   swa he nu gyt dyde!"
        Beowulf maþelode,   bearn Ecþeowes:
     "We þæt ellenweorc   estum miclum,
     feohtan fremedon,   frecne geneðdon

927 fahne] With the e altered from o?   936 gehwylcum] ge hwylcne   941
ær] ær A, ęr B   947 me] me A, ne (later altered to me) B   949 nænigra]
ænigre   954 dom] Not in MS.

960 eafoð uncuþes. Uþe ic swiþor
þæt ðu hine selfne geseon moste,
feond on frætewum fylwerigne.
Ic hine hrædlice heardan clammum
on wælbedde wriþan þohte,
965 þæt he for mundgripe minum scolde
licgean lifbysig, butan his lic swice.
Ic hine ne mihte, þa metod nolde,
ganges getwæman, no ic him þæs georne ætfealh,
feorhgeniðlan; wæs to foremihtig
970 feond on feþe. Hwæþere he his folme forlet
to lifwraþe last weardian,
earm ond eaxle. No þær ænige swa þeah
feasceaft guma frofre gebohte;
no þy leng leofað laðgeteona,
975 synnum geswenced, ac hyne sar hafað
mid nydgripe nearwe befongen,
balwon bendum. Ðær abidan sceal
maga mane fah miclan domes,
hu him scir metod scrifan wille."
980 Ða wæs swigra secg, sunu Eclafes,
on gylpspræce guðgeweorca,
siþðan æþelingas eorles cræfte
ofer heanne hrof hand sceawedon,
feondes fingras. Foran æghwylc wæs,
985 stiðra nægla gehwylc, style gelicost,
hæþenes handsporu hilderinces,
egl; unheoru. Æghwylc gecwæð
þæt him heardra nan hrinan wolde
iren ærgod, þæt ðæs ahlæcan
990 blodge beadufolme onberan wolde.
Ða wæs haten hreþe Heort innanweard
folmum gefrætwod. Fela þæra wæs,
wera ond wifa, þe þæt winreced,

963 hine] him 965 mundgripe] hand gripe 974 leofað] leofað A,
leofad B 976 mid nydgripe] inmid gripe 985 stiðra] steda 986
hilderinces] hilde at the end of a page, followed by [.]ilde rinces at the beginning of the next page

gestsele gyredon. Goldfag scinon
995 web æfter wagum, wundorsiona fela
secga gehwylcum þara þe on swylc starað.
Wæs þæt beorhte bold tobrocen swiðe,
eal inneweard irenbendum fæst,
heorras tohlidene. Hrof ana genæs,
1000 ealles ansund, þe se aglæca,
fyrendædum fag, on fleam gewand,
aldres orwena. No þæt yðe byð
to befleonne, fremme se þe wille,
ac gesecan sceal sawlberendra,
1005 nyde genydde, niþða bearna,
grundbuendra gearwe stowe,
þær his lichoma legerbedde fæst
swefeþ æfter symle. þa wæs sæl ond mæl
þæt to healle gang Healfdenes sunu;
1010 wolde self cyning symbel þicgan.
Ne gefrægen ic þa mægþe maran weorode
ymb hyra sincgyfan sel gebæran.
Bugon þa to bence blædagande,
fylle gefægon; fægere geþægon
1015 medoful manig magas þara
swiðhicgende on sele þam hean,
Hroðgar ond Hroþulf. Heorot innan wæs
freondum afylled; nalles facenstafas
þeodscyldingas þenden fremedon.
1020   Forgeaf þa Beowulfe bearn Healfdenes
segen gyldenne sigores to leane;
hroden hildecumbor, helm ond byrnan,
mære maðþumsweord manige gesawon
beforan beorn beran. Beowulf geþah
1025 ful on flette; no he þære feohgyfte
for sceotendum scamigan ðorfte.
Ne gefrægn ic freondlicor feower madmas

1004 gesecan] ge sacan   1016 -hicgende] hiegeade *A*, hicgende *B*   1020
bearn] brand   1022 hildecumbor] hilte cumbor   1024 beforan] *With
the* o *altered from* e   Beowulf] beowulf *with the* b *altered from* w   1026
sceotendum] scotenum

golde gegyrede   gummanna fela
in ealobence   oðrum gesellan.
1030 Ymb þæs helmes hrof   heafodbeorge
wirum bewunden   walu utan heold,
þæt him fela laf   frecne ne meahton
scurheard sceþðan,   þonne scyldfreca
ongean gramum   gangan scolde.
1035 Heht ða eorla hleo   eahta mearas
fætedhleore   on flet teon,
in under eoderas.   þara anum stod
sadol searwum fah,   since gewurþad;
þæt wæs hildesetl   heahcyninges,
1040 ðonne sweorda gelac   sunu Healfdenes
efnan wolde.   Næfre on ore læg
widcuþes wig,   ðonne walu feollon.
Ond ða Beowulfe   bega gehwæþres
eodor Ingwina   onweald geteah,
1045 wicga ond wæpna,   het hine wel brucan.
Swa manlice   mære þeoden,
hordweard hæleþa,   heaþoræsas geald
mearum ond madmum,   swa hy næfre man lyhð,
se þe secgan wile   soð æfter rihte.
1050   Ða gyt æghwylcum   eorla drihten
þara þe mid Beowulfe   brimlade teah
on þære medubence   maþðum gesealde,
yrfelafe,   ond þone ænne heht
golde forgyldan,   þone ðe Grendel ær
1055 mane acwealde,   swa he hyra ma wolde,
nefne him witig god   wyrd forstode
ond ðæs mannes mod.   Metod eallum weold
gumena cynnes,   swa he nu git deð.
Forþan bið andgit   æghwær selest,
1060 ferhðes foreþanc.   Fela sceal gebidan
leofes ond laþes   se þe longe her
on ðyssum windagum   worolde bruceð.
   Þær wæs sang ond sweg   samod ætgædere

1031 walu] walan   1037 in under] munder *A*, in under (*altered from*
munder) *B*   1051 brimlade] brim leade

fore Healfdenes hildewisan,
1065 gomenwudu greted, gid oft wrecen,
ðonne healgamen Hroþgares scop
æfter medobence mænan scolde
be Finnes eaferum, ða hie se fær begeat,
hæleð Healfdena, Hnæf Scyldinga,
1070 in Freswæle feallan scolde.
Ne huru Hildeburh herian þorfte
Eotena treowe; unsynnum wearð
beloren leofum æt þam lindplegan,
bearnum ond broðrum; hie on gebyrd hruron,
1075 gare wunde. Þæt wæs geomuru ides!
Nalles holinga Hoces dohtor
meotodsceaft bemearn, syþðan morgen com,
ða heo under swegle geseon meahte
morþorbealo maga, þær heo ær mæste heold
1080 worolde wynne. Wig ealle fornam
Finnes þegnas nemne feaum anum,
þæt he ne mehte on þæm meðelstede
wig Hengeste wiht gefeohtan,
ne þa wealafe wige forþringan
1085 þeodnes ðegna; ac hig him geþingo budon,
þæt hie him oðer flet eal gerymdon,
healle ond heahsetl, þæt hie healfre geweald
wið Eotena bearn agan moston,
ond æt feohgyftum Folcwaldan sunu
1090 dogra gehwylce Dene weorþode,
Hengestes heap hringum wenede
efne swa swiðe sincgestreonum
fættan goldes, swa he Fresena cyn
on beorsele byldan wolde.
1095 Ða hie getruwedon on twa healfa

1068 be] *Not in MS.* 1070 Freswæle] fr es wæle *with the* r *altered from some other letter, one letter erased after* r, *and* es *written on an erasure* 1073 lindplegan] hild plegan 1077 syþðan] sywðan *A,* syþðan *B* 1079 heo] he mæste] moste *with the* o *dotted beneath for deletion and* æ *written above by the same hand* 1081 feaum] fea *with* ū *added above the line by the same hand* 1085 ðegna] ðegne

fæste frioðuwære. Fin Hengeste
elne, unflitme aðum benemde
þæt he þa wealafe weotena dome
arum heolde, þæt ðær ænig mon
1100 wordum ne worcum wære ne bræce,
ne þurh inwitsearo æfre gemænden
ðeah hie hira beaggyfan banan folgedon
ðeodenlease, þa him swa geþearfod wæs;
gyf þonne Frysna hwylc frecnan spræce
1105 ðæs morþorhetes myndgiend wære,
þonne hit sweordes ecg seðan scolde.
Ad wæs geæfned ond icge gold
ahæfen of horde. Herescyldinga
betst beadorinca wæs on bæl gearu.
1110 Æt þæm ade wæs eþgesyne
swatfah syrce, swyn ealgylden,
eofer irenheard, æþeling manig
wundum awyrded; sume on wæle crungon.
Het ða Hildeburh æt Hnæfes ade
1115 hire selfre sunu sweoloðe befæstan,
banfatu bærnan ond on bæl don
eame on eaxle. Ides gnornode,
geomrode giddum. Guðrinc astah.
Wand to wolcnum wælfyra mæst,
1120 hlynode for hlawe; hafelan multon,
bengeato burston, ðonne blod ætspranc,
laðbite lices. Lig ealle forswealg,
gæsta gifrost, þara ðe þær guð fornam
bega folces; wæs hira blæd scacen.
1125 Gewiton him ða wigend wica neosian,
freondum befeallen, Frysland geseon,
hamas ond heaburh. Hengest ða gyt
wælfagne winter wunode mid Finne
eal unhlitme. Eard gemunde,

1104 frecnan] frecnen 1106 seðan] syððan 1107 Ad] að 1109
beadorinca] *With the first* a *added above the line by the same hand* 1110
wæs] *Followed by the words* on bæl gearu *erased* 1117 eame] earme 1128-
1129 Finne eal] finnel

1130 þeah þe he ne meahte   on mere drifan
hringedstefnan;   holm storme weol,
won wið winde,   winter yþe beleac
isgebinde,   oþðæt oþer com
gear in geardas;   swa nu gyt deð,
1135 þa ðe syngales   sele bewitiað,
wuldortorhtan weder.   Ða wæs winter scacen,
fæger foldan bearm.   Fundode wrecca,
gist of geardum;   he to gyrnwræce
swiðor þohte   þonne to sælade,
1140 gif he torngemot   þurhteon mihte
þæt he Eotena bearn   inne gemunde.
Swa he ne forwyrnde   woroldrædenne,
þonne him Hunlafing   hildeleoman,
billa selest,   on bearm dyde,
1145 þæs wæron mid Eotenum   ecge cuðe.
Swylce ferhðfrecan   Fin eft begeat
sweordbealo sliðen   æt his selfes ham,
siþðan grimne gripe   Guðlaf ond Oslaf
æfter sæsiðe,   sorge, mændon,
1150 ætwiton weana dæl;   ne meahte wæfre mod
forhabban in hreþre.   Ða wæs heal roden
feonda feorum,   swilce Fin slægen,
cyning on corþre,   ond seo cwen numen.
Sceotend Scyldinga   to scypon feredon
1155 eal ingesteald   eorðcyninges,
swylce hie æt Finnes ham   findan meahton
sigla, searogimma.   Hie on sælade
drihtlice wif   to Denum feredon,
læddon to leodum.   Leoð wæs asungen,
1160 gleomannes gyd.   Gamen eft astah,
beorhtode bencsweg;   byrelas sealdon
win of wunderfatum.   Þa cwom Wealhþeo forð
gan under gyldnum beage,   þær þa godan twegen
sæton suhtergefæderan;   þa gyt wæs hiera sib ætgædere,
1165 æghwylc oðrum trywe.   Swylce þær Unferþ þyle

1130 ne] *Not in MS.*   1135 bewitiað] *With the* b *written by the same hand above* g *erased*   1151 roden] hroden   1165 Unferþ] hun ferþ (*with a letter erased after* þ?)

æt fotum sæt frean Scyldinga; gehwylc hiora his ferhþe
              treowde,
þæt he hæfde mod micel, þeah þe he his magum nære
arfæst æt ecga gelacum. Spræc ða ides Scyldinga:
"Onfoh þissum fulle, freodrihten min,
1170 sinces brytta! Þu on sælum wes,
goldwine gumena, ond to Geatum spræc
mildum wordum, swa sceal man don.
Beo wið Geatas glæd, geofena gemyndig,
nean ond feorran þu nu hafast.
1175 Me man sægde þæt þu ðe for sunu wolde
hererinc habban. Heorot is gefælsod,
beahsele beorhta; bruc þenden þu mote
manigra medo, ond þinum magum læf
folc ond rice, þonne ðu forð scyle
1180 metodsceaft seon. Ic minne can
glædne Hroþulf, þæt he þa geogoðe wile
arum healdan, gyf þu ær þonne he,
wine Scildinga, worold oflætest;
wene ic þæt he mid gode gyldan wille
1185 uncran eaferan, gif he þæt eal gemon,
hwæt wit to willan ond to worðmyndum
umborwesendum ær arna gefremedon."
Hwearf þa bi bence þær hyre byre wæron,
Hreðric ond Hroðmund, ond hæleþa bearn,
1190 giogoð ætgædere; þær se goda sæt,
Beowulf Geata, be þæm gebroðrum twæm.
  Him wæs ful boren ond freondlaþu
wordum bewægned, ond wunden gold
estum geeawed, earmreade twa,
1195 hrægl ond hringas, healsbeaga mæst
þara þe ic on foldan gefrægen hæbbe.
Nænigne ic under swegle selran hyrde
hordmaððum hæleþa, syþðan Hama ætwæg
to þære byrhtan byrig Brosinga mene,

1200 sigle ond sincfæt;   searoniðas fleah
Eormenrices,   geceas ecne ræd.
þone hring hæfde   Higelac Geata,
nefa Swertinges,   nyhstan siðe,
siðþan he under segne   sinc ealgode,
1205 wælreaf werede;   hyne wyrd fornam,
syþðan he for wlenco   wean ahsode,
fæhðe to Frysum.   He þa frætwe wæg,
eorclanstanas   ofer yða ful,
rice þeoden;   he under rande gecranc.
1210 Gehwearf þa in Francna fæþm   feorh cyninges,
breostgewædu   ond se beah somod;
wyrsan wigfrecan   wæl reafedon
æfter guðsceare,   Geata leode,
hreawic heoldon.   Heal swege onfeng.
1215 Wealhðeo maþelode,   heo fore þæm werede spræc:
"Bruc ðisses beages,   Beowulf leofa,
hyse, mid hæle,   ond þisses hrægles neot,
þeodgestreona,   ond geþeoh tela,
cen þec mid cræfte   ond þyssum cnyhtum wes
1220 lara liðe;   ic þe þæs lean geman.
Hafast þu gefered   þæt ðe feor ond neah
ealne wideferhþ   weras ehtigað,
efne swa side   swa sæ bebugeð,
windgeard, weallas.   Wes þenden þu lifige,
1225 æþeling, eadig.   Ic þe an tela
sincgestreona.   Beo þu suna minum
dædum gedefe,   dreamhealdende.
Her is æghwylc eorl   oþrum getrywe,
modes milde,   mandrihtne hold;
1230 þegnas syndon geþwære,   þeod ealgearo,
druncne dryhtguman   doð swa ic bidde."

1200 fleah] fealh   1209 he] *Added above the line by the same hand*   1212
reafedon] reafeden   1218 þeodgestreona] þeo ge streona   1221 Hafast]
hafast *A*, hawast *B*   1223 side] *Originally* wide, *but the* w *altered to* si
and the original i *dotted beneath for deletion*   bebugeð] bebugeð *A*, be buged
(*with the second* e *altered from* a) *B*   1229 hold] heol *with* e *crossed out*

Eode þa to setle.   þær wæs symbla cyst;
druncon win weras.   Wyrd ne cuþon,
geosceaft grimme,   swa hit agangen wearð
1235 eorla manegum,   syþðan æfen cwom
ond him Hroþgar gewat   to hofe sinum,
rice to ræste.   Reced weardode
unrim eorla,   swa hie oft ær dydon.
Bencþelu beredon;   hit geondbræded wearð
1240 beddum ond bolstrum.   Beorscealca sum
fus ond fæge   fletræste gebeag.
Setton him to heafdon   hilderandas,
bordwudu beorhtan;   þær on bence wæs
ofer æþelinge   yþgesene
1245 heaþosteapa helm,   hringed byrne,
þrecwudu þrymlic.   Wæs þeaw hyra
þæt hie oft wæron   an wig gearwe,
ge æt ham ge on herge,   ge gehwæþer þara,
efne swylce mæla   swylce hira mandryhtne
1250 þearf gesælde;   wæs seo þeod tilu.

Sigon þa to slæpe.   Sum sare angeald
æfenræste,   swa him ful oft gelamp,
siþðan goldsele   Grendel warode,
unriht æfnde,   oþþæt ende becwom,
1255 swylt æfter synnum.   Þæt gesyne wearþ,
widcuþ werum,   þætte wrecend þa gyt
lifde æfter laþum,   lange þrage,
æfter guðceare.   Grendles modor,
ides, aglæcwif,   yrmþe gemunde,
1260 se þe wæteregesan   wunian scolde,
cealde streamas,   siþðan Cain wearð
to ecgbanan   angan breþer,
fæderenmæge;   he þa fag gewat,
morþre gemearcod,   mandream fleon,
1265 westen warode.   Þanon woc fela

1234 grimme] grimne   1236 Hroþgar] *With the* h *altered from* b? (*Zupitza*)   1245 heaþosteapa] *Originally* heaþo stoapa, *but the second* o
blotted in the course of correction and e *written above by a different hand*   1246
þeaw] wear *A*, þeaw *B*   1261 Cain] camp   1265 woc] woc *A*, woe *B*

geosceaftgasta; wæs þæra Grendel sum,
heorowearh hetelic, se æt Heorote fand
wæccendne wer wiges bidan.
þær him aglæca ætgræpe wearð;
1270 hwæþre he gemunde mægenes strenge,
gimfæste gife ðe him god sealde,
ond him to anwaldan are gelyfde,
frofre ond fultum; ðy he þone feond ofercwom,
gehnægde helle gast. þa he hean gewat,
1275 dreame bedæled, deaþwic seon,
mancynnes feond, ond his modor þa gyt,
gifre ond galgmod, gegan wolde
sorhfulne sið, sunu deað wrecan.
 Com þa to Heorote, ðær Hringdene
1280 geond þæt sæld swæfun. þa ðær sona wearð
edhwyrft eorlum, siþðan inne fealh
Grendles modor. Wæs se gryre læssa
efne swa micle swa bið mægþa cræft,
wiggryre wifes, be wæpnedmen,
1285 þonne heoru bunden, hamere geþuren,
sweord swate fah swin ofer helme
ecgum dyhttig andweard sireð.
þa wæs on healle heardecg togen
sweord ofer setlum, sidrand manig
1290 hafen handa fæst; helm ne gemunde,
byrnan side, þa hine se broga angeat.
Heo wæs on ofste, wolde ut þanon,
feore beorgan, þa heo onfunden wæs.
Hraðe heo æþelinga anne hæfde
1295 fæste befangen, þa heo to fenne gang.
 Se wæs Hroþgare hæleþa leofost
on gesiðes had be sæm tweonum,
rice randwiga, þone ðe heo on ræste abreat,
blædfæstne beorn. Næs Beowulf ðær,

1278 deað] þeod   1282 gryre] gry *at the end of a line with* r *erased after it,*
then re *at the beginning of the next line*   1285 þonne] þōn *with* e *erased*
after it   bunden] *With the first* n *altered from* m *by erasure*   1287 dyhttig]
dyhttig *A*, dyttig *B*

1300 ac wæs oþer in   ær geteohhod
aefter maþðumgife   mærum Geate.
Hream wearð in Heorote;   heo under heolfre genam
cuþe folme;   cearu wæs geniwod,
geworden in wicun.   Ne wæs þæt gewrixle til,
1305 þæt hie on ba healfa   bicgan scoldon
freonda feorum.   Þa wæs frod cyning,
har hilderinc,   on hreon mode,
syðþan he aldorþegn   unlyfigendne,
þone deorestan   deadne wisse.
1310 Hraþe wæs to bure   Beowulf fetod,
sigoreadig secg.   Samod ærdæge
eode eorla sum,   æþele cempa
self mid gesiðum   þær se snotera bad,
hwæþer him alwalda   æfre wille
1315 æfter weaspelle   wyrpe gefremman.
Gang ða æfter flore   fyrdwyrðe man
mid his handscale   (healwudu dynede),
þæt he þone wisan   wordum nægde
frean Ingwina,   frægn gif him wære
1320 æfter neodlaðum   niht getæse.
Hroðgar maþelode,   helm Scyldinga:
"Ne frin þu æfter sælum!   Sorh is geniwod
Denigea leodum.   Dead is Æschere,
Yrmenlafes   yldra broþor,
1325 min runwita   ond min rædbora,
eaxlgestealla,   ðonne we on orlege
hafelan weredon,   þonne hniton feþan,
eoferas cnysedan.   Swy[lc] scolde eorl wesan,
æþeling ærgod,   swylc Æschere wæs!
1330 Wearð him on Heorote   to handbanan
wælgæst wæfre;   ic ne wat hwæder

1302 in] on *with the o dotted beneath for deletion and i written above by the same
hand*   1308 -þegn unlyfigendne] þegum lyfig- endne *A*, þegnun lyfi ndne
B, Unlifigendne *Conybeare*   1310 Hraþe] hraþe *A*, hrade *B*   1314 hwæ-
þer] hwæþre   alwalda] alf walda   1318 nægde] hnægde   1320 neod-
laðum] neod laðu   1329 æþeling] *Not in MS.*   1331 hwæder] hwæþer

atol æse wlanc   eftsiðas teah,
fylle gefægnod.   Heo þa fæhðe wræc
þe þu gystran niht   Grendel cwealdest
1335 þurh hæstne had   heardum clammum,
forþan he to lange   leode mine
wanode ond wyrde.   He æt wige gecrang
ealdres scyldig,   ond nu oþer cwom
mihtig manscaða,   wolde hyre mæg wrecan,
1340 ge feor hafað   fæhðe gestæled
(þæs þe þincean mæg   þegne monegum,
se þe æfter sincgyfan   on sefan greoteþ),
hreþerbealo hearde;   nu seo hand ligeð,
se þe eow welhwylcra   wilna dohte.
1345 Ic þæt londbuend,   leode mine,
selerædende,   secgan hyrde
þæt hie gesawon   swylce twegen
micle mearcstapan   moras healdan,
ellorgæstas.   Ðæra oðer wæs,
1350 þæs þe hie gewislicost   gewitan meahton,
idese onlicnæs;   oðer earmsceapen
on weres wæstmum   wræclastas træd,
næfne he wæs mara   þonne ænig man oðer;
þone on geardagum   Grendel nemdon
1355 foldbuende.   No hie fæder cunnon,
hwæþer him ænig wæs   ær acenned
dyrnra gasta.   Hie dygel lond
warigeað, wulfhleoþu,   windige næssas,
frecne fengelad,   ðær fyrgenstream
1360 under næssa genipu   niþer gewiteð,
flod under foldan.   Nis þæt feor heonon
milgemearces   þæt se mere standeð;
ofer þæm hongiað   hrinde bearwas,
wudu wyrtum fæst   wæter oferhelmað.
1365 Þær mæg nihta gehwæm   niðwundor seon,
fyr on flode.   No þæs frod leofað

1333 gefægnod] ge frægnod   1344 welhwylcra] *With an* s *inserted between*
hwylc *and* ra *by a later* (*modern?*) *hand*   1354 nemdon] nemdod *AB*
1358 windige] windige *A*, windig *B*   1362 standeð] stanðeð

gumena bearna, þæt þone grund wite;
ðeah þe hæðstapa hundum geswenced,
heorot hornum trum, holtwudu sece,
1370 feorran geflymed, ær he feorh seleð,
aldor on ofre, ær he in wille
hafelan hydan. Nis þæt heoru stow!
þonon yðgeblond up astigeð
won to wolcnum, þonne wind styreþ,
1375 lað gewidru, oðþæt lyft drysmaþ,
roderas reotað. Nu is se ræd gelang
eft æt þe anum. Eard git ne const,
frecne stowe, ðær þu findan miht
felasinnigne secg; sec gif þu dyrre.
1380 Ic þe þa fæhðe feo leanige,
ealdgestreonum, swa ic ær dyde,
wundnum golde, gyf þu on weg cymest."
    Beowulf maþelode, bearn Ecgþeowes:
"Ne sorga, snotor guma; selre bið æghwæm
1385 þæt he his freond wrece, þonne he fela murne.
Ure æghwylc sceal ende gebidan
worolde lifes; wyrce se þe mote
domes ær deaþe; þæt bið drihtguman
unlifgendum æfter selest.
1390 Aris, rices weard, uton raþe feran
Grendles magan gang sceawigan.
Ic hit þe gehate, no he on helm losaþ,
ne on foldan fæþm, ne on fyrgenholt,
ne on gyfenes grund, ga þær he wille.
1395 Ðys dogor þu geþyld hafa
weana gehwylces, swa ic þe wene to."
    Ahleop ða se gomela, gode þancode,
mihtigan drihtne, þæs se man gespræc.

1372 hydan] *Not in MS.*   1378 findan] finda n *with a letter erased between* a *and* n   1382 wundnum] wun dini *or* wun dmi   1383 Ecgþeowes] ecgþeo æs *A*, Ecgþeo wes *B*   1386 æghwylc] æghryle *A*, æghwylc *B*   1388 drihtguman] driht gumen *with the* e *dotted beneath for deletion and a* written *above by the same hand*   1390 raþe] hraþe   1391 gang] *With the final* g *added above the line by a different hand*   1398 gespræc] ge spræc *A*, ge spręc *B*

þa wæs Hroðgare hors gebæted,
1400 wicg wundenfeax. Wisa fengel
geato*lic* gende; gumfeþa stop
lindhæbbendra. Lastas wæron
æfter waldswaþum wide gesyne,
gang ofer grundas, þær heo gegnum for
1405 ofer myrcan mor, magoþegna bær
þone selestan sawolleasne
þara þe mid Hroðgare ham eahtode.
Ofereode þa æþelinga bearn
steap stanhliðo, stige nearwe,
1410 enge anpaðas, uncuð gelad,
neowle næssas, nicorhusa fela.
He feara sum beforan gengde
wisra monna wong sceawian,
oþþæt he færinga fyrgenbeamas
1415 ofer harne stan hleonian funde,
wynleasne wudu; wæter under stod
dreorig ond gedrefed. Denum eallum wæs,
winum Scyldinga, weorce on mode
to geþolianne, ðegne monegum,
1420 oncyð eorla gehwæm, syðþan Æscheres
on þam holmclife hafelan metton.
Flod blode weol (folc to sægon),
hatan heolfre. Horn stundum song
fuslic *f*[yrd]leoð. Feþa eal gesæt.
1425   Gesawon ða æfter wætere wyrmcynnes fela,
sellice sædracan, sund cunnian,
swylce on næshleoðum nicras licgean,
ða on undernmæl oft bewitigað
sorhfulne sið on seglrade,
1430 wyrmas ond wildeor; hie on weg hruron,
bitere ond gebolgne, bearhtm ongeaton,
guðhorn galan. Sumne Geata leod
of flanbogan feores getwæfde,

1401 geatolic] geatolic *A*, geato. *B*   1404 þær heo] *Not in MS.*   1424
fyrdleoð] .....leod *A*, f...leod *B*   gesæt] ge seah *with* eah *crossed out*
and æt *written above by the same hand*

yðgewinnes, þæt him on aldre stod
1435 herestræl hearda; he on holme wæs
sundes þe sænra, ðe hyne swylt fornam.
Hræþe wearð on yðum mid eoferspreotum
heorohocyhtum hearde genearwod,
niða genæged, ond on næs togen,
1440 wundorlic wægbora; weras sceawedon
gryrelicne gist. Gyrede hine Beowulf
eorlgewædum, nalles for ealdre mearn.
Scolde herebyrne hondum gebroden,
sid ond searofah, sund cunnian,
1445 seo ðe bancofan beorgan cuþe,
þæt him hildegrap hreþre ne mihte,
eorres inwitfeng, aldre gesceþðan;
ac se hwita helm hafelan werede,
se þe meregrundas mengan scolde,
1450 secan sundgebland since geweorðad,
befongen freawrasnum, swa hine fyrndagum
worhte wæpna smið, wundrum teode,
besette swinlicum, þæt hine syðþan no
brond ne beadomecas bitan ne meahton.
1455 Næs þæt þonne mætost mægenfultuma
þæt him ðn ðearfe lah ðyle Hroðgares;
wæs þæm hæftmece Hrunting nama.
þæt wæs an foran ealdgestreona;
ecg wæs iren, atertanum fah,
1460 ahyrded heaþoswate; næfre hit æt hilde ne swac
manna ængum þara þe hit mid mundum bewand,
se ðe gryresiðas gegan dorste,
folcstede fara; næs þæt forma sið
þæt hit ellenweorc æfnan scolde.
1465 Huru ne gemunde mago Ecglafes,
eafoþes cræftig, þæt he ær gespræc
wine druncen, þa he þæs wæpnes onlah
selran sweordfrecan. Selfa ne dorste
under yða gewin aldre geneþan,

1438 genearwod] *About two letters erased between* ge *and* nearwod   1450
geweorðad] ge weorðad *A*, geweordad *B*

1470 drihtscype dreogan; þær he dome forleas,
    ellenmær[ð]um. Ne wæs þæm oðrum swa,
    syðþan he hine to guðe gegyred hæfde.
    Beowulf maðelode, bearn Ecgþeowes:
    "Geþenc nu, se mæra maga Healfdenes,
1475 snottra fengel, nu ic eom siðes fus,
    goldwine gumena, hwæt wit geo spræcon,
    gif ic æt þearfe þinre scolde
    aldre linnan, þæt ðu me a wære
    forðgewitenum on fæder stæle.
1480 Wes þu mundbora minum magoþegnum,
    hondgesellum, gif mec hild nime;
    swylce þu ða madmas þe þu me sealdest,
    Hroðgar leofa, Higelace onsend.
    Mæg þonne on þæm golde ongitan Geata dryhten,
1485 geseon sunu Hrædles, þonne he on þæt sinc starað,
    þæt ic gumcystum godne funde
    beaga bryttan, breac þonne moste.
    Ond þu Unferð læt ealde lafe,
    wrætlic wægsweord, widcuðne man
1490 heardecg habban; ic me mid Hruntinge
    dom gewyrce, oþðe mec deað nimeð."
    Æfter þæm wordum Wedergeata leod
    efste mid elne, nalas ondsware
    bidan wolde; brimwylm onfeng
1495 hilderince. Ða wæs hwil dæges
    ær he þone grundwong ongytan mehte.
    Sona þæt onfunde se ðe floda begong
    heorogifre beheold hund missera,
    grim ond grædig, þæt þær gumena sum
1500 ælwihta eard ufan cunnode.
    Grap þa togeanes, guðrinc gefeng
    atolan clommum. No þy ær in gescod
    halan lice; hring utan ymbbearh,
    þæt heo þone fyrdhom ðurhfon ne mihte,

1471 -mærðum] [....]um MS., mærdam A B   1481 hondgesellum] With
the letters se added above the line by the same hand   1488 Unferð] hunferð
1495 hilde-] hib de A, hil de B

1505 locene leoðosyrcan laþan fingrum.
    Bær þa seo brimwylf, þa heo to botme com,
hringa þengel to hofe sinum,
swa he ne mihte, no he þæs modig wæs,
wæpna gewealdan, ac hine wundra þæs fela
1510 swencte on sunde, sædeor monig
hildetuxum heresyrcan bræc,
ehton aglæcan. Ða se eorl ongeat
þæt he in niðsele nathwylcum wæs,
þær him nænig wæter wihte ne sceþede,
1515 ne him for hrofsele hrinan ne mehte
færgripe flodes; fyrleoht geseah,
blacne leoman, beorhte scinan.
    Ongeat þa se goda grundwyrgenne,
merewif mihtig; mægenræs forgeaf
1520 hildebille, hond sweng ne ofteah,
þæt hire on hafelan hringmæl agol
grædig guðleoð. Ða se gist onfand
þæt se beadoleoma bitan nolde,
aldre sceþðan, ac seo ecg geswac
1525 ðeodne æt þearfe; ðolode ær fela
hondgemota, helm oft gescær,
fæges fyrdhrægl; ða wæs forma sið
deorum madme, þæt his dom alæg.
    Eft wæs anræd, nalas elnes læt,
1530 mærða gemyndig mæg Hylaces.
Wearp ða wundenmæl wrættum gebunden
yrre oretta, þæt hit on eorðan læg,
stið ond stylecg; strenge getruwode,
mundgripe mægenes. Swa sceal man don,
1535 þonne he æt guðe gegan þenceð
longsumne lof, na ymb his lif cearað.

1505 leoðo-] leoðo *A*, leodo *B*   1506 brimwylf] brim wyl   1508 þæs] þæm   1510 swencte] swecte   1513 in] *Not in MS.*   1517 scinan] sciman *A*, scinan *B*   1520 hond] hord   sweng] swenge   1522 Ða] da *A*, ða *B*   1525 ðeodne] ðeodne *A*, deoðne *B*   1531 Wearp] *With the* r *added above the line by the same hand*   wundenmæl] wundel mæg *with the* g *crossed out and* l *written above it*

Gefeng þa be eaxle   (nalas for fæhðe mearn)
Guðgeata leod   Grendles modor;
brægd þa beadwe heard,   þa he gebolgen wæs,
1540 feorhgeniðlan,   þæt heo on flet gebeah.
Heo him eft hraþe   andlean forgeald
grimman grapum   ond him togeanes feng;
oferwearþ þa werigmod   wigena strengest,
feþecempa,   þæt he on fylle wearð.
1545 Ofsæt þa þone selegyst   ond hyre seax geteah,
brad ond brunecg,   wolde hire bearn wrecan,
angan eaferan.   Him on eaxle læg
breostnet broden;   þæt gebearh feore,
wið ord ond wið ecge   ingang forstod.
1550 Hæfde ða forsiðod   sunu Ecgþeowes
under gynne grund,   Geata cempa,
nemne him heaðobyrne   helpe gefremede,
herenet hearde,   ond halig god
geweold wigsigor;   witig drihten,
1555 rodera rædend,   hit on ryht gesced
yðelice,   syþðan he eft astod.
    Geseah ða on searwum   sigeeadig bil,
eald sweord eotenisc,   ecgum þyhtig,
wigena weorðmynd;   þæt wæs wæpna cyst,
1560 buton hit wæs mare   ðonne ænig mon oðer
to beadulace   ætberan meahte,
god ond geatolic,   giganta geweorc.
He gefeng þa fetelhilt,   freca Scyldinga
hreoh ond heorogrim   hringmæl gebrægd,
1565 aldres orwena,   yrringa sloh,
þæt hire wið halse   heard grapode,
banhringas bræc.   Bil eal ðurhwod
fægne flæschoman;   heo on flet gecrong.
Sweord wæs swatig,   secg weorce gefeh.
1570 Lixte se leoma,   leoht inne stod,
efne swa of hefene   hadre scineð

1541 andlean] handlean   1542 togeanes] *With the* a *added above the line
by the same hand*   1543 oferwearp] ofer wearf *A*, ofer wearp *B*   1545
seax] seaxe   1546 ond] *Not in MS.*   1559 wæs] *Not in MS.*

rodores candel. He æfter recede wlat;
hwearf þa be wealle, wæpen hafenade
heard be hiltum. Higelaces ðegn,
1575 yrre ond anræd. Næs seo ecg fracod
hilderince, ac he hraþe wolde
Grendle forgyldan guðræsa fela
ðara þe he geworhte to Westdenum
oftor micle ðonne on ænne sið,
1580 þonne he Hroðgares heorðgeneatas
sloh on sweofote, slæpende fræt
folces Denigea fyftyne men
ond oðer swylc ut offerede,
laðlicu lac. He him þæs lean forgeald,
1585 reþe cempa, to ðæs þe he on ræste geseah
guðwerigne Grendel licgan
aldorleasne, swa him ær gescod
hild æt Heorote. Hra wide sprong,
syþðan he æfter deaðe drepe þrowade,
1590 heorosweng heardne, ond hine þa heafde becearf.
   Sona þæt gesawon snottre ceorlas,
þa ðe mid Hroðgare on holm wliton,
þæt wæs yðgeblond eal gemenged,
brim blode fah. Blondenfeaxe,
1595 gomele ymb godne, ongeador spræcon
þæt hig þæs æðelinges eft ne wendon
þæt he sigehreðig secean come
mærne þeoden; þa ðæs monige gewearð
þæt hine seo brimwylf abroten hæfde.
1600 Ða com non dæges. Næs ofgeafon
hwate Scyldingas; gewat him ham þonon
goldwine gumena. Gistas setan
modes seoce ond on mere staredon,
wiston ond ne wendon þæt hie heora winedrihten
1605 selfne gesawon. þa þæt sweord ongan
æfter heaþoswate hildegicelum,
wigbil wanian. þæt wæs wundra sum,

1575 Næs] *With the æ altered from e by the same hand*   1592 wliton] wliton
A, wlitom B   1599 abroten] abreoten   1602 setan] secan

    þæt hit eal gemealt   ise gelicost,
    ðonne forstes bend   fæder onlæteð,
1610 onwindeð wælrapas,   se geweald hafað
    sæla ond mæla; þæt is soð metod.
    Ne nom he in þæm wicum, Wedergeata leod,
    maðmæhta ma, þeh he þær monige geseah,
    buton þone hafelan ond þa hilt somod
1615 since fage. Sweord ær gemealt,
    forbarn brodenmæl; wæs þæt blod to þæs hat,
    ættren ellorgæst se þær *in*ne swealt.
    Sona wæs on sunde se þe ær æt sæcce gebad
    wighryre wraðra, wæter up þurhdeaf.
1620 Wæron yðgebland eal gefælsod,
    eacne eardas, þa se ellorgast
    oflet lifdagas ond þas lænan gesceaft.
      Com þa to lande lidmanna helm
    swiðmod swymman; sælace gefeah,
1625 mægenbyrþenne þara þe he him mid hæfde.
    Eodon him þa togeanes, gode þancodon,
    ðryðlic þegna heap, þeodnes gefegon,
    þæs þe hi hyne gesundne geseon moston.
    Ða wæs of þæm hroran helm ond byrne
1630 lungre alysed. Lagu drusade,
    wæter under wolcnum, wældreore fag.
    Ferdon forð þonon feþelastum
    ferhþum fægne, foldweg mæton,
    cuþe stræte. Cyningbalde men
1635 from þæm holmclife hafelan bæron
    earfoðlice heora æghwæþrum,
    felamodigra; feower scoldon
    on þæm wælstenge weorcum geferian
    to þæm goldsele Grendles heafod,
1640 opðæt semninga to sele comon
    frome fyrdhwate feowertyne
    Geata gongan; gumdryhten mid

1617 ellorgæst] *With the letters* or *altered from* en *by the same hand*   inne]
mne *A*, inne *B*   1618 sæcce] *With the first* c *added above the line by the same hand*

modig on gemonge   meodowongas træd.
Ða com in gan   ealdor ðegna,
1645 dædcene mon   dome gewurþad,
hæle hildedeor,   Hroðgar gretan.
Þa wæs be feaxe   on flet boren
Grendles heafod,   þær guman druncon,
egeslic for eorlum   ond þære idese mid,
1650 wliteseon wrætlic;   weras on sawon.
Beowulf maþelode,   bearn Ecgþeowes:
"Hwæt! we þe þas sælac,   sunu Healfdenes,
leod Scyldinga,   lustum brohton
tires to tacne,   þe þu her to locast.
1655 Ic þæt unsofte   ealdre gedigde
wigge under wætere,   weorc geneþde
earfoðlice;   ætrihte wæs
guð getwæfed,   nymðe mec god scylde.
Ne meahte ic æt hilde   mid Hruntinge
1660 wiht gewyrcan,   þeah þæt wæpen duge;
ac me geuðe   ylda waldend
þæt ic on wage geseah   wlitig hangian
eald sweord eacen   (oftost wisode
winigea leasum),   þæt ic ðy wæpne gebræd.
1665 Ofsloh ða æt þære sæcce,   þa me sæl ageald,
huses hyrdas.   Þa þæt hildebil
forbarn brogdenmæl,   swa þæt blod gesprang,
hatost heaþoswata.   Ic þæt hilt þanan
feondum ætferede,   fyrendæda wræc,
1670 deaðcwealm Denigea,   swa hit gedefe wæs.
Ic hit þe þonne gehate,   þæt þu on Heorote most
sorhleas swefan   mid þinra secga gedryht
ond þegna gehwylc   þinra leoda,
duguðe ond iogoþe,   þæt þu him ondrædan ne þearft,
1675 þeoden Scyldinga,   on þa healfe,
aldorbealu eorlum,   swa þu ær dydest."
Ða wæs gylden hilt   gamelum rince,
harum hildfruman,   on hand gyfen,

1668 heaþoswata] *With the first* a *added above the line by the same hand*

enta ærgeweorc; hit on æht gehwearf
1680 æfter deofla hryre Denigea frean,
wundorsmiþa geweorc, ond þa þas worold ofgeaf
gromheort guma, godes ondsaca,
morðres scyldig, ond his modor eac,
on geweald gehwearf woroldcyninga
1685 ðæm selestan be sæm tweonum
ðara þe on Scedenigge sceattas dælde.
    Hroðgar maðelode, hylt sceawode,
ealde lafe, on ðæm wæs or writen
fyrngewinnes, syðþan flod ofsloh,
1690 gifen geotende, giganta cyn
(frecne geferdon); þæt wæs fremde þeod
ecean dryhtne; him þæs endelean
þurh wæteres wylm waldend sealde.
    Swa wæs on ðæm scennum sciran goldes
1695 þurh runstafas rihte gemearcod,
geseted ond gesæd hwam þæt sweord geworht,
irena cyst, ærest wære,
wreoþenhilt ond wyrmfah. Ða se wisa spræc
sunu Healfdenes (swigedon ealle):
1700 "þæt, la, mæg secgan se þe soð ond riht
fremeð on folce, feor eal gemon,
eald ᚦweard, þæt ðes eorl wære
geboren betera! Blæd is aræred
geond widwegas, wine min Beowulf,
1705 ðin ofer þeoda gehwylce. Eal þu hit geþyldum healdest,
mægen mid modes snyttrum. Ic þe sceal mine gelæstan
freode, swa wit furðum spræcon. Ðu scealt to frofre
                                        weorþan

eal langtwidig leodum þinum,
hæleðum to helpe. Ne wearð Heremod swa
1710 eaforum Ecgwelan, Arscyldingum;
ne geweox he him to willan, ac to wælfealle

1686 Scedenigge] *With the first g altered from n*   1704 Beowulf] beowolf
(*with f altered from r*) A, Beovulf B   1707 freode] freode *or* freoðe? *See
Note*   frofre] *With the second f added by a later hand*   weorþan] *With
the þ written on d erased?*   1711 geweox] *With the first e written above the
line by the same hand*

ond to deaðcwalum   Deniga leodum;
breat bolgenmod   beodgeneatas,
eaxlgesteallan,   oþþæt he ana hwearf,
1715 mære þeoden,   mondreamum from.
Ðeah þe hine mihtig god   mægenes wynnum,
eafeþum stepte,   ofer ealle men
forð gefremede,   hwæþere him on ferhþe greow
breosthord blodreow.   Nallas beagas geaf
1720 Denum æfter dome;   dreamleas gebad
þæt he þæs gewinnes   weorc þrowade,
leodbealo longsum.   Ðu þe lær be þon,
gumcyste ongit;   ic þis gid be þe
awræc wintrum frod.   Wundor is to secganne
1725 hu mihtig god   manna cynne
þurh sidne sefan   snyttru bryttað,
eard ond eorlscipe;   he ah ealra geweald.
Hwilum he on lufan   læteð hworfan
monnes modgeþonc   mæran cynnes,
1730 seleð him on eþle   eorþan wynne
to healdanne,   hleoburh wera,
gedeð him swa gewealdene   worolde dælas,
side rice,   þæt he his selfa ne mæg
for his unsnyttrum   ende geþencean.
1735 Wunað he on wiste;   no hine wiht dweleð
adl ne yldo,   ne him inwitsorh
on sefan sweorceð,   ne gesacu ohwær
ecghete eoweð,   ac him eal worold
wendeð on willan   (he þæt wyrse ne con),
1740 oðþæt him on innan   oferhygda dæl
weaxeð ond wridað.   Þonne se weard swefeð,
sawele hyrde;   bið se slæp to fæst,

1713 beodgeneatas] *A letter (a?) erased between* ge *and* neatas   1718
ferhþe] *With the* h *added above the line by a different hand*   1719 breost-
hord] *With the* e *added above the line by the same hand*   1734 for] for *A*,
not in B   unsnyttrum] *With the letters* un *added above the line by the same
hand*   1735 Wunað] wunad *A*, wunað *B*   1736 adl] adl *A*, adl (*the*
l *added later by Thorkelin*) *B*   1737 sefan] sefað *AB*   1741 weaxeð]
weaxed *AB*

bisgum gebunden,   bona swiðe neah,
se þe of flanbogan   fyrenum sceoteð.

1745 þonne bið on hreþre   under helm drepen
biteran stræle   (him bebeorgan ne con),
wom wundorbebodum   wergan gastes;
þinceð him to lytel   þæt he lange heold,
gytsað gromhydig,   nallas on gylp seleð

1750 fædde beagas,   ond he þa forðgesceaft
forgyteð ond forgymeð,   þæs þe him ær god sealde,
wuldres waldend,   weorðmynda dæl.
Hit on endestæf   eft gelimpeð
þæt se lichoma   læne gedreoseð,

1755 fæge gefealleð;   fehð oþer to,
se þe unmurnlice   madmas dæleþ,
eorles ærgestreon,   egesan ne gymeð.
Bebeorh þe ðone bealoNIð,   Beowulf leofa,
secg betsta,   ond þe þæt selre geceos,

1760 ece rædas;   oferhyda ne gym,
mære cempa.   Nu is þines mægnes blæd
ane hwile.   Eft sona bið
þæt þec adl oððe ecg   eafoþes getwæfeð,
oððe fyres feng,   oððe flodes wylm,

1765 oððe gripe meces,   oððe gares fliht,
oððe atol yldo;   oððe eagena bearhtm
forsiteð ond forsworceð;   semninga bið
þæt ðec, dryhtguma,   deað oferswyðeð.
Swa ic Hringdena   hund missera

1770 weold under wolcnum   ond hig wigge beleac
manigum mægþa   geond þysne middangeard,
æscum ond ecgum,   þæt ic me ænigne
under swegles begong   gesacan ne tealde.
Hwæt, me þæs on eþle   edwenden cwom,

1748 he lange] he to lange *with* to *partly erased*   1753 endestæf] *There was room for about four letters (perhaps* ende *erased) before* stæf, *at the beginning of the line*   1754 læne] lane *A,* læne *B*   1755 fehð] *With the* ð *added above the line by another hand*   1770 beleac] be leac *A,* be *B (B omits* -leac...mid-)   1771 middangeard] mid dan geard *A,* ðan geard *B (see the preceding note)*   1774 edwenden] ed wendan

1775 gyrn æfter gomene,   seoþðan Grendel wearð,
ealdgewinna,   ingenga min;
ic þære socne   singales wæg
modceare micle.   þæs sig metode þanc,
ecean dryhtne,   þæs ðe ic on aldre gebad
1780 þæt ic on þone hafelan   heorodreorigne
ofer ealdgewin   eagum starige!
Ga nu to setle,   symbelwynne dreoh
wigge weorþad;   unc sceal worn fela
maþma gemænra,   siþðan morgen bið."
1785   Geat wæs glædmod,   geong sona to
setles neosan,   swa se snottra heht.
þa wæs eft swa ær   ellenrofum
fletsittendum   fægere gereorded
niowan stefne.   Nihthelm geswearc
1790 deorc ofer dryhtgumum.   Duguð eal aras.
Wolde blondenfeax   beddes neosan,
gamela Scylding.   Geat unigmetes wel,
rofne randwigan,   restan lyste;
sona him seleþegn   siðes wergum,
1795 feorrancundum,   forð wisade,
se for andrysnum   ealle beweotede
þegnes þearfe,   swylce þy dogore
heaþoliðende   habban scoldon.
Reste hine þa rumheort;   reced hliuade
1800 geap ond goldfah;   gæst inne swæf
oþþæt hrefn blaca   heofones wynne
bliðheort bodode.   Ða com beorht scacan
      * * *   scaþan onetton,
wæron æþelingas   eft to leodum
1805 fuse to farenne;   wolde feor þanon
cuma collenferhð   ceoles neosan.
Heht þa se hearda   Hrunting beran

1775 gyrn] *With the* n *added above the line by the same hand*   1790 dryht-
gumum] *With the* h *altered from some other letter*   1796 beweotede] be
weotene   1797 dogore] *With the* e *added in a different ink*   1802 Ða
com] ða com B, *a space* A   1805 farenne] [...]ene ne *MS.,* arene ne *A,*
farene ne *B*   1806 collen-] colen *A,* col len *B*

sunu Ecglafes,   heht his sweord niman,
leoflic iren;   sægde him þæs leanes þanc,
1810 cwæð, he þone guðwine   godne tealde,
wigcræftigne,   nales wordum log
meces ecge;   þæt wæs modig secg.
Ond þa siðfrome,   searwum gearwe
wigend wæron;   eode weorð Denum
1815 æþeling to yppan,   þær se oþer wæs,
hæle hildedeor   Hroðgar grette.
     Beowulf maþelode,   bearn Ecgþeowes:
"Nu we sæliðend   secgan wyllað,
feorran cumene,   þæt we fundiaþ
1820 Higelac secan.   Wæron her tela
willum bewenede;   þu us wel dohtest.
Gif ic þonne on eorþan   owihte mæg
þinre modlufan   maran tilian,
gumena dryhten,   ðonne ic gyt dyde,
1825 guðgeweorca,   ic beo gearo sona.
Gif ic þæt gefricge   ofer floda begang,
þæt þec ymbsittend   egesan þywað,
swa þec hetende   hwilum dydon,
ic ðe þusenda   þegna bringe,
1830 hæleþa to helpe.   Ic on Higelac wat,
Geata dryhten,   þeah ðe he geong sy,
folces hyrde,   þæt he mec fremman wile
wordum ond worcum,   þæt ic þe wel herige
ond þe to geoce   garholt bere,
1835 mægenes fultum,   þær ðe bið manna þearf.
Gif him þonne Hreþric   to hofum Geata
geþingeð, þeodnes bearn,   he mæg þær fela
freonda findan;   feorcyþðe beoð
selran gesohte   þæm þe him selfa deah."
1840   Hroðgar maþelode   him on ondsware:
"Þe þa wordcwydas   wigtig drihten

1815 æþeling] *Two or three letters erased after this word*   1816 hæle] helle
1821 bewenede] *With the* n *altered from* r   1830 Higelac] hige lace   wat]
With the t *altered from* c *in a different ink*   1833 wordum] weordum
1836 Hreþric] hreþrinc   1837 geþingeð] geþinged

on sefan sende;   ne hyrde ic snotorlicor
on swa geongum feore   guman þingian.
þu eart mægenes strang   ond on mode frod,
1845 wis wordcwida.   Wen ic talige,
gif þæt gegangeð,   þæt ðe gar nymeð,
hild heorugrimme,   Hreþles eaferan,
adl oþðe iren   ealdor ðinne,
folces hyrde,   ond þu þin feorh hafast,
1850 þæt þe Sægeatas   selran næbben
to geceosenne   cyning ænigne,
hordweard hæleþa,   gyf þu healdan wylt
maga rice.   Me þin modsefa
licað leng swa wel,   leofa Beowulf.
1855 Hafast þu gefered   þæt þam folcum sceal,
Geata leodum   ond Gardenum,
sib gemæne,   ond sacu restan,
inwitniþas,   þe hie ær drugon,
wesan, þenden ic wealde   widan rices,
1860 maþmas gemæne,   manig oþerne
godum gegretan   ofer ganotes bæð;
sceal hringnaca   ofer heafu bringan
lac ond luftacen.   Ic þa leode wat
ge wið feond ge wið freond   fæste geworhte,
1865 æghwæs untæle   ealde wisan."
    Ða git him eorla hleo   inne gesealde,
mago Healfdenes,   maþmas XII;
het hine mid þæm lacum   leode swæse
secean on gesyntum,   snude eft cuman.
1870 Gecyste þa   cyning æþelum god,
þeoden Scyldinga,   ðegn betstan
ond be healse genam;   hruron him tearas,
blondenfeaxum.   Him wæs bega wen,

1846a þæt] þ *altered from* w *by the same hand*   1852 gyf] gyf *A*, gif *B*
1853 modsefa] nod sefa *A*, mod sefa *B*   1854 Beowulf] beo þulf *A*, Beo
vulf *B*   1857 gemæne] ge mænum   1860 manig] ma mg *A*, ma nig *B*
1861 gegretan] geg ret tan   1862 sceal] *With a second* l *erased at the end
of the word*   heafu] hea þu   1868 hine] inne   1872 be] *With the* e
added above the line by the same hand

ealdum infrodum, oþres swiðor,
1875 þæt hie seoðða[n no] geseon moston,
modige on meþle. [W]æs him se man to þon leof
þæt he þone breostwylm forberan ne mehte,
ac him on hreþre hygebendum fæst
æfter deorum men dyrne langað
1880 beorn wið blode. Him Beowulf þanan,
guðrinc goldwlanc, græsmoldan træd
since hremig; sægenga bad
agendfrean, se þe on ancre rad.
Þa wæs on gange gifu Hroðgares
1885 oft geæhted; þæt wæs an cyning,
æghwæs orleahtre, oþþæt hine yldo benam
mægenes wynnum, se þe oft manegum scod.
Cwom þa to flode felamodigra,
hægstealdra heap, hringnet bæron,
1890 locene leoðosyrcan. Landweard onfand
eftsið eorla, swa he ær dyde;
no he mid hearme of hliðes nosan
gæs[tas] grette, ac him togeanes rad,
cwæð þæt wilcuman Wedera leodum
1895 scaþan scirhame to scipe foron.
Þa wæs on sande sægeap naca
hladen herewædum, hringedstefna,
mearum ond maðmum; mæst hlifade
ofer Hroðgares hordgestreonum.
1900 He þæm batwearde bunden golde
swurd gesealde, þæt he syðþan wæs
on meodubence maþme þy weorþra,
yrfelafe. Gewat him on naca
drefan deop wæter, Dena land ofgeaf.
1905 Þa wæs be mæste merehrægla sum,
segl sale fæst; sundwudu þunede.

1875 hie] he   1876 Wæs] þæs A, *not in* B   1883 agendfrean] aged frean
þe] we A, þe B   1889 heap] *Not in MS.*   1893 gæstas] gæs *followed by*
a space A, ... B   1894 cwæð] cwæð A, ... B   1895 scaþan]
sca wan A, sca þan B   1902 maþme] maþma   weorþra] weo rþre
1903 naca] nacan

No þær wegflotan   wind ofer yðum
siðes getwæfde;   sægenga for,
fleat famigheals   forð ofer yðe,
1910 bundenstefna   ofer brimstreamas,
þæt hie Geata clifu   ongitan meahton,
cuþe næssas.   Ceol up geþrang
lyftgeswenced,   on lande stod.
Hraþe wæs æt holme   hyðweard geara,
1915 se þe ær lange tid   leofra manna
fus æt faroðe   feor wlatode;
sælde to sande   sidfæþme scip,
oncerbendum fæst,   þy læs hym yþa ðrym
wudu wynsuman   forwrecan meahte.
1920 Het þa up beran   æþelinga gestreon,
frætwe ond fætgold;   næs him feor þanon
to gesecanne   sinces bryttan,
Higelac Hreþling,   þær æt ham wunað
selfa mid gesiðum   sæwealle neah.
1925   Bold wæs betlic,   bregorof cyning,
heah in healle,   Hygd swiðe geong,
wis, welþungen,   þeah ðe wintra lyt
under burhlocan   gebiden hæbbe,
Hæreþes dohtor;   næs hio hnah swa þeah,
1930 ne to gneað gifa   Geata leodum,
maþmgestreona.   Mod þryðo wæg,
fremu folces cwen,   firen ondrysne.
Nænig þæt dorste   deor geneþan
swæsra gesiða,   nefne sinfrea,
1935 þæt hire an dæges   eagum starede,
ac him wælbende   weotode tealde
handgewriþene;   hraþe seoþðan wæs
æfter mundgripe   mece geþinged,

1908 sægenga] *With the second g altered from* t *by the same hand*   1910
bundenstefna] bunden stefne *with the final* e *marked for deletion and a* written
above *by the same hand*   1914 Hraþe] hreþe *with the first* e *marked for dele-*
tion and a written above *by the same hand*   1918 oncerbendum] oncear
bendum   1926 heah in] hea

þæt hit sceadenmæl   scyran moste,
1940 cwealmbealu cyðan.   Ne bið swylc cwenlic þeaw
    idese to efnanne, þeah ðe hio ænlicu sy,
    þætte freoðuwebbe feores onsæce
    æfter ligetorne leofne mannan.
    Huru þæt onhohsnode Hemminges mæg;
1945 ealodrincende oðer sædan,
    þæt hio leodbealewa læs gefremede,
    inwitniða, syððan ærest wearð
    gyfen goldhroden geongum cempan,
    æðelum diore, syððan hio Offan flet
1950 ofer fealone flod be fæder lare
    siðe gesohte; ðær hio syððan well
    in gumstole, gode, mære,
    lifgesceafta lifigende breac,
    hiold heahlufan wið hæleþa brego,
1955 ealles moncynnes mine gefræge
    þone selestan bi sæm tweonum,
    eormencynnes.   Forðam Offa wæs
    geofum ond guðum, garcene man,
    wide geweorðod, wisdome heold
1960 eðel sinne; þonon Eomer woc
    hæleðum to helpe, Hemminges mæg,
    nefa Garmundes, niða cræftig.
    Gewat him ða se hearda mid his hondscole
    sylf æfter sande sæwong tredan,
1965 wide waroðas.   Woruldcandel scan,
    sigel suðan fus.   Hi sið drugon,
    elne geeodon, to ðæs ðe eorla hleo,
    bonan Ongenþeoes burgum in innan,
    geongne guðcyning godne gefrunon

1939 sceadenmæl] *With the* d *altered from* ð *by erasure*   moste] *The second hand of the MS. begins with this word*   1944 onhohsnode] on hohsnod *with the* s *added by a later hand*   Hemminges] hem ninges   1947 syððan] fyððan *A*, syððan *B*   1951 syððan] *With the* n *added by the same hand* 1956 þone] þæs   1959 wide geweorðod] widege weorðod *A*, wida weordod *B*   1960 Eomer] geomor   1961 Hemminges] hem inges

1970 hringas dælan. Higelace wæs
  sið Beowulfes snude gecyðed,
  þæt ðær on worðig wigendra hleo,
  lindgestealla, lifigende cwom,
  heaðolaces hal to hofe gongan.
1975 Hraðe wæs gerymed, swa se rica bebead,
  feðegestum flet innanweard.
  Gesæt þa wið sylfne se ða sæcce genæs,
  mæg wið mæge, syððan mandryhten
  þurh hleoðorcwyde holdne gegrette,
1980 meaglum wordum. Meoduscencum hwearf
  geond þæt healreced Hæreðes dohtor,
  lufode ða leode, liðwæge bær
  hæleðum to handa. Higelac ongan
  sinne geseldan in sele þam hean
1985 fægre fricgcean (hyne fyrwet bræc,
  hwylce Sægeata siðas wæron):
  "Hu lomp eow on lade, leofa Biowulf,
  þa ðu færinga feorr gehogodest
  sæcce secean ofer sealt wæter,
1990 hilde to Hiorote? Ac ðu Hroðgare
  widcuðne wean wihte gebettest,
  mærum ðeodne? Ic ðæs modceare
  sorhwylmum seað, siðe ne truwode
  leofes mannes; ic ðe lange bæd
1995 þæt ðu þone wælgæst wihte ne grette,
  lete Suðdene sylfe geweorðan
  guðe wið Grendel. Gode ic þanc secge
  þæs ðe ic ðe gesundne geseon moste."
  Biowulf maðelode, bearn Ecgðioes:
2000 "Þæt is undyrne, dryhten Hige[lac],

1978 syððan] iððan A, syððan B   1979 holdne] *With the* n *altered from* e
gegrette] *With the* r *altered from some other letter*   1981 þæt healreced]
þæt reced *with* side *added above the line after* þæt *by the same hand but with a
different ink*   1983 hæleðum] hæ nū *with a letter* (ð?) *erased after* æ   1991
widcuðne] wið cuðne   2000 Higelac] hife *with a space after it* A, hige....
with lac *added later above the dots* B

[micel] gemeting,　monegum fira,
hwyl*c* [orleg]hwil　uncer Grendles
wearð on ðam wange,　þær he worna fela
Sige*scyld*ingum　sorge gefremede,
2005 yrmðe to aldre.　Ic ðæt eall gewræc,
swa *be*gylpan ne þearf　Grendeles maga
[æ]*n*[ig] ofer eorðan　uhthlem þone,
se ðe lengest leofað　laðan cynnes,
f[acne] bifongen.　Ic ðær furðum cwom
2010 to ðam hringsele　Hroðgar gretan;
sona me se mæra　mago Healfdenes,
syððan he modsefan　minne cuðe,
wið his sylfes sunu　setl getæhte.
Weorod wæs on wynne;　ne seah ic widan feorh
2015 under heofones hwealf　healsittendra
medudream maran.　Hwilum mæru cwen,
friðusibb folca,　flet eall geondhwearf,
bædde byre geonge;　oft hio beahwriðan
secge [sealde],　ær hie to setle geong.
2020 Hwilum for [d]*u*guðe　dohtor Hroðgares
eorlum *on* ende　ealuwæge bær;
þa ic Freaware　*flet*sittende
nemnan hyrde,　þær hio [næ]*g*led sinc
hæleðum sealde.　Sio gehaten [is],
2025 geong, goldhroden,　gladum suna Frodan;
[h]*a*fað þæs geworden　wine Scyldinga,
rices hyrde,　ond þæt ræd talað,
þæt he mid ðy wife　wælfæhða dæl,

2002 hwylc] hwyle *with a space after it A*, hwylce.. *B*　　2003 on ðam]
ondū *A*, onðam *B*　　2004 Sigescyldingum] sige scyl di ngū *A*, sige..
ðingum *B*; *in the MS. the second* i *of the word is altered from* u　　2005
yrmðe] yrmðe *A*, yrind.. *B*　　2006 swa begylpan] swabe gylpan *A*,
swal.. gylpan *B*　　ne] *Not in MS.*　　2007 ænig] en.. *B, a space A*　　2008
se ðe] sede *A*, seðe *B*　　2009 facne] fæ *with a space after it A*, fer.. *B*
2020 for duguðe] for gude.... *A*, for ....uguðe *B*　　2021 on] on *B, a
space A*　　2022 fletsittende] *So A and B, but see Note*　　2023 nægled]
gled *A*, ...gled *B; see Note*　　2024 is] ...se *B, a space A*　　2026 hafað]
iafað *AB* (*with* ia *in B added later by Thorkelin*)　　2028 mid] *With the* d
altered from ð

sæcca gesette. Oft seldan hwær
2030 æfter leodhryre lytle hwile
bongar bugeð, þeah seo bryd duge!
Mæg þæs þonne ofþyncan ðeodne Heaðobeardna
ond þegna gehwam þara leoda,
þonne he mid fæmnan on flett gæð,
2035 dryhtbearn Dena, duguða biwenede;
on him gladiað gomelra lafe,
heard ond hringmæl Heaðabeardna gestreon
þenden hie ðam wæpnum wealdan moston,
oððæt hie forlæddan to ðam lindplegan
2040 swæse gesiðas ond hyra sylfra feorh.
þonne cwið æt beore se ðe beah gesyhð,
eald æscwiga, se ðe eall ge[m]a[n],
garcwealm gumena (him bið grim *se*fa),
onginneð geomormod geong[um] cempan
2045 þurh hreðra gehygd higes cunnian,
wigbealu weccean, ond þæt word acwyð:
'Meaht ðu, min wine, mece gecnawan
þone þin fæder to gefeohte bær
under heregriman hindeman siðe,
2050 dyre iren, þær hyne Dene slogon,
weoldon wælstowe, syðða*n* Wiðergyld læg,
æfter hæleþa hryre, hwate Scyldungas?
Nu her þara banena byre nathwylces
frætwum hremig on flet gæð,
2055 morðres gylpeð, ond þone maðþum byreð,
þone þe ðu mid rihte rædan sceoldest.'
Manað swa ond myndgað mæla gehwylce
sarum wordum, oððæt sæl cymeð
þæt se fæmnan þegn fore fæder dædum
2060 æfter billes bite blodfag swefeð,

2032 ðeodne] ðeoden 2037 Heaðabeardna] heaða bearna 2041
gesyhð] gesyhð *A*, gesyhd *B* 2042 geman] ge *followed by a space A*, ge
nam. (*with* na *added later*) *B* 2043 grim sefa] grim fa *A*, grimme.. fa
(*with the second* m *added later by Thorkelin*) *B*, grim sefa (?) *Conybeare*
2051 syððan] syððan *B, not in A*, syððan *Conybeare* 2055 gylpeð]
gylwed *A*, gylped *B*

ealdres scyldig;   him se oðer þonan
losað [li]*f*igende,   con him land geare.
Þonne bioð [a]*b*rocene   on ba healfe
aðsweord eorla;   [syð]ðan Ingelde
2065 weallað wælniðas,   ond him wiflufan
æfter cearwælmum   colran weorðað.
Þy ic Heaðobeardna   hyldo ne telge,
dryhtsibbe dæl   Denum unfæcne,
freondscipe fæstne.   Ic sceal forð sprecan
2070 gen ymbe Grendel,   þæt ðu geare cunne,
sinces brytta,   to hwan syððan wearð
hondræs hæleða.   Syððan heofones gim
glad ofer grundas,   gæst yrre cwom,
eatol, æfengrom,   user neosan,
2075 ðær we gesunde   sæl weardodon.
Þær wæs Hondscio   hild onsæge,
feorhbealu fægum;   he fyrmest læg,
gyrded cempa;   him Grendel wearð,
mærum maguþegne   to muðbonan,
2080 leofes mannes   lic eall forswealg.
No ðy ær ut ða gen   idelhende
bona blodigtoð,   bealewa gemyndig,
of ðam goldsele   gongan wolde,
ac he mægnes rof   min costode,
2085 grapode gearofolm.   Glof hangode
sid ond syllic,   searobendum fæst;
*s*io wæs orðoncum   eall gegyrwed
deofles cræftum   ond dracan fellum.
He mec þær on innan   unsynnigne,
2090 dior dædfruma,   gedon wolde
manigra sumne;   hyt ne mihte swa,

2062 lifigende] figende *A*, .eigende *B*   2063 bioð] bioð *A*, biod *B*   abro-
cene] orocene *A*, .orocene B, brocene (?) *Conybeare*   2064 aðsweord]
With the d *altered from* ð *by erasure?*   2067 Heaðobeardna] heaðo bearna
2076 hild] hilde   2079 maguþegne] magū þegne   2085 gearofolm]
geareo folm *A B*   2087 sio] fio *A*, sio *B*   2088 deofles] dieofles *A*,
deofles *B*   2090 wolde] *An erasure of about eight letters after this word*

syððan ic on yrre   uppriht astod.
To lang ys to reccenne   hu i[c ð]*am* leodsceaðan
yfla gehwylces   ondlean forgeald;
2095 þær ic, þeoden min,   þine leode
weorðode weorcum.   He on weg losade,
lytle hwile   lifwynna bre[a]c;
hwæþre him sio swiðre   swaðe weardade
hand on Hiorte,   ond he hean ðonan
2100 modes geomor   meregrund gefeoll.
Me þone wælræs   wine Scildunga
fættan golde   fela leanode,
manegum maðmum,   syððan mergen com
ond we to symble   geseten hæfdon.
2105 þær wæs gidd ond gleo.   Gomela Scilding,
felafricgende,   feorran re*h*te;
hwilum hildedeor   hearpan wynne,
gomenwudu grette,   hwilum gyd awræc
soð ond sarlic,   hwilum syllic spell
2110 rehte æfter rihte   rumheort cyning.
Hwilum eft ongan,   eldo gebunden,
gomel guðwiga   *gi*oguðe cwiðan,
hildestrengo;   hreðer [in]*n*e weoll,
þonne he wintrum frod   worn *g*emunde.
2115 Swa we þær inne   ondlangne dæg
niode naman,   oððæt niht becwom
oðer to yldum.   þa wæs eft hraðe
gearo gyrnwræce   Grendeles modor,
siðode sorhfull;   sunu deað fornam,
2120 wighete Wedra.   Wif unhyre
hyre bearn gewræc,   beorn acwealde
ellenlice;   þær wæs Æschere,

2092 uppriht] upp rihte *A*, uppriht *B*   2093 hu ic ðam] huiedā *A*, hui
B   2094 ondlean] hon[.....] *MS.*, hondlean *A*, hondlan *B*   2097
breac] bræc *A*, brec *altered from* brene *B*   2106 rehte] relite *A B*, rehtlice
Conybeare   2108 gomenwudu] go mel wudu *A B*   2112 gioguðe] gioguðe
A, glogude *B*   2113 inne] mne *A*, . .me *B*   2114 gemunde] *So A and B,
but see Note*   2115 inne] mne *or* inne?   dæg] deg *A*, dæg *B*   2120
wif] *An* h *erased between this word and* unhyre

frodan fyrnwitan,   feorh uðgenge.
Noðer hy hine ne moston,   syððan mergen cwom,
2125 deaðwerigne,   Denia leode,
bronde forbærnan,   ne on bæl hladan
leofne mannan;   hio þæt lic ætbær
feondes fæð[mum   un]der firgenstream.
Þæt wæs Hroðgar[e]   hreowa tornost
2130 þara þe leodfruman   lange begeate.
Þa se ðeoden mec   ðine life
healsode hreohmod,   þæt ic on holma geþring
eorlscipe efnde,   ealdre geneðde,
mærðo fremede;   he me mede gehet.
2135 Ic ða ðæs wælmes,   þe is wide cuð,
grimne gryrelicne   grundhyrde fond;
þær unc hwile wæs   hand gemæne,
holm heolfre weoll,   ond ic heafde becearf
in ðam guðsele   Grendeles modor
2140 eacnum ecgum,   unsofte þonan
feorh oðferede.   Næs ic fæge þa gyt,
ac me eorla hleo   eft gesealde
maðma menigeo,   maga Healfdenes.
Swa se ðeodkyning   þeawum lyfde.
2145 Nealles ic ðam leanum   forloren hæfde,
mægnes mede,   ac he me [maðma]s geaf,
sunu Healfdenes,   on [min]ne sylfes dom;
ða ic ðe, beorncyning,   bringan wylle,
estum geywan.   Gen is eall æt ðe
2150 lissa gelong;   ic lyt hafo
heafodmaga   nefne, Hygelac, ðec."
   Het ða in beran   eaforheafodsegn,
heaðosteapne helm,   hare byrnan,

2126 bronde] *Originally written twice, but the first* bronde *erased*   bæl]
bęl   hladan] *Altered from* blædan (*Zupitza*)   2128 fæðmum under]
fæð *followed by a wide space and then by* der *A*, fædrungu ðer (*with* ungu
added later) B   2129 Hroðgare] hroð *followed by a space A*, Hrodgar..
B   2131 mec] mic *A*, mec *B*   2135 is] *With the* s *altered from* c *by the
same hand*   2136 grimne] grimme   2139 guð-] *Not in MS.*   2146
maðmas] *is preceded by a space A*, ...is B

guðsweord geatolic, gyd æfter wræc:
2155 "Me ðis hildesceorp Hroðgar sealde,
snotra fengel, sume worde het
þæt ic his ærest ðe est gesægde;
cwæð þæt hyt hæfde Hiorogar cyning,
leod Scyldunga lange hwile;
2160 no ðy ær suna sinum syllan wolde,
hwatum Heorowearde, þeah he him hold wære,
breostgewædu. Bruc ealles well!"
Hyrde ic þæt þam frætwum feower mearas
lungre, gelice, last weardode,
2165 æppelfealuwe; he him est geteah
meara ond maðma. Swa sceal mæg don,
nealles inwitnet oðrum bregdon
dyrnum cræfte, deað ren[ian]
hondgesteallan. Hygelace wæs,
2170 niða heardum, nefa swyðe hold,
ond gehwæðer oðrum hroþra gemyndig.
Hyrde ic þæt he ðone healsbeah Hygde gesealde,
wrætlicne wundurmaððum, ðone þe him Wealhðeo geaf,
ðeod[nes] dohtor, þrio wicg somod
2175 swancor ond sadolbeorht; hyre syððan wæs
æfter beahðege breost geweorðod.
  Swa bealdode bearn Ecgðeowes,
guma guðum cuð, godum dædum,
dreah æfter dome, nealles druncne slog
2180 heorðgeneatas; næs him hreoh sefa,
ac he mancynnes mæste cræfte
ginfæstan gife, þe him god sealde,
heold hildedeor. Hean wæs lange,
swa hyne Geata bearn godne ne tealdon,
2185 ne hyne on medobence micles wyrðne

2159 Scyldunga] *With* ld *altered from* in   2167 oðrum] oðrum *A,* odr....
B   2168 renian] re *followed by a space A,* ren... *B*   2170 niða] mða *A,*
niða.. *B*   2171 gehwæðer] gehwæðer *A,* ge hwæder *B*   2176 æfter]
æft *A,* æft *B*   breost] brost   2177 Swa bealdode] swab dode *A,* swa
beal dode *B*   2178 guðum] guð *A,* guðum *B*

[drih]ten Wedera   gedon wolde;
swyðe [wen]don   þæt he sleac wære,
æðeling unfrom.   Edwenden cwom
tireadigum menn   torna gehwylces.

2190   Het ða eorla hleo   in gefetian,
heaðorof cyning,   Hreðles lafe
golde gegyrede;   næs mid Geatum ða
sincmaðþum selra   on sweordes had;
þæt he on Biowulfes   bearm alegde
2195   ond him gesealde   seofan þusendo,
bold ond bregostol.   Him wæs bam samod
on ðam leodscipe   lond gecynde,
eard, eðelriht,   oðrum swiðor
side rice   þam ðær selra wæs.
2200   Eft þæt geiode   ufaran dogrum
hildehlæmmum,   syððan Hygelac læg
ond Heardrede   hildemeceas
under bordhreoðan   to bonan wurdon,
ða hyne gesohtan   on sigeþeode
2205   hearde hildefrecan,   Heaðoscilfingas,
niða genægdan   nefan Hererices,
syððan Beowulfe   brade rice
on hand gehwearf;   he geheold tela
fiftig wintra   (wæs ða frod cyning,
2210   eald eþelweard),   oððæt an ongan
deorcum nihtum   draca rics[i]an,
se ðe on heaum hofe   hord beweotode,
stanbeorh steapne;   stig under læg,
eldum uncuð.   Þær on innan giong

2186 drihten] . . . . . .nten (*with* dri *added later by Thorkelin and the first*
n *altered to* h) B, *a space* A   Wedera] wereda   2192 mid] mid A, mið
B   2193 on] n *preceded by a space* A, on B   2196 bam] am *preceded by
a space* A, bam B   2197 lond] cond A, lond B   2200 Eft] eft A, æft B
2202 Heardrede] hearede   2207–2252] *See Note*   2209 wintra] wintru
freshened up from original wintra (*Zupitza*)   2210 an] ón *freshened up
from original* án (*Zupitza*)   2211 ricsian] rics an A, ric an (*with* s *inserted
later by Thorkelin*) B   2213 steapne] stearne *freshened up from original*
steapne (*Zupitza*)

2215 niða nathwylc, se [ðe] n[e]h gefeng
 hæðnum horde, hond [.........],
 since fahne. He þæt syððan [....],
 þ[eah] ð[e he] slæpende besyre[d] wu[r]de
 þeofes cræfte; þæt sie ðiod onf[and],
2220 b[u]folc beorna, þæt he gebolge[n] wæs.
  Nealles mid gewealdum wyrmhord abræc
 sylfes willum, se ðe him sare gesceod,
 ac for þreanedlan þ[eow] nathwylces
 hæleða bearna heteswengeas fleah,
2225 ærn[es] þearfa, ond ðær inne feal[h],
 secg synbysig, sona onfunde
 þæt [þær] ðam gyste [gry]rebroga stod;
 hwæðre [earm]sceapen [..............
 ....]sceapen
2230 [..........], þa hyne se fær begeat.
 Sincfæt [.....]; þær wæs swylcra fela
 in ðam eorð[hu]se ærgestreona,
 swa hy on geardagum gumena nathwylc,
 eormenlafe æþelan cynnes,
2235 þanchycgende þær gehydde,
 deore maðmas. Ealle hie deað fornam
 ærran mælum, ond se an ða gen
 leoda duguðe, se ðær lengest hwearf,
 weard winegeomor, wende þæs ylcan,
2240 þæt he lytel fæc longgestreona
 brucan moste. Beorh eallgearo
 wunode on wonge wæteryðum neah,
 niwe be næsse, nearocræftum fæst.

2217 fahne] fac ne *with* h *written above* c   2221 gewealdum] ge weoldū
freshened up from original ge wealdū (*Zupitza*)   wyrmhord abræc] wyrm
horda cræft   2224 fleah] fleoh *freshened up from original* fleah (*Zupitza*)
2225 fealh] weal[.] *freshened up from original* feal[ ] *MS.* (*Zupitza*), weall *A B*
2226 onfunde] mwatide   2230 fær] fǽs *freshened up from original* fǽr?
(*Zupitza*)   2232 -huse] se *B, a space A*   2237 se] si *freshened up from
original* se? (*Zupitza*)   2239 weard] feard *A*, weard *B*   wende] rihde
freshened up from original wende (*Zupitza*)   ylcan] yldan *with the* d
altered from c *by a later hand*   2242 wæter-] weter *A*, wæter *B*

Þær on innan bær   eorlgestreona
2245 hringa hyrde   hordwyrðne dæl,
fættan goldes,   fea worda cwæð:
"Heald þu nu, hruse,   nu hæleð ne moston,
eorla æhte!   Hwæt, hyt ær on ðe
gode begeaton.   Guðdeað fornam,
2250 feorhbealo frecne,   fyra gehwylcne
leoda minra,   þara ðe þis lif ofgeaf,
gesawon seledream.   [Ic] nah hwa sweord wege
oððe fe[ormie]   fæted wæge,
dryncfæt deore;   dug[uð] ellor sceoc.
2255 Sceal se hearda helm   [hyr]sted golde
fætum befeallen;   feormynd swefað,
þa ðe beadogriman   bywan sceoldon,
ge swylce seo herepad,   sio æt hilde gebad
ofer borda gebræc   bite irena,
2260 brosnað æfter beorne.   Ne mæg byrnan hring
æfter wigfruman   wide feran,
hæleðum be healfe.   Næs hearpan wyn,
gomen gleobeames,   ne god hafoc
geond sæl swingeð,   ne se swifta mearh
2265 burhstede beateð.   Bealocwealm hafað
fela feorhcynna   forð onsended!"
    Swa giomormod   giohðo mænde
an æfter eallum,   unbliðe hwe[arf]
dæges ond nihtes,   oððæt deaðes wylm
2270 hran æt heortan.   Hordwynne fond
eald uhtsceaða   opene standan,

2244 innan] innon *freshened up from original* innan (*Zupitza*)   2245
hordwyrðne] hard wyrðne (*or* fyrðne?) *MS.*, hard fyrdne *AB*   2246 fea]
fec *freshened up from original* fea (*Zupitza*)   2247 moston] mæstan
freshened up from original mostun *or* moston? (*Zupitza*)   2250 feorhbealo]
reorh bealc *freshened up from original* feorh bealo (*Zupitza*)   fyra] fyrena
2251 þara] þana   lif] *Not in MS.*   2253 feormie] f *followed by a space A,*
fe... *B*   2254 sceoc] seoc   2261 wigfruman] wigfwu man *A,* wig fru
man *B,* wigfruman *Conybeare*   2266 forð] feo[..] *with a dot (for deletion?)*
under e *MS.* (*Zupitza*), feorð *AB*   2268 hwearf] hwe[...] *MS.,* hpeir *A,*
not in B

se ðe byrnende biorgas seceð,
nacod niðdraca, nihtes fleogeð
fyre befangen; hyne foldbuend
2275 [swiðe ondræ]da[ð]. He gesecean sceall
[ho]r[d on h]rusan, þær he hæðen gold
waɼað wintrum frod, ne byð him wihte ðy sel.
  Swa se ðeodsceaða þreo hund wintra
heold on hrusan hordærna sum,
2280 eacencræftig, oððæt hyne an abealch
mon on mode; mandryhtne bær
fæted wæge, frioðowære bæd
hlaford sinne. Ða wæs hord rasod,
onboren beaga hord, bene getiðad
2285 feasceaftum men. Frea sceawode
fira fyrngeweorc forman siðe.
  Þa se wyrm onwoc, wroht wæs geniwad;
stonc ða æfter stane, stearcheort onfand
feondes fotlast; he to forð gestop
2290 dyrnan cræfte dracan heafde neah.
Swa mæg unfæge eaðe gedigan
wean ond wræcsið, se ðe waldendes
hyldo gehealdeþ! Hordweard sohte
georne æfter grunde, wolde guman findan,
2295 þone þe him on sweofote sare geteode,
hat ond hreohmod hlæw oft ymbehwearf
ealne utanweardne, ne ðær ænig mon
on þære westenne; hwæðre wiges gefeh,
bea[du]we weorces, hwilum on beorh æthwearf,
2300 sincfæt sohte. He þæt sona onfand
ðæt hæfde gumena sum goldes gefandod,
heahgestreona. Hordweard onbad

2272 byrnende] byrnende B, *not in A*, byrnende *Conybeare* 2277 win-
trum] wintrum B, *not in A* 2279 hrusan] hrusam 2283 sinne] *With
the second* n *added above the line by the same hand* 2293 gehealdeþ] *With
the* þ *altered from* w 2296 hlæw] hlæwū 2297 utan-] ucan A, utan B
2298 þære] þære B, *a space A* wiges] hilde 2299 beaduwe] be[. . .]
at the end of a line MS., bea *followed by a space AB* 2300 onfand] on
fand A, on fanð B

earfoðlice   oððæt æfen cwom;
wæs ða gebolgen   beorges hyrde,
2305 wolde se laða   lige forgyldan
drincfæt dyre.   Þa wæs dæg sceacen
wyrme on willan;   no on wealle læg,
bidan wolde,   ac mid bæle for,
fyre gefysed.   Wæs se fruma egeslic
2310 leodum on lande,   swa hyt lungre wearð
on hyra sincgifan   sare geendod.
   Ða se gæst ongan   gledum spiwan,
beorht hofu bærnan;   bryneleoma stod
eldum on andan.   No ðær aht cwices
2315 lað lyftfloga   læfan wolde.
   Wæs þæs wyrmes wig   wide gesyne,
nearofages nið   nean ond feorran,
hu se guðsceaða   Geata leode
hatode ond hynde;   hord eft gesceat,
2320 dryhtsele dyrnne,   ær dæges hwile.
Hæfde landwara   lige befangen,
bæle ond bronde,   beorges getruwode,
wiges ond wealles;   him seo wen geleah.
   Þa wæs Biowulfe   broga gecyðed
2325 snude to soðe,   þæt his sylfes ham,
bolda selest,   brynewylmum mealt,
gifstol Geata.   Þæt ðam godan wæs
hreow on hreðre,   hygesorga mæst;
wende se wisa   þæt he wealdende
2330 ofer ealde riht,   ecean dryhtne,
bitre gebulge.   Breost innan weoll
þeostrum geþoncum,   swa him geþywe ne wæs.
Hæfde ligdraca   leoda fæsten,
ealond utan,   eorðweard ðone
2335 gledum forgrunden;   him ðæs guðkyning,
Wedera þioden,   wræce leornode.
Heht him þa gewyrcean   wigendra hleo

2305 se laða] fela ða   2309 egeslic] *An erasure of several letters after this*
word, at the end of a line   2314 No ðær] noðær *A*, neðer *B*   2322
getruwode] *With the* t *altered from* g *by erasure*   2325 ham] him

eallirenne, eorla dryhten,
wigbord wrætlic; wisse he gearwe
2340 þæt him holtwudu he[lpan] ne meahte,
lind wið lige. Sceolde lændaga
æþeling ærgod ende gebidan,
worulde lifes, ond se wyrm somod,
þeah ðe hordwelan heolde lange.
2345 Oferhogode ða hringa fengel
þæt he þone widflogan weorode gesohte,
sidan herge; no he him þa sæcce ondred,
ne him þæs wyrmes wig for wiht dyde,
eafoð ond ellen, forðon he ær fela
2350 nearo neðende niða gedigde,
hildehlemma, syððan he Hroðgares,
sigoreadig secg, sele fælsode
ond æt guðe forgrap Grendeles mægum
laðan cynnes. No þæt læsest wæs
2355 hondgemot[a], þær mon Hygelac sloh,
syððan Geata cyning guðe ræsum,
freawine folca Freslondum on,
Hreðles eafora hiorodryncum swealt,
bille gebeaten. Þonan Biowulf com
2360 sylfes cræfte, sundnytte dreah;
hæfde him on earme [ana] XXX
hildegeatwa, þa he to holme [be]ag.
Nealles Hetware hremge þorf[t]on
feðewiges, þe him foran ongean
2365 linde bæron; lyt eft becwom
fram þam hildfrecan hames niosan.
Oferswam ða sioleða bigong sunu Ecgðeowes,
earm anhaga, eft to leodum;
þær him Hygd gebead hord ond rice,
2370 beagas ond bregostol, bearne ne truwode
þæt he wið ælfylcum eþelstolas
healdan cuðe, ða wæs Hygelac dead.

2341 lændaga] þend daga 2347 þa] þā 2355 hondgemota] *See Note*
2363 þorfton] þorf *followed by a space A,* þorf .on *B* 2366 hild-] hild *B,*
not in A

No ðy ær feasceafte findan meahton
æt ðam æðelinge ænige ðinga,
2375 þæt he Heardrede hlaford wære
oððe þone cynedom ciosan wolde;
hwæðre he him on folce freondlarum heold,
estum mid are, oððæt he yldra wearð,
Wedergeatum weold. Hyne wræcmæcgas
2380 ofer sæ sohtan, suna Ohteres;
hæfdon hy forhealden helm Scylfinga,
þone selestan sæcyninga
þara ðe in Swiorice sinc brytnade,
mærne þeoden. Him þæt to mearce wearð;
2385 he þær for feorme feorhwunde hleat
sweordes swengum, sunu Hygelaces,
ond him eft gewat Ongenðioes bearn
hames niosan, syððan Heardred læg,
let ðone bregostol Biowulf healdan,
2390 Geatum wealdan. þæt wæs god cyning!
    Se ðæs leodhryres lean gemunde
uferan dogrum, Eadgilse wearð
feasceaftum freond, folce gestepte
ofer sæ side sunu Ohteres,
2395 wigum ond wæpnum; he gewræc syððan
cealdum cearsiðum, cyning ealdre bineat.
Swa he niða gehwane genesen hæfde,
sliðra geslyhta, sunu Ecgðiowes,
ellenweorca, oð ðone anne dæg
2400 þe he wið þam wyrme gewegan sceolde.
    Gewat þa XIIa sum torne gebolgen
dryhten Geata dracan sceawian.
    Hæfde þa gefrunen hwanan sio fæhð aras,

2381 forhealden] *Originally* forgolden, *but* go *altered to* ea *and* h *inserted
above the line*   2383 ðe] *At the end of a line, and repeated at the beginning
of the next line*   2385 þær] þær *A*, bær *B*   for feorme] orfeorme   2386
sweordes] sweore des *A*, sweor des *B*   2387 him] hū *A*, him *B*   2398
geslyhta] geslyhta *A*, geslyh.. *B*   2400 wyrme] *With the* r *altered from
some other letter*   2401 XIIa] .xii. *with* a *added above by the same hand*

bealonið biorna;   him to bearme cwom
2405 maðþumfæt mære   þurh ðæs meldan hond.
Se wæs on ðam ðreate   þreotteoða secg,
se ðæs orleges   or onstealde,
hæft hygegiomor,   sceolde hean ðonon
wong wisian.   He ofer willan giong
2410 to ðæs ðe he eorðsele   anne wisse,
hlæw under hrusan   holmwylme neh,
yðgewinne;   se wæs innan full
wrætta ond wira.   Weard unhiore,
gearo guðfreca,   goldmaðmas heold,
2415 eald under eorðan.   Næs þæt yðe ceap
to gegangenne   gumena ænigum!
Gesæt ða on næsse   niðheard cyning,
þenden hælo abead   heorðgeneatum,
goldwine Geata.   Him wæs geomor sefa,
2420 wæfre ond wælfus,   wyrd ungemete neah,
se ðone gomelan   gretan sceolde,
secean sawle hord,   sundur gedælan
lif wið lice,   no þon lange wæs
feorh æþelinges   flæsce bewunden.
2425 Biowulf maþelade,   bearn Ecgðeowes:
"Fela ic on giogoðe   guðræsa genæs,
orleghwila;   ic þæt eall gemon.
Ic wæs syfanwintre,   þa mec sinca baldor,
freawine folca,   æt minum fæder genam;
2430 heold mec ond hæfde   Hreðel cyning,
geaf me sinc ond symbel,   sibbe gemunde.
Næs ic him to life   laðra owihte,
beorn in burgum,   þonne his bearna hwylc,
Herebeald ond Hæðcyn   oððe Hygelac min.
2435 Wæs þam yldestan   ungedefelice
mæges dædum   morþorbed stred,
syððan hyne Hæðcyn   of hornbogan,

2428 sinca baldor] sinta baldor *A*, sinca baldor (*with* -a *and* bal- *added later by Thorkelin*) *B*   2429 fæder] fæder *A*, fædor *B*   2433 in] m *A*, in *B*   2435 ungedefelice] *With an erasure (the perpendicular stroke of an* f?) *after the first* e

his freawine, flane geswencte,
miste mercelses ond his mæg ofscet,
2440 broðor oðerne blodigan gare.
Þæt wæs feohleas gefeoht, fyrenum gesyngad,
hreðre hygemeðe; sceolde hwæðre swa þeah
æðeling unwrecen ealdres linnan.
Swa bið geomorlic gomelum ceorle
2445 to gebidanne, þæt his byre ride
giong on galgan, þonne he gyd wrece,
sarigne sang, þonne his sunu hangað
hrefne to hroðre, ond he him helpe ne mæg,
eald ond infrod, ænige gefremman.
2450 Symble bið gemyndgad morna gehwylce
eaforan ellorsið; oðres ne gymeð
to gebidanne burgum in innan
yrfeweardas, þonne se an hafað
þurh deaðes nyd dæda gefondad.
2455 Gesyhð sorhcearig on his suna bure
winsele westne, windge reste
reote berofene. Ridend swefað,
hæleð in hoðman; nis þær hearpan sweg,
gomen in geardum, swylce ðær iu wæron.
2460 Gewiteð þonne on sealman, sorhleoð gæleð
an æfter anum; þuhte him eall to rum,
wongas ond wicstede. Swa Wedra helm
æfter Herebealde heortan sorge
weallende wæg. Wihte ne meahte
2465 on ðam feorhbonan fæghðe gebetan;
no ðy ær he þone heaðorinc hatian ne meahte
laðum dædum, þeah him leof ne wæs.
He ða mid þære sorhge, þe him swa sar belamp,
gumdream ofgeaf, godes leoht geceas,
2470 eaferum læfde, swa deð eadig mon,
lond ond leodbyrig, þa he of life gewat.

2448 hroðre] *With the* ð *added above the line, apparently by a different hand*
helpe] helpa[.] *MS.,* hel wan *A,* helpan *B*   2464 weallende] weal linde
AB, Weallende *Conybeare*   2466 heaðorinc] *With the* n *added above the*
line in a different ink   2468 swa] sio

Þa wæs synn ond sacu   Sweona ond Geata
ofer [w]*id* wæter,   wroht gemæne,
herenið hearda,   syððan Hreðel swealt,
2475 oððe him Ongenðeowes   eaferan wæran
frome, fyrdhwate,   freode ne woldon
ofer heafo healdan,   ac ymb Hreosnabeorh
eatolne inwitscear   oft gefremedon.
þæt mægwine   mine gewræcan,
2480 fæhðe ond fyrene,   swa hyt gefræge wæs,
þeah ðe oðer his   ealdre gebohte,
heardan ceape;   Hæðcynne wearð,
Geata dryhtne,   guð onsæge.
þa ic on morgne gefrægn   mæg oðerne
2485 billes ecgum   on bonan stælan,
þær Ongenþeow   Eofores niosað.
Guðhelm toglad,   gomela Scylfing
hreas hildeblac;   hond gemunde
fæhðo genoge,   feorhsweng ne ofteah.
2490 Ic him þa maðmas,   þe he me sealde,
geald æt guðe,   swa me gifeðe wæs,
leohtan sweorde;   he me lond forgeaf,
eard, eðelwyn.   Næs him ænig þearf
þæt he to Gifðum   oððe to Gardenum
2495 oððe in Swiorice   secean þurfe
*wyr*san wigfrecan,   weorðe gecypan.
Symle ic him on feðan   beforan wolde,
ana on orde,   ond swa to aldre sceall
sæcce fremman,   þenden þis sweord þolað,
2500 þæt mec ær ond sið   oft gelæste.
Syððan ic for dugeðum   Dæghrefne wearð
to handbonan,   Huga cempan;
nalles he ða frætwe   Frescyninge,
breostweorðunge,   bringan moste,
2505 ac in compe gecrong   cumbles hyrde,

2473 ofer wid] ofer rid *A*, ofer.. *B*   2478 gefremedon] ge ge fremedon
2488 hildeblac] blac   2496 wyrsan] wyrsan *A*, ... *B*   2498 ana]
With the second a *added above the line by the same hand*   2503 Frescyninge]
fres cyning   2505 compe] cempan

æþeling on elne; ne wæs ecg bona,
ac him hildegrap heortan wylmas,
banhus gebræc. Nu sceall billes ecg,
hond ond heard sweord, ymb hord wigan."
2510 Beowulf maðelode, beotwordum spræc
niehstan siðe: "Ic geneðde fela
guða on geogoðe; gyt ic wylle,
frod folces weard, fæhðe secan,
mærðu fremman, gif mec se mansceaða
2515 of eorðsele ut geseceð."
Gegrette ða gumena gehwylcne,
hwate helmberend, hindeman siðe,
swæse gesiðas: "Nolde ic sweord beran,
wæpen to wyrme, gif ic wiste hu
2520 wið ðam aglæcean elles meahte
gylpe wiðgripan, swa ic gio wið Grendle dyde.
Ac ic ðær heaðufyres hates wene,
oreðes ond attres; forðon ic me on hafu
bord ond byrnan. Nelle ic beorges weard
2525 forfleon fotes trem, ac unc furður sceal
weorðan æt wealle, swa unc wyrd geteoð,
metod manna gehwæs. Ic eom on mode from
þæt ic wið þone guðflogan gylp ofersitte.
Gebide ge on beorge byrnum werede,
2530 secgas on searwum, hwæðer sel mæge
æfter wælræse wunde gedygan
uncer twega. Nis þæt eower sið
ne gemet mannes, nefne min anes,
þæt he wið aglæcean eofoðo dæle,
2535 eorlscype efne. Ic mid elne sceall
gold gegangan, oððe guð nimeð,
feorhbealu frecne, frean eowerne!"
Aras ða bi ronde rof oretta,

2514 mærðu] mærðū 2520 elles] elles *A*, ellas *B* 2521*b* wið] wið *A*,
wid *B* 2522 ic] *Added above the line by the same hand* 2523 oreðes
ond attres] reðes 7 hattres 2525 forfleon] ofer fleon furður] *Not in
MS.* 2533 nefne] nefu *A*, nef... *with* ne *added later B* 2534 þæt] wat

heard under helme,   hiorosercean bær
2540 under stancleofu,   strengo getruwode
anes mannes.   Ne bið swylc earges sið!
Geseah ða be wealle   se ðe worna fela,
gumcystum god,   guða gedigde,
hildehlemma,   þonne hnitan feðan,
2545 stondan stanbogan,   stream ut þonan
brecan of beorge.   Wæs þære burnan wælm
heaðofyrum hat;   ne meahte horde neah
unbyrnende   ænige hwile
deop gedygan   for dracan lege.
2550 Let ða of breostum,   ða he gebolgen wæs,
Wedergeata leod   word ut faran,
stearcheort styrmde;   stefn in becom
heaðotorht hlynnan   under harne stan.
Hete wæs onhrered,   hordweard oncniow
2555 mannes reorde;   næs ðær mara fyrst
freode to friclan.   From ærest cwom
oruð aglæcean   ut of stane,
hat hildeswat.   Hruse dynede.
Biorn under beorge   bordrand onswaf
2560 wið ðam gryregieste,   Geata dryhten;
ða wæs hringbogan   heorte gefysed
sæcce to seceanne.   Sweord ær gebræd
god guðcyning,   gomele lafe,
ecgum unslaw;   æghwæðrum wæs
2565 bealohycgendra   broga fram oðrum.
Stiðmod gestod   wið steapne rond
winia bealdor,   ða se wyrm gebeah
snude tosomne;   he on searwum bad.
Gewat ða byrnende   gebogen scriðan,
2570 to gescipe scyndan.   Scyld wel gebearg
life ond lice   læssan hwile
mærum þeodne   þonne his myne sohte,
ðær he þy fyrste,   forman dogore

2542 se ðe] seðe *A*, sede *B*   2545 stondan] stodan   2564 unslaw] un
gl aw *with a letter erased between* l *and* a   2566 wið] wid *A*, vid *B*   2568
searwum] *With the* r *added above the line by the same hand*

wealdan moste   swa him wyrd ne gescraf
2575 hreð æt hilde.   Hond up abræd
Geata dryhten,   gryrefahne sloh
incgelafe,   þæt sio ecg gewac
brun on bane,   bat unswiðor
þonne his ðiodcyning   þearfe hæfde,
2580 bysigum gebæded.   Þa wæs beorges weard
æfter heaðuswenge   on hreoum mode,
wearp wælfyre;   wide sprungon
hildeleoman.   Hreðsigora ne gealp
goldwine Geata;   guðbill geswac,
2585 nacod æt niðe,   swa hyt no sceolde,
iren ærgod.   Ne wæs þæt eðe sið,
þæt se mæra   maga Ecgðeowes
grundwong þone   ofgyfan wolde;
sceolde ofer willan   wic eardian
2590 elles hwergen,   swa sceal æghwylc mon
alætan lændagas.   Næs ða long to ðon
þæt ða aglæcean hy   eft gemetton.
Hyrte hyne hordweard   (hreðer æðme weoll)
niwan stefne;   nearo ðrowode,
2595 fyre befongen,   se ðe ær folce weold.
Nealles him on heape   handgesteallan,
æðelinga bearn,   ymbe gestodon
hildecystum,   ac hy on holt bugon,
ealdre burgan.   Hiora in anum weoll
2600 sefa wið sorgum;   sibb æfre ne mæg
wiht onwendan   þam ðe wel þenceð.
Wiglaf wæs haten   Weoxstanes sunu,
leoflic lindwiga,   leod Scylfinga,
mæg Ælfheres;   geseah his mondryhten
2605 under heregriman   hat þrowian.
Gemunde ða ða are   þe he him ær forgeaf,

2579 hæfde] *With the* æ *altered from* e *by the same hand*   2580 bysigum]
With b *on an erasure (of* f*?)*   weard] *With the* d *altered from* ð *by erasure*
2588 grundwong] *With the* o *altered from* a (*Zupitza*)   2589 ofer] *Not in*
MS.   2592 aglæcean] aglægcean *with the second* g *partly erased*   2596
handgesteallan] heand gesteallan

wicstede weligne Wægmundinga,
folcrihta gehwylc, swa his fæder ahte.
Ne mihte ða forhabban; hond rond gefeng,
2610 geolwe linde, gomel swyrd geteah,
þæt wæs mid eldum Eanmundes laf,
suna Ohteres. þam æt sæcce wearð,
wrǣcca[n] wineleasum, Weohstan bana
meces ecgum, ond his magum ætbær
2615 brunfagne helm, hringde byrnan,
eald sweord etonisc; þæt him Onela forgeaf,
his gædelinges guðgewædu,
fyrdsearo fuslic, no ymbe ða fæhðe spræc,
þeah ðe he his broðor bearn abredwade.
2620 He frætwe geheold fela missera,
bill ond byrnan, oððæt his byre mihte
eorlscipe efnan swa his ærfæder;
geaf him ða mid Geatum guðgewæda,
æghwæs unrim, þa he of ealdre gewat,
2625 frod on forðweg. þa wæs forma sið
geongan cempan, þæt he guðe ræs
mid his freodryhtne fremman sceolde.
Ne gemealt him se modsefa, ne his mæges laf
gewac æt wige; þæt se wyrm onfand,
2630 syððan hie togædre gegan hæfdon.
  Wiglaf maðelode, wordrihta fela
sægde gesiðum (him wæs sefa geomor):
"Ic ðæt *mæl* geman, þær we medu þegun,
þonne we geheton ussum hlaforde
2635 in biorsele, ðe us ðas beagas geaf,
þæt we him ða guðgetawa gyldan woldon
gif him þyslicu þearf gelumpe,
helmas ond heard sweord. Ðe he usic on herge geceas
to ðyssum siðfate sylfes willum,
2640 onmunde usic mærða, ond me þas maðmas geaf,

2612 Ohteres] ohtere   2613 wræccan] wræcca *A*, vr... *B*   Weohstan]
weoh stanes   2628 mæges] mægenes   2629 þæt] þa   2632 sefa]
With the f *altered from* w   2633 mæl geman] mæl geman *A*, ...geman *B*
2634 we geheton] wegeton *A*, vigheton *B*, geheton *Conybeare*

þe he usic garwigend   gode tealde,
hwate helmberend,   þeah ðe hlaford us
þis ellenweorc   ana aðohte
to gefremmanne,   folces hyrde,
2645 for ðam he manna mæst   mærða gefremede,
dæda dollicra.   Nu is se dæg cumen
þæt ure mandryhten   mægenes behofað,
godra guðrinca;   wutun gongan to,
helpan hildfruman,   þenden hyt sy,
2650 gledegesa grim.   God wat on mec
þæt me is micle leofre   þæt minne lichaman
mid minne goldgyfan   gled fæðmie.
Ne þynceð me gerysne   þæt we rondas beren
eft to earde,   nemne we æror mægen
2655 fane gefyllan,   feorh ealgian
Wedra ðeodnes.   Ic wat geare
þæt næron ealdgewyrht,   þæt he ana scyle
Geata duguðe   gnorn þrowian,
gesigan æt sæcce;   urum sceal sweord ond helm,
2660 byrne ond beaduscrud,   bam gemæne.''
Wod þa þurh þone wælrec,   wigheafolan bær
frean on fultum,   fea worda cwæð:
"Leofa Biowulf,   læst eall tela,
swa ðu on geoguðfeore   geara gecwæde
2665 þæt ðu ne alæte   be ðe lifigendum
dom gedreosan.   Scealt nu dædum rof,
æðeling anhydig,   ealle mægene
feorh ealgian;   ic ðe fullæstu.''
Æfter ðam wordum   wyrm yrre cwom,
2670 atol inwitgæst,   oðre siðe
fyrwylmum fah   fionda nios[i]an,

2646 dæg] *Added above the line by the same hand*   2562 fæðmie] fæðmię
2656 geare] geare *A*, gear *B*   2658 Geata] geaca *A*, geata *B*   2659
sceal] *Added in the margin by the same hand*   2660 beaduscrud] byrdu
scrud   2661 wælrec] *With the* e *altered from* æ *by erasure*   2662 cwæð]
cwæð *A*, cvæd *B*   2671 fyrwylmum] *With the* l *altered from* r   niosian]
mosum *A*, niosnan *with three dots below* nan *B*

laðra manna; ligyðum for.
Born bord wið rond, byrne ne meahte
geongum garwigan geoce gefremman,
2675 ac se maga geonga under his mæges scyld
elne geeode, þa his agen [wæs]
gledum forgrunden. Þa gen guðcyning
m[ærða] gemunde, mægenstrengo sloh
hildebille, þæt hyt on heafolan stod
2680 niþe genyded; Nægling forbærst,
geswac æt sæcce sweord Biowulfes,
gomol ond grægmæl. Him þæt gifeðe ne wæs
þæt him irenna ecge mihton
helpan æt hilde; wæs sio hond to strong,
2685 se ðe meca gehwane, mine gefræge,
swenge ofersohte, þonne he to sæcce bær
wæpen wundrum heard; næs him wihte ðe sel.
Þa wæs þeodsceaða þriddan siðe,
frecne fyrdraca, fæhða gemyndig,
2690 ræsde on ðone rofan, þa him rum ageald,
hat ond heaðogrim, heals ealne ymbefeng
biteran banum; he geblodegod wearð
sawuldriore, swat yðum weoll.
Ða ic æt þearfe gefrægn þeodcyninges
2695 andlongne eorl ellen cyðan,
cræft ond cenðu, swa him gecynde wæs.
Ne hedde he þæs heafolan, ac sio hand gebarn
modiges mannes, þær he his mæges healp,
þæt he þone niðgæst nioðor hwene sloh,
2700 secg on searwum, þæt ðæt sweord gedeaf,
fah ond fæted, þæt ðæt fyr ongon
sweðrian syððan. Þa gen sylf cyning
geweold his gewitte, wællseaxe gebræd
biter ond beaduscearp, þæt he on byrnan wæg;
2705 forwrat Wedra helm wyrm on middan.
Feond gefyldan (ferh ellen wræc),

2675 under] under *A*, und *B*   2687 wundrum] wundū   2694 gefrægn]
Not in MS.   2698 mæges] mægenes   2703 his] *Followed by another* his
partly erased

    ond hi hyne þa begen   abroten hæfdon,
    sibæðelingas. Swylc sceolde secg wesan,
    þegn æt ðearfe! Þæt ðam þeodne wæs
2710 siðast sigehwila   sylfes dædum,
    worlde geweorces. Ða sio wund ongon,
    þe him se eorðdraca   ær geworhte,
    swelan ond swellan; he þæt sona onfand,
    þæt him on breostum   bealonið[e] weoll
2715 attor on innan. Ða se æðeling giong
    þæt he bi wealle   wishycgende
    gesæt on sesse; seah on enta geweorc,
    hu ða stanbogan   stapulum fæste
    ece eorðreced   innan healde.
2720 Hyne þa mid handa   heorodreorigne,
    þeoden mærne, þegn ungemete till
    winedryhten his   wætere gelafede,
    hilde sædne, ond his hel[m] onspeon.
    Biowulf maþelode   (he ofer benne spræc,
2725 wunde wælbleate; wisse he gearwe
    þæt he dæghwila   gedrogen hæfde,
    eorðan wyn[ne]; ða wæs eall sceacen
    dogorgerimes, deað ungemete neah):
    "Nu ic suna minum   syllan wolde
2730 guðgewædu, þær me gifeðe swa
    ænig yrfeweard   æfter wurde
    lice gelenge. Ic ðas leode heold
    fiftig wintra; næs se folccyning,
    ymbesittendra   ænig ðara,
2735 þe mec guðwinum   gretan dorste,
    egesan ðeon. Ic on earde bad
    mælgesceafta, heold min tela,
    ne sohte searoniðas, ne me swor fela

2710 siðast sigehwila] siðas sige hwile   2712 eorð-] eorð *A*, eord *B*   2714
bealoniðe] bealomð *A*, bealo niði *B*   2716 wishycgende] *With the* w
altered from s   2719 healde] healde *A*, heald *B*   2722 winedryhten]
wine dryhī *A*, wine dryht *B*   2723 helm] helo *A*, heb *B*   2727 wynne]
wym *A*, wyni *B*   2728 dogorgerimes] *With the* s *added (by a different hand?)*

aða on unriht. Ic ðæs ealles mæg
2740 feorhbennum seoc gefean habban;
for ðam me witan ne ðearf waldend fira
morðorbealo maga, þonne min sceaceð
lif of lice. Nu ðu lungre geong
hord sceawian under harne stan,
2745 Wiglaf leofa, nu se wyrm ligeð,
swefeð sare wund, since bereafod.
Bio nu on ofoste, þæt ic ærwelan,
goldæht ongite, gearo sceawige
swegle searogimmas, þæt ic ðy seft mæge
2750 æfter maððumwelan min alætan
lif ond leodscipe, þone ic longe heold."
Ða ic snude gefrægn sunu Wihstanes
æfter wordcwydum wundum dryhtne
hyran heaðosiocum, hringnet beran,
2755 brogdne beadusercean under beorges hrof.
Geseah ða sigehreðig, þa he bi sesse geong,
magoþegn modig maððumsigla fealo,
gold glitinian grunde getenge,
wundur on wealle, ond þæs wyrmes denn,
2760 ealdes uhtflogan, orcas stondan,
fyrnmanna fatu feormendlease,
hyrstum behrorene; þær wæs helm monig
eald ond omig, earmbeaga fela
searwum gesæled. Sinc eaðe mæg,
2765 gold on grund[e], gumcynnes gehwone
oferhigian, hyde se ðe wylle.
Swylce he siomian geseah segn eallgylden
heah ofer horde, hondwundra mæst,
gelocen leoðocræftum; of ðam leoma stod,
2770 þæt he þone grundwong ongitan meahte,
wræte giondwlitan. Næs ðæs wyrmes þær
onsyn ænig, ac hyne ecg fornam.

2751 þone] *With a horizontal stroke erased above* n   2755 beadusercean]
With the second e *altered from* æ   under] urder   2759 ond] 7 *altered from
some other letter?* (*Zupitza*)   2765 grunde] grund *AB*   2769 leoma]
leoman   2771 wræte] wræce

Ða ic on hlæwe gefrægn hord reafian,
eald enta geweorc, anne mannan,
2775 him on bearm hladon bunan ond discas
sylfes dome; segn eac genom,
beacna beorhtost. Bill ær gescod
(ecg wæs iren) ealdhlafordes
þam ðara maðma mundbora wæs
2780 longe hwile, ligegesan wæg
hatne for horde, hioroweallende
middelnihtum, oððæt he morðre swealt.
Ar wæs on ofoste, eftsiðes georn,
frætwum gefyrðred; hyne fyrwet bræc,
2785 hwæðer collenferð cwicne gemette
in ðam wongstede Wedra þeoden
ellensiocne, þær he hine ær forlet.
He ða mid þam maðmum mærne þioden,
dryhten sinne, driorigne fand
2790 ealdres æt ende; he hine eft ongon
wæteres weorpan, oððæt wordes ord
breosthord þurhbræc. * * *
gomel on giohðe (gold sceawode):
"Ic ðara frætwa frean ealles ðanc,
2795 wuldurcyninge, wordum secge,
ecum dryhtne, þe ic her on starie,
þæs ðe ic moste minum leodum
ær swyltdæge swylc gestrynan.
Nu ic on maðma hord mine bebohte
2800 frode feorhlege, fremmað gena
leoda þearfe; ne mæg ic her leng wesan.
Hatað heaðomære hlæw gewyrcean
beorhtne æfter bæle æt brimes nosan;
se scel to gemyndum minum leodum
2805 heah hlifian on Hronesnæsse,

2775 hladon] hlod[..] *MS.*, holdon *A*, hlodon *B*, hlodon *Conybeare*   2777
Bill] *With the second* l *added by a different hand*   2781 horde] *Originally*
hogode, *but the* g *erased and the second* o *altered to* r   2785 gemette] *With
the second* t *altered from* e? (*Zupitza*)   2793 giohðe] giogoðe   sceawode]
With the w *altered from* p   2799 mine] minne

þæt hit sæliðend   syððan hatan
Biowulfes biorh,   ða ðe brentingas
ofer floda genipu   feorran drifað."
   Dyde him of healse   hring gyldenne
2810 þioden þristhydig,   þegne gesealde,
geongum garwigan,   goldfahne helm,
beah ond byrnan,   het hyne brucan well:
"Þu eart endelaf   usses cynnes,
Wægmundinga.   Ealle wyrd forsweop
2815 mine magas   to metodsceafte,
eorlas on elne;   ic him æfter sceal."
Þæt wæs þam gomelan   gingæste word
breostgehygdum,   ær he bæl cure,
hate heaðowylmas;   him of hreðre gewat
2820 sawol secean   soðfæstra dom.
   Ða wæs gegongen   guman unfrodum
earfoðlice,   þæt he on eorðan geseah
þone leofestan   lifes æt ende
bleate gebæran.   Bona swylce læg,
2825 egeslic eorðdraca   ealdre bereafod,
bealwe gebæded.   Beahhordum leng
wyrm wohbogen   wealdan ne moste,
ac hine irenna   ecga fornamon,
hearde, heaðoscearde   homera lafe,
2830 þæt se widfloga   wundum stille
hreas on hrusan   hordærne neah.
Nalles æfter lyfte   lacende hwearf
middelnihtum,   maðmæhta wlonc
ansyn ywde,   ac he eorðan gefeoll
2835 for ðæs hildfruman   hondgeweorce.
Huru þæt on lande   lyt manna ðah,
mægenagendra,   mine gefræge,
þeah ðe he dæda gehwæs   dyrstig wære,
þæt he wið attorsceaðan   oreðe geræsde,
2840 oððe hringsele   hondum styrede,
gif he wæccende   weard onfunde

2814 forsweop] for speof   2819 hreðre] hwæðre   2821 guman] gumū
2828 hine] him

buon on beorge.   Biowulfe wearð
dryhtmaðma dæl   deaðe forgolden;
hæfde æghwæðer   ende gefered
2845 lænan lifes.   Næs ða lang to ðon
þæt ða hildlatan   holt ofgefan,
tydre treowlogan   tyne ætsomne.
Ða ne dorston ær   dareðum lacan
on hyra mandryhtnes   miclan þearfe,
2850 ac hy scamiende   scyldas bæran,
guðgewædu,   þær se gomela læg,
wlitan on Wilaf.   He gewergad sæt,
feðecempa,   frean eaxlum neah,
wehte hyne wætre;   him wiht ne speow.
2855 Ne meahte he on eorðan,   ðeah he uðe wel,
on ðam frumgare   feorh gehealdan,
ne ðæs wealdendes   wiht oncirran;
wolde dom godes   dædum rædan
gumena gehwylcum,   swa he nu gen deð.
2860   Þa wæs æt ðam geongan   grim ondswaru
eðbegete   þam ðe ær his elne forleas.
Wiglaf maðelode,   Weohstanes sunu,
sec, sarigferð   (seah on unleofe):
"Þæt, la, mæg secgan   se ðe wyle soð specan
2865 þæt se mondryhten   se eow ða maðmas geaf,
eoredgeatwe,   þe ge þær on standað,
þonne he on ealubence   oft gesealde
healsittendum   helm ond byrnan,
þeoden his þegnum,   swylce he þrydlicost
2870 ower feor oððe neah   findan meahte,
þæt he genunga   guðgewædu
wraðe forwurpe,   ða hyne wig beget.
Nealles folccyning   fyrdgesteallum
gylpan þorfte;   hwæðre him god uðe,
2875 sigora waldend,   þæt he hyne sylfne gewræc
ana mid ecge,   þa him wæs elnes þearf.
Ic him lifwraðe   lytle meahte

2844 æghwæðer] æg hwæðre   2854 speow] speop   2860 geongan]
geongū   ondswaru] 7 swaru *A*, and swarn *B*

ætgifan æt guðe,   ond ongan swa þeah
ofer min gemet   mæges helpan;
2880 symle wæs þy sæmra,   þonne ic sweorde drep
ferhðgeniðlan,   fyr unswiðor
weoll of gewitte.   Wergendra to lyt
þrong ymbe þeoden,   þa hyne sio þrag becwom.
Nu sceal sincþego   ond swyrdgifu,
2885 eall eðelwyn   eowrum cynne,
lufen alicgean;   londrihtes mot
þære mægburge   monna æghwylc
idel hweorfan,   syððan æðelingas
feorran gefricgean   fleam eowerne,
2890 domleasan dæd.   Deað bið sella
eorla gehwylcum   þonne edwitlif!"
    Heht ða þæt heaðoweorc   to hagan biodan
up ofer ecgclif,   þær þæt eorlweorod
morgenlongne dæg   modgiomor sæt,
2895 bordhæbbende,   bega on wenum,
endedogores   ond eftcymes
leofes monnes.   Lyt swigode
niwra spella   se ðe næs gerad,
ac he soðlice   sægde ofer ealle:
2900 "Nu is wilgeofa   Wedra leoda,
dryhten Geata,   deaðbedde fæst,
wunað wælreste   wyrmes dædum.
Him on efn ligeð   ealdorgewinna
sexbennum seoc;   sweorde ne meahte
2905 on ðam aglæcean   ænige þinga
wunde gewyrcean.   Wiglaf siteð
ofer Biowulfe,   byre Wihstanes,

2881 fyr unswiðor] fyrun swiðor (*with* u *altered from* a?)   2882 Wergendra] fergen dra   2884 Nu] hu   2885 eowrum cynne] *Written above an erasure, apparently of the same words*   2890 dæd] *Originally* dæl, *but the* l *marked for deletion and* d *added by the same hand*   2891 edwitlif] *With the* d *added above the line by the same hand*   2902 wælreste] *About five letters* (bennū?) *erased between* wæl *and* reste; r *of* reste *altered from some other letter*   2904 sexbennum] siex bennū   2905 aglæcean] *With the* c *altered from* g *by erasure*

eorl ofer oðrum unlifigendum,
healdeð higemæðum heafodwearde
2910 leofes ond laðes. Nu ys leodum wen
orleghwile, syððan underne
Froncum ond Frysum fyll cyninges
wide weorðeð. Wæs sio wroht scepen
heard wið Hugas, syððan Higelac cwom
2915 faran flotherge on Fresna land,
þær hyne Hetware hilde genægdon,
elne geeodon mid ofermægene,
þæt se byrnwiga bugan sceolde,
feoll on feðan, nalles frætwe geaf
2920 ealdor dugoðe. Us wæs a syððan
Merewioingas milts ungyfeðe.
Ne ic to Sweoðeode sibbe oððe treowe
wihte ne wene, ac wæs wide cuð
þætte Ongenðio ealdre besnyðede
2925 Hæðcen Hrepling wið Hrefnawudu,
þa for onmedlan ærest gesohton
Geata leode Guðscilfingas.
Sona him se froda fæder Ohtheres,
eald ond egesfull, ondslyht ageaf,
2930 abreot brimwisan, bryd ahredde,
gomela iomeowlan golde berofene,
Onelan modor ond Ohtheres,
ond ða folgode feorhgeniðlan,
oððæt hi oðeodon earfoðlice
2935 in Hrefnesholt hlafordlease.
Besæt ða sinherge sweorda lafe,
wundum werge, wean oft gehet
earmre teohhe ondlonge niht,
cwæð, he on mergenne meces ecgum

2911 underne] under   2916 genægdon] ge hnægdon   2921 Merewioingas milts] mere wio ingasmilts *with* sm *altered from* nn   2922 to]
te   2923 ne wene] *Added above the line by the same hand*   2929 ondslyht]
hond slyht   2930 bryd ahredde] bryda heorde   2931 iomeowlan] io
meowla *followed by a space A*, io meowlan *B*

2940 getan wolde, sum on galgtreowum
fuglum to gamene. Frofor eft gelamp
sarigmodum somod ærdæge,
syððan hie Hygelaces horn ond byman,
gealdor ongeaton, þa se goda com
2945 leoda dugoðe on last faran.
Wæs sio swatswaðu Sweona ond Geata,
wælræs weora wide gesyne,
hu ða folc mid him fæhðe towehton.
Gewat him ða se goda mid his gædelingum,
2950 frod, felageomor, fæsten secean,
eorl Ongenþio, ufor oncirde;
hæfde Higelaces hilde gefrunen,
wlonces wigcræft, wiðres ne truwode,
þæt he sæmannum onsacan mihte,
2955 heaðoliðendum hord forstandan,
bearn ond bryde; beah eft þonan
eald under eorðweall. þa wæs æht boden
Sweona leodum, segn Higelaces
freoðowong þone forð ofereodon,
2960 syððan Hreðlingas to hagan þrungon.
þær wearð Ongenðiow ecgum sweorda,
blondenfexa, on bid wrecen,
þæt se þeodcyning ðafian sceolde
Eafores anne dom. Hyne yrringa
2965 Wulf Wonreding wæpne geræhte,
þæt him for swenge swat ædrum sprong
forð under fexe. Næs he forht swa ðeh,
gomela Scilfing, ac forgeald hraðe
wyrsan wrixle wælhlem þone,
2970 syððan ðeodcyning þyder oncirde.
Ne meahte se snella sunu Wonredes
ealdum ceorle ondslyht giofan,

2940 galgtreowum] galg treowu   2941 fuglum] *Not in MS.*   2946
Sweona] swona   2948 fæhðe] *With the h added above the line by the same
hand*   2958 Higelaces] hige lace   2959 forð] ford   2961 Ongenðiow]
With the w added by a different hand   sweorda] sweordū   2972 ond-
slyht] hond slyht

ac he him on heafde   helm ær gescer,
þæt he blode fah   bugan sceolde,
2975 feoll on foldan; næs he fæge þa git,
ac he hyne gewyrpte,   þeah ðe him wund hrine.
Let se hearda   Higelaces þegn
bradne mece,   þa his broðor læg,
eald sweord eotonisc,   entiscne helm
2980 brecan ofer bordweal;   ða gebeah cyning,
folces hyrde,   wæs in feorh dropen.
Ða wæron monige   þe his mæg wriðon,
ricone aræron,   ða him gerymed wearð
þæt hie wælstowe   wealdan moston.
2985 þenden reafode   rinc oðerne,
nam on Ongenðio   irenbyrnan,
heard swyrd hilted   ond his helm somod,
hares hyrste   Higelace bær.
H[e ðam] frætwum feng   ond him fægre gehet
2990 leana [mid] leodum,   ond gelæste swa;
geald þone guðræs   Geata dryhten,
Hreðles eafora,   þa he to ham becom,
Iofore ond Wulfe   mid ofermaðmum,
sealde hiora gehwæðrum   hund þusenda
2995 landes ond locenra beaga   (ne ðorfte him ða lean oðwitan
mon on middangearde),   syððan hie ða mærða geslogon,
ond ða Iofore forgeaf   angan dohtor,
hamweorðunge,   hyldo to wedde.
Þæt ys sio fæhðo   ond se feondscipe,
3000 wælnið wera,   ðæs ðe ic wen hafo,
þe us seceað to   Sweona leoda,
syððan hie gefricgeað   frean userne
ealdorleasne,   þone ðe ær geheold
wið hettendum   hord ond rice
3005 æfter hæleða hryre,   hwate Scildingas,
folcred fremede   oððe furður gen
eorlscipe efnde.   Nu is ofost betost

2978 bradne] brade   2989 He ðam] h . d . . B, a space A   2990 gelæste]
gelæsta   2993 ofermaðmum] *With the* u *altered from* a *by erasure*   2996
syððan] syðða   3000 wen] *Not in MS.*   3007 efnde] *With the* f *inserted
later, apparently by the same hand*   Nu] me

þæt we þeodcyning   þær sceawian
ond þone gebringan,   þe us beagas geaf,
3010 on adfære.   Ne scel anes hwæt
meltan mid þam modigan,   ac þær is maðma hord,
gold unrime   grimme gecea[po]d,
ond nu æt siðestan   sylfes feore
beagas [geboh]te.   þa sceall brond fretan,
3015 æled þeccean,   nalles eorl wegan
maððum to gemyndum,   ne mægð scyne
habban on healse   hringweorðunge,
ac sceal geomormod,   golde bereafod,
oft nalles æne   elland tredan,
3020 nu se herewisa   hleahtor alegde,
gamen ond gleodream.   Forðon sceall gar wesan
monig, morgenceald,   mundum bewunden,
hæfen on handa,   nalles hearpan sweg
wigend weccean,   ac se wonna hrefn
3025 fus ofer fægum   fela reordian,
earne secgan   hu him æt æte speow,
þenden he wið wulf   wæl reafode."
     Swa se secg hwata   secggende wæs
laðra spella;   he ne leag fela
3030 wyrda ne worda.   Weorod eall aras;
eodon unbliðe   under Earnanæs,
wollenteare   wundur sceawian.
Fundon ða on sande   sawulleasne
hlimbed healdan   þone þe him hringas geaf
3035 ærran mælum;   þa wæs endedæg
godum gegongen,   þæt se guðcyning,
Wedra þeoden,   wundordeaðe swealt.
Ær hi þær gesegan   syllicran wiht,
wyrm on wonge   wiðerræhtes þær
3040 laðne licgean;   wæs se legdraca

3012 geceapod] gecea followed by a space A, ge cea .... B, gecea...d Conybeare   3016 mægð] With the g inserted between æ and ð by the same hand
3032 wundur] wundu A, wundur B   3035 ærran] ærrun with the u altered
from a by erasure (Zupitza), or possibly ærran with part of a accidentally
obscured   3040 laðne] laðm followed by a space A, ladn.. B, laðne..
Conybeare

grimlic, gry[refah], gledum beswæled.
Se wæs fiftiges fotgemearces
lang on legere, lyftwynne heold
nihtes hwilum, nyðer eft gewat
3045 dennes niosian; wæs ða deaðe fæst,
hæfde eorðscrafa ende genyttod.
Him big stodan bunan ond orcas,
discas lagon ond dyre swyrd,
omige, þurhetone, swa hie wið eorðan fæðm
3050 þusend wintra þær eardodon.
Þonne wæs þæt yrfe, eacencræftig,
iumonna gold galdre bewunden,
þæt ðam hringsele hrinan ne moste
gumena ænig, nefne god sylfa,
3055 sigora soðcyning, sealde þam ðe he wolde
(he is manna gehyld) hord openian,
efne swa hwylcum manna swa him gemet ðuhte.
Þa wæs gesyne þæt se sið ne ðah
þam ðe unrihte inne gehydde
3060 wræte under wealle. Weard ær ofsloh
feara sumne; þa sio fæhð gewearð
gewrecen wraðlice. Wundur hwar þonne
eorl ellenrof ende gefere
lifgesceafta, þonne leng ne mæg
3065 mon mid his [ma]gum meduseld buan.
Swa wæs Biowulfe, þa he biorges weard
sohte, searoniðas; seolfa ne cuðe
þurh hwæt his worulde gedal weorðan sceolde.
Swa hit oð domes dæg diope benemdon
3070 þeodnas mære, þa ðæt þær dydon,
þæt se secg wære synnum scildig,
hergum geheaðerod, hellbendum fæst,
wommum gewitnad, se ðone wong strude,
næs he goldhwæte gearwor hæfde
3075 agendes est ær gesceawod.
Wiglaf maðelode, Wihstanes sunu:

3060 wræte] wræce   3065 magum] ...gum B, a space A   3073 strude]
strade

"Oft sceall eorl monig   anes willan
wræc adreogan,   swa us geworden is.
Ne meahton we gelæran   leofne þeoden,
3080 rices hyrde,   ræd ænigne,
þæt he ne grette   goldweard þone,
lete hyne licgean   þær he longe wæs,
wicum wunian   oð woruldende;
heold on heahgesceap.   Hord ys gesceawod,
3085 grimme gegongen;   wæs þæt gifeðe to swið
þe ðone þeodcyning   þyder ontyhte.
Ic wæs þær inne   ond þæt eall geondseh,
recedes geatwa,   þa me gerymed wæs,
nealles swæslice   sið alyfed
3090 inn under eorðweall.   Ic on ofoste gefeng
micle mid mundum   mægenbyrðenne
hordgestreona,   hider ut ætbær
cyninge minum.   Cwico wæs þa gena,
wis ond gewittig;   worn eall gespræc
3095 gomol on gehðo   ond eowic gretan het,
bæd þæt ge geworhton   æfter wines dædum
in bælstede   beorh þone hean,
micelne ond mærne,   swa he manna wæs
wigend weorðfullost   wide geond eorðan,
3100 þenden he burhwelan   brucan moste.
Uton nu efstan   oðre siðe,
seon ond secean   searogimma geþræc,
wundur under wealle;   ic eow wisige,
þæt ge genoge   neon sceawiað
3105 beagas ond brad gold.   Sie sio bær gearo,
ædre geæfned,   þonne we ut cymen,
ond þonne geferian   frean userne,
leofne mannan,   þær he longe sceal
on ðæs waldendes   wære geþolian."
3110 Het ða gebeodan   byre Wihstanes,
hæle hildedior,   hæleða monegum,

3078 adreogan] a dreogeð   3086 þeodcyning] *Not in MS.*   3100 burh-
welan] *With the b altered from þ by erasure*   3101 siðe] *Not in MS.*   3102
searogimma] searo

boldagendra, þæt hie bælwudu
feorran feredon, folcagende,
godum togenes: "Nu sceal gled fretan,
3115 weaxan wonna leg wigena strengel,
þone ðe oft gebad isernscure,
þonne stræla storm strengum gebæded
scoc ofer scildweall, sceft nytte heold,
feðergearwum fus flane fulleode."
3120 Huru se snotra sunu Wihstanes
acigde of corðre cyninges þegnas
syfone [to]somne, þa selestan,
eode eahta sum under inwithrof
hilderinca; sum on handa bær
3125 æledleoman, se ðe on orde geong.
Næs ða on hlytme hwa þæt hord strude,
syððan orwearde ænigne dæl
secgas gesegon on sele wunian,
læne licgan; lyt ænig mearn
3130 þæt hi ofostlic[e] ut geferedon
dyre maðmas. Dracan ec scufun,
wyrm ofer weallclif, leton weg niman,
flod fæðmian frætwa hyrde.
þa wæs wunden gold on wæn hladen,
3135 æghwæs unrim, æþeling boren,
har hilderinc to Hronesnæsse.
Him ða gegiredan Geata leode
ad on eorðan unwaclicne,
helmum behongen, hildebordum,
3140 beorhtum byrnum, swa he bena wæs;
alegdon ða tomiddes mærne þeoden
hæleð hiofende, hlaford leofne.

3117 strengum] stren *with* gū *added above the line by the same hand* 3119
feðergearwum] fæder gearwum 3121 cyninges] cyniges 3122 syfone]
syfone *B, a space A* 3124 hilderinca] hilde rinc 3133 hyrde] *Written
twice, but the second* hyrde *erased* 3134 þa] þ 3135 æþeling] æþelinge
3136 hilderinc] hilde *followed by a blank space sufficient for two letters; possibly one letter has been erased after* hilde 3139 helmum] helm 3142
hlaford] hlafor *A,* hlaford *B*

Ongunnon þa on beorge   bælfyra mæst
wigend weccan;   wud[u]rec astah,
3145 sweart ofer swioðole,   swogende leg
wope bewunden   (windblond gelæg),
oðþæt he ða banhus   gebrocen hæfde,
hat on hreðre.   Higum unrote
modceare mændon,   mondryhtnes cw[e]alm;
3150 swylce giomorgyd   [Ge]at[isc] meowle
[. . . . .]   bundenheorde
[so]ng sorgcearig   s[w]iðe geneahhe
þæt hio hyre [heofun]g[da]gas   hearde ond[r]ede,
wælfylla worn,   werudes egesan,
3155 hynðo ond h[æ]f[t]nyd.   Heofon rece swe[a]lg.
Geworhton ða   Wedra leode
hleo on hoe,   se wæs heah ond brad,
wægliðendum   wide gesyne,
ond beti[m]bredon   on tyn dagum
3160 beadurofes becn,   bronda lafe
wealle beworhton,   swa hyt weorðlicost
foresnotre men   findan mihton.
Hi on beorg dydon   beg ond siglu,
eall swylce hyrsta,   swylce on horde ær
3165 niðhedige men   genumen hæfdon,
forleton eorla gestreon   eorðan healdan,
gold on greote,   þær hit nu gen lifað
eldum swa unnyt   swa h[it ær]or wæs.
þa ymbe hlæw riodan   hildediore,

3144 wudurec] wud   rec A, wud. . .ec B   3145 swioðole] swicðole   leg]
let AB   3147 hæfde] hæfd A, hæfde B   3149 cwealm] cw   aln A,
. . .lm B   3150 Geatisc] iat preceded by space for one letter and followed
by "traces of two letters, the first like s or i or a much distorted g, the second
e, c, or o" (Smith); above the line are written the letters an' (i.e. Latin anus)
3151 bundenheorde] bunden hear followed by some illegible letters MS. (Smith),
-unden heor- MS. (Zupitza), unden hiord A, unden heorde B   3152
swiðe] See Note   3154 worn] wonn   3155 hynðo] hyðo or hyðo (see
Note)   3157 hleo on hoe] See Note   3168 hit æror] he ::.e :.or MS.
(Smith), hi ::::r MS. (Zupitza), hi followed by a space A, hi. . . B; see Note

3170 æþelinga bearn, ealra twelfe,
woldon [ceare] cwiðan ond kyning mænan,
wordgyd wrecan ond ymb w[er] sprecan;
eahtodan eorlscipe ond his ellenweorc
duguðum demdon, swa hit ged[efe] *bið*
3175 þæt mon his winedryhten wordum herge,
ferhðum freo*ge*, þonne he forð scile
of lichaman [læded] weorðan.
Swa begnornodon Geata leode
hlaforde*s* [hr]yre, heorðgeneatas,
3180 cwædon þæt he wære wyruldcyninga
*m*anna mildust ond mon[ðw]ærust,
leodum liðost ond lofgeornost.

3170 twelfe] twelfa   3171 ond kyning] *See Note*   3172 wordgyd]
wordgyd *MS.* (*Zupitza*), wordgyð *MS.* (*Smith*), wordgyd *AB*   3174
bið] bið *B, not in A*   3176 freoge] freog *A,* freogen *B*   3179 hlafordes]
hlafor *followed by a space A,* hla fordes *B*   3180 wyruldcyninga] wyruld
cyning (*see Note*)   3181 manna] monne *B, not in A*

JUDITH

gifena in ðys ginnan gru*n*d*e*. Heo ðar ða gearwe funde
mundbyrd æt ðam mæran þeodne,   þa heo ahte mæste
                      þearfe,
hyldo þæs hehstan deman,   þæt he hie wið þæs hehstan
                      brogan
5 gefriðode, frymða waldend.   Hyre ðæs fæder on roderum
torhtmod tiðe gefremede,   þe heo ahte trumne geleafan
a to ðam ælmihtigan.   Gefrægen ic ða Holofernus
winhatan wyrcean georne   ond eallum wundrum þrymlic
girwan up swæsendo.   To ðam het se gumena baldor
10 ealle ða yldestan ðegnas;   hie ðæt ofstum miclum
ræfndon, rondwiggende,   comon to ðam rican þeodne
feran, folces ræswan.   Þæt wæs þy feorðan dogore
þæs ðe Iudith hyne,   gleaw on geðonce,
ides ælfscinu,   ærest gesohte.
15   Hie ða to ðam symle   sittan eodon,
wlance to wingedrince,   ealle his weagesiðas,
bealde byrnwiggend*e*.   Þær wæron bollan steape
boren æfter bencum gelome,   swylce eac bunan ond orcas
fulle fletsittendum;   hie þæt fæge þegon,
20 rofe rondwiggende,   þeah ðæs se rica ne wende,
egesful eorla dryhten.   Ða wearð Holofernus,
goldwine gumena,   on gytesalum,
hloh ond hlydde,   hlynede ond dynede,
þæt mihten fira bearn   feorran gehyran
25 hu se stiðmoda   styrmde ond gylede,
modig ond medugal,   manode geneahhe
bencsittende   þæt hi gebærdon wel.
   Swa se inwidda   ofer ealne dæg
dryhtguman sine   drencte mid wine,
30 swiðmod sinces brytta,   oðþæt hie on swiman lagon,

oferdrencte his duguðe ealle,   swylce hie wæron deaðe
                                                      geslegene,
agotene goda gehwylces.   Swa het se gumena aldor
fylgan fletsittendum,   oðþæt fira bearnum
nealæhte niht seo þystre.   Het ða niða geblonden
35 þa eadigan mægð   ofstum fetigan
to his bedreste   beagum gehlæste,
hringum gehrodene.   Hie hraðe fremedon,
anbyhtscealcas,   swa him heora ealdor bebead,
byrnwigena brego,   bearhtme stopon
40 to ðam gysterne,   þær hie Iudithðe
fundon ferhðgleawe,   ond ða fromlice
lindwiggende   lædan ongunnon
þa torhtan mægð   to træfe þam hean,
þær se rica hyne   reste on symbel
45 nihtes inne,   nergende lað,
Holofernus.   þær wæs eallgylden
fleohnet fæger   ymbe þæs folctogan
bed ahongen,   þæt se bealofulla
mihte wlitan þurh,   wigena baldor,
50 on æghwylcne   þe ðær inne com
hæleða bearna,   ond on hyne nænig
monna cynnes,   nymðe se modiga hwæne
niðe rofra   him þe near hete
rinca to rune gegangan.   Hie ða on reste gebrohton
55 snude ða snoteran idese;   eodon ða stercedferhðe,
hæleð heora hearran cyðan   þæt wæs seo halige meowle
gebroht on his burgetelde.   þa wearð se brema on mode
bliðe, burga ealdor,   þohte ða beorhtan idese
mid widle ond mid womme besmitan.   Ne wolde þæt
                                             wuldres dema
60 geðafian, þrymmes hyrde,   ac he him þæs ðinges gestyrde,
dryhten, dugeða waldend.   Gewat ða se deofulcunda,
galferhð gumena ðreate   *   *   *

---

32 aldor] *With* b *erased before* a   47 ymbe] 7 ymbe   54 gebrohton]
gebrohten *with the second* e *dotted beneath for deletion and* o *written above by
the same hand*

bealofull his beddes neosan, þær he sceolde his blæd
forleosan
ædre binnan anre nihte; hæfde ða his ende gebidenne
65 on eorðan unswæslicne, swylcne he ær æfter worhte,
þearlmod ðeoden gumena, þenden he on ðysse worulde
wunode under wolcna hrofe. Gefeol ða wine swa druncen
se rica on his reste middan, swa he nyste ræda nanne
on gewitlocan. Wiggend stopon
70 ut of ðam inne ofstum miclum,
weras winsade, þe ðone wærlogan,
laðne leodhatan, læddon to bedde
nehstan siðe. Þa wæs nergendes
þeowen þrymful, þearle gemyndig
75 hu heo þone atolan eaðost mihte
ealdre benæman ær se unsyfra,
womfull, onwoce. Genam ða wundenlocc
scyppendes mægð scearpne mece,
scurum heardne, ond of sceaðe abræd
80 swiðran folme; ongan ða swegles weard
be naman nemnan, nergend ealra
woruldbuendra, ond þæt word acwæð:
"Ic ðe, frymða god ond frofre gæst,
bearn alwaldan, biddan wylle
85 miltse þinre me þearfendre,
ðrynesse ðrym. Þearle ys me nu ða
heorte onhæted ond hige geomor,
swyðe mid sorgum gedrefed. Forgif me, swegles ealdor,
sigor ond soðne geleafan, þæt ic mid þys sweorde mote
90 geheawan þysne morðres bryttan; geunne me minra
gesynta,
þearlmod þeoden gumena. Nahte ic þinre næfre
miltse þon maran þearfe. Gewrec nu, mihtig dryhten,
torhtmod tires brytta, þæt me ys þus torne on mode,
hate on hreðre minum." Hi ða se hehsta dema
95 ædre mid elne onbryrde, swa he deð anra gehwylcne

---

85 þearfendre] þearf *at the end of a line, followed by* fendre *at the beginning
of the next line*   87 heorte] heorte ys   90 me] *Added above the line by
the same hand*

herbuendra þe hyne him to helpe seceð
mid ræde ond mid rihte geleafan. Þa wearð hyre rume
                                              on mode,
haligre hyht geniwod; genam ða þone hæðenan mannan
fæste be feaxe sinum, teah hyne folmum wið hyre weard
100 bysmerlice, ond þone bealofullan
listum alede, laðne mannan,
swa heo ðæs unlædan eaðost mihte
wel gewealdan. Sloh ða wundenlocc
þone feondsceaðan fagum mece,
105 heteþoncolne, þæt heo healfne forcearf
þone sweoran him, þæt he on swiman læg,
druncen ond dolhwund. Næs ða dead þa gyt,
ealles orsawle; sloh ða eornoste
ides ellenrof oðre siðe
110 þone hæðenan hund, þæt him þæt heafod wand
forð on ða flore. Læg se fula leap
gesne beæftan, gæst ellor hwearf
under neowelne næs ond ðær genyðerad wæs,
susle gesæled syððan æfre,
115 wyrmum bewunden, witum gebunden,
hearde gehæfted in hellebryne
æfter hinsiðe. Ne ðearf he hopian no,
þystrum forðylmed, þæt he ðonan mote
of ðam wyrmsele, ac ðær wunian sceal
120 awa to aldre butan ende forð
in ðam heolstran ham, hyhtwynna leas.
    Hæfde ða gefohten foremærne blæd
Iudith æt guðe, swa hyre god uðe,
swegles ealdor, þe hyre sigores onleah.
125 Þa seo snotere mægð snude gebrohte
þæs herewæðan heafod swa blodig
on ðam fætelse þe hyre foregenga,
blachleor ides, hyra begea nest,
ðeawum geðungen, þyder on lædde,
130 ond hit þa swa heolfrig hyre on hond ageaf,
higeðoncolre, ham to berenne,
Iudith gingran sinre. Eodon ða gegnum þanonne

þa idesa ba   ellenþriste,
oðþæt hie becomon,   collenferhðe,
135 eadhreðige mægð,   ut of ðam herige,
þæt hie sweotollice   geseon mihten
þære wlitegan byrig   weallas blican,
Bethuliam.   Hie ða beahhrodene
feðelaste   forð onettan,
140 oð hie glædmode   gegan hæfdon
to ðam wealgate.   Wiggend sæton,
weras wæccende   wearde heoldon
in ðam fæstenne,   swa ðam folce ær
geomormodum   Iudith bebead,
145 searoðoncol mægð,   þa heo on sið gewat,
ides ellenrof.   Wæs ða eft cumen
leof to leodum,   ond ða lungre het
gleawhydig wif   gumena sumne
of ðære ginnan byrig   hyre togeanes gan,
150 ond hi ofostlice   in forlæton
þurh ðæs wealles geat,   ond þæt word acwæð
to ðam sigefolce: "Ic eow secgan mæg
þoncwyrðe þing,   þæt ge ne þyrfen leng
murnan on mode.   Eow ys metod bliðe,
155 cyninga wuldor;   þæt gecyðed wearð
geond woruld wide,   þæt eow ys wuldorblæd
torhtlic toweard   ond tir gifeðe
þara læðða   þe ge lange drugon."
    Þa wurdon bliðe   burhsittende,
160 syððan hi gehyrdon   hu seo halige spræc
ofer heanne weall.   Here wæs on lustum.
Wið þæs fæstengeates   folc onette,
weras wif somod,   wornum ond heapum,
ðreatum ond ðrymmum   þrungon ond urnon
165 ongean ða þeodnes mægð   þusendmælum,
ealde ge geonge.   Æghwylcum wearð

---

134 hie] hie hie   141 wealgate] *With the letters* weal *written above the line
by the same hand*   142 heoldon] heoildon *with* il *altered from* r   144
Iudith] iudithe   150 forlæton] for lęton *with the second* o *altered from* e
165 þeodnes] þeoðnes

men on ðære medobyrig   mod areted,
syððan hie ongeaton   þæt wæs Iudith cumen
eft to eðle,   ond ða ofostlice
170 hie mid eaðmedum   in forleton.
    Þa seo gleawe het,   golde gefrætewod,
hyre ðinenne   þancolmode
þæs herewæðan   heafod onwriðan
ond hyt to behðe   blodig ætywan
175 þam burhleodum,   hu hyre æt beaduwe gespeow.
Spræc ða seo æðele   to eallum þam folce:
"Her ge magon sweotole,   sigerofe hæleð,
leoda ræswan,   on ðæs laðestan
hæðenes heaðorinces   heafod starian,
180 Holofernus   unlyfigendes,
þe us monna mæst   morðra gefremede,
sarra sorga,   ond þæt swyðor gyt
ycan wolde,   ac him ne uðe god
lengran lifes,   þæt he mid læððum us
185 eglan moste;   ic him ealdor oðþrong
þurh godes fultum.   Nu ic gumena gehwæne
þyssa burgleoda   biddan wylle,
randwiggendra,   þæt ge recene eow
fysan to gefeohte.   Syððan frymða god,
190 arfæst cyning,   eastan sende
leohtne leoman,   berað linde forð,
bord for breostum   ond byrnhomas,
scire helmas   in sceaðena gemong,
fyllan folctogan   fagum sweordum,
195 fæge frumgaras.   Fynd syndon eowere
gedemed to deaðe,   ond ge dom agon,
tir æt tohtan,   swa eow getacnod hafað
mihtig dryhten   þurh mine hand."
    Þa wearð snelra werod   snude gegearewod,
200 cenra to campe.   Stopon cynerofe
secgas ond gesiðas,   bæron sigeþufas,
foron to gefeohte   forð on gerihte,

hæleð under helmum, of ðære haligan byrig
on ðæt dægred sylf. Dynedan scildas,
205 hlude hlummon. Þæs se hlanca gefeah
wulf in walde, ond se wanna hrefn,
wælgifre fugel. Wistan begen
þæt him ða þeodguman þohton tilian
fylle on fægum; ac him fleah on last
210 earn ætes georn, urigfeðera,
salowigpada sang hildeleoð,
hyrnednebba. Stopon heaðorincas,
beornas to beadowe, bordum beðeahte,
hwealfum lindum, þa ðe hwile ær
215 elðeodigra edwit þoledon,
hæðenra hosp. Him þæt hearde wearð
æt ðam æscplegan eallum forgolden,
Assyrium, syððan Ebreas
under guðfanum gegan hæfdon
220 to ðam fyrdwicum. Hie ða fromlice
leton forð fleogan flana scuras,
hildenædran, of hornbogan,
strælas stedehearde; styrmdon hlude
grame guðfrecan, garas sendon
225 in heardra gemang. Hæleð wæron yrre,
landbuende, laðum cynne,
stopon styrnmode, stercedferhðe,
wrehton unsofte ealdgeniðlan
medowerige; mundum brugdon
230 scealcas of sceaðum scirmæled swyrd,
ecgum gecoste, slogon eornoste
Assiria oretmæcgas,
niðhycgende, nanne ne sparedon
þæs herefolces, heanne ne ricne,
235 cwicera manna þe hie ofercuman mihton.
Swa ða magoþegnas on ða morgentid
ehton elðeoda ealle þrage,
oððæt ongeaton ða ðe grame wæron,

207 Wistan] westan   234 ricne] rice

ðæs herefolces   heafodweardas,
240 þæt him swyrdgeswing   swiðlic eowdon
weras Ebrisce.   Hie wordum þæt
þam yldestan   ealdorþegnum
cyðan eodon,   wrehton cumbolwigan
ond him forhtlice   færspel bodedon,
245 medowerigum   morgencollan,
atolne ecgplegan.   þa ic ædre gefrægn
slegefæge hæleð   slæpe tobredon
ond wið þæs bealofullan   burgeteldes
werigferhðe   hwearfum þringan,
250 Holofernus.   Hogedon aninga
hyra hlaforde   hilde bodian,
ærðon ðe him se egesa   on ufan sæte,
mægen Ebrea.   Mynton ealle
þæt se beorna brego   ond seo beorhte mægð
255 in ðam wlitegan træfe   wæron ætsomne,
Iudith seo æðele   ond se galmoda,
egesfull ond afor.   Næs ðeah eorla nan
þe ðone wiggend   aweccan dorste
oððe gecunnian   hu ðone cumbolwigan
260 wið ða halgan mægð   hæfde geworden,
metodes meowlan.   Mægen nealæhte,
folc Ebrea,   fuhton þearle
heardum heoruwæpnum,   hæfte guldon
hyra fyrngeflitu,   fagum swyrdum,
265 ealde æfðoncan;   Assyria wearð
on ðam dægeweorce   dom geswiðrod,
bælc forbiged.   Beornas stodon
ymbe hyra þeodnes træf   þearle gebylde,
sweorcendferhðe.   Hi ða somod ealle
270 ongunnon cohhetan,   cirman hlude
ond gristbitian,   gode orfeorme,
mid toðon torn þoligende.   þa wæs hyra tires æt ende,
eades ond ellendæda.   Hogedon þa eorlas aweccan
hyra winedryhten;   him wiht ne speow.

249 werigferhðe] weras ferhðe   251 hilde] hyldo

275 Þa wearð *sið* ond late   sum to ðam arod
þara beadorinca,   *þæt* he in þæt burgeteld
niðheard neðde,   swa hyne nyd fordraf.
Funde ða on bedde   blacne licg*an*
his goldgifan   gæstes gesne,
280 lifes belidenne.   He þa lungre gefeoll
freorig to foldan,   ongan his feax teran,
hreoh on mode,   ond his hrægl somod,
ond þæt word acwæð   to ðam wiggendum
þe ðær unrote   ute wæron:
285   "Her ys geswutelod   ure sylfra forwyrd,
toweard getacnod   þæt þære tide ys
mid niðum neah geðrungen,   þe *we* sculon nyde losian,
somod æt sæcce forweorðan.   Her lið sweorde geheawen,
beheafdod healdend ure."   Hi ða hreowigmode
290 wurpon hyra wæpen of dune,   gewitan him werigferhðe
on fleam sceacan.   Him mon feaht on last,
mægeneacen fol*c*,   oð se mæsta dæl
þæs heriges læg   hilde gesæged
on ðam sigewonge,   sweordum geheawen,
295 wulfum to willan   ond eac wælgifrum
fuglum to frofre.   Flugon ða ðe lyfdo*n*,
laðra lindwerod.   Him on laste for
sweot Ebrea   sigore geweorðod,
dom*e* gedyrsod;   him feng dryhten god
300 fægre on fultu*m*,   frea ælmihtig.
Hi ða fromlice   fagum swyrdum,
hæleð higerofe,   herpað worhton
þurh laðra gemong,   linde heowon,
scildburh scæro*n*.   Sceotend wæron
305 guðe gegremede,   guman Ebrisce;
þegnas on ða tid   þearle gelyste
gargewinnes.   Þær on greot gefeoll
se hyhsta dæl   heafodgerimes

279 goldgifan] *With the* o *altered from* u? 287 nyde] *Not in MS.* 292 mægeneacen] *With the* a *of* -eacen *added above the line by the same hand* 297 lindwerod] lind *followed by one or more letters; see Note* 298 sigore] *Added above the line by the same hand*

Assiria ealdorduguðe,
310 laðan cynnes. Lythwon becom
cwicera to cyððe. Cirdon cynerofe,
wiggend on wiðertrod, wælscel on innan,
reocende hræw. Rum wæs to nimanne
londbuendum on ðam laðestan,
315 hyra ealdfeondum unlyfigendum
heolfrig herereaf, hyrsta scyne,
bord ond bradswyrd, brune helmas,
dyre madmas. Hæfdon domlice
on ðam folcstede fynd oferwunnen
320 eðelweardas, ealdhettende
swyrdum aswefede. Hie on swaðe reston,
þa ðe him to life laðost wæron
*c*wicera cynna. Þa seo cneoris eall,
mægð*a* mærost, anes monðes fyrst,
325 wlanc, wundenlocc, *w*agon ond læddon
to ðære beorhtan byrig, Bet*h*uliam,
helmas ond hupseax, hare byrnan,
guðsceorp gumena golde gefrætewod,
mærra madma þonne mon ænig
330 asecgan mæge searoþoncelra;
eal þæt ða ðeodguman þrymme geeodon,
cene under cumblum on compwige
þurh Iudithe gleawe lare,
mægð modigre. Hi to mede hyre
335 of ðam siðfate sylfre brohton,
eorlas æscrofe, Holofernes
sweord ond swatigne helm, swylce eac side *b*yrnan
gerenode readum golde, ond eal þæt se rinca baldor
swiðmod sinces ahte oððe sundoryrfes,
340 beaga ond beorhtra maðma, hi þæt þære beorhtan idese
ageafon gearoþoncolre. Ealles ðæs Iudith sægde
wuldor weroda dryhtne, þe hyre weorðmynde geaf,
mærðe on moldan rice, *swy*lce eac mede on heofonum,
sigorlean *in swegles wuldre, þæs þe heo ahte soðne geleafan*

345 *to ðam ælmihtigan;   huru æt þam ende ne tweode*
þæs leanes þe heo lange gyrnde.   Ðæs sy ðam leofan drihtne
wuldor to widan aldre,   þe gesceop wind ond lyfte,
roderas ond rume grundas,   swylce eac reðe streamas
ond swegles dreamas,   ðurh his sylfes miltse.

NOTES

ABBREVIATIONS IN THE NOTES

For Conybeare and Zupitza, see Bibliography, Part I. For other names unaccompanied by any more specific reference, see Bibliography, Part II. For names followed by "tr.," see Bibliography, Part IV.

Note that in Parts II and IV of the Bibliography there are separate listings for Beowulf and Judith.

Andrew. Postscript on Beowulf.

Anglia Beibl. Beiblatt zur Anglia.

Anz. fdA. Anzeiger für deutsches Altertum.

Archiv. Archiv für das Studium der neueren Sprachen und Literaturen.

Beitr. Beiträge zur Geschichte der deutschen Sprache und Literatur.

Bonner Beitr. Bonner Beiträge zur Anglistik.

Bos.-Tol. Bosworth-Toller, Anglo-Saxon Dictionary.

Cosijn, Aant. Aanteekeningen op den Beowulf.

Eng. Stud. Englische Studien.

Ettmüller, Sc. Engla and Seaxna Scopas and Boceras.

Foster. Judith: Studies in Metre, Language and Style.

Grein, Bib. Bibliothek der angelsächsischen Poesie.

Grein, ed. Grein's separate edition of Beowulf (1867).

Grein, Spr. Sprachschatz der angelsächsischen Dichter.

Grein-Köhler. Sprachschatz der angelsächsischen Dichter, revised ed. by Köhler.

Holthausen, AEW. Altenglisches etymologisches Wörterbuch.

Hoops. Kommentar zum Beowulf.

Hoops, Bwst. Beowulfstudien.

Indog. Forsch. Indogermanische Forschungen.

JEGPh. Journal of English and Germanic Philology.

Kemble II. The notes on the text in Kemble's Beowulf, Volume II (1837).

Klaeber Misc. Studies in English Philology . . . in Honor of Frederick Klaeber (Minneapolis, 1929).

Kock, JJJ. Jubilee Jaunts and Jottings.

MLN. Modern Language Notes.

MLQuart. Modern Language Quarterly.

MLRev. Modern Language Review.

Mod. Phil. Modern Philology.

N.E.D. New English Dictionary (Oxford English Dictionary).

Pope. The Rhythm of Beowulf.

Schücking, Svk. Die Grundzüge der Satzverknüpfung im Beowulf.

Sievers-Brunner. Altenglische Grammatik (Halle, 1942).

Tidskrift. Tidskrift for Philologi og Pædagogik.

Trautmann, BVE. Berichtigungen, Vermutungen und Erklärungen zum Beowulf.

Trautmann, FH. Finn und Hildebrand.

Williams, FE. The Finn Episode in Beowulf.

ZfdA. Zeitschrift für deutsches Altertum.

ZfdPh. Zeitschrift für deutsche Philologie.

NOTES ON BEOWULF

1-50

Beowulf] For a general survey of the literary problems presented by this poem, see Introd., p. xxxiii. 1 in geardagum] Dependent not on *gefrunon* but on *þrym*: "the glory of the Spear-Danes in days of yore." For the word order, cf. ll. 74f., 575f., 2484f., 2694f. (as emended), 2752ff., 2773f., Judith 246f.; other examples are cited by Sievers, Beitr. XII, 191, note 1. 2 þeodcyninga] Probably a variation of *Gardena*, and Trautmann, Holthausen, and Klaeber so punctuate it. See also Hoops, p. 2. But Schücking, Sedgefield, Chambers, and von Schaubert, following most of the earlier edd., take *Gardena* as dependent on *þeodcyninga*. 3 ða] Hoops, Bwst., p. 89, construes ða as an adverb, here and in l. 99 (and presumably also in l. 189, which he does not mention). Kock, Anglia LXIV, 99f., cites *swa þa foremeahtige folces ræswan*, Genesis 1669, where *þa* is followed by the strong form of the adjective and is therefore undoubtedly an adverb. But as Klaeber sensibly remarks, Eng. Stud. LXVIII, 113, Genesis 1669 does not prove anything for the passages in Beowulf. It is possible, then, that ða is a demonstrative pronoun, here and in ll. 99, 189. 4 sceaþena þreatum] Parallel to *monegum mægþum*. Trautmann's interpretation, "mit scharen von kriegern," though followed by Sedgefield, Verse-Book, p. 141, is unlikely. 6 eorlas] In spite of Kock's attempt, Anglia XXVII, 219f., to defend the MS. *eorl* as a collective noun ("terrified many a warrior"; cf. *eorl*, l. 795, and *æþelinge*, l. 1244), all recent edd. except von Schaubert adopt Kemble's emendation to *eorlas*, plural object of *egsode*, on both metrical and stylistic grounds. Klaeber, Mod. Phil. III, 249, would retain *eorl*, but in his edition he emends to *eorlas*. Grienberger, Beitr. XXXVI, 94f., and Bos.-Tol., Supp., p. 184, take *egsode* in an absolute sense, with *eorl* as subject. Elsewhere, however, *egsian* is regularly transitive; see the examples in Sievers, Berichte über die Verhandlungen der . . . Gesellschaft der Wissenschaften zu Leipzig XLVII, 188f. For a complete discussion of the problem of this half-line, see Sievers, Beitr. XXIX, 560ff. Sewell, [London] Times Literary Supplement, Sept. 11, 1924, p. 556, would read *Eorlas* as a proper noun, referring to the Heruli or Erulians; but as Klaeber (3 ed.) points out, a tribal name is extremely unlikely here. Syððan, etc.] The punctuation here follows Schücking; see also his Svk., p. 1. Since this clause serves as antecedent of *þæs*, l. 7b, it seems naturally to belong to the same sentence. The traditional punctuation puts a comma after l. 6a and a semicolon after l. 7a. See also Kock, Anglia XLII, 99. 9 þara] Holder (2 ed.) and later edd., except Socin and von Schaubert, omit *þara*, following Sievers, Berichte über die Verhandlungen der . . . Gesellschaft der Wissenschaften zu Leipzig LXVII, 190. But the metrical arguments for the omission of this word are not as convincing as they once were, and the argument from syntax (the infrequency of *se, seo, þæt* as a definite article in the early poetry) is refuted by *ymbesittendra ænig ðara*, l. 2734, where *ðara* is required by the meter.   **11 gomban]** This word is also found in Genesis 1978; the nom. sing. form is not recorded but was probably *gombe*, feminine.   See Holthausen, AEW., p. 123, s.v. *gambe*.   **12 æfter]** "Coming after him," Klaeber, Mod. Phil. III, 445.   Cf. l. 2731.   **14 fyrenðearfe]** Schücking emends to *fyrnþearfe*, "Elend der Vorzeit," following an oral suggestion by Dr. Hans Krauel.   But *fyren-* may be used as an intensive prefix (cf. *fyrenearfeða*, Genesis 709, parallel to *hearma*, and *firinquala*, "of terrible torment," Heliand 4918), and that is evidently its function here, where "dire need, dire distress" seems to have been the intended meaning.   On this use of *fyren-* see Hoops, p. 8, and J. Weisweiler, Indog. Forsch. XLI (1923), 33ff.   **15]** In l. 15*b*, Grundtvig, tr., p. 267, restored to *aldor[le]ase*, apparently following a suggestion by Rask (see the footnote in Grundtvig's edition), and so most later edd.   In l. 15*a*, exception may be taken to *þæt* as a relative, since *fyren-ðearfe* is feminine.   Holder (1 ed.), Trautmann, and most later edd. therefore emend the MS. *þ* to *þa*, following Bouterwek, Cædmon's des Angelsachsen biblische Dichtungen I, cv, and Sievers, Beitr. IX, 136.   Thorkelin, Kemble (2 ed.), and Klaeber emend to *þe*, the uninflected relative.   So also Andrew, p. 139.   Holthausen (2–4 ed.) retains *þæt* as a conjunction by emending to *aldorleaste*, "lack of a lord," in l. 15*b*, thus providing an object for *drugon.*   Holthausen (1, 7, 8 ed.), reading *aldorlease*, emends to *þa* in l. 15*a*.   Chambers, retaining *þæt*, takes *hwile* as object of *drugon*, translating, "that . . . they had . . . experienced a long time of sorrow"; so also Holthausen (5, 6 ed.).   But *lange* (or *lytle*) *hwile* is regularly adverbial, as in ll. 2030, 2097, 2159, 2780.   Kock, Anglia XLII, 100, XLV, 123, would construe *drugon* as intransitive, "that they had lived without a lord," and so von Schaubert in her edition.   The verb *drēogan* is recorded several times in intransitive use, as in l. 2179, Genesis 2284, Azarias 3, but the usual intransitive meaning, "to be employed, be busy" (Bos.-Tol., p. 212), does not fit here.   In view of the parallels adduced by Klaeber, Anglia L, 108 (ll. 831, 1858, Judith 158, etc.), it seems best to emend.   For other apparent examples of MS. *þ* for either *þa* or *þe*, see J. M. Hart, MLN. I (1886), 175ff.; Chambers, Beowulf: an Introduction, p. 305, note 1, and the other references given in Klaeber's note.   **16 Him]** "To him," that is, to the *eafera* of l. 12.   **18 Beowulf]** See l. 53, note.   **18*b*–19]** Taking l. 18*b* as a parenthesis avoids the need of emending the MS. *eafera* in l. 19*a*.   So Grundtvig, Grein, ed., Heyne (4 ed.), Wülker, Holder (1 ed.), Wyatt, Sedgefield, Chambers, Klaeber, Hoops, p. 9, and von Schaubert.   Kemble emended to *eaferan*, dependent on *blæd*, in l. 19*a*, and so many edd., most recently Trautmann, Holthausen, and Schücking.   Sievers, Beitr. IX, 135, cites Fates of the Apostles 6ff., *Lof wide sprang . . . þeodnes þegna*, as apparently imitated from the passage in Beowulf.   But for a defence of the MS. reading here (with l. 18*b* in parentheses), see Bugge, Tidskrift VIII, 41f.; Klaeber, Eng. Stud. XXXIX, 428; Kock, Anglia XLV, 107.   **20 geong guma]** Restored by Grein, ed., and so all later edd. except Heyne (1 ed.) and Arnold.   **21 bearme]** For a fuller account of the readings of transcripts A and B, see Malone, PMLA

LXIV, 1191f. The word [bea]rme was first restored by Bouterwek, Cædmon's des Angelsachsen biblische Dichtungen I, cv ("in des Vaters Schutze," p. cvii), and so Holder, Holthausen (2–6 ed.), Chambers, Klaeber, and von Schaubert. Thorpe also restored bearme but read fæder-bearme as a compound. Of the other restorations which have been made, ærne (Grein, Bib.), inne (Grein, ed.), and wine (Grundtvig, note; Kock, Anglia XLV, 107f.) do not fill the gap in the MS. and may be rejected without further consideration. Trautmann's leofne, "sustenance" (cf. Andreas 1123) is unlikely on syntactical grounds (see Sievers, Beitr. XXIX, 307f.); Kemble's feorme, recently revived by Mezger, MLN. LIX, 113f. ("through splendid gifts from his father's [possessions]"), gives double alliteration in the second half-line and is otherwise doubtful. For a more complete survey of these suggested restorations, see Chambers, note.   24 leode] Usually explained as nom. plur., parallel to wilgesipas; the verbs gewunigen and gelæsten are also parallel, with hine the object of both: "that in [his] old age [his] dear companions may in turn (eft) abide with him, . . . [his] people stand by him." Kock, Anglia XLII, 100, calling attention to the dative construction after gelæstan in Andreas 411f., Maldon 11f., would take leode as dat. sing., "follow their prince." But Klaeber, MLN. XXXIV, 129, Anglia L, 109f., points out that the accusative is found after gelæstan in Beow. 2500 and Guthlac 376, and that it is doubtful whether the singular leod, "prince," could stand without a qualifying genitive; cf. ll. 341, 348, 625, etc. It is best, then, to retain the older interpretation, with leode construed as nom. plur.   25 gehwære] Trautmann, Holthausen, Schücking, and Sedgefield emend to gehwam, following Sievers, Beitr. X, 485. Cf. nihta gehwæm, l. 1365, where also the dependent noun is feminine.   26 to gescæphwile] "At the time appointed by fate." For this meaning of to, cf. to þam ærdæge, Exodus 198, and such phrases as to midre nihte. See also Klaeber, Anglia L, 110.   28 faroðe] Krapp, Mod. Phil. II, 405ff., would emend to waroðe, "shore," here and in l. 1916. But in l. 1916 the alliteration strongly supports the MS. faroðe; see Klaeber, Anglia XXVIII, 455. Cf. also the use of faroð in Andreas 236, 255, 1658. Thorkelin had previously read waroðe here in l. 28, perhaps as a misreading of the MS., but not in l. 1916.   31] The MS. form of l. 31, with no apparent object for ahte, has given rise to a great variety of interpretations and emendations. Attempts to emend the text have, on the whole, not been convincing and have not found favor with the editors. Grein, Bib., suggested þrage for the MS. ahte, and so also Sievers, Beitr. IX, 136 (who suggested the alternative possibility of the loss of some words before lange), and Cosijn, Aant., p. 1. Cf. longe þrage, l. 54. Rieger, ZfdPh. III, 381, would emend to lif landfruma in l. 31a; Kluge, Beitr. IX, 188f., suggested lændagas ahte in l. 31b, and so Holder (1 ed.); Lübke, Anz. fdA. XIX, 341, would read land leodfruma lange ahte. Bright, MLN. X, 85, suggested þenden wordum geweald in l. 30a, with geweald the object of ahte, and this emendation was approved by Child, MLN. XXI, 175ff. Sedgefield, MLRev. V, 286, and in his edition, suggests that the poet or scribe, while writing l. 31, may have thought that he had written þenden worda geweald in l. 30a. It is in fact surprising that worda geweald (or wordes geweald, as in l. 79) has not been proposed as an emendation. Klaeber, Mod. Phil. III, 446, suggested that *hi* (= the *gesiþas?*) is to be supplied in sense, and Holthausen (2–5 ed.) prints *hi* after *lange*. Other emendations have been less promising: Trautmann, BVE., p. 126, proposed *langre æhte* in l. 31*b*, and in his edition he read *langan æhte*, "so lange er mit worten waltete . . . des vieljährigen besitzes." Kock, Anglia XXVII, 221ff., would read *lan geahte*, with *lan* explained as a variant form of *læn* and *geahte* as the preterite of *geāgan*, "to possess" (see Bos.-Tol., Supp., p. 285); he translates, "possessed the grant," i.e., either the land or the transitory life granted him by God. The verb *geāgan*, however, would normally have a perfective or ingressive meaning, "took possession of," rather than a durative meaning; see Klaeber, Mod. Phil. III, 447. Patzig, Anglia XLVII, 97, would read *lange tahte*, with the rather obscure translation, "der liebe Landesfürst lange angegeben hatte." Holthausen (8 ed.) emends to *landriht ahte*, but in the addenda to this edition, Archiv CLXXXVII (1950), 125, he suggests *landgē āhte*; on the form *-gē* (= German *Gau*), recorded in Anglo-Saxon only in Kentish place names, see O. Ritter, Eng. Stud. LXII (1927), 110ff. Holthausen (1, 7 ed.), like Sievers (cited above), would assume a lacuna in the MS., but he would put it after l. 31*b*. Bugge, Beitr. XII, 79, would put l. 31 in parentheses, after l. 32, with an accusative *hringedstefnan* understood as object of *ahte*. Most edd., however, preserve the text unaltered. Heyne and Socin assume an object *geweald* to be carried over in thought from *weold*, l. 30; similarly Sedgefield, MLRev. V, 286, suggests that an object *word* is to be understood, *ahte* merely repeating the idea of *weold*. (See also his alternative proposal, cited above.) Schücking, Eng. Stud. XXXIX, 100f., and in his edition, would take *swa*, l. 29*b*, as a relative pronoun, with *bæd* and *ahte* parallel; but for objections to this construction, see Klaeber, Eng. Stud. XXXIX, 429. Hoops, Bwst., pp. 13ff., takes *lange* as acc. plur. of an adjective *lang*, translating, "solange . . . der liebe Landesfürst Angehörige hatte." Such an adjective is, however, not elsewhere recorded, and Holthausen, Anglia Beibl. XLIII, 358, points out that we should expect *gelange* rather than *lange*. See also Girvan, MLRev. XXVIII, 245. E. von Schaubert, Anglia LXII, 182ff., and in her edition, takes *lange ahte* as an absolute participial construction in the nominative, translating, "nachdem der liebe Landesfürst lange besessen war (nachdem sie den lieben Landesfürsten lange besessen hatten)." She would also give similar explanations of ll. 936*a*, 2035*b*, 2106*a*, and 3115*a*; see the notes on these lines. In view of the passages (Phoenix 79f., Riming Poem 9*b*, Ruin 5f., etc.) which she discusses in Philologica: The Malone Anniversary Studies (Baltimore, 1949), pp. 31ff., as well as such half-lines as *wer unwundod*, Genesis 183, and *folc ferende*, Exodus 45, which have always occasioned difficulties of interpretation, it is possible that such a construction is to be assumed for Anglo-Saxon. It must, however, be remembered that the two cases of a nominative absolute which are attested in Gothic (*jah waurþans dags gatils*, Mark vi. 21, which corresponds to a genitive absolute in the original Greek, and *jah wlits is auralja bibundans*, John xi. 44) are the only completely unambiguous examples of this construction in the Old Germanic languages. And here in Beow. 31 the assumption of an absolute participial construction requires us to accept an analogical past participle

*āht (beside the regular āgen), of which the MS. ahte would be a weak nom. sing.
masculine with weakened ending. It is best to leave the MS. reading unaltered, though none of the explanations is entirely convincing. 33 isig]
Since there is no other indication that the time is winter, many commentators
have doubted the relevance of īsig, "icy," here. A figurative meaning, "shining like ice," is also doubtful. A number of alternative forms, most of them
unrecorded in Anglo-Saxon, have been suggested: īcig (or ītig or īfig), "shining,"
by Trautmann, BVE., p. 127; īsig or īsig, "rushing forward" (cf. O. Icel. eisa,
"to dash"), by Holthausen, Anglia Beibl. XIV, 82f., and similarly Krogmann,
Anglia LVI, 438f.; īsig, "ready," by Trautmann in his edition and in Bonner
Beitr. XVII, 151f.; ȳsig, "ausgeschöpft, bailed out" (cf. M.H.G. æsen, ōsen),
by Grienberger, Beitr. XXXVI, 95; ītig, "splendid" (cf. O. Icel. ītr), by Hollander, MLN. XXXII, 246f.; ūrig, "water-splashed, spray-drenched," by
Sedgefield, MLRev. XXVII, 448. But for a defence of īsig, "icy," see Sievers,
Beitr. XXVII, 572, XXXVI, 422ff. 43 læssan] For læssum, dat. plur.:
"with lesser gifts." 44 þon] The edd., except Arnold, Trautmann, Klaeber,
and von Schaubert, emend to þonne, as elsewhere in the poem. 46 umbor-
wesende] Ettmüller and Trautmann emend to umborwesendne. But the
participle, when used predicatively, is often uninflected; cf. cnihtwesende, l. 372,
and see Sievers-Brunner, § 305, note 1. 47 geldenne] Kemble and all
later edd., except Grundtvig, restore g[yl]denne. But Malone, PMLA LXIV,
1192, suggests the restoration ge[l]denne, and this reading is to be preferred on
the evidence of the Thorkelin transcripts, both of which have ge-. Nowhere
else in Beowulf, however, do we find a form with e for etymological ȳ, unless
trem, l. 2525, is one (cf. trym, Maldon 247, which may be a late form of trem).
48b-49a] With the pronoun object hine to be supplied in sense in l. 48b:
₍they let the sea carry [him], gave [him] into the possession of the ocean."

51–100

51 selerædende] So Kemble II and most later edd.; cf. l. 1346a. Malone,
Anglia LIII, 335f., defends the MS. selerædenne as a legitimate form, plural of
*seleræden, "hall-ruler" (from an earlier selerædend). Von Schaubert retains
selerædenne in her text. See the notes on ll. 106, 1026, 1142. 53 Beowulf
Scyldinga] "Beowulf of the Scyldings"; cf. ll. 374, 676, 1069, 1191, 1202. K.
Fuhr, Die Metrik des westgerm. Allitterationsverses (Marburg, 1892), p.
49, and Kaluza, Metrik des Beowulfliedes, p. 56, would emend to Beowulf
Scylding for metrical reasons, and so Trautmann. Child, MLN. XXI, 198f.,
suggests that the original text had Beaw (or Beow) Scyldinga. Pope, p. 365,
also suggests Beow Scyldinga. It is quite possible that Beaw (or Beow) was the
original form of the name of the Danish prince, both here and in l. 18, since the
West Saxon genealogies (most conveniently available in Klaeber, 3d ed., pp.
254f.) give Beaw (Beauu, Beo, Beowius) as the name of the son of Scyld. 56
oþþæt] Von Schaubert begins a new sentence with oþþæt, which she takes as an
adverb, following E. Glogauer, Die Bedeutungsübergänge der Konjunktionen
in der ags. Dichtersprache (Leipzig, 1922), pp. 29ff. See ll. 1414, 1740, 2039,
2210, notes. But for well-grounded objections to Glogauer's interpretation, see

Klaeber, Anglia Beibl. LII (1941), 217f. Other edd. adopt the punctutation in the text, with ll. 55b–56a taken as a parenthesis. **58** guðreouw] Bugge, ZfdPh. IV, 192f., suggested guðrof, as in l. 608. glæde Scyldingas] "The lordly Scyldings." See Klaeber, Anglia XXIX, 379; Hoops, Bwst., pp. 91f. The word glæde is also taken as an adjective by Sedgefield ("radiant," 3 ed., note), Chambers ("gracious. lordly"), and von Schaubert. Other edd. take it as an adverb ("auf gnädige, freundliche Weise," Heyne), but then the construction is very awkward. **60** ræswan] So Kemble II and most later edd., either as dat. sing., parallel to Ðæm, l. 59a (as by Heyne, Trautmann, Holthausen, and Klaeber), or, less probably, as nom. plur., parallel to feower bearn (as by Kemble, Grein, Spr. II, 369, and apparently by Chambers). But Arnold, Wülker, Holder (1 ed.), Socin, Wyatt, Schücking, Sedgefield (1, 2 ed.), and von Schaubert retain the MS. ræswa, nom. sing., as referring only to Heorogar. **62]** The MS. reads hyrde ic þ elan cwen. There is no damage to the text at this point, but some words have obviously been omitted by a scribe. The early edd. accepted the MS. elan as a Germanic feminine name; the usual reading of l. 62 was hyrde ic þæt Elan cwen [Ongenþeowes wæs], an arrangement which is still found in Sedgefield (1 ed.). But as early as 1841 Grundtvig, Brage og Idun IV, 500, note, had identified the letters elan as part of the gen. sing. form of the name Onela (the Swedish king of ll. 2616, 2932, the son of Ongentheow). The gap in the text, then, is before elan and not after cwen. Bugge, Tidskrift VIII, 43, proposed to read hyrde ic þæt [. . . . wæs On]elan cwen, and so Wülker, Holder (1 ed.), Holthausen (2–6, 8 ed.), Chambers, Schücking (11–14 ed.), Klaeber, and von Schaubert. The lady's name is now believed to have been Yrse, O. Icel. Yrsa (see especially M. G. Clarke, Sidelights on Teutonic History during the Migration Period [Cambridge, 1911], pp. 82ff.; H. M. Belden, MLN. XXVIII [1913], 149, note 2; Malone, in Klaeber Misc., pp. 153ff.), but as yet no editor has ventured to put her name into the text. Holthausen, note, suggests Hyrde ic [eorlas cweðan], þæt [heo wæs On]elan cwen, assuming that a line containing the name of Onela's wife has been lost before l. 62. A less probable emendation is hyrde ic þæt [Sigeneow wæs Sæw]elan cwen, first proposed by Kluge, Eng. Stud. XXII, 144ff., and based on the marriage of Signy, daughter of Halfdan, to Sævil, in the Hrólfs saga Kraka. So Holder (2 ed.), Socin (7 ed.), Holthausen (1 ed.), Schücking (8–10 ed.), and Sedgefield (2 ed.). The reading adopted by Holthausen (7 ed.), hyrde ic, þæt [Signi wæs Seaf]elan cwen, is a variation of the same idea. **63** Heaðoscilfingas] A gen. sing. in -as, as in ll. 2453, 2921, Wanderer 44, and possibly Riddle 11, 4. healsgebedda] On the form of this word (a weak noun in -a with feminine meaning), cf. manscaða, l. 1339, foregenga, Judith 127, and see Sievers-Brunner, §278, note 4, and Kluge, Beitr. VIII, 532f. **67** bearn] From be-irnan, "it occurred to him in his mind." For other examples of this verb, see Bos.-Tol., p. 98 (s.v. be-yrnan). **68** þæt healreced] Most of the early edd. and Wülker, Holder, Trautmann, Sedgefield supply he before healreced. But the omission of a pronoun subject in a subordinate clause is not uncommon in Beowulf; cf. ll. 286, 300, etc., and see A. Pogatscher, Anglia XXIII (1900), 265ff. **69–70]** The word æfre in l. 70b marks l. 70 as the end of a comparative construction, and Grein, Bib., and later edd. (except Grundtvig, Heyne, Wülker, and Socin) emend the MS. *þone*; Trautmann emends to *þon*, the other edd. to *þonne*. In l. 69, a comparative form of the adjective is to be expected, and several emendations have been proposed: Schönbach, Anz. fdA. III, 42, suggested emending *micel* to *mare*; Trautmann reads *medoærn micel ma gewyrcean*, "ein grosses methaus, ein grösseres errichten"; Bright, MLN. XXVII, 181ff., *medoærn micle* (or *micele*) *mare gewyrcean*; Holthausen (4, 5 ed.) *medoærn micle merre* (= *mǣrre*) *gewyrcean*. Holthausen (2, 3, 6–8 ed.) assumes a loss after l. 69. If an emendation is to be made (and it is quite possible that the MS. reading is wrong, the scribe having been confused by *micel* in l. 67), then Schönbach's *mare* is the simplest and best. But most edd. do not emend, and W. Horn, Archiv CXIV (1905), 363, Anglia XXIX, 130f., and Hoops, Bwst., pp. 92f., plausibly take ll. 69–70 as a mixture of two constructions. E. Koeppel, Eng. Stud. XXX (1902), 376f., cites two seventeenth-century examples of *than* without a preceding comparative. The MS. reading of Elene 646b–647, *þæt wæs fær mycel . . . þonne . . .*, provides an analogous case and probably should not have been emended in the present edition (Records II, 84). A prose example of this construction, cited by Bugge, ZfdPh. IV, 193, is *he swiðe þæs londes fæstenum truwode þonne his gefeohte & gewinne* in the Epistle of Alexander to Aristotle (ed. S. Rypins, Three Old English Prose Texts, 26, 9ff.). The use of *god . . . þonne* in Psalm 117, 8–9 (Paris Psalter), is due, as Bright, loc. cit., has shown, to the literal translation of a hebraism in the Latin text of the Psalter. **70** yldo] For *ylda*, gen. plur., "children of men." Other examples of gen. plur. in -*o* are *hynðo*, ll. 475, 593, *medo*, l. 1178. See also E. Sievers, Beitr. IX (1884), 230; Klaeber, MLN. XVI, 33f. **73**] The precise meaning of this line is obscure, except that it seems to express a limitation on the power of the king, and Cosijn, Aant., pp. 2f., would reject it as a later insertion. Sedgefield, Chambers, and Klaeber take *folcscare* as referring to the public land, the "folk-share," following J. M. Kemble, Codex Diplomaticus Aevi Saxonici II (London, 1840), ix. But elsewhere in the poetry *folcscearu* means "nation, tribe of people"; see Bos.-Tol., p. 298; Supp., p. 229. **76** on fyrste] "In due time, punctually." See Klaeber, Anglia L, 111, who cites *on tid*, Andreas 214. **79**] "He who possessed (or exerted) widely the power of his word," i.e., power exercised by means of his word. Cf. *his fingra geweald*, l. 764. **82** horngeap] "Wide-gabled"; see Miller, Anglia XII, 396ff.; Hoops, Eng. Stud. LXIV, 207ff., Bwst., p. 93. **83** lenge] Rieger, ZfdPh. III, 382f., would take *lenge* as an adjective, equivalent in meaning to *gelenge*, *gelang*. But *gelenge* means "belonging (to)," and *gelang* means "pertaining (to), dependent (on)," and neither of these meanings fits the present passage. Most later edd. take *lenge* as an adjective meaning "at hand, ready, bevorstehend, nahe," and so Hoops, pp. 24f. There are, however, no parallels for this meaning. (In Maxims I, 120, *wiþ god lenge* probably means "pertaining to God"; Guthlac 20, often cited as a parallel, is to be read *lenge hu sel*, with *lenge* an adverb.) Wyatt, also taking *lenge* as an adjective, translates it "long." Holthausen (2 ed.) emends to *longe*. The alternative construction is to take *lenge* as a variant of *leng*, the comparative of the adverb, and to translate, "nor was it [the time] very far [distant], when . . ." For the form *lenge*, cf. Guthlac 20, 138, Juliana 375. We should, however, expect *lang*, *long* rather than *leng(e)*; cf. ll. 2591, 2845. Neither of the two interpretations of *lenge* can be accepted without strong reservations, and an editor cannot be blamed for not making up his mind. Klaeber, Mod. Phil. III, 246, took *lenge* as the comparative of the adverb, but in his edition he says that it is more probably an adjective; Sedgefield (1, 2 ed.) took *lenge* as an adjective, but more recently (3 ed., note) he has explained it as a variant form of *leng*. 84 ecghete] So Grein, Bib., and all later edd. Krogmann, Eng. Stud. LXVIII, 318, would retain the MS. *secghete*, in spite of the lack of alliteration. aþumsweorum] The MS. *aþum swerian*, which gave great difficulty to the early edd., was first correctly explained by Bugge, Tidskrift VIII, 44ff., as for *aþumsweorum*, dat. plur., "for son-in-law and father-in-law" (a dvandva-compound like *suhtergefæderan*, l. 1164). Bugge and the edd. who immediately followed him, though accepting this interpretation, retained the MS. spelling *aþumswerian*, and so also Chambers and von Schaubert. Trautmann, however, emended to *aþumsweorum*, and so Holthausen (1–7 ed.), Schücking, and Sedgefield (1, 2 ed.). Binz, Anglia Beibl. XIV, 359, proposed to read *aþumsweoran*, dat. plur., as closer to the MS., and so Klaeber, Sedgefield (3 ed.), Hoops, p. 25, and Holthausen (8 ed.). But there is no particular virtue in the *-an* of the MS.; the scribe was confused by *aþum*, which he took to mean "with oaths" (cf. *aðum benemde*, l. 1097), and accordingly expected *swerian* to follow. There is no reason for believing that the original text had *-an* rather than *-um*. 86 ellengæst] Grein, Bib., and Rieger, ZfdPh. III, 383, suggested emending *ellen-* to *ellor-*, and so Trautmann, Holthausen (1 ed.), and Sedgefield. This emendation is tempting, especially since in l. 1617 the scribe, having first written *ellen-*, altered it to *ellor-*; it may be that a similar correction should have been made here. On the second element of this compound (*-gæst* or *-gæst?*), see l. 102, note. earfoðlice] Kock, Anglia XLII, 102, would take *earfoðlice* as an adjective, and would regard *earfoðlice þrage* as the equivalent of *earfoðþrage*, l. 283, and of *earfoðhwile*, Seafarer 3. So also Hoops, p. 27. But as Klaeber, Mod. Phil. III, 254, showed, *þrage* is to be taken by itself as meaning "hard or disagreeable time," as in l. 2883, Juliana 453, 464, Guthlac 1350, etc. The traditional interpretation of *earfoðlice* as an adverb is therefore better; see Klaeber, MLN. XXXIV, 131, who cites l. 2303 as a parallel. 92 worhte] Restored by Kemble and all later edd. 93 swa] The equivalent of *swa swa*, *swa wide swa*, *swa side swa*. See Kock, Anglia XLII, 102f., and Ericson, Eng. Stud. LXV, 343f. Ericson translates, "as far as the water encircles it." The fuller form of the same construction is to be found in l. 1223 and Andreas 333. 98 þara ðe . . . hwyrfaþ] For this construction, with *þara ðe* subject of a relative clause, see E. A. Kock, The English Relative Pronouns (Lund, 1897), pp. 19ff.; Woolf, MLQuart. IV, 50f. Here and in ll. 785, 937, the verb of the relative clause is plural; elsewhere in Beowulf the verb is singular, ll. 843, 996, 1051, 1407, 1461, etc. See l. 206, note. 99 ða] See l. 3, note. 100 an] See *anne*, l. 2410, and note.

101–150

101 fremman] Restored by Kemble and all later edd.   helle] Bugge, Beitr. XII, 80, pointing out that although Grendel is a fiend of hell (cf. ll. 788, 1274), he does not live in hell, would emend to *feond on healle*. So also Socin (5 ed.), Trautmann, and Holthausen (8 ed.). Cf. *healðegnes hete*, l. 142, where some edd. emend to *helðegnes*. But Cosijn, Aant., p. 3, minimizing the significance of the preposition, would take the MS. *feond on helle* as the equivalent of *helle gast*. Klaeber, Mod. Phil. III, 258, translates, "hellish fiend."   102] Andrew, p. 65, would take l. 102 as a parenthesis, with *mearcstapa* in apposition to *feond on helle*.   gæst] This form, both as a separate word and as the second element of a compound, occurs thirteen times in Beowulf, once (l. 1893) being restored by the edd.   In many of these cases it is difficult to tell whether the word is *gǣst* (= *gāst*, "spirit, demon") or *gǣst* (= *giest*, "stranger, visitor"). In ll. 1800, 1893, where it refers to Beowulf and his men, it is of course *gǣst*; it is, on the other hand, certainly *gǣst* in l. 1123, where it is used of the funeral fire.   In ll. 2312, 2670, 2699, where it refers to the dragon, recent edd., except Holthausen, take it as (-)*gǣst* (Sedgefield prints -*gǣst* in l. 2699, but in his glossary takes it as for -*giest*).   In ll. 86, 102, 1331, 1349, 1617, 1995, 2073, where it is used of Grendel and his kin, recent editors agree on (-)*gǣst* (except Chambers, who reads *gǣst* in l. 2073).   The distinction assumed by the edd. is probably valid; it is to be noted that whereas Grendel is called *gāst* in ll. 133, 1274, and *ellorgāst* in ll. 807, 1621, he is never called a *giest*, and that whereas the dragon is called *gryregiest* in l. 2560, he is never called a *gāst*.   Rieger, ZfdPh. III, 383, would, however, read -*gǣst* in ll. 86, 1331, 1995.   For further discussions of this problem, see Chambers, note, and Hoops, pp. 29f.   104 fen ond fæsten] Mackie, MLRev. XXXIV, 516, suggests that l. 104a is an example of hendiadys, "the fastness of the fens" (with *fen* taken as acc. plur.). See ll. 619, 1195, notes.   The nouns *fen* and *fæsten* also occur together in the Letter of Alexander to Aristotle (ed. S. Rypins, Three Old English Prose Texts, 30, 20–31, 1), *ða cwom þær semninga sum deor of þæm fenne & of ðæm fæstene*. 106ff.] The punctuation here is very difficult.   Most edd. begin a new sentence with l. 107a; so, for example, Wülker, Socin, Wyatt, Holder (2 ed.), Schücking, Sedgefield (1, 2 ed.), and Chambers.   Sedgefield (3 ed.) puts only a comma after *hæfde* and a semicolon after *cynne*.   Similarly, Klaeber and von Schaubert have no punctuation after *hæfde* and a dash after *cynne*, thus beginning a new clause with l. 107b.   Sievers, Beitr. IX, 136f., disturbed by the genitive *þæs þe* in l. 108b, apparently parallel to *þone cwealm*, l. 107b, would take ll. 107b–108a as a parenthesis; he translates the rest of the passage, "seit ihn gott mit dem ganzen geschlechte Cains geächtet hatte, . . . weil dieser den Abel erschlagen."   So also Holder (1 ed.) and Holthausen, Anglia Beibl. X, 266.   Holthausen (2–8 ed.) puts ll. 107b–108b within dashes, thus making l. 109a follow immediately after l. 107a.   The punctuation in the text, which follows Sedgefield (3 ed.) and Hoops, p. 31, takes l. 107a as meaning "among (or with) the race of Cain." This seems better than taking l. 107a with what follows, since in the latter case

(translating, "he avenged that crime against the race of Cain") we would expect *on* rather than *in*.   106 him] Trautmann emends *him* to *hine*, following a suggestion by Grundtvig, to provide an accusative object for *forscrifan*; see his note in BVE., p. 130. But for a defence of the dative after *forscrifan*, see Sievers, Beitr. XXIX, 311.   scyppend] Although the final *d* was added by a different hand, it is probably genuine. But Malone, Anglia LIII, 335f., would accept the uncorrected reading *scyppen* as a legitimate variant of *scyppend*, and von Schaubert reads *scyppen* in her text. See l. 51, note.   108 þæs þe] Klaeber, Anglia Beibl. XL, 25f., points out that *(ge)wrecan* can be followed by the genitive as well as by the accusative; both constructions are found here, accusative *(þone cwealm)* and genitive *(þæs þe)*. Cf. *uncre hearmas . . . laðes*, Genesis 759f.   109] In l. 109a, *he* is Cain; in l. 109b, *he* is God.   112 orcneas] "Evil spirits, spirits of hell." For the meaning of this word, see R. Jente, Die mythologischen Ausdrücke im altengl. Wortschatz (Heidelberg, 1921), p. 137; W. Krogmann, Anglia LVI, 40ff.; Hoops, Bwst., pp. 17ff., and the references given there.   113 gigantas] For an account of the readings of transcripts A and B, see Malone, PMLA LXIV, 1193, who concludes that the *-ga-* of *gigantas* was a conjecture by Thorkelin, introduced by him into both transcripts at a late date. In any case, it seems to be the only possible reading and has been accepted by all edd.   115 neosian] Followed by both a genitive object *(hean huses)* and an indirect question introduced by *hu*: "He went to explore . . . the high house, to find out how . . ." Klaeber, Anglia LXIII, 400ff., compares *abidan . . . miclan domes, hu*, etc., ll. 977ff., and Guthlac 236f. For the indirect question after *neos(i)an*, cf. Genesis 855f., Guthlac 350ff.   120 wonsceaft] "Misfortune, misery," parallel to *sorge*. Sievers, Beitr. IX, 137, rejecting this parallelism on stylistic grounds, would emend to *wonsceaft weras*, with *weras* the subject of *cuðon*. This emendation is adopted by Holder, Socin, Trautmann, and Holthausen. But for a defence of the MS. *wera*, see Kock, Anglia XLV, 108f.   Wiht unhælo] Holthausen (2–6 ed.), Schücking, and von Schaubert, following Kemble II and Thorpe, put a comma after l. 120a, thus making *wiht unhælo*, "aught of misfortune," parallel to *sorge* and *wonsceaft*. But, as Klaeber, Anglia XXXV (1912), 252, points out, *Grim ond grædig* would be a very abrupt beginning of the next sentence. Sedgefield takes ll. 119b–120b as a parenthesis, apparently construing *grim ond grædig*, "the grim and greedy one," as the subject of *Fand*, l. 118, as well as of *wæs*, l. 121. Rieger, ZfdPh. III, 383f., beginning the new sentence with l. 120b, would emend to *Wiht unfælo*, "the evil creature" (see Bos.-Tol., p. 1103). Trautmann emends to *Wiht onhæle*, "Der unheimliche wicht." But Heyne, following a suggestion by H. Leo, took *unhælo* as gen. sing., "the creature of evil," and so Grein, ed., Socin, Chambers, Klaeber, Holthausen (7, 8 ed.), and Hoops, p. 33.   126 on uhtan mid ærdæge] Cf. Andreas 235, 1388, Elene 105. The phrase *mid ærdæge* repeats the idea of *on uhtan*; see Malone, Anglia LV, 269.   128ff.] Heinzel, Anz. fdA. XV, 189, would take ll. 128–131 as a parenthesis, thus referring *hie*, l. 132a, back to *gumum*, l. 127b: "Then Grendel's war-might was revealed to men . . . , after they beheld the track of the hateful one."   128 wiste] "Feasting," here used figuratively for "joy, good fortune." Cf.

Wunað he on wiste, l. 1735. With this interpretation we have a clear antithesis between *wist* and *wop*. See Cosijn, Aant., pp. 3f.; Kock, Anglia XXVII, 223. **130 ærgod]** Not "good of old, formerly good," as Bryan, Mod. Phil. XXVIII, 157ff., explains it, but rather "very good," here and in ll. 989, 1329, 2342, 2586. See Hoops, Bwst., pp. 20ff. The implication is that the atheling (or the sword) has been proved good by long experience. The Modern English "good old sword," etc., conveys the same idea; see N.E.D., s.v. *old*, 8. **131 ðryð-swyð]** An adjective, "strong in might," and so also in l. 736, "the mighty one." The verb *þolode* is probably intransitive, as in l. 2499, Maldon 307, Resignation 118, and Riddle 16, 8. Klaeber's construction, Mod. Phil. III, 242, with *þegnsorge* object of both *þolode* and *dreah*, is less likely. **133 wergan gastes]** "Of the accursed spirit," here and in l. 1747. For other examples of this adjective (the form of the nom. sing. masculine is uncertain), see Bos-Tol., p. 1177, s.v. *wearg*. For the etymology (which is disputed), see the summary in Hoops, p. 34, and the references there cited. **136 morðbeala]** For *morðbealu*, acc. sing. neuter, and Trautmann and Sedgefield so emend, following Rieger, ZfdPh. III, 384. The half-line means "more (additional) murder," and not "greater murder (than on the preceding night)"; see Klaeber, Mod. Phil. III, 449f. ond no mearn fore] "And did not shrink from it." Cf. l. 1537, Maldon 96. **139 gerumlicor]** An adverb *gerumlice* is not found elsewhere, but the adjective *gerum* occurs in Genesis 759, Daniel 290. Grein, Bib., read *elles hwær ge rum-licor*, "elsewhere and further away," but no later edd. have followed him. sohte] Supplied by Grein and most later edd. Wülker supplied *rymde*, with double alliteration in the second half-line. Andrew, p. 143, suggests that the scribe took *ræste* (= *reste*) to be the verb. **142 healðegnes]** Trautmann, Sedgefield, and Holthausen (8 ed.) emend to *helðegnes*, following Ettmüller, tr., and Bugge, Beitr. XII, 80. In l. 719, *healðegnas* refers to the Geats. Cf. *feond on helle*, l. 101, where the emendation to *healle* has been proposed. For a defence of the MS. reading in l. 142, see Klaeber, Mod. Phil. III, 450. H. Marquardt, Die altenglischen Kenningar (Halle, 1938), p. 193, takes *healðegnes* as an objective genitive, "[Grendel's] hatred toward the retainer," but this seems unlikely. **143]** Schücking, taking *se* as a demonstrative, punctuates l. 143b as a separate sentence; similarly, von Schaubert puts a semicolon after *fæstor*. See also Schücking, Svk., p. 131. **145 ana]** Andrew, p. 82, would take *ana* as a scribal error for *an*, "one against all." Cf. *an æfter eallum*, l. 2268. But *ana*, "alone," as in ll. 425, 431, 888, etc., is unobjectionable. **146b]** Sievers, Beitr. IX, 137, would take l. 146b as a parenthesis, with a colon after *tid*, l. 147a. That is, the hall was empty for twelve years. So Holder (1 ed.), Holthausen (1–6 ed.). But Holthausen (7, 8 ed.), beginning a new sentence with *Wæs*, punctuates *Wæs seo hwil micel, XII wintra tid: torn geþolode*, etc. Other edd. take l. 147a with what follows, as in the text. Schücking prints l. 146b as a separate sentence. **148 Scyldinga]** Suggested by Grundt-vig, tr., p. 269, and so all later edd. **149 secgum]** To supply the word which has been omitted from the MS., various readings have been proposed. Kemble (2 ed.), following a suggestion by Thorpe, supplied *syððan*, and so Thorpe, Grein, Bib., Grundtvig, Arnold, Wülker, Holder, Socin, Wyatt, Sedgefield, and

Chambers. Bugge, Beitr. XII, 367, would supply *sarcwidum*. Trautmann, BVE., pp. 132f., proposed to read *sarleoðum wearð* as the whole of l. 149*b* (that is, he would regard the MS. *forðam* as a scribal error for *sarleoðum*); in his edition he reads *sarspellum*. Sievers, Beitr. XXIX, 313, suggested *for ðam socnum wearð* (cf. l. 1777), and so Holthausen (1 ed.). Holthausen (2-5 ed.) reads *forðan sona wearð*. Klaeber, JEGPh. VI, 191, and Schücking, Eng. Stud. XXXIX, 101f., would supply *secgum*, as a variation of *ylda bearnum*, and so in their editions. Holthausen (6 ed.) and von Schaubert also supply *secgum*; Holthausen (7, 8 ed.) reads *forðan socnum wearð*. Recently Andrew, p. 147, has proposed to supply *gesyne*, a variation of *undyrne cuð*; cf. the close parallel in l. 1255. Of all these proposals, *secgum* and *gesyne* are stylistically the best, as furnishing variations of other words in the same passage. But *secgum* has been preferred in the text, because of the unlikelihood of *gesyne . . . gyddum*.   **150** undyrne cuð] The same half-line occurs at l. 410. Schücking, Sedgefield, and Chambers take *undyrne* as an adverb in both places. But Klaeber, Anglia XXVIII, 440, Kock, Anglia XLII, 104, and Hoops, p. 36, take *undyrne* and *cuð* as asyndetic synonyms; Kock translates, "manifest and known." Cf. *frome fyrdhwate*, ll. 1641, 2476, *ealdum infrodum*, l. 1874, and the succession of five adjectives in Andreas 526-527*a*.

151-200

151 gyddum geomore] Klaeber, JEGPh. VI, 190f., calls this a "suspiciously harsh collocation" and suggests the emendation *gihðu geomore*, "sorrowful grief (affliction)." Trautmann emends to *gyddum geomrum*, "durch jammernde reden." Andrew, p. 81, has recently suggested *gyddum geomorod*, "bewailed in song," parallel to l. 150*b*, but the verb *geomrian* apparently does not occur in transitive use. The MS. reading is perfectly acceptable and is retained in all the editions except Trautmann's. We may translate, "sadly with (by means of) songs," or (following Kock, Anglia XLII, 104), "through solemn songs [and] sadly."   **154** sibbe] Not instr. sing., as the older edd., Grein-Köhler, p. 605, and Sievers, Beitr. XXIX, 316f., took it, but acc. sing., object of *wolde*. See Bugge, Beitr. XII, 82; Kock, Anglia XLIV, 98f.; Hoops, p. 37. As a parallel to *sibbe . . . wið manna hwone*, Hoops cites Guthlac 1262, *sibbe wiþ þe*. In the present passage the verb *wolde* is to be construed with both *sibbe* and *feorhbealo feorran*: "he did not wish peace, did not wish to banish life-bale."   **156** fea] A variant spelling of *feo*, dat. sing. of *feoh*, "property, money." The edd., except Chambers, Klaeber, and von Schaubert, normalize to *feo*. For the phrase *feo þingian*, "to settle (a dispute or feud) with money," i.e., to pay wergild, cf. l. 470.   **157** nænig witena] Holthausen (2-6 ed.) and Sedgefield (1, 2 ed.) transpose to *witena nænig*, to obtain a more normal alliteration, but Sievers, Beitr. X, 286, correctly classes l. 157*a* under type A3, with alliteration on the second stress. Trautmann suggests *wigena* for the MS. *witena*, here and in l. 266.   **158** to] For the construction *wenan . . . to*, cf. ll. 525, 600f., 1396, 2922f., also (with other verbs) ll. 188, 909, 1206f., 1272, etc. The preposition expresses the direction of the expectation or the desire, rather than the direction of the fulfillment. See Kock, Anglia XXVII, 223f.

banan] So Kemble and later edd., except Grundtvig.   **159** ac se] As a restoration of the letters lost from the MS., Thorpe (in Kemble II) suggested [*Atol*] *æglæca*, and so most of the older edd., together with Sedgefield and Chambers.   But *Atol æglæca*, beginning a new sentence, is rather abrupt and does not provide any logical relation of l. 159 to what precedes.   Rieger, ZfdPh. III, 384, proposed [*ac se*] *æglæca*, and so Holder, Trautmann, Holthausen, Schücking, Klaeber, and von Schaubert.   **161** seomade ond syrede] "Lurked and plotted," or perhaps, as Klaeber, Mod. Phil. III, 450, suggests, "kept on plotting, or ambushing."   The form *syrede* is preterite of *syrwan, sirwan* (see Bos.-Tol., p. 877), a derivative of *searu*.   sinnihte] No certain example of the nom. sing. of this word is recorded.   Schücking and Sedgefield take *sinnihte* to be acc. plur. (of extent of time) of *sinniht*, feminine; Klaeber takes it as dat. sing. of *sinniht*.   But Grein-Köhler, p. 614, and Bos.-Tol., Supp., p. 703, assume a neuter noun *sinnihte* (*ja*-stem); so also Girvan, Beowulf and the Seventh Century, p. 10, who takes the form in the text to be acc. sing.   **163** helrunan] "Wizards, magicians"?   For the meaning of this word, see especially Bugge, ZfdPh. IV, 194; R. Jente, Die mythologischen Ausdrücke im altengl. Wortschatz (Heidelberg, 1921), pp. 166, 330; Hoops, p. 38.   **164** Swa fela fyrena] Not "so many crimes," as the older edd. interpreted it.   The word *swa* is rather to be construed separately and translated, "thus, in this way"; see Klaeber, Anglia XXVIII, 447.   **168–169**] The principal questions involved in the interpretation of these lines are: Is *he*, l. 168a, Grendel or Hrothgar?   Does *gifstol* refer to Hrothgar's throne or to God's?   What does *gretan* mean?   What is the subject of *wisse*, l. 169b?   It is impossible to give here a complete survey of opinion on these points, but the principal lines of argument will be briefly summarized.   In the first place, *he*, l. 168a, is almost certainly Grendel, and most edd. and commentators so explain it.   Holtzmann, Germania VIII, 489f., Trautmann, BVE., pp. 135f., Sievers, Beitr. XXIX, 319, and Tinker, MLN. XXIII, 239, take *he* as referring to Hrothgar.   But Grendel, as the subject of the preceding lines, would most naturally be referred to here, and the words *for metode*, "on account of the Lord," also point to Grendel as the one who was prevented from approaching the *gifstol* (cf. l. 711, *godes yrre bær*). If, then, *he* is Grendel, the *gifstol* is probably Hrothgar's throne (and so most commentators) rather than God's throne of Grace (as Sedgefield, for example, explains it), since we have no reason for believing that Grendel was desirous of religious experience.   Assuming that *he* is Grendel and that the *gifstol* is Hrothgar's throne, then *gretan* may mean either "approach (in the character of a retainer)" or "attack."   Wülker, Anglia I, 185f., and Kölbing, Eng. Stud. III, 92, took *gretan* as meaning "attack."   But if *mapðum*, l. 169a, is a variation of *gifstol*, as it seems to be, then *gretan* more probably means "approach"; that is, Grendel could not approach the *gifstol*, as retainers do, in order to receive his share in the distribution of treasure.   So far, most recent edd. are agreed; but l. 169b, by far the most difficult part of this passage, is open to a variety of interpretations, because we cannot be sure what *myne* means.   Taking God as the subject of *wisse*, Klaeber, JEGPh. VIII, 254f., translates, "nor did he [God] take thought of him"; similarly, Schücking (9–14 ed.), note, "noch dachte er

(Gott) an ihn." Taking Grendel as the subject, Kölbing, loc. cit., translates, "noch wusste er etwas von seiner [i.e., God's] absicht"; Bos.-Tol., p. 703, "and knew not his purpose"; Chambers, note, "he knew not His [i.e., God's] mind." Cosijn, Aant., p. 5, takes l. 169*b* as meaning "nor had he any joy in it" [i.e., in the *gifstol*]; Crawford, MLRev. XXIII, 336, "nor [was he permitted] to work his will upon it [the *gifstol*]" (or "have his pleasure in it"); Hoops, p. 39, "noch schenkte er ihm [the *gifstol*?] Beachtung," "noch kümmerte er sich darum." Klaeber (3 ed.), second supplement (1950), p. 465, would translate, "nor did he feel (affection) gratitude for it." Trautmann, taking Hrothgar as the subject of *wisse* (as of *moste*), translates, "noch wusste er seine [God's] absicht" (cf. Kölbing's translation, above); Holtzmann, Germania VIII, 489f., also taking Hrothgar as the subject, translates, "er . . . konnte seine Lust nicht an ihm [the *gifstol*] haben." The word *myne* (*mine*) apparently occurs also in Wanderer 27, where the solitary one is seeking a new lord, *þone þe in meoduhealle mine wisse*. In this, the MS. reading, the second half-line is too short, and the emendation adopted in this edition, *min mine wisse*, "took (kind) thought of me" (Records III, 288f.), is based on the passage of Beowulf now under consideration. In the interest of consistency, therefore, it is advisable to adopt Klaeber's earlier translation here, "nor did he [God] take thought of him." Among the more enlightening discussions of this passage are those by Kock, Anglia XXVII, 225f. (see also Kock, JJJ., pp. 7f.) and Estrich, JEGPh. XLIII, 384ff. Kock explains the passage as follows: "[Grendel] could not partake in the festivities of the day, not step, like the others, before the precious throne to salute the Monarch (and receive his gifts); for he was prevented by the Creator, a stranger to Him." Estrich translates: "he [Grendel] could not approach [or attack] the throne, the treasure, because of God: he did not know God's love," and explains the passage as a reflection of the old belief that the *gifstol*, "as a symbol of semi-divine royalty," was sacrosanct.   **171 brecða]** Probably nom. plur. of a feminine noun *brecð*, "breaking," not elsewhere attested except in the compounds *æbrecð*, *edorbrecð*. So Hoops, p. 39, and Klaeber. But Dietrich, ZfdA. XI, 410f., assumed a noun *brecða*, masculine, and so Holthausen, Schücking, Sedgefield, and Chambers.   **171–172 Monig . . . rune]** "Many a powerful one often sat in council." Trautmann suggests *rinca* for the MS. *rice*. For the change in number in l. 172*b*, see Woolf, MLQuart. IV, 54f.   **175 hærgtrafum]** Kemble and other early edd. emend the MS. *hrærg* to *hearg-*, Grundtvig, Grein, ed., Heyne (2–4 ed.), and later edd. to *hærg-*. The compound *heargtræf* ("idol-sanctuary"?) does not occur elsewhere.   **176 wigweorþunga]** Gen. plur. or acc. plur. (either case may be found after *gehatan*), "idol-worshippings."   **177 gastbona]** The "soul-killer," i.e., the devil; on this term, see especially Klaeber, Anglia XXXV (1912), 249f.; Hoops, Bwst., pp. 24ff.   **184 þurh sliðne nið]** Sedgefield translates, "in fierce enmity" (to God); Mackie, MLRev. XXXIV, 516f., "owing to dreadful wickedness," citing *þurh nædran niþ*, Phoenix 413. For another interpretation, "in dire distressful wise" (Clark Hall's prose translation), see Klaeber, Archiv CXV, 178.   **186 wihte gewendan]** Parallel to l. 185*b*, "not to expect comfort, (not) to change in any way," with *wihte* taken as a dat. sing. used adverbially (cf. ll. 1514, 1995, etc.) and *gewendan* as intransitive, as in Elene 617, Solomon and Saturn 152, 500. Cf. also *gewendan mid wihte*, Genesis 428. Rieger, ZfdPh. III, 385, taking *gewendan* as transitive, proposed the emendation *wite*, "punishment, torment," for the MS. *wihte*. Trautmann, BVE., pp. 136f., and in his edition, emends ll. 185*b*–186*a* to *frofre ne wene wihte gewinnan*, "trost wähne er nicht zu gewinnen." 189 ठa] See l. 3, note. mælceare] "The sorrow of this time"; see Sievers, Beitr. XXIX, 320ff., and Chambers, note. Trautmann unnecessarily emends to *modceare*, which occurs with *seað* in ll. 1992f. 190 seað] The verb *sēoðan*, "to boil," is regularly transitive in Anglo-Saxon and Middle English, both as an item of cooking terminology and in figurative use, as here; see Bos.-Tol., p. 866; N.E.D., s.v. *seethe*, 1. Hrothgar, then, kept his sorrow boiling, he nursed his wrath to keep it warm. Kock, Anglia XLII, 104f., XLIV, 99f., would take *seoðan* as intransitive, with *mælceare* instrumental: "seethed in care, was tormented by care." In support of this interpretation, previously adopted by Trautmann, Kock cites ll. 1992f., where he construes *modceare* as parallel to *sorhwylmum*. But see Klaeber, Archiv CXXVI (1911), 351, MLN. XXXIV, 131f., Anglia L, 115f. 194 þæt] Anticipating the true object, *Grendles dæda*. fram ham] We would say "at home," but for the Old Germanic idiom, see Sievers, Beitr. XI (1886), 361f., Beitr. XII, 188ff.; Hoops, pp. 42f. A close parallel in meaning to the present passage is to be found in *feorran gefricgean*, l. 2889. 195 mid Geatum] Malone, Anglia LV, 270, would take *mid Geatum* as a variation of *ham*, l. 194*a*. But this interpretation ignores the unity of *god mid Geatum*, which is an alliterative filler like *geong in geardum*, l. 13, *ædre mid yldum*, l, 77, etc.

201–250

201*b*] "Since he had need of men," referring to Hrothgar. The causal use of *þa* which is evident in this passage is not found in l. 2876, *þa him wæs elnes þearf*, where *þa* is sufficiently translated by "when." Here in l. 201 Trautmann emends the MS. *þa* to *þe*, with *þe him* introducing a relative clause, "dem männer nötig waren," but he retains *þa* in l. 2876. 204 higerofne] So Rask (in Grundtvig, tr., p. 270) and all later edd. except Grundtvig. This must certainly have been the reading of the MS.; the forms in transcripts A and B are convincingly explained by Malone, PMLA LXIV, 1194f. hæl sceawedon] "Inspected the omens." Müllenhoff, in R. von Liliencron and K. Müllenhoff, Zur Runenlehre (Halle, 1852), p. 28, cites O.H.G. *heil scouwōn*. Sedgefield, MLRev. V, 286, suggested *hæl gēeawedon*, "gave him a farewell greeting," and so in his 1st ed.; in his 2d ed. he retains the MS. reading, but in his 3d ed. he emends to *hæle scēawedon*, "gazed at the warrior." 206 þara þe] For this construction, with *þara þe* object of a relative clause, see E. A. Kock, The English Relative Pronouns (Lund, 1897), pp. 23ff. Here *þara* agrees with *leoda*, which Kock takes to be "a kind of partitive genitive" governed by *cempan gecorone*. For the use of *þara þe* as subject of a relative clause, see l. 98, note. 207 XVna sum] For *fiftēna*, *fiftȳna sum*, "one of fifteen." Cf. *XIIa*, l. 2401. 208f.] The *secg*, the *lagucræftig mon*, is now usually taken to be Beowulf, who is represented as showing the men the way to the shore. Lawrence, JEGPh. XXIII, 297, thinks it more probable that Beowulf "indicated the headlands and rocks in the passage leading out of the haven." Chambers, following a suggestion by J. H. G. Grattan, takes the passage in a general sense, as meaning that Beowulf "was their pilot on this expedition." As Lawrence remarks, the sequence of events need not be strictly logical. The older view (Thorpe, Grein, Heyne) was that the *lagucræftig mon* is not Beowulf but a professional pilot, and this may after all be correct. Grundtvig, note, would put ll. 208b–209a in parentheses, making *landgemyrcu* an object of *sohte*, and this punctuation is approved by Gering, ZfdPh. XII, 124.   **210** Fyrst forð gewat] Grundtvig, note, suggested *fyrd*, "troop of warriors," for the MS. *fyrst*, and so Holthausen, Literaturblatt XXI, 64; Trautmann emends to *Fleot*, "vessel."   **219** antid] The earlier edd. explained this word as *āntīd*, "hora prima"; so doubtfully Grein, Spr. I, 34, who compares *nōntīd*, "hora nona." Cosijn, Beitr. VIII, 568, took the word as for *and-tīd*, i.e., the same, or corresponding, hour of the next day. So Heyne, Holder, Socin, and Trautmann. Most recent edd. follow Sievers's explanation, Beitr. XXIX, 322ff., "a fixed time, a proper time." Cf. *āndaga*, "a fixed day," *āndagian*, "to appoint a day." Sievers takes *opres dogores* as an adverbial phrase, but these words may be dependent on *antid*. See l. 605, note.   **223b–224a]** The MS. *eoletes* has never been convincingly explained. It is of course possible to assume a noun *eolet*, unrecorded elsewhere, meaning either "sea" or "journey." But on the whole the edd. have been inclined to emend rather than to explain *eoletes*. In l. 223b, objections have been raised to the MS. *liden*, since the verb *līðan*, "to go (especially by sea), to sail," is not recorded as a transitive verb elsewhere in Anglo-Saxon. Thorpe emended the MS. *sund liden* to *sundlida*, "sea-sailer" (i.e., ship), and so several later edd. Since the emendations in l. 223b and l. 224a are closely interrelated, it is best to treat them together. Thorpe, reading *sundlida* in l. 223b, emended to *ealade*, gen. sing., in l. 224a and translated, "then was the sea-sailer at the end of its watery way" (cf. *ealada*, Andreas 441); as an alternative he suggested *yðlade*. Trautmann, reading *sundlida* in l. 223b, emends to *eosetes* in l. 224a, translating, "am ende der fahrt"; but no such noun as *eoset* is recorded. Holthausen (3–5 ed.) reads *sundlida* and *eoledes* (gen. sing. of **ēo-lod*, with *-lod* a weakened form of *-lād* used as a neuter; see his note in ZfdPh. XLVIII, 129); Holthausen (7 ed.), retaining the MS. *sund liden*, emends *eoleces* (= *ēa-lāces*, see Eng. Stud. LXIX, 433). In his 8th ed., retaining *sund liden*, Holthausen emends to *eoflotes* (= *ēa-flotes*). In Die neueren Sprachen, 1910, Ergänzungsband, p. 127, Holthausen suggested emending to *eares*, "of the sea." Sedgefield (1 ed.) follows the MS. but suggests that *eoletes* is nom. sing.; in his 2d ed. he emends to *sundlida* but retains *eoletes* as gen. sing.; in MLRev. XVIII, 471f., and in his 3d ed., reading *sundlida*, he further emends to *eateles*, translating, "at the end of the terrible (sea)." Whitbread, MLRev. XXXVII, 481, suggests *eotelre sæ*, gen. sing., "of the fierce sea," as an improvement on Sedgefield's last reading. Mackie, MLRev. XXI, 301, had suggested *þa wæs sundlidan* (dat. sing.) *eoletes æt ende* as an impersonal construction, "then it was at the end of the sea to the ocean-traveller"; similarly Andrew, p. 149, *þa wæs sundlidan ealad æt* *ende,* with *ealad* explained as nom. sing., "when for the ship the voyage was ended." Von Schaubert, note, suggests *eo leten æt ende,* translating, "das Wasser an seiner äussersten Grenze (am Strande) zurückgelassen." With all these possibilities at hand, it is still doubtful that the MS. needs to be emended, and Schücking, Chambers, Klaeber, and Holthausen (6 ed.) do not emend. For *līðan* in transitive use, cf. *ena meri līðan,* "to traverse a sea," Heliand 2233, as well as three examples of the transitive use of O. Icel. *līða* in Cleasby-Vigfusson, Icelandic-English Dict., p. 390, s.v. *līða* A. II; see also Dunstan, MLRev. XX, 317f. Among the various attempts to explain the unemended *eoletes,* the following are deserving of mention: C. M. Lotspeich, JEGPh. XL, 1 f. (*eolete* < **el-wite,* "foreign journey"); Prokosch, in Klaeber Misc., p. 202 (*ēa-letes,* "sea-voyage"); Krogmann, Anglia LVIII, 351ff. (*ēolet,* a term for the sea derived from a plant-name **ēol,* "Angelica silvestris," cognate with O. Icel. *jöll*); A. C. Bouman, Neophilologus XXXV (1951), 239f. (*eolete* < **eolhete,* "the pasture of the elk, " or, figuratively, "the pasture-land of the ship"). **226 hrysedon**] Taken by most edd. as intransitive, "their shirts of mail rattled." Trautmann, however, would construe it transitively, with *Wedera leode* the subject of this verb as well as of *sældon* and *þancedon.* So also Andrew, p. 48. This interpretation gives a much smoother reading but is probably wrong; the intransitive function of *hryssan* here is supported by Andreas 127, *garas hrysedon* (parallel to *guðsearo gullon*). The punctuation in the text, with ll. 226b–227a in parentheses, follows Socin and Holder (2 ed.); cf. the similar punctuation of Andreas 127 in this edition (Records II, 6). **230 se þe . . . scolde**] "Whose office it was" (Chambers, note). **237 Hwæt . . . searohæbbendra**] "What manner of shield-possessors . . .?" Cf. *Hwæt . . . freomanna,* Genesis 2175f., *Hwæt . . . manna,* Elene 902, and see Bos.-Tol., Supp., p. 575 (s.v. *hwā,* I, 2d). **240b**] There is no damage to the MS. at this point, the missing matter having been omitted by the scribe. The reading of the MS. is clearly *le wæs,* rather than *ic wæs,* as most of the earlier edd. believed. Bugge, Beitr. XII, 83, suggested [*Hwile ic on weal*]*le wæs,* with *wealle* at the end of l. 240b and *wæs* in l. 241a. Other commentators and edd. put both *le* and *wæs* at the end of l. 240b. Trautmann read [*Ic on hyl*]*le wæs.* Sievers, Anglia XIV, 146, proposed [*Hwæt! ic hwi*]*le wæs,* and so Holthausen, Sedgefield (2, 3 ed.), Chambers, and Klaeber. Kaluza, Metrik des Beowulfliedes, p. 47, would read simply [*Ic hwi*]*le wæs,* and so Holder (2 ed.), Socin (6, 7 ed.), Schücking, and von Schaubert. Either of these last two readings is acceptable. **242 þe**] Most of the earlier edd. (including Grein, Bib., and Heyne) emended to *þæt* or to *þæt þe.* But *þe* is for *þȳ,* instr. sing., "so that"; cf. *þy ðine wordcwidas weorðan gefelde,* Psalm 50, 53 (Records VI, 90). **242-243 on land Dena . . . sceðþan**] "Do injury against the land of the Danes," with *sceðþan* used in the absolute sense, as in *Regnþeof ne læt on sceade sceþþan,* Resignation 15f. (Records III, 215). Klaeber, Mod. Phil. III, 257, suggests that *sceðþan* is the equivalent of *sæcce secean* (*to Hiorote*), l. 1989. **244-245a**] "Never have warriors attempted to come here more openly." So most edd. But Bugge, Tidskrift VIII, 290, construed *cuman* as a noun (cf. l. 1806) and translated *ongunnon* as "advanced." So also Holthausen. Chambers, note, taking *cuman* as "possibly a noun," translates,

"Never have strangers, warriors, made themselves more at home." Klaeber, Anglia XXVIII, 439, adopts Bugge's interpretation but takes *ongunnon* in the sense of "behaved"; in his edition, however, he construes *cuman* as an infinitive. **245** ne ge leafnesword] Most of the earlier edd., together with Ettmüller and Holthausen (2–7 ed.) read *ne geleafnesword*. So also Klaeber, Anglia XXVIII, 440 (but not in his edition). This reading is acceptable if *cuman*, l. 244, is taken as a noun, but otherwise we lack a subject for *wisson*. It is possible that ll. 245b–247a are a question, and Holthausen (7 ed.) punctuates them as such. **246** gearwe] Either an adverb, "with certainty," or (as Klaeber, note, suggests) an error for *gearo*, predicate adjective modifying *leafnesword*. **247** maga gemedu] "The consent of my compatriots" (Kock, Anglia XLVI, 75ff.). The form *gemedu* is acc. plur. of *gemēde*, neuter, for which see Bos.-Tol., Supp., p. 369. **249** seldguma] Kock's translation, "no menial is he, this man adorned with weapons," Anglia XLV, 109, comes close to the meaning of ll. 249b–250a, although "menial" is too strong a word for *seldguma*. In the interpretation of *seldguma*, most edd. follow Bugge, Tidskrift VIII, 290f., who explained *seld-* as "hall, palace," and the compound as "hall-man," i.e., retainer. The word then means the same thing as *selesecg*, Wanderer 34, or *healþegn*. Klaeber, Anglia XXIX, 379, and Kock, loc. cit., point out that *wæpnum geweorðad* goes with *þæt*, not with *seldguma*. Bright, MLN. XXXI, 84, reviving the old interpretation which took *seld-* as meaning "seldom, rare, superior," would emend to *Is þæt seldguma*. **250** næfne] So Kemble (2 ed.) and later edd., except Grundtvig.

251–300

252 ær] "Rather than that ...." See Sievers, Beitr. XXIX, 329ff., and cf. l. 1371, Elene 676, Juliana 255. **253** leassceaweras] The older edd., except Kemble and Grundtvig, emended to *lease sceaweras*, and so Wülker, Holder, Socin, and Wyatt. But later edd., except Trautmann, have accepted the compound, following A. Pogatscher, Anz.fdA. XXV (1899), 12. See also Klaeber, Anglia XXIX, 379f. The usual translation of *leassceaweras* is "deceitful observers," i.e., spies, but Mezger, MLN. LXVI, 38, would define it as "observers whose lineage or home is not known," citing O. Icel. *lausamaðr*, "vagabond." Trautmann emends to *leafsceaweras*, "observers with permission." Holthausen (1–3 ed.) reads *swa leassceaweras*; see his note in ZfdPh. XXXVII, 113. **255** minne] So Kemble II and later edd. **258** se yldesta] "The chief, the senior member of the party." Cf. l. 363, Genesis 1670, Andreas 763, etc. **260** gumcynnes] Klaeber, note, suggests that this is a genitive of specification; he translates, "as to race." Other commentators take *gumcynnes* as dependent on *leode*, "people of the race of the Geats." **262** Wæs min fæder] For metrical reasons, a number of emendations have been proposed for this half-line: *Wæs min fæder [monegum]*, Trautmann, BVE., pp. 141f.; *Wæs min fæder [foldan]*, Trautmann in his edition; *Wæs min fæder [on foldan]*, Holthausen, ZfdPh. XXXVII, 113, and in his 1st ed.; *Wæs min [frod] fæder*, Holthausen (2 ed.) and Sedgefield (2 ed.); *Wæs min fæder folcum* [*feor*] *gecyþed*, Holthausen (3–7 ed.). But for a defence of the MS. reading as metrically regular, see Sedgefield, MLRev. XXVIII, 226. A similar half-line is l. 2048a. **266 witena**] See l. 157, note. **272b–273**] The punctuation in the text, with *gif . . . hyrdon* in parentheses, follows Hoops, p. 51, and Kiaeber, Eng. Stud. LXVIII, 114. The meaning is, "if what we have heard is true." **275 dædhata**] The MS. reading gives perfectly good sense, with *dædhata* explained as "deed-hater," i.e., one who manifests his hate through his deeds. For the idea, cf. ll. 2466f. But Kluge, Beitr. IX, 188, proposed to read *dædhwata* (cf. Daniel 352, Elene 292, Juliana 2, etc.), and so Holder (1 ed.). Trautmann emends to *deaðscapa*. **276 þurh egsan**] Klaeber, Mod. Phil. III, 451, takes this not as "through terror," but as "in a terrible manner"; cf. *þurh hæstne had*, l. 1335. This is similar to his interpretation of *þurh sliðne nið*, l. 184. **280 edwendan**] Infinitive, parallel to *cuman*, with *bisigu* nom. sing. Translate, "if for him the affliction of woes should ever change, remedy come again." No other example of the verb *edwendan* is cited in Bos.-Tol., but the form *edwendende* occurs in the interlinear Regius Psalter (ed. F. Roeder, Halle, 1904) as a translation of *rediens*, Psalm lxxvii. 39. Bugge, Tidskrift VIII, 291f., proposed to emend to the noun *edwenden*, as in l. 2188 (and by emendation in l. 1774), and so Holder (1 ed.), Holthausen, Sedgefield, Chambers, note, and Klaeber. This emendation involves taking *bisigu* as gen. sing., dependent on both *edwenden* and *bot*. For a defence of the MS. reading, see Hoops, Bwst., p. 96. **282 wurðaþ**] Grein, Bib., and ten Brink, Beowulf, p. 49, suggested *wurðan*, and Ettmüller read *weorðan*, apparently taking the word as parallel to *edwendan* and *cuman*. Andrew, p. 45, also prefers *wurðan*. But the MS. *wurðaþ* is more probably parallel to *oferswyðeþ*, l. 279: "how he will overcome the fiend, . . . and the surgings of sorrow will become cooler." **286b**] Sievers, Beitr. IX, 137, would supply *he* after *ðær*, and so Holthausen and Sedgefield. But for the omission of the pronoun here, see l. 68, note. **287b–289**] Most edd. begin the coastguard's speech at l. 287b, as in the text, but Schücking (9–14 ed.) and Holthausen (3–5 ed.) begin it at l. 290. The latter arrangement is very awkward, involving a long parenthesis before the beginning of the speech. **288 gescad witan**] "To know how to distinguish," i.e., to understand. There is no exact parallel in Anglo-Saxon, but in Old Saxon we have *uuissun im thingo gisked*, Heliand 653. For contrasting views on the meaning of the sentence, see Klaeber (3 ed.), p. 139, and Mackie, MLRev. XXXIV, 517. **299 godfremmendra . . . bið**] "To whomsoever of the brave ones it will be granted," Klaeber, Mod. Phil. III, 250. The words *godfremmendra swylcum* are logically parallel to *leofne mannan*, but grammatically, in the relative clause, *swylcum* is dative after *gyfeðe*. For other examples of *swylc* in a relative clause, see E. A. Kock, Kontinentalgermanische Streifzüge (Lunds Universitets Årsskrift, N.F., Avd. 1, Bd. 15, Nr. 3, Lund, 1919), pp. 24f. Grundtvig suggested emending to *guðfremmendra*, as in l. 246, and so Holtzmann, Germania VIII, 490, Heyne (2–4 ed.), and Holder (1 ed.). **300a**] Sievers, Beitr. IX, 137, would supply *he* after *þæt*, and so Sedgefield. Holthausen, who adds *he* in l. 286, does not do so here. See l. 68, note.

301–350

302 sale] So Heyne (2–4 ed.) and most later edd., following Ettmüller, Sc., Grundtvig, note, and Holtzmann, Germania VIII, 490. Malone, Eng. Studies XVIII, 257, would retain the MS. *sole* as early evidence for the rounding of Anglo-Saxon *ā*.   **304 ofer hleorberan]** The emendation to *ofer hleorbergan* ("over the cheek-guards"; cf. *cinberge*, Exodus 175), first made by Ettmüller and later proposed independently by Gering, ZfdPh. XII, 123, gives the expected sense and is adopted by Holder and all later edd. except Trautmann and Sedgefield (1, 2 ed.). So also Hoops, p. 54. Trautmann less plausibly emends to *ofer helmum wera*. Sedgefield (2 ed.) reads *ofer hleoþu bēran*, with *scionon*, l. 303, taken as a variant form of *scīenan*, "bright," weak acc. plur., modifying *eoforlic*; he translates, "they bore the bright boar-images over the hillsides." But it is by no means certain that an emendation is necessary here. Reading *hleor beran* as two words, Sedgefield (1 ed.) took *beran* as an infinitive dependent on *gewiton*, l. 301, and *scionon* as an adjective. This interpretation, which involves punctuating ll. 301*b*–303*a* as a parenthesis, is improbable if only because it requires taking *ofer* with the accusative *hleor* in a place-where construction. Grein, ed., reading *hleorberan* as a compound, took it as dat. sing. of a feminine noun *hlēorbere*, "was auf dem Gesicht getragen wird, Helmvisier?" Heyne (2–4 ed.) assumed a masculine *hlēorbera*, "Wangenträger" (i.e., the part of the helmet which covers the cheeks). Malone, JEGPh. XXIX, 233, would assume a noun *hlēorbere*, feminine, the element *-bere* to be identified with M.E. *bęre*, "pillowcase" (cf. Chaucer, Book of the Duchess 254, and *pilwebeer*, Canterbury Tales A 694); the compound *hlēorbere* would then mean "cheek-covering." The M.E. form *bęre* seems not to be related to the Anglo-Saxon verb *beran*, but the attempt by Hoops, Bwst., pp. 27ff., to demonstrate a French origin for it is unconvincing (see Holthausen, Anglia Beibl. XLIII, 358, and Malone, Medium Ævum II, 58f.), and Malone's suggestion remains a plausible etymology of the Middle English word. In view of this and other possible explanations of *hleorberan*, no emendation has been made in the text.   **305*b*–306*a*]** In these two difficult half-lines, the principal problem is the disposal of the MS. *ferh wearde*. Is this a compound, "life-watch," or is it two separate words, *ferh* being a variant form of *fearh*, "boar"? A second problem is the interpretation (or emendation) of the MS. *grummon*. That the MS. *ferh* is for *fearh* and refers to the *eoforlic*, the boar-image on the helmet, was first suggested by Grein, Bib.; see also Spr. I, 282. This interpretation was rejected by Cosijn, Aant., p. 7, who pointed out that *fearh* means "porcellus, pig," and not "boar"; but it is accepted by Heyne, Socin, Wyatt, Sedgefield (1, 2 ed.), Holthausen (6, 7 ed.), and Hoops, p. 55. The other explanation of the MS. *ferh wearde*, as a compound, is accepted by most of the earlier edd., by Bugge, ZfdPh. IV, 195f., and by Holder, Holthausen (2–5 ed.), Schücking, Chambers, Klaeber, Sedgefield (3 ed.), and von Schaubert. Now, if *ferh* is for *fearh*, "boar," it is the subject of *heold* and is probably modified by *guþmod*; but the MS. *grummon*, if a plural form of a verb, does not fit this interpretation. Malone, JEGPh. XXIX, 233, explains *grummon* as the dat. plur. of an adjective *grum, citing Old Danish grum, "fierce, cruel," and Modern English grum, "surly" (the latter form, however, is not attested before the seventeenth century). Bright, MLN. X, 85f., accepting ferh as meaning "boar," would emend to grimmon, an adverbial dat. plur., "The boar held guard, grimly warlike of mood." Sedgefield (1, 2 ed.), also emending to grimmon, dat. plur., translates, "the warlike boar kept guard over the fierce ones." So also Kock, Anglia XLVI, 77ff. Prokosch, in Klaeber Misc., p. 200, would assume a triple compound guþmodgrimmon, dat. plur., "grim with battle courage." If, on the other hand, we accept a compound ferhwearde, then the subject of heold is probably Eoforlic, l. 303b, which is plural and is subject of the plural verb scionon. Imelmann, however, Eng. Stud. LXVII, 325ff., would take guþmod, referring to the coastguard, as the subject of heold. In either case, we can end the sentence with the emended form grimmon ("The boar-figures shone, . . . kept, warlike of mind, life-watch over the fierce ones," or, following Imelmann, "The boar-figures shone . . . ; the [man] warlike of mind kept guard over the fierce ones"), or we can begin a new sentence with guþmod (on this latter possibility, see below). Still another alternative is the emendation proposed by Bugge, Beitr. XII, 83f., guþmodgum men for the MS. guþmod grummon in l. 306a. This tempting reading is adopted by Holthausen (2 ed.), Schücking, Chambers, and Klaeber (1 ed.). Chambers translates, "the gleaming and tempered [helm] held guard of life over the valiant man." Trautmann emends to Færwearde, "boat-watch" (previously suggested by Cosijn, Aant., p. 7), and alters the MS. grummon to grim-mon, "warrior"; he translates, "Bootwache hielt ein kampfmutiger krieger." Holthausen (1 ed.), also reading færwearde in l. 305b, emends grummon to gummon (cf. l. 1028); Holthausen (3–5 ed.) returns to the MS. ferhwearde but reads gummon, as referring to Beowulf. Carleton Brown, PMLA LIII, 910f., would read færwearde with Trautmann and gummon with Holthausen, translating, "a warlike man held boat-watch." Bryan, JEGPh. XIX, 84, retaining the MS. grummon ("roared"?), takes eoforlic as subject; but this interpretation involves a double shift in the number of the verb, from scionon to heold to grummon. Mackie, MLRev. XXXIV, 517, would emend to guþbord grummon, "the shields growled," taking ferh wearde heold, "a small pig kept guard," as a parenthesis. Furuhjelm, Anglia LVII, 318ff., suggests that grummon is the preterite plural of a strong transitive grimman (see Bos.-Tol., Supp., p. 487, s.v. grimman III) and translates, "the boar(figure)s excited the battle-mood (i.e., the courage) of Beowulf and his men." Finally, it is possible to begin a new sentence with l. 306a, retaining grummon as the preterite of the intransitive grimman. The usual meaning of grimman, "to rage, roar, make a loud noise," as in Genesis 793 and Riddle 2, 5, is inappropriate here, but the translation given by Bos.-Tol., Supp., p. 487, "martial minds were fierce," is worthy of consideration. With some such interpretation in mind, Kemble (2 ed.) emended to Guðmode, nom. plur. masculine, and so Thorpe, Grein, Bib., Heyne, Arnold, Holder (1 ed.), Socin, and Holthausen (7 ed.). All these proposals make an editor's choice difficult, but it is at least probable that the MS. grummon is to be emended to grimmon, dat. plur. If ferhwearde is taken as a compound, the translation, "the guþmod (that is, either the coastguard, as Imelmann explains it, or the boar-figures) maintained life-guard over the fierce ones," gives a likely meaning with the least violence to the recorded text.   **307** sæl timbred] Suggested by Kemble II, and so Grein and most later edd.   **308** ongyton] The spelling with -*on*, found also in *bregdon*, l. 2167, *buon*, l. 2842, *forlæton*, Judith 150, and *tobredon*, Judith 247, may be accepted as a legitimate variant of the infinitive ending; for other examples, see Bugge, ZfdPh. IV, 221.   **312** hof] So Kemble (2 ed.) and later edd., for the MS. *of*.   **314** guðbeorna sum] The coastguard, who has accompanied Beowulf and his men to this point.   **320** wisode] Intransitive, with *stig* the subject; cf. ll. 292, 402, etc., and Andreas 985. The verb is used transitively in l. 208 and in Andreas 381, 488, etc.   **322** hringiren] Now usually explained as a coat of mail made of rings, the equivalent of *hringnet*, l. 1889. The word is then a variation of *guðbyrne*. See Hoops, p. 58. Heyne's old interpretation, "ring-decorated sword," is defended by Hübener, Literaturblatt LVI, 242.   **323ff.**] According to Andrew, pp. 9f., the *þa...furðum* clause must mean "as soon as they reached the hall" and is best taken with *bugon ða to bence*; he would therefore begin a new sentence with l. 323*b* and put a comma after *cwomon*, l. 324*b*. But all edd. punctuate as in the text, with no serious difficulties of interpretation. Trautmann emends *furðum* to *furður*.   **330** ufan græg] "Gray (when looked at) from above," referring to the metal tip of the spear. Cf. *æftan hwit*, Brunanburh 63, *hindan grene*, Phoenix 293, etc., and see Sievers, Beitr. XII, 199.   **332** æþelum] So Grein and later edd., as required by the alliteration. The half-line means, "inquired concerning their lineage." Cf. l. 392, where *æþelu* is acc. plur. **338** Wen] For *wene*, with omission of the final -*e* before a following vowel, as also in l. 442. (But in ll. 525, 1184 we find the full form *wene*.) Other instances of omission of final -*e* occur in ll. 668 (*eotonweard*), 1932 (*firen*), 2600 (*sibb*), 2940 (*sum*), and in *slæp* (= *slæpe*), Deor 16. It seems unnecessary to print an apostrophe in such cases, though some edd. do so, e.g., Schücking, Klaeber, and von Schaubert.   **339** higeþrymmum] On the reading of transcript B, see Malone, PMLA LXIV, 1196.   **344** sunu] The edd., except Wyatt, Schücking, Chambers, Klaeber, Holthausen (3–8 ed.), and von Schaubert, emend to *suna*. But for *sunu* as dat. sing., cf. Christ 210, 635, and perhaps also Beow. 1808.   **345** min] Andrew, p. 123, taking exception to *min* as an alliterating word, suggests emending to *micel*. See l. 655, note. **348** þæt] Andrew, p. 35, claiming that *þæt* "cannot . . . be used, in a mere statement of identity, to refer to a person," would emend either to *he* or to the relative *ðe*. He suggests that the MS. *þ* stands for *ðe*. See l. 15, note.

351–400

357 anhar] Bugge, Tidskrift VIII, 71, 303, and ZfdPh. IV, 197, defended the MS. reading *unhar*, explaining *un-* as an intensifying prefix. Of the later edd., Schücking and von Schaubert accept this interpretation. Trautmann emends to *anhar*, and so Holthausen, Chambers, and Klaeber; cf. *ansund*, l. 1000, Lord's Prayer II, 89. Trautmann, BVE., p. 147, had previously proposed the emendation *unhror*, "infirm." Sedgefield (1 ed.) suggested that the MS. *unhar* may mean "with hair not yet white." In his 2d ed., p. 254, he suggested *inhar*, the *in-* being an intensifying prefix as in *infrod*, ll. 1874, 2449; in his 3d ed., he puts *inhar* into the text. See also his note in MLRev. XXVIII, 226. It is most probable that the MS. reading is an error for *anhar*; cf. Dream of the Rood 117, where the MS. *unforht* is emended to *anforht* (Records II, 64), and *uncyðig*, Elene 960, where a similar emendation might well have been made on the basis of *oncyðig*, Elene 724. **358** for eaxlum] The equivalent of the preposition *for(e)*, "before"; see Thomas, MLRev. XXII, 70. **359** he] Andrew, p. 57, condemning *he* on stylistic grounds, suggests that it is an error for *hi* (= *him*); cf. *con him land geare*, l. 2062, and *cuðe him soð genog*, Guthlac 295. **363** þone yldestan] See l. 258, note. **366** wordum wrixlan] Not "to exchange words," i.e., to converse, but rather "to make variations with words," i.e., to speak in connected discourse. See Hoops, p. 60. Cf. l. 874, where no dialogue is involved. **367** glædman] On the evidence of its use as a gloss of Latin *hilaris* (Wright-Wülker, Anglo-Saxon and Old English Vocabularies I, 171, 40), Bugge, Beitr. XII, 84f., accepted this word as an adjective, and so most later edd., glossing it either as "cheerful" or as "kind, gracious." Holthausen (1, 2 ed.) and Sedgefield (1, 2 ed.) emend to *glædmod*, as Grundtvig had suggested. Sedgefield (3 ed.) emends to *glæd min Hroðgar*; see his note in MLRev. XXVII, 448. The same emendation has more recently been proposed by Andrew, p. 149. **368** wiggetawum] The second element of this word is apparently a variant form of *-geatwum*; it also occurs in *guðgetawa*, l. 2636. In l. 395 the MS. has still another form, *-geatawum*. Sievers, Beitr. X, 273f., suggested emending to *-geatwum*, *-geatwa* in ll. 368, 2636, for metrical reasons, and so Holthausen (1–6 ed.), Schücking, and Sedgefield. In this proposal Sievers, to whom credit is usually given, was anticipated by Heyne (2–4 ed.) and, in l. 368, by Ettmüller. But Pope, p. 322, gives cogent grounds for believing that the *a* of the noun *-getawe* is short, and in that case there is no metrical objection to the MS. reading. In l. 395, also, the form *-geatawum* is possibly an error for *-getawum*; see the note on that line. **372** cnihtwesende] Ettmüller emended to *cniht wesendne*, Trautmann to *cnihtwesendne*. But see l. 46, note. **373** ealdfæder] Recent edd., except Trautmann, Chambers, and Sedgefield (3 ed.), read *ealdfæder* as a compound, but the meaning of the term is open to question. It usually means either "grandfather" or "forefather" (see Bos.-Tol., p. 227, Supp., p. 166); Old Saxon *aldfader*, Heliand 3375, 3396, means "patriarch." But we know from ll. 262f., 529, 631, etc., that Ecgtheow was Beowulf's own father. On the other hand, in Maldon 218 the phrase *min ealda fæder*, spoken by Ælfwine and referring to Ealhelm, cannot mean "my old father," since Ælfwine's father was Ælfric (l. 209). The best way out of the difficulty here in Beow. 373 is to gloss *ealdfæder* as "late father," and Schücking, Eng. Stud. LV, 89ff., gives a lengthy justification of this meaning, both for *ealdfæder* and for *ærfæder*, l. 2622. **374** to ham forgeaf] "Gave in marriage." The expression as it stands here is unique, but for a similar use of *to hame*, cf. Genesis 1720f. Other examples are cited by Klaeber, Anglia L, 120. **375** eafora] Suggested by Grundtvig, tr., p. 272, and so Kemble and most later edd.   **378** Geata] Explained by Klaeber, Mod. Phil. III, 452, as objective genitive, "presents (not "tribute") for the Geats." The proposed emendations, *hyder* for the MS. *þyder* in l. 379a (Cosijn, Aant., p. 7), or *Geatum* for *Geata* (Thorpe, Arnold, Bugge, Beitr. XII, 85f., Trautmann, and Andrew, p. 78), are therefore unnecessary.   **379** XXXtiges] For *þritiges*, the letters -*tig*- being superfluous. From the fact that the letters *XXX* are at the end of fol. 140a and *tiges* at the top of fol. 140b, we need not assume that the scribe wrote more than he intended; cf. the similar spelling *XXXtig* on fol. 125a, l. 11, of the MS. (S. Rypins, Three Old English Prose Texts, 21, 11).   **387** sibbegedriht] Is this word subject or object of *seon*? Bugge, Beitr. XII, 86, and Klaeber take it as subject of *seon*, referring to the Geats, with "me" understood as object. The other alternative, preferred by most commentators, is to take *sibbegedriht* as object of *seon*, referring to the Danes, with a pronoun "them," object of *hat*, to be understood in l. 386b.   Bright, MLN. X, 87, suggested emending to *hat þæt in ga seo sibbegedriht*, with *seo* to be taken as the definite article, as in Exodus 214. Reading *seo* in l. 387a, as Bright does, makes *sibbegedriht* nom. sing. and necessitates the further emendation in l. 386b. The form *sibbegedriht*, which occurs also in l. 729, is unusual, and Holthausen emends to *sibbgedriht*, following ten Brink, Beowulf, p. 53. Cf. Exodus 214, Guthlac 1372, Phoenix 618. Most of the early edd. and Grein-Köhler, pp. 129, 605, read *sibbe gedriht* as two words, with *sibbe* gen. sing.   **389–390**] It is probable that two half-lines were omitted by a scribe at this point, though Trautmann, by emending l. 390b to *Duruweard him abead*, manages to make one line of what other edd. print as two. To fill the apparent gap, Grein, Bib., supplied *þa wið duru healle Wulfgar eode* as ll. 389b-390a, and so most later edd. But Klaeber, Anglia L, 120, pointed out that *to duru* would be more natural than *wið duru*, and in his 3d ed. he supplies *þa to dura eode widcuð hæleð*. Von Schaubert supplies *þa to dura healle Wulfgar eode*. A possible objection to all these readings, first pointed out by Carleton Brown, PMLA LIII, 911, is that the verb *eode* never ends a half-line in Beowulf, though it does so in other poems; accordingly, Klaeber, Anglia LXIII, 406, proposed to supply *þa to* (or *wið*) *dura efste widcuð hæleð*. Andrew, p. 142, suggests [*þa he wið duru æthwearf, Wulfgar hæleðum*] *word inne abead*, but this reading, with a dependent clause, is less likely.   **395** guðgeatawum] See l. 368, note. Here in l. 395 the MS. reading gives double alliteration in the second half-line, and -*geatwum* is no improvement in this respect. It may be that the scribe intended -*getawum*, as in l. 368, and Grein, Bib., Holder, Trautmann, Klaeber (3 ed.), von Schaubert, and Holthausen (8 ed.) emend to -*getawum*, following Ettmüller, Sc.; so also Bugge, Tidskrift VIII, 64, Rieger, ZfdPh. III, 386, and Hoops, Bwst., p. 10. Holthausen (1–7 ed.) and Klaeber (1 ed.) emend to *guðsearwum*.   **397** onbidan] Such was apparently the intention of the scribe. The first stroke of the *m* was less completely erased than the others, and some edd. (most recently Holthausen, Schücking, and von Schaubert) give *onbidian* as the MS. reading.   **398** worda geþinges] "The result of words," with *geþinges* gen. sing. after *onbidan*. For this meaning of *geþinge*, cf. ll. 525, 709, Andreas 1598.

401–450

402*b*] For metrical reasons, Sievers, Beitr. X, 256, suggested omitting *þa* and taking l. 402*b* as a parenthesis; so Holder (2 ed.), Holthausen, and Klaeber (1 ed.). Sedgefield (2, 3 ed.) also omits *þa* but punctuates with a comma before l. 402*b* and no punctuation after it. Bugge, Beitr. XII, 86, suggested *þam secg wisode*, and so Andrew, p. 49, who translates, "those for whom B. led the way hastened...." But a relative construction seems unlikely here. 403*b*] A half-line has been omitted here by the scribe. Grein, Bib., restored *hygerof eode* as l. 403*b*, and so most later edd. Klaeber supplies *heaþorinc eode*; Sedgefield (3 ed.) and von Schaubert supply *eode hildedeor*. Carleton Brown, PMLA LIII, 911f., pointing out, as against the readings of Grein and Klaeber, that *eode* never ends a half-line in Beowulf (see also ll. 389–390, note), would supply *hygeþyhtig geong*; Klaeber, Anglia LXIII, 406, suggests *herewisa geong*, and Andrew, p. 142, *herewisa for*. 404 heoðe] Thorpe (in Kemble, 2 ed.) suggested *heorðe*, dat. sing. of *heorð*, "hearth," and so Holder (1 ed.), Holthausen (1–6 ed.), Sedgefield (1, 2 ed.), and Klaeber. Hoops, p. 64, objects that *æt heorðe* or *be heorðe* would be more usual than *on heorðe*; a similar objection to *on heorðe* had previously been made by Bugge, Beitr. XII, 86. But the examples with *æt* and *be* cited by Bos.-Tol., p. 531, are rather late, and the poet, if he intended *heorðe*, may have been thinking of a hearth in the center of the hall, the *langeldr* of the Scandinavian writers (see Cleasby-Vigfusson, Icelandic-English Dict., p. 126, s.v. *eldr* II). Klaeber, Anglia Beibl. LIV/LV, 173, defends *on heorðe* as referring to the fireplace and its surroundings. Other suggested emendations are *on hleoðe*, "within hearing distance" (Bugge, Beitr. XII, 86), *on heaþe*, "amid his band of retainers" (Sedgefield, 3 ed.), and *on Heorte* (Holthausen, Anglia Beibl. XLIV, 226, and in his 8th ed.). The emendation to *heorðe* has much to commend it but is not absolutely necessary, since the existence of a noun *heoðu* is attested by the compound *helheoðo* ("the precincts of hell"?), Christ and Satan 699. Holthausen, Anglia Beibl. LIV/LV, 27f., retaining *heoðe*, would assume a noun *hēoð*, "interior"; in Christ and Satan 699 he would emend to *helheoð seo dreorig*, with *seo* explained as a verb. 407 Wæs] For *Wes*, imperative. Cf. *þæs*, l. 411, and *spræc*, l. 1171. 409 Grendles þing] "[This] affair of Grendel." The word *ðing* in l. 426, often cited as a parallel, does not have quite the same meaning. See ll. 425–426, note. 411 þæs] For *þes*, nom. sing. masculine. See l. 407, note. 414 hador] Usually explained as *hādor*, a noun meaning "brightness." No such noun is recorded elsewhere, but the adjective *hādor*, "bright, clear," as in l. 497, is not infrequent in the poetry, and an abstract noun derived from it would not be unlikely; see Kock, Anglia XLV, 110f., and Mackie, MLRev. XXXIV, 517f. Grein, Bib., emended to *haðor*, glossed "receptaculum" in Spr. II, 40 (s.v. *heaðor*); this word occurs twice in the Riddles, as *heaþore*, dat. sing., Riddle 20, 13, and as *headre*, also dat. sing., Riddle 65, 3. Socin, Trautmann, Holthausen (1–5, 8 ed.), Schücking, and Sedgefield (3 ed.) emend to *haðor*, following Grein, and Pope, p. 323, also advocates this reading. Sedgefield (1 ed.) emended to *hador under heofene*, translating, "after the bright evening light is hidden under the sky"; Sedgefield (2 ed.) reads *under heofene hador*, with commas before and after. But the MS. reading need not be emended, nor need *hador* mean "brightness"; if *headre* can stand for *heaðore* in Riddle 65, 3, then *hador* can be a legitimate variant of *haðor* here.   **418 minne]** So Grein, Bib., and most later edd. Von Schaubert, retaining the MS. *mine*, explains *cræft* as acc. sing. feminine; see l. 2181, note. Another possibility would be the emendation to *mines*, modifying *mægenes*.   **419 of searwum]** Cf. *searoniða(s)*, ll. 582, 3067, and *searogrim*, l. 594, where no implication of treachery is to be found. But the frequent use of *searu* in the sense of "artifice, plot" (see Bos.-Tol., p. 852) makes it likely that such a meaning was in the poet's mind here. Kock's translation, "from insidious fights," Anglia XLV, 111, is probably the best that can be found.   **420 þær]** Rieger, ZfdPh. III, 399, proposed *þæra*, gen. plur.: "the enemies, of whom I bound five." But for *þær* as used here, cf. ll. 513, 550.   **fife]** Since Beowulf later (l. 575) claims to have killed nine of the nickers, some commentators have taken the MS. *fife* to be an error for *fifel*, "sea monster." Grein, Bib., was the first to make this suggestion, citing l. 104. Bugge, Beitr. XII, 367f., proposed *þær ic on fifelgeban* (with *-geban* explained as an old form of *geofon*, "ocean"). Trautmann reads *fifla gebann*, "den heerbann der Fiflen."   **423 wean ahso-don]** "They were looking for trouble." Cf. *wean ahsode*, l. 1206. Klaeber, MLN. XVI, 29f., compares the use of *secan* in ll. 1989, 3001.   **424 gramum]** This construction, with dative object of *forgrindan*, is not elsewhere found in Anglo-Saxon.   **wið Grendel]** The preposition *wið* is construed with the dative in ll. 425, 426, and to remove the inconsistency of case, Kemble II, Ettmüller, Trautmann, and Holthausen (1, 2 ed.) emend here to *wið Grendle*. So also Krüger, Beitr. IX, 571, and Andrew, pp. 62f. But a similar incon-sistency occurs in ll. 1977f.; see the note on these lines.   **425–426 gehegan ðing]** For this legal term, "to hold a meeting," cf. Andreas 157, 930, Maxims I, 18.   **428 bene]** Used in the sense of "favor (granted in answer to a peti-tion)," a meaning of *bēn* not recorded in Bos.-Tol. Klaeber, Anglia L, 121, compares Ælfric's Lives of Saints (ed. W. W. Skeat), I, 80, 516, *ac uton swa þeah biddan þas bena æt gode.*   **431–432]** The MS. reading *þ ic mote ana minra eorla gedriht 7 þes hearda heap* is meaningless. Kemble II suggested transferring *ond* to the beginning of l. 431b, as in the text, and so Grein and later edd. But Andrew, p. 150, points out that the *gedryht* phrase is elsewhere found with *mid*, ll. 357, 633, 662, 1672. Thorpe had supplied *mid* at the beginning of l. 431b but had left *ond* in l. 432a.   **434 wæpna ne recceð]** "Has no regard for weapons." This may mean either that Grendel does not fear weapons, or that he has no love for them, no desire to possess them himself. See Cosijn, Aant., p. 8. The latter meaning, which seems the more probable, is supported by Daniel 201, Descent into Hell 37, Riddle 77, 5, Meters 12, 31, etc.   **435–436]** The punctuation in the text, with ll. 435b–436b taken as a parenthesis, follows Arnold and Sedgefield.   **440 gelyfan]** Earle translates as "resign himself to," which is evidently the intended meaning. Klaeber, Mod. Phil. III, 452, cites ll. 685b-687 as illustrating the general sentiment of the present passage.   **442 Wen]** See l. 338, note.   **443 guðsele]** Bugge,

Tidskrift VIII, 47f., suggested *goldsele,* and so Holthausen (1 ed.).   Geotena]
For *Geata,* "of the Geats," and Trautmann, Holthausen (1 ed.), Schücking, and
Sedgefield (3 ed.) so emend. Grein, Bib., Grundtvig, Heyne, Wülker, Socin,
Wyatt, and Sedgefield (1, 2 ed.) emend to *Geatena.* But for *eo* as a variant
spelling of *ēa,* cf. *abreot,* 1. 2930, and for the weak gen. plur. form, cf. the forms
Eotena, ll. 1072, 1088, 1141 (as well as the analogical dat. plur. *Eotenum,*
ll. 902, 1145), beside the strong form *Eota* (*lond*) in the Alfredian translation
of Bede's Ecclesiastical History, Book IV, ch. 16 (ed. T. Miller, I, 308, 11).
Rieger, ZfdPh. III, 400f., suggests that the form *Geotena* here is due to scribal
confusion between the Geats and the Jutes. This, then, would be the reverse
of what we find in Bede, Book I, ch. 15 (ed. T. Miller, I, 52, 4ff.), where the
forms *Geatum, Geata* are applied to the Jutes. (Another explanation of the
Geat- forms in the Bede is given by Kemp Malone, MLRev. XX [1925], 1 ff.)
445 mægen Hreðmanna] The MS. has *mægen hreð manna.* The earlier edd.
analysed this as *mægen Hreðmanna,* "the host of the Hreth-men" (all but
Grundtvig taking it as referring to the Danes), and so Heyne, Wülker, Holder,
Socin, Wyatt, Holthausen (1, 2 ed.), and Chambers. Schücking, Eng. Stud.
XXXIX, 102, and in his edition, reads *mægenhreð manna,* "the pride of men."
In his rejection of *mægen Hreðmanna,* Schücking was guided largely by Schröder's
observation, ZfdA. XLIII, 366, that (except for adjectives in *un-*) the second
element of a compound does not alliterate in preference to the first. Holthausen
(3–6 ed.), Klaeber (1 ed.), and von Schaubert follow Schücking. Trautmann had emended to *mægenþryð manna.* But it is tempting to find a tribal
name in this line, as a variation of *Geotena leode,* and Malone, JEGPh. XXVII,
323, has argued in favor of the old reading *mægen Hreðmanna,* taking the
Hreðmen to be the Geats. He equates *Hreðmen* with the name *Hreiðgotar*
of the Old Norse sources (cf. also the forms *Hreðgotum* and *Hræda here,* Widsith
57, 120) and argues that the name *Hreiðgotar* originally referred to the Gautar
in southern Sweden, only later being applied to tribes south of the Baltic.
These arguments are too complicated to be adequately dealt with here, but see
Malone's earlier discussions in The Literary History of Hamlet I, 151ff., PMLA
XL (1925), 812f., and MLRev. XX (1925), 8ff. Malone's identification of the
Hreðmen with the Geats was rejected by A. Johannson, Acta Philologica
Scandinavica VII (1932), 119ff., who pointed out, among other considerations,
that in Widsith 57f. the words *Hreðgotum* and *Geatum* appear to refer to different
tribes. But Klaeber (3 ed.) and Holthausen (7, 8 ed.) read *mægen Hreðmanna,*
with Malone's interpretation. If *mægen Hreðmanna* is the proper reading,
it is very unlikely that it refers to the Danes, since l. 444*b* is a formula complete
in itself, and l. 445*a* must therefore be taken as a variation of l. 443*b.* Cf.
ll. 1238, 1381, 1676, 1891, and see Schücking, Svk., p. 31, and Klaeber, note.
It should be observed that Schücking's reading *mægenhreð manna* is not an
"emendation" (as Malone, PMLA XL, 812, and Eng. Studies XV, 150, calls
it), since here, as elsewhere in Beowulf, the spacing of the manuscript affords
no clue to the proper word division; see Introd..p. xix. Schücking's reading has,
in fact, much to commend it, and a choice between it and *mægen Hreðmanna* is
difficult.   **445–446** minne ... hafalan hydan] Not "to bury me," as many

edd. (including Sedgefield and Chambers) have explained it, but rather "to cover my head," an allusion to the custom, prevalent in Scandinavian antiquity, of covering the head of a corpse at the time of burial. See Konrath, Archiv XCIX, 417 f., and Hoops, Eng. Stud. LIV, 19ff., who points out that in Bede's Ecclesiastical History, Book IV, chapter 19, St. Æthelthryth, abbess of Ely, who died in 679, is represented as having been buried in this fashion. The relevant words in the Latin text, part of the narrative of the translation of St. Æthelthryth to the church at Ely sixteen years after her death, are *Sed et discooperto vultus indumento, monstraverunt mihi etiam vulnus incisurae . . . curatum* (ed. C. Plummer, I, 245, 32ff.). A different explanation of *hafalan hydan* has recently been given by Mezger, MLN. LXVI, 36ff., who regards it as a reference to the custom, attested by Scandinavian sources, of cutting off the head of one's enemy in the course of the blood feud.   **447** dreore] So Kemble II and later edd., following Grundtvig, tr., p. 273. Thorkelin, retaining the MS. *deore fahne*, had translated, "cruore imbuta."   **450** morhopu] Cf. *fenhopu*, l. 764. For the element *-hop* in both these compounds, see the first definition in the N.E.D. s.v. *hope*, sb.², "a piece of enclosed land, e.g. in the midst of fens or marshes, or of waste land generally," and particularly the quotation from *c*1200 with its reference to *unam hopam marisci* (=*fenhop*?).

451–500

451 feorme] The usual meaning of *feorm* is "food, sustenance," but Klaeber, note, suggests that the word here means "taking care of, disposal"; that is, the Danes will not need to have a funeral for Beowulf if Grendel overcomes him. See also Gering, ZfdPh. XII, 124, and Cosijn, Aant., pp. 8f., who explains *ne . . . leng* as meaning "not at all."   **454** Hrædlan] Gen. sing. of *Hrædla*, a weak variant of *Hreðel* (gen. sing. *Hreðles*), the usual and more original form of the name. In l. 1485 the strong gen. sing. *Hrædles* occurs. We find a similar variation between *Hræd-* and *Hreð-* in the forms *Hræda here*, Widsith 120, and *Hreðgotan*, Widsith 57, *Hreða here*, Elene 58; here, however, the form in *Hræd-* is apparently the older. On the variation between *Hreðel* and *Hrædla*, see especially Bugge, ZfdPh. IV, 197f., and G. Binz, Beitr. XX (1895), 164; on *Hræda here* and *Hreðgotan* in Widsith, see Malone, Widsith, pp. 168f. **457** For gewyrhtum] The MS. *fere fyhtum*, which makes some sense if *fere* is taken as the equivalent of *for* ("For fighting's sake," Arnold), does not alliterate, and various emendations have been proposed. Thorpe, Arnold, and Schücking, reading *Fore fyhtum*, emend *wine* to *freond*, following Ettmüller, Sc.; an objection to this reading, pointed out by Klaeber, Anglia Beibl. XXIV, 290, is that *freond* does not occur as a vocative in Anglo-Saxon poetry. Carleton Brown, PMLA LIII, 912, proposed *Fore fyhtum þu, freowine Beowulf*. But *wine min* is a standard formula, as in ll. 530, 1704, Genesis 824, etc., and most edd. therefore retain *wine* in l. 457b and provide an alliterating word in l. 457a. Grundtvig suggested emending to *For werefyhtum*, "for defensive fights," and so Grein, ed., Ettmüller (*werefeohtum*), Wülker, Holder, Socin, Wyatt, and von Schaubert. Hoops, Eng. Stud. LXX, 77ff., also accepts this emendation, as explaining better than any other the MS. reading *fere fyhtum*. Klaeber (3 ed.), second supplement (1950), p. 466, suggests that if *For werefyhtum* is to be adopted, *þu* is to be dropped or transferred to the second half-line. Grein, Bib., read *Fore wyhtum* ("wegen der Wichte, der Dämonen ... ?" Spr. II, 704), and similarly Holthausen (7, 8 ed.) reads *Fer wyhtum*. Cf. l. 3038, where *wiht* is used of the dragon. Holthausen (1, 2 ed.) emends to *For wælslyhtum*; Holthausen (3–6 ed.) to *For* (or *Fer*) *wigum*; Sedgefield (1, 2 ed.) to *Fore wyrhtum*, "for good cause." Trautmann emends to *For gewyrhtum* ("because of deeds done," Klaeber, JEGPh. VI, 191f.), and so Chambers, Klaeber, and Sedgefield (3 ed.). Of all these proposals, Trautmann's seems the least open to objection and has been adopted in the text. As Sievers pointed out, Beitr. IX, 138, we expect in this half-line a concept parallel to that of l. 458*a*. Reading *For gewyrhtum*, we may translate, "On account of deeds done (that is, of gratitude for what I did for your father) and on account of good will, you have sought us."   **459** Gesloh þin fæder, etc.] Klaeber, MLN. XVI, 28f., translates, "thy father brought about (or, brought on his head) by fight the greatest feud," and suggests that *fæhðe* is to be taken as gen. plur. The usual perfective meaning of *geslēan* is "to win, obtain, achieve by fighting" (cf. l. 2996, Widsith 38f., 44, Brunanburh 3f., etc.), but this meaning is less appropriate here. For metrical reasons, Holthausen (1–7 ed.), Sedgefield (1, 2 ed.), and Schücking (10–14 ed.) emend to *þin fæder gesloh*.   **461** Wedera] A reference to the Geats is in order here, and the alliteration indicates the proper emendation. Grundtvig first proposed *Wedera*, and so Heyne (2–4 ed.) and most later edd. Holthausen (8 ed.) reads *wigana* as a variant form of *wigena*; see also his note in Studia Neophilologica XIV, 160. The meaning of ll. 461*b*–462 seems to be that the Geats were forced to disown Ecgtheow because of their fear of a feud with the Wylfings; see Klaeber, Anglia XXVIII, 440. But Malone, MLQuart. I, 39f., would emend to *Wulgara*, gen. plur. of a form *Wulgaras* (< **Wulgwaras*), a name for the Wylfings; he suggests that Ecgtheow was a Wylfing by birth, who was banished by his own people after the slaying of Heatholaf in order to forestall an act of vengeance by Heatholaf's kinsmen. But *herebroga* as a term for private vengeance seems somewhat forced.   **465** Deniga] So Thorpe and later edd., except Grundtvig, Heyne, Ettmüller, Socin, Schücking, and von Schaubert, who retain the MS. *Deninga*.   **466** ginne] This emendation, first made by Ettmüller, Sc., is adopted by Arnold, Holder, Socin (6, 7 ed.), Trautmann, Holthausen, and Klaeber. Schücking and von Schaubert retain *gimme* as a variant form of *ginne*. Grein, Grundtvig, Heyne, Wülker, Socin (5 ed.), Wyatt, and Chambers retain *gimme* as the first element of a compound adjective *gimmerice*, "jewel-rich"; but, as Hoops, p. 73, points out, the combining form of *gim* is always *gim-*, never *gimme-*. Sedgefield emends to *gumena rice*.   **470** Siððan þa fæhðe] With *ic* to be supplied in sense from l. 471. That is, Hrothgar paid a wergild on behalf of Ecgtheow, who in return swore certain oaths (l. 472*b*), the nature of which is not quite clear. Malone, MLQuart. I, 38, believes that Ecgtheow entered Hrothgar's service; it is, however, possible that the obligations which he assumed were less specific.   feo þingode] See *fea þingian*, l. 156, and note.   **475** hynðo] Gen. plur.,

parallel to *færniða*. See l. 70, note.   **479** þone dolsceaðan] Andrew, p. 93,
would take this phrase in a generic sense, as meaning "any rash assailant."
But the reference is clearly to Grendel.   **485** þonne dæg lixte] A variation
of *on morgentid*. See Klaeber, Archiv CXV, 179.   **487** heorudreore] On
the reading of transcript A, see Malone, PMLA LXIV, 1196.   **488** þe þa
deað fornam] Holthausen, Chambers, Klaeber, and von Schaubert take *þe*
as a causal conjunction, and so also Hoops, p. 74. See Klaeber, Mod. Phil.
III, 453, who translates, "since death had taken them away," citing ll. 1435f.
and Riddle 9, 11f. E. A. Kock, The English Relative Pronouns (Lund, 1897),
p. 57, translates, "in proportion as death took those away." The older interpretation (as found, for example, in Heyne) took *þe* as a relative.   **489b–
490a**] The MS. reads 7 *on sæl meoto sige hreð secgū*. As elsewhere in the
manuscript, the spacing gives no clue to the proper word division; see Introd.,
p. xix. In the interpretation of l. 489b the edd. and commentators divide into
two main groups, those who read *ond on sæl meoto*, with *sæl* taken as a noun,
and those who read *ond onsæl meoto*, with *onsæl* taken as a verb. Disregarding
the early edd., we may begin with Körner, Eng. Stud. II, 250f., who explained
sæl as a noun, "joy," and *meoto* as a verb, translating, "sei nur auf heiterkeit
bedacht, auf den ruhm, der dir nebst deinen mannen aus deinem siege erwachsen
wird." Körner is followed by Kock, Anglia XLII, 105, XLIV, 100, who,
adopting Klaeber's emendation of *meoto* to *meota* (see below), translates, "think
on joy, on conquest's glory for the men." Similarly Moore, JEGPh. XVIII,
205f., who, retaining the MS. *meoto*, translates, "think of good fortune, victory-
renown to men." So also Holthausen (3–5 ed.) and apparently von Schaubert.
This interpretation takes *meoto* (*meota*) as the imperative of *metgian, metian*,
"meditate" (Bos-Tol., p. 682), which however is not elsewhere followed by *on*.
Earlier Klaeber, JEGPh. VI, 192f., reading *on sæl meota* in l. 489b, had translated *on sæl* as "joyfully" (see *on lust*, l. 618, and note), and had emended
secgum, l. 490a, to *secga*: "joyfully think of the victory-fame of men." So also
Holthausen (2 ed.). Holthausen, ZfdPh. XXXVII, 114, adopting Kluge's
emendation to *sigehreðgum*, l. 490a (see below), and the reading *on sælum*,
suggested by Kemble II, made a further emendation of his own, *weota* (imperative of a verb *witian*, "to determine"; cf. *weotode*, l. 1936) for the MS. *meoto*.
The resulting reading, *ond on sælum weota sigehreðgum secgum*, etc., he translates, "und im glück (wohlsein) bestimme den siegberühmten männern, wie
dich dein sinn treibt." So also Holthausen (1 ed.). Whitbread, MLRev.
XXXVII, 481, also reading *on sælum*, emends the MS. *meoto* to *eowa*. With
further emendations in l. 490a, his reading is *ond on sælum eowa sige* (acc.
plur.) *Hreðsecga*, "in gladness reveal the victorious achievements of the Geats."
Schücking, Eng. Stud. XXXIX, 103, and in his edition, accepts Holthausen's
weota but otherwise retains the MS. reading, translating *on sæl* as "bei gele-
genheit"; his translation of the entire passage is "und wenn die günstige gele-
genheit da ist, bestimme den leuten siegruhm," etc. Sedgefield (1 ed.) emends to
ond on sæl mota, "speak, when the time suits," and, since the verb *mōtian* is
intransitive, reads *sigehreðig secgum* in l. 490a; in his 2d ed. he emends to
ond on sælum teo sigehreð secgum, "joyfully award victory to warriors"; in his

3d ed. he reads *ond on sæl ne ofteoh sigehreð secgum*, "Do not at this moment (or on this occasion) withhold thy glory (*i.e.*, thy glorious presence) from the warriors." Andrew, p. 147, proposes a more violent alteration of the text, *ond on sæl meotod sigehreð sele*, "and may God in due time grant glory." Finally, two commentators take *sæl* to mean "hall," Patzig, Anglia XLVII, 97f., who emends to *on sæle beota* and translates, "Sprich gross vom Siegesruhm im Saale den Männern," and Du Bois, MLN. L, 89, who translates, "and in the hall reckon on victory for men [over Grendel]." Holthausen (8 ed.) adopts Patzig's *beota* but retains the MS. *on sæl*. So much for the interpretations of this passage which read *sæl* as a noun; those which read *onsæl* as a verb, "untie, unloose," i.e., "reveal," are almost as many and varied, beginning with Dietrich, ZfdA. XI, 411. If *onsæl* is a verb, then *meoto* (if that is indeed the correct reading) is probably the object, parallel to *sigehreð*. So Bugge, Tidskrift VIII, 292, who took *meoto* as acc. plur. of a noun *met*, neuter, the equivalent of *gemet*; the words *onsæl meoto* would then mean "speak courteous, well-chosen words." Similarly Trautmann, BVE., p. 154, and in his edition. Heyne (4 ed.), Socin, Wyatt, Holder (2 ed.), and Chambers, also reading *onsæl meoto*, take *meoto* as acc. plur. of a neuter noun *met*, "thought, intention." Grein, Spr. II, 240, Hoops, Bwst., pp. 33ff., and Klaeber (3 ed.) follow Dietrich in assuming a noun *me(o)tu*, feminine, related to *metgian* and to Gothic *miton* and meaning "thought." See also Klaeber, MLN. XXXIV, 132. Holthausen, who in his 2d–5th ed. had read *sæl* as a noun (see above), later read *onsæl* as a verb; in Anglia Beibl. XL, 90, he emends to *onsæl meotod*, "reveal fate" (cf. Waldere I, 19), and so in his 6th ed. In Anglia Beibl. XLII, 249f., he retains the MS. *onsæl meoto*, with *meoto* taken as an adverbial gen. plur. of *met*, and translates, "verkünde massvoll (mit Mass) den Männern Siegruhm." In his 7th ed. he reads *onsæl meodogal*, with *meodogal* an adjective. Kluge, Beitr. IX, 188, retaining *onsæl meoto* and translating "entseile die etikette" (following H. Leo in Heyne, 1–3 ed.), in l. 490a emends the MS. *sigehreð secgum* to *sigehreð(e)gum*, "to the victorious ones," and so Holder (1 ed.). Bright, MLN. XXXI, 217ff., emended *meoto* to *mętto*, citing the compound *ofermętto* and translating, "disclose . . . what thou hast in mind." An ingenious proposal has been made by Imelmann, Eng. Stud. LXV, 195f., who would read *onsæl me to*, translating, "enthülle mir Deinen Ruhm (unter) den Männern"; see also his further note in Eng. Stud. LXVI, 321ff. But it seems most likely that *meoto* is correct and that it is a noun, however it is to be translated. The general meaning of ll. 489–490 is apparently "Sit down now to the feast and tell us about yourself, as your mind may inspire you." For a more complete survey of the scholarship on these lines, see Imelmann, Eng. Stud. LXV, 190ff., and Hoops, Bwst., pp. 33ff. **496 wered]** Such a noun is found nowhere else, but the adjective *weorod, wered*, "sweet," is not infrequent (see Bos.-Tol., p. 1193), and the edd. explain *wered* here as meaning "sweet drink." **498 duguð]** Holthausen, Archiv CV, 366, would emend to *duguðe*, gen. sing., with *duguðe Dena ond Wedera* explained as a variation of *hæleða*. Klaeber, Archiv CVIII, 370, retaining the MS. *duguð*, explains *hæleða . . . duguð* as an example of an "apparently incongruent parallel construction," as in ll. 642ff., Andreas 869f.,

Exodus 326ff., etc. These interpretations presuppose that *duguð* has the usual meaning, "body of retainers." Cosijn, Aant., p. 10, however, took *duguð* ("splendor, glory"? see Grein-Köhler, p. 132, s.v. *duguð* 4) as a variation of *dream*, citing *duguðe ond dreamas*, Homiletic Fragment II, 11 (Records III, 224). Cf. also *help ond hælu hæleþa cynne, duguð ond drohtað*, Guthlac 683f.
499 Unferð] This name occurs four times in Beowulf, here and in ll. 530, 1165, 1488, and although wherever it alliterates it alliterates with a vowel, it is invariably spelled with initial *H*-. Rieger, ZfdPh. III, 414, proposed to emend to *Unferð*, and so all later edd. except Heyne, Ettmüller, Arnold, Wülker, and Sedgefield. There can be no doubt that this was the form intended by the poet, and the scribe's use of *Hun*- in this name is commonly attributed to the influence of names in *Hūn*-, such as *Hunbeorht, Hunfrith, Hunlaf*, etc. Three other names (all, to be sure, non-Germanic) which are regularly spelled with *H*- in the manuscripts likewise have vocalic alliteration, *Heliseus*, Juliana 25, 160, 673, *Holofernus*, Judith 7, 21, 46, etc., and *Herodes*, Andreas 1324, Fates of the Apostles 36, Juliana 293; cf. also *Hebreos*, Daniel 1 (elsewhere spelled with *E*-). These non-Germanic names are left unemended in the present edition, but it seems best to emend to *Unferð* here and elsewhere in Beowulf. In Beowulf, also, the common nouns *ondlean*, "reward, requital," and *ondslyht*, "onslaught," are invariably spelled with initial *h*- in the manuscript, ll. 1541, 2094, 2929, 2972.

501–550

501 onband beadurune] "Unbound a battle-rune," i.e., began a quarrel. For this use of *-rūn*, cf. *wælrune (hygerune) ne mað*, Elene 28, 1098, and *eahtian inwitrune*, Juliana 609f. **Beowulfes sið]** Holthausen (7, 8 ed.) emends to *beornes sið*. **505 gehedde]** For *gehēgde*, preterite subjunctive, "should perform, carry out," and Holthausen (2–8 ed.) so emends. Holthausen (1 ed.), Klaeber, and Sedgefield (3 ed.) emend to *gehede* (= *gehēgde*); Schücking and von Schaubert retain the MS. *gehedde* as a variant form of *gehēgde*. **510ff. inc ... belean ... sorhfullne sið]** The same construction (dative of person and accusative of thing) as with the simple verb *lēan*; cf. *Ðone siðfæt him ... logon*, l. 202f. **516 wylmum]** The MS. *wintrys wylm* is too short for a half-line, and we expect a dative here, parallel to *yþum*. The emendation in the text follows Kluge's suggestion, adopted by Holder (1 ed.), Klaeber, Holthausen (6–8 ed.), and von Schaubert. Cf. *yðum stilde, wæteres wælmum*, Andreas 451f. Möller, Das altenglische Volksepos I, 131, II, xxiii, emended to *þurh wintrys wylm* on the model of l. 1693, and so Holthausen (1–5 ed.), Sedgefield (1, 2 ed.). This reading, however, obscures the parallelism in ll. 515b-516a. Other recent edd. emend to *wintrys wylme*, following Thorpe. **519 Heaþoræmas]** Grein and most later edd. emend the MS. *heaþoræmes* to either *Heaþoræmas* or *Heaþoreamas*, as proposed by P. A. Munch in 1850; see his Samlede Afhandlinger II (Christiania, 1874), 371. For the latter form, cf. Widsith 63. Malone, Anglia LIV, 98, and Hoops, p. 79, would retain the ending in *-es* as a late weakening of the acc. plur. ending; so also Klaeber (3 ed.) and von Schaubert. **520 Ⓡ]** For *eþel*, as also in ll. 913, 1702 (Ⓡ*weard*).

524 Beanstanes] Bugge, ZfdPh. IV, 198, suggested *Beahstan* as the proper form of this name, and so Holder (1 ed.) and Holthausen (7, 8 ed.). The name *Beahstan, Beagstan* occurs several times in charters and other documents; see Searle, Onomasticon Anglo-Saxonicum, p. 83. As an alternative, Bugge proposed *Banstan*; so also Krüger, Beitr. IX, 572f., who explains the form as meaning "einen wie bein und stein harten." **525** to þe] Not "for you," as we might expect, but "from you, at your hands." See l. 158, note. wyrsan geþingea] Both words are gen. plur. after *wene*. For the meaning of *geþingea*, see l. 398, note. Rieger, Germania IX, 303, ZfdPh. III, 389, would emend to *geþinges*, and so Holder (1 ed.), Trautmann, Holthausen (1, 2, 7, 8 ed.), and Sedgefield. **530** Unferð] See l. 499, note. **534** earfeþo] Because *earfeþo*, "hardships," is not a natural parallel to *merestrengo*, Heyne (1–3 ed.), glossary, suggested emending to *eafoð*, "power, might." Bugge, ZfdPh. IV, 198, proposed *eafeðo*, acc. plur., and so Heyne (4 ed.), Holder (1 ed.), Trautmann, and Sedgefield (3 ed.). Cf. l. 902, where the MS. *earfoð* is apparently an error for *eafoð*. Other edd. retain the MS. *earfeþo*, and Bryan, JEGPh. XIX, 85, points out that this reading is supported by *nearoþearfe dreah*, l. 422. **535** gecwædon] "Agreed"; see Bos.-Tol., Supp., p. 307, s.v. *ge-cweþan* IV (1). **540** hronfixas] Schücking, Bedeutungslehre, pp. 55f., pointing out that whales were unlikely opponents for Beowulf and his rival, suggests *horn-* for the MS. *hron-*, citing Andreas 370. **543** no] As Andrew, p. 46, remarks, the MS. *no*, rather than *ne*, is surprising here in the coordinate clause. Most edd. put a comma after l. 543a, as in the text, but Wyatt, Sedgefield, and Chambers punctuate with a semicolon, producing a rather abrupt effect. Cf. *no . . . no*, ll. 972–974, where this difficulty is not felt. **544** Ða] Andrew, p. 87, would read *Swa* for the MS. *ða*. Cf. ll. 99, 144, 189, etc. **548** ondhwearf] The MS. has 7 *hwearf*. Grein took *hwearf* as an adjective, "versatilis, volubilis"; see Spr. II, 118. So also Ettmüller and Wülker. Other edd. read *ondhwearf* as a verb, "turned." A more regular form would be *onhwearf*, as in Christ 618, and Trautmann, Holthausen (3–8 ed.), and Sedgefield (3 ed.) so emend.

551–600

552b] Holthausen supplies *þæt me* before *on*, following Sievers, Beitr. IX, 138. But for a defence of the MS. reading, with *licsyrce*, l. 550b, parallel to *beadohrægl* and *gefremede* parallel to *læg*, see Kock, Anglia XLV, 112f. **562** Næs] A variant form of *nealles, nalæs*, opening a new sentence as in ll. 43, 1076, etc. Holthausen (1, 2 ed.) emends to *nalæs*. It is possible, but not necessary, to explain *Næs*, l. 2262, in the same way. **563b–564a**] Holthausen (7, 8 ed.) emends to the subjunctive forms *þegen* and *ymbsæten*, following Sievers's unpublished edition of the poem. **565** mecum] Plural with singular meaning, since Beowulf presumably had only one sword. For similar plurals, cf. *sweordum*, l. 567, *bearnum ond broðrum*, l. 1074, *hiltum*, l. 1574, *eacnum ecgum*, l. 2140, and probably also *mundum*, l. 1461. **566** be yðlafe] "Among the leavings of the waves," i.e., the sand? See Bugge, Beitr. XII, 88f., and Cosijn, Aant., pp. 11f. But Hoops, Bwst., pp. 98f., takes *be yðlafe* as meaning simply "along the shore"; he cites Exodus 585f., where the *yðlaf* is apparently to be distinguished from the *sælaf*. **567** sweordum] So Kemble and most later edd. Malone, PMLA LXIV, 1197, suggests that the MS. had *sweodū*, as in transcript A. **568** ymb brontne ford] "Across the high sea." This sense of *ford* is not found elsewhere in Anglo-Saxon, but it follows naturally from the general meaning of the word, "a path through the water from one body of land to another." T. B. Haber, A Comparative Study of the Beowulf and the Æneid (Princeton, 1931), p. 69, points out that Virgil uses the Latin *vadum* eighteen times with this meaning. With the adjective *bront* as applied to the sea, we may compare *heare sæ*, gen. sing. (emended from J's reading *heah sæ*), Meters 11, 3, as well as the Latin *altum* (*mare*) and the use of the Old Icelandic cognate *brattr* to refer to lofty waves. Since elsewhere in Anglo-Saxon *bront* is applied only to ships (l. 238, Andreas 273, Elene 238), Sedgefield, MLRev. V, 286f., and in his edition, takes *brontne* as an absolute adjective here, "around the high one," i.e., the ship, and emends *ford* to *forð*, "henceforth" (cf. l. 948, Widsith 43). Holthausen, Archiv CV, 366f., had previously proposed to emend *brontne* to *bradne*, and so Trautmann. **570b**] Holder and Holthausen treat l. 570b as a parenthesis. The question is whether it was the light of dawn, or the subsiding of the waves, which enabled Beowulf to see the shore. **573b**] For this phrase, cf. Andreas 460, Christ and Satan 282. **574a** Hwæþere] In spite of the similar use of *Hwæþre* in l. 890, Bugge, Tidskrift VIII, 48, proposed to emend to *Swa ðær*. Trautmann emends to *þeah þe*, introducing a subordinate clause. But see Sievers, Beitr. IX, 138, who defends the MS. reading. **574b**] To avoid the double alliteration in the second half-line, Rieger, ZfdPh. VII, 8f., proposed to read *mece* for the MS. *sweorde*. Holthausen, ZfdPh. XXXVII, 114, would read *abreat* for the MS. *ofsloh*, and so in his 1st ed. E. von Schaubert, Literaturblatt LVII, 27f., and in her edition, defends the double alliteration here and in ll. 1151b, 2916b; she would also recognize double alliteration in ll. 1251b, 1351b, although in these last two half-lines it is possible to regard *sum* and *oðer* as nonalliterating words. **577** mannon] For *mannan*, acc. sing. of *manna*, Bos.-Tol., p. 669. Other examples of -*on* for -*an* are *hæfton*, l. 788, *haton*, l. 849, and *balwon*, l. 977. **581** wadu] So Kemble II and most later edd., following Grundtvig, tr., p. 275. **583** brogan] Construed by most edd. (including Schücking, Sedgefield, and von Schaubert) as acc. sing.; Klaeber takes it as either acc. sing. or acc. plur., and in Mod. Phil. III, 238, explains *searoniða* and *billa brogan* as equivalent terms of variation expressed by different grammatical forms. But *brogan* is best construed as a genitive, grammatically parallel to *searoniða*. Wyatt, Chambers, and Hoops, p. 83, take it as gen. sing., but Kock, Anglia XLIV, 100f., with less probability, as a gen. plur. in -*an*. Translate: "Not at all have I heard tell, concerning you, of such insidious conflicts, of [such] terror of swords." **586** fela] It is evident that a word has been omitted by the scribe, and Grein and most later edd. supply *fela*. Kluge, Beitr. IX, 188, suggested *geflites*, and so Holder (1 ed.), Holthausen (1–6 ed.), Schücking (9, 10 ed.), and Chambers. **593** hynðo] For *hynða*, gen. plur. (as also in l. 475), parallel to *gryra*, l. 591. Kock, Anglia XLII, 105, points out that ll. 809ff. and ll. 2003ff. also contain a form of *gefremman* together with *fela* and two parallel genitives; he compares the similar constructions in ll. 164ff. and Guthlac 585f. **596 eower leode]** The form *eower* is here used as a possessive dependent on *leode*, gen. sing. The feminine *leod*, in the sense of "people, tribe," is usually plural, as in ll. 205, 634, 938, etc., but here, as well as in l. 599 and in Genesis 2075, it is used in the singular. Ettmüller, Sc., emended to *eowra leoda*; in his edition he reads *eowerra leoda*. Trautmann, Holthausen (1, 2 ed.), and Sedgefield, accepting *leode* as gen. sing., emend to *eowre leode*; see Trautmann's note in BVE., pp. 157f. **599 lust wigeð]** On this phrase, see especially Moore, JEGPh. XVIII, 207f., who translates, "has (the object of) his desire, has his own way." For the use of *wegan* here, he cites ll. 1931f., Fates of the Apostles 86f., Guthlac 60f., and Gifts of Men 2f. For *lust* in the sense of "object of one's desire," Moore cites the Alfredian Boethius (ed. W. J. Sedgefield, 88, 17f.), *gif he þonne lust begite ond þæt þurhtio þæt he þonne getiohhad hæfð*, and the use of the word as a gloss of Latin *desiderium*, Psalm lxxvii. 29, in the Vespasian Psalter (ed. H. Sweet, Oldest English Texts, p. 297). Kemble II suggested *on lust wigeð*, "he fights at his pleasure" (cf. l. 618), and so Heyne (3, 4 ed.), Holder (1 ed.), Socin (5 ed.), and Wyatt. Socin (6, 7 ed.) and Holthausen (1, 2, 7 ed.) also supply *on* but read *wigeð*, glossed by Socin under a verb *wegan*, "to fight" (cf. *gewegan*, l. 2400, and O. Icel. *vega*), by Holthausen under *wegan*, "to carry." **600 sendeþ]** The meaning of this verb is not immediately apparent, and a number of emendations have been proposed. Holthausen, Anglia Beibl. X, 267, proposed *swenceþ*, and so Holthausen (1, 2 ed.) and Sedgefield (3 ed.); Trautmann, BVE., p. 158, and in his edition, reads *swelgeþ*; Sedgefield (1, 2 ed.) emends to *serweþ*, as a form of *sierwan* (cf. l. 161); Kemble (2 ed.) reads *onsendeð*, and Mackie, MLRev. XXXIV, 518, also advocates this reading, citing l. 2266. Imelmann, Eng. Stud. LXVI, 324ff., proposed *snedeþ* (= *snædeþ*), and this is accepted by Klaeber (3 ed.) and Hoops, Bwst., pp. 99f. But, as E. von Schaubert points out, Literaturblatt LVII, 28, such a form as *snēdeþ*, with *ē* as the *i*-mutation of Anglo-Saxon *ā*, West Gmc. *ai*, would be unparalleled in Beowulf. Holthausen (7, 8 ed.) emends to *snædeþ*, but in the addenda to his 8th ed., Archiv CLXXXVII, 125, he would read *swendeþ*. This last reading, previously adopted by Ettmüller, had been advocated by Holthausen in Literaturblatt XVI, 82, but had been withdrawn by him in Anglia Beibl. X, 267. The verb *swendan* is not recorded in Anglo-Saxon, but cf. O.H.G. *swentan*, M.H.G. *swenden*, "to destroy." Schücking, Eng. Stud. XXXIX, 103f., proposed to retain the MS. *sendan* as the equivalent of *forsendan*, l. 904. Klaeber, Anglia Beibl. XL, 24f., points out that Old Icelandic *senda* occurs in the Poetic Edda (Hávamál, st. 145, *veiztu hvé biðja skal, veiztu hvé blóta skal? veiztu hvé senda skal, veiztu hvé soa skal?*), apparently as a synonym of *soa* and *blóta*, both of which mean "to kill, to sacrifice." See also H. Falk, Arkiv för nordisk Filologi V (1889), 111f. In view of this Icelandic parallel, we are probably justified in retaining the MS. *sendeþ* in the sense of "put to death."

601–650

603 guþe] Taken by most edd. and by Hoops, p. 84, as dat. sing., "in battle," but by Klaeber, Mod. Phil. III, 453, Holthausen (2–8 ed.), and Sedgefield as

acc. sing., parallel to *eafoð ond ellen*.   **605** oþres dogores] Adverbial, or
dependent on *morgenleoht?* See l. 219, note.   **608** geoce] Acc. sing., object
of *gelyfde*. Cf. ll. 627f., 909, 1272f., and Waldere II, 27, *helpe gelifeð*.   **613**
cynna] Gen. plur. of *cyn*, "what is fitting, etiquette," a noun formed from the
adjective *cyn*, "suitable, proper"; see Bos.-Tol., Supp., p. 140, s.v. *cyn*, adj.
Cf. *cynnum* in the Paris Psalter, Psalm 138, 1, 1, and perhaps also *cynna*,
Genesis 2433.   **617** bæd hine bliðne] With ellipsis of the verb "to be," as in
ll. 1783f., 1855ff., 2363, 2659f., etc.   But Sedgefield, MLRev. XXVII, 448f.,
and in his 3d ed., pointing out that there is no other example of the omission
of "to be" after *biddan*, emends to *bædde hine bliðne*, "pressed him, glad (to
accept)." Grundtvig suggested emending the MS. *bliðne* to *bliðsian*, "to be
joyful"; similarly, Trautmann emends to *bliðsan*.   **618** on lust] For *on*
with the accusative in semi-adverbial use, as here, cf. *on sped*, l. 873, *on gylp*,
l. 1749, etc.   **619** symbel ond seleful] Mackie, MLRev. XXXIV, 516,
suggests that this is an example of hendiadys, "the tankard of drink." See ll.
104, 1195, and notes.   **627** gelyfde] See l. 608, note. Here *frofre*, acc.
sing., is the object.   **630** guþe] Gen. sing.; cf. *siðes gefysde*, Elene 260.
634–635 þæt ic . . . geworhte] "That I would altogether win the good will of
your people." See Kock, Anglia XLII, 106, who cites *Nu þu willan hæfst,
hyldo geworhte heofoncyninges*, Genesis 504f.   **643**] Sedgefield transposes
the two halves of this line, and it is true that ll. 643a–644a, as they stand in
the MS., do not hang together very well. Gering, ZfdPh. XII, 124, proposed
the preterite *þeat* for the MS. *þeod*, with *sweg* taken as the subject; but *þeotan*
usually means "to howl." Andrew, pp. 73f., would emend *þeod* to *þeoda*,
gen. plur., dependent on *þryðword*, translating, "then was uttered once more
the proud speech of a glad people, the clamour of the victor-folk."   **644**
semninga] "At last, after a while," as also in ll. 1640, 1767. See Kock,
Anglia XLV, 113f.   **646–647** wiste . . . geþinged] Hrothgar knew that battle
was determined upon at the high hall, but whether it was Beowulf or Grendel
whose intention it was to give battle, is not clear. Klaeber believes that
Grendel was the one who was determined upon a fight; so also Hoops, Bwst., pp.
100f., who points out that the phrase *to þæm heahsele* fits Grendel rather than
Beowulf. On the other hand, Malone, JEGPh. XXIX, 234f., Medium Ævum
II, 61f., taking *þæm ahlæcan* as the equivalent of *wið þæm ahlæcan*, believes that
it was Beowulf who intended to bring about a fight. Cf. ll. 424b–426a. According to Mackie, MLRev. XXXIV, 518, *geþingan* here means "to determine
to come"; he takes *hilde* as instr. sing. and translates, "He knew (it) determined
to (by) the monster to come with battle to the high hall." But ll. 1836f. and
Judgment Day I, 5, which Mackie cites in support of his interpretation, are not
exactly parallel to the present passage. Malone's interpretation seems to fit the
context best; as he points out, it may be inferred from ll. 600b–601a that
Grendel was not expecting a fight. But it is not necessary to take *þæm ahlæcan*
as the equivalent of *wið þæm ahlæcan*, since *þæm ahlæcan . . . geþinged* may
mean "appointed, destined for the monster"; cf. *heleþum geþinged*, Menologium
164.   **648ff.**] The MS. reads *geseon meahton* in l. 648b. Klaeber and
Hoops, p. 87, who believe that Grendel was the one who was intent on battle

in the high hall (see the preceding note), retain the MS. reading and take ll. 648ff. as referring to Grendel; that is (taking *opðe* as *op ðe,* "until"), Grendel had meditated battle from morning until evening. But most edd. prefer to insert *ne* after *geseon,* following Ettmüller, Sc., and Thorpe, and to take ll. 648ff. as defining the time (night) when the fight is to take place. Bugge, Tidskrift VIII, 57, explained *opðe* as the equivalent of *ond,* here and in l. 2475. Prokosch, in Klaeber Misc., p. 198, note, rejecting *ne,* would take *siððan* as an adverb: "(and that) after that they would (either) see once more the light of the sun, (or) darkening night over all . . . ." Similarly Hope Traver, Archiv CLXVII, 253ff., who characterizes ll. 648ff. as "Hrothgar's dramatic visualization of the consequences for them all of the battle itself." Andrew, Medium Ævum VIII, 205, also rejecting *ne,* would emend *opðe,* l. 649a, to *opre* and would translate, "when once they could see the sun's light darkening with another nightfall." But the addition of *ne,* as in the text, seems to do best justice to the poet's intention. Even so, the thought is somewhat roundabout, and as Klaeber remarks, we should expect the word *leng* somewhere in l. 648.

651–700

652 Gegrette] Suggested by Grundtvig, tr., p. 276, and so Grein, Bib., Socin (6, 7 ed.), and later edd. Other early edd. supplied a word after *þa;* Grein, ed., Ettmüller, and Wülker supplied *glædmod,* Heyne (2–4 ed.) and Socin (5 ed.) supplied *giddum.* **653 ond him hæl abead]** "And wished him good luck." Cf. *hælo,* l. 2418. Here the verb *abead* has two meanings and two objects: Hrothgar wished Beowulf good luck, committed to him the custody of the wine-hall. Cosijn's suggestion *healle,* in Holder (2 ed.), is therefore unnecessary. **655 ænegum men]** Andrew, p. 123, taking exception to the alliteration of *ænegum* in preference to the noun *men,* suggests the omission of *men.* See l. 345, note. **665 kyningwuldor]** "The glory of kings," i.e., God. For this compound as the equivalent of *cyninga wuldor,* see Klaeber, Mod. Phil. III, 454. Thorpe, Grundtvig, Grein, Heyne, Arnold, Wülker, Holder (1 ed.), Socin (5 ed.), Wyatt, Holthausen (2 ed.), and. Sedgefield emend to *kyninga wuldor,* following a suggestion by Kemble II. Trautmann emends to *Hæfde kyning wraðum,* with *wraðum* parallel to *Grendle.* **667 sundornytte beheold]** With change of subject: "he (that is, Beowulf) discharged a special service around the lord of the Danes." Cf. l. 494b. **668 eotonweard abead]** "He offered (i.e., maintained) a giant-watch," a watch against the giant. The form *eotonweard* is for *eotonwearde,* acc. sing., with elision of the final *-e;* see l. 338, note. In spite of the reasonableness of the MS. reading, several emendations have been proposed. Trautmann, BVE., p. 161, and his edition, emended to *eoton weard abad,* taking *weard* as the subject and translating, "den riesen erwartete der hüter"; the verb *abidan,* however, normally takes a genitive object. Sedgefield (1, 2 ed.) emended to *abad* but read *eotonweard* as a compound; he translates, "the watcher against the monster (i.e., Beowulf) stayed behind." In MLRev. XXVIII, 226, and in his 3d ed., Sedgefield reads *eoton weard abreat,* "the guardian (Beowulf) destroyed the giant." **670 hyldo]** Gen. sing., parallel to *modgan mægnes*, both being objects of *truwode*. For the genitive after *truwian*, cf. l. 2953, Guthlac 1161; elsewhere in the poetry this verb is followed by the dative.   **677 herewæsmun**] For *herewæstmum*, dat. plur. In accordance with the two common meanings of *wæstm*, we should translate as either "in battle-fruits" (i.e., in the results won by fighting; cf. *þines gewinnes wæstme*, Psalm 127, 2, 1) or "in battle-stature" (with plural for singular, as in l. 565). Cosijn, Aant., p. 13, proposed to emend to *hereræsum*, "in battle-onslaughts"; Trautmann, BVE., p. 162, and in his edition, emends to *herewæpnum*.   **678 guþgeweorca**] Genitive of specification, parallel to *an herewæsmun*.   **680 þeah ... eal**] "Although." For a brief comment on this construction, see Bugge, ZfdPh. IV, 203.   **681 Nat he þara goda**] "He does not know of those advantages, that . . . . " This meaning is assured by a similar passage in Ælfric's Catholic Homilies (ed. B. Thorpe, I, 190, 31f.), *þæt folc ne cuðe ðæra goda, þæt hi cwædon, þæt he God wære*. For the genitive after *nytan*, see Bos.-Tol., Supp., p. 656, and G. Shipley, The Genitive Case in Anglo-Saxon Poetry (Baltimore, 1903), p. 50.   **684 he**] So Kemble (2 ed.) and all later edd.   **685 ofer**] This is the only certain example of *ofer* in the sense of "without," although in Daniel 73 the word may have this meaning.   **692 eardlufan**] "[His] beloved home," an abstract compound used in a concrete sense. Cf. *wæteregesan*, l. 1260, *Hordwynne*, l. 2270, *eðelwyn*, l. 2493, etc.   **694 hie ... to fela micles**] "By far (*micles*) too many of them." The word *fela* is not elsewhere found in apposition with a pronoun, but this construction is not uncommon with *sume*; see Klaeber, Mod. Phil. III, 455, and Bos.-Tol., p. 934, s.v. *sum* II (2). Klaeber (3 ed.), supplement (1941), p. 455, suggests that *fela* is to be taken as an adverb. Thorpe suggested *hyra* for the MS. *hie*, and Kluge, Beitr. IX, 189, Holder (1 ed.), and Sedgefield emend *hie ær* to *hiera*. In l. 696a, *leode* is acc. sing., parallel to *hie*.   **698**] On the readings of this line in the Thorkelin transcripts, see Malone, PMLA LXIV, 1197, who believes that the words *that hie* in transcript B, added at a much later date, were based on transcript A rather than on the manuscript itself.   **frofor**] The noun *frofor* is regularly feminine, and this is the only occurrence in the poetry of *frofor* as an acc. sing. form; the expected reading would be *frofre* (as in l. 1273 and elsewhere), but only Trautmann emends. In Lord's Prayer III, 1 (Records VI, 77), we find the gen. sing. *frofres*; for other apparently masculine forms in late texts, see Bos.-Tol., p. 340, Supp., p. 269.

701–750

702 wideferhð] The reports of the MS. reading given by transcript A (*ride-*) and by Conybeare, p. 143 (*side-*), probably represent misreadings of a MS. *wide-*. See Malone, PMLA LXIV, 1197, who points out that in transcript A the letter *r* frequently appears in place of a *w* of the manuscript. All edd. read *wideferhð*, following Grundtvig, tr., p. 277. Cf. ll. 937, 1222, Genesis 906, etc.   **706 hie ne**] Because of *anum*, l. 705a, and *he*, l. 708a, the plural object here has seemed unnatural to some commentators. An emendation to *hine ne* was suggested by both Grein, Bib., and Grundtvig, and was approved by Gering, ZfdPh. XII, 124. Holthausen (1 ed.) reads *hine ne* in his text. But the MS. *hie*, with *yldum* as antecedent, gives perfectly satisfactory sense. **707** *scynscaþa*] Because of the irregular alliteration (of *s-* with *sc-*) in the MS. reading of this line, Grein, Bib., suggested *scin-* for the MS. *syn-*, and Grein, ed., Trautmann, Holthausen, Schücking, Chambers, Klæber, and von Schaubert emend to *scinscaþa* or *scynsc(e)aþa*, "demonic enemy." Cf. *scinnum*, l. 939. On the other hand, there is no such objection to *synscaðan* in l. 801. The principle underlying the emendation to *scin-*, *scynscaþa* here, stated by Schröder, ZfdA. XLIII, 365f., is the same as has been used to support Schücking's reading *mægenhreð manna* in l. 445; see the note on that line. **708** *wraþum on andan*] "For vexation to hostile ones"; see Klaeber, Anglia LXIII, 409f., who cites l. 2314, Daniel 713, Elene 969, Guthlac 773, and Wanderer 105. The opposite of *on andan* is *on willan*, as in l. 2307. **709** *beadwa*] Kemble II suggested *beadwe*, gen. sing., and so Thorpe, Arnold, and Holthausen (1–6 ed.). **710a**] Grendel's approach to the hall is alluded to three times, in ll. 702f., 710f., and 720f. Apparently to soften the effect of this repetition, Bugge, Beitr. XII, 368, proposed to put a comma after l. 709*b* and to read *ða of more com*, in a subordinate clause, in l. 710*a*. So also Holthausen (1 ed.). But this arrangement ignores the highly dramatic effect of the triple use of *com*. Hoops, pp. 91f., points out that the poet tells us the time when Grendel came, the place whence he came, and the goal of his journey. **713a**] On the reading of transcript B, see Malone, PMLA LXIV, 1198. **714** *to þæs þe*] "To the place where . . . ." Cf. ll. 1967, 2410, Andreas 1059, etc. **719** *hæle*] Most of the older edd. explained this word as *hæle*, either acc. sing. or acc. plur. of *hæle*, "warrior"; so also, more recently, von Schaubert. This reading, however, gives too short a half-line, and Schücking, Eng. Stud. XXXIX, 104, and in his edition, emends to *hæleðas*. Sievers, Beitr. X, 275, suggested *hæle*, and so Holthausen, Anglia XXIV, 267f., either construing the word as dat. sing. of *hæl*, "omen," and explaining *heardran hæle* as adverbial, "with worse omen" (cf. M.E. *to wroþer hele, to uvele hele*, etc.), or taking it as gen. sing. of *hælu*, "health," with *heardran hæle* explained as genitive of quality. Holthausen (1, 7, 8 ed.), Trautmann, Sedgefield, and Chambers read *hæle* with various interpretations (e.g., "zu grösserem unheile," Trautmann; "with sterner greeting," Sedgefield). Klaeber, also reading *heardran hæle*, takes it as acc. sing., "worse luck." Holthausen (2 ed.) emends to *heardran hilde* (see his note in Anglia Beibl. XVIII, 77); Holthausen (3–6 ed.) reads *heardran hælescipes*. The reading *hæle* satisfies sense and meter but does not provide the expected variation of *healðegnas*. Bugge, Beitr. XII, 368, reading *hæle* as acc. sing., would emend in l. 719*b* to *helþegn onfand*, the *helþegn*, nom. sing., then being Grendel. **722** *æthran*] In the MS. the letters *an* are clearly visible, with a letter before them which may be *n*, *m*, or *r*; Kölbing, Archiv LVI, 97, and Wülker, however, report all of *hran* as visible except the lower part of *r*. Most edd., including Schücking and Sedgefield, read simply *hran*. There was, however, room in the MS. for several more letters, at the beginning of the line. Grundtvig, tr., p. 277, read [*æthr*]*an*, apparently following a suggestion by Rask (see the footnote in Grundtvig's edition), and so Chambers, Klaeber, and von Schaubert. Zupitza, Holder (1 ed.), Trautmann, and Holthausen restore [*gehr*]*an*. Klaeber, note, suggests [onhr]an. Any of these last three readings is acceptable, since any of the three compound verbs may govern the dative. Mackie, MLRev. XXXIV, 518f., accepting [gehr]an in the sense of "pushed," explains that Grendel "pushed [the door] in and broke it down, even though it was *fyrbendum fæst . . .*" **723** gebolgen] The text is so restored by all recent edd., following Grundtvig, tr., p. 277. This reading fits the extent of the missing matter better than [a]bolgen, restored by Kemble, Thorpe, Ettmüller, Arnold, Wülker, and Socin (5 ed.). The pronoun *he*, not in either of the Thorkelin transcripts, is reported by Conybeare, p. 143. **729** sibbegedriht] Holthausen emends to *sibbgedriht*, following ten Brink, Beowulf, p. 53. See l. 387, note. **730** magorinca] Möller, Das altenglische Volksepos II, xxvii, and ten Brink, Beowulf, p. 53, would emend to *magoþegna* to avoid the repetition of *rinca* in l. 728b and here. **736** þryðswyð] See l. 131, note. **738** under færgripum] Klaeber, note, and Hoops, p. 93, understand *under* as denoting attendant circumstance: "with [his] sudden attacks." But Cosijn's old interpretation, Aant., p. 14, which takes *under* as denoting duration, has much in its favor; cf. *under þæm gewinne*, "in the course of the struggle," Orosius (ed. H. Sweet, 46, 7), and the other examples given by Bos.-Tol., p. 1096, s.v. *under* I (3f). **739** Ne þæt] Grundtvig suggested *No þær*, and Holthausen (1, 2 ed.) and Schücking (8 ed.) read *No þæt*; see Holthausen's note in ZfdPh. XXXVII, 115. But for a justification of the MS. *ne*, see Klaeber, Eng. Stud. XXXIX, 430. **741** unwearnum] "Without hindrance," an adverbial form from the noun *wearn*, "hindrance, obstacle, refusal." For other examples of this type, see l. 1072, note. This meaning of *unwearnum* is much more likely than "greedily," accepted by Hoops, pp. 93f., following R. Schuchardt, Die Negation im Beowulf (Berlin, 1910), p. 14. **743** sona] Schücking, in Britannica, Max Förster zum 60. Geburtstage, pp. 87f., suggests doubtfully the possibility that *sona* here, as well as in ll. 750, 1497, 1591, is the equivalent of *sona swa*, introducing a subordinate clause. Such a construction would require a comma after l. 745a, with corresponding punctuation in the other passages cited. **745ff.**] The subject of *ætstop*, *nam*, and *ræhte* is Grendel; in l. 748b the subject changes, and *he* is Beowulf. There can be no doubt that *feond*, l. 748a, refers to Grendel; see E. Kölbing, Eng. Stud. XXIII (1897), 306, and Trautmann, BVE., pp. 166f. Cassidy, MLN. L, 88f., would begin a new clause with l. 747a, taking *rinc* (i.e., Beowulf) as nom. sing. and the subject of *ræhte*; he would also emend to *togeanes* in l. 747b (see the note on that line). He would, then, apparently take *ræhte togeanes feond* as meaning "[Beowulf] reached toward the fiend." An objection to Cassidy's reading is that *togeanes* regularly governs the dative and only very rarely the accusative (see Bos.-Tol., pp. 998f.); this objection does not hold for the MS. *ongean*, which governs the accusative when motion is involved, as here. Cassidy's interpretation is possible, but stylistic considerations (particularly the appearance of *he* in l. 748b, which seems to introduce a new subject) favor the older interpretation, with Grendel the subject of *ræhte*. **747** ræhte ongean] For metrical reasons, Sievers, Beitr. X, 265, proposed *ræhte togeanes*, and so Holthausen (1–7 ed), Schücking, Sedgefield (1, 2 ed.), and Chambers. Trautmann, BVE.,

p. 167, suggested *him ræhte ongean*, and so in his edition; Sedgefield, MLRev. XXVIII, 226f., and in his 3d ed., reads *ond ræhte ongean*. The word *ræhte* begins a new line in the MS., and it is possible that *him* or *ond* stood at the end of the preceding line, after the erasure.   Pope, p. 372, suggests that the illegible letters at the end of the preceding line were not intentionally erased but were accidentally obscured; he would restore to [*him swa*] *ræhte ongean*.   So also Holthausen (8 ed.).   **749** inwitþancum] "With hostile intent" (Wyatt, Klaeber).   It has been objected that *inwit-*, which normally implies malice, does not fit Beowulf's character, and that if *inwitþancum* is adverbial, then *onfeng* has no object.   Sedgefield (3 ed.) supplies *him* before *onfeng*, as object of the verb.   Kock, Anglia XLV, 115, takes *inwitþancum* as dat. sing. of an adjective *inwitþanc*, here used as a noun, "(one) with wicked thought," the object of *onfeng*.   The word had previously been explained in this way by Grein (see the translation "malitiosus" in Spr. II, 145) and by Heyne.   Cosijn, Aant., p. 14, proposed *inwitþanc(u)lum*, dat. sing. of an adjective *inwitþancol*; so also, more recently, Hoops, Bwst., pp. 102f., Andrew, p. 71, and Holthausen (8 ed.).   wið earm gesæt] Splitter, MLN. LXIII, 118ff., taking *he*, l. 748*b*, as referring to Grendel, would translate, "[Grendel] set (or leaned) him [Beowulf] against his (Grendel's) arm."   Such a meaning of *gesittan* would, however, be unparalleled.   C. S. Brown, Jr., PMLA LV, 621ff., taking *he* to be Beowulf, would interpret l. 749*b* as meaning that Beowulf used an arm-lock on Grendel.   But there seems to be no good reason for departing from the usual interpretation, "[Beowulf] sat up, leaning against his [own] arm," which is supported by the close parallel in Christ and Satan 430f., *wið earm gesæt, hleonade wið handa*.   **750** Sona]   See l. 743, note.

751–800

752 eorþan sceata] Adverbial gen. plur., parallel to *middangeardes*.   The MS. reading *sceat ta*, with two *t*'s, one at the end of a line and the other at the beginning of the next line, was probably due to the carelessness of the scribe.   Cf. l. 986, where *hilde-* is similarly repeated, and l. 1282, where the MS. *gry re* is corrected from *gryr re*.   elran] The adjective *elra*, "other" (related to Latin *alius* and Gothic *aljis*), is not elsewhere recorded, unless *eldran*, Psalm 147,9,1 (where *Ne . . . eldran cynne* translates the Latin *Non . . . omni nationi*), is a variant form.   Kluge, Eng. Stud. XXII, 145, suggested emending to *eldran*, "older," and so Holder (2 ed.); but for objections to this, see Klaeber, Mod. Phil. III, 252.   Trautmann emends to *oþrum*.   **758** goda] The alliteration in this line is somewhat irregular, since in the older poetry a verb does not ordinarily alliterate in preference to a noun or adjective.   Rieger, ZfdPh. VII, 24, would therefore emend to *modega*.   Holder, Trautmann, Holthausen, Schücking, Sedgefield, and Chambers read *modga*, following Rieger.   Ettmüller had previously emended to *mæra*.   But a parallel to the alliteration here is to be found in l. 1537; see the note on that line.   **760** fingras burston] See Tinker, MLN. XXIII, 239f., Lyons, MLN. XLVI, 443f., both of whom think the fingers were Grendel's, and Clarke, MLRev. XXIX, 320, who thinks the

fingers were Beowulf's.   **762 þær]** It is highly probable that the MS. had
þær and that the form *hwær* (later crossed out in pencil) in transcript B was
no more than a conjecture by Thorkelin. See Malone, PMLA LXIV, 1198.   The
early edd. read *hwær*, following Thorkelin's edition, and so Holder, Wyatt, Socin
(6, 7 ed.), and Schücking.   But the close parallel in l. 797*b* favors *þær*, "if,"
the restoration adopted by Ettmüller, Sc., and most later edd.   **763** widre
gewindan] Here *widre* is acc. sing. neuter comparative of the adjective, "to reach
by flight . . . a more remote place"; see Klaeber, Mod. Phil. III, 263.   The
prefix *ge-* then has the same perfective function in *gewindan* as in *gesæt*, l. 633,
gebeag, l. 690, etc.   **764** fenhopu] See l. 450, note.   **765-766** þæt . . .
þæt . . .] Sievers, Beitr. IX, 138, would explain the MS. *þæt*, l. 766*a*, as a scribal
error for *þone*, since the antecedent *sið* is masculine.   Most edd. take *þæt* as a
conjunction, as in l.735, with *ateah* intransitive.   But Kock, Anglia XLII,
106ff., defends *þæt* as a relative pronoun, citing parallels to show that a relative
clause attached to a demonstrative *þæt* would begin with *þæt*.   Chambers
(rev. ed., 1920, p. 255), Klaeber, and Hoops, pp. 96f., accept this explanation.
For the phrase *sið ateon*, cf. Guthlac 301f., Genesis 2094 (*wigsið*).   **769**
ealuscerwen] More has been written about this word than any other in Beowulf.
The one certain thing about it is that, like *meoduscerwen* in Andreas 1526, it
has the figurative meaning of "terror, distress."   Because of the occurrence
of *meoduscerwen* in Andreas, no emendation of *ealuscerwen* (except *ealuscerpen*,
accepted by several edd. on the basis of what was once supposed to be the reading in Andreas) has ever been suggested.   It is generally agreed that the specific
meaning of *ealu-*, *meoduscerwen* is either "dispensing of ale" or "deprivation of
ale," but in our uncertainty as to the etymology and significance of *-scerwen*,
no final choice between these meanings has ever been achieved.   Most edd.
accept the meaning "dispensing of ale."   For arguments in favor of this interpretation, see especially Bugge, Tidskrift VIII, 293ff.; Klaeber, Anglia Beibl.
XXII, 372f., Eng. Stud. LXVI, 1ff., Eng. Stud. LXVII, 24ff.; Holthausen,
Anglia Beibl. XXXIV, 89f.; Imelmann, Eng. Stud. LXVI, 331ff.   Among the
points that are made in favor of "dispensing of ale" are: (1) that in Andreas
meoduscerwen seems to have the same reference as *biter beorþegu*, "bitter beer-
drinking," l. 1533, and must therefore mean "dispensing of mead," used in
an ironic sense of the flood that engulfed the Marmedonians; (2) that "to
deprive" is *bescerwan*, not *scerwan*, and that therefore the meaning "deprivation
of ale" is impossible.   Imelmann, while accepting *ealuscerwen* as "dispensing
of ale," thinks the word may indicate not a calamity, but something hoped for
by the Danes, that is, the restoration of beer-drinking to them through the
death of Grendel; he cites ll. 823*b*–824 as a possible parallel to ll. 767*b*–769*a*.
This last interpretation, however, is in contradiction of the accepted sense of
meoduscerwen in Andreas.   The other meaning, "deprivation of ale," has been
accepted by Socin, Wyatt, Schücking, and Chambers, and has been more recently upheld by Crawford, MLRev. XXI, 302f., Hoops, Eng. Stud. LXV,
177ff. (but see his note in Eng. Stud. LXVI, 3ff.), and Krogmann, Eng. Stud.
LXVI, 346, LXVII, 15ff.   See also F. Liebermann, Archiv CXLIII (1922),
247f.   Krogmann's argument is chiefly on etymological grounds, but he also

points out that *ealuscerwen* must be the equivalent of *atelic egesa*, l. 784, and echoes Chambers' argument that deprivation of ale was apparently "synonymous with the greatest distress." Hoops defends *scerwan* as an equivalent of *bescerwan* and cites *mægþum meodosetla ofteah*, l. 5, as a possible parallel in meaning to *eorlum ealuscerwen wearð*. Kock, Anglia XLV, 105ff., argues for the meaning "thinning," or "eking out," of ale. But the weight of the evidence, and particularly the passage in Andreas, seems to favor the meaning "dispensing of ale," in an ironic sense. It is of course true, as Krogmann remarks, that we should begin with the Beowulf passage rather than with the passage in Andreas, since Beowulf is the older poem; on the other hand, it is possible from the context to guess at the meaning of the word in Andreas, but not in Beowulf. Klaeber, Eng. Stud. LXXIII, 185ff., who inclines (contrary to his earlier opinion) to the meaning "deprivation of ale" in the Beowulf passage, makes an ingenious attempt to reconcile the two possible translations of *ealuscerwen* by suggesting that the Andreas-poet understood the word in Beowulf in the general sense of "deadly terror" but misinterpreted the precise meaning of the compound as "dispensing of ale" and so applied it in Andreas. Lumiansky, JEGPh. XLVIII, 116ff., has called attention to the "great difference in purpose and tone" between the two passages; although he accepts the general meaning "ale-, mead-serving," he argues that there is no need to use one passage in explaining the other. In Beowulf he would translate, "to [the minds of] all the Danes . . . came [the thought of] ale-serving," that is, regret at the prospect of the cessation of ale-serving if the hall is destroyed. But "[the thought of] ale-serving" as a translation of *ealuscerwen* seems to put too great a burden on the verb *wearð*. In Anglia Beibl. XL, 28f., Klaeber suggests a popular (proverbial?) origin for the phrases involving *ealu-*, *meoduscerwen*, which we cannot recover. This suggestion is rendered highly probable by the parallels from later literature cited by Whitbread, MLRev. XXXVII, 481, particularly the proverbial couplet quoted in the Peterborough Chronicle for 1075, *þær wes þæt bryd eala mannum to beala*. In a recent note, Holthausen, Anglia Beibl. LIV/LV, 28, has proposed to connect *ealu-* not with "ale," but with the word *alu* which occurs in Scandinavian runic inscriptions and possibly in personal names compounded with A.S. *Ealu-*, O.Icel. *Öl-* and which seems to mean "good luck." The word *ealuscerwen* would then mean "taking away of good luck." This explanation assumes a misunderstanding by the poet of Andreas, who took *ealu-* to mean "ale." **770 renweardas]** "The occupants of the hall," with *ren-* taken as a variant form of *ærn-*, *ern-*. This interpretation, proposed independently by H. Weyhe, Beitr. XXX (1905), 59, note, and Klaeber, JEGPh. VI, 193, is accepted by later edd. except Sedgefield (2, 3 ed.). The earlier edd. had taken *ren-* as for *regn-* (as in *regnhearde*, l. 326) and had explained the compound as "mighty guardians." **779 mid gemete]** The translation "by any ordinary means" seems to do best justice to the noun *gemet* as used here. But Klaeber, Mod. Phil. III, 455f., defends Thorpe's old translation, "in any wise," citing parallels from the prose. Because of the unusual alliteration (on the second stress of a B-type half-line), Holthausen (1 ed.) emends to *þæt hit mid gemete æfre*; Holthausen (2–8 ed.) emends to *ænig manna* in l. 779b, giving the line vocalic alliteration. This latter reading is approved by Pope, p. 238. But for other B-type half-lines with a similar alliterative pattern, cf. ll. 3027a, 3056a, and possibly also ll. 459a, 1514a.   **780** betlic ond banfag] Grundtvig, tr., p. 278, proposed *betlic* for the MS. *hetlic*, and so Ettmüller, Sc., and later edd., except Arnold. Cf. l. 1925. Prokosch, in Klaeber Misc., p. 203, would retain the MS. *hetlic* as the equivalent of *hetelic*, as in l. 1267; but this interpretation, which seems to require taking the two adjectives as modifying *manna ænig*, is unconvincing. Holthausen, Anglia Beibl. XLIV, 226, suggests *bōnfāg* for the MS. *banfag*, citing *bōn*, "ornament," Bos.-Tol., Supp., p. 101.   **782** swaþule] The noun *swaþul* is not elsewhere recorded, unless it is a variant of *swioðole* (MS. *swicðole*), l. 3145. On the meaning "flame, heat," accepted by most edd., see especially Chambers, note. Bouterwek, ZfdA. XI, 82ff., suggested that *swaþul* is an error for *swaluð* (= *sweoloð*, as in l. 1115); Thorpe had previously emended *swaþule* to *swaloðe*. Trautmann reads *on staþule*, "auf der stätte," following a suggestion by Grundtvig.   **782b–783a**] Kock, JJJ., p. 8, translates, "the din arose in manner strange and strong," taking *niwe* and *geneahhe* as parallel adverbs; he would explain *neode geneahhe*, Juliana 24, and *nearwe geneahhe*, Elene 1157, in the same way. The traditional interpretation of Beow. 783a takes *niwe* as an adjective, "startling" or "unheard-of."   **785** of wealle . . . gehyrdon] It is clear that it was the Danes who were on the *weall* (see *fram ham*, l. 194, and note), but it is uncertain what the *weall* was. The most reasonable suggestion is that by Lawrence, JEGPh. XXIII, 297, "that the Danes in their fright may have taken refuge on the wall surrounding the *tūn*." The verb *gehyrdon* takes part in two constructions; it has the direct object *wop* and is also followed by *andsacan* and *hæfton*, accusative subjects of the infinitives *galan* and *wanigean*.   **788** hæfton] For *hæftan*, acc. sing. See l. 577, note. A weak variant of *hæft*, "captive," is not elsewhere recorded, and Holthausen (1–5 ed.) emends to *hæftling*, as in Andreas 1342 and Juliana 246; see his note in ZfdPh. XXXVII, 124.   Heold hine fæste] The older edd., except Grundtvig, read *Heold hine to fæste*, and so Wülker, Holder, Socin, Trautmann, Schücking, and Sedgefield (1, 2 ed.).   The word *to* is reported by Conybeare, p. 143, but is not in either of the Thorkelin transcripts.   At the end of the line in in the MS., after *hine*, there was apparently room for *to*, but if the word originally stood there, no trace of it is left.   There is nothing in the context which makes *to fæste* a probable reading, and Wyatt, Holthausen, Chambers, Klaeber, Sedgefield (3 ed.), and von Schaubert omit *to*.   **794–795** genehost . . . eorl] "Many a warrior," with collective force, and with the singular verbs *brægd* and *wolde*; in l. 797b the number changes to the plural.   **797** ðær] For *ðær*, "if," cf. ll. 762, 2573, 2730, Genesis 388, 797, Exodus 152, etc. The usual construction is with the subjunctive, and Holthausen (7, 8 ed.) emends to *meahten*, following Sievers's unpublished edition of the poem.

801–850

801 sawle secan] Trautmann emends to *sawle seocan*, "(the one) sick in spirit," to provide an object for *heawan*. This is a possible interpretation, but Trautmann's emendation is unnecessary, since the MS. *secan* can be retained as a variant form of *sēocan*; see l. 2863, note. All other edd. take *secan* as an infinitive, parallel to *heawan*.   þone synscaðan] Because of the anacoluthon, many of the early edd. supply *þæt* before *þone*, following Ettmüller, Sc.   So also Sedgefield and Holthausen (7, 8 ed.).   Other recent edd. follow the MS., putting a colon after l. 801*a*.   In the present edition, however, the colon is used only to introduce a quotation, and therefore a comma is used here.   804] "But he [Grendel] had put an enchantment on victory-weapons."   For this meaning of *forswerian*, see Bos.-Tol., Supp., p. 254; Klaeber, Anglia L, 195; Thomas, MLRev. XXII, 70. Sedgefield (1, 2 ed.) takes *forswerian* in the modern meaning "to forswear, renounce" (which is apparently not recorded in Anglo-Saxon), with *he* referring to Beowulf.   So also Laborde, MLRev. XVIII, 202ff., who believes that the passage "merely repeats Beowulf's resolve to trust to his handgrip alone."   Cf. ll. 435ff.   But Sedgefield (3 ed.) is doubtful of his earlier interpretation and gives "to lay a spell on" as an alternative meaning of the verb.   810 myrðe] Taken by Holthausen and most other recent edd. as from a feminine *mierð(u)*, "injury, damage," related to the verb *mierran*. This meaning had previously been assigned by Grein, Spr. II, 271.   See also Klaeber, Anglia L, 195f.; Hoops, pp. 101f.   But Lawrence, MLN. XXV, 156, defends the older interpretation (as in Heyne, Holder, Wyatt, and Chambers) which takes the word as a form of *myrhð*, "joy"; he translates, "much of the joy of his heart, of crime against the race of men."   It is at least clear that *myrðe* is parallel to *fyrene*.   Klaeber (3 ed.) and Hoops take *myrðe* and *fyrene* as gen. plur. with late weakened ending, following Malone, Anglia LIV, 98; but *fela* can govern a gen. sing., as in *uncuþes fela*, l. 876, *ealfela eotena cynnes*, l. 883, *wyrmcynnes fela*, l. 1425, *fela goldes*, Resignation 101, etc.   811 wæs] Kemble (2 ed.) and most later edd. supply *wæs* to complete the sense.   So also Hoops, Bwst., p. 103.   See l. 1559, note.   But Grundtvig, Grein, ed., Wülker, Wyatt, Holder (2 ed.), Trautmann, Chambers, Klaeber (1 ed.), and von Schaubert retain the MS. reading, with or without parentheses around l. 811*b*.   According to Chambers, note, the addition of *wæs* "appears to be a distinct enfeeblement of the MS. reading," but he does not explain how he would interpret the line without *wæs*.   Trautmann puts a comma after *he*, with no parentheses, and translates, "er, der Gott feindliche," parallel to *se*, l. 809*b*.   This is not an impossible reading.   822ff.] Andrew, p. 54, would put a comma after *dægrim* and regard ll. 822–823*a* and ll. 823*b*–824 as coordinate clauses dependent on *wiste*.   But such a construction seems very forced.   All edd. punctuate as in the text.   833 þæt wæs tacen sweotol] Klaeber, Mod. Phil. III, 456, translates, "that was clearly proved," and in Anglia XXV (1902), 280, he cites analogous expressions from the prose.   835*b*–836*a*] Most recent edd. punctuate as in the text, following Grundtvig, with ll. 835*b*–836*a* taken as a parenthesis and with *grape* construed as gen. sing. dependent on *eal*.   So also Bugge, Tidskrift VIII, 49, and Hoops, p. 103.   But Socin (6, 7 ed.), Schücking, Sedgefield, and Holthausen (7, 8 ed.) take *Grendles grape* as parallel to *hond* . . . , *earm ond eaxle*, and limit the parenthesis to l. 835*b*.   836 under geapne hrof] Grundtvig, tr., p. 279, restored *hr[of]*, apparently following Rask (see the footnote in Grundtvig's edition), and so all later edd. Miller, Anglia XII, 396ff., would emend to *horn*, citing l. 82; he translates, "under the wide gable."   **841** laþes lastas Thomas, MLRev. XXII, 71, would explain *lastas* as referring to the hand, arm, and shoulder of ll. 834f. But the usual interpretation, "tracks, footprints," is certainly correct; cf. l. 132, where there is no question of hands or arms, and especially l. 1402 and Riddles 51,2; 95,11. In the last two examples cited, *lastas* is synonymous with *swaþu, swaþe*.   **843** þara þe . . . sceawode] See l. 98, note.   **845** niða ofercumen] For metrical reasons, Kaluza, Metrik des Beowulfliedes, p. 82, suggested *niða oferwunnen*; Holthausen (2–6 ed.) emends to *niða genæged* (cf. ll. 1439, 2206), Holthausen (7, 8 ed.) to *mid niðe ofercumen*. **846** feorhlastas] "Life-tracks," i.e., "tracks of (failing) life" (so Heyne, Chambers, Klaeber, and others; see Klaeber, Anglia XXVIII, 445), or merely "bloody tracks" (so Hoops, Bwst., p. 104). Grein, Bib., and Trautmann emend to *feorlastas*; see Trautmann's note in BVE., p. 171.   **847**] Cosijn, Aant., pp. 14f., would omit *on*, citing l. 1422, *Flod blode weol*. But Klaeber, MLN, XVI, 30ff., pointing out the close syntactical relationship of *wæs* to *on blode*, translates, "There was bloody the surging water." That is, *brim weallende* is parallel to *atol yða geswing*, and *on blode* is parallel to *eal gemenged*.   **849** haton heolfre] So all recent edd., following Grein, Bib., Rieger, ZfdPh. III, 389f., and Cosijn, Aant., p. 14. Cf. l. 1423. The reading of the earlier edd. was *hat on heolfre*. For *haton* as a variant spelling of *hatan*, see l. 577, note.   **850** deog] For this word, not elsewhere recorded in Anglo-Saxon, several emendations have been suggested. Sievers, Beitr. IX, 138, proposed to read *deop* as a noun, as in l. 2549, Exodus 281, and elsewhere, explaining *deaðfæge deop* as meaning "the bloody abyss." So Holder, Trautmann (who also emends to *deahfage*, "dye-stained"), and Holthausen (7, 8 ed.). Bugge, Beitr. XII, 89f., adopting Sievers' *deop*, would emend the MS. *deaðfæge* to *deaðfæges*, dependent on *heorodreore*. Cosijn, Aant., pp. 14f., also reading *deop*, would emend *deað-fæge* to *deaðfage*, "death-stained," and so more recently Andrew, p. 96, and Holthausen (8 ed.); this emendation was, however, foreshadowed by Sievers's interpretation of *deaðfæge*. Zupitza, Archiv LXXXIV, 124f., suggested *deaf*, preterite of *dūfan*, "to dive," in pluperfect sense, and so Schücking and Sedgefield. Holthausen (2–6 ed.) and Klaeber (1 ed.) read *deof* as a Northern variant of *deaf*, following Trautmann, BVE., p. 172. But the MS. *deog* was explained by H. Leo (in Heyne, 1 ed.) as preterite, in pluperfect use, of a verb **dēagan*, "to lie concealed" (related to the O.H.G. past participle *tougan*); so also, more recently, E. E. Wardale, MLRev. XXIV, 62f., who cites A.S. *dēagol, dīegel*, "secret," as a related word. For another etymological justification of the MS. *deog*, see Krogmann, Eng. Stud. LXVIII, 317f., who assumes a verb **dēan* (< **dēahan*), "to rage." See also H. M. Flasdieck, Anglia LX (1936), 267. Whitbread's emendation, MLRev. XXXVII, 481f., to *deaðdæge ne gefeag*, "he did not rejoice in his day of death," is unnecessarily remote from the MS. reading.

851–900

855 ridan] Infinitive, dependent on *gewiton*, l. 853, and not preterite plural, as Kluge, Beitr. IX, 189, explained it.   **856** blancum] Etymologically the noun *blanca* is perhaps "white horse" (see Holthausen, AEW., p. 26), but in the poetry it seems to mean any kind of horse. Cf. Elene 1184, Riddle 22,18. **867** cystum cuðe] Probably parallel to *fægere* and referring to the roads rather than to the horses. Cf. the parallelism in ll. 1633f., and see Trautmann, BVE., p. 172; F. Panzer, Studien zur germanischen Sagengeschichte I (Munich, 1910), 282, note 3; Klaeber, Anglia L, 196. **868** gilphlæden] Not "covered with glory, renowned," as Klaeber, Mod. Phil. III, 456, translated it, but rather "laden with glorious words" (Chambers, note), "stored with glorious deeds" (Bryan, JEGPh. XIX, 85). Then *gilphlæden* is synonymous with *gidda gemyndig*. Trautmann emended unnecessarily to *gliwhlæden*. **870–871** word . . . gebunden] The *cyninges þegn* "found other words properly bound together." The older interpetation by Rieger and Bugge (see below), by which ll. 870*b*–871*a* are a parenthesis, is now generally rejected. It is widely held that the word *oþer* here means "new" and that this passage provides evidence for the improvisation of lays in Anglo-Saxon times. See especially Hoops, Bwst., pp. 49ff.; Klaeber (3 ed.), p. 158. But this assumption has recently been called into question by Eliason, Philological Quarterly XXXI, 171ff. Heyne, Socin, Klaeber, and von Schaubert take *soðe gebunden* as meaning "in good alliterative verse," and Klaeber, Anglia L, 196, cites Sir Gawain and the Green Knight 35, *with lel letteres loken*. Hoops also accepts this meaning. The alternative interpretation, "linked with truth," accepted by Schücking, Sedgefield, and others, is less probable. Rieger, ZfdPh. III, 390, and Bugge, ZfdPh. IV, 203, would take ll. 870*b*–871*a* as a parenthesis and emend *secg* to *secgan*. This reading requires us to construe *word* as the subject of *fand*, "[one] word found another." Klaeber (1 ed.), Holthausen (7 ed.), and von Schaubert put ll. 870*b*–871*a* within dashes but retain the MS. *secg* as a variation of *cyninges þegn*. This reading, with *cyninges þegn* and *secg* parallel subjects, makes a long and awkward construction. Klaeber (3 ed.) and Holthausen (1–6, 8 ed.) follow the traditional interpretation, by which *cyninges þegn* is the subject of *fand*. More recently, however, Klaeber (3 ed.), second supplement (1950), pp. 466f., has returned to his earlier punctuation. **872** styrian] "To treat of, discuss." For this unusual meaning of *styrian*, Cosijn, Beitr. XIX, 455 (in his note on Genesis 2495), cites a close parallel in Byrhtferth's Manual (ed. S. J. Crawford, 182, 17f.), *nu ne lyst us þas þing leng styrian*. **873** on spged] See l. 618, note. spel gerade] Holthausen (5–7 ed.) reads *spelgerade* as a compound, acc. sing. of a noun *spelgerād*, "narrative." In this reading he followed a suggestion by Sievers, cited by Schücking (10–14 ed.), glossary. But Holthausen (8 ed.) reads *spel gerade*, with the other edd. **874ff.**] The sentence which begins with *Welhwylc* seems impossibly long and complicated, but there is no place where it can be conveniently divided. Most edd. put a semicolon after l. 874*a* and begin the sentence at l. 867*b*. **875** Sigemundes] So Grein, Ettmüller, Wülker, Holder, Socin, and later edd., except Chambers and von Schaubert, who retain the dative *Sigemunde*. Chambers translates, "concering Sigemund, concerning his deeds of valour." Malone, Eng. Studies XV, 150, would retain *Sigemunde* and take *ellendædum* as a dative of accompaniment, "with mighty deeds." But the emendation is slight, particularly in view of the following *s*-, and gives a more probable reading.   **876*b*–877**] These three half-lines are all parallel to *Welhwylc*, l. 874*b*.   **878 þara þe**] See l. 206, note.   As Klaeber, note, points out, the genitive here is probably due to the partitive idea suggested by *uncuþes fela*, l. 876.   **879 fyrena**] The corrected form *fyrena* does not prove that *fæhðe* is also gen. plur., with weakened ending.   We may translate (beginning at l. 876*b*), "much of what is unknown, . . . of those things which the children of men did not know at all, of hostility and of crimes." **880 swulces**] The spelling *u* for *y* is infrequent before the twelfth century, but it appears twice in the Vercelli Book, in *wunn*, Andreas 1713, and *wurd*, Fates of the Apostles 42.   **893 aglæca**] Mackie's translation of *aglæca* as "monster-warrior" or "giant-warrior," MLRev. XXXIV, 519, and his statement that the word as used here "implies a rather hostile attitude on the part of the poet," are not borne out by the total evidence.   Whether *āglæca* originally meant "warrior," as suggested by Holthausen, Indog. Forsch. XX (1907), 316, or "one inspiring fear," as M. Brie, Eng. Stud. XLI (1910), 24f., would explain it, it is clear that in the historical period of Anglo-Saxon it did not need to have any more specific meaning than "formidable (one)."   Cf. l. 2592, where the word is applied to both Beowulf and the dragon, and especially the reference to *Beda, se æglæca lareow*, in Byrhtferth's Manual (ed. S. J. Crawford, 74, 15). **895 gehleod**] Most edd. emend to the regular form *gehlod*, but Chambers, Klaeber, and von Schaubert retain the MS. *gehleod* and explain it as an analogical form on the model of the *ēo*-preterites; cf. the forms *weox* beside *wox*, preterite of *weaxan*, and *speon* beside *spon*, preterite of *spanan* (Sievers-Brunner, §392, notes 4–5).   **897 hat**] Scherer, Zeitschrift für die österreichischen Gymnasien XX, 110, proposed to read *hate* as instrumental, "in his heat," and so Trautmann.   **900 he þæs ær onðah**] "He had prospered with respect to that."   Cosijn, Beitr. VIII, 568, proposed *he þæs aron þah*, "he throve with honors," citing *weorðmyndum þah*, l. 8, and so Holder, Socin (5 ed.), Trautmann, Holthausen (1–5 ed.), and Sedgefield (3 ed.).   The punctuation in the text, with l. 900*b* taken as a parenthesis, follows Müllenhoff, ZfdA. XIV, 202; see also Klaeber, Mod. Phil. III, 457.   Holder, Socin, Wyatt, and Trautmann begin a new sentence with *siððan*, putting a comma after l. 902*a*.   Sedgefield also begins a new sentence with *siððan* but construes the word as an adverb, putting a semicolon after l. 902*a*.

901–950

902 eafoð] Suggested by J. Grimm, Andreas und Elene (Cassel, 1840), p. 101, for the MS. *earfoð*, and so Grein and most later edd.   Cf. ll. 602, 2349.   **902–903 mid Eotenum . . . on feonda geweald**] Rieger, ZfdPh. III, 399f., and Bugge, Beitr. XII, 45, explained this word as *eotenum*, dat. plur. of *eoton*, "giant." Bugge translates, "unter den riesen."   This interpretation is accepted by Wyatt, Trautmann, Holthausen (1, 2 ed.), and Chambers.   Other recent edd. read *Eotenum* as a proper name, referring to the Jutes.   The most usual translation of *mid Eotenum* is "among the Jutes"; see, for example, Hoops, p. 116, who takes *on feonda geweald* as meaning "into the power of devils," as in l. 808.

That is, Heremod, who was in exile among the Jutes, was treacherously betrayed to death. But Kock, Anglia XLV, 117, would take *mid Eotenum* and *on feonda geweald* as parallel terms; he explains that "Heremod was among the Danes when he was treacherously sent to the Jutes." Similarly, Malone, Anglia LV, 268, would construe *mid Eotenum* as a variation of *feonda*, translating, "he was betrayed into the power of his enemies the Euts." But the historical allusion here is so obscure that grammatical analysis is difficult. For the form *Eotenum* (on the analogy of the gen. plur. *Eotena*), see l. 443, note.

905 lemede] Many of the early edd., and more recently Trautmann and Holthausen, emend to *lemedon*, following Grundtvig, tr., p. 280, in order to secure agreement with the plural subject *sorhwylmas*. But since we find singular verb with plural subject in ll. 2163f. and also in l. 1408 (if *bearn* is plural, as seems likely), it is possible that such lack of concord is to be accepted as a feature of Anglo-Saxon poetic style. On these passages, see Woolf, MLQuart. IV, 49f.

908 sið] Does this word mean "journey, expedition" (its usual meaning), or does it mean "fate" (as Kock, Anglia XLV, 117, takes it)? Or may it not simply mean "way (of doing things)," as apparently in ll. 2532, 2541? That is, it was Heremod's conduct which was lamented by his followers. The obscurity of the allusion makes it impossible to judge. **909** bote gelyfde] See l. 608, note. Here *bote* is accusative object of *gelyfde*, and *to*, l. 909a, goes with *him*.

910 þæt þæt ðeodnes bearn] Since a definite article before a noun qualified by the genitive of another noun is rare in Beowulf (only here and in l. 2059), Barnouw, Textkritische Untersuchungen, p. 22, suggests that the second *þæt* is an erroneous repetition by the scribe. See l. 2059, note. **911** fæderæþelum onfon] Thorpe, Grein, Bib., Grundtvig, Arnold, and Wyatt read *fæder æþelum* as two words, "his father's preeminence," and Trautmann emends to *fædereþlum onfon*, "des vaters länder empfangen." But cf. *fæderæðelo*, Exodus 361. **913** 8] See l. 520, note. **913b–915**] In l. 913b, *He* refers to Beowulf; in l. 915b, *hine* is Heremod. Schücking, Eng. Stud. XXXIX, 105, compares *He . . . he*, ll. 1207ff. **915** gefægra] Kemble II and Grein, Bib., suggested *gefrægra*, "more famous," as comparative of *gefræge*; this emendation was revived, after many years, by Sedgefield (3 ed.). For a defence of the MS. form, apparently the comparative of an elsewhere unrecorded adjective *gefæg*, "pleasing, dear," see Klaeber, Anglia XXVIII, 440f. **916** fealwe] The adjective *fealu* is not elsewhere used to describe a road. W. E. Mead, PMLA XIV (1899), 198, suggests that *fealwe* in the present passage means "covered with pale yellow sand or gravel," an interpretation which is supported by the phrase *on fealwum ceosle*, "on the fallow sand," in Ælfric's Catholic Homilies (ed. B. Thorpe, II, 138,14). Cosijn, Aant., p. 16, would emend to *fealwum*, dat. plur., modifying *mearum*. Cf. l. 865. **918** scofen ond scynded] The morning was "moved forward and hastened (to its close)." The verb *scyndan* is usually intransitive, as in l. 2570, but its use here as a transitive verb is admirably paralleled by the interlinear Rushworth gloss to Matthew xxiv.22 (ed. W. W. Skeat, The Gospel according to Saint Matthew [Cambridge, 1887], p. 197, foot of page), *and þær ne wære scynde þa dagas . . . ah . . . beoþ scynde uel scorte þa dagas* (translating *Et nisi breviati fuissent dies illi . . . sed . . . brevia-*

buntur dies illi). Mackie's interpretation of both *scofen* and *scynded* as intransitive, "had hastened," MLRev. XXXIV, 519f., is therefore unnecessary.
924 medostigge mæt] The earlier edd. and some later ones read *medostig gemæt*, but Holder (2 ed.), Holthausen, Sedgefield (2, 3 ed.), Schücking (9–14 ed.), Chambers, Klaeber, and von Schaubert read *medostigge mæt*, as in the text. Whereas *metan* is found elsewhere in the sense of "traverse" (cf. ll. 514, 1633, Exodus 104, Elene 1262), the compound *gemetan* does not appear to have had this meaning.   **926** on stapole] Explained by Miller, Anglia XII, 398f., as "on the steps," apparently a flight of steps leading up to the hall. Cf. M.E. *stōpel*, with lengthened grade of the vowel, for which the N. E. D., s. v. *stopel*, gives one quotation with this meaning. Addy, Notes & Queries CLII, 363ff., suggests that "there was an upper chamber annexed to Hrothgar's hall, that chamber having a separate entrance from without"; but the evidence which he cites for such a structure, from the Bayeux Tapestry, is too late to prove anything for Beowulf. Child, MLN. VIII, 504ff., defends the older interpretation of *stapol* in the more usual meaning "pillar, post, stake." This meaning, though probable in l. 2718, does not fit here. It is at least certain that Hrothgar is standing outside the hall, looking up at Grendel's hand, which is displayed *under geapne hrof* (l. 836).   **930** grynna] A variant form of *gyrna*, gen. plur. of *gyrn*, "grief, affliction." Cf. *grynsmiðas*, Andreas 917.   **936** wea . . . gehwylcum] So Holthausen (3–6, 8 ed.), Schücking (10–14 ed.), Chambers, Klaeber, and Hoops, p. 120, following Kemble II and Thorpe. Klaeber, Eng. Stud. XLII, 326, translates, "ein weit geschobenes (weitgehendes, grosses) weh für einen jeden der ratgeber," comparing Genesis 2813ff. Numerous attempts have been made to preserve the MS. *gehwylcne* through emendation or interpretation of the first half-line. Bugge, Beitr. XII, 90, would supply *hæfde* in sense, retaining *witena gehwylcne* as the direct object of *hæfde widscofen*. So also Wyatt, who translates, "woe [had] scattered each councillor." Trautmann prints *hæfde* in his text, at the beginning of l. 936a, and emends *widscofen* to *wiðscofen*; so also Holthausen (2 ed.). The construction with *hæfde*, either supplied or understood, requires putting a semicolon or colon at the end of l. 935b. Schücking (8, 9 ed.) would take *widscofen* in the sense of "having scattered," citing *druncne*, l. 1231, and *geclungne*, Phoenix 226, as similar in function. Sedgefield emends l. 936a rather violently; in his 1st ed. he reads *wea wide sceaf witena gehwylcne*, in his 2d ed., *wean wide scufon witena gehwylcne* (in both editions translating, "misfortune drove afar . . ."); in his 3d ed. Sedgefield emends to *Nu is wea wiðscofen* in l. 936a and accepts Kemble's *gehwylcum* in l. 936b.   Holthausen (7 ed.) makes no emendation but assumes a loss from the text after *gehwylcne*, following Sievers's unpublished edition of the poem (see Literaturblatt LIX, 164). Grein, ed., took l. 936, without emendation, as a nominative absolute construction, translating, p. 176, "da Wehe an jeden herangebracht war." A similar interpretation has been advanced by E. von Schaubert, Anglia LXII, 177ff., who explains l. 936a as a nominative absolute, "(als) das Unglück weitging (gross war)," and would make *witena gehwylcne* a variation of *weana . . . bote*, translating, "Das war unlängst, dass ich (mir) nicht erwartete, Abhilfe irgendwelcher Übel je zu erleben (erwarten),

. . . einen Ratgeber unter denen, die nicht erwartet hatten, dass," etc. So
also in her edition. See l. 31, note. Neither this nor any of the other attempts
to rescue the MS. *gehwylcne* can be called successful, and Kemble's *gehwylcum*
is therefore adopted in the text.   **943** ðone magan] "Such a son." Klaeber,
Anglia XXVIII, 442, note, cites *ðone bealonið*, l. 1758, as a parallel; see the
note on that line.   **946** bearngebyrdo] Gen. sing., "with respect to child-
bearing." For *este* with the genitive in this construction, cf. *ealra . . . ara este*,
Genesis 1508f.   **947** secg betsta] For metrical reasons, Sievers, Beitr. X, 312,
proposed *secga*, and so most later edd. But Sedgefield (3 ed.) reads *secg betosta*
(see his note, MLRev. XXVIII, 227); similarly Pope, p. 320, suggests *secg
betesta*. Holthausen (7, 8 ed.) retains *secg* but puts *me* at the end of l. 947a.
Wyatt, Klaeber (3 ed.), and von Schaubert retain the MS. reading, arranging
as in the text. Trautmann adopts Sievers's *secga betsta* in his text; in BVE.,
p. 175, he had suggested *secg se betsta* as an alternative. The same metrical
insufficiency is found in ll. 1759a, 1871b. Since we have three similar cases, all
involving the superlative *betsta(n)*, it seems best to dispose of them in some
other way than by emendation.   me] On the reading of transcript B, see
Malone, PMLA LXIV, 1200.   **949** nænigra] The alliteration indicates that
the MS. *ænigre* is to be emended to a form of *nænig*, and Grein, Bib., and most
later edd. emend to *nænigra*, gen. plur., modifying *wilna*. So also Bugge,
ZfdPh. IV, 203f. Trautmann reads *nænge* (used adverbially, "nicht . . .
irgendwie"); Holthausen (2, 4–8 ed.) and Sedgefield (1, 2 ed.) emend to *nænges*
(with *wilna* dependent on it), following Trautmann's alternative suggestion,
BVE., p. 175. Hoops, pp. 121f., would read *nænigre* as gen. plur. with weakened
ending, following Malone, Anglia LIV, 97f., and so Klaeber (3 ed.) and von
Schaubert.

951–1000

954 dædum gefremed] For metrical reasons, Trautmann emended to *dædum
geæfned*; Holthausen, Literaturblatt XXI, 64, suggested *mid dædum gefremed*,
and so Holthausen (2, 8 ed.), Sedgefield (1 ed.), and Chambers; Holthausen
(3–7 ed.) reads *dædum gefremedne*, but an accusative form is difficult to justify
here, since *þe*, l. 953b, is probably dative. Andrew, p. 138, suggests *dædum
gefered*, citing l. 1221.   dom] Supplied by Kemble (2 ed.) and all later edd.,
to complete the half-line. Cf. Andreas 541, Christ 405.   **957** Ecþeowes]
Ecg- as the first element of a personal name is spelled *Ec-* here and in *Eclafes*,
l. 980. Many edd., including Holthausen and Klaeber, normalize. In l. 263
the scribe originally wrote *ec þeow* but later corrected it to *ecg þeow*.   **962**
feond on frætewum] Grundtvig, tr., p. 281, proposed *feond on fæterum*, "the
fiend in fetters," and Bugge, Beitr. XII, 90, would read *feond þone frætgan*,
"the proud fiend," citing Juliana 284. But we need not hold the Beowulf
poet to strict logic here; he is thinking of Grendel as being "equipped for battle," whatever that may have involved in Grendel's case.   **963** hine] So
Thorpe and later edd., except von Schaubert, for the MS. *him*. Malone, Eng.
Studies XVIII, 257f., would retain *him* as a late accusative form, and so von
Schaubert in her text. See l. 2828, note.   **965** mundgripe] So Kemble and

all later edd., except Grundtvig and Arnold, to provide alliteration.   **967 Ic]**
Andrew, pp. 97f., would emend to *ac*, with a comma after l. 966*b*.   See l. 1994,
note.   **968b]** Most edd. put a semicolon or period afteɪ l. 968*a*, but Holthausen,
Klaeber, and von Schaubert put l. 968*b* within commas, and Kock, Anglia
XLIII, 304f., translates, "however eagerly I clung to him."   See also Kock,
Anglia XLVI, 83f.; Klaeber, Anglia L, 197f.   Kock would also explain *no he þæs*
(MS. *þæm*) *modig wæs*, l. 1508, and *no þon lange wæs . . . bewunden*, ll. 2423f.,
in the same way; see the notes on these lines.   **976 mid nydgripe]** For the
MS. *inmid gripe*, which does not alliterate, Thorpe read *in niðgripe*, "in hostile
gripe," and so Grein, Heyne (1–3 ed.), Ettmüller, Arnold, and Sedgefield.
Grundtvig, p. 209, suggested *in nydgripe*, and so Bugge, Tidskrift VIII, 49f.,
Heyne (4 ed.), and most later edd.; Klaeber and von Schaubert read *in nidgripe*,
as closer to the MS. reading.   Schücking ʼand Holthausen (3–8 ed.) read *mid
nydgripe*; see Schücking's note in Eng. Stud. XXXIX, 105f.   This last is probable the best reading.   The agent or instrument after *befon* is regularly expressed by the instrumental alone, as in ll. 2274, 2321, 2595, etc., but for *mid*
in this construction, cf. *mid handa befeng*, Exodus 416.   **977 balwon]** For
balwum, dat. plur. of *bealu*, adjective.   For the ending -*on*, see l. 577, note.
980 Eclafes] See l. 957, note.   **982 eorles cræfte]** The word *cræfte* is usually
explained as instrumental, "by means of (or, as a result of) the power of the
warrior," i.e., of Beowulf.   Malone, Anglia LVII, 315, would explain *cræfte*
as dative of accompaniment, translating, "after they beheld the hand and fingers
of the foe and the strength of the hero."   But cf. *þeofes cræfte*, l. 2219, and
sylfes cræfte, l. 2360, where there is no idea of accompaniment.   For a salutary
expression of doubt that the dative of accompaniment is to be recognized in
such passages as this, see Klaeber (3 ed.), second supplement (1950), p. 467.
983 ofer heanne hrof] The men gazed "up to the high roof" or "in the direction
of the high roof."   See Klaeber, Mod. Phil. III, 256, who cites *ofer wolcna hrof*,
Elene 89, as a parallel.   The position of the hand has not been changed since
l. 836.   **985 stiðra nægla gehwylc]** The MS. *steda nægla gehwylc* is difficult to
interpret.   Schücking, Chambers, and von Schaubert, retaining *steda*, explain
this half-line as meaning "each of the places of the nails," that is, the places
where nails would be on a human being.   So also Pope, pp. 313f.   Clarke,
MLRev. XXIX, 320, suggests that *steda nægla* may be a kenning for "finger-
tips."   But *steda nægla gehwylc* shows an unusual word-order and is otherwise
stylistically suspect; also, as Klaeber, Beitr. LXXII, 120, points out, the
plural of *stede* appears nowhere else in Anglo-Saxon poetry.   Ettmüller emended
steda to *stiðra*, and so Sievers, Beitr. IX, 138f., Trautmann, Holthausen, and
Klaeber.   With this emendation, the half-line makes excellent sense, "each of
the stiff nails," and although it is rather long, it is identical in metrical structure with *oncyð eorla gehwæm*, l. 1420.   It is, however, possible that *gehwylc*
is an unintentional repetition of *æghwylc* in the preceding line, and Ettmüller,
Sievers, loc. cit., Trautmann, and Holthausen omit *gehwylc*, following a suggestion by Thorpe, reading simply *stiðra nægla*.   Klaeber, Archiv CXV, 179, also
would omit *gehwylc*, but in his edition he retains it.   Sedgefield (1, 2 ed.) reads
stiðnægla gehwylc; Sedgefield (3 ed.) emends more extensively to *studunægla*

gehwylc, translating *studunægla* . . . *style gelicost* as "like the steel of timber-nails." Holthausen (2-8 ed.) and Chambers take ll. 984*b*-985*b* to be a parenthesis, with *handsporu* parallel to *fingras*.   986 handsporu] Rieger, ZfdPh. III, 390f., would emend to *handsperu*, "hand-spears," and Holthausen (2-6 ed.) reads *handspeoru*. Other edd. take the MS. *handsporu* as nom. sing. of a strong feminine noun, "hand-spur," although the word for "spur" is elsewhere *spora*, *spura*, weak masculine. Grundtvig suggested emending to -*spora*, and so Grein, ed., Ettmüller, Wülker, Sedgefield (3 ed.), and Holthausen (7, 8 ed.). 987 egl] Apparently for *eglu*, nom. sing. feminine of the adjective *egle*, "loathsome, horrid"; see Grein-Köhler, p. 880. For other cases of elision of a final vowel, see l. 338, note. Grein, Wyatt, Sedgefield, Chambers, and von Schaubert construe *egl* as a noun, "talon, claw," and so also Bos.-Tol., Supp., p. 184; but this meaning is very doubtful.   988 heardra] Taken by the edd. as gen. plur., "of the brave ones," dependent on *nan* . . . *iren ærgod*. Laborde, MLRev. XVIII, 203, construes *heardra* as nom. sing. of the comparative, translating, "no excellent blade (even) of the harder sort"; but since *iren* is neuter, this meaning would require emendation to *heardre*.   989*b*-990] Grundtvig, note, and Sievers, Beitr. IX, 139, would emend the MS. *þæt* to *þe*, referring back to *him*, l. 988*a*, and so Holthausen (1-5 ed.) and Sedgefield; with this reading the sentence refers to Beowulf rather than to Grendel. Klaeber and von Schaubert explain *þæt* as a conjunction, "(in such a way) that." But *þæt* is more probably a relative pronoun, the neuter *iren* being the antecedent. In l. 990*b* Sievers, loc. cit., suggested the emendation *aberan mihte*, regarding the MS. *wolde* as a careless repetition of *wolde* in l. 988*b*. Holthausen (1-5 ed.) follows Sievers. In Literaturblatt XXI, 64, Holthausen had suggested *scolde* in l. 990*b*, and so Trautmann in his text. But for the MS. *onberan*, "to weaken," cf. *breosthord* [*wæs*] *onboren*, Guthlac 944. The meaning of *onberan* in Beow. 2284, *onboren beaga hord*, "the hoard of rings [was] diminished," is clearly a variation of the same meaning. Cf. also the gloss *Imminutus*, *onboren* in Wright-Wülker, Anglo-Saxon and Old English Vocabularies I, 430, 12. Kock's translation of *onberan* as "to act on, to cut, to bite," Anglia XLVI, 79, is unconvincing. Translate, "everyone said that no trusty sword of the brave ones would touch him [Grendel], that would weaken the bloody battle-hand of the monster." 991-992 Ða wæs haten . . . gefrætwod] The usual construction after *hatan* is the infinitive rather than the past participle; cf. ll. 198f., 1035f., 2190ff. Trautmann therefore emended *haten* to *handum*, getting rid of the *hatan* construction altogether. Kluge, Beitr. IX, 189, had previously proposed *hroden*, "ornamented," for the MS. *haten*. Sedgefield (1 ed.) emends *haten hreþe* to *haton hreþre*, "with hot heart (i.e., with zeal)"; in his 2d ed. he reads Ða *wæs hat on hreþre*; *Heort innan wearð*, etc. (see also his note in MLRev. V, 287); in his 3d ed. he reads Ða *wæs haten hraðe* in l. 991*a* and emends to *gefrætwan* in l. 992*a*. Holthausen (8 ed.), retaining the MS. reading of l. 991*a*, emends to *gefrætwan* in l. 992*a*. Bugge, Beitr. XII, 90f., had previously proposed to read *gefrætwon* as an infinitive. For the verb *gefrætwan*, beside the more usual *gefrætwian*, see Grein-Köhler, p. 217. Holthausen (1, 2 ed.) assumes the loss of a line after l. 991. Other recent edd. retain the MS. reading. Cosijn, Aant., pp. 17f., suggests that the infinitive *beon* is to be understood in l. 992*a*; he cites the similar construction after *hyrde* in Andreas 360f., *ic ne hyrde . . . ceol gehladenne*, where also *beon* is apparently to be supplied in sense. Klaeber, Archiv CXXVI (1911), 355, suggests that the use of the past participle here is a Latinism. J. F. Royster, JEGPh. XVII (1918), 89, note 28, puts a comma after *hreþe* (as had Chambers in his text) and explains the passage as a mixed construction, the use of *gefrætwod* being due to a shift in the poet's mind from the giving of the order to the state of Heorot which resulted from the order. **991 hreþe]** This form, which also occurs in Meters 25, 47, is usually explained as a variant of *hraþe*, "quickly," and Sedgefield (3 ed.) emends to *hraðe* (see the preceding note). Malone, Anglia LXV, 229, suggests reading *Hrēþe*, "for the Geat," i.e., for Beowulf. See l. 445, note. But Klaeber, Anglia Beibl. LIV/LV, 277, pointing out that the preparations for the banquet were not made for Beowulf alone, defends *hreþe* as an adverb. **996 þara þe . . . staraið]** See l. 98, note. **998]** Holthausen (2 ed.), p. viii, proposed *eal inneweard fæst irenbendum*, apparently for metrical reasons, and so Holthausen (3–5 ed.). **1000 þe]** Thorpe, Grein, Bib., Heyne, Arnold, Socin, Wyatt, Trautmann, Holthausen, and Sedgefield emend to *þa*, following Ettmüller, Sc.; Grundtvig suggested *þonne*. Other edd. retain *þe* as "when"; see Schücking, Svk., pp. 7, 57f. There seem to be no other certain examples in the poetry of *þe*, "when" (though *þe* in l. 2468 is possibly one), but examples from the prose are cited by Arthur Adams, The Syntax of the Temporal Clause in O.E. Prose (New York, 1907), pp. 26ff.

1001–1050

1002 þæt] To provide a reference for this word, Rieger, ZfdPh. III, 391, would supply *deað* at the beginning of l. 1003*a*, as object of *befleonne*; Holthausen, ZfdPh. XXXVII, 116, would supply *fyll*. But *þæt* anticpates ll. 1004ff. **1004 gesecan]** So most recent edd., following Kemble II and Sievers, Beitr. X, 291. Wyatt, retaining the MS. *gesacan*, glosses it as "gain by strife," a meaning first proposed by Grein, ed. Schücking (8–10 ed.), also retaining *gesacan*, takes it as meaning "to struggle (against)"; this unlikely sense had previously been assigned to *gesacan* by Bos.-Tol., p. 433. Brett, MLRev. XIV, 7, would retain *gesacan* as meaning "gain, for all his striving, in spite of his striving." But the emendation, besides giving better sense, is strongly supported by the meter. The subject of *gesecan* is implied in l. 1003*b*; the object is *stowe*, on which the genitives *sawlberendra*, *niþða bearna*, and *grundbuendra* are dependent. **1005 genydde]** Acc. sing. feminine, modifying *stowe*. Klaeber translates, "the place forced (upon him) by necessity," citing Christ 68f. The emendation to *genyded*, first made by Kemble II, is therefore unnecessary. **1009 gang]** Apparently a variant of *geong*, preterite of *gangan*, as also in ll. 1295, 1316. Cf. *gangan*, preterite plural, Psalm 54,12,5. Grein-Köhler, p. 263, assigns these forms to an infinitive **gingan*; Krogmann, Anglia LVII, 216f., assigns them to **gungan*. **1011 þa]** Taken as an adverb, "then," by Schücking, Svk., p. 108, Kock, Anglia XLVI, 181, Klaeber, note, and Hoops, p. 127. Schücking cites l. 2192*b*. But Malone, Anglia LVII, 316, would explain *þa* as a demonstrative adjective:

"I have not heard of that tribe behaving better. . . . "   1015 magas þara]
For the MS. þara, ten Brink, Beowulf, p. 73, suggested wæron, with a semicolon
after l. 1015a; this proposal was repeated by Klaeber, Anglia XXVIII, 442.
Holthausen (2–5 ed.), Schücking, Sedgefield, Chambers, and Klaeber (1 ed.)
adopt this emendation, either reading wæron or trying to achieve a closer approxi-
mation to the MS. reading with wæran, waron, or waran.   Trautmann emends
to þwære, "friendly," following J. Hornburg, Archiv LXXII (1884), 372f.
Patzig, Anglia XLVII, 99, suggests magas deore.   But the MS. þara is acceptable if we assume, with Wyatt, note, that the antecedent is implied in blædagande, l. 1013b.   Kock, Anglia XLVI, 75ff., translates, "Their countrymen,
the valiant ones, Hroðgar and Hroðulf, took in courtly manner many a cup of
mead within the lofty hall."   For magas in the sense of "compatriots," cf.
maga gemedu, l. 247.   Bugge, Beitr. XII, 91, also taking þara as referring to
blædagande, would punctuate ll. 1014–1015 as a parenthesis, and so Socin and
Holder (2 ed.); with this punctuation the blædagande would be Hrothgar and
Hrothulf, and magas þara would apparently be the retainers.   Bugge's interpretation is therefore the reverse of Kock's.   1020ff.] Most of the early edd.,
together with Wyatt, Chambers, and Klaeber, put a colon or semicolon after
byrnan, l. 1022, and this punctuation is approved by Cosijn, Aant., p. 18, and
Hoops, p. 128.   The punctuation with a semicolon (or colon) after maðþumsweord, l. 1023, recommended by Sievers, Beitr. IX, 139, and adopted by Holthausen (1–7 ed.) and Sedgefield, is hardly possible, since it fails to provide an
object for beran.   (To be sure, one could cite Finnsburh 5a as evidence that
beran does not require an object.)   The punctuation in the text seems most
satisfactory.   It is adopted by Holthausen (8 ed.), who, however, puts a colon
after leane instead of a semicolon.   If we put the semicolon after byrnan, we
have five gifts instead of the four specified in l. 1027; we have a segen, a hildecumbor, a helm, a byrne, and a maðþumsweord.   Of these, the segen and the
hildecumbor are undoubtedly the same thing.   Punctuating as in the text, we
have first a statement that Beowulf was given a segen, then a further statement
that the hildecumbor (i.e., the aforementioned segen), plus a helmet, a corselet,
and a sword, were brought into Beowulf's presence.   1020 bearn] So Grundtvig, tr., p. 282, and most later edd.   See Prokosch, in Klaeber Misc., p. 203.
But recently two attempts have been made to preserve the MS. brand.   Hertha
Marquardt, Anglia LX, 391ff., points out that the poet never uses the bearn
formula for Hrothgar, though he uses it for others.   She would take brand
Healfdenes as the equivalent of Healfdenes hildewisa, l. 1064, explaining brand
as meaning "one who carries a sword."   So also von Schaubert.   But helm,
"protector" (as in ll. 371, 456, etc.), which Dr. Marquardt cites as a parallel
to brand in this sense, is hardly adequate support for her interpretation, since the
development of helm from "protection" to "one who affords protection" is
remote from the semantic development which she assumes for brand.   Kuhn,
JEGPh. XLII, 82ff., would explain brand Healfdenes as object of forgeaf, the
subject being unexpressed.   He translates, "[Someone, clearly Hroðgar], gave
then, to Beowulf, the sword of Healfdene."   For the omission of the subject,
he cites l. 2892, Maldon 62, etc.   But bringing a sword into the picture at this

point would make *maðþumsweord*, l. 1023, a rather awkward repetition.   **1022 hildecumbor]** The MS. *hiltecumbor* has been explained as "staff-banner" (Sedgefield, 1, 2 ed., and Chambers) and as "an ensign having a hilt" (Bos.-Tol., p. 536). But although a weak feminine *hilte*, "hilt, handle," is recorded, the usual word is *hilt*, strong masculine or neuter, and *hilte-* as a combining form is therefore doubtful. The emendation to *hiltcumbor*, suggested to Holder by Cosijn and adopted by Holder (2 ed.) and Klaeber (1 ed.), takes care of the objections based on the form of the MS. reading, but it is not at all clear what a banner with a hilt would be. The emendation *hildecumbor*, first made by Ettmüller, Sc., is approved by Rieger, ZfdPh. III, 391f., Sievers, Beitr. XXXVI, 420, and Hoops, p. 128, and has been adopted by Grein, Bib., Arnold, Trautmann, Holthausen, Schücking (10–14 ed.), Sedgefield (3 ed.), Klaeber (3 ed.), and von Schaubert.   **1024 geþah]** Apparently a variant spelling of *geþeah* (cf. ll. 618, 628), preterite of *geþicgan*, "to partake." See Klaeber, Anglia LXIII, 414. The form *geþah* also appears as a corrected reading in Widsith 65.   **1026 sceotendum]** So Kemble II and most later edd., for the MS. *scotenum*. This emendation is approved by Rieger, ZfdPh. III, 392, and by Hoops, p. 128. Cf. ll. 703, 1154. Kluge, Beitr. VIII, 533, would retain *scotenum* as dat. plur. of a weak masculine *scota*, noun of agency from *scēotan*; this form, with the ending in *-num*, would be similar to *Eotenum*, ll. 902, 1145. So Holder, Socin, and Wyatt. But *for scotenum* is too short for a full half-line, and emendation of some sort seems desirable. Malone, Anglia LIII, 335f., would read *sc(e)otenum* as dat. plur. of **scēoten*, a variant form of *scēotend*. See his similar explanation of the MS. *seleræðenne* in l. 51. Von Schaubert reads *scōtenum*, with Malone's interpretation.   **1031 walu]** For the MS. *walan*, Grein, Wyatt, Holthausen, Chambers, Schücking (9–14 ed.), Klaeber, and von Schaubert read *wala* as subject of *heold*, following Ettmüller, Sc. But Bugge, Beitr. XII, 369, emended to *walu* (as Sievers, Beitr. X, 257, had previously done, without comment), and so Trautmann and Sedgefield. The quotations given s.v. *walu*, "ridge, bank(?)," and *dīc-walu* in Bos.-Tol., p. 1163, Supp., p. 151, clearly show that this word is a strong feminine and that *walu* is the proper form here. The reference of the word is undoubtedly to a band of metal surrounding the helmet. The object of *heold* is *heafodbeorge*.   **1032 fela laf . . . meahton]** To remedy the lack of agreement, Grein, Heyne, Ettmüller, Wülker, Holder, Socin, and Holthausen (1, 7, 8 ed.) emend the MS. *laf* to the plural *lafe*, following a suggestion by Grundtvig; this emendation is approved by Kock, Anglia XLVI, 77f. Kemble II, Thorpe, Trautmann, Holthausen (2 ed.), Schücking, Sedgefield, and Klaeber emend *meahton* to the singular *meahte*, retaining *laf*, and so also Bugge, Beitr. XII, 91f. Holthausen (3–6 ed.), Chambers, and von Schaubert retain the MS. reading in spite of the lack of agreement; Chambers, note, points out that *laf*, as a collective noun, may conceivably have a plural verb. For other examples of lack of agreement, see l. 905, note. The form *fela* is a variant of *feola*, gen. plur. of *fēol*, "file."   **1033 scurheard]** Apparently "hard (or hardened) in the storm of battle." Cf. Andreas 1133 and *scurum heardne*, Judith 79. Sedgefield (3 ed.), note, and Colgrave, MLRev. XXXII, 281, suggest that the poet was misled by *regnheard*, l. 326, taking *regn-* in that word to mean "rain"; this explanation of *scurheard* seems, however, less likely. On the meaning of *scurheard*, see especially Palmer, MLN. VIII, 121f.; Krapp, MLN. XIX, 234; Klaeber, Anglia LXIII, 414.   1037 in under eoderas] This apparently means simply "into the hall." Cf. Genesis 2447, 2489, and the Old Saxon *undar ederos*, Heliand 4943. For the development of this meaning, as well as of the meaning "protector, prince" (found in Beow. 428, 663, 1044), see G. Neckel, Beitr. XLI (1916), 163ff.   anum] Cosijn, Aant., p. 18, suggested *on anum*, and so Holthausen (2–5 ed.).   1046–1048 Swa . . . swa] Kock, Anglia XLII, 108f., takes the second *swa* as introducing a consecutive clause; *Swa manlice . . .*, *swa* would then mean "in such a manly way . . ., that . . . ." But Schücking, Svk., p. 33, takes *swa*, l. 1048, as meaning "such as" and does not connect it with *Swa* in l. 1046.   1048 lyhð] Third singular present indicative of *lēan*, "to blame, find fault with"; cf. *logon*, l. 862, *log*, l. 1811. Sievers, Beitr. X, 269, would supply *ne* before *lyhð*, for metrical reasons, citing *ne* in l. 1460, and so Holthausen (1, 2, 8 ed.). The form *lyhð*, however, was undoubtedly dissyllabic at the time when Beowulf was written.

1051–1100

1051 þara þe . . . teah] See l. 98, note.   brimlade] So Kemble and later edd. 1055 swa he, etc.] The grammatical structure here is somewhat confused, but the sequence of thought, beginning at l. 1053*b*, is fairly clear: Hrothgar paid a wergild for the one of Beowulf's men whom Grendel had killed, as he (Grendel) would have killed more if he had had the opportunity. It is unnecessary to begin a new main clause with l. 1055*b*, as Schücking and Holthausen (2–8 ed.) do.   1056 him] Malone, JEGPh. XXIX, 235f., taking *wyrd* as a variant form of *weorod*, "band of men," explains *him* as dat. sing. referring to Grendel. But *him* is more probably dat. plur., referring to Beowulf's comrades. In the light of *Ic him þæt forstonde*, Riddle 16, 8, we may translate, "if wise God and the courage of the man had not averted fate from them." Cf. also *ne magon ge him þa wic forstondan*, "you may not keep those dwellings from him," Guthlac 702, which is, however, not so close a parallel. See also Hoops, p. 131.   1063–1070] Many edd. consider the Finnsburh episode to be a formal quotation and therefore put quotation marks around it. Grein, Ettmüller, Arnold, Wülker, Holder (1 ed.), Wyatt, and Chambers begin the quotation at l. 1068*a*; Heyne, Socin, Holder (2 ed.), Trautmann, and Holthausen (2 ed.) begin it at l. 1069*a*; Holthausen (5, 6 ed.) begins it at l. 1069*b*. Holthausen (1, 7 ed.) and Sedgefield (1, 2 ed.), beginning the episode with l. 1068*a*, indicate a loss from the text before this line. Schücking and Holthausen (3, 4 ed.) begin the quotation with *Ne huru*, l. 1071*a*. The majority of the early edd., together with Klaeber, Sedgefield (3 ed.), von Schaubert, and Holthausen (8 ed.), omit quotation marks, and this seems the preferable course. See Lawrence, PMLA XXX, 399ff.; Hoops, Bwst., pp. 55f.; Girvan, Proc. of the British Academy XXVI, 334.   Lawrence and Hoops point out that the transition from the narrative of Beowulf to the content of the episode is as gradual here as in ll. 867ff., where the story of Sigemund is introduced; if any further argument against the use of quotation marks is needed, it may be found in the inability of the edd. to agree on the proper place to put them.   The details of the interpretation of these lines and the suggested emendations of l. 1068*a* are treated in the following notes. 1064 Healfdenes hildewisan] Usually explained as meaning "Healfdene's battle-leader" and as referring to the military post held by Hrothgar before his father's death.   As an alternative, Chambers, note, suggests taking *hildewisan* as dat. plur., "referring to the old captains who had fought under Healfdene."   Traut-mann emends to *Healf-Dena*, "of the Half-Danes" (see his note in FH., p. 11), and Malone, JEGPh. XXV, 116, also suggests that *Healf-Dena* was the original reading.   In ELH X, 258f., Malone retains the MS. *Healfdenes* but translates as "Hrothgar's champions," explaining *Healfdenes* as a dynastic rather than a personal name.   1065 oft] Trautmann emends to *eft*, following Lübke, Anz.fdA. XIX, 342.   But *gid oft wrecen* may mean "many a lay [was] recited." See Sievers, Beitr. XXIX, 571, who points out the similar use of *oft* in ll. 2018, 2478.   1066 healgamen] "Hall-joy," that is, a hall entertainment, in the present instance a recitation.   This word is direct object of *mænan*, "to utter," and there is no reason to emend to *on healgamen*, as suggested by Andrew, p. 79.   Williams, FE., p. 11, would translate *healgamen* as "(a tale of) hall-play," referring to the narrative of the slaughter in Finn's hall.   Similarly Malone, ELH X, 258ff., who translates *healgamen . . . mænan* as "to tell about the hall-sport," that is, about the fight.   Trautmann, BVE., p. 183, and in his edition, emends *healgamen* to *healguma*, parallel to *scop*; this reading is of no importance and is mentioned here only because of its bearing on Trautmann's emendation to *eaferan* in l. 1068 (see the following note).   1068–1070] The MS. *finnes eaferum*, l. 1068*a*, if it is not a scribal error, raises serious difficulties of inter-pretation.   Grein, Wyatt, and Chambers, beginning a new sentence with l. 1068*a*, explain *eaferum* as instrumental, and Chambers, note, translates, "At the hands of the children of Finn . . . ."   Similarly Malone, JEGPh. XXV, 157, "At the hands of Finn's men."   Green, PMLA XXXI, 759ff., also beginning a new sentence here, explains *eaferum* as dative of agency and regards ll. 1068*b*–1069*a* as a parenthesis; he translates, "By Finn's battle-fighters—when onset befell them, The heroes of Half-Danes,—Hnæf . . . was fated to fall."   Kock, Anglia XLII, 109, defends *feallan sumum* in the sense of "to fall by someone." Williams, FE., pp. 19ff., and Malone, Anglia LVII, 313ff., ELH X, 258ff., take *eaferum* as dative of accompaniment.   But *Finnes eaferum*, either as instru-mental or as dative, in this position at the head of the sentence is very ques-tionable stylistically.   It is more probable that l. 1068 is a continuation of the sentence which begins at l. 1063 and that only a comma is to be put after *scolde*, l. 1067*b*.   Thorpe, in Kemble (2 ed.), suggested that the preposition *be* is to be supplied before *Finnes*, and so Thorpe in his edition, Klaeber, and Hoops, Bwst., pp. 55ff.   With this emendation, the text means "when Hrothgar's scop was to utter hall-entertainment concerning the sons of Finn."   Socin supplied *fram* after *eaferum*, but this emendation, though recently advocated by Mackie, MLRev. XXXIV, 520, is less likely.   Trautmann, BVE., p. 183, sug-gested that the MS. *eaferum* is an error for *eaferan*, object of *mænan*, and Holthausen (2–4 ed.) and Schücking emend to *eaferan*.   In Trautmann's own case the reading *eaferan* did no harm, since he simultaneously emended *heal-gamen*, l. 1066, out of existence (see the preceding note). But when *healgamen* is retained, the emendation to *eaferan* gives *mænan* two quite incongruous objects, *healgamen* and *eaferan*. And in spite of the attempt by Klaeber, Anglia XXVIII, 443, to justify *eaferan*, this reading must be rejected. E. von Schaubert, Literaturblatt LVII, 29f., and in her edition, retains *eaferum*, assuming a verb *mænan* meaning "to turn (something, accusative) toward (something, dative), to devote (to)," and translates, "als Hrōþgārs Hofsänger sich verpflichtet fühlte, die Unterhaltung . . . den Mannen Finns zuzuwenden." Sedgefield (3 ed.) supplies a line, *cwæð, him ealdres wæs ende gegongen*, between l. 1067 and l. 1068, the pronoun *him* then being parallel to *eaferum*. Of all these proposals, Thorpe's addition of *be* seems most in accord with the style of the poem and has been adopted in the text. A further problem is the syntactical relationship of l. 1068 to the two following lines. Heyne, Socin, Holder (2 ed.), Trautmann, Holthausen (2 ed.), Sedgefield, and Klaeber (1 ed.) begin a new sentence with *Hæleð*, putting either a colon or a period at the end of l. 1068*b*. But Schücking, Eng. Stud. XXXIX, 106, objected to this punctuation, proposing to return to the practice of Grein and other early edd. and to take *hæleð . . . scolde* as a second, asyndetic dependent clause introduced by *ða*: "when danger befell them, [when] the warrior of the Half-Danes was destined to fall," etc. Hoops, Bwst., pp. 55ff., Klaeber (3 ed.), von Schaubert, and Holthausen (8 ed.) follow Schücking's arrangement. In Eng. Stud. LV, 92ff., Schücking pointed out that elsewhere in Beowulf *scolde* immediately preceded by the infinitive occurs only at the end of a subordinate clause (ll. 10*b*, 85*b*, 230*b*, 1034*b*, 1260*b*, etc.). This rule is not quite without exception; the clause ending with l. 1106*b* is an independent clause (though Schücking says that it is not). But the weight of the evidence is in favor of Schücking's punctuation, which is accordingly adopted in the present text. The pronoun *hie*, l. 1068*b*, refers to Finn's men and not to the Danes. 1071–1072 Ne huru . . . treowe] "Truly Hildeburh had no reason to praise the good faith of the Eotens." That is, she had reason to condemn their treachery. Most commentators, identifying the Eotens either as the Jutes, presumably allied with the Frisians, or as an alternative name for the Frisians, accept this interpretation, following Bugge, Beitr. XII, 29. The litotes involved here is discussed by Klaeber, Anglia LXIII, 414f., who cites Elene 918f., Guthlac 239f., 421, 1356f., and Brunanburh 39f. as similar examples of this rhetorical figure. 1072 unsynnum] Grundtvig, note, suggested *unsynnigum*, and Holthausen, Anglia Beibl. X, 273, *unsynngum*, dat. plur. of *unsynnig*, parallel to *leofum* in the next line. But this emendation, adopted by Trautmann and Holthausen (1–5 ed.), is unnecessary. The form *unsynnum*, "guiltlessly," is generally accepted as an adverbial instrumental of the noun, compounded with *un-*; other examples of this type of compound are *unwearnum*, l. 741, *unrædum*, Phoenix 403, *unsnyttrum*, Guthlac 859, Juliana 145, 308, etc. See Kock, Anglia XLVI, 79f. 1073 lindplegan] So Kemble and all later edd., except Grundtvig, to provide alliteration. 1074 bearnum ond broðrum] Hildeburh apparently lost only one brother (Hnæf) and one son in the fight. For the use of the plural here, see l. 565, note. on gebyrd]

Usually translated, "to their fate." Cosijn, Aant., p. 18, would, however, trans-late, "in turn, one after the other," and so doubtfully Bos.-Tol., Supp., p. 301 (s.v. *ge-byrd* VIII). Cosijn compares *on gebyrd faran an æfter anum*, Solomon and Saturn 386f., where he apparently takes *on gebyrd* and *an æfter anum* as equivalent terms. But there is no reason for believing that *on gebyrd* means the same as *an æfter anum*, and the passage from Solomon and Saturn seems rather to reinforce the meaning "to their fate" which is generally assumed in Beow. 1074. In a gloss of Latin *conditio* in MS. Harley 3376 (Wright-Wülker, Anglo-Saxon and Old English Vocabularies, I, 213, 2ff.), *gebyrd* appears together with *gescæp*, *gewyrd*, and *gescæft* and is apparently to be regarded as synonymous with them. **1079 heo]** So Thorpe and all later edd. except Chambers, following Ettmüller, Sc. Chambers retains the MS. *he*, as referring to Finn, and begins the new sentence with l. 1079*b*, putting only a comma after *wynne*. Williams, FE., pp. 34ff., would also retain *he*, with a similar interpretation. But ll. 1079*b*–1080*a* seem rather to belong with what precedes. Although the masculine pronouns which are sometimes used to refer to Grendel's mother (see l. 1260, note) have been left unemended in the text, it seems proper to emend here, where Hildeburh is the apparent reference. **1083 wig . . . gefeohtan]** Klaeber, JEGPh. XIV, 548, translates, "he could not at all give fight to Hengest," taking *wig* as cognate accusative. Malone, JEGPh. XXV, 157, translates, "so that he could not . . . in any wise fight out the fight with Hengest," bringing out more clearly the perfective sense of *gefeohtan*. Either of these translations is possible. The usual perfective meaning of *gefeohtan*, "to obtain by fighting," hardly permits *wig* as a direct object. Rieger, Lesebuch, emends to *wiht Hengeste wið gefeohtan*, "to obtain anything (*wiht*) by fighting against Hengest," and so Ettmüller, Holthausen (1 ed.). See also Rieger's note in ZfdPh. III, 394f. Holder (1 ed.), Holthausen (3–5, 7 ed.) accept Rieger's *wið* in l. 1083*b* but retain *wig* in l. 1083*a*. Klaeber, Anglia XXVIII, 443f., proposed to read *wig Hengeste wiht gebeodan*, citing ll. 601ff. and Andreas 217ff. So also Holthausen (2 ed.). But no emendation is necessary. **1084 forþringan]** Nearly all edd. translate this verb as "to rescue, protect," following Grein, Spr. I, 332. There is, however, no evidence for such a meaning of *forþringan*, and the most probable translation is "to drive out, expel." See Carleton Brown, MLN. XXXIV, 181ff.; Williams, FE., pp. 166ff.; Malone, JEGPh. XXV, 115. A similar meaning of *forþringan* is found in the passage *ne seo ylde þa geogoðe ne forþringe*, "nor shall age displace youth," Benedictine Rule (ed. A. Schröer), 115, 6f. Lines 1084–1085*a* then mean "nor drive out by battle the wretched survivors of the thanes of the prince." This translation involves emending the MS. *ðegne*, l. 1085, to *ðegna*; see the following note. **1085 ðegna]** The emendation to *ðegna*, as gen. plur. dependent on *wealafe*, was first proposed by Carleton Brown, MLN. XXXIV, 181ff., and is adopted by Sedgefield (3 ed.). Mackie, MLRev. XXXIV, 520f., would retain *ðegne* as a variant form of *ðegna* with weakening of the unstressed vowel. Moore, JEGPh. XVIII, 208f., retains *ðegne* as dat. sing., parallel to *Hengeste*, l. 1083, apparently regarding l. 1084 as parenthetical. Malone, JEGPh. XXV, 157, also retaining *ðegne* as dat. sing., translates, "nor expel the survivors by battle with the king's thane [i.e., Hengest]." Similarly

Malone, ELH X, 266.   In Eng. Studies XV, 150, however, Malone explains *ðegne* as dative of accompaniment, grammatically attached to *wealafe*.   Hoops, Bwst., pp. 57f., explains *ðegne* as dative of interest.   None of these interpretations of the MS. *ðegne* is convincing, and the emendation to *ðegna* is to be preferred on stylistic grounds.   1085*b*–1086*a*] In these lines *hig, hie* refer to the Frisians and *him* to Hengest's men; in l. 1087*b*, on the other hand, *hie* refers to the Danes.   1086–1087 oðer flet . . . , healle ond heahsetl] Bugge, Beitr. XII, 29, translated *oðer flet* as "eine andere halle," but this rendering seems inconsistent with the implications of *healfre geweald*. Heusler, Anz. fdA. XLI, 32, suggests that the *oðer flet* and the second high-seat presumably assigned to the Danes are to be equated with the *úæðri bekkr,* "the lower (or southern) bench," and the *annat öndvegi,* "the second high-seat," mentioned in Icelandic texts (see Cleasby-Vigfusson, Icelandic-English Dict., pp. 56f., s.v. *bekkr*; pp. 764f., s.v. *önd-vegi*). Heusler translates, "dass sie ihnen (die Friesen den Dänen) die ganze eine bankbühne der halle nebst dem (zugehörigen) hochsitz einräumen sollten," and calls attention to the Ynglinga saga, chap. 37, where such an arrangement is made by King Granmar for his visitor king Hjörvarth.   But Heusler's translation, in so far as it takes *healle* as gen. sing., dependent on *oðer flet eal,* is improbable. As Klaeber, Anglia L, 230, says, *healle* "has all the appearance of being the variation of *flet.*"   Also, in a half-line like *healle ond heahsetl* the two nouns are normally parallel in syntax. See also Hoops, Bwst., pp. 58ff., where "hall-space" is suggested as the meaning of *healle*.   In any case, there is no longer any reason to believe that a second hall was put at the disposal of the Danes; both Danes and Frisians were undoubtedly to be entertained in the same hall.   1087 healfre] Thorpe, Trautmann, Holthausen (1–5 ed.), and Sedgefield emend to *healfne,* as modifier of *geweald,* following a suggestion by Ettmüller, Sc.   But the MS. *healfre* is gen. sing. feminine, referring back to *healle*: "control of half [the hall]."   1088 wið Eotena bearn] "As compared with the sons of the Eotens" or "together with the sons of the Eotens"?   Either of these translations is possible.   But Heusler, Anz. fdA. XLI, 32, translates ll. 1087*b*–1088, "so dass es ihnen (den Dänen) vergönnt war, der halben (halle) zu walten gegenüber den kindern der Eoten," and similarly Malone, JEGPh. XXV, 157, "so that they [Danes] should have control of the half [of the hall] opposite the sons of the Euts."   1097 elne, unflitme] "Strongly and indisputably," Kock, Anglia XLII, 109. The meaning of *unflitme* is not certain, but most commentators connect it with the verb *flītan,* "to strive, contend."   For the -*me* suffix, cf. *unhlitme,* also of uncertain meaning, in l. 1129.   Grundtvig suggested emending to *unhlytme* in the present passage, and Holthausen (1 ed.) reads *unhlitme.*   Trautmann, FH., p.24, and in his edition, emends to *elne unblinne,* "mit unablässigem eifer." Mackie, MLRev. XXXIV, 521, would emend to *unflitne,* instr. sing. of *unfliten,* past participle of *flītan* with the negative prefix; he translates, "with undisputed zeal," "earnestly and sincerely."   1099 þæt] Klaeber, Anglia XXVIII, 444, taking ll. 1099*b*–1101 as referring to the Danes, translates *þæt* as "on condition that" and *þonne,* l. 1104, as adversative, "on the other hand."   See also Klaeber, Eng. Stud. LXVIII, 114, Beitr. LXXII, 121f., and his 3d ed., note.   But these lines more probably refer to the Frisians and describe a second concession on the part of Finn (the first having been described in ll. 1098–1099a). In that case, *þæt*, l. 1099b, is parallel to *þæt*, l. 1098a. See Malone, JEGPh. XXV, 158, 163; Hoops, Bwst., p. 60. A similar explanation is given by Williams, FE., pp. 65f.

1101–1150

1101 ne ... gemænden] "Nor should they [the Frisians] ever mention it." For this meaning of *gemænan*, see Bos.-Tol., Supp., p. 364. The verbs *bræce* and *gemænden* are then syntactically parallel, in spite of the difference in number.   **1102 ðeah]** Apparently used in the sense of *þæt*, and Trautmann emends to *þæt*. But Malone, JEGPh. XXV, 158, translates literally, "nor ... should they [Frisians] ever mention it, although they [Danes] ... were following the slayer of their king." Similarly Malone, ELH X, 266.   **1104 frecnan]** So Thorpe, Grein, Bib., Heyne, and most later edd.   **1106 seðan]** Unless the MS. *syððan* is a verb, there is no infinitive dependent on *scolde*. Most of the earlier edd. assumed a verb *syððan*, "to avenge," and cited the MS. *seðe*, Genesis 1525, as a form of the same verb. So, for example, Grein, Spr. II, 423 (s.v. *seððan*), Heyne, Holder, Socin, Wyatt, and Schücking (8 ed.). But the MS. *seðe* in Genesis 1525 is probably to be emended to *sece*, as in the present edition (Records I, 47), and therefore gives little support to a verb *syððan* here. Holthausen (1, 2, 6 ed.), retaining *syððan* as an adverb, assumes the loss of a line after l. 1106; the same suggestion had previously been made by Sievers, Beitr. IX, 139. Schücking (9–14 ed.) and von Schaubert also retain *syððan* as an adverb, with *myndgiend wesan* or the like to be supplied in sense. See Schücking's note, Eng. Stud. XLII, 109f. This explanation is accepted by Hoops, Bwst., pp. 60f., but is rejected by Klaeber, Anglia LXIII, 416. An explanation of *syððan* similar to Schücking's is given by Moore, in Klaeber Misc., pp. 208ff., who cites other examples of the ellipsis of a verb and considers the MS. reading of l. 1106 to justify some such interpretation as "Then the sword's edge should attend to (deal with) it later." Kock, Anglia XLII, 109, would assume a verb *syððan*, related to *seoðan* and meaning "to atone." Similarly Malone, ELH X, 266. Trautmann, FH., p. 19, suggested emending to *sehtan*, "to settle, adjust," or *seman*, with the same meaning. Trautmann and Sedgefield (1, 2 ed.) adopt *sehtan* in their texts, and this emendation is approved by Carleton Brown, PMLA LIII, 912. The verb *sehtan* is, however, probably a loan from the Scandinavian (see E. Björkman, Scandinavian Loan-Words in Middle English I [Halle, 1900], 100), and one would not expect to find it in the early poetry. Imelmann, Deutsche Literaturzeitung XXX, 998, suggested *scyran*, citing l. 1939; this reading, however, would give an irregular alliteration. Klaeber, JEGPh. VIII, 255f., proposed to emend to *seðan*, suggesting that this verb, which regularly means "to declare, testify, prove," here means "to decide, settle." Klaeber and Sedgefield (3 ed.) emend to *seðan* in their texts. Holthausen (3–5 ed.) emends to *swyðan*, "to make strong" (i.e., to affirm?); see also his note in ZfdPh. XLVIII, 130. Holthausen (7, 8 ed.) reads *sidian*, "to arrange," following Sievers's unpublished edition of the poem; see Holthausen's note, Literaturblatt LIX, 164.   Cf. the verbs *besidian*, *gesidian*, "to regulate, arrange," Bos.-Tol., Supp., pp. 83, 411, as well as the noun *sydung*, Bos.-Tol., p. 962.   These words, however, do not occur in the poetry.   None of the proposed emendations is entirely convincing, but in the absence of any dependable evidence for a verb *syððan*, it seems best to put the most likely of the emendations, Klaeber's *seðan*, into the text.   1107 Ad] Suggested by Grundtvig, tr., p. 283, and adopted by Klaeber, Holthausen (6, 7 ed.), and Sedgefield (3 ed.).   This emendation is supported by *Æt þæm ade*, l. 1110, as well as by *Sie sio bær . . . geæfned*, ll. 3105f.   See also Klaeber, JEGPh. VIII, 256, Anglia L, 230f., Sedgefield, MLRev. XXVII, 449, and Hoops, p. 139. The scribe who wrote *að* was apparently still thinking of the oaths sworn by Finn in l. 1097.   icge] The meaning of this word is not known.   It may, however, be the same word as *incge-*, l. 2577, and *inge-*, Exodus 142, 190.   Brett, MLRev. XIV, 2, suggests that the root-meaning "mighty" would fit well in all three passages.   A connection with *idge*, Phoenix 407, is less likely.   As in the other passages cited, a number of emendations have been proposed here. Bugge, Beitr. XII, 30, would emend the MS. *7 icge gold* to *ondiege gold*, citing the Gothic adverb *andaugjo*, "openly."   Sedgefield (1 ed.), following Bugge, emends to *andiege gold*, explaining *andiege* either as an adverb, "openly," or as an adjective, "confronting the eye," i.e., ready.   Sedgefield (3 ed.) emends to *ondlicge gold*, "gold lying stored."   In MLRev. XXVII, 449, Sedgefield had proposed the more violent emendation to *æðelinga gold*.   Holthausen (2 ed.) reads *itge* for the MS. *icge*, explaining it (1 ed., note) as a weak form of an adjective **itig* (cf. the suggestion made by Hollander for the MS. *isig* in l. 33); similarly Holthausen, Eng. Stud. LXXIV, 324f. Holthausen (3–5 ed.) reads *icge* as the equivalent of *idge*, "eagerly," on the basis of *idge*, Phoenix 407.   Bouman, Acta Philologica Scandinavica X, 143f., would explain *icge* as a Kentish form, the equivalent of *ecge*, "by (on) the spearpoint."   But it seems more likely that *icge* represents an adjective.   None of the proposals already mentioned is especially convincing; for other suggestions, which are less promising and which therefore need not be summarized here, see Singer, Beitr. XII, 213f.; Holthausen, Anglia Beibl. XIII, 363f.; Grienberger, Anglia XXVII, 331f.; Klaeber, JEGPh. VIII, 256; R. E. Zachrisson, Studia Neophilologica I (1928), 75; Malone, ELH X, 266f.   1112b–1113] That is, the funeral ceremony was not only for Hnæf but also for the other warriors who had been killed in the fight.   Line 1113b, "certain ones had fallen in the battle," accounts for the presence of the other dead warriors.   Klaeber, Anglia XXVIII, 444f., Mod. Phil. III, 248, explains *sume* as an example of litotes, the equivalent of "a good many."   1115 sunu] Acc. sing.   See l. 1074, note, and Hoops, p. 140.   1116 banfatu] Other compounds of *ban-* denoting the body are also used in the plural, even with singular meaning; so *banlocan*, l. 818, and *banhus*, l. 3147.   But *bancofan*, l. 1445, is dat. sing., and the number of *banlocan*, l. 742, is uncertain. 1117 eame on eaxle] If the MS. *earme* is retained, there are some difficulties of interpretation.   Grein, Heyne, Wülker, Socin, Wyatt, Holder (2 ed.), Schücking, Chambers, and von Schaubert take *earme* as weak nom. sing. feminine, modifying *ides*.   So also Williams, FE., pp. 75f., 110, and Malone, JEGPh.

XXV, 158, ELH X, 270. Other commentators begin a new sentence with l. 1117*b*. Thorpe emended *eaxle* to *axe*, translating, "and on the pile be done the luckless ones to ashes"; this emendation was approved by Rieger, ZfdPh. III, 395, who, however, translated, "die armen in die asche." Schröer, Anglia XIII, 334, retaining the MS. reading, would take *on eaxle* as meaning "beside him (i.e., Hnæf)." A similar interpretation had been adopted by J. Grimm in 1849; see his Kleinere Schriften II (Berlin, 1865), 262. Boer, ZfdA. XLVII, 134f., suggested *earm ond eaxle*, "arm and shoulder," referring to the entire body of the son. In support of this unlikely emendation he cited ll. 835*a*, 972*a*; he might also have cited l. 745*a*. Holthausen, Beitr. XVI, 549f., proposed to read *eame on eaxle*, "at his uncle's shoulder," as in the text. This slight emendation, which satisfies all the requirements of the passage, is adopted by Trautmann, Holthausen, Sedgefield, and Klaeber.   1118 Guðrinc astah] This probably means "the warrior ascended"; that is, the body, perhaps of Hnæf but more probably of the unnamed son of Hildeburh, was placed on the pyre. See Bugge, Tidskrift VIII, 50f., who cites Vafþrúðnismál, st. 54, in the Poetic Edda, *hvat mælti Óðinn áðr á bál stigi . . . ?* "what did Odin say before he ascended the pyre?" Grundtvig, tr., p. 284, and in his edition, emended to *guðrec*; Grein, ed., and Trautmann read *guðreoc*, "battle-smoke." Grein, Bib., suggested *guðhring*, doubtfully glossed as "clamor," Spr. I, 535. Sedgefield emends to *guðhring* but glosses it as "spiral of smoke." But no emendation is necessary. In ll. 1114–1118*a* we are told that Hildeburh ordered her son's body to be put on the pyre beside his uncle's; in l. 1118*b* we learn that it was actually placed there.   1119 Wand to wolcnum] Holthausen (7, 8 ed.) supplies *ða* after *Wand*, following Sievers's unpublished edition of the poem.   1120 for hlawe] Holthausen, ZfdPh. XXXVII, 116, suggested emending to *for hrawe*, "on account of the body," and so in his 1st ed. Grundtvig suggested *from hlawe*, and so Trautmann, who translates, "prasselte vom hügel." Other less probable suggestions are made by Klaeber, Eng. Stud. XXXIX, 463. But there is no reason for rejecting the MS. reading if we take *for* as the equivalent of *fore* and translate, "in front of the (burial-)mound." See Chambers, note.   1122 laðbite] Probably nom. plur., parallel to *bengeato*. So Schücking (9–14 ed.), Klaeber, and von Schaubert; see also Schücking's note in Eng. Stud. XLII, 110. Most other edd. take *laðbite* as dat. sing. after *ætspranc*, with no comma after l. 1121*b*.   1125 wigend] Usually explained as referring to the Frisian warriors; see, for example, Hoops, p. 141. On the other hand, Williams, FE., pp. 78ff., and Malone, JEGPh. XXV, 158, Mod. Phil. XLIII, 83ff., take the word as referring to the Danes. But, as Hoops points out, *wica* (or *hames*) *neos(i)an* and similar phrases always mean "to go home" (cf. ll. 125, 2366, 2388, etc.), and *wica neosian* is therefore not applicable to the Danes here.   1126 Frysland geseon] We would expect Finnsburh, an estate of the king of the Frisians, to be in Frisia. Many commentators have therefore been puzzled by the apparent statement that the warriors, leaving Finnsburh, go to visit Frisia. See, for example, Girvan, Proc. of the British Academy XXVI, 344ff. Therefore Boer, ZfdA. XLVII, 136ff., would emend *Frysland* to *Frysan*, "the Frisians," parallel to *wigend*, with no comma after l. 1126*b*. Malone, Mod.

Phil. XLIII, 83ff., who considers the *wigend* to be Danes (see the preceding note), would take *geseon* in a perfective meaning and translate, "they departed [from the pyre] to see the last of Frisia"; that is, the Danes entered upon the last stage of their stay in Frisia. In support of this interpretation, Malone cites *gesawon*, l. 2252. But it is not necessary to insist on an exact literal meaning for every word in this passage, and the traditional interpretation of *Frysland geseon*, "to visit [their homes elsewhere in] Frisia," seems unobjectionable. Malone, ELH X, 274, apparently abandoning his earlier interpretation, translates simply, "The warriors . . . went to Frisia." Klaeber, JEGPh. VI, 193f., remarks that if, on the evidence of this passage, we are to assume that Finnsburh is not in Frisia, we may as well conclude from Brunanburh 55f. that Dublin is not in Ireland. See also Klaeber, Beitr. LXXII, 122f. **1127 heaburh]** Finnsburh (if this is indeed a place name, as is doubted by some commentators, notably by Trautmann, FH., p. 50, and by Magoun, ZfdA. LXXVII, 65f.) was apparently not Finn's chief stronghold but a *ham* (cf. l. 1147) like th one at Wimborne which was occupied by Æthelwold in his rising against his cousin Edward the Elder (Anglo-Saxon Chronicle, 901). **1128–1129 mid Finne eal unhlitme]** The MS. *mid finnel unhlitme*, which is deficient as regards both sense and meter, has been variously emended. Kemble (2 ed.) read *mid Finne* as the end of l. 1128, and so most later edd. This leaves the *-l* of the MS. *finnel* to be explained, as well as the word *unhlitme*, which is apparently an adverb. Kemble (2 ed.) read *elne unhlitme* as l. 1129a (probably on the model of l. 1097a), and so Holder (2 ed.), Socin (6, 7 ed.), Holthausen (1–5, 7 ed.), Schücking, and Chambers. Heyne and Socin (5 ed.) read *ealles unhlitme*; Klaeber, Holthausen (6, 8 ed.), and von Schaubert read *eal unhlitme*. Grein, ed., Ettmüller, Wülker, Holder (1 ed.), Wyatt, and Sedgefield read *elne*, with Kemble, but emend *unhlitme* to *unflitme*, as in l. 1097a, following Thorpe. Prokosch, in Klaeber Misc., p. 200, approves the emendation to *unflitme* and would read either *elne* or *eal* at the beginning of the line; he translates, "quite without quarrel." But there is no need to emend *unhlitme*. This word, not elsewhere recorded, is to be connected with *hlytm*, "casting of lots," and the related words, and means "without casting of lots"; that is, Hengest, having no choice, was forced to remain with Finn. Cf. *on hlytme*, l. 3126. **1130 þeah þe he ne meahte]** The MS. has only *þeah þe he meahte*, but the context seems to demand a negative. Grundtvig, tr., p. 284, suggested supplying *ne* after *he*, and so in his edition. This emendation is adopted by Heyne, Wülker, Holder, Socin, Wyatt, Holthausen (1–3 ed.), Schücking (8, 9 ed.), and Sedgefield. Grein and Holthausen (5–8 ed.) emend the MS. *he* to *ne*, thus reading *þeah þe ne meahte*. (The reading *þeah ne meahte* in Grein, ed., was apparently due to an oversight; see Wülker, note.) Hoops, p. 142, would also read *þeah þe ne meahte*. Trautmann reads *þeah he ne meahte*. Klaeber, Anglia Beibl. XXII, 373f., omitting the negative, would take *gemunde, þeah þe* as similar in meaning to *þohte . . . , gif*, ll. 1139f.; see his 1st ed., note, where he explains that Hengest "thought longingly of his home, if . . . [speculating whether . . . , wishing for a chance to sail]." Malone, JEGPh. XXV, 158, also accepting the MS. reading, translates, "He longed for home, wondered whether he could drive his ring-prowed ship upon the waters." Similarly Malone, ELH X, 274. Schücking (10-14 ed.), Holthausen (4 ed.), and von Schaubert also follow the MS., with Klaeber's interpretation. But Klaeber (3 ed.) reads *þeah þe ne meahte*, with Grein. The weight of probability is on the side of the negative construction; without the negative, the logical relationship of ll. 1131*b*–1133*a* to what precedes is very slight. Whether we assume that the scribe has omitted the negative or take the MS. *he* as a scribal error for *ne*, seems immaterial. **1134–1135** swa nu gyt deð, þa ðe] The MS. reading of this passage gives the impression that the subject of the singular *deð* is also the antecedent of the plural relative *þa ðe* in the next line. To avoid this apparent lack of congruence, Thorpe emended *deð* to the plural *doð*, translating, "so now yet do those who constantly watch a happy moment." Cosijn, Aant., pp. 19f., independently proposed the emendation *doað*, and so Trautmann (*doð*), Holthausen (2–8 ed.), and Schücking. Sedgefield, retaining *deð*, emends *þa* to *þam*; see also his note, MLRev. V, 287, where he translates, "as it (the year) still does (come) to those who are continually watching the seasons." Bugge, Beitr. XII, 30f., proposed to put l. 1135 after l. 1141, construing *Eotena bearn* as the antecedent of *þa . . . bewitiað* and taking *sele* as *sĕle*, "hall"; he translates, "die welche unablässig den saal bewachen." But, as Cosijn pointed out, the present tense in l. 1135 forbids putting this line after l. 1141. Boer, ZfdA. XLVII, 138f., apparently accepting Cosijn's *doað*, suggested taking ll. 1131*b*–1133*a* as a parenthesis, with l. 1134*b* then referring back to ll. 1129*b*–1131*a*; that is, Hengest thought of his home, as others do who are in the same situation. This punctuation is accepted by Schücking, Eng. Stud. XXXIX, 106, and adopted in his edition. Chambers, Klaeber, and von Schaubert, together with Hoops, p. 143, avoid the incongruence in these lines by taking *wuldortorhtan weder* as a variation of *oþer . . . gear* and as the antecedent of the preceding relative clause. We may then translate, "until another year came, as it still does, the gloriously bright weathers which always observe the (proper) seasons." **1135** sele] A variant form of *sæle*, acc. plur. of *sæl*, "time, season." This noun is found with both masculine and feminine endings. **1140** þurhteon] "Carry through (to its conclusion)." This meaning is preferable to "bring about," adopted by many edd. **1141** þæt . . . gemunde] The meaning of this line is not immediately clear, and a number of emendations have been proposed. Thorpe emended *þæt* to *þæs*. Sievers, Beitr. XII, 193, in citing this line, emended *þæt* to *þær*, without comment, and translated, "wo wie er wusste die helden sich befanden." So also Holthausen (3, 7 ed.). Cosijn, Beitr. XXI, 26, proposed to supply *wið* before *Eotena*, the word *þæt* as a relative then referring back to *torngemot*. This emendation is adopted by Sedgefield and by Holthausen (4–6 ed.). Klaeber, Eng. Stud. XXXIX, 430f., suggested emending *þæt he* to *þætte* and taking *gemunde* as a plural subjunctive form without final *-n*, the subject of the verb then being *Eotena bearn*: "dass die Kinder der E. in ihrem inneren daran denken würden." Trautmann, FH., pp. 24f., and in his edition, emends *inne* to *irne*, "dass er der Friesen mit dem eisen gedächte," and this reading is accepted by Hoops, Bwst., p. 64, Klaeber (3 ed.), and Holthausen (8 ed.). But it is at least doubtful that such a form as *irne* would have been possible in so early a text as Beowulf, and the uncontracted form *irenne* would give an exceptional metrical type. No emendation is necessary in this line if *þæt . . . inne* is taken as the equivalent of a relative, following E. A. Kock, The English Relative Pronouns (Lund, 1897), p. 35. Cf. *þæt . . . on,* Daniel 418, Christ 326f., *þæt . . . ymb,* Riddle 23, 11, and probably also *þæt . . . þurh,* Judith 48f. This interpretation is adopted by Chambers and von Schaubert, also by Malone, JEGPh. XXV, 158, who translates, "in which he would be mindful of the children of the Euts." Schücking translates *inne* as "darin" (that is, in the battle), taking *þæt* as a conjunction, and similarly Kock, Arkiv för nordisk Filologi XXXIX, 187f. This construction is possible but is less convincing than Kock's earlier interpretation. Williams, FE., pp. 91f., and Girvan, Proc. of the British Academy XXVI, 352, explain *Eotena bearn* as nom. sing. and a variation of *he,* making the improbable assumption that the Eotens are Danes and that the *Eotena bearn* is Hengest. 1142-1145] These four lines, though not so obscure as many other passages in Beowulf, are of fundamental importance in the reconstruction of the Finnsburh story and consequently have received more critical attention than perhaps they would otherwise merit. The traditional interpretation of the passage, as represented for example by Lawrence, PMLA XXX, 417ff., Ayres, JEGPh. XVI, 292f., and R. W. Chambers, Beowulf: an Introduction, pp. 252f., 285f., has been vigorously disputed by Malone, JEGPh. XXV, 158f., MLN. XLIII, 300ff., ELH X, 276ff., but has recently been defended by Brodeur, The Climax of the Finn Episode. In the present discussion the traditional lines of argument are followed for the most part, but with certain modifications which are required by Malone's findings. The first problem which confronts us is the question whether or not l. 1142 begins a new sentence. All recent edd. except Schücking and von Schaubert put either a period or a semicolon at the end of l. 1141, thus beginning a new main clause with *Swa,* l. 1142a, which is construed as an adverb. Schücking puts only a comma after l. 1141b and a period after l. 1142b, taking *swa* as a conjunction and l. 1142 as the end of the sentence which begins with *Fundode,* l. 1137b (or, in his punctuation, with *Ða wæs,* l. 1136b). He translates (in his glossary), "ohne dass er die Bedingung versagte (d.h. bräche), d.h. ohne dass er seine Schwüre bräche." That is, Hengest was meditating how he might perform his duty of revenge without breaking the oath he had made to Finn. Von Schaubert adopts Schücking's punctuation but explains *woroldrædenne* as a variant form of *woroldrædende,* "lord" (following Malone, Anglia LIII, 335f.; see the note on that word, below), and applies it to Finn. She translates (in her note), "ohne dem Fürsten (Finn) abzusagen." Malone, JEGPh. XXV, 158f., with an interpretation quite different from Schücking's, also takes *swa* as a conjunction; he puts a comma after l. 1141b, with no period until the end of l. 1145, and translates, "since he did not prevent his lord when he [Hnæf] laid in his [Hengest's] lap Hunlafing, the battle-gleamer, the best of bills; its edges were known to the Euts." In a footnote Malone defends the punctuation with a comma after l. 1141b, pointing out that "the use of an adverbial *swa* to introduce a negative clause is excessively rare." Further evidence to the same effect is presented by E. E. Ericson, in Studies in Honor of Hermann Collitz (Baltimore, 1930), pp. 159-175, who claims that in his collection of representative examples of *swa* in negative clauses, "there is not a single clear case of adverbial (non-conjunctive) *swa* in the initial position." By "clear case" he presumably means an unambiguous case. But the punctuation of clauses beginning with *þa, swa,* and similar words is notoriously difficult—so much so that one is frequently tempted to resort to the coin-tossing technique suggested by Ericson, p. 168. And in two of the *swa*-clauses which Ericson discusses (both of them, to be sure, from the late Genesis B), *swa* seems to be an adverb rather than a subordinating conjunction. These are the clause beginning with Genesis 289*b*, which Ericson classifies as a causal clause, and the one beginning with Genesis 733*b*, which he calls a clause of result. In both of these negative clauses *swa* is best translated as "therefore," introducing a new sentence. Brodeur, The Climax of the Finn Episode, pp. 293ff., defends this meaning of *swa* in Genesis 289*b*; what he says of this passage is, in general, also applicable to the other. Thus, while we must agree with Malone's statement that negative clauses with initial adverbial *swa* are rare, we cannot accept Ericson's conclusion that they do not exist. And in Beow. 1142ff. the older punctuation, with *Swa* explained as an adverb at the beginning of a new sentence, seems clearly superior to the interpretations by Schücking, von Schaubert, and Malone. In ll. 1137ff. we learn that Hengest is meditating revenge against Finn; in ll. 1142ff. the narrative proceeds: "Therefore he did not refuse the obligation imposed by custom, when Hunlafing (or Hunlaf, which is a possible emendation) put into his lap the battle-flame, the best of swords, the edges of which were well known among the Eotens." For the details of this interpretation, see the following notes. The more general questions involved are discussed in the Introd., p. xlviii. 1142 forwyrnde] The verb *forwyrnan,* "to refuse," is regularly construed with the genitive of the thing refused and the dative of the person to whom it is refused. Cf. *Me þæs forwyrnde,* Genesis 2221; *þæt he his lichoman* (dat. sing.) *wynna forwyrnde,* Guthlac 163f.; *þy læs eow wiþerfeohtend weges forwyrnen,* Juliana 664f. In Beow. 1142 (if the interpretation accepted by Lawrence and Ayres is correct; see the following note) there is no dative of the person, but *woroldrædenne* is apparently genitive of the thing. Sanderlin, MLN. LIII, 501ff., supporting Malone's explanation of *woroldrædenne* as dat. sing., "earthly ruler" (see the following note), gives statistics to show that if *woroldrædenne* is dat. sing., it must denote a person rather than an abstract idea. But this tells us nothing new, and if *woroldrædenne* is gen. sing., Sanderlin's statistics are irrelevant to the present passage. See Brodeur, The Climax of the Finn Episode, pp. 302-313. woroldrædenne] The MS. *woroldrædenne* can be explained as gen. sing. of a feminine abstract noun *woroldrǣden* meaning "law (or custom) of the world," semantically similar to *folcrǣden* and *landrǣden,* both of which mean "law (or custom) of a people or nation." Möller, Das altenglische Volksepos I, 68, suggested the emendation *worodrædenne,* translating, "so wehrte er dem willen der gefolgschaft nicht." This emendation was adopted by Socin in his edition. Bugge, Beitr. XII, 31ff., approved of Möller's reading but interpreted it differently, as meaning that Hengest did not refuse allegiance to Finn; he apparently took this line as a further reference to the agreement in ll. 1095ff., a very unlikely supposition.

Sedgefield (2, 3 ed.), also reading *worodrædenne*, glosses it as "troop-service."
Trautmann, FH., p. 25, and in his edition, emends to *wraðrædenne*, "assistance,
support"; a noun *wraðræden* is possible, on the model of *gafolræden, weorcræ-
den*, and the like, but is not elsewhere recorded. Malone, The Literary History
of Hamlet I, 22, emends to *woroldrædende*, "earthly ruler, king"; in JEGPh.
XXV, 159, with the same reading, he explains l. 1142 as meaning that Hengest
"did not prevent his lord" (i.e., Hnæf) when the latter bestowed upon him the
gift of a sword. In Anglia LIII, 335f., Malone would retain the MS. *woroldrædenne* as a variant form of *woroldrædende*; cf. his similar explanation of the MS.
selerædenne, l. 51. Von Schaubert also translates *woroldrædenne* as "prince"
but applies it to Finn; see the note on ll. 1142–1145, above. Klaeber, Anglia
LVI, 421f., proposed *worodrædende*, translating, "So, then, he did not refuse
[sc. it, i.e. *torngemotes*] to the ruler of the host" (i.e., to Finn); in his 3d ed. he
reads *weorodrædende*, with the same interpretation. It should be noted that
Malone's and von Schaubert's readings, as well as Klaeber's emendation just
cited, are dat. sing. (the usual case of the person after *forwyrnan*) rather than
gen. sing. But there is no need of a reference to a king (either Hnæf or Finn)
at this point. The MS. *woroldrædenne*, if taken as gen. sing. and as meaning
"law of the world," "obligation imposed by custom," or the like, provides satisfactory sense. Williams, FE., pp. 95f., translates *woroldrædenne* as "the uni-
versal obligation," that is, the duty of revenge. Klaeber, JEGPh. XIV, 546f.,
translated l. 1142, "he did not refuse [him, i.e., Hūnlāfing] the condition (stipu-
lation)," and so in his 1st ed. The translation by Clark Hall, MLN. XXV,
114, "He did not run counter to the way of the world," is acceptable, but Hall's
suggestion that this is to be interpreted from the religious point of view, as
meaning that Hengest fell into temptation, is less probable. Lawrence's
paraphrase in PMLA XXX, 418, "he did his worldly duty" (that is, the duty of
revenge), expresses in general terms the import of the passage. Ayres's rendering in JEGPh. XVI, 292, "he did not *thus* prove recreant to his duty," amounts
to the same thing but is somewhat more literal. For a discussion of the meaning of *woroldræden*, which supports the interpretation adopted here, see Brodeur,
The Climax of the Finn Episode, pp. 313–330.   **1143** Hunlafing] This word
is usually identified, following Cosijn, Aant., p. 20, as the name of the warrior
who gave the sword to Hengest. Bugge, Beitr. XII, 32f., had previously read
it as two words, *Hun Lafing*, taking *Hun* as a personal name (cf. Widsith 33)
and *Lafing* as a sword name (cf. *Hrunting*, the name of Hunferth's sword, ll.
1457, 1490, etc., and *Nægling*, Beowulf's sword, l. 2680). So also Socin, Holder
(2 ed.), Trautmann, Schücking (8 ed.), and Sedgefield (1 ed.). But in view of
the discovery, in Arngrímur Jónsson's epitome of the lost Skjöldunga saga (ed.
A. Olrik, Aarbøger for Nordisk Oldkyndighed og Historie, 2d Series, IX [1894],
107), of the names Hunleifus, Oddleifus, and Gunnleifus, borne by three of the
six sons of King Leifus of Denmark and to be equated with the Anglo-Saxon
names Hunlaf, Ordlaf, and Guthlaf, the reading *Hun Lafing* has been regarded
as untenable. The passage in Arngrímur was first pointed out by H. M. Chadwick, The Origin of the English Nation (Cambridge, 1907), p. 52, note, and its
significance for Beow. 1143 was first shown by R. Huchon, Revue germanique

III (1907), 626, note. Axel Olrik, Danmarks Heltedigtning I (Copenhagen, 1903), 60 (translated in The Heroic Legends of Denmark [New York, 1919], pp. 145f.), reading *Hunlafing* as a compound, had explained it as a sword name, "the sword owned by Hunlaf." This interpretation, previously suggested by Rieger, ZfdPh. III, 396ff. (who took Finn to be the subject of *dyde*) and by R. Koegel, Geschichte der deutschen Litteratur bis zum Ausgange des Mittelalters, Vol. I, Part 1 (Strassburg, 1894), p. 167, is followed by Malone, MLN. XLIII, 300ff., and by Hoops, pp. 144f. Malone shows that everywhere else in Beowulf a patronymic in *-ing* either is accompanied by the true name (ll. 4, 1923, 2925, 2965) or serves as a variation of it (l. 877, where *Wælsinges* is equivalent to *Sigemundes*, two lines above), but never occurs alone. Nor, he argues, can *Hunlafing* be a true personal name like *Hemming* and *Swerting*. He therefore concludes that *Hunlafing* is a sword name. Elsewhere (see the preceding note) he identifies this sword as one given by Hnæf to Hengest. Brodeur, The Climax of the Finn Episode, pp. 330–355, attempts by means of analogous expressions, both in Anglo-Saxon and Old Norse (patronymic formulas involving *sunu, bearn, eafora*, etc.; *burr, sonr, dóttir*, etc.) to demonstrate the possibility that *Hunlafing* is a patronymic, but the evidence which he presents proves nothing for patronymics in *-ing*. It must, however, be pointed out that neither is there any parallel in Anglo-Saxon to a sword name *Hunlafing* with the meaning "the sword of Hunlaf," since the two other sword names in Beowulf, *Hrunting* and *Nægling*, do not mean "the sword of Hrunt, of Nægl," and there is no evidence that Mimming, Waldere's sword, was ever the property of Mimir. On this last point, see Brodeur, The Climax of the Finn Episode, pp. 332f. The argument from silence is hardly valid against *Hunlafing* either as a personal name or as a sword name, in view of the infrequency of names in *-ing* in the Old Germanic languages. On the whole, it seems unlikely that *Hunlafing* is a patronymic. But if this name cannot have the specific meaning "the son of Hunlaf," there seems to be no reason why it may not be taken in the more general sense "one of the kin of Hunlaf," as suggested by Klaeber, Anglia LVI, 422f. Klaeber cites *gamela* (*Gomela*) *Scylding*, ll. 1792, 2105, as a possible parallel; the form *Merewioingas*, l. 2921, apparently a genitive singular, may also be cited. In spite of Malone's arguments, it is difficult to believe that *Hunlafing* is a sword name. If we interpret it as such, then we are forced to make *woroldrædenne* mean something which in all probability it does not mean, in order to provide a subject for *dyde*. If *Hunlafing* is not acceptable as a personal name, the emendation to *Hunlaf* (which gives us a regular half-line of type A3) is always available. 1146 ferhðfrecan] "Bold in spirit," weak acc. sing., modifying *Fin*. So most commentators. But Williams, FE., pp. 102f., suggests taking *ferhðfrecan* as gen. sing., dependent on *sweordbealo*; he translates (p. 110), "the cruel sword-bale of the bold-minded hero" (i.e., of Hengest). Carleton Brown, PMLA LIII, 912f., proposed to emend to *ferhðfrēcen* as a noun, "mortal peril," in apposition to *sweordbealo slīðen*. The same suggestion had previously been made by Trautmann, FH., p. 27, but in his edition Trautmann retained the MS. reading. 1148–1149 grimne gripe . . . sorge] Here *grimne gripe* and *sorge* are evidently parallel objects of *mændon*, "after Guthlaf and Oslaf lamented the fierce attack . . . , their [resulting] sorrow." The significance of l. 1149a has been disputed. Ayres, JEGPh. XVI, 293, Hoops, p. 145, and Klaeber (3 ed.), p. 232, note 2, believe that the words æfter sæsiðe refer to the original voyage of Hnæf and his men to Frisia; Klaeber compares æfter deaðdæge dom, l. 885. On the other hand, Klaeber (1 ed.), p. 220, Williams, FE., pp. 101f., Malone, JEGPh. XXV, 169, ELH X, 282f., and Brodeur, Essays and Studies (Univ. of California Publications in English, Vol. XIV), p. 27, take these words as referring to a voyage made by Guthlaf and Oslaf during the truce for the purpose of bringing reinforcements. Williams, Malone, and Brodeur further believe that grimne gripe . . . , sorge mændon, ætwiton weana dæl refer to a report made by Guthlaf and Oslaf to the Danes at home.   1150 ætwiton weana dæl] However we interpret the preceding lines, it is probable that here Guthlaf and Oslaf are represented as imputing to Finn the blame for all their troubles. The alternative explanation, that they imputed these woes to Hengest (since they had been unable to perform their duty of revenge because of the truce by which he had bound them) is possible but less likely. 1150–1151 ne meahte . . . hreþre] The verb forhabban is usually taken as intransitive, "restrain itself, forbear" (cf. l. 2609), and mod as nom. sing. There is, however, less agreement as to whose mod is referred to. Bugge, Tidskrift VIII, 295, Beitr. XII, 36, interprets the text as meaning that Guthlaf and Oslaf could not restrain themselves; he translates, "Ihr unruhiger mut konnte sich in ihrer brust nicht zurückhalten." This interpretation is accepted by Chambers, Klaeber, and Hoops, p. 146. Ayres, JEGPh. XVI, 293f., on the other hand, thinks that it was Hengest who could not restrain himself. Malone, JEGPh. XXV, 159 (who assumes that Guthlaf and Oslaf made a voyage to their homeland for reinforcements; see the note on ll. 1148–1149), takes wæfre mod as referring to the Danes at home: "the restless spirit [of the Danes] could not restrain itself in the breast." Similarly Malone, ELH X, 282. Cosijn, Aant., pp. 20f., had identified the wæfre mod as Finn's and had explained the passage as meaning that Finn could not restrain his anger; it is difficult, however, to see the relevance of such a statement at this point. Williams, FE., p. 102, suggests the translation, "His [Finn's] flickering spirit had no power to restrain itself in the body"; that is, Finn was unable to remain alive. Similarly Carleton Brown, PMLA LIII, 913, who, however, construes forhabban transitively, as in Exodus 488, and translates, "Nor could he [Finn] retain his flickering spirit in his breast." Of all these many interpretations, that by Bugge seems on the whole the most probable. It is, however, not impossible that Ayres's explanation of the passage is the correct one, although Hengest has not been the subject of a sentence since l. 1142.

1151–1200

1151 roden] So Holder, Holthausen, Sedgefield, Schücking (10–14 ed.), Chambers, and Klaeber, following Bugge, Tidskrift VIII, 64, 295. This emendation was independently proposed by Sievers, Beitr. IX, 139 (see his note, ibid., p. 370), and is defended by Klaeber, Anglia XXVIII, 445. Von Schaubert, like the early edd., retains the MS. *hroden*, "covered, decorated." See l. 574*b*, note. From the point of view of meaning there can be no objection to *hroden* (cf. *onhread*, Genesis 2932), but the double alliteration in the second half-line is very questionable in so early a poem. For this use of *rēodan*, "to redden," cf. Exodus 413, Andreas 1003. A superfluous initial *h-* was written by the scribe in Beow. 1318*b* also.   1152 feorum] This use of *feorh* in the sense of "(dead) body" is paralleled by *feorh cyninges*, l. 1210, and by *feonda feorh*, Genesis 2065.   Holthausen's proposed emendation *dreore*, Literaturblatt XXI, 64, ZfdPh. XXXVII, 116, is therefore unnecessary.   1156 swylce] Trautmann and Holthausen emend to *swylc*, to secure agreement with the neuter *ingesteald*. But the plural *swylce* may have been suggested by the collective sense of *eal ingesteald*. Cf. *beaduþreata mæst, . . . swylce . . .*, Elene 31f.   1157 Hie] Nom. plur., referring to the Danes. The proposal by Andrew, p. 51, to take *hie* (= Hildeburh) as the object of *feredon* is much less likely.   1161 beorhtode] Sedgefield, MLRev. V, 287, and in his edition, emends to *beorhtmode*, "made a noise," citing *breahtmian*, Bos.-Tol., Supp., p. 104; for the *-eo-* in his emended form, he cites *beorhtme*, Elene 205. But although the verb *beorhtian* is elsewhere found only with reference to a visual image, the adjective *beorht* describes a voice in *beorhte stefne*, Gifts of Men 94. Cf. also *stefn . . . heaðotorht*, Beow. 2552f., *torhtan reorde*, Daniel 510.   1165 Unferþ] See l. 499, note.   1171 spræc] For *sprec*, imperative. See l. 407, note.   1172*b*] Heyne, Holder, Socin, Holthausen, and Sedgefield take *swa* as an adverb and put a period, colon, or semicolon after l. 1172*a*. Cf. l. 1534*b*, where *swa* undoubtedly introduces a new main clause. But for the punctuation in the text, adopted by Wyatt, Trautmann, Schücking, Chambers, Klaeber, and von Schaubert, cf. the similar construction in ll. 2590*b*–2591*a*, and see Schücking, Svk., p. 31.   1174 þu nu hafast] Although the alliteration seems to assure a main stress for *nu*, Ettmüller, Sc., supplied *friþu* after *nu*, as object of *hafast*; similarly Grein, Ettmüller, Heyne, Wülker, Holder, Socin, Wyatt, and Schücking (8 ed.) supply either *friðu* or *freoðu* after *nu*. Holthausen (7 ed.) supplies *frioðu* and in l. 1174*a* transposes the two adverbs to read *feorran ond nean*, following Sievers's unpublished edition of the poem; see his note in Literaturblatt LIX, 165. Trautmann supplies *genog* after *nu*. Carleton Brown, PMLA LIII, 913f., and Holthausen, Anglia Beibl. LIV/LV, 30, suggest *freode*, "friendship." This reading had previously been proposed but rejected by Patzig, Anglia XLVII, 99, who considered it more probable that *nu* is an error for *neode* (cf. l. 2116). Schücking (9–14 ed.) indicates a gap in the text after *nu* but supplies nothing. Kock, Anglia XLVI, 80, suggests that the missing concept is "people"; he translates (with a semicolon after l. 1173*b*), "from near and far thou now hast people here." Bugge, Beitr. XII, 92, suggested that a line was lost after l. 1174 and proposed to supply *secgas ætsomne in sele þam hean*. Sievers, Eng. Stud. XLIV, 296f., assumes a loss but would put it before l. 1174; he also suggests adding *þe* before *þu* (see Trautmann's similar reading, below). Klaeber also thinks it possible that a line has dropped out, either before or after l. 1174. In JEGPh. VIII, 256f., Klaeber had proposed to emend *hafast* to *lufast*, translating, "You love now (from) near and far"; that is, Hrothgar loves both his own people and the Geatish hero whom he has adopted. Trautmann, BVE., p. 191, suggested the addition of a relative *þa* or *þe* before *þu*, making a relative clause with *geofena* the antecedent; he translates, "der gaben eingedenk, welche du nun hast." Sedgefield supplies *þe*; so also Holthausen (5, 6 ed.), who, however, assumes the loss of a line before l. 1174. But retaining the MS. reading, we may still take l. 1174*b* as a relative clause, with Trautmann's interpretation, in spite of the lack of an expressed relative pronoun; so Holthausen (2, 3, 8 ed.) and Chambers.   1176 hererinc] So Kemble (2 ed.) and later edd., except Grundtvig, who took the MS. *hereric* to be a proper name, as in l. 2206. In Beow. 2466 the original reading *heaðo ric* is corrected (in a different ink but apparently in a contemporary hand) to *heaðo rinc*, and it is possible that a similar correction should have been made here. Grienberger, Beitr. XXXVI, 92, suggested that in the present passage the MS. *hereric* might be retained as a common noun, "heerkönig," and similarly Malone, Anglia LXIII, 103, JEGPh. L, 19ff., who translates as "army commander," referring to Beowulf. In l. 2466 Malone would accept the uncorrected reading *heaðoric*; see the note on that line. An Anglo-Saxon noun *-ric*, "ruler, commander," would be cognate with Gothic *reiks*, which has the same meaning, but would have no cognates in Old West Germanic, since German nouns like *Wüterich*, *Fähnrich*, and the like are of later origin. The explanation of the MS. reading given by Grienberger and Malone is tempting, but until further evidence for a noun *-ric* in Anglo-Saxon is forthcoming, emendation is probably the safer course.   1178 medo] For *mēda*, gen. plur. See l. 70, note.   1180 metodsceaft] Kock, Anglia XLV, 117f., points out that elsewhere in the poem (ll. 1077, 2815) *metodsceaft* seems to mean only "fate in the shape of death." He would therefore put a comma after l. 1179*b*, taking *forð* (with *faran* or *gewitan* to be supplied in sense) and *metodsceaft seon* as variations of the same idea. But for the punctuation in the text, cf. Genesis 1742f.   1185 uncran eaferan] Dat. plur.; for similar forms in *-an*, cf. *læssan*, l. 43, *ærran*, l. 907, *feorhgeniðlan*, l. 2933, etc.   1187 umborwesendum ær] For metrical reasons, Bugge, Beitr. XII, 92, would transfer *ær* to the end of l. 1186*a*, leaving only *umborwesendum* here. Trautmann, BVE., p. 191, would omit *ær* entirely.   1194 earmreade] "Arm-ornaments." Grein, Bib., emended to *earmhreade*, and so Heyne, Ettmüller, Wülker, Holder, Socin, Wyatt, Schücking (10–14 ed.), and Klaeber. This is etymologically the proper form of the second element of the compound, which is related to the verb **hrēodan*, "to decorate" (recorded only in the past participle form *hroden*). Other edd., including Holthausen, Schücking (8, 9 ed.), Sedgefield, Chambers, and von Schaubert, retain the MS. reading as a variant form of *-hreade*.   1195 hrægl ond hringas] Mackie, MLRev. XXXIV, 516, suggests that this is an example of hendiadys, "the ringed coat of mail." See ll. 104, 619, notes. Schücking also takes *hrægl ond hringas* as meaning a ringed coat of mail. Another, stylistically less likely, possibility is to take *hringas* as a variation of *earmreade*; so Klaeber, Mod. Phil. III, 242f. In any case, three gifts seem to be enumerated here, the arm-ornaments, the corselet, and the collar.   1197 Nænigne] For metrical reasons, Trautmann, BVE., p. 192, suggested *Nænne*, and so Holthausen (2, 5–8 ed.).   1198 hordmaððum] Grein and most later

edd. emend the MS. *mad mum* either to *-maððum* or to *-maðum*.   Grundtvig
suggested *-maðm*, and so Trautmann, Holthausen (2–8 ed.), Schücking, and
Sedgefield (1, 2 ed.); Chambers emends to *-madm*.   The last of these is closest
to the MS. reading; but although we find *madmas*, ll. 385, 472, 1027, etc., and
madma, ll. 36, 41, the *-d-* does not seem to occur in the nom. sing. or acc. sing.
And if we are going to emend at all, we may as well go all the way and read
-maððum (*-mapðum*), which is the regular acc. sing. form in Beowulf.   **1199**
þære] So Ettmüller, Sc., and later edd., for the MS. *here*.   Cf. Judith 326 and
the other examples of *to* (*in*) *þære byrhtan byrig* cited by Klaeber, Anglia LXIII,
418.   Malone, Widsith, p. 152, defends *here* as an Anglo-Saxon precursor of
Middle English *here*, "their," referring to the Brosings.   But a form *here*,
"their," though found in the Peterborough Chronicle under 1123 (ed. C. Plummer, I, 251, 28), would be extremely unusual in English of the end of the tenth
century.   **1200** sincfæt] "Precious setting"; cf. *goldfæt*, Phoenix 303, and see
the remarks by Klaeber in JEGPh. VI, 194.   fleah] So Heyne (1–3 ed.),
Socin, and all later edd. except von Schaubert, following Leo, Beowulf, p. 44,
and Grundtvig.   This emendation is accepted by Cosijn, Beitr. VIII, 569, and
Bugge, Beitr. XII, 69.   Hintz, JEGPh. XXXIII, 98ff., argues for the retention
of the MS. *fealh* and translates, "he reached (or incurred, or penetrated to) the
treacherous envy (or malignity) of Eormanaric."   Similarly Malone, Widsith,
p. 151, who translates, "he incurred the enmity of Ermanric," and Bos.-Tol.,
p. 275 (s.v. *felgan*), "he underwent the guileful enmity of Ermanric."   But,
as Cosijn and Bugge pointed out, *feolan* is elsewhere found only in intransitive
use.   The half-line *floh her Otachres nid*, "he fled the anger of Odoaker," in the
Old High German Hildebrandslied, l. 18, is often cited as a parallel to the
emended reading in the present passage.   See also Klaeber, Anglia LXIII,
417, who cites a similar passage in the Alfredian Bede (ed. T. Miller, 208, 7f.),
þa he þær wrecca wæs ond Rædwaldes feondscipe fleah.

1201–1250

1201 geceas ecne ræd] Klaeber, note, and Hoops, pp. 150f., interpret these words
as meaning that Hama became a good Christian.   Similarly Chambers, who
cites *ece rædas*, l. 1760, Exodus 516, and explains the phrase as meaning "coun-
sel such as will lead to eternal benefit."   See also Bugge, Beitr. XII, 70.   But
according to Malone, Eng. Studies XV, 150f., and Widsith, pp. 151f., l. 1201*b*
means simply that Hama died.   Malone compares l. 2469*b*.   The historical
basis of this passage is extremely obscure; see Introd., p. xlvi, note 16.   **1202**
hring] That is, apparently, the *healsbeag* referred to in l. 1195.   **1203** nyhstan
siðe] "On [that] last occasion."   Cf. l. 2511, Judith 73.   **1206** wean ahsode]
See l. 423, note.   For the preposition *to* after *ahsian*, see l. 158, note.   **1208**
eorclanstanas] The first element of this compound usually appears as *eorcnan-*;
cf. Elene 1024, Phoenix 603, and the passages cited in Bos.-Tol., Supp., p. 191.
It is spelled *eorcan-* in Ruin 36, and *eorclan-* in the Blickling Homilies (ed. R.
Morris, 149, 3).   **1210** feorh] Sievers, Beitr. IX, 139, suggested emending to
feoh.   Trautmann emends to *feorm*, translating, "die habe des königs."   But

feorh may mean "body, corpse," as it does in l. 1152.   See Bugge, Beitr. XII, 92.
That is, the body of the king, with his armor and the gold collar, passed into
the possession of the Franks.   Schücking, Eng. Stud. LV, 97ff., and Klaeber,
Anglia L, 198, explain *feorh* as meaning "life," and Klaeber cites Battle of Maldon 125.   **1212** wyrsan] This word, here and in l. 2496, must mean "hostile"
(or perhaps merely "foreign"), since it is unlikely that the victorious Franks
would be referred to as "inferior."   reafedon] So Ettmüller, Sc., and most
later edd.   **1213** guðsceare] Holtzmann, Germania VIII, 494, proposed to
emend to *guðceare*, as in l. 1258.   **1214** hreawic heoldon] There are two possible interpretations of these words.   Klaeber, Anglia L, 198f., Anglia Beibl.
L, 331, takes *Geata leode* as subject of *heoldon*, "the bodies of the Geats covered
the battlefield."   Cf. *hlimbed healdan*, l. 3034.   On the other hand, Kock,
Anglia XLVI, 80f., would explain *hreawic healdan* as the equivalent of *wælstowe
wealdan*, ll. 2051, 2984.   This interpretation involves taking *wyrsan wigfrecan*
as subject of *heoldon*, with *Geata leode* a variation of *wæl*.   Malone, Eng. Studies
XXI, 116, with a similar interpretation, translates, "[the Franks] plundered the
slain after the battle-carnage, plundered the men of the Geatas, held the place
of corpses."   A choice between these alternatives is difficult, but probability
seems slightly to favor the construction assumed by Kock and Malone, and a
comma is therefore put after *leode* in the text.   Heal swege onfeng] Usually
taken in its literal meaning, "the hall received the noise"; that is, the men in the
hall were noisily jubilant over the bestowal of the gifts in ll. 1193ff.   Cosijn,
Beitr. VIII, 569f., and Aant., p. 21, would emend to *Healsbege onfeng*, assuming
that Wealhtheow received the collar and gave it to Beowulf, making a presen-
tation speech.   So also Holder and Trautmann; the latter translates, "Er
empfing den halsreif," making Beowulf, rather than Wealhtheow, the subject.
Sedgefield (3 ed.) reads *Heals bege onfeng*; that is, Beowulf's neck received the
collar, bestowed by Wealhtheow.   Andrew, p. 139, supports this interpretation,
citing ll. 688b–689a.   **1218** þeodgestreona] So Kemble (2 ed.) and later edd.,
following Grundtvig, tr., p. 285.   When the scribe wrote *þeo ge streona*, he may
have been thinking ahead to *geþeoh*.   **1219** cen þec mid cræfte] "Make yourself known by means of your strength."   There is no exact parallel to this use
of *cennan*, but see the quotations s.v. *cennan* II in Bos.-Tol., p. 150, and Supp.,
p. 121.   There were apparently two separate verbs, *cennan*, "to beget, bear
(a child)," found in ll. 12, 943, and *cennan*, "to declare, make known"; for the
etymologies, see Holthausen, AEW., p. 46.   **1222** ealne] Andrew, p. 141,
suggests *ealle*, modifying *weras*.   **1224** windgeard, weallas] The reference of
windgeard is not entirely clear.   Kemble emended l. 1224a to *windge eardweallas*,
translating, "the windy walls of the land."   So also Thorpe, Heyne (1 ed.),
Arnold, Wülker, Holder, Wyatt, Socin (6, 7 ed.), and Sedgefield (1, 2 ed.).
Ettmüller, Sc., emended to *windige weallas*, and Heyne (2–4 ed.), Socin (5 ed.),
Trautmann, Holthausen (1, 2, 7, 8 ed.), and Sedgefield (3 ed.) follow him, reading either *windige* or *windge*.   Retaining the MS. reading, Schücking explains
windgeard as a synonym of *sæ*.   So Chambers, Holthausen (3–6 ed.), Klaeber,
and von Schaubert.   For a justification of this reading, see Krackow, Archiv
CXI, 171f., and for Scandinavian parallels to the kenning *windgeard*, see Kock

Anglia XLII, 110. Klaeber, Anglia Beibl. XXIV, 290, suggests that *wind-geard* is accusative, parallel to *weallas*; he explains *windgeard, weallas* as of the same asyndetic type as *wudu, wælsceaftas*, l. 398. But in Anglia L, 199, he accepts *windgeard* as a variation of *sæ*. Prokosch, in Klaeber Misc., p. 200, would read *windgeardweallas* as a triple compound, "the walls of the home of the wind," i.e., the coasts. This is possible, but *windgeard* as a variation of *sæ* seems more likely.   1226 suna] Thorpe, Grein, Ettmüller, and Arnold emended to *sunum*, since Wealhtheow had two sons (l. 1189). Other edd. retain *suna*, as referring only to Hrethric, the elder of the two sons and the heir apparent.   1231 doð] Most of the older edd., as well as Holder, Socin, Wyatt, and Schücking, take *doð* as imperative plural; with this interpretation of the verb, the first half-line may be vocative, as Holder, Socin, and Wyatt construe it, or it may be a variation of *þegnas* and *þeod*, as Schücking takes it to be. Sievers, Beitr. IX, 139f., doubting that an imperative "Do as I command!" would be addressed to all the warriors, would emend to *do*, imperative singular, spoken to Beowulf alone. So Holthausen (1–6, 8 ed.), Sedgefield, and Klaeber (1 ed.). Kluge, Beitr. IX, 189, would retain *doð* as plural imperative by explaining *dreamhealdende*, l. 1227, as vocative, addressed to the entire assembly; he would then emend *is*, l. 1228, to *si*, and *syndon*, l. 1230, to *sin*, both the resulting forms being hortatory subjunctive. Holder and Trautmann accept Kluge's reading. But *doð* as indicative seems more probable. Malone, MLN. XLI, 466f., translates, "the retainers, flushed with wine, do as I ask." A similar interpretation had previously been advocated by Kock, Anglia XLIV, 246f. Klaeber (3 ed.), Holthausen (7 ed.), and von Schaubert also take *doð* as indicative; see especially Klaeber's note in Anglia L, 199. Whether we are to assume irony here (as Hoops, p. 153, and Malone do) is at least doubtful.   1234 geosceaft] This word certainly means "fate" and may be, as Kluge, Beitr. VIII, 533f., explained it, a variant form of *gesceaft*, with stress on the prefix (cf. *-geatwe* beside *-getawa*). Or *geo-* is perhaps the adverb *geó*, "formerly, of old." Chambers suggests that the compound may mean "fate ordained of old," and similarly Hoops, p. 154. Cf. *geosceaftgasta*, l. 1266.   grimme] So Ettmüller, Sc., and most later edd., to agree with the feminine *geosceaft*.   1235ff.] The punctuation in the text seems preferable to the arrangements adopted by Wyatt and Chambers, who begin a new sentence with *syððan* and put only a comma after *ræste*, and by Schücking and Sedgefield, who make ll. 1235b–1237a a separate sentence. See Kock, Anglia XLVI, 81.   1240 Beorscealca sum] Lawrence, JEGPh. X, 638, would take *sum* as singular, referring only to Æschere (cf. ll. 1251b, 1294b). There can be no doubt that grammatically *sum* is singular, but the interpretation adopted by Kock, Anglia XXVII, 219, note 3, and Klaeber, Mod. Phil. III, 457, "many a one of the beer-drinkers," is supported by the plural *Setton* in l. 1242. See also Klaeber's notes in Anglia XLVI (1922), 233f., and Anglia L, 200. A similar plural use may be assumed for *æþelinge*, l. 1244.   1247 an wig gearwe] "Ready for battle." So most of the early edd., also Socin, Wyatt, Schücking, Klaeber, and von Schaubert. In Mod. Phil. III, 458, Klaeber compares the accusatives in *on bæl gearu*, l. 1109 ("ready to be placed on the pyre"), *in gefeoht gearo*, Gifts of Men 90, *gearu . . . on* *willsið*, Elene 222f., and *on sið gearu*, Guthlac 1175. For further discussion in support of this reading (with l. 1247*a* taken as type A3), see Klaeber, Anglia LXIII, 418, and Beitr. LXXII, 123f.   Cosijn, Beitr. VIII, 570, suggested the compound *andwiggearwe*, "ready for defence."   Cf. *ondwiges heard*, Guthlac 176, and perhaps also *ymbe antwig*, Exodus 145.   The form *andwiggearwe*, with Cosijn's interpretation, is approved by Carleton Brown, PMLA LIII, 914, and adopted by Holthausen (7, 8 ed.).   Similarly, Holder, Holthausen (1–6 ed.), and Sedgefield read *anwiggearwe*, with *an-* taken as the equivalent of *and-*.   Ettmüller, Grein, ed., and Chambers read *ānwiggearwe*, "prepared for single combat," and this reading is approved by Prokosch, in Klaeber Misc., p. 201.   **1248 ge . . . þara]** "Both at home and in the field, as well as on both [of these two occasions]." The logic of this line may be questioned, but little is gained by omitting the third *ge*, as Ettmüller, Sc., Holder, and Schücking (8 ed.) did.   See Klaeber, JEGPh. VI, 194f.   **1249–1250]** Andrew, pp. 96f., would put only a comma after l. 1250*a*, explaining ll. 1249–1250*a* as a clause dependent on l. 1250*b*: "whensoever need befel their liege lord were those warriors loyal." This is possible, but the punctuation in the text is more in accord with Anglo-Saxon poetic style.

1251–1300

1257 lange þrage] The exaggeration in this phrase has often been pointed out. If we connect it with *lifde*, as is usually done, then *lange þrage*, "a long time," must refer to the one night which Grendel's mother lived after her son's death. Malone, Eng. Studies XV, 151, would connect *lange þrage* with *widcup*.   Andrew, p. 149, would emend *æfter*, l. 1258, to *iecte*, with no comma after *þrage*; he translates, "added to the long spell of anxious war."   **1258 guðceare]** Trautmann emends to *guðsceare*, as in l. 1213.   **1260 se]** Masculine pronouns are used several times to refer to Grendel's mother, *se þe* here and in l. 1497, *he* in ll. 1392, 1394.   In l. 1379, she is called *felasinnigne secg*.   No emendation of the pronouns is called for, since elsewhere in Beowulf we find the relative *se*, *se þe* with feminine antecedent, ll. 1887 (*yldo*), 2421 (*wyrd*), 2685 (*hond*), and perhaps l. 1344 (*hand*).   **1261 Cain]** So Kemble (2 ed.) and later edd., following Grundtvig, tr., p. 286.   The scribe must have been unfamiliar with the story of Cain; in l. 107 he at first wrote *cames*, later altering it to *caines*.   **1266 geosceaftgasta]** See l. 1234, note.   **1267 heorowearh]** See the note on *grundwyrgenne*, l. 1518.   **1269f.]** The pronouns *him* and *he* refer not to Grendel, who has been the subject of the preceding sentence, but to the *wer* of l. 1268. In l. 1274*b* the subject shifts back to Grendel.   **1271 gimfæste]** For *ginfæste*, "ample"; the assimilation of *-n-* before a labial is found also in *hlimbed*, l. 3034. **1272 are gelyfde]** See l. 608, note.   Here *are*, *frofre*, and *fultum* are all objects of *gelyfde*.   **1278 sunu]** For *suna*, gen. sing.   **deað]** So Heyne (3, 4 ed.) and most later edd., following a suggestion by Ettmüller, Sc.   But Holthausen (2–8 ed.), Klaeber, and von Schaubert emend to *deoþ*, *deoð*, as closer to the MS. reading, and it is in fact likely that the scribal confusion goes back to a Northumbrian form *deoð*, which some scribe copied as *ðeod*.   **1280 sona]** If *edhwyrft* is taken in its usual meaning of "return," an ellipsis of some kind must be assumed here; Bos.-Tol., Supp., p. 178, translates, "a return to the old state of things." Holthausen (1–6 ed.) emends *sona* to *socna*, gen. plur. of *sōcn*, "visitation"; see his note in ZfdPh. XXXVII, 117.   **1284 be]** "In comparison with" (Wyatt). Holthausen, note, points out that logically we should expect *wæpnedmonnes*, genitive, instead of the dative *wæpnedmen*.   **1285 geþuren]** Grein, Bib., and Spr. I, 474, suggested *geþrūen*, and so Sievers, Beitr. X, 458, Trautmann, Holthausen, Schücking, Sedgefield, Chambers, and Klaeber, for metrical reasons.   But the form *geþuren* occurs also in Riddle 91,1, and in Meters 20, 134 the original form *geþruen* is corrected to *geþuren*.   The word is apparently a form of *(ge)þweran*, "to beat or mix together," used here, as in Riddle 91,1, in the meaning "to forge."   **1287 dyhttig]** Since both the Thorkelin transcripts show *-tt-* in this word (although A has an *-h-* where B has not), Malone, PMLA LXIV, 1201, is probably right in his assumption that the MS. had the reading *dyhttig*.   **1291 þa hine]** Grein, Bib., suggested *þe hine*, "whom," to provide a subject for *gemunde*. This emendation was approved by Bugge, Tidskrift VIII, 296, and Rieger, ZfdPh. III, 401f., and is adopted by Heyne (3, 4 ed.), Holder (1 ed.), Socin, and Holthausen (8 ed.).   Trautmann, also emending *þa* to *þe*, omits *hine*.   But for a defence of the construction in the MS., with no subject for *gemunde*, see A. Pogatscher, Anglia XXIII (1900), 296f., who cites Nine Herbs Charm 25f. (Records VI, 119) as a similar instance.   **1292b]** For the punctuation in the text, with a comma after *þanon*, see Kock, Anglia XLVI, 81f.   An infinitive, "to go," parallel to *beorgan*, is to be understood in l. 1292b.   **1295 gang]** See l. 1009, note.

1301–1350

1302 under heolfre] Apparently dependent on *folme* rather than on *genam*. Cosijn, Aant., p. 14, takes the phrase as meaning "covered with blood," and so Klaeber, note, and Hoops, p. 159, who cite *blodge beadufolme*, l. 990. Bugge, Beitr. XII, 92f., suggested emending to *under hrof*; Miller, Anglia XII, 399f., would read *under heofe*, "amid the wailing." Grundtvig suggested *under heolstre*, and so Trautmann.   **1314 hwæþer]** So Trautmann, Holthausen, Sedgefield, and Klaeber. That the MS. *hwæþre* is a scribal error, and not a variant form of the conjunction *hwæþer*, was first pointed out by Sievers, ZfdPh. XXI, 357. A similar scribal error is to be found in the MS. *æghwæðre*, l. 2844.   **1316 Gang]** See l. 1009, note.   **1317 handscale]** This is the only recorded example of *-scalu* as a variant form of *-scolu* (for the latter form, cf. l. 1963). Thorpe, Wyatt, and Holthausen emend to *-scole*.   **1318 nægde]** Grein and most later edd. either emend to *nægde* or explain *hnægde* as a variant spelling of *nægde*. The meaning is clearly "accosted, addressed"; cf. Exodus 23, Guthlac 1227.   **1320 æfter neodlaðum]** As a dat. sing. form the MS. *-laðu* would be very irregular. Ettmüller, Wülker, Holthausen (1–6 ed.), Sedgefield, and Klaeber emend to *neodlaðum*; Holthausen (7, 8 ed.) emends to *neodlaðe*, following Sweet, Reader. Cosijn's emendation, Beitr. VIII, 570, to *neadlaðum* (= *nydlaðum*, dat. plur., "oppressive hostilities") is unnecessary. Klaeber, Archiv CXV, 179f., translates *æfter neodlaðum* as "nach seinem (Hroð-

gars) Wunsche"; Mackie, MLRev. XXXIV, 521f., who retains the MS. reading, would translate, "in accordance with my earnest desire," explaining ll.
1319*b*–1320 as the equivalent of "I hope you have slept well." Cf. *freondlaþu*,
l. 1192 (where *-laþu* means "invitation"; cf. the verb *laðian*), and *wordlæðe*,
acc. sing., "eloquence," Andreas 635, *wordlaþe*, Christ 664.   **1327** *þonne
hniton feþan*] Cosijn, Aant., p. 22, would punctuate this half-line as a parenthesis, making *we*, l. 1326, the subject of *cnysedan* as well as of *weredon*.   **1329**
æþeling] Supplied by Grein, ed., Heyne (2–4 ed.), and most later edd., to fill
the half-line.   Grundtvig had previously supplied *ædeling*, probably a mis-
print for *æðeling*.   The phrase *æþeling ærgod* also occurs in ll. 130, 2342.   **1331**
hwæder] For the MS. *hwæþer*, Grein, Bib., suggested *hwider*, and so Wülker,
Socin (5 ed.), and Sedgefield (3 ed.); this emendation was also approved by
Bugge, Beitr. XII, 93.   Grein, ed., emended to *hwæder*, and so Heyne (2–4 ed.),
Wyatt, Trautmann, Sedgefield (1, 2 ed.), Schücking (10–14 ed.), Chambers,
Klaeber, Holthausen (7, 8 ed.), and von Schaubert.   The latter reading is to be
preferred.   Max Deutschbein, Beitr. XXVI (1901), 201, cites the forms *þæder*
(= *þider*) and *hwæder* from MS. B of the Alfredian Bede; for other examples of
hwæder (or *hweder*), see Bos.-Tol., p. 570.   The usual form *hwider* is probably
analogical, on the model of *hider*; cf. Gothic *hwadre*, "whither," beside *hidre*,
"hither."   **1333** *gefægnod*] So Kemble II and most later edd., including
Holder, Holthausen, Sedgefield, Klaeber, and von Schaubert.   Thorpe and
Trautmann emend to *gefrefrod*, "comforted."   Heyne, Socin, Wyatt, Schücking, and Chambers retain the MS. *gefrægnod* in the sense of "made famous,"
a meaning not elsewhere attested for *gefrægn(i)an*, which ordinarily means
"to ask, inquire."   On the other hand, *gefægnian* is elsewhere intransitive; it is,
however, found several times as a synonym of *geblissian* (see Bos.-Tol., p. 389),
which occurs in transitive use.   **1333f.** *þa fæhðe . . . þe*] "The fight in which
. . . ."   For similar uses of the relative *þe*, cf. *ðone . . . dæg þe*, "the day on
which . . . ," ll. 2399f.; *on þa dune . . . ðe*, "to the hill on which . . . ," Elene 717.
See also Schücking, Svk., pp. 57f.   **1337ff.**] The structure of ll. 1337*b*–1344
is rather confused, but it can be made less so by putting ll. 1341–1342 within
parentheses, as in the text.   This punctuation assumes, with Schücking, Sedgefield (2, 3 ed.), and von Schaubert, that *fæhðe* and *hreþerbealo hearde* are parallel objects of *hafað . . . gestæled*.   The traditional interpretation of the passage
takes *hreþerbealo hearde* as nom. sing.; so, for example, Klaeber (who calls
these words a "loosely connected, semi-exclamatory noun phrase") and Hoops,
p. 162.   Kock, Anglia XLVI, 82f., would explain *hreþerbealo hearde* as object of
greoteþ, which is by no means impossible.   But the parenthesis gives a more
probable reading.   A free rendering of the passage (beginning at l. 1339*b*) is:
"[she] wished to avenge her kinsman, and she has carried her revenge a long
way (as it may seem to many a warrior, he who weeps in his heart after the
treasure-giver), [this] hard heart-bale," etc.   **1340** *hafað . . . gestæled*] "Has
revenged," with *fæhðe* and *hreþerbealo hearde* as objects; see the preceding note.
For this meaning of *(ge)stælan*, see Kock, Anglia XXVII, 229ff., who explains
(ge)stælan hwæt on hwone as meaning "to lay something to somebody's charge,"
hence "to call him to account for it, avenge it on him."   Cf. *fæhðe ic wille on*

weras stælan, Genesis 1351f., also Beow. 2484f., Christ 1372ff. In the present passage the *on* phrase is missing, as in Christ and Satan 638f.   **1344** se þe] Ettmüller, Sc., emended to *seo*, and so Grein, Bib., Ettmüller, and Holthausen, because of the feminine antecedent *hond*. See l. 1260, note. But here the masculine pronoun may refer to Æschere (the *sincgyfa* of l. 1342) rather than to the grammatical antecedent. See E. Nader, Anglia XI (1889), 471.

1351–1400

1351 onlicnæs] The MS. *onlic næs* may rest on a misunderstanding by a scribe, and most edd. emend to *onlicnes*. Holder, following Sweet, Reader, reads *idese onlic* for l. 1351a and emends the MS. *næs* to *wæs*, putting it at the beginning of l. 1351b; Holder punctuates l. 1352 as a parenthesis. Holthausen and Sedgefield (3 ed.) read simply *idese onlic*, omitting the *næs* of the MS.; this emendation was first proposed by Grundtvig, tr., p. 287.   **1354** nemdon] So Kemble (2 ed.) and later edd., for the *nemdod* of the Thorkelin transcripts, which may well have been the reading of the MS.   **1363** hrinde] For this adjective, not elsewhere recorded in Anglo-Saxon, Wülker, Socin (5 ed.), and Wyatt read *hrimge*, following R. Morris, Blickling Homilies (London, 1880), pp. vi–vii, who pointed out the phrase *hrimige bearwas* in a very similar passage in the seventeenth Blickling Homily (ed. R. Morris, 209, 32f.). Cosijn, Beitr. VIII, 571, proposed *hrimde* as the equivalent of *hrimige*, and so Holthausen (7, 8 ed.). Sedgefield emends to *hringde*, "standing in a ring" (or "gnarled"); similar suggestions had previously been made by G. Sarrazin, Beitr. XI (1886), 163, note, and by Bos-Tol., p. 561, s.v. *hrind*. But the explanation of the MS. *hrinde* by E. M. Wright, Eng. Stud. XXX, 341ff., is undoubtedly correct and has been adopted by all later edd. Citing the dialect word *rind*, which occurs both as noun, "hoar-frost," and as adjective, "frozen to death" (J. Wright, Eng. Dialect Dict. V, 116), she explains the MS. *hrinde* as for *hrindede*, inflected past participle of a verb **hrindan*, "to cover with hoar-frost."   **1365** mæg] With a subject *man* to be understood. Grein, ed., Heyne (2, 3 ed.), and Wülker supplied *man* in their texts, but Bugge, Tidskrift VIII, 51, calls attention to Old Icelandic *þar má sjá undr*, "there [one] may see a strange thing," as a parallel to the MS. reading here. Cf. also *mæg cweðan* (a translation of *dici potest*) in the Tanner MS. of the Alfredian Bede (ed. T. Miller, 406, 26); on that passage, see Klaeber, Anglia XXVII (1904), 428.   **1367** þæt þone grund wite] Sedgefield supplies *he* after *þæt*.   **1370f.** ær . . . ær . . .] "He will sooner give up his life . . . before he will go in."   **1372** hydan] Supplied by Kemble II and most later edd.; cf. l. 446, where, to be sure, the situation is different. Holthausen, note, suggests *beorgan*, as in l. 1293, and so Klaeber in his text; see Klaeber's note in Anglia LXIII, 419f.   **1374**] The punctuation here, with a comma after *styreþ*, follows Kock, Anglia XLV, 118, who takes *lað gewidru* as a variation of *wind*, with *styreþ* intransitive, like *styredon* in Andreas 374. For the usual interpretation, by which *lað gewidru* is construed as object of *styreþ*, see Klaeber, Anglia L, 201f.; Hoops, p. 165.   **1375** drysmaþ] "Becomes gloomy"? For this verb, which is not recorded elsewhere, Sedgefield,

MLRev. XXVII, 449, suggested *ðrysmaþ*, "stifles, grows oppressive," and so in his 3d ed. This emendation has also been proposed independently by C. L. Wrenn, Trans. of the Philological Soc. 1943, p. 18, who cites the noun *þrosm*. **1376 reotað**] Sedgefield (3 ed.) emends to *recað*, " 'are smoking,' i.e., are charged with fine spray." If *reotað* is retained, the meaning of the half-line must be "the heavens lament." Elsewhere in the poetry *rēotan* refers to weeping; cf. Christ 835, 1229, Fortunes of Men 46. Klaeber, Anglia L, 202, cites Old Icelandic parallels for the weeping of the heavens. **1379 felasinnigne secg**] As a half-line alliterating in *s*, *felasinnigne secg* is irregular, since elsewhere *fela-* as the first element of a compound invariably alliterates. See especially Klaeber, Anglia LXIII, 420. Heyne (2–4 ed.), Holder, Socin, Trautmann, Schücking, Chambers, Sedgefield, Klaeber, and Holthausen (8 ed.) omit *fela-*. Holthausen (1–6 ed.) retains *fela* in his text but prints it as the last word of a line which once stood between l. 1378 and l. 1379, the remainder of which has been lost; see his note in ZfdPh. XXXVII, 117. In Literaturblatt LIX, 165, Holthausen would assume a loss from the text after *felasinnigne*, suggesting that the original reading was *felasinnigne [feond in helle, sarigne] secg*. Holthausen (7 ed.) adopts this reading. Andrew, Medium Ævum VIII, 205f., would omit *secg* altogether and emend to *sele sinnigne* or, preferably, to *sele sinnigra*, "the hall of the evil ones." Malone, MLRev. XXV, 191, and Hoops, Bwst., p. 12, defend the MS. reading, and von Schaubert retains *felasinnigne* in her text. It is probable that something is wrong with the text here, but Heyne's omission of *fela-* is not the best solution of the difficulty, since the scribe was always more likely to omit than to add to his copy. In view of the many possibilities, the text has not been emended. **1382 wundnum**] For the MS. *wun dini* or *wun dmi*, Grein and later edd., except Holder (2 ed.), Holthausen, Chambers, and von Schaubert, emend to *wundnum*, following Ettmüller, Sc. Chambers, note, and Hoops, p. 166, defend the form *wundini* as a survival of the early instrumental ending and urge its retention. But if this explanation of the MS. reading is correct, it is odd that we have no other early endings of this sort in the poem. The emendation to *wundnum* puts less of a strain on probability. **1390 raþe**] The alliteration indicates that *raþe* was the original form here. In l. 1975*a*, also, the form *Hraðe* may be for an original *Raðe*, but it is possible that l. 1975*a* is of type A3 and that *Hraðe* was not intended to alliterate. In l. 724 the MS. has *raþe* with alliteration in *r*. Elsewhere in the poem where this word partakes of the alliteration, ll. 991 (*hreþe*), 1576, 1914, 1937, it is spelled with *hr-* and alliterates in *h*; the same is true of the comparative *hraþor*, l. 543. **1392 he**] See l. 1260, note. **helm**] Thorpe, in Kemble (2 ed.), suggested emending to *holm*, and so Ettmüller, Arnold, and Holder. This emendation is also approved by Cosijn, Aant., p. 23, who takes *gyfenes grund* as a variation. But the MS. *helm* may mean "protection, refuge"; cf. *helme [g]edygled* (parallel to *heolstre gehyded*), Homiletic Fragment II, 13 (Records III, 224). **losaþ**] The verb *losian* usually means "to be lost, to perish," but here, as elsewhere in Beowulf (ll. 2062, 2096), it means "to escape." **1396b**] "As I expect of you" (Kock, Anglia XXVII, 223f.). See l. 158, note. **1399 gebæted**] Usually translated "bridled," since *(ge)bætan* is apparently a causative verb related to *bítan*. But Bos.-Tol., Supp., pp. 62, 291, translates *bǽtan* as "to spread a covering, to saddle a horse," and *gebǽtan* (1) as "to bridle and saddle a horse"; the latter is probably the intended meaning here. See Carleton Brown, PMLA LIII, 914f.; Klaeber, Anglia Beibl. LIV/LV, 175.

1401–1450

1401 gende] For *gengde*, "went," which is the MS. reading in l. 1412. **1404** þær heo gegnum for] The MS. *gegnum for* is too short for a half-line, and several emendations have been suggested. Sievers, Beitr. IX, 140, proposed to supply *þær heo* before *gegnum*; Cosijn, Aant., p. 24, suggested *gegnunga* for *gegnum*, with the subject of *for* to be understood as Grendel's mother. Klaeber, JEGPh. VI, 195, would supply *swa* before *gegnum*, and so in his edition; as an alternative Klaeber suggested *gegnum ferde*, and so Schücking (9–14 ed.). Kock, Anglia XLIV, 247, favors *swa*. Hoops, Bwst., p. 108, would retain the MS. reading, minimizing the metrical difficulty. Von Schaubert, who also retains the MS. reading, cites other examples of half-lines with only three syllables (ll. 25*b*, 386*b*, 528*b*, 629*b*, 1036*b*, etc.); but each of these contains a contracted form which was probably dissyllabic when the poem was written. Sievers's reading, adopted by Socin, Holder (2 ed.), Trautmann, Holthausen, Schücking (8 ed.), Sedgefield, and Chambers, seems the most desirable emendation. Bugge's *hwær heo*, Beitr. XII, 94, is less likely. **1407** eahtode] Thorpe suggested *ealgode*, "defended," and so Trautmann in his text. The recorded meanings of *eahtian* do not seem to fit the context. On the lack of agreement in *þara þe . . . eahtode*, see l. 98, note. **1408** bearn] Whether this word is singular (referring to Hrothgar or to Beowulf) or plural (referring to the entire company) has been much disputed. The verb is singular, but that in itself is not conclusive, since other examples of lack of agreement are to be found; cf. ll. 904f., 2163f., and see Woolf, MLQuart. IV, 49f. Lawrence, JEGPh. XXIII, 298, who takes *bearn* as singular, explains it as the antecedent of *He* in l. 1412. But Andrew, p. 51, says that *He*, l. 1412, is correct only if *bearn* is plural, the king thus being distinguished from his escort. Cf. l. 748, where *he* introduces a new subject. Chambers, note, would refer *bearn*, singular, to either Hrothgar or Beowulf. Klaeber, Mod. Phil. III, 259f., Anglia L, 202, and Hoops, p. 169, explain *bearn* as plural, citing l. 3170, where *æþelinga bearn* is certainly plural. Hoops regards *Ofereode . . . æþelinga bearn* as the equivalent of *gumfeþa stop*, l. 1401. **1413** wong sceawian] A very close parallel to this passage is provided in Genesis 2593ff., *ac him Loth gewat . . . wic sceawian, oðþæt hie . . . eorðscræf fundon*. Mackie, MLRev. XXXIV, 522, would take *sceawian* in the present passage (and presumably also in Genesis 2595) not with the usual interpretation, "to survey (the plain)," but as meaning "to look out for (the place)"; he cites *hæl sceawedon*, l. 204, as a similar use of the verb. **1414** oþþæt] Von Schaubert puts a semicolon after l. 1413*b*, taking *oþþæt* as an adverb. See l. 56, note. **1418** winum] Trautmann and Schücking (8 ed.) emend to *wigum*. Holthausen (1 ed.), note, suggested *witenum*. But for *wine* (*winas*), plural, in the sense of "men, people," see Klaeber, JEGPh. VI, 195; Kock,

Anglia XLII, 111ff.   Klaeber points out that in *winia bealdor*, l. 2567, the word *winia* refers to the retainers; Kock further cites Andreas 198, Genesis 1847, 2699, 2735, etc.   **1424** fyrdleoð] Restored by Bouterwek, ZfdA. XI, 92, and so Grein, Heyne, Wülker, and later edd.   **1428** bewitigað] "Perform"; see Klaeber, Anglia LXIII, 420.   **1431** bearhtm ongeaton] As Cosijn pointed out, Aant., p. 24, we might expect *sið ðan* before *bearhtm*.   As the text stands, we have hysteron proteron; it is the noise which causes the water-monsters to flee.   **1434** yðgewinnes] Parallel to *feores* and taken by most edd. in its literal meaning "wave-strife," i.e., "(power of) swimming." But Mackie, MLRev. XXXIV, 522, would translate, "the strife of the waves, the battling waves," the meaning which the word has in l. 2412.   **1436** ðe hyne swylt fornam] Holthausen, Chambers, Klaeber, and von Schaubert translate ðe as "because." G. W. Small, PMLA XLV (1930), 369, suggests that ðe is temporal, "as death seized him." But this is more probably a relative construction, "whom death took away." See l. 488, note, and Hoops, p. 171.   **1440** wægbora] This word is not elsewhere recorded; it certainly refers to some kind of sea-beast, but the etymology is uncertain.   The usual translation, which goes back to Grein, Spr. II, 643, is "wave-bearer"; this interpretation assumes a connection with the verb *beran*. See Sievers, Anglia XIV, 134f.   But Schröer, Anglia XIII, 335, explains the word as "wave-guardian, wave-ruler," citing *mundbora* and similar compounds; Holthausen, Anglia Beibl. XIV, 49, explains it as "wave-disturber," Klaeber as "wave-roamer," Sedgefield (3 ed.), note, as "wave-lifter."   Several emendations have been proposed.   Trautmann emended to *wægfara*, "wogengänger," and so Holthausen (1, 2 ed.); Klaeber, Eng. Stud. XXXIX, 463, suggested *wægdeor*, which is rather far from the reading of the MS.; Holthausen, Anglia Beibl. XXI, 300f., would emend to *wægþora*, related to *þweran*, "to stir."

1451–1500

1451 freawrasnum] "With splendid chains" (or "bonds"), apparently referring to the *walu* of l. 1031.   Holthausen (1, 2 ed.) emends to *freoðowrasnum*, "with protective chains"; see his note in ZfdPh. XXXVII, 124.   **1454** brond ne beadomecas] Cosijn, Aant., p. 24, suggested *bro(g)dne beadomecas*, and so Trautmann, Holthausen (1–5 ed.), and Sedgefield.   **1458** an foran] Bos.-Tol., Supp., p. 233, suggests that *foran* is to be translated as "in the front rank."   With *an* as used here, cf. *an cyning*, l. 1885.   The meaning of the entire line is "that was an outstandingly fine old treasure."   **1459** atertanum fah] "Decorated with poison-twigs," referring either to the process of etching a design on a sword (by means of pieces of wood dipped in acid?) or to a twiglike pattern produced by the etching process.   Cosijn, Beitr. VIII, 571, proposed *atertærum* (= *ātertēarum*) *fah*, and so Holthausen (1, 2 ed.).   Trautmann emends to *atertacnum fah*.   In Aant., p. 24, Cosijn compares *earh ættre gemæl*, Andreas 1331, which describes the point of a spear.   **1461** mid mundum] It is not necessary to assume that the sword was a two-handed one, since the plural form can be explained in the same way as *mecum*, l. 565; see the note on that line.   In any case, a sword grasped *mid mundum* is not nearly so startling as the book written *þam handum twam*, in the Metrical Epilogue to MS. 41 of Corpus Christi College, Cambridge (Records VI, 113).   bewand] The verb *bewindan* usually means "to bind, wrap, encircle"; but for the meaning "to grasp," cf. l. 3022, where *mundum bewunden* is a variation of *hæfen on handa*.   For the lack of agreement in *þara þe . . . bewand*, see l. 98, note.   1462 gryresiðas] Andrew, p. 73, would emend to *gryresiða*, adverbial genitive, arguing that the nouns *gryresiðas* and *folcstede* are not the same in kind and should not be in apposition.   But for *gryresiðas* as object of *gegan*, cf. *gegan . . . sorhfulne sið*, ll. 1277f.   1465ff.] The edd. punctuate with a comma after *druncen*, l. 1467, as in the text, and with either a period or a semicolon after *sweordfrecan*, l. 1468.   But Carleton Brown, PMLA LIII, 915, would put a semicolon after *druncen* and a comma after *sweordfrecan*; this punctuation, he says, emphasizes Unferth's cowardice rather than his magnanimity.   1470b–1471a] According to Mackie, MLRev. XXXIV, 522f., this is an early example of *þær* in the meaning "in that, on that account"; see N.E.D., s.v. *there*, 6.b, the earliest citation of which is from Chaucer.   Mackie suggests the translation, "in that (respect) he missed glory, the fame of heroism."   Such a meaning fits here, but not in l. 972, which Mackie considers an analogous case.   1471 ellenmærðum] So Thorpe, Grein, ed., and later edd.   1481 hondgesellum] Since a noun *gesella*, "companion," does not occur elsewhere in Anglo-Saxon, Grundtvig suggested emending to *hond-gesteallum*, and so Holthausen (1–4 ed.).   If an emendation is to be made, *-geseldum*, suggested by Holthausen, note, would be closer to the MS. reading.   1485 Hrædles] See l. 454, note.   1486 gumcystum godne] "Good by reason of his manly virtues." Cf. l. 2543 and *cystum cuðe*, l. 867.   1487 breac] With a genitive object *his* to be understood.   1488 Unferð] See l. 499, note.   1489 wægsweord] Usually interpreted as "a sword with wavy ornamentation"; for such swords in Old Germanic times, see the references in Hoops, p. 174.   1495 Ða wæs hwil dæges] "Then it was a [good] part of the day," i.e., a good part of the day had passed before he could see the bottom. Cf. ll. 2319b–2320, which apparently mean "he hastened to the hoard . . . before a [good] part of the day [had passed]."   The interpretation of *hwil dæges* as "daytime," proposed by Andrew, pp. 98f., has little to commend it.   1497 Sona] See l. 743, note.   se ðe] See l. 1260, note.   1498 hund missera] Mackie, MLRev. XXXVI, 97, suggests that these words mean merely "for a very long time." See l. 2994, note.   1500 ælwihta] For *elwihta*, gen. plur. of *elwiht*, "alien creature." This is a different word from *ælwihta*, Andreas 118, which is a variant form of *eallwihta*, as in Genesis 113, 978, Andreas 1603.

1501–1550

1504 fyrdhom] Holthausen (1, 2 ed.) and Sedgefield emend to *fyrdhoman*, following a suggestion by Ettmüller, Sc. But the strong form *-hom* (beside the weak *-homa*) is found in *byrnhomas*, Judith 192.   1506 brimwylf] So Kemble (2 ed.) and most later edd.   1508 no he þæs modig wæs] "No matter how brave he was." See l. 968b, note, and Kock, Anglia XLVI, 83f. The emendation to *þæs* had already been suggested by Grundtvig and adopted by Heyne (2–4 ed.),

Holder, Socin, Holthausen (1–5, 7, 8 ed.), and Schücking (8, 9 ed.); but Heyne, Socin, and Schücking missed the point of the construction and (together with many edd. who retain the MS. *þæm*) put *no* at the end of the first half-line. Other emendations which have been proposed, such as *þeah*, adopted by Grein, Ettmüller, Arnold, Wülker, Wyatt, and Chambers, and *þær*, suggested by Cosijn, Aant., p. 24, and adopted by Schücking (10–14 ed.) and Sedgefield, are no longer of value, in view of Kock's convincing explanation of the passage. **1510** swencte] Suggested by Kemble II and adopted by Thorpe, Grein, and later edd. **1511** bræc] "Tried to break"? So Klaeber, note, and Mod. Phil. III, 261, note 1. See *wehte*, l. 2854, and note. **1512** aglæcan] This word may be either subject (nom. plur.) or object of *ehton*. If, as seems the more probable, it is the object, it may be either gen. sing. or acc. sing., since both cases appear after *ehtan* to designate the object of pursuit. For the possibility that *aglæca* is applied to Beowulf here, see l. 893, note. **1513** in] Supplied by Thorpe, Grein, and later edd., except Holder, to complete the sense. **1514** nænig wæter] Holthausen, Literaturblatt XXI, 61, ZfdPh. XXXVII, 117, and in his edition, transposes to *wæter nænig* for metrical reasons. Martin, Eng. Stud. XX, 295, suggested *wætera* for the MS. *wæter*, with no transposition. **1516** fyrleoht] "A fiery light" (Mackie, JEGPh. XXXVII, 461). This is the same *leoht* which is mentioned in l. 1570. **1518** Ongeat] Andrew, p. 137, calls the repetition of the verb *ongeat* "intolerable." He would explain ll. 1512b–1517 as a subordinate clause and emend *ongeat*, l. 1518, to *ongean*, preposition, beginning the main clause: "then against the hag of the abyss he let drive with his battle-bill." But the resulting word order is surely more intolerable than the repetition of *ongeat*. grundwyrgenne] In spite of the similar compound *brimwylf* in ll. 1506, 1599, the word -*wyrgen* apparently does not mean "she-wolf," as many edd. have glossed it. Nor, in spite of *heorowulfas*, Exodus 181, does -*wearh* in *heorowearh*, Beow. 1267, mean "wolf." On the meaning of *wearh* (masculine) and *wyrgen* (feminine), "the accursed one, the outcast," see Klaeber, Anglia XXXV (1912), 253, who cites *wearhtreafum*, Elene 926, used with reference to hell. It is to be noted that the Old Icelandic cognate, *vargr*, "wolf," may also mean "outlaw." **1519b–1520a**] "He gave a mighty impetus to his battle-sword" (Klaeber, Mod. Phil. III, 458). **1520** hond sweng ne ofteah] The emendation *hond*, for the MS. *hord*, is made by Grein and all later edd., following Bouterwek, ZfdA. XI, 92. Trautmann emended *swenge* to the acc. sing. *sweng*, and so Schücking (9–14 ed.), Sedgefield (2, 3 ed.), Holthausen (5–8 ed.), Klaeber, and von Schaubert. Trautmann made this emendation principally for metrical reasons (see his note in Bonner Beitr. XVII, 147f.), but it is also necessary for the sense, since *ofteon*, "to withhold," though it may take either the accusative (as in l. 2489) or the genitive (as in l. 5) of the thing withheld, never takes a direct object in the dative. Bouterwek, loc. cit., had also emended the MS. *swenge* to *sweng* but had read *hondsweng* as a compound; this reading is defensible, but the analogy of ll. 2488b–2489 makes it probable that here also *hond* is the subject. **1530** Hylaces] Explained by Klaeber, Mod. Phil. III, 458, as a variant of *Hyglaces*. Cf. *Wilaf* for *Wiglaf*, l. 2852. The form *Hyglac*, without the medial -*e*-, was probably the regular form in the original text; see Sievers, Beitr. X, 463f., who cites similar forms from the Liber Vitae Dunelmensis and other early documents.   **1531** wundenmæl] So Kemble (2 ed.) and later edd., except Grundtvig.   **1537** be eaxle] Rieger, ZfdPh. VII, 24, proposed to emend to *be feaxe*, "by the hair," to regularize the alliteration, and so Holder (1 ed.), Trautmann, Holthausen, Schücking, Sedgefield, and Chambers.   Holthausen, Anglia Beibl. LIII, 272f., cites *feaxfang*, "(the act of) seizing by the hair," in the laws of Æthelberht of Kent. But for another example of alliteration on the verb alone, cf. l. 758.   **1541** andlean] See l. 499, note.   Arnold, Wülker, Wyatt and Sedgefield retain the MS. *handlean, hondlean* here and in l. 2094, but Sedgefield glosses the word under *andlēan*; other recent edd. emend.   **1543–1544**] Elsewhere in Anglo-Saxon the verb *oferweorpan* is transitive, and the most natural course here would be to take Grendel's mother as the subject of *oferwearp* and *wigena strengest* (i.e., Beowulf) as object.   But *feþecempa*, which can hardly be anything else than a variation of *wigena strengest*, is nominative. Cosijn, Aant., pp. 24f., explaining *oferwearp* as transitive and *werigmod* as referring to Grendel's mother, emended to *feþecempan*, following a suggestion by Ettmüller, Sc.   He also, quite unnecessarily, emended *strengest* to *strengel*, "chief, ruler," a word which is found in l. 3115.   Trautmann and Sedgefield (3 ed.) adopt the emendation to *feþecempan*; Trautmann, Holthausen (1, 2 ed.), and Sedgefield (1, 3 ed.) adopt the emendation to *strengel*.   Ettmüller, Sc., also suggested supplying *hine*, reflexive, before *þa*, l. 1543a, which would permit retaining the nominative *feþecempa*.   So Sedgefield (2 ed.).   But although *oferweorpan* as an intransitive verb is not attested in Anglo-Saxon, there is evidence for this use in Middle English.   Klaeber, Anglia L, 203f., and M. Ashdown, MLRev. XXV, 78, cite the line *min herte overwerpes* ("is overturned, upset") in the Middle English MS. Harley 2253 (ed. G. L. Brook, 58, 12).   See also the quotations in the N.E.D. s.v. *overthrow, v.,* 5.   Brett, MLRev. XIV, 7, and H. Logeman, Leuvensche Bijdragen XVII (1925), 3ff., also accept an intransitive use of *oferwearp* here.   This seems the best interpretation of the passage: Beowulf, weary of mind, stumbled and fell down.   **1545** seax] So Ettmüller, Sc., and most later edd. Cf. l. 2610, Solomon and Saturn 166.   A dative object of *getēon*, "to draw," is hardly conceivable.   **1546** ond] Supplied by Grundtvig, note, and so Heyne (2–4 ed.) and later edd., except Arnold, Wülker, Holder (1 ed.), and Wyatt.   Cf. *brad and bruneccg*, Battle of Maldon 163.   **1550** Hæfde] Subjunctive: "[He] would have perished . . . ."

1551–1600

1552 gefremede] Indicative, parallel to *geweold*, l. 1554.   See Kock, Anglia XLV, 115f.; Hoops, Bwst., p. 109.   Then *nemne* means "except that"; cf. *næfne*, l. 1353.   **1554–1556**] The edd. vary widely in the punctuation of this passage.   Heyne, Wülker, Socin, and Schücking put only a comma after *wigsigor* but a semicolon after *drihten*; similarly Trautmann, who puts a period after *drihten*, beginning a new sentence with *Rodera*.   Chambers and von Schaubert put commas after both *wigsigor* and *drihten*, taking *halig god, witig drihten*, and *rodera rædend* as parallel subjects of both *geweold* and *gesced*.   So also Kock,

Anglia XLIV, 248. Holthausen and Klaeber punctuate ll. 1554–1556 as in the text. Most edd. put a comma after *yðelice*, with no punctuation after l. 1555*b*. Schücking, however, taking *syððan* as an adverb, puts a semicolon after l. 1555*b*, and Holder (1 ed.), Wyatt, and Holthausen (7, 8 ed.) put either a semicolon or a colon after *yðelice*, following Sievers, Beitr. IX, 140. Kock, loc. cit., also favors a semicolon after *yðelice*. But the meaning of ll. 1554*b*–1556 is that God settled the fight in a just way after Beowulf had got on his feet again. See Klaeber, note, and Eng. Stud. XXXIX, 431. Sedgefield, beginning a new sentence with *syððan*, puts only a comma after l. 1556*b*.   **1557 on searwum**] The most usual interpretation of these words, "among other arms" (adopted, for example, by Grein, Spr. II, 434, Schücking, Sedgefield, and Chambers), has the least to commend it. Other translations are: "fully equipped, ready" (modifying *bil*); "[he] in his armor" (cf. ll. 249, 2530, 2568, 2700); "in battle, during the fight." The last two of these are the most probable, and a choice between them is difficult. Hoops, pp. 178f., who prefers "in battle," compares *of searwum*, l. 419.   **1559 wæs**] Supplied by Kemble (2 ed.) and most later edd. Grundtvig, tr., p. 290, suggested supplying *wæs* before *þæt*. Von Schaubert retains the MS. reading. See l. 811, note.   **1563 þa fetelhilt**] Hoops, pp. 179, 182, takes *þa*, here and in l. 1614, as the definite article and assumes that *hilt*, elsewhere masculine or neuter, is feminine in these two passages. In l. 1614 *þa* is certainly an article, but here it is more probably an adverb.   **1568*b***] Andrew, pp. 74f., would supply *þæt* before *heo*, putting only a comma after l. 1568*a*. Cf. l. 1540.   **1582–1583 fyftyne men and oðer swylc**] That is, fifteen men plus fifteen more. Cf. ll. 122f., where Grendel seizes thirty men in their sleep.   **1584 laðlicu lac**] Holthausen (4–8 ed.) supplies *ful* before *laðlicu*, for metrical reasons.   **1585 to ðæs þe**] Elsewhere in Beowulf (ll. 714, 1967, 2410) *to þæs þe* follows a verb of motion and means "to (the point) where." Here, however, such a meaning is impossible. Chambers, translating *to ðæs þe* as "until" (referring back to ll. 1572ff.), punctuates ll. 1575*b*–1585*a* as a long parenthesis, but this arrangement does not help us much, since *to ðæs þe* is no more appropriate after *wæpen hafenade* than after *lean forgeald*. So also Sedgefield in his note, although in his text he seems to make a parenthesis of ll. 1585*b*–1590*a* rather than of the preceding passage. Hoops, p. 180, explains *to ðæs þe* as meaning "so that." Trautmann emends *to ðæs þe* to *þa*, which gives good sense at the cost of some violence to the MS. reading. One is tempted to believe that some of the text, containing a verb of motion, has been lost before l. 1585*b*.   **1589–1590**] The pronoun *he*, subject of *þrowade*, refers to Grendel; in the next line, the subject of *becearf* is Beowulf. Trautmann emends l. 1590*b* to *þe hine heafde becearf*, "(the hard battle-blow) which cut off his head." The emendation to *þe hine* is also advocated by Andrew, p. 45. **1591 Sona**] See l. 743, note.   **1598 þa ðæs monige gewearð**] "Many agreed in thinking . . ." (Hubbard, JEGPh. XVII, 119f.). Here *gewearð* is used impersonally, and *monige* is acc. plur. Cf. Christ and Satan 254, where, however, there is no genitive of the thing. On impersonal *geweorðan*, found also in Beow. 1996, 2026, and Judith 260, see Klaeber, JEGPh. XVIII (1919), 257ff.   **1599 abroten**] So Kemble II and later edd.

1601–1650

1602 setan] Grundtvig, tr., pp. 290f., suggested emending the MS. *secan* to *sæton,* and so Grein, Bib., and Heyne (1 ed.). Grein, ed., emended to *setan,* and so the later edd. **1604** wiston] This verb is best taken as a variant form of *wyscton,* "wished"; that is, they wished and (but) did not expect that they would see their lord again. See Bugge, Tidskrift VIII, 51f.; Cosijn, Beitr. VIII, 571; Klaeber, Mod. Phil. III, 458, Anglia L, 204; Whitbread, MLRev. XXXVII, 482. The two verbs *wyscan* and *wenan* also appear together in Guthlac 76. Klaeber, Archiv CXXVI (1911), 356, cites Milton's "He wish'd, but not with hope" (Paradise Lost, IX, 422). Of the edd., Thorpe, Grundtvig, Arnold, and Holthausen (1 ed.) emend to *wyscton* or *wiscton,* following Kemble II, while Holder, Socin, Holthausen (2–8 ed.), Schücking, Sedgefield, Chambers, Klaeber, and von Schaubert retain *wiston* but explain it as "wished." Attempts to interpret *wiston* as preterite of *witan* have not been successful. Bush, MLN: XXXVI, 251, would translate, "they knew and did not merely expect . . ."; Thomas, MLRev. XVII, 63, apparently with a similar interpretation in mind, translates, "they were as certain as they could be." But, as has often been pointed out, the retainers would hardly have been *modes seoce* if they had been sure of Beowulf's return. Wyatt takes this passage as a blending of two constructions, *wiston . . . þæt hie . . . ne gesawon* and *ne wendon þæt hie . . . gesawon;* as an alternative he suggests that *ne* has dropped out of the text after *selfne* in l. 1605: "they knew, and did not merely expect, that they should not see their lord himself again." This, however, seems only slightly more plausible than Bush's interpretation. **1610** wælrapas] Kemble and some other early edd. emended to *wægrapas,* following a suggestion by Grundtvig, tr., p. 291. Most later edd. connect the first element of the compound with *wæl,* "deep pool, gulf," translating as "water-fetters" or the like. But E. A. Kock, in Klaeber Misc., pp. 19f., would explain the word as *wælrāpas,* "quelling chains," citing *wælbende,* l. 1936, and *wælclommum,* Genesis 2128. So also Hoops, p. 182. Trautmann had previously translated *wælrapas* as "die todesseile." But *wælrapas* is clearly a variation of *forstes bend* in the preceding line. **1614** þa hilt] See l. 1563, note. Here it seems necessary to take *hilt* either as acc. sing. feminine or as acc. plur. neuter. The assumption of a plural with singular meaning receives some support from the plural use of the feminine *hilte* in Judges iii.22 (ed. S. J. Crawford, The Old English Version of the Heptateuch, 403, 7), *swa þæt þa hiltan eodon in to þam innoðe,* translating the Latin *ut capulus sequeretur ferrum in vulnere.* **1616b–1617**] "The blood was so hot, [so] poisonous the alien spirit which died there within." That is, *ættren* is a predicate adjective parallel to *hat.* But Klaeber, note, suggests taking *ættren* as attributive, *ættren ellorgæst,* "the poisonous alien spirit," then being a variation of *blod.* The passage is usually interpreted as referring to Grendel, but the sword had also been in contact with Grendel's mother. **1619** wighryre] Grein, Spr. II, 702, and Cosijn, Aant., p. 25, suggested emending to *wiggryre.* But the MS. reading is quite satisfactory: Beowulf had experienced (lived to see) the battle-death of the hostile ones. For the plural *wraðra,* cf. *hyrdas,* l. 1666, and *feon-*

dum, l. 1669. Since it is unlikely that Beowulf would be speaking of the dead Grendel as well as of his mother, these words are probably to be explained as plurals with singular meaning. See l. 565, note.   1624*b*–1625 sælace . . . þara þe] Trautmann suggested emending to *sælaca*, gen. plur., to provide an antecedent for *þara þe*, and so Holthausen, ZfdPh. XXXVII, 117, and in his edition. This reading involves taking the variation *mægenbyrþenne* as gen. sing. But *gefēon*, "to rejoice," may be followed by the instrumental as well as by the genitive. Bugge, Beitr. XII, 95, would emend *þara* to *þære*, and so Socin in his text. Malone, Anglia LIV, 97f., and Klaeber, note, explain *þara* as a late variant of *þære*. But Hoops, p. 183, accepts *þara* as gen. plur. and, retaining *sælace*, explains *þara þe* as a stereotyped use of the partitive genitive. Ettmüller and Trautmann omit *þara* in their texts, and so also Andrew, pp. 127f. **1633** mæton] Sedgefield (3 ed.) unnecessarily emends to *metan* as infinitive after *Ferdon*. See *bæron*, l. 1889, and note.   **1634** Cyningbalde] Grein, Ettmüller, Trautmann, Holthausen (1, 2 ed.), and Sedgefield emend to *cynebalde*, on the model of *cynegod*, *cynerof*, etc. So also Cosijn, Aant., p. 25. Bugge, Beitr. XII, 369, suggested *cyningholde*, citing *dryhtenhold* and *þeodenhold*. But Klaeber, Mod. Phil. III, 459, cites *bregorof*, l. 1925, as a compound similar to *cyningbald*.   **1636** æghwæþrum] It should be noted that this word is not the equivalent of *æghwylcum*. The line apparently means "with difficulty for each of two [pairs] of them," i.e., for each pair of men. Four men carried the burden, presumably two on a side. See Hoops, p. 183. According to Andrew, p. 99, the text means that the burden was too heavy for "either of two," i.e., for any pair, and that therefore four bearers had to be used.   **1640** semninga] See l. 644, note.   **1644** Ða com in gan] Andrew, p. 150, points out that after *com* the infinitive *gangan* is more usual than *gan*, and he would assume that the MS. *gan* here is an error for *gangan*. Holthausen and Schücking had previously emended to *gangan* for metrical reasons. Cf. ll. 324, 710f., 1640ff., 1973f., Daniel 149ff., 735f., etc. We also find *gangan* regularly after forms of *gewītan*, as in Genesis 858, 1049f., 1345, etc. But one (and the only?) parallel to *com . . . gan* is to be found in Beow. 1162f.   **1649** for eorlum ond þære idese mid] "Before the warriors and also before the lady," i.e., Wealhtheow. See Malone, Anglia LV, 271, who explains *idese mid* as a variation of *eorlum*.

1651–1700

1656 wigge . . . weorc] Cosijn, Aant., p. 25, would emend *wigge* to *wig* and (following Thorpe) *weorc* to *weorce*, taking *wig* as the object of *geneþde* and *weorce* as an adverb parallel to *earfoðlice*. Klaeber, Eng. Stud. XXXIX, 463f., accepts the emendation to *wig* but explains the word as a variation of *þæt* in the preceding line; putting a semicolon after *wætere*, he retains the MS. *weorc* as object of *geneþde*. He also suggests the possibility of putting *weorc geneþde* within parentheses. In his edition Klaeber retains the MS. reading in both half-lines, construing *wigge* as dat. sing.; he does not offer a translation. Other edd., except Trautmann, retain *wigge* (or *wige*) with varying interpretations. Hoops, Bwst., p. 110, and von Schaubert take *wigge*, "in battle," as a variation of *unsofte*. 1657*b*–1658] In spite of the indicative *wæs*, this passage looks very much like ll. 1550–1552, and one is tempted to translate, "immediately the battle would have been separated (i.e., ended), except that God protected me." See the notes on ll. 1550, 1552. Kock, Anglia XLV, 115ff., preserves the indicative function of *wæs* by translating, "a stop was almost put to my encounter, but God protected me." For *ætrihte*, "immediately," see Klaeber, Anglia L, 204f. Grundtvig suggested emending the MS. *guð* to *guðe*, gen. sing., and so Trautmann, Holthausen (1, 7, 8 ed.), and Sedgefield; this reading, also accepted by Bugge, Tidskrift VIII, 52, presupposes the translation, "immediately I was (or "would have been") separated from battle"; cf. ll. 479, 1433, 1763, 1908, etc. But the MS. *wæs guð getwæfed* is supported by the uses of *getwæfan* in *him se mæra* (i.e., God) *mod getwæfde*, Genesis 53, and *ferhð getwæfde*, Exodus 119, as well as by similar uses of the related verb *getwæman*, especially the passage *Beo ælc sacu getwæmed*, cited by Bos.-Tol., p. 461, from the laws of Æthelred. 1663 oftost wisode] Holder (2 ed.), Holthausen, and Sedgefield emend *oftost* to *oft*, for metrical reasons, following Sievers, Beitr. X, 256. Here God is the subject of *wisode*, which is used intransitively, as in ll. 292, 320, 370, etc. 1664 ðy wæpne] For the instrumental after *gebregdan*, cf. l. 2703. Elsewhere in Beowulf this verb is transitive. 1665 þa me sæl agealed] "When the opportunity offered itself to me." Cf. *þa him rum ageald*, l. 2690. 1667 swa] The equivalent of *sona swa*, "when." See Ericson, Eng. Stud. LXV, 347ff. Other examples of this temporal use of *swa*, cited by Ericson, are in Genesis 552, 574, Elene 128, 207, Juliana 253, etc. 1674 him] "For them," that is, for the retainers; *eorlum*, l. 1676, is parallel. Cf. Waldere I, 19, *ic ðe metod ondred*, "I feared God for you," i.e., on your account. In the present passage the object of *ondræde* is *aldorbealu*, l. 1676. 1675 on þa healfe] "From that quarter" (Chambers, note), i.e., from Grendel and his mother. 1677 gylden hilt] Holder (2 ed.) and Holthausen read *Gyldenhilt* as a compound, the name of the sword, following Kluge, Eng. Stud. XXII, 145. So also Andrew, p. 132. A compound word would give a more regular alliteration. But it is merely the hilt, and not the entire sword, which is being given to Hrothgar; cf. ll. 1614, 1687. 1681 ond] Holthausen and Sedgefield omit *ond*, following Müllenhoff, ZfdA. XIV, 213, and Bugge, ZfdPh. IV, 201f. It must be admitted that the emendation gives a smoother reading. 1684 on geweald gehwearf] This is a very awkward repetition of *on æht gehwearf*, l. 1679, but there is no reason for believing, with Cosijn, Aant., p. 25, that ll. 1681*b*–1684*a* are an interpolation. 1686 ðara þe ... dælde] See l. 98, note. 1688–1689 or ... fyrngewinnes] Kock, Anglia XLVI, 84, translates, "an exposition of the ancient struggle," "all about the old contest." But for possible objections to this interpretation, see Klaeber, Anglia L, 205ff., who points out that when *or* (or *ord*) has the meaning claimed by Kock, it is usually accompanied by *ende*, as in Andreas 649, Elene 590, Juliana 353, etc. Certainly in Beow. 2407, *ðæs orleges or*, the word *or* means merely "beginning"; cf. also Riddle 3, 59. 1689–1693] The edd. vary considerably in the punctuation of this passage. Most early edd. put either a semicolon or a colon after *fyrngewinnes*, taking *syðþan* either as a conjunction introducing a subordinate clause (l. 1691*a* then being the main clause) or as an adverb. But Wyatt, Sedgefield, Chambers, Holthausen (7, 8 ed.), Klaeber (3 ed.), and von Schaubert put a comma after *fyrngewinnes*, taking the *syðþan* clause as explanatory of *or . . . fyrngewinnes*. This construction involves giving *syðþan* the unusual meaning "when" (or, more freely, "in which"); see Kock, Anglia XLVI, 84ff., and Hoops, p. 187. Then *frecne geferdon* is best taken as a parenthesis. See also l. 2356, note. **1691 frecne geferdon**] The proper translation is undoubtedly "they suffered terribly" (Klaeber, note); cf. the close parallel in Christ and Satan 61f., *Habbað we alle . . . lyðre gefered*. Crawford, MLRev. XXIII, 207f., cites *Geþencean þa ealderas hu frecedlice . . . Heli se sacerd geferde* (= *memores periculi Heli sacerdotis*), in the Enlarged Rule of Chrodegang (ed. A. S. Napier, 18, 11ff.). The other translation of *geferan* which has been proposed, "to act, behave" (see Lawrence, JEGPh. X, 638, "they behaved impiously"; Kock, Anglia XLVI, 86, "they had acted boldly"), is unsubstantiated. In Andreas 516, which Kock cites as a parallel, *geferan* means "to pass through (a journey)." **1696 hwam**] "For whom."

1701–1750

1702 ꝥweard] For *eþelweard*. See l. 520, note. **1702–1703 þæt . . . betera**] For the absolute use of the comparative, as here, see Klaeber, Mod. Phil. III, 251f. Bugge, Tidskrift VIII, 52f., following an oral suggestion by P. A. Munch, would emend to *þæt þe eorl nære geboren betera*, "that there never has been born a better warrior than you," and so Trautmann in his text. **1705–1706**] The phrase *mid . . . snyttrum* is a variation of *geþyldum*. See Kock, Anglia XLVI, 86f., and Malone, Anglia LV, 271, who translates, "Thou holdest it, strength, altogether in steadfastness and prudence of spirit." For the meaning of *geþyldum*, cf. Gifts of Men 79f., where *geþyld* is parallel to *fæstgongel ferð*. **1707 freode**] Zupitza reads the MS. as *freoðe*, Wülker and Chambers as *freode*. Of these two readings, *freode*, "friendship," is more probable than *freoðe*, "peace," and is adopted by all recent edd. Cf. l. 2476, Andreas 390, Genesis 1026, etc. **1708 langtwidig**] This adjective is not elsewhere recorded, but *-twidig* is apparently related to Old Saxon *twiðôn*, "to grant" (*tuithos*, second person singular, Heliand 2752C, corresponding to *tugithos* in MS. M). See Holthausen, AEW., p. 356, where other cognates are cited. The adjective is usually explained as meaning "long-granted, granted for a long time," but Mackie, MLRev. XXXIV, 523, would assume an active meaning, "long-time granting, long-time helpful." **1710 eaforum Ecgwelan**] The children of Ecgwela are certainly the Danes, though the identity of Ecgwela is not known. Schaldemose, note, Holtzmann, Germania VIII, 495, and Müllenhoff, Beovulf, p. 50, suggest emending *eaforum* to *eafora*, parallel to *Heremod*. But this change, as Chambers remarks, leaves us little wiser about either Heremod or Ecgwela. Malone, Anglia LVI, 436f., would explain *Ecgwela* as "sword-vexer," a kenning for "shield," used as a name for Scyld. **1716ff.**] Most edd. put a semicolon or colon after *from*, l. 1715b, and a comma after l. 1718a, taking ll. 1718b–1719a as the main clause to which ll. 1716a–1718a are subordinate. But Schücking, Klaeber (3 ed.), Holthausen (7, 8 ed.), and von Schaubert put a comma after *from* and begin a new sentence with *Hwæþere*, l. 1718*b*. On this latter punctuation, see Schücking, Svk., p. 23, and Hoops, pp. 188f., who point out the antithesis between *ana hwearf* and *ofer ealle men forð gefremede*. But the older punctuation provides an equally clear antithesis between the advantages which God gave to Heremod (ll. 1716–1718*a*) and Heremod's failure to benefit by them (ll. 1718*b*–1722*a*). To be sure, there is no other passage in Beowulf in which *hwæþ(e)re* serves to introduce a main clause following a concessive subordinate clause, but Daniel 232*b*–234*a* provides a valid parallel to the interpretation adopted here. **1720 æfter dome]** "In pursuit of glory, for the sake of glory." Cf. l. 2179, Genesis 282, 291. **1723 þe]** "For your sake," or perhaps better, "for your benefit." **1726 snyttru]** Kock, Anglia XLVI, 87, takes this word as instrumental, parallel to *þurh sidne sefan*; he cites Elene 313 and *unsnyttro*, Elene 1285. So also Holthausen (6, 7 ed.). But for a defence of the traditional interpretation, with *snyttru* parallel to *eard* and *eorlscipe*, see Klaeber, Anglia L, 207. **1728 on lufan]** The meaning of this phrase has been much discussed, and a number of emendations have been proposed. Grundtvig suggested emending to *on luste*. Trautmann reads *on lustum*, partly for metrical reasons; Holthausen (3, 4 ed.) reads *on luston*, Holthausen (5, 6 ed.) *on lustan*. Holthausen (1 ed.), note, suggested *on heahlufan*, and so Sedgefield (1 ed.), who translates, "in exalted love." Holthausen (2 ed.) emends to *on hyhte*, Sedgefield (2, 3 ed.) to *on hlisan*, "in glory." Retaining the MS. reading, Kock, Anglia XLVI, 88f., explains *lufan* as for *lufne*, dat. sing. of a noun *lufen*, related to the verb *læfan* and meaning "that which has been granted," "estate held by grant." Cf. *eard* (*ham*, *eðel*) *alefan to æhte*, Christ and Satan 115f., 277f. The MS. form *lufan*, Kock thinks, has been influenced by *lufu*, "love." He also explains *lufen*, l. 2886, as nom. sing. of the same noun. In the present passage he translates, "Sometimes he lets a high-born man's desire be altogether bent on tenancy." Holthausen (7, 8 ed.) reads *on lufene*, apparently accepting this explanation by Kock. Chambers, taking the MS. *lufan* as a form of *lufu*, "love," suggests that *on lufan . . . hworfan* means "to wander in delight"; similarly Klaeber, Eng. Stud. XXXIX, 464, "in wonne wandeln (sich befinden)." But Klaeber, Anglia L, 207f., thinks it possible that *lufan* is the equivalent of *eardlufan*, l. 692; he points out that the word *eard* is used in l. 1727. So also Hoops, Bwst., pp. 110ff., who explains *lufan* as "dear home, dwelling." This interpretation is inviting, but Kock's also deserves serious consideration. **1733 his]** "Of it," that is, of the *side rice*. See Klaeber, Archiv CXV, 180f. **1734 for his unsnyttrum]** Transcript A has *for his unsnyttrum*; transcript B has only *his unsnyttrum*. See Malone, PMLA LXIV, 1203, who suggests that the word *for* had crumbled away in the MS. by the time transcript B was made. Thorkelin in his edition followed A, including *for* in his text, and so most of the early edd. But Zupitza, apparently through an oversight, omitted *for* in his report of A, and Wyatt, Sedgefield, Chambers, Klaeber, and von Schaubert read only *his unsnyttrum*, with difficulties of interpretation. **1736 adl]** On the readings of the Thorkelin transcripts, see Malone, PMLA LXIV, 1204. **1737 sefan]** So Kemble and all later edd., following Grundtvig, tr., p. 292. The *sefað* of the two Thorkelin transcripts was in all probability the reading of the

MS. Zupitza incorrectly reported *sefad* as the reading of A. gesacu]
Grein, ed., Wülker, Trautmann, Holthausen, and Sedgefield emend to *gesaca*,
"adversary." Other edd. retain *gesacu* as the equivalent of *sacu*, "strife, con-
tention." **1738** eoweð] Kock, Anglia XLVI, 90, takes this verb as intransitive,
"shows itself," with *gesacu* and *ecghete* parallel subjects. Chambers and von
Schaubert accept this interpretation. But *īewan* (*ȳwan*, *ēowan*) is regularly
transitive, though some of its compounds (*ætīewan*, *oðīewan*) are used both
transitively and intransitively. See Klaeber, Anglia L, 208, who cites l. 276,
Judith 240, Genesis 2056, etc. **1739** he þæt wyrse ne con] Schücking, Chambers, and Holthausen (7, 8 ed.) begin a new sentence with this half-line; other
recent edd. put a semicolon after l. 1739*a*. But a parenthesis seems the most
probable construction here; cf. the similar parenthesis in l. 1746. Translate,
"he does not know the worse [part]," i.e., wickedness. **1740**] Von Schaubert
begins a new sentence with *oðþæt*. See l. 56, note. Here in l. 1740, as well as
in l. 2039, *oðþæt* is the first word of a section in the MS., but even so, her de-
parture from the traditional punctuation is highly questionable. **1741**
weaxeð] So Kemble and later edd., for the *weaxed* of the Thorkelin transcripts.
1742 to fæst] Holthausen (7, 8 ed.) emends to *to þon fæst*. Sedgefield and Chambers punctuate l. 1742*b* as a parenthesis, connecting *bisgum gebunden* with *se
weard . . . , sawele hyrde*. **1747** wom wundorbebodum] Parallel to *biteran
stræle*, with l. 1746*b* to be taken as a parenthesis. So Holthausen (1–6, 8 ed.),
Schücking, Chambers, Klaeber, Sedgefield (3 ed.), and von Schaubert. See
Klaeber, Archiv CVIII, 368ff. Kock, Anglia XLIV, 101f., translates, "wondrous perverse messages," i.e., the promptings of the devil. But Trautmann,
Sedgefield (1, 2 ed.), and Holthausen (7 ed.) follow the older edd. in connecting
l. 1746*b* with what follows, putting a comma after l. 1746*a* and no punctuation
after l. 1746*b*. This punctuation is, however, very doubtful, since elsewhere
(as in l. 1758) *bebeorgan* takes the accusative of the thing guarded against; see
Bos.-Tol., Supp., p. 66. **1749** on gylp] See l. 618, note. **1750** fædde]
Thorpe and later edd. emend to *fætte*, the usual spelling of the word. Cf. ll.
333, 1093, 2102, etc. But *fædde* may perhaps be retained as a variant form; see
fædan gold[e]*s*, Husband's Message 36, and note.

1751–1800

1755 fehð oþer to] "Another inherits (the treasure)." The similar construction
fon to rice, "to succeed (by inheritance) to the throne," is frequent in the Anglo-
Saxon Chronicle. See Schröer, Anglia XIII, 336; Cosijn, Aant., pp. 26f.
1757 egesan ne gymeð] "Pays no heed to fear, disregards fear," a continuation
of the idea of *unmurnlice*. See Klaeber, Anglia XXVIII, 455; Anglia L, 208.
The object *egesan* may be either gen. sing. or acc. sing. Kock's interpretation,
Anglia XLII, 114, which explains *egesan* as dat.-instr. sing., corresponding to
unmurnlice, and *madmas* and *ærgestreon* as objects of both *dæleþ* and *ne gymeð*,
is less convincing. **1758** ðone bealonið] "Such wickedness." See Barnouw,
Textkritische Untersuchungen, p. 29, and cf. ðone magan, l. 943. **1759**
secg betsta] Sievers, Beitr. X, 312, proposed *secga betsta*, for metrical reasons,

and so most later edd. This reading had previously been suggested by Thorpe in Kemble (2 ed.). Heyne (2–4 ed.) and Socin (5 ed.) read *secg se betsta*, following Grundtvig, note. Sedgefield (3 ed.) reads *secg betosta*; similarly Pope, p. 320, would read *secg betesta*. Wyatt, Klaeber (3 ed.), and von Schaubert retain the MS. reading. See ll. 947, 1871, and notes. þæt selre geceos] "Choose the better [part]." Cf. *þæt wyrse*, l. 1739. **1766b** oððe] Pope, pp. 343f., would omit this word, either explaining the verbs *forsiteð* and *forsworceð* as transitive (with *atol yldo* the subject of both, and *eagena bearhtm* the object) or beginning a new sentence with *eagena*. But for objections to Pope's proposal, see Klaeber, Beitr. LXXII, 124. **1767** forsiteð ond forsworceð] Although these verbs are found elsewhere in both transitive and intransitive use, most edd. accept an intransitive meaning in the present passage, "the brightness of the eyes diminishes and grows dark." **1770–1771** ond hig . . . mægþa] "And protected them against many tribes by fighting." See Kock, Anglia XLII, 114. The striking parallel in the Benedictine Office, Psalm 34,3 (Records VI, 82), *Heald me . . . and wige beluc wraðum feondum*, was first pointed out by Heyne. **1772** æscum ond ecgum] Parallel to *wigge*, l. 1770. **1774** edwenden] Suggested by Grein, Bib., and so most later edd. **1777** þære socne] Gen. sing., dependent on *modceare*. See Hoops, p. 193, who compares ðæs *modceare*, l. 1992. The word *socn* here implies not only a visit (by Grendel) but also an assault; cf. *hāmsōcn*, from which comes the "hamesucken" of Scots law, the crime of assaulting a person in his own house. **1783** wigge weorþad] The edd. differ in the word division of this half-line. The MS. divides as *wigge weorþad*, but this fact is not conclusive; see Introd., p. xix. Grein, Bib., reads *wigge weorþad*, and so Arnold, Wyatt, Holder (2 ed.), Schücking, Chambers, and von Schaubert. Hoops, p. 193, also reads *wigge weorþad*. Kemble read *wiggeweorþad* as a compound, and so Grundtvig, Grein, ed., Heyne, Wülker, Klaeber, and Holthausen (6 ed.). Cf. the similar compound *lyftgeswenced*, l. 1913. Ettmüller, Holder (1 ed.), Socin, Trautmann, Holthausen (1–5, 7, 8 ed.), and Sedgefield emend to *wigge* (or *wige*) *geweorþad*, and this emendation is approved by Cosijn, Beitr. VIII, 571f. The reading adopted in the text follows the precedent of Elene 1195, in Records II, 99. **1784** gemænra] Kock, Anglia XLII, 115f., would emend to *gemæne*, the form which would normally occur in the predicate position. But Klaeber, MLN. XXXIV, 132f., explains the MS. *gemænra* as the result of attraction to the preceding word. There is no need to emend here, as there is in l. 1857. **1789** niowan stefne] "Anew, again," a variation of *eft*, l. 1787. For this expression (from *stefn*, "time, turn," not from *stefn*, "voice"), cf. l. 2594, Genesis 1555, 1886, etc. **1792** unigmetes] Apparently a late form of *ungemetes*. Thorpe and most later edd. emend to *ungemetes*, but Holder (2 ed.), Holthausen (2–8 ed.), Schücking, Klaeber, and von Schaubert retain the MS. form. Sedgefield (3 ed.) emends to *ungemete*, citing ll. 2420, 2721. **1796** for andrysnum] Most edd. assume a noun *and-rysnu*, "courtesy, etiquette," related to the adjective *gerisne* and the verb *gerisan*, "to be fitting." But Moore, JEGPh. XVIII, 209f., would explain the MS. *andrysnum* as a form of the noun *on-drysnu*, *an-drysnu*, "fear, reverence" (Bos.-Tol., p. 749), reviving the old translation of Thorpe and of Bos.-Tol., p. 41, "from reverence." be-

weotede] So Kemble II and all later edd., following Grundtvig, tr., p. 293.
1797 þegnes] Sedgefield assumes a collective sense for this word, citing the following plural *heaþoliðende*. So also Hoops, p. 194. But Thomas, MLRev.
VI, 267, points out that Beowulf would naturally have a special attendant assigned to him. Similarly, it is not necessary to explain *þy dogore* as used in a generic sense, "in those days," as Klaeber does, since it may mean merely "on that particular day." The meaning of ll. 1794ff. is that one of the Danes showed Beowulf where to sleep, one who was assigned to attend to Beowulf's needs, such an attendant as was fitting for the sea-warriors (Beowulf and the other Geats) to have. 1798 heaþoliðende] The dat. plur. of this word is found in l. 2955 (where it is a variation of *sæmannum*) and in Andreas 426. It is tempting to translate *heaþoliðende* as "seafarers" (cf. *brimliðende, sæliðende*, etc.), particularly in view of the MS. *heaþu* in l. 1862, where a word for "sea" is clearly indicated. But *heaþu* in l. 1862 is probably to be emended; see the note on that line. Most recent edd. follow Kluge, Beitr. IX, 190, in taking *heaþo* in its usual sense of "war" and translating *heaþoliðende* as "war-seafarers, sea-warriors." But for a defence of *heaþu-*, "sea," see G. P. Krapp, Andreas and the Fates of the Apostles (Boston, 1906), p. 104.

1801–1850

1803a] Nothing is lost from the MS. at this point, but it is apparent that a half-line has dropped out of the text, and several readings of l. 1803a have been proposed. Sievers, Anglia XIV, 137f., would supply *scima æfter sceadwe*, and so Holder (2 ed.), Trautmann, Holthausen, Schücking, Chambers, and von Schaubert. Similarly Klaeber, who supplies *scima ofer sceadwa*. Sedgefield (1 ed.) supplies *scima scyndan*, Sedgefield (2 ed.) *scima scynded*. With less probability, Heyne (2–4 ed.) and Socin assumed a loss both before and after *scacan* and read *Ða com beorht sunne scacan ofer grundas;* similarly Sedgefield (3 ed.), who however reads *sigel* instead of *sunne*. 1805 farenne] So Kemble (2 ed.) and later edd. 1808 sunu] Whether this word is nom. sing. or dat. sing. (as in l. 344), or even acc. sing., depends on who *se hearda* is in the preceding line. Kock, Anglia XLVI, 90, assumes that *se hearda* is Beowulf and that Beowulf is the logical subject of all the finite verbs in ll. 1807–1812a. He explains *sunu* as acc. sing. and *Heht . . . Hrunting beran* as parallel to *heht his sweord niman*. That is, Beowulf asked Unferth to take back his sword Hrunting. This seems less likely than the interpretation given by Hoops, Bwst., p. 113, who, also assuming that Beowulf is the subject, takes *sunu* as dat. sing. That is, Beowulf ordered Hrunting to be brought to Unferth, asked him to take back his sword. Both of these interpretations require us to explain *leanes*, l. 1809, as the equivalent of a form *lænes*, gen. sing. of *læn*, "loan, grant." Müllenhoff, ZfdA. XIV, 215, with an interpretation very similar to Kock's, had proposed to emend to *lænes*, and so Ettmüller, Holder, Wyatt, Trautmann, and Holthausen (7, 8 ed.). Elsewhere in the extant texts, however, *læn* is regularly feminine, and, as Klaeber (3 ed.), second supplement (1950), p. 468, points out, it seems not to have been a poetic word in Anglo-Saxon, occurring in the poetry only in Genesis 601, 692 as a loan from Old Saxon. Klaeber, Mod. Phil. III, 460f., and in his edition, takes *sunu Ecglafes*, i.e., Unferth, as the subject of the sentence: "Then the brave son of Ecglaf had Hrunting brought, bade [him, i.e., Beowulf] take his sword, the precious weapon." Beowulf is then the subject of *sægde*, l. 1809, and of the following verbs. This interpretation is attractive in that it permits us to explain the MS. *leanes* as gen. sing. of *lēan*, "reward"; on the other hand, Hoops's interpretation of the passage has the advantage of not requiring a change of subject at l. 1809b.   heht his sweord niman] Grundtvig suggested supplying *hine* after *heht*, and so Holthausen (2–8 ed.). Apparently Holthausen accepts Klaeber's interpretation of ll. 1807ff.; see the preceding note.   **1810** þone guðwine] "The battle-friend," i.e., the sword.   **1813** Ond] Sedgefield omits this word. It is hardly possible, for stylistic reasons, to put ll. 1813–1814a in the same sentence with what precedes, but either *Ond þa siðfrome* or *þa siðfrome* is an awkward beginning for a new sentence. Ettmüller's old emendation, *Sona þa siðfrome*, is perhaps worthy of consideration. Trautmann, Schücking, and Chambers put only a comma after *wæron*, taking *þa* to be a subordinating conjunction, "when." But *þa* is more probably an adverb, "then," and most edd. take it as such.   **1816** hæle hildedeor] This phrase refers to Beowulf and is parallel to *æþeling*, not to *se oþer*. Similarly, *grette* is parallel to *eode*, l. 1814. On the problem of punctuation in this passage, see Kock, Anglia XLVI, 90f., and Klaeber, Anglia L, 209. Normal punctuation would require a comma after *hildedeor*, but as Klaeber points out, a comma there would be ambiguous. Kemble II and all later edd. read *hæle* for the MS. *helle*.   **1821** willum bewenede] "Entertained in accordance with our desires"? Kock, Anglia XLIV, 102, takes *tela* and *willum* as parallel adverbs, translating, "well and pleasantly (after our desire)." But Mackie, MLRev. XXXIV, 523, citing *hringum wenede*, l. 1091, thinks it more likely that *willum* is used here in its concrete sense; he translates, "We have been well honoured here with desirable gifts."   **1822-1823** owihte ... maran] Kock, Anglia XLVI, 91f., would take *owihte* and *maran* together, translating as "any more, at all greater." He points out that elsewhere *owihte* as an absolute instrumental invariably stands in a clause with a comparative; cf. l. 2432, Andreas 800, Christ 248, 343. Kock's interpretation seems more satisfactory than taking *owihte* by itself and translating, "by any means."   **1825** guðgeweorca] Grein, Bib., Heyne, Wyatt, Trautmann, and Chambers explain *guðgeweorca* as dependent on *gearo*. Kock, Anglia XLVI, 91, cites *gearo gyrnwræce*, l. 2118, and *gearo ... willan þines*, Juliana 49f., as parallels. But Klaeber, Anglia L, 210, points out that in such a construction the qualifying genitive never precedes *gearo*. He suggests the possibility that *guðgeweorca* is to be construed with *tilian*, parallel to *modlufan maran*. In his 1st ed. Klaeber, following Cosijn, Aant., p. 38 (note on l. 2791), takes *guðgeweorca* as an instrumental genitive, like *niða* in ll. 845, 1439, 2206. Hoops, p. 198, who construes *owihte*, l. 1822, as an independent instrumental (see the preceding note), would explain *guðgeweorca* as dependent upon it, translating, "durch irgend etwas ... von

Kriegstaten." So also Sedgefield and von Schaubert. But *owihte* and *guðgeweorca* are rather far apart. **1828 hetende]** A more regular spelling would be *hettende*, and so Grein, Bib., Arnold, Trautmann, Holthausen, Schücking, and Sedgefield (2, 3 ed.). **hwilum dydon]** The MS. reading gives an unusually short A-type half-line, and Sievers, Beitr. X, 498, would emend to *hwilum dædon*; this emendation is made by Trautmann, Holthausen (*dēdon*), and Schücking. Sedgefield (2, 3 ed.) emends to *hwilum ðydon*, explaining *ðydon* as preterite of *ðīen, ðȳwan*, "to oppress." But the form *þywað* occurs in the preceding line, and it is unlikely that the same verb would be used here. **1829 þusenda]** For *þusendu*, acc. plur. **1830-1831 Higelac . . . dryhten]** The MS. *higelace* must be construed as parallel to *dryhten*, in spite of the difference in case. Trautmann, Holthausen, and Sedgefield (3 ed.) emend to *Higelac* in l. 1830b, retaining the MS. *dryhten*. Cf. l. 2650, where *on*, in a similar function, takes the accusative *mec*. On the other hand, Ettmüller, Holder, and Sedgefield (1 ed.), retaining *Higelace*, emend *dryhten* to *dryhtne*. Sedgefield (2 ed.) transposes to *Ic wat on Higelace* in l. 1830b, apparently for metrical reasons, and emends to *dryhtne* in l. 1831a. Schücking, Chambers, Klaeber, and von Schaubert retain the MS. reading in both places. But in view of *on mec*, l. 2650, the emendation to *Higelac* seems justified. **1832 fremman]** "Support"; cf. Andreas 934, where *fremman* is a synonym of *fyrþran*. **1833 wordum ond worcum]** The MS. reads *weordum 7 worcum*. Thorpe and all later edd. emend *weordum* to *wordum*. Thorpe, Grein, Bib., Grundtvig, Ettmüller, Arnold, Wülker, Socin, Wyatt, Schücking, Chambers, Klaeber, and von Schaubert emend *worcum* to *weorcum*. But no emendation of *worcum* is necessary, except on the supposition that a form *weorcum* in the scribe's original caused him to write the MS. *weordum*. Cf. *worda ond worca*, l. 289; *wordum ne worcum*, l. 1100. **herige]** Lübke, Anz. fdA. XIX, 342, suggested *nerige* for the MS. *herige*, and so Sedgefield (3 ed.). But *herige* probably means "show [my] esteem by deeds," perhaps even "assist, help"; see Klaeber, Mod. Phil. III, 261, Anglia L, 210; Kock, Anglia XLVI, 92; Hoops, Bwst., pp. 114f. **1836 Hreþric]** So Thorpe and all later edd., following Grundtvig, tr., p. 294. Apparently the scribe who wrote the MS. *hreþrinc* was not expecting a proper name. **1837 geþingeð]** So Heyne and later edd., following Grein, Spr. I, 471. The phrase *him geþingan* means "to decide (to go)"; see Cosijn, Aant., p. 28, and Kock, Anglia XLVI, 93, who translates it as "make arrangements (by negotiation, message, announcement) for oneself to go, or to come," "appoint to go, or to come." Cf. the close parallel in Judgment Day I, 5 (Records III, 212), *Hafað him geþinged hider þeoden user.* **1838b-1839]** "Far countries are better sought by him who himself is worthy," that is, one who is worthy (such as Hrethric) will be better treated in a foreign country than one who is not worthy. **1840]** As this line stands in the MS. it has, contrary to the usual rule, alliteration on the unstressed pronoun *him*. Holthausen (2-6 ed.) supplies *helm Scyldinga, eorl æðelum god* between l. 1840a and l. 1840b; see his note in ZfdPh. XXXVII, 125. But for a defence of the MS. reading, see Kock, Anglia XLVI, 93f.; Hoops, Bwst., pp. 115f. Klaeber, note, cites l. 543*b* as a similar instance of alliteration on *him*. **1850 þe]** Heyne, Socin, Wyatt, Trautmann, Schücking, Sedgefield (1, 2 ed.), Chambers, and von Schaubert take this word as dative of comparison, "than you." G. W. Small, The Germanic Case of Comparison (Philadelphia, 1929), pp. 38ff., also favors this interpretation, citing a number of examples of the dative of comparison from other poems (Elene 505f., 565, 1109, Christ 1188, 1241, 1651, etc.). But Klaeber, note, points out that a dative (or instrumental) with a comparative does not occur elsewhere in Beowulf. See also his comments in Anglia Beibl. XLVIII (1937), 162, where he suggests that though the dative of comparison cannot be called un-Germanic, its use in the Cynewulfian poems was perhaps reinforced by Latin models. Klaeber and Holthausen take *þæt þe* as the equivalent of *þætte*; cf. l. 858, where *þætte* occurs in a similar context, and *þæt ðe*, l. 1846, which is certainly the equivalent of *þætte*. But in Anglia LXIII, 421, Klaeber says that "it is impossible to prove or disprove that *þe* is = *þē*."

1851–1900

1854 leng swa wel] We should expect a comparative after *swa* here, as in *leng swa swiðor*, Genesis 989. Grein, Spr. II, 498 (s.v. *swā* 3), emended the MS. *wel* to *sel*; Ettmüller emended to *bet*. Bugge, Beitr. XII, 96, approving *sel*, also suggested *bet*, apparently independently of Ettmüller. Socin, Trautmann, Holthausen, Schücking, and Sedgefield emend to *sel*, with Grein. But Klaeber, note, and Hoops, p. 200, are probably right in accepting the MS. reading as a mixed construction (*licað leng swa sel* combined with *licað wel*); see ll. 69–70, note. **1857 gemæne]** So Sievers, Beitr. IX, 140, and later edd. It is impossible to explain the MS. reading as the result of attraction, as in l. 1784. **1861 gegretan]** So Thorpe and most later edd. The verb *sceal*, l. 1855, has three infinitives dependent on it, *restan*, l. 1857, *wesan*, l. 1859, and *gegretan*, in addition to the infinitive "to be" which must be understood in l. 1857*a*. **1862 heafu]** Attempts have been made to explain the MS. *heaþu* as "sea," the meaning which is required here, but there is no unambiguous evidence for such a noun. The first element of the compound *heaþoliðende* has been interpreted as "sea," but probably wrongly; see l. 1798, note. Sarrazin, Beowulf-Studien, p. 27, would explain the MS. *heaþu* as "war" and translate *ofer heaþu* as "after the war." Cf. *ofer eald gewin*, l. 1781. But *heaþu-*, "war," though frequent in compounds, does not seem to exist as an independent word in West Germanic. Kluge, Beitr. IX, 190, proposed the emendation to *heafu* (plural of *hæf*, "sea," found in l. 2477), and so all later edd. except Socin and Wyatt. **1864 fæste geworhte]** "Firmly disposed." For other examples of *gewyrcan* in this sense, see Bos.-Tol., Supp., p. 460, s.v. *ge-wyrcan*, V; Klaeber, Mod. Phil. III, 461. **1865 ealde wisan]** Explained by most commentators as an adverbial phrase in the accusative, "after the old fashion, according to the ancient custom." For this construction see J. E. Wülfing, Die Syntax in den Werken Alfreds des Grossen I (Bonn, 1894), 268. But Kock, Anglia XLVI, 94, would explain *wisan* not as acc. sing. of *wise*, "manner," but as acc. plur. of *wisa*, "leader," parallel to *leode*, l. 1863; he translates, "their aged leaders wholly free of blame." This interpretation is favored by Hoops, p. 201. See also Klaeber, Anglia LXIII, 421. Sedgefield (3 ed.) takes *ealde wisan* as acc. sing., parallel to *leode*, and translates, "I know the old custom (*i.e.* long-established friendship) to be in every respect blameless." 1868 hine] So Thorpe and later edd. 1871 ðegn betstan] For metrical reasons, H. Schubert, De Anglo-Saxonum arte metrica (Berlin, 1870), p. 41, and Sievers, Beitr. X, 232, suggested emending the MS. ðegn to ðegna, and so Wülker, Holder (2 ed.), and most later edd. Sedgefield (3 ed.) emends to ðegn betostan; similarly Pope, p. 372, suggests ðegn betestan. Wyatt, Klaeber (3 ed.), and von Schaubert retain the MS. reading. See ll. 947, 1759, and notes. Kemble (2 ed.) had emended to the gen. plur. here and (following Thorpe's suggestion) in l. 1759, but he left *secg*, l. 947, unaltered. 1873 Him wæs bega wen] "He expected both [things]," i.e., that he would see Beowulf again, and that he would not see Beowulf again. But one of the two expectations was stronger (l. 1874b). Cf. *bega on wenum*, etc., ll. 2895ff. 1875 hie] Thorpe and all later edd. read either *hi* or *hie*, as required by the plural verb, following Grundtvig, tr., p. 294. Kluge, Beitr. IX, 190, would take *geseon* in a reflexive sense, "to see one another again." He compares *þæs ðe hie onsundne æfre moston geseon under sunnan*, Andreas 1012f. So also Chambers, note. But *hie* may be the object in both passages, the pronoun subject being unexpressed; see A. Pogatscher, Anglia XXIII (1900), 273, 299. Mackie, MLRev. XXXIV, 523, would retain the MS. *he* and emend *moston* to *moste*. Then supplying the required negative (see the following note) and omitting the comma after l. 1875b, he would translate, "that he (Hrothgar) might never again see the brave men (Beowulf and his comrades) in the assembly." This proposal by Mackie is worthy of serious consideration. The chief argument against it is that throughout this passage (ll. 1866–1887) nothing is said of Beowulf's comrades. seoððan no] The letters seoðða are all that are now visible in the MS., but there seems to have been room for three or four more letters, now lost, at the end of the line. It is apparent that at least seoðða[n] is to be restored. It is also likely, in view of Hrothgar's tears, l. 1872b, that there was a negative particle somewhere in l. 1875. That is, Hrothgar wept because he did not expect that he and Beowulf would see each other again. Bugge, Beitr. XII, 96, and Sievers, Anglia XIV, 139ff., proposed to restore *na* after seoðða[n], and so Trautmann, Holthausen (1–6, 8 ed.), Sedgefield, Chambers, and von Schaubert. Klaeber restores *no*, which is much more frequent in the MS. than *na*. Holthausen (7 ed.) puts the negative in the second half-line: *þæt hie seoðða[n] geseon ne moston.* 1880 beorn] For *bearn*, "burned." Grein, Ettmüller, Wyatt, and Chambers emend to *bearn*, a form not elsewhere found in the poetry; Thorpe, Holder (2 ed.), Socin (6, 7 ed.), Trautmann, Holthausen, Schücking, Sedgefield, and Klaeber (1 ed.) emend to *born*, as in Guthlac 938, 964, 980. But the form *beorn*, which is also found as a corrected reading in Christ 540, may be retained as a late West Saxon variant of *bearn*, *born*; see Thomas, MLRev. XXII, 72. Most of the early edd. retain *beorn*, and so also Klaeber (3 ed.) and von Schaubert. 1880b]

Sedgefield unnecessarily supplies *Gewat* at the beginning of this half-line.   **1883**
agendfrean] So Kemble (2 ed.) and later edd.   **1887** se] Grundtvig, note,
Ettmüller, and Holthausen emend to *seo*, following a suggestion by Grein, Bib.,
in order to secure agreement with the antecedent *yldo*. But see l. 1260, note.
1889 hægstealdra] Ettmüller, Holthausen (1, 2 ed.), and Sedgefield emend to
hægstealda, since this word is usually a noun. So also Björkman, Anglia Beibl.
XXX, 122. But *hægstealdra* as gen. plur. occurs also in Genesis 1862.   heap]
Supplied by Grein, Bib., and most later ed., to complete the half-line.
bæron] Sievers, Beitr. X, 224, suggested emending to *beran*, infinitive after
Cwom. So also Trautmann and Sedgefield (3 ed.); Holthausen (1–6 ed.)
emends to *beron*, as a variant form of the infinitive. There appears to be a dot
in the MS. under the *a* of *bæron*, which (as Sievers suggests) may have been
intended for a mark of deletion; but Wülker and Zupitza do not mention this
dot, and it may be accidental. For the MS. *Cwom . . . bæron*, which is
stylistically unobjectionable, cf. *Ferdon . . . mæton*, ll. 1632f.   **1892** nosan]
Cf. l. 2803. This weak noun, *nōse* (or *nōsa?*), "promontory," is apparently a
different word from the strong feminine *nosu*, "nose." See Holthausen, AEW.,
p. 238, and Pope, p. 357, both of whom assume a long root vowel in this word.
But Hoops, Bwst., p. 116, assumes a weak feminine *nŏse*, "promontory," and
so Klaeber (3 ed.) and von Schaubert.   **1893** gæstas grette] Grundtvig, tr.,
p. 294, suggested the restoration *gæs[tas ne] grette*, and so Kemble (1 ed.).
Grein, ed., read *gæs[tas] grette*, accepting Grundtvig's plural form *gæstas* but
omitting the *ne*, and so all later edd. except Arnold, who restored *gæs[t ne] grette*,
following Kemble (2 ed.) and Thorpe. Grein, Bib., restored *gæs[t ge]grette*, a
reading recently revived by Andrew, p. 150. The singular *gæst* has the advantage of providing an antecedent for *He* in l. 1900, but other considerations
favor the plural *gæstas*.   **1894-1895**] "He said that the bright-armored
warriors went to their ships welcome to the Geats"; that is, he paid a compli-
ment to the visitors by predicting that they would be warmly welcomed at
home. Malone's suggestion, Eng. Studies XV, 151, that *Wedera leodum* is
dative of accompaniment, serving as a variation of *scaþan*, is less likely.   **1896**
sægeap] "Wide-bosomed." See Hoops, Eng. Stud. LXIV, 211.

1901–1950

1902 maþme þy weorþra] So Thorpe (who, however, read *madme*) and most
later edd. The meaning is "he was . . . more honored on account of that
treasure." Sedgefield (1, 2 ed.), emending to *weorþra*, retains *maþma* as gen.
plur. but does not offer a translation. Malone, Anglia LIV, 97f., explains the
MS. *maþma þy weorþre* as an example of late confusion between unstressed
vowels.   **1903** Gewat him on naca] The MS. reads *gewat him on nacan*.
With this reading, *on* is an unstressed preposition, and since the line requires
vocalic alliteration, it is necessary to emend. Grein, Heyne, Ettmüller, Wülker,
and Socin emend *nacan* to *yŏnacan*; Sedgefield and Holthausen (8 ed.) supply
eft before *on*. But Rieger's proposal, ZfdPh. III, 402, to emend the MS.
nacan to *naca*, subject of *Gewat*, thus making *on* a stressed adverb, is entirely

convincing and is adopted by Holder (1 ed.), Holthausen (2–7 ed.), Schücking, Chambers, Klaeber, and von Schaubert. For this adverbial use of *on*, cf. *ræsdon on sona*, Andreas 1334; *þæt þu . . . miht on treddian*, Psalm 65, 5, 4f., etc.   **1913** lyftgeswenced] Rieger, ZfdPh. III, 405, and Trautmann suggest emending to *lyfte geswenced*. Cf. *wigge weorþad*, l. 1783, where, however, some edd. assume a compound *wiggeweorþad*, similar in formation to *lyftgeswenced*.   on lande stod] Sievers, Beitr. IX, 141, proposed to supply *þæt he* before *on*, and so Holder, Holthausen, and Sedgefield. Cf. l. 404. **1914** geara] For *gearu*, "ready."   **1915** leofra manna] Genitive object of *wlatode*, "looked out (for)." Bugge, Beitr. XII, 97, cites the similar construction after the Old Icelandic cognate *leita* and after Anglo-Saxon *wilnian, gyrnan, wyscan, abidan*, etc.   **1916** faroðe] See l. 28, note.   **1917** sidfæþme] Thorpe, Grundtvig, Arnold, and Sedgefield (3 ed.) emend to *sidfæþmed*, as in l. 302. But cf. *widfæðme scip*, Andreas 240.   **1918** oncerbendum] So Thorpe and later edd., for the MS. *oncear-*, following Grundtvig, tr., p. 295. The only other compound of *ancor-*, "anchor," found in the poetry is also spelled irregularly, *oncyrrapum*, Whale 14. In each case the scribe may have been thinking of another word—of the verb *oncierran* in Whale 14, and of (an unrecorded) *cearbendum* here.   **1923** wunað] Thorpe emended to *wunode*, and Grein, Arnold, Wülker, Holder, Trautmann, and Holthausen (2 ed.) read either *wunode* or *wunade*. Sievers, Beitr. IX, 141, suggested that ll. 1923*b*–1924 are to be taken as direct discourse. But in the very next sentence we find a similar change (*wæs . . . hæbbe*) from preterite in the main clause to present in the subordinate clause; cf. also ll. 1311ff., 2484ff., etc. Holthausen supplies *he* after *þær*.   **1925** bregorof] Thorpe, Grein, Ettmüller, Arnold, Wülker, Wyatt, Schücking, Sedgefield, and Chambers read *brego rof* as two words, and Wyatt, p. 163, translates, "the prince [was] a brave king." But the compound is more probable: "The hall was excellent, royally brave the king." Kock, Anglia XLII, 116, would explain *brego-* as an intensifying prefix, citing *Cyningbalde*, l. 1634.   **1926** heah in healle] If the MS. *hea healle* is retained, it is best taken as meaning "high [were] the halls"; so Wyatt, Trautmann, Chambers, Klaeber (1 ed.), and von Schaubert. But the plural *healle*, following the singular *bold*, seems unlikely. Malone, MLN. LVI, 356, would put a comma after *hea* and explain *healle* as a dative of accompaniment, translating, "the king renowned, high, the hall even so." Schücking, following von Grienberger, Zeitschrift für die österreichischen Gymnasien LVI, 750, assumes a compound *heahealle*, locative instrumental, "in der Herrscherhalle." But in a place-where construction of this kind we expect a preposition. Cf. *hludne in healle*, l. 89; *in þæm guðsele*, l. 443, and as an emended reading in l. 2139; *in þæm winsele*, l. 695, etc. Sedgefield accordingly emends to *on heahealle*. Holder reads *on heanhealle*, following a suggestion by Kluge, and so Holthausen (3, 4 ed.). Heyne (2–4 ed.) and Socin emend to *hea on healle*, explaining *hea* as nom. sing.; Kock, Anglia XLII, 116, proposed *heah on healle*, and so Holthausen (5, 6 ed.) and Klaeber (3 ed.). Holthausen (7 ed.) emends to *heah in healle*, and this reading is adopted in the text of the present edition. The reading of Holthausen (8 ed.), *heard in healle*, is also well worthy of consideration. **1927ff.**] Trautmann begins a new sentence with l. 1927*b*, explaining ll. 1927*b*–1929*a* as a subordinate clause dependent on ll. 1929*b*–1931*a*. So also Malone, MLN. LVI, 356. Sedgefield similarly puts a semicolon after l. 1927*a*. Cf. the punctuation adopted in the present text for ll. 1716ff. But here the antithesis seems to be between l. 1927*a* and ll. 1927*b*– 1929*a*. That is, Hygd was wise and accomplished in spite of her youth. The other interpretation, that in spite of her youth she was not mean or stingy with gifts, would be strange indeed, since youth is traditionally more open-handed than crabbed age. **1928 hæbbe**] Thorpe and Holthausen (1, 2 ed.) emend to *hæfde*. But see l. 1923, note. **1931 Mod þrýðo wæg**] The reading of the MS. is *mod þrýðo wæg*. The chief problems in the interpretation of this passage are: (1) Are we to read *modþrýðo* as a compound, or *mod þrýðo* as two words? (2) Is (-)*þrýðo* as nom. sing. a possible form? (3) What does *wæg* mean? Whatever our answers may be to the first two of these questions, it is reasonably certain (as Grundtvig, note, first pointed out) that there is a proper name— either *Modþrýðo* or *þrýðo* or something else—in l. 1931*b* and that this woman is being contrasted with Hygd, who has been the subject of the preceding lines. Grundtvig read *mod þrýðo* as two words, and so Suchier, Beitr. IV, 501, Heyne (3, 4 ed.), Arnold, Wülker, Holder, Socin, Wyatt, Trautmann, and von Schaubert. But Grein, Jahrb. für rom. und eng. Lit. IV, 279ff., proposed to read *Modþrýðo* as a compound. With either of these readings, the proper name is most naturally taken as subject of *wæg* and parallel to *fremu folces cwen*. But objections have been raised (principally by Hart, MLN. XVIII, 117f., and Holthausen, ZfdPh. XXXVII, 118) to (-)*þrýðo* as a nom. sing. feminine form, since -*u*, -*o* would normally be dropped after a long root syllable and since elsewhere we find -*þrýð* (not -*þrýðu*, -*þrýðo*) as the second theme of Anglo-Saxon feminine names. Schücking, Eng. Stud. XXXIX, 108f., therefore proposed to emend to *þrýðe*, gen. sing., dependent on *Mod*, and to supply *ne* after it. With this reading Hygd is still the subject: "she, the good queen of the people, did not have the pride of Thryth." So also Schücking in his edition, followed by Holthausen (2–5, 8 ed.), Chambers, and Klaeber (1 ed.). This reading, however, is rejected by Kock, Anglia XLIV, 102f. Holthausen, ZfdPh. XXXVII, 118, proposed to read *modþrýðe*, acc. plur., as a common noun, citing *higeþrýðe wæg*, Genesis 2240, and so in his 1st edition. This emendation is adopted by Sedgefield, who translates, "The bold folk-queen displayed arrogance, a grievous sin." See also the remarks by K. Sisam, Rev. of Eng. Studies XXII (1946), 266, note. But if the *fremu folces cwen* is to form a contrast to Hygd, who is mentioned by name, we expect her to be mentioned by name also. A new approach to this problem was made by Imelmann, Forschungen, pp. 462f., who suggested the reading *Mod þrýð o wæg*, construing *þrýð* as the subject of *wæg* and *Mod*, "passion," as the object, and translating *o* as "always." So also Holthausen (6 ed.). Hoops, Bwst., pp. 64ff., undoubtedly influenced by Imelmann's proposal, would read *Modþrýð o wæg*, translating, "M. übte immer . . . schrecklichen Frevel," and so Holthausen (7 ed.). As an alternative, Hoops suggested a return to Grein's old reading, *Modþrýðo wæg* (with *Modþrýðo* nom. sing.), and so Klaeber (3 ed.). A choice between these alternatives is difficult but must be made, since one reading or another must be put into the text. The objections raised by Klaeber, Anglia L, 233ff., to Imelmann's reading *Mod þrýð o wæg* (that this use of *o* is stylistically very questionable, and that "always" is hardly borne out by ll. 1944ff.) also apply to Hoops's *Modþrýð o wæg*. The two most probable readings are still Grundtvig's *mod þrýðo wæg* (with *þrýðo* the subject of *wæg* and *mod* the object, parallel to *firen ondrysne*) and Grein's *Modþrýðo wæg*. The argument from alliteration in favor of *Modþrýðo wæg* and against *mod þrýðo wæg* is hardly valid, since there are other half-lines in Beowulf (ll. 1323*b*, 1441*b*) in which a proper name, the subject of a clause, does not alliterate. Objections to a nom. sing. (-)*þrýðo* have been noted above. Klaeber, Anglia XXVIII, 452, suggested that *þrýðo* is a short (hypocoristic) form for such a name as *þrýðgifu*, and Holthausen, Anglia Beibl. XLII (1931), 341, has accepted this view. Such an explanation is valid for *þrýðo*, but if applied to *Modþrýðo* (Klaeber's reading in his 3d ed.) it requires us to assume that the original name, of which this is a shortening, was trithematic. All things considered, the reading *Mod þrýðo wæg*, as in the text, occasions fewest misgivings. Translate: "Thryth, the proud (?) queen of the people, showed arrogance, carried on terrible crime." For this use of *wæg*, cf. *heteniðas wæg*, l. 152. The emphatic position of *Mod* is to be explained by the strong antithesis between this passage and the preceding one. A similar interpretation is given by E. von Schaubert, Anglia LXII, 173ff., who, however, reads *firenondrysne*, a compound noun, in l. 1932*b*. Malone, MLN. LVI, 356, reads *mod þrýðo wæg* but explains *þrýðo* as gen. sing., translating, "the good folk-queen [i.e., Hygd] had weighed the arrogance and terrible wickedness of Thryth." But, as Klaeber points out, Anglia Beibl. LIV/LV, 277, such a meaning of *wegan* is not recorded in Anglo-Saxon and is probably too modern in conception. For a more extensive account of the scholarship on this half-line, see Hoops, Bwst., pp. 64ff. **1932 fremu]** The adjective *freme*, which is not recorded elsewhere, is variously translated as "good, excellent" (Klaeber), "brave, excellent" (Chambers), "hervorragend, herrlich" (Heyne, Socin, Schücking), "good, strenuous, bold" (Bos.-Tol., p. 332). If the *folces cwen* is Hygd, as a few scholars have assumed (see the preceding note), then the meaning "good, excellent" fits; if, as others believe, it is Thryth, then "strenuous, bold," or perhaps even "proud, overbearing," is an appropriate meaning. Mackie, MLRev. XXXIV, 523f., would translate as "imperious," and Hoops, p. 213, as "hochfahrend, herrisch, stolz." The word is apparently an *i*-stem adjective from the same root as *fram, from*, "strenuous, valiant, bold." In favor of the meaning "proud, imperious" is the fact, pointed out by Kock, Anglia XLIV, 103, that Old Icelandic *framr*, cognate with Anglo-Saxon *fram*, can mean both "valorous" and "overbearing." Cosijn, Beitr. VIII, 572, suggested emending *fremu* to *frecnu* (nom. sing. feminine of *frēcne*, "savage, wicked"), and so Holder. Bugge, ZfdPh. IV, 206f., proposed to explain *fremu* as an irregular spelling of *framu* (nom. sing. feminine of the adjective *fram*), and Holthausen (1, 2 ed.) emends to *fromu*. Similarly, Sedgefield reads *freomu*; cf. Genesis 2794, Exodus 14, where *freom* is apparently a variant form of *fram*.   firen ondrysne] Acc. sing., "terrible crime," parallel to *Mod*. For the elision of final -*e* in *firen*, see l. 338, note. Grein, Bib., Suchier, Beitr. IV, 502, and Heusler, Anz.fdA. XLI, 33, read *firen-ondrysne* as a compound adjective, "nimis terribilis," "überaus grausam," "übers mass furchtgebietende." E. von Schaubert, Anglia LXII, 175ff., and in her edition, assumes a compound noun *firen-ondrysne*; she identifies the second element of this word not as *on-drysnu*, "fear, awe," but as *and-rysnu*, "courtesy, etiquette" (see l. 1796, note), and therefore translates the compound as "ungeheuerlicher, unerhörter Brauch." But *firen ondrysne*, as two words, is accepted by all other recent edd.   1934 nefne sinfrea] "Except as husband" (?). So Schücking, following Grein, Jahrbuch für rom. und eng. Lit. IV, 283, and Cosijn, Beitr. XIX, 454 (note on Genesis 2240). A noun *sinfrēa*, "husband," is not elsewhere recorded but may be assumed on the model of *sinhīwan*, "a married couple." Grundtvig and other early edd. read *nefne sin frea*, "except her lord," and so Wyatt, Holthausen (*frega*), and Chambers. But as Sedgefield (3 ed.) points out, Thryth is not the subject of the sentence, and therefore *sīn*, which elsewhere in Beowulf is reflexive, would hardly be in order here. Von Schaubert, note, explains *sinfrea* as "father," following R. C. Boer, in Handelingen van het 3de Nederlandsche Philologen-Congres (Groningen, 1902), pp. 84ff., and Stefanović, Anglia XXXV, 523, Eng. Stud. LXIX, 18f.   1935 þæt hire an dæges . . . starede] "That he should stare upon her by day." So Grein, Heyne (2–4 ed.), Ettmüller, Wülker, Socin, Wyatt, Holder (2 ed.), Schücking (8–10 ed.), Chambers, Holthausen (3–8 ed.), Klaeber, and von Schaubert. See also Cosijn, Beitr. XIX, 454 (note on Genesis 2240), and Hoops, pp. 213f. Elsewhere *starian* is followed by *on* with the accusative (as in ll. 996, 1485, 1780f., etc.), and Holthausen (2 ed.) therefore emends *hire* to *hie*. But for examples in the prose of *on* with the dative after other verbs of looking (*lōcian*, *besēon*), see Klaeber, Archiv CXXIII (1909), 417, note; Anglia L, 237, note 2; Eng. Stud. LXVIII, 114. Several unnecessary emendations have been proposed: Bugge, Tidskrift VIII, 296f., following an oral suggestion by P. A. Munch, suggested *andēges*, "eye to eye, full in the face" (cf. Gothic *andaugjō*), and so Holder (1 ed.); Sedgefield (1, 2 ed.) and Schücking (11–14 ed.) read *andæges*, with the same meaning. Sedgefield, MLRev. XXVIII, 227, suggests *on egesan*, "with intimidating mien," and so in his 3d ed.   1938 æfter mundgripe] "After the arrest." See Bugge, ZfdPh. IV, 207; Suchier, Beitr. IV, 501f.   1940 cwealmbealu] Mackie, MLRev. XXXIV, 524, would explain *cwealmbealu* as the subject of *cȳðan*, parallel to *sceadenmæl*. He translates, "That the damascened blade might make the matter manifest, his miserable death make it known." This seems, however, less likely than the usual interpretation, which takes *cwealmbealu* as object of *cȳðan*.   1942 onsæce] A form of *onsēcan*, "to deprive a person (accusative) of something (genitive)." Klaeber (3 ed.), p. lxxvii, explains the *æ*, here as well as in *higemæðum*, l. 2909, and *æht*, l. 2957, as an alteration of original *ǣ*. A close parallel, pointed out by Rieger, ZfdPh. III, 403f., is to be found in Juliana 678f., *þær XXX wæs ond feowere eac feores onsohte*. Chambers glosses *onsæce* as a form of *onsacan*, and so also Kock, Anglia XLVI, 94f., who explains *mannan feores onsacan* as meaning "to bring an accusation against a man in which his life is concerned," "to try to take his life." This meaning, however, is unsubstantiated, and *onsacan* regularly means "to resist, to deny, to renounce." **1943** æfter ligetorne] "After a pretended injury" (Bugge, ZfdPh. IV, 208), with *lige-* taken as a variant form of *lyge*, "lie." **1944** onhohsnode] The MS. *onhohsnod* cannot be interpreted as a past participle, and Thorpe's emendation to *onhohsnode* is adopted by most later edd. The usual interpretation of this word follows Bugge, Tidskrift VIII, 302f., who connects it with *hōh-sinu*, "hamstring, hock-sinew," and translates, "restrained, weakened." That is, the kinsman of Hemming put a stop to Thryth's bad conduct. Kock, Anglia XLVI, 95, would connect *onhohsnian* with *hyge* and would translate, "thought on, considered, took to heart." Dietrich, ZfdA. XI, 413ff., suggested a connection with *husc*, "scorn," and so also, much later, Holthausen, Literaturblatt LIX, 165. Sedgefield (3 ed.) emends to *huru þæs hohs onwod*, explaining *hohs* as a variant form of *husc* and translating, "Scorn for such conduct filled the kinsman of Hemming (Offa)." Hemminges] Most edd. normalize to *Hemminges*, here and in l. 1961. For the recorded forms of this name, in Anglo-Saxon and elsewhere, see Suchier, Beitr. IV, 511f.; Sievers, Beitr. X, 501f.; G. Binz, Beitr. XX (1895), 172; E. Björkman, Nordische Personennamen in England (Halle, 1910), pp. 67f. But Malone, Anglia LXIII, 104f., defends *Hemming* and *Heming* as legitimate variants of the name, suggesting that the form *Hemming* itself goes back to an earlier form with *-mn-*. **1945** ealodrincende oðer sædan] Klaeber, note, translates, "beer-drinking men related further"; Hoops, p. 215, "Biertrinkende Männer sagten noch andres, d.h. sagten weiter." See also Klaeber, Mod. Phil. III, 244. This interpretation, which goes back to Cosijn, Aant., pp. 28f., may be supported by *word oþer fand*, l. 870. But the context seems rather to demand Suchier's old translation, Beitr. IV, 502, "Biertrinkende erzählten andres." That is, the warriors had a different story to tell, that Thryth had mended her ways after her marriage to Offa. So also Andrew, pp. 99f.

1951–2000

1956 þone] So Thorpe, Heyne (1, 4 ed.), Bugge, ZfdPh. IV, 208f., and later edd., for the MS. *þæs*. **1960** Eomer] Thorpe and most later edd. emend the MS. *geomor* to either *Eomer* or *Eomær*, the name of Offa's grandson in the Mercian genealogy (Anglo-Saxon Chronicle, 755). The emendation to *Eomær* was proposed independently by J. Bachlechner, Germania I (1856), 298. Edith Rickert, Mod. Phil. II (1904), 54ff., defends *geomor* as an adjective, and so also Malone, Germanic Rev. XIV, 235f., who would read *þon ongeomor woc*, "when he woke, the sad one," taking *ongeomor* as an intensive adjective compound, "very sad." **1961** Hemminges] See l. 1944, note. Here the MS.

has *hem inges* with a space between *m* and *i*, but apparently nothing has been erased. **1967 to ðæs ðe]** See l. 714, note. **1972 þæt ðær]** Holthausen (7, 8 ed.), following Sievers's unpublished edition of the poem, supplies *he* after *þæt*, with a comma at the end of the half-line. *worðig]* In the poetry this word is recorded only here and (in the form *weorþige*) in Psalm 54, 10, 1, but it is common in the charters. See Bos.-Tol., p. 1267. **1975 Hraðe]** See l. 1390, note. **1977–1978 wið sylfne ... wið mæge]** For the inconsistency in case, cf. ll. 424ff., where also *wið* governs first the accusative, then the dative. Andrew, pp. 62f., would emend *sylfne* to *sylfum*. **1978 mandryhten]** It is impossible to tell whether this word is acc. sing., object of *gegrette*, Beowulf being carried over as subject from l. 1977*b*, or whether it is nom. sing., subject of *gegrette*, the adjective *holdne* (i.e., Beowulf) then being the object. Klaeber, Mod. Phil. III, 461, would take it as accusative, citing Beowulf's address to Hrothgar in ll. 407ff. So also Trautmann, Schücking, Hoops, p. 218, and von Schaubert. Sedgefield, on the other hand, construes it as a nominative. **1981 healreced]** The scribe originally wrote merely *reced*, then later added *side* above the line. To provide the proper alliteration, Kemble suggested *healreced*, and so Thorpe and most later edd. Cf. l. 68. But Holthausen (1–4 ed.), retaining *side reced*, suggests that two half-lines have been lost between l. 1981*a* and l. 1981*b*; see also his note in ZfdPh. XXXVII, 119. In his later editions, Holthausen reads *healreced*. Grein, Bib., Grundtvig, Heyne (2–4 ed.), and von Schaubert read *hwearf geond þæt reced* as l. 1981*a*; this arrangement, however, leaves l. 1980*b* too short. The hook under *e* in the MS. *reced* is also found in the MS. *bel*, l. 2126, and *fæðmie*, l. 2652. It also appears, for no apparent reason, under the *æ* of *sæcce*, l. 1989. In the present text, *bel* is interpreted as *bæl* (the usual form of the word), but in *reced* and *fæðmie* the hook seems to have no phonetic significance. **1983 hæleðum]** The scribe apparently first wrote *hæðnum*, then erased the ð but did not complete the intended correction. Socin, Holder (2 ed.), Schücking, Chambers, and von Schaubert read *Hænum* as a tribal name, explained by Bugge, Beitr. XII, 9ff., as for *Hæðnum, dat. plur., "men of the heath," and corresponding to the form *Heinir* (< *Heiðnir) of the Scandinavian texts, which refers to the inhabitants of the Norwegian district of Hedemarken. Cf. Widsith 81, where the form *hæðnum* has usually been explained as a proper name. But the MS. *hæ num* here in Beow. 1983 seems insufficient evidence for the assumption of a tribal name. Grein, Bib., emended to *hælum*, dat. plur. of *hæle*, "warrior," and so Heyne (2–4 ed.), Wülker, Holder (1 ed.), Wyatt, and Sedgefield (1, 2 ed.). But there is no other example of *hæle* in the plural (unless *hæle*, l. 719, is one), the plural cases being formed from *hæleð(-)*. See J. Platt, Beitr. IX (1884), 368f.; Sievers-Brunner, §290. Trautmann emended to *hæleþum*, and so Holthausen, Klaeber, Sedgefield (3 ed.), and Hoops, pp. 218f. This emendation is also accepted by E. Björkman, Studien über die Eigennamen im Beowulf (Halle, 1920), pp. 55f. **1990 Ac]** For *Ac* used to introduce a question, with no suggestion of an antithesis, cf. Solomon and Saturn 230, 282, 302, 336, etc., and see Cosijn, Aant., p. 29. **1992–1993 modceare ... seað]** See *mælceare ... seað*, ll. 189f., and notes. **1994 ic]** Andrew, p. 52, suggests that *ic* is an error for *ac.* See l. 967, note.   **1996-1997** lete Suðdene ... geweorðan guðe]   The same impersonal use of *geweorðan,* with accusative of the person and genitive of the thing, as in ll. 1598, 2026.   Here *Suðdene* is the accusative and *guðe* the genitive.   Bugge, Beitr. XII, 97, translates, "Du solltest die Süd-Dänen selbst über die bekämpfung Grendels einig werden lassen"; similarly, Klaeber, JEGPh. XVIII (1919), 264f., "that you should let the Danes themselves agree as to the fight," or (less literally and with decision translated into action) "attend to [settle] the fighting."   Hubbard's suggested translations, JEGPh. XVII, 120ff., "that you leave to the South Danes themselves the war against Grendel" or "that you let the South-Danes alone in their war against Grendel" (see also Cosijn, Aant ⁻ 30), are less idiomatic.   **2000** Higelac]   On the reading of transcript B, see Malone, PMLA LXIV, 1206, who suggests that *-lac* was a late conjecture by Thorkelin.

2001-2050

2001 micel]   Grein and nearly all later edd. restore *mære.*   But Moore, JEGPh. XVIII, 210, points out that the regular form (not known in Grein's time) of the strong nom. sing. feminine would be *mæru,* as in l. 2016.   Holthausen (6 ed.) and von Schaubert restore *mæru.*   Klaeber restores *micel,* citing ll. 2354*b*–2355*a.*   Andrew, pp. 39f., arguing against an adjective in this half-line, would read [*on ða*] *gemeting,* "as regards that encounter."   **2002** orleghwil]   So Thorpe, Grein, and later edd.   **2004-2005** sorge ... yrmðe]   These two words are evidently parallel genitives, dependent on *worna fela.*   See Kock, Anglia XLII, 105; Malone, Anglia LIV, 97; Hoops, Bwst., p. 117.   Malone and Hoops explain them as gen. plur. with weakened ending.   But if *worna fela* may be taken as the equivalent of *fela,* then *sorge* and *yrmðe* can equally well be gen. sing.; see l. 810, note.   The alternative construction, adopted by most edd., by which *yrmðe* is acc. sing. and therefore not parallel to *sorge,* is less probable on stylistic grounds.   **2006** ne]   Nothing is lost from the MS. at this point, but it is apparent that a negative has dropped out of the text. Kemble and most of the early edd., together with Socin, Wyatt, Schücking (8 ed.), and Sedgefield (1, 2 ed.), read *swa ne gylpan þearf,* following Grundtvig, tr., p. 296.   Grein, ed., Ettmüller, Wülker, Holder (1 ed.), Holthausen, Schücking (9–14 ed.), Chambers, Klaeber, and von Schaubert read *swa begylpan ne þearf.*   Sedgefield (3 ed.) reads *swa he gylpan ne þearf.*   The evidence of the Thorkelin transcripts, that the first letter of the word following *swa* had an ascending stroke, rules out Grundtvig's *swa ne gylpan þearf.*   Also, as Klaeber points out, Eng. Stud. XXXIX, 431, the simplex *gylpan* would be very unusual as a transitive verb, being regularly followed by the genitive or the dative.   Cf. ll. 586, 2055, etc.   The verb, then, was undoubtedly *begylpan,* as in transcript A, and Grein's addition of *ne* after *begylpan* is the proper emendation.   Schücking and Holthausen (7, 8 ed.) begin a new sentence with l. 2006*a,* and this punctuation is approved by Hoops, Bwst., p. 117; but the punctuation in the text seems preferable, with ll. 2006ff. explained as a clause of result. **2007** ænig]   Restored by Kemble, Thorpe, Grein, and later edd., except Trautmann, who restores *æfre*. Nothing can be done with the *en* . . of transcript B. 2009 facne] Most early edd. restore *f*[*ær*]*bifongen* as a compound, apparently combining the readings of the two Thorkelin transcripts. Grundtvig suggested *f*[*enne*] *bifongen*, and so Heyne (3, 4 ed.), Socin, and Wyatt. Bugge, Beitr. XII, 97, proposed *f*[*acne*] *bifongen*, as in Juliana 350 (where the phrase refers to the devil), and so Schücking, Sedgefield, Chambers, Klaeber, and von Schaubert. Trautmann and Holthausen restore *f*[*læsce*] *bifongen*, as in Guthlac 994, Phoenix 259, 535, etc. The parallel in Juliana 350 argues strongly in favor of *f*[*acne*]. 2018 bædde] Klaeber, Mod. Phil. III, 461, suggested emending to *bælde*, as a variant form of *bylde*, "encouraged," and so Holthausen (2–6 ed.), Schücking, and Klaeber (1 ed.). But Kock, Anglia XLVI, 95f., and Hoops, Bwst., p. 117, defend the MS. *bædde* as a form of *bædan*, "to urge, to invite (to drink)." Klaeber (3 ed.), Holthausen (7, 8 ed.), and von Schaubert accept the MS. reading. 2019 sealde] Restored by Thorpe, Grein, and later edd. Cf. l. 2024*a*. hie] The more regular form would be *hio* (with the *io*-diphthong characteristic of the second scribe of the MS.), and so Grein, Grundtvig, and later edd., except Holthausen (2–8 ed.), Schücking, Chambers, Klaeber, and von Schaubert. But cf. *sie*, reported by the Thorkelin transcripts in l. 2219. 2020 for duguðe] On the reading of transcript A, see Malone, PMLA LXIV, 1206. 2021 on ende] "Consecutively, continuously, from end to end" (Klaeber, note); "to all in succession" (Bos.-Tol., Supp., p. 188, s.v. *ende* II.9d). Malone, Mod. Phil. XXVII, 257, translates *eorlum on ende* as "to all the warriors," apparently considering it a variation of *for duguðe*. 2022 Freaware] Malone's identification of Freawaru with Ruta, the sister of Rolvo Krake and the wife of Biarco in Book II of Saxo Grammaticus (The Literary History of Hamlet I, 84ff., Klaeber Misc., pp. 150f., Mod. Phil. XXVII, 258), and his reconstruction of the Scandinavian form of her name as *Hrūt* are of little significance for the textual criticism of Beowulf, since in all probability the name *Freawaru* was the invention of the Anglo-Saxon poet. See Hoops, p. 222, and Malone, ELH VII, 39ff. fletsittende] On the reading of transcript B, see Malone, PMLA LXIV, 1206, who suggests that *flet-* was added later by Thorkelin and taken from A. 2023 nægled] Restored by Grein and most later edd. Grein, Bib., Holthausen, Sedgefield, and von Schaubert read *nægledsinc* as a compound. Malone, PMLA LXIV, 1206, suggests that in transcript B the *-g-* of *-gled* was added later by Thorkelin and taken from A. 2024 is] Most of the early edd. restored *wæs*, with Kemble, but Holder restored *is*, following a suggestion by Kluge, and so the later edd., except Socin (5 ed.). 2026 hafað . . . Scyldinga] "The friend of the Scyldings has made up his mind as to that (decided on the policy) . . . ," Klaeber, JEGPh. XVIII (1919), 261. For this construction, *geweorðan* used impersonally with accusative of the person and genitive of the thing, see ll. 1598, 1996f., and notes. An interesting parallel to the present passage is Andreas 307f., *Hu gewearð þe þæs . . . ðæt ðu sæbeorgas secan woldes?* "How did you make up your mind to seek the sea-hills?" On the reading *iafað* in the Thorkelin transcripts, see Malone, PMLA LXIV, 1206. 2029 gesette] Present subjunctive, "that he should settle a deal of deadly feuds, of hostilities." For *gesettan* in this sense (apparently borrowed from legal terminology), cf. *þæt þis æfre gesett spæc wære*, "that this should forever be a settled suit," in a document of about the year 961 (W. de G. Birch, Cartularium Saxonicum III, 285). Sedgefield (2 ed.) emends the MS. *gesette* to *gesehte*, with the same meaning. **Oft seldan hwær**] The apparent contradiction in *Oft seldan* has given rise to much discussion and to a number of emendations, of which only the most reasonable will be mentioned here. Heyne, Wülker, Socin, and Wyatt supplied *no* after *Oft*, making the half-line mean "Often, not at all seldom"; as an alternative Heyne suggested the addition of *nalæs*. Sedgefield, MLRev. V, 287, and in his edition, emends more violently to *Oft selð* (= *sælð*) *onhwearf*, putting a semicolon after l. 2030a: "Often has fortune changed after the fall of a prince." But *Oft* is convincingly explained by Kock, Anglia XXVII, 233ff., who takes it in a general sense, meaning "As a rule (on the whole)." We may then translate, "As a rule, seldom anywhere does the deadly spear turn aside [even] for a little while after the fall of a prince, though the bride may be good." That is, international marriages intended to compose feuds are rarely successful in achieving that end. Klaeber, Anglia L, 211, suggests that *Oft seldan hwær* has resulted from the blending of two concepts, (1) "often (always, as a rule) the spear will rest only a short time," and (2) "it seldom happens that the spear rests for any length of time." **2030 lytle hwile**] Accusative of extent of time; cf. l. 2097, where the phrase means "(only) for a short time," and *lytel fæc*, l. 2240. The translation "[even] for a little while" given in the preceding note follows Hoops, Bwst., pp. 72f. Kock, Anglia XXVII, 235, translates, "a little time (when some time has elapsed) after the fall of the prince"; this rendering is less probable and is complicated by Kock's attempt (in Anglia XLIII, 303f.) to construe *lytle* as an instrumental governing a genitive *hwile*. **2032ff.**] The chief difficulty in this passage is the disposition of *dryhtbearn Dena*, l. 2035a, which is discussed in the note on that line. The most satisfactory translation of ll. 2032–2035, which follows Klaeber and Hoops, is: "That may then be a vexation to the lord of the Heathobards [i.e., to Ingeld] and to each of the warriors of that tribe, when he [i.e., Ingeld] goes with the lady [i.e., Freawaru] into the hall, [to wit:] the noble sons of the Danes, splendidly entertained (or, the noble sons of the Danes, the warriors entertained); on them are resplendent the heirlooms of the ancestors [of the Heathobards]," etc. That is, it was the sight of the Danish warriors, arrayed in the trappings of the dead Heathobards, which aroused the ire of Ingeld and his men. For the details of this interpretation, see the following notes. For a fuller account of the scholarship on these lines than is possible here, see E. von Schaubert, Anglia LXII, 179ff. **2032 ðeodne**] So Kemble, Thorpe, Ettmüller, Holder, Trautmann, Holthausen (1–4, 7, 8 ed.), Sedgefield, and Klaeber, as dative of the person after *ofþyncan*, parallel to *gehwam* in the next line. Malone, Anglia LXIII, 106, would retain the MS. *ðeoden* as a variant form of *ðeodan*, dat. sing. of a noun *ðeoda*. But the MS. *ðeoda* in Widsith 11, which he cites as evidence for such a noun, is emended by most edd. to *þeodna*, gen. plur. of *þeoden*, since the partitive gen. plur. is usual with *gehwylc*. Von Schaubert retains *þeoden* as dat. sing. of *þeoden*. **2034 he**] That is, Ingeld, the lord of the Heathobards. The alternative interpretation, which takes *he* as referring to a Dane (the *dryhtbearn* of l. 2035), is less likely. The *fæmne* is evidently Freawaru. 2035 dryhtbearn Dena] The word *dryhtbearn* has often been explained as a singular. Rieger, ZfdPh. III, 404f., Klaeber, Mod. Phil. III, 255, Moore, in Klaeber Misc., pp. 210f., and Girvan, MLRev. XXVIII, 246, explain it as referring to an unidentified Dane, the *he* of l. 2034, who escorts the princess into the hall. This interpretation has been most recently adopted by E. von Schaubert, Anglia LXII, 181f., and in her edition. Trautmann and Sedgefield take *dryhtbearn* as referring to the princess herself, the *fæmne* of the preceding line. But neither of these identifications is entirely satisfactory, and it seems more probable that *dryhtbearn* is plural. Kock, Anglia XLVI, 173f., explains *dryhtbearn Dena* and *duguða biwenede* as parallel to *flett* in the preceding line; to these three parallel terms Malone, MLRev. XXIV, 322f., would add a fourth, *fæmnan* (taking *mid*, l. 2034a, as meaning "to"), and would translate, "when he [Ingeld] goes to the maiden, to the hall, to the noble children of the Danes, to the well-cared-for retainers." See also Malone, Mod. Phil. XXVII, 257ff., Anglia LV, 270, Anglia LXIII, 107f. But it is doubtful that *mid* can mean "to," in spite of the observations of Kock and Malone on *mid Eotenum*, l. 902. It is also far from certain that the action is represented as taking place at the Danish court; see Introd., p. liii. Klaeber, note, taking *dryhtbearn* as nom. plur., suggests that l. 2035 is "a loosely joined elliptic clause indicating the cause of the king's displeasure." This seems the most satisfactory disposition of this line; see the translation in the note on ll. 2032ff. duguða biwenede] The word *duguða* may be an instrumental gen. plur., "entertained with gifts," or more freely, "splendidly entertained." For this use of the genitive, cf. *niða*, ll. 845, 1439, 2206. Or *duguða* may be nom. plur., a variation of *dryhtbearn*, and it is so construed by Hoops, Bwst., pp. 73f., and Klaeber (3 ed.). In either case, *biwenede* is nom. plur. of the past participle. E. von Schaubert, Anglia LXII, 181f. (who takes *dryhtbearn* as a variation of *he*, l. 2034), explains *duguða biwenede* as an absolute participial construction in the nominative; she translates, "wenn die (beiden) Gefolgsscharen [i.e., Danes and Heathobards] bewirtet werden." So also in her edition. See l. 31, note. Grein emended to *duguða bi werede*, "among the troop of warriors," and so Ettmüller, Wülker, Holder, Chambers, and Holthausen (8 ed.). This emendation was also approved by Bugge, Beitr. XII, 98. Holthausen (1–3 ed.) read *duguðe bi werede*, explaining *duguðe* as gen. sing., but otherwise with an interpretation similar to Grein's. 2038–2040] These inept lines were apparently intended to convey the idea that the precious possessions now being displayed by the Danish warriors had been the property of the Heathobards of an older generation as long as they had been able to wield weapons, that is, until they lost both their lives and their treasure in battle. Von Schaubert begins a new sentence with *oððæt*, which she construes as an adverb. See l. 56, note. 2040 swæse gesiðas] Their swords, according to Hoops, Bwst., p. 74. 2041 se ðe beah gesyhð] The word *beah* is explained by Klaeber as meaning "ornament, precious thing," the equivalent of *maðþum*, l. 2055, and referring to a sword, the *mece* of l. 2047. See his note in Mod. Phil. III, 462. So also Hoops, Bwst., pp. 75f., who points out that in l. 2635 ðas beagas apparently means the same thing as ða guðgetawa and helmas ond heard sweord. But Malone, JEGPh. XXXIX, 80f., Anglia LXV, 227ff., Anglia Beibl. LII, 179f., is doubtful that the singular beah can mean "sword." He explains the word as preterite singular of būgan, "to flee"; then, accepting the reading genam in l. 2042b (see the following note) and treating gesyhð, l. 2041b, as two words, ge, "and," and syhð (= segð), "says," he translates, "Then he who bowed ... speaks at beer and says, he the old spearman, he who took [i.e., endured] all," etc. With this reading, syhð, "says," is parallel to cwið. A fundamental objection to Malone's interpretation is that it involves the inclusion in a single half-line of a subordinate clause followed by the second part of a compound main clause. No half-line of this type is found elsewhere in the entire body of Anglo-Saxon poetry, and in view of the normally unitary structure of the Old Germanic half-line, such an exceptional construction, if it occurred, would merit the deepest suspicion. In Beowulf, for example, two verbs in the same half-line connected by a coordinating conjunction are invariably parallel (ll. 161a, 600a, 658a, 918a, 1337a, 1604a, 1696a, 1741a, etc., fifteen cases in all). It is improbable, then, that beah is a verb. Klaeber, Anglia Beibl. LI, 206f., attempting to reconcile the meaning "sword" with the more usual meaning of beah, "ring," suggests that here the word means "sword-ring" or "hilt-ring." Holthausen (5 ed.), note, had previously explained beah as "Griffring." The emendations of beah which have been proposed (bill, suggested by Grein, Bib.; ba, referring to Freawaru and a singular dryhtbearn, proposed by Bugge, Beitr. XII, 98; bearn, proposed by Holthausen, ZfdPh. XXXVII, 119, as a variant form of beorn) are unnecessary. **2042** geman] So Thorpe and all later edd., following Grundtvig, tr., p. 296. Malone, JEGPh. XXXIX, 80f., Anglia LXV, 227ff., accepts genam, the reading of transcript B and of Thorkelin's edition, and translates, "he who took [i.e., endured] all." See also his note in PMLA LXIV, 1206f. But no such meaning as "endure" is recorded for Anglo-Saxon geniman, and the parallels from Modern English which Malone cites in JEGPh. XXXIX, 80, prove nothing for the older language. The aged warrior with a keen memory of past events is a familiar figure in heroic literature. **2043** grim sefa] On the reading of transcript B, see Malone, PMLA LXIV, 1207. **2044** geongum] Restored by Kemble (1 ed.) and most later edd. Trautmann's geong[an] cempan is also possible if it is taken as a dative. The accusative geong[ne], restored by Kemble (2 ed.), Thorpe, Heyne, Socin, and Schücking, following Grundtvig, tr., p. 296, is very doubtful, since the direct object of cunnian is the genitive higes. **2045** þurh hreðra gehygd] Kock, Anglia XLVI, 174, takes this phrase as parallel to geomormod, translating, "sad in his soul, and guided by the promptings of his heart." So also Hoops, pp. 228f. Klaeber, on the other hand, connects þurh hreðra gehygd with higes cunnian, suggesting that it emphasizes the intensity with which the young warrior's mind is searched; see also his note in Anglia L, 212. **2048** þone þin fæder] For the metrical form of this half-line, see l. 262, note. Here Holthausen (2 ed.) and Sedgefield (2 ed.) emend to þone þin frod fæder, Holthausen (3–7 ed.) to þone þin fæder fæge.

2050] Von Schaubert puts the question mark after *slogon* and begins a new sentence with l. 2051*a*, following a suggestion by Schücking, Eng. Stud. LIII, 469f. Other recent edd. punctuate as in the text.

2051–2100

2051 Wiðergyld] Grein, Bib., Heyne, and Socin read *wiðergyld* as a common noun, "vengeance." But in view of parallels such as ll. 2201*b*, 2388*b*, etc., there can be no doubt that this is a proper name. The *Wiþergield* of Widsith 124 is, according to Malone (Widsith, p. 197), the same person, though there is nothing in the text of Widsith which connects him with the Heathobards. **2056 þone þe]** The verb *rædan*, "to possess, to have disposition (of)," regularly takes a dative or instrumental object. The accusative here has undoubtedly resulted from attraction to *þone maðþum* in the preceding line. See Klaeber, note; Hoops, p. 229. **2059 se fæmnan þegn]** Barnouw, Textkritische Untersuchungen, p. 23, would read *fæmnanþegn* as a compound, to avoid the use of a definite article with a noun preceded by a dependent genitive. See l. 910, note. But *fæmnan-* as a combining form is not recorded (though *fæmnen-* occurs beside *fæmn-* in the compound adjective *fæmn(en)lic*, "virginal," Bos.-Tol., p. 265, Supp., p. 198). The only compound noun with *fæmne* as the first element is *fæmnhad*, with *fæmn-* as the combining form; *fæmnan had*, Christ 92, Christ and Satan 493, is properly printed as two words. A genitival compound with the meaning "the thane of the lady" would also be in contradiction to the rule stated by C. T. Carr, Nominal Compounds in Germanic (London, 1939), p. 324, that "it is impossible to make a compound of two words between which there is no permanent relation." Malone, Mod. Phil. XXVII, 259, accepting the compound *fæmnanþegn*, would translate as "maiden-thane," that is, a warrior who has had no experience in battle. But in an appositional compound of this type, the genitive *fæmnan-* would be inexplicable. Furthermore, the idea of a "maiden-thane" is a modern one, at least in English; the N.E.D. does not record this use of *maiden* (as in *maiden-knight*, etc.) earlier than 1603 (s.v. *maiden*, B.5.d). In view of the similar phrase *þæt ðeodnes bearn* in l. 910, we are justified in printing *se fæmnan þegn* here, with *fæmnan* gen. sing. **2061 se oðer]** I.e., the slayer. **2062 lifigende]** Restored by Heyne (2–4 ed.) and most later edd. **2063 abrocene]** Both the Thorkelin transcripts read *orocene*, but the initial *o* in this reading probably reflects a *b* in the MS., and Conybeare, p. 148, doubtfully reported *brocene* as the MS. reading. Kemble restored [*ab*]*rocene*; this reading is adopted by Zupitza in his transcript and by all later edd., except Wülker, Socin, Wyatt, and Schücking, who restore [*b*]*rocene* with Thorpe. There was apparently more space in the MS. than can be accounted for by the reading [*b*]*rocene*, and [*ab*]*rocene* is therefore to be preferred. **2064 aðsweord]** "Oath-swearing." The element *-sweord* is not "sword," but a derivative of *swerian*, "to swear." See Hoops, p. 230. **syððan]** Restored by Kemble and all later edd. Arnold and Schücking begin a new sentence with this word. **2065 wiflufan]** The plural here is unusual, and there is no exact parallel to it. In *lufena to leane*,

Resignation 116 (Records III, 218), the plural is justified as denoting love directed to more than one person; in *lufum ond lissum*, Genesis 1949, 2738, and *lufena ond lissa*, Guthlac 1076, the word "love" is attracted into the plural by the following *lissum, lissa*.   **2067-2069a**] "Therefore I do not consider the favor of the Heathobards, their great alliance, [to be] sincere toward the Danes, their friendship [to be a] firm [one]."   **2076** hild] So Heyne (3, 4 ed.) and later edd., except Wülker, following Holtzmann, Germania VIII, 496, and Rieger, ZfdPh. III, 405. Malone, Anglia LVII, 315, would retain the MS. *hilde* as a dative of accompaniment grammatically attached to *feorhbealu*, translating, "life-bale and battle." But surely this is carrying the dative of accompaniment too far! The natural construction here is *hild*, parallel to *feorhbealu*.   **2079** maguþegne] So Kemble (2 ed.) and later edd., except Wülker, who reads *magumþegne* with the MS. Cf. the similar scribal error in l. 2514.   **2085** gearofolm] On the reading of transcript B, see Malone, PMLA, LXIV, 1208.   Glof] Apparently "pouch, bag," or a large glove used as a bag. Thomas's explanation of *glof* as Grendel's hand, MLRev. XVII, 63f., has little to commend it. Laborde, MLRev. XVIII, 202, points out that a large glove was a characteristic property of trolls and suggests that "Grendel used his glove as a game-bag." See also Hoops, Bwst., p. 118.   **2088**] The two instrumentals *deofles cræftum* and *dracan fellum* do not present a natural parallel, and Trautmann and Holthausen (1 ed.) emended *ond* to *of*. But Klaeber, Mod. Phil. III, 240, cites Juliana 574ff.   **2090-2091** gedon . . . sumne] Grendel wished to make Beowulf "one of many," that is, to kill him as he had killed so many of the Danish warriors.   **2093** hu ic ðam] On the readings of the Thorkelin transcripts, see Malone, PMLA LXIV, 1208.   **2094** ondlean] See l. 1541, note.   **2096** weorðode weorcum] Kock, Anglia XLVI, 92f., translates, "helped by my works." See *herige*, l. 1833, and note. But Hoops, Bwst., p. 118, who accepts the meaning "help" in l. 1833, prefers here the traditional interpretation, "honored, exalted."   **2097** breac] In spite of the reading *bræc* in transcript A, it is almost certain that *breac* was the reading of the MS. See the instructive analysis of this point by Malone, PMLA LXIV, 1208f.

2101–2150

2105ff.] Whether the *gomela Scilding* of l. 2105b, the *hildedeor* of l. 2107a, the *rumheort cyning* of l. 2110b, and the *gomel guðwiga* of l. 2112a are all the same person is a question which cannot be answered with certainty. Chambers, note, says: "Since it is Hrothgar who speaks in ll. 2105–6, and again in ll. 2109–10, it seems natural to assume that he is the *hilde-dēor* who plays the harp in l. 2107." But it is not necessary to assume that the *gomela Scilding* of l. 2105b is the king. Kock, Anglia XLVI, 175f., who points out that this part of Beowulf's speech is apparently a report of the action of ll. 1013–1233a, calls particular attention to ll. 1063ff., where the entertainment is ascribed to Hrothgar's *scop*. See also Hoops, Bwst., pp. 118f. There can be no doubt that the *rumheort cyning* is Hrothgar, and the *hildedeor* of l. 2107 may also be the king.

But it is also likely that the *gomela Scilding* is the *scop* referred to in the earlier passage. If *eft*, l. 2111, means "in turn" (as in l. 56), then we may assume that the *gomel guðwiga* of l. 2112 is not Hrothgar, though he may be the same person as the *gomela Scilding*. The sequence is then, in all probability, as follows: (1) an old *scop* recites a lay of bygone times, perhaps the story of Finnsburh; (2) King Hrothgar also recites a lay; (3) either the *scop* or another aged warrior recites a poem, more in the lyric than the heroic vein, lamenting his lost youth and vigor.   **2106 felafricgende**] The early edd., together with Wülker, Holder, Socin, Wyatt, and Trautmann, read *fela fricgende* as two words. This reading, to be translated as "asking many questions," is defended by Kock, Anglia XLVI, 175f., who cites other passages where both the asking of questions and the giving of information are referred to. Cf. especially Order of the World 14–15 (Records III, 164), *a fricgende ... ond secgende*, and the Old Icelandic Hávamál, st. 28, *Fróðr sá þykkisk er fregna kann ok segja it sama*, "Learned does he seem who can ask and likewise tell." E. von Schaubert, Anglia LXII, 186, also reading *fela fricgende*, would explain it as an absolute participial construction in the nominative, "als (da) viele [danach] fragten," and so in her edition, where she treats this half-line as a parenthesis. But other recent edd. agree in accepting a compound *felafricgende*, "widely experienced, well informed." With such a meaning we would, to be sure, expect *gefricgan* rather than *fricgan*. But for a justification of the compound, with *-fricgan* in a perfective sense, see Klaeber, Mod. Phil. III, 262, and Hoops, Bwst., pp. 119f.   **2108 gomenwudu**] So Kemble and most later edd., following Grundtvig, tr., p. 297. The *gomel wudu* of the Thorkelin transcripts may well have been the reading of the MS.   **2109 sarlic**] Holthausen (2–6 ed.) emends to *searolic*, following a suggestion by Grein, Bib. But the MS. *sarlic* is appropriate as describing the "old, unhappy, far-off things" which were a common subject of Old Germanic heroic song. Schücking's suggestion, Eng. Stud. XXXIX (1908), 12f., that the *hildedeor* recited an elegy, similar to the *sorhleoð* of l. 2460, is less probable.   **2114 gemunde**] On the reading of transcript B, see Malone, PMLA LXIV, 1209, who points out that the letters *ge-* in B were added many years later and must have been taken from A rather than from the MS.   **2116 niode naman**] "Took [our] pleasure," or, more literally, "received [the object of our] desires." For *nēod*, *niod*, "desire," cf. Genesis 835, Andreas 158, Guthlac 329, etc.   **2124 Noðer**] This form is also found in Fortunes of Men 38; it is likely that *No þær*, Guthlac 421 (printed as two words in Records III, 61), is a variant of the same word. Andrew, p. 84, suggests *No ðy ær*, as in ll. 754, 1502, 2081, etc.   **2126 bæl**] See l. 1981, note.   **2128 fæðmum under**] The word [*un*]*der* was first restored by Kemble, *fæð*[*mum*] by Grein, ed.   **2130 þara þe ... begeate**] See l. 98, note.   **2131 ðine life**] "By your life," i.e., as Hygelac's life was dear to Beowulf. See Bugge, Beitr. XII, 369f. Heyne, following a suggestion by H. Leo, emended to *þine lyfe*, "by your [Hygelac's] permission." This is an ingenious reading, but unnecessary.   **2136 grimne**] So Thorpe and later edd., except Grundtvig.   **2137 þær ... gemæne**] That is, they were in close physical contact. Chambers, like the earliest edd., reads *handgemæne* as a compound, citing the German *handgemein werden*; but the impersonal construction which results from this reading is very much open to question. 2139 guðsele] Nothing has been lost from the MS. between *ðam* and the *s-* of *sele*, but the lack of alliteration indicates that at least one syllable has dropped out of the text. Thorpe, Holthausen, Sedgefield, Klaeber, and von Schaubert emend to *guðsele*, as in l. 443. Other edd. read *grundsele*, following Grundtvig, tr., p. 297; cf. *grundwong*, ll. 1496, 2770. Either reading may have been intended by the poet. 2146 maðmas] Restored by Kemble, following Grundtvig, tr., p. 297; all later edd. restore either [*maðma*]*s* or [*madma*]*s*. 2147 on minne sylfes dom] "According to my own choice." The restoration to [*min*]*ne*, first made by Kemble, is supported by *selfes* (*sylfes*) *dome*, ll. 895, 2776, *on eowerne agenne dom*, Andreas 339, etc. Grundtvig's suggested restoration [*sin*]*ne*, though adopted by Heyne, is very improbable. Kock, Anglia XXVII, 235f., cites the *sjálfdæmi* or *eindæmi* of Old Icelandic law, the arrangement by which the aggrieved party in a dispute is permitted by his adversary to choose what satisfaction he is to receive. 2150 lissa gelong] For metrical reasons, several emendations have been proposed. Holthausen, Anglia Beibl. X, 269, suggested *gelenge* for the MS. *gelong*, and so Trautmann, Holthausen (1, 2 ed.), Schücking (8 ed.), and Sedgefield (1, 2 ed.); but Klaeber, JEGPh. VIII, 257, points out that the uses of *gelong*, "at hand, dependent (on)," and *gelenge*, "belonging (to), related (to)," are entirely different. In Literaturblatt XXI, 61, Holthausen proposed *gelong lissa*, and so Schücking (9 ed.) and Holthausen (5, 6 ed.); to this emendation it may be objected that elsewhere (l. 1376, Andreas 979, Christ 152, 365, etc.) *gelang*, *gelong* regularly comes at the end of the half-line. Schücking (10–14 ed.), following an oral suggestion by Sievers, reads *lissa gelongra*, and so Holthausen (4 ed.). Kock, Anglia XLII, 117, doubts that *gelong* can be used attributively, but cf. the inflected form in Guthlac 251f., *me on heofonum sind lare gelonge*. Klaeber, JEGPh. VIII, 257, suggested *minra lissa gelong*, and so in his 1st ed.; this emendation is adopted by Chambers, Holthausen (3, 7, 8 ed.), and Sedgefield (3 ed.). Klaeber (3 ed.) and von Schaubert accept the MS. reading, which is supported by *leofes gelong*, Guthlac 313, in a context very similar to the present passage.

2151–2200

2152 eaforheafodsegn] Heyne (4 ed.), Socin, Wyatt, Schücking, Chambers, Klaeber, and von Schaubert read *eafor*(,) *heafodsegn* as two words, assuming the same asyndetic relationship of two nouns which we find in *wudu, wælsceaftas*, l. 398, and *ides, aglæcwif*, l. 1259. For a justification of this reading, see Klaeber, Mod. Phil. III, 462. But as Cosijn remarked, Aant., p. 31, it is not at all clear what a noun *heafodsegn*, without *eafor*, would mean. Lines 47f., cited by von Schaubert, note, are hardly relevant to the present passage. A possible, though unlikely, reading would be *eaforheafod, segn*. It seems best to assume a triple compound here, meaning "boar-head banner"; such triple compounds are excessively rare, but *wulfheafedtreo*, Riddle 55, 12, is an example. Most early edd. print *eaforheafodsegn* here, and so also Trautmann, Holthausen (2–7 ed.), and Sedgefield. See also Mackie, MLRev. XXXIV, 524; C. T. Carr, Nominal Compounds in Germanic (London, 1939), pp. 199f. Holder (1 ed.) and Holthausen (8 ed.) emend to *ealdor heafodsegn*, following a suggestion by Kluge, and explain *ealdor* as the subject of *Het*; this reading, however, is open to the same objections as *eafor, heafodsegn*.   2157] This line has been much discussed, but the interpretation which I find most convincing is that recently advanced by Andrew, p. 100. Taking *his* as referring not to Hrothgar (as it is usually taken) but to the *hildesceorp*, Andrew explains that the passage means "he bade me mention to thee the gift of the byrnie first, because Herogar once possessed it." For the objective genitive after *est*, cf. l. 2165f., *est . . . meara ond maðma.* Hoops, pp. 236f., also regarding *his* as an objective genitive, would take *est* in the sense of "origin," translating, "dass ich dir zuerst dessen Vermachung (dh. Herkunft, Geschichte) mitteilte." A similar suggestion had previously been made by Klaeber, Mod. Phil. III, 462f., who explained *his est* as "its transmission." But neither of these meanings of *est* is substantiated, and the parallel in ll. 2165f. clearly favors Andrew's interpretation. The most usual rendering of l. 2157, "that I should first express to you his [Hrothgar's] good will," admits no logical connection between it and the following lines.   2164 lungre, gelice] Parallel adjectives, "swift [and] all alike." See Kock, Anglia XLII, 117; Anglia XLIV, 103f.   last weardode] For the singular verb with plural subject, cf. ll. 904f. (and probably also l. 1408), and see Woolf, MLQuart. IV, 49f. The usual meaning of *last weardian* is "to remain behind" (as in l. 971, Christ 496, Guthlac 1338, etc.; cf. also *swaðe weardade*, Beow. 2098), but in the present passage *last weardode* must mean "followed."   2168 renian] Restored by Kemble II and most later edd. Cf. the parallel in Genesis 2676ff., *hu geworhte ic þæt, . . . þæt þu me . . . searo renodest?* "how have I deserved that, that you should prepare a trap for me?"   2174 ðeodnes] First restored by Kemble.   2176 breost] So Thorpe and later edd.   2177 bealdode] "Bore himself boldly" (Chambers, p. 183) would be the natural translation, since the verbs in *-ian* are for the most part intransitive. Cf. the transitive *byldan*, "to make bold," l. 1094. But Mackie, MLRev. XXXIV, 524, suggests that *bealdian* is used transitively here; he would translate, "In this way the son of Ecgtheow encouraged (others) by acts of generosity."   2179 æfter dome] See l. 1720, note.   2181 mæste cræfte] This phrase is usually construed as instrumental, "with the greatest strength." Klaeber (3 ed.), note, suggests the translation, "with the greatest self-control." But Hoops, Bwst., pp. 76ff., would explain *mæste cræfte* as acc. sing. feminine, parallel to *ginfæstan gife*, and so von Schaubert. Cf. ll. 1270f., where *gimfæste gife* is a variation of *mægenes strenge*. Hoops points out that although in Anglo-Saxon *cræft* is regularly masculine, O.H.G. *kraft* is feminine, and Old Saxon *kraft* varies between masculine and feminine. Klaeber, Eng. Stud. LXVIII, 115, suggests that the MS. *cræft mine* in l. 418, which is usually emended to *cræft minne*, may be valid evidence for a feminine *cræft* in Anglo-Saxon. Hoops would also take *ac* as meaning "and yet." With his interpretation, we may translate, "[Beowulf's] spirit was not fierce, and yet he had of all mankind the greatest strength, the ample endowment, which God gave to him." But little is gained by this interpretation, since construing *mæste cræfte* as instrumental also gives good sense and avoids the hazardous assumption of a feminine *cræft* in Anglo-Saxon. In any case, there is little doubt that this characterization of Beowulf is intended as a contrast to that of Heremod in ll. 902ff., 1709ff.   **2186** drihten Wedera]   So Trautmann, Holthausen (3–8 ed.), Sedgefield (2, 3 ed.), Chambers, and Klaeber, following Cosijn, Aant., p. 31.   The MS. *wereda*, retained by the other edd., gives a possible but very unlikely meaning, since *drihten wereda* or *wereda drihten*, "Lord of Hosts," is regularly applied to God and not, as here, to an earthly prince.   On the reading of transcript B, see Malone, PMLA LXIV, 1211, who believes that the letters *drih-* in B's reading represent a late conjecture on Thorkelin's part and were not derived directly from the MS.   **2187** wendon]   Restored by Grein and later edd., except Arnold.   **2187–2188** sleac . . . unfrom]   Kock, Anglia XLVI, 176, explains *sleac* and *unfrom* as parallel adjectives and *æðeling* as a variation of *he*; he translates, "that he, the noble youth, was slack and feeble." Hoops, p. 239, would accordingly put a comma after *æðeling*, as Trautmann had previously done.   Most edd., however, punctuate as in the text.   **2195** seofan þusendo]   I.e., seven thousand hides of land.   This explanation was first given by Kluge, Beitr. IX, 191f., following a suggestion by Leo, Beowulf, p. 101, note 2.   Klaeber, Anglia XXVII (1904), 411f., cites similar instances of the omission of the noun *hyda* in the Alfredian Bede.   As Kluge pointed out, the number "seven thousand" is not to be taken literally, being probably due to considerations of meter and alliteration.   The size of a hide is difficult to estimate and seems to have varied considerably, but according to Kluge's calculations seven thousand hides would have amounted to about 2300 sq. km., or about 890 sq. mi. See l. 2994, note.   **2196b–2199**]   That is, both Hygelac and Beowulf were the possessors of inherited (*gecynde*) land, but Hygelac, who as the king was of higher rank, had more such land than Beowulf. In l. 2199b, *þam* is the equivalent of *þam þe* (as also in l. 2779), and Ettmüller, Sedgefield, and Holthausen (7, 8 ed.) supply *þe*.   Grundtvig had previously emended *þær* to *þe*.

2201–2250

2201 syððan]   See l. 2356, note.   **2202** Heardrede]   So Thorpe and most later edd., following Grundtvig, tr., p. 298, in accordance with ll. 2375, 2388. hildemeceas]   Bouterwek, ZfdA. XI, 102, would read *hildemecgas*, "warriors," as in l. 799.   Cf. l. 587, where it is Unferth who is the *bana*, and not his weapon. **2205** hildefrecan]   The noun *hild* is unlike other *jō*-stem nouns in that its combining form varies between *hilde-* and *hild-*.   Before a metrically long syllable in the second element, we have *hilde-* (as in *hildebord, hildefrōfor, hildesæd*, etc.); before a metrically short syllable, we have *hild-* (as in *hildfruma, hildlata*, etc.).   See H. Weyhe, Beitr. XXX (1905), 79ff.; C. T. Carr, Nominal Compounds in Germanic (London, 1939), pp. 289ff.   In conformity with this rule, we elsewhere find *hildfrecan* without the *-e-* (l. 2366, Andreas 126, 1070).   Here in Beow. 2205 Grundtvig, Holthausen, Schücking, Klaeber, and von Schaubert emend to *hildfrecan*. So also Sievers, Beitr. X, 305, for metrical reasons. The only other exceptions to the rule stated above are *hildegicelum*, l. 1606 (where the -*e*- is necessary to the meter), and *hildbedd*, Andreas 1092. **2207*a*]** The conjunction "that" is to be supplied in sense at the beginning of this half-line, completing the construction begun by *Eft þæt geiode*, l. 2200. See Chambers, note. Wyatt and Chambers punctuate with a dash after l. 2206*b*, Holthausen (1–6 ed.) with a colon, Klaeber with a dash and a colon. Sedgefield (3 ed.) puts a comma after l. 2206*b*, but a colon after l. 2201*a*. The punctuation in the text, which seems adequate to the situation, follows Sedgefield (1, 2 ed.) and von Schaubert. Other edd. put a period after l. 2206*b*, leaving *Eft þæt geiode* hanging in mid-air. **2207–2252]** Fol. 182, which begins with *Beowulfe*, l. 2207, and apparently ended with [*Ic*], l. 2252, is in very bad condition. According to Zupitza, much of this folio has been "freshened up by a later hand," not always correctly. Sedgefield (3 ed.), p. 135, calls Zupitza's statement "inaccurate," asserting that there is no evidence in the MS. to support it. It is possible, however, that signs of "freshening up" of the folio which were evident seventy years ago, when Zupitza studied the MS., have since disappeared, and there is therefore no reason for dismissing his "original" readings, which are recorded below the text in the present edition. Besides Zupitza's report of the MS., use has been made of readings reported by Sedgefield, Chambers, and others who have studied the MS. in detail. The readings given by Sedgefield (3 ed.), made with the help of an ultraviolet lamp, deserve special confidence. **2209 ða]** Thorpe, Holthausen (1, 2 ed.), and Sedgefield emend unnecessarily to *ðæt*. So also Rieger, ZfdPh. III, 406, who considers this line to be the closing passage of a lay. The punctuation in the text, with ll. 2209*b*–2210*a* taken as a parenthesis, goes back to Grein and to Bugge, ZfdPh. IV, 210. **2210 oððæt]** Von Schaubert begins a new sentence with this word, which she construes as an adverb. See l. 56, note. **2211 ricsian]** On the reading of transcript B, see Malone, PMLA LXIV, 1213, who points out that B's -*s*- was added by Thorkelin at a later time and suggests that it was taken from transcript A rather than from the MS. **2212 on heaum hofe]** This reading is adopted on the authority of Sedgefield (3 ed.), note. Other readings based on an inspection of the MS. are *hæþe* (Sievers, Beitr. XXXVI, 418, from the collation which he made in the winter of 1870–1871), *on heaðohlæwe* (Zupitza), and *on heaum hope* (Chambers, note). For the noun *hop* involved in Chambers's reading, see Bos.-Tol., Supp., p. 558. Kock, Anglia XLVI, 176f., apparently without benefit of the MS. itself, had earlier suggested *on heaum hofe*, translating, "in [his] high abode." Cf. *of þam hean hofe* (i.e., from the Ark), Genesis 1489. **2213–2214]** Trautmann begins a new sentence with *Stanbeorh steapne*, putting a period after *uncuð*. Andrew, p. 73, also beginning a sentence with l. 2213*a*, would put only a comma after *uncuð*, taking l. 2214*b* as the first words of a dependent clause; he translates, "There lay a pathway beneath a lofty barrow, whereinto went some man. . . ." The more usual interpretation construes *stanbeorh steapne* as a variation of *hord*. Schücking, beginning a sentence with l. 2213*b*, puts only a comma after *uncuð*;

other edd. punctuate as in the text, with either a colon or semicolon after *steapne* and a period or semicolon after *uncuð*.   **2215b**]   According to Sedgefield (3 ed.), both the *n*- and the -*h* of *n*[*e*]*h* are "fairly distinct." The reading *gefeng*, reported by Wülker and Zupitza, is adopted by all later edd. except Sedgefield and Klaeber. There is a vertical line above the *f* in the MS., regarded by Zupitza as accidental, which makes the *f* look very much like a *þ*. Sedgefield, who reads *geþrang* in his text, suggests (3 ed., note) that "the copyist had begun to write a *þ* but finished it as an *f*." Klaeber's reading *gefealg* is improbable, judging by the facsimile.   **2216b–2217a**]   The restoration of these two half-lines depends to a large extent on whether we read *fahne* or *fah ne* (the *ne* belonging to l. 2217b). If we read *fahne*, then we must assume that there was a masculine noun in l. 2216b; with *fah ne* the choice of restorations is not so restricted. On the problem of *fahne* or *fah ne*, see the next note. Trautmann restores *Hond* [*wæge nam, sigle*] *since fach* for ll. 2216b–2217a. Klaeber accepts Trautmann's restoration of l. 2216b but reads [*sid*], *since fah* for l. 2217a. There is not enough room in the MS. for the old reading suggested by Bugge, Beitr. XII, 100, *hond* [*ætgenam seleful*] *since fah*. The edd. who read *fahne* in l. 2217a do not, as a rule, attempt the restoration of l. 2216b; Holthausen (6–8 ed.), however, reads *hond* [*maððum nam*], *since fahne*. In view of these various possibilities, no restoration is made in the text, either in l. 2216b or in l. 2217b.   **2217b**]   Some of the restorations which have been proposed involve a negative in this half-line and therefore necessitate reading *fah*, rather than *fahne*, at the end of l. 2217a. Bugge, Beitr. XII, 100, restored *ne he þæt syððan* [*ageaf*], the pronoun *he* referring to the thief. Klaeber, Anglia XXVIII, 445f., would read *ne he þæt syððan* [*bemað*], "nor did he (the dragon) afterwards conceal it," and so in his edition. Trautmann's restoration *Ne him þæt syððan* [*hreaw*], "nor did it grieve him (the dragon) later," involves the emendation of the MS. *he* to *him* and seems inconsistent with the dragon's reaction in ll. 2296f., 2304ff., etc. Sedgefield (2, 3 ed.) and Holthausen (6–8 ed.), who read *fahne* in l. 2217a, restore *he þæt syððan* [*wræc*].   **2218**]   All recent edd. restore as in the text, following Zupitza, note, in l. 2218a and Kluge (in Holder, 2 ed.) in l. 2218b. According to Sedgefield, the letters *wu-* of *wurde* are "still just visible."   **2219b**]   The restoration *onf*[*and*], first proposed by Grein, ed., is accepted by most later edd. Holder (2 ed.), following a suggestion by Kluge, emended the *sie* of the text (based on the Thorkelin transcripts) to the more normal *sio*, and so Trautmann, Holthausen, Sedgefield, and Chambers. Chambers, note, suggests that *sio* was the original reading of the MS., before the freshening up of the page. But cf. *hie*, l. 2019.   **2220a**]   There is apparently room for only one letter (not *i*) between *b*- and *folc*, at the beginning of this half-line. Bugge, Beitr. XII, 100, suggested *b*[*y*]*folc*, the equivalent of a noun *bifolc*, "neighboring people"; such a noun is not recorded, but *bifylce* has this meaning. Trautmann restores *b*[*u*]*folc*, and so Sedgefield, Chambers, Holthausen (6–8 ed.), and von Schaubert. Malone, JEGPh. XXVII, 318ff., would read *b*[*u*] *folcbeorna*, translating, "the band of warriors and their dwelling found that out, that he was angry." A choice between *b*[*u*]*folc beorna* and *b*[*u*] *folcbeorna* is difficult, but the alliteration favors the former reading. Kluge's *b[urh]folc* (in Holder, 2 ed.) and Klaeber's *b[ig]folc* are both too long for the space in the MS.   **2220b]** In spite of the reading *hege bolge* in both the Thorkelin transcripts, it is clear from Zupitza's facsimile that *bolge-* was followed in the MS. by another letter, undoubtedly *-n*. According to Zupitza, the *-n* is "faded."   **2221 wyrmhord abræc]** This emendation of the MS. *wyrm horda cræft*, suggested to Holthausen by Kaluza, is adopted by Holthausen (2–8 ed.), Schücking, Sedgefield, Chambers, Klaeber, and von Schaubert. Trautmann emended to *wyrmhord astread*, a reading which was independently suggested by Klaeber, Mod. Phil. III, 463. Cf. *hwa þæt hord strude*, l. 3126.   **2223 þeow]** Kemble, Grein, Heyne (1–3 ed.), Ettmüller, Zupitza, Holder, Socin (6, 7 ed.), Trautmann, Holthausen (1–6 ed.), and Schücking restore *þ[egn]*; Arnold, Heyne (4 ed.), Wülker, Socin (5 ed.), Wyatt, Sedgefield, Chambers, Klaeber, Holthausen (7, 8 ed.), and von Schaubert restore *þ[eow]*, following a suggestion by Grundtvig. Lawrence, PMLA XXXIII, 551ff., JEGPh. XXIII, 298f., argued that the culprit was a warrior (*þegn*), fleeing from the vengeance of someone whom he had wronged, who stole from the dragon's hoard in order to obtain objects of value with which he might compose the feud. The other alternative, that the thief was a runaway slave (*þeow*), has been defended by Bugge, ZfdPh. IV, 210, and Hubbard, Univ. of Wisconsin Studies in Lang. and Lit., No. 11, pp. 8–11. Klaeber, Anglia L, 213f., and Hoops, p. 243, also favor the latter interpretation. As has often been observed, both *heteswengeas fleah*, l. 2224, and *hæft hygegiomor*, l. 2408, point to a slave rather than to a freeman. It is also to be noted that in l. 2401 Beowulf is represented as going *twelfa sum* (i.e., with eleven others) to seek the dragon; the discoverer of the hoard, who was the thirteenth man in the party (l. 2406), is not deemed worthy of being included in the count of Beowulf's companions.   **2225 ærnes]** Restored by Zupitza and all later edd. According to Sedgefield (3 ed.), the letters *ærn-* are "faintly visible."   **fealh]** Restored by Grein and later edd., except Wülker. The last letter was probably *h* in the MS., rather than *l*, as in the Thorkelin transcripts.   **2226 onfunde]** The MS. *mwatide* is meaningless; as Zupitza suggests, it probably resulted from the inaccurate freshening up of a partly illegible word in the MS. The probable sense, so far as we can judge from the inadequate context, is either "it became evident" or "[the *secg synbysig*] soon discovered." Either Wyatt's *Sona getidde*, "Soon it happened," or *Sona þæt geiode*, the reading of Sedgefield (2 ed.), gives a suitable meaning, but neither is very close to the form in the MS. Other readings, none of them entirely convincing, are *Sona in þa tide* (Ettmüller and Heyne, 4 ed.), *Wæs sona in þa tide* (Grein, ed., and others), *Sona inwlatode*, "Soon he gazed in" (Thorpe and others, including Schücking, Chambers, and von Schaubert), *Sona he* [the dragon] *wagode* (Holthausen), *sona he þa eode* (Sedgefield, 1 ed.), *þonan swat iode* (Sedgefield, 3 ed.), and *sona him witad* (Whitbread, MLRev. XXXVII, 483). From the paleographical point of view the most satisfactory emendation of *mwatide* is *onfunde*, as in the text. This reading supposes that the *m-* of the MS. represents an inaccurate freshening up of *on-* in the original text (part of which may have been illegible), that *-w-* represents an original -*f*-, and that -*ati*- represents an original -*un*-. For a fuller discussion of this reading, see my note in MLN. LXVII, 242ff.   **2227**] The restoration in l. 2227*a*, first made by Grein, ed., is adopted by Wülker, Holder, Holthausen, and Sedgefield (3 ed.). In l. 2227*b*, [*gry*]*rebroga*, adopted by all recent edd., was first restored by Grein, Bib. According to Sedgefield (3 ed.), the -*re*- of *gryre*- is "faintly visible" in the MS.   **2228-2230**] Klaeber's restoration of these lines,

> hwæðre [earm]sceapen   [atolan wyrme
> wræcmon ætwand   (him wæs wroht] sceapen)
> [fus on feðe],   þa hyne se fær begeat,

is as good a guess as anyone is likely to achieve. Kemble's [*earm*]*sceapen*, l. 2228*a*, adopted by most later edd., is practically certain. The words *þa hyne*, l. 2230, are printed in this edition on the authority of Sedgefield (3 ed.), who says they are "very faint" in the MS.   **2231a**] Several restorations are possible here. Heyne (2-4 ed.), Socin, Wyatt, Holder (2 ed.), Trautmann, and Chambers restore *geseah*; Holthausen (2-8 ed.) restores *genom*; Sedgefield (3 ed.) restores *sohte*, which had previously been suggested by Grein, Bib. **2232** eorðhuse] Restored by Zupitza and most later edd. The reading *eorðsele*, adopted by Holder (2 ed.) and Trautmann, following a suggestion by Kluge, ignores the evidence of transcript B that the next to the last letter of this word was -*s*-.   **2237** se] So Kemble II and all later edd. except Grundtvig and von Schaubert, who read *si*. Malone, Eng. Studies XV, 151, also accepts *si*. But according to Zupitza the reading of the MS., which now looks like *si*, may originally have been *se*. Elsewhere in the less legible portions of the text written by the second scribe, the letter *e* sometimes looks very much like *i*. See l. 2464, note.   **2239** weard] According to Zupitza, the last letter of this word was originally ð, but the crossbar of the ð was not freshened up with the rest of the letter. Chambers and Sedgefield (3 ed.), however, have been unable to find any trace of the crossbar. Either *weard* or *wearð* makes good sense, but *weard* is stylistically to be preferred as providing a variation of *se an*, l. 2237. Of the recent edd., Trautmann, Schücking, Chambers, Klaeber, Holthausen (6-8 ed.), Sedgefield (3 ed.), and von Schaubert read *weard*; only Holthausen (2-5 ed.) and Sedgefield (1, 2 ed.) read *wearð*. ylcan] Sedgefield (1 ed.) was the first to point out that the *d* of the MS. *yldan* has been clumsily altered from *c* by a later hand. The proper reading is undoubtedly *ylcan*.   **2240** longgestreona] Apparently "long-guarded treasure," the equivalent of *ærgestreon* or *ealdgestreon* (Hoops, p. 243). Sievers, Anglia XIV, 141f., translates, "einen in langer zeit gesammelten, angehäuften schatz, d.h. das resultat langen sammelns." Thorpe emended the MS. *long* to *leng*, "longer," reading *leng gestreona* as two words, and so Ettmüller, Arnold, and Trautmann; this emendation was also accepted by Rieger, ZfdPh. III, 407. Bugge, Beitr. XII, 102, suggested *længestreona*, citing *þas lænan gestreon*, Fates of the Apostles 83. Schröer, Anglia XIII, 343f., would read *londgestreona*.   **2243** niwe] Thorpe and Sedgefield (3 ed.) read *niwel*, and Trautmann *niwol*, "low, deep down," for the MS. *niwe*. But there is nothing wrong with *niwe*. It need hardly be pointed out that the grave-mound was "new," not at the time of the action of Beowulf, but at the time (*on geardagum*, l. 2233) when the treasure was placed in it.   2245 hordwyrðne] Grein, Heyne, Arnold, Wülker, Socin, Wyatt, and Holder (2 ed.) read *hardfyrdne* with the Thorkelin transcripts, explaining it as "difficult to carry," that is, heavy.   The adjective *heard*, however, does not seem to have meant "difficult" in Anglo-Saxon. Bugge, Beitr. XII, 102, suggested *hordwynne dæl*, citing l. 2270, and so Holthausen (1, 2 ed.); the emendation to *hord-* had already been made by Bouterwek, ZfdA. XI, 98.   Schücking reads *hord, wyrðne dæl* with no comma after *dæl.*   Klaeber, Eng. Stud. XXXIX, 431, suggested *hordwyrðne dæl*, and so Sedgefield, Chambers, Holthausen (3–8 ed.), Klaeber, and von Schaubert. 2248–2249 hyt . . . begeaton] The meaning is that the gold which is now being buried was once obtained from the earth, and *on ðe* is therefore properly translated as "in you" rather than "on you."   For a discussion of this passage, see Mackie, MLRev. XXXVI, 95.   2250 fyra] Kemble II emended the MS. *fyrena* to *fira*, Thorpe to *fyra*, and so the later edd., except Grundtvig.

2251–2300

2251 þara ðe . . . ofgeaf] See l. 98, note. Here it is noteworthy that the singular verb *ofgeaf* is parallel to the following plural *gesawon*. The emendation *þara*, for the MS. *þana*, was first made by Kemble II.   lif] Nothing is lost from the MS. here, but the alliteration requires the addition of a word. Kemble II supplied *lif*, and so most later edd.   Holthausen (3–8 ed.) supplies *leoht* (see his note in Die neueren Sprachen, 1910, Ergänzungsband, p. 127), and this reading is preferred by Carleton Brown, PMLA LIII, 915.   2252 gesawon seledream] A continuation of the idea of l. 2251*b*. Kock, Anglia XLII, 118, translates, "who left this life, had seen (had seen the last of, had done with) the joy in hall." He compares ll. 2725ff. and the Virgilian *fuimus Troes, fuit Ilium.* This seems the best explanation of l. 2252*a*, which has given a great deal of trouble to the edd. and has inspired several emendations. Rieger, ZfdPh. III, 408, suggested *gesiþþa seledream*, "the hall-joy of comrades," parallel to *lif*, and Holthausen (1–3 ed.) reads *gesiþa.* Trautmann emends to *secga seledream*, and so Klaeber (1 ed.) and Holthausen (6–8 ed.); see Klaeber's note in Eng. Stud. XXXIX, 465. Bugge, Beitr. XII, 102, suggested *geswæfon seledreamas*, assuming that the two illegible letters in the MS. after *seledream* (see the following note) were *-as.* Cf. *swæfon seledreamas*, Exodus 36. So also Carleton Brown, PMLA LIII, 915f., who, however, would emend the MS. *þana*, l. 2251*b*, to *þam*, beginning a new sentence, and translate, "For the one who forsook this light, the hall-joys slept." This reading involves taking *nah*, l. 2252*b*, as third person singular, with no pronoun before it.   Ic nah] Most edd. begin l. 2252*b* with *Nah*, the subject being unexpressed.   But there seem to have been two letters, now illegible, after the MS. *sele dream* at the end of fol. 182*b*. Bugge's reading (see the preceding note) assumes that these illegible letters were part of the preceding word.   But Holthausen, Sedgefield, and Chambers restore *Ic*, as in the text. 2253 feormie] Restored by Grein and most later edd. The indications in the MS. are that the fourth letter of the word had a descending stroke. **2254** duguð] First restored by Kemble II, who, however, read *duguð bið ellorseoc.* Grein and later edd. also restore *dug[uð].* **2255** hyrsted golde] Kemble and most later edd. restore *[hyr]sted golde,* "adorned with gold," as in the text, following Grundtvig, tr., p. 299. But Kock, Anglia XLII, 118, Anglia XLVI, 177, would read *hyrstedgolde* as a compound, parallel to *fætum;* he compares *wæpnedmen,* l. 1284, and *fætedsinces,* Andreas 478. So also Klaeber. If Kock's reading is right, we should probably read *hyrstedgold* as a compound in Genesis 2156. **2256** feormynd] For *feormiend,* and Grein, Bib., Heyne, Socin, and Schücking so emend. **2261** æfter wigfruman] Klaeber, JEGPh. VI, 197, explains *æfter* as meaning "behind," "following," hence "along with," and this interpretation is accepted by Chambers and by Sedgefield (3 ed.). The older view, that *æfter* is used in a temporal sense here, as in l. 2260a, is defended by Kock, Anglia XLVI, 179f. But Klaeber, Anglia L, 214f., points out that *æfter wigfruman* cannot be separated from *faran* and that *hæleðum be healfe* is presumably a variation of it. **2262** healfe] Grundtvig, Ettmüller, Sedgefield (1 ed.), and Holthausen (7, 8 ed.) emend to *healse.* This reading had earlier been proposed by Grundtvig, tr., p. 300, as an emendation of *Hæleþum be heals* in Thorkelin's edition. But cf. *Him be healfe,* Battle of Maldon 152. Næs] Thorpe, Wülker, and most later edd. emend to *nis,* to secure agreement with the present tense forms which follow. So also Bugge, ZfdPh. IV, 212. But Klaeber explains the MS. *næs* as an adverb, the equivalent of *nealles,* as in l. 562, and would supply "is" in sense. So also Hoops, p. 246, and von Schaubert. Holthausen (8 ed.) supplies *bið* after *næs.* Schücking, Eng. Stud. LV, 97, points out that if *næs* is to be emended, then *nis þær* (as in l. 2458) would be a more probable emendation than *nis.* **2266** fela feorhcynna] "Many kinds of living creatures," and not merely "many races of men," as most edd. explain it. See Mackie, MLRev. XXXVI, 95, who cites *Feorhcynna fela,* Maxims I, 14 (Records III, 157), and the use of *cynn* in Beow. 98. **2268** hwearf] Transcript A reads *hweir,* an impossible form. Kemble printed *hweop* in his text (whether as a reading of the MS. or as a conjecture, is not certain), and so Grein, Bib., Grundtvig, Heyne, Wülker, Zupitza, Socin, Wyatt, and Schücking (8 ed.). But the usual meaning of *hwōpan,* "to threaten," is not particularly appropriate here. Grein, Spr. II, 123 (s.v. *hvōpan*), suggested *weop,* "wept," and so Holder, Trautmann, Holthausen (1, 2 ed.), and Schücking (9, 10 ed.). But *hwe[arf],* the reading of Grein, Sedgefield, Schücking (11–14 ed.), Chambers, Holthausen (3–8 ed.), Klaeber, and von Schaubert, is much more probable. The *-r* in the reading *hweir* of transcript A may be taken as supporting *hwe[arf].* There seems to have been sufficient room in the MS. for three letters after *hwe-.* **2269b]** Ettmüller supplies *him* after *oððæt.* In any case, *him* must be supplied in sense. **2275a]** The restoration in the text, adopted by all recent edd., was first made by Zupitza. **2275b–2276a]** "It is his nature to seek a hoard in the earth." Cf. the frequent use of *sceal* with this meaning in Maxims I (Records III, 156ff.) and Maxims II (Records VI, 55ff.). **2276** hord on hrusan] Restored by Zupitza, and so all later edd. The restoration *[hea]r[h on h]rusan,* by Grein, ed., also fits the evidence of the MS. but is less likely from the point of view of meaning. **2278b**] See l. 3050a and note. **2283b–2284a**] "Then was the hoard discovered, the hoard of precious objects diminished." See Hubbard, Univ. of Wisconsin Studies in Lang. and Lit., No. 11, pp. 14f. For the meaning assigned to *onberan*, "to diminish," see ll. 989b–990, note. To avoid the repetition of *hord*, Holthausen, ZfdPh. XXXVII, 120, would emend to *hlæw* in l. 2283b, and so Holthausen (1 ed.) and Sedgefield. Bugge, ZfdPh. IV, 212, suggested *beaga dæl* in l. 2284a. **2284** getiðad] Here used impersonally, with genitive of the thing (*bene*) and dative of the person (*men*). See Klaeber, Eng. Stud. XXXIX, 466f. **2287** wroht wæs geniwad] Klaeber, Mod. Phil. III, 463, points out that this half-line does not mean "strife was renewed" (the usual meaning of *genīwian*), but rather "strife (quarrel) arose which previously did not exist." He compares *heaf wæs geniwad*, Exodus 35. **2288** stonc] "Moved rapidly." This verb *stincan*, cognate with Gothic *stigqan*, "to thrust, push, attack," and Old Icelandic *stökkva*, "to leap, spring," is also found in Riddle 29, 12, *Dust stonc to heofonum*. The verb *stincan*, "to emit an odor," is apparently unrelated. Sedgefield's explanation of *stonc* as a variant form of *stong*, "snapped, stabbed," in MLRev. XXVIII, 229, and in his 3d ed., is improbable. **2289** he to forð gestop] Usually explained as "he (the thief) had stepped too far forward." Hoops, Bwst., pp. 120f., suggests that this half-line is the equivalent of a relative clause and translates, "die Fussspur des Feindes, der zu weit vorgeschritten war." But it seems more idiomatic to take *to* not as the intensifying adverb, but as an adverb of direction. Cf. ll. 1785, 2648, and especially Battle of Maldon 150, *þæt se* [the spear] *to forð gewat*, where the meaning "too far forward" is quite inappropriate, since it would have been unreasonable to expect the spear to stop before it reached its target. Klaeber, Archiv CXV, 181, defends this interpretation of *to*, but in his edition he defines it as "too." **2292b–2293a**] Kock, Anglia XLII, 118f., construes the relative ðe not as the subject of the subordinate clause, but as the object. He translates, "a man . . ., whom the Almighty's loving-kindness shields." So also Klaeber, note, and von Schaubert. It is, however, possible that *se* and ðe are to be taken together, "he who retains the favor of the Lord." Cf. *agan hyldo heofoncyninges*, Genesis 473f., and *habban his hyldo*, Genesis 567, 625. **2295** sare] Cosijn, Aant., pp. 33f., would emend to *sar*, since *getēon*, "to appoint, arrange," is regularly transitive. Cf. Daniel 111, 235, Andreas 14, Maxims I, 5f., 70, etc. So also Holthausen, Schücking, and Sedgefield. Chambers and von Schaubert, retaining the MS. *sare*, assume that this noun is feminine here and in l. 2468. But *sare* need not be a noun at all, since *getēon* is used absolutely in *swa unc wyrd geteoð*, l. 2526. See Klaeber, Anglia L, 215, who suggests that in these two passages *getēon* means "to deal with." **2296** hlæw] So Kemble (2 ed.) and most later edd., for the MS. *hlæwū*. **2297** ealne utanweardne] For metrical reasons Holthausen (1–5, 8 ed.) emends to *eal utanweard*, following Sievers, Beitr. X, 305f., who suggested that *hlæw* was an old neuter. In his Altgermanische Metrik (Halle, 1893), p. 134, Sievers suggested *ealne utweardne*, and so Schücking. Trautmann, Klaeber (1 ed.), and

Holthausen (6, 7 ed.) read *ealne utanweard*, and this emendation is preferred by Pope, pp. 323f. Sedgefield (2, 3 ed.) reads *ealne utan*. ne ðær ænig mon] Grein supplied the verb *wæs* after *ne*, and so Ettmüller and Holder (1 ed.); as an alternative, Grein, Bib., suggested *næs* for the MS. *ne*, and so Holder (2 ed.), Trautmann, Schücking, Holthausen (3–8 ed.), and Chambers. Sedgefield (2, 3 ed.) supplies *wearð* after *ne*, which is less likely. Still another possibility would be *fand*, which in this position would have neither stress nor alliteration (cf. unstressed *cuþe*, l. 359, *sohte*, l. 376, etc.). But Hoops, p. 248, cites *Næs hearpan wyn*, l. 2262 (with *Næs* taken as an adverb, and with the verb understood), as a syntactical parallel to the MS. reading here. **2298** wiges] So Schücking, Holthausen (3–8 ed.), Chambers, Klaeber, and von Schaubert, for the MS. *hilde*, which does not alliterate. Trautmann had previously emended *hilde* to *wiges* but had also emended the MS. *gefeh* to *georn*, producing the reading *wiges georn*, "the one eager for battle," as the subject of *gehwearf*. Rieger, ZfdPh. III, 408, Holthausen (1, 2 ed.), and Sedgefield assume one or more gaps in the MS. text of ll. 2298–2299. Andrew, p. 151, would emend *hilde* to *he wide*; from the paleographical point of view this is an excellent emendation, but the combination of *wide* with the verb *gefeon* arouses doubts. **2299** beaduwe weorces] Kemble (2 ed.) and most later edd. restore *bea[du]weorces*, which is, however, too short for a normal half-line. Holthausen (1, 2 ed.), Schücking (8 ed.), and Sedgefield supply *georn* after *beaduweorces*; this reading was first proposed by Holthausen in Anglia XXI, 366, where as an alternative he suggested *biter beaduweorces*, citing Riddle 33, 6. Trautmann supplies *bysig* after *beaduweorces*. All these emendations sacrifice the variation *wiges . . . beaduweorces*. Klaeber, JEGPh. VIII, 257f., suggested *beaduwe weorces* (the *-du-* being a restoration, the *-we* an emendation), and so in his edition; he cites *guðe ræs*, ll. 2356, 2626, beside the more usual *guðræs*. Klaeber's reading is adopted by Schücking (9–14 ed.), Holthausen (3–8 ed.), Chambers, and von Schaubert, and is approved by Pope, p. 319. The letters *-we* must be considered an emendation rather than a restoration, since there was room in the MS. for only two letters after *bea-*, at the end of a line.

2301–2350

2301 gefandod] Here *fandian* means "to examine, explore"; in l. 2454 it means "to experience." **2305** se laða] So Bugge, ZfdPh. IV, 212f., and most later edd. Von Schaubert retains the MS. *fela ða*, in spite of the lack of alliteration. **2307** læg] Grundtvig, tr., p. 300, proposed to emend to *leng*; Cosijn, Aant., p. 34, would read *læng* as closer to the MS. reading. Kemble II and all later edd. except von Schaubert adopt one or the other of these emendations. But Moore, in Klaeber Misc., pp. 211f., would retain the MS. *læg*, placing a comma after it. The emendation to *leng*, *læng*, though to our way of thinking a stylistic improvement, is by no means necessary, and the MS. reading is therefore retained in the present text, following Moore and von

Schaubert. For the parallelism *læg, bidan wolde,* cf. *bugan sceolde, feoll,* ll. 2918f.   **2320** ær dæges hwile] See l. 1495, note.   **2325** ham] So all edd. except Heyne, Wülker, and Holder, following Grundtvig, tr., p. 301. Conybeare, p. 150, erroneously reported *ham* as the MS. reading.   **2334** ealond] Not necessarily "island," but rather "land by the sea." See Bugge, Tidskrift VIII, 68, Beitr. XII, 5. Krapp, Mod. Phil. II, 403f., commenting on *igland, ealand* in Andreas 15, 28, suggested that to the insular Anglo-Saxon all foreign lands were "water lands," that is, lands reached by water. Sedgefield (1 ed.) unnecessarily emends the MS. *ealond utan* to *eal utanweard,* citing l. 2297. eorðweard] This compound is usually taken as meaning "land-property," that is, "region of earth, locality." Klaeber glosses it as "earth-guard, stronghold." The second element, *-weard,* can hardly be the masculine *weard,* "guardian," which always refers to a living being. It is tempting to find a parallel in *flodweard,* "sea-wall, wall of waves," Exodus 494, but that word, a compound with *weard,* "guard, watch," is feminine. Sedgefield (1, 3 ed.) emends to *eorðweall,* "earth-wall, rampart." Elsewhere in the poem, however (ll. 2957, 3090), *eorðweall* refers to the dragon's barrow.   **2336** leornode] "Pondered, devised"? So Hoops, Bwst., p. 121, who cites *Leorna þe seolfa and geþancmeta þine mode,* Genesis 1916f. Holthausen, note, cites the Anglo-Saxon translation of Gregory's Pastoral Care (ed. H. Sweet), 435, 23f., *and ðeah geleornað ðæt he deð ðæt yfel,* where the Latin original, with a different construction, has *mala . . . ex deliberatione perpetrare.*   **2338** eallirenne] The absence of a masculine noun here has often been remarked. Bugge, Tidskrift VIII, 56, suggested supplying *scyld* after *eallirenne.* Holthausen, Literaturblatt XXI, 61, would emend to *irenne scyld,* adding *scyld* and omitting *eall,* and so Holthausen (1, 2, 8 ed.) and Schücking (8, 9 ed.). Holthausen (3, 4 ed.) emends to the improbable *wigena hleo scyld* in l. 2337b, retaining the MS. *eallirenne* in l. 2338a. Kock, Anglia XLII, 119f., would emend to *ealliren ner,* "a covering, all iron," citing the noun *gener,* "refuge." So also Holthausen (5, 6 ed.). J. H. G. Grattan (in Chambers, note) explains the MS. *eallirenne* as a weak neuter form used absolutely, "that thing all of iron." Hoops, Bwst., pp. 121f., also explains the word as a weak neuter but takes it as modifying *wigbord.* Holthausen (7 ed.) emends to *eallirenen,* neuter of an adjective form in *-en,* like *gylden, stænen,* etc.; but *iren* itself, with no suffix, is the regular adjective form. The most convincing explanation of the MS. reading is that given by Klaeber, Eng. Stud. XXXIX, 465, who believes that the poet first thought of *scyld* and accordingly wrote *eallirenne,* but then in the next line shifted to the neuter *-bord.* As Klaeber says, the MS. reading gives such an appearance of genuineness that one is loath to emend.   **2341** lændaga] So Kemble II and later edd., following Grundtvig, tr., p. 301. This emendation, apparently based on l. 2591, satisfies both alliteration and meaning. **2347** him þa] So Kemble II and later edd., except Grundtvig, Wülker, and Holder (1 ed.), for the MS. *hī þā* (= *him þam*).   **2348** ne . . . dyde] "Nor did he hold the battle(-power) of the dragon in any esteem at all."

2351–2400

2351 syððan] See l. 2356, note. **2353** Grendeles mægum] "The kin of Grendel," apparently including both Grendel and his mother. **2354** laðan cynnes] Trautmann and Holthausen (1, 6–8 ed.) emend to *laðan cynne* (dat. sing., a variation of *mægum*), following a suggestion by ten Brink, Beowulf, v. 151. This reading is defended by Kock, Anglia XLVI, 178, and Andrew, p. 78. There can be no doubt that the emended reading is stylistically superior, but that the poet intended it is less certain. **2355** hondgemota] This reading, adopted by Kemble and most later edd., is to be regarded as a restoration rather than as an emendation. Both the Thorkelin transcripts read *hond gemot*, but in all likelihood there was an -a in the MS., at the end of the line, which had been lost by Thorkelin's time. **2356** syððan] If the conjunction *syððan* has here its usual meaning "since, after," then there is an inconsistency between l. 2355b and the following lines. Kock, Anglia XLVI, 84ff., is therefore probably right in taking *syððan* as the equivalent of *þær* in the preceding line and translating it as "when" or, more freely, "where, in which." Kock would also translate *syððan* as "when" in ll. 1689, 2201, and 2351, but in at least the last two of these passages the meaning "after" is more probable. guðe ræsum] Hoops, Bwst., p. 123, would assume a compound *guðeræs* here and in l. 2626, citing *hilderæs*, l. 300. But he overlooked the fact that whereas before a metrically long syllable the combining form of *hild* is *hilde-* (see l. 2205, note), the combining form of *guð* is always *guð-*, never *guðe-*. **2358** hiorodryncum] "With sword-drinks." Cf. *heoru*, "sword," l. 1285, Maxims I, 200. The exact metaphor is obscure. Krüger, Beitr. IX, 574f., and Edith Rickert, Mod. Phil. II (1904), 67, picture the sword as the drinker. But the reverse may be intended; that is, the slain warrior may be thought of as doing the drinking. This latter alternative is supported by *mandrinc* (referring to an arrow shot), Riddle 23, 13. **2361** ana] Restored by all recent edd., following Grein, Bib. **2362** beag] Kemble (2 ed.) and all later edd., except Grundtvig and Trautmann, restore [st]ag. But there is no other example of *to holme stigan*, though we have *on holm gestah* in l. 632. Trautmann restored [be]ag, "turned, withdrew," and this reading has more recently been proposed by Malone, Eng. Studies XV, 151, who believes that "the booty is spoken of to bring out Beowulf's prowess in battle, not in swimming." Klaeber, Anglia Beibl. L, 332, finds it "hard to believe that the poet would have spoken of Beowulf's 'flight.'" But after all, there can be little doubt that the Geats were defeated in the battle and that Beowulf lived to fight again. **2367** sioleða] The word *sioloð* is not recorded elsewhere, but *sioleða bigong* is undoubtedly a kenning for "sea." For a probable etymology of *sioloð* (which connects it with a Germanic **sīl-*, **sĭl-*, "still, or gently flowing, water"), see Bugge, ZfDPh. IV, 214; Hoops, Bwst., pp. 123f. Sedgefield, MLRev. XXVIII, 229, and in his 3d ed., emends *sioleða* to *solewa*, gen. plur. of *sol*, *solu*, "miry place, shallow pond" (see Bos.-Tol., p. 894); but his justification of this reading is not convincing. **2370** bearne] That is, to Heardred. **2373ff.**] Beowulf had no desire to usurp the throne, but merely to give advice and support to the young Heardred until the latter became old enough to rule. It was only after Heardred's death (ll. 2384ff.) that Beowulf succeeded to the throne. The *feasceafte*, l. 2373, are the Geatish people, destitute of leadership after the death of Hygelac.   **2373** findan] "Succeed in obtaining (from Beowulf)"; see Bos.-Tol., Supp., p. 219, s.v. *findan* II (2), especially the citation from Gregory's Dialogues.   **2377** him] Thorpe, Grein, and later edd., except von Schaubert, emend the MS. *hi* (= *him*) to *hine*. But Mackie, MLRev. XXXVI, 95, calls attention to the intransitive construction of *healdan* with dative of the person and instrumental of the thing, with the meaning "to perform for a person the action suggested by the noun" (Bos.-Tol., Supp., p. 519, s.v. *healdan* B.IV). Cf. Guthlac 729, 736, Daniel 505, etc. In the present instance *him* is the dative of the person, while *freondlarum* and *estum* are parallel instrumentals. **2381** forhealden] Cosijn, Aant., p. 35, explains *forhealdan* here as meaning "to commit an offence toward, to fall short in one's duty to (someone)." This is apparently an extension of the meaning "to disregard, neglect" (Bos.-Tol., Supp., p. 245, s.v. *for-healdan* II).   **2383** þara ðe ... brytnade] See l. 98, note.   **2384** Him ... wearð] "That became the limit (of time) for him"; that is, Heardred lost his life as a result of it. For other examples of *mearc* in the sense of "limit (of time)," see Genesis 1719, Christ and Satan 499.   **2385** for feorme] So Holder, Socin, Holthausen, and later edd., following Möller, Das altenglische Volksepos I, 111. The meaning is "on account of hospitality."   feorhwunde] Kock, JJJ., p. 9, explains *feorhwunde* and *swengum* as parallel instrumental objects of *hleat*. This construction is also found in *leanum hleotan*, Christ 783. But the accusative and genitive are more common as objects of *hleotan* than the instrumental, and either may have been intended here: "he obtained his life-wound through blows of the sword."   **2394** ofer sæ side] Schücking (8–10 ed.) reads *ofer sæsiðe*, "after a sea journey," following Schröder, ZfdA. XLIII, 366f. But as Klaeber, Eng. Stud. XXXIX, 432, points out, with this meaning we would expect *ofer* with the accusative, as in ll. 736, 1781.   sunu Ohteres] That is, Eadgils.   **2395–2396** he gewræc ... cearsiðum] Most edd. take *he* as referring to Eadgils, following Müllenhoff, ZfdA. XIV, 228. We expect an object for *gewræc*, as in ll. 107, 2005, etc. Cosijn, Aant., p. 35, would therefore emend to *cealde cearsiðas*, acc. plur., in l. 2396a. Trautmann emends *cealdum* to *cwealm*, acc. sing., "death." Andrew, p. 51, suggests that *he* is a scribal error for *hine*. Other commentators supply an object "it" (that is, Eadgils's exile) in sense, thus achieving an adequate meaning.   **2400** gewegan] "To fight." For the etymology of this verb (which is unrelated to *wegan*, "to move," but is cognate with the noun *wiga*, "warrior," and with the Old Icelandic verb *vega*, "to fight, slay"), see Hoops, pp. 256f., and the references given there.

2401–2450

2401 XIIa] For *twelfa*. See *XVna*, l. 207, and note.   **2410** to ðæs ðe] See l. 714, note.   anne] Thorpe, Ettmüller, and Arnold emended to *ana*, "alone"; Schröer, Anglia XIII, 345, proposed to assume an adverb *ane*, with the same meaning. But *an* in a demonstrative sense, meaning "the one previously mentioned" (in this case the *eorðsele*), is well authenticated; cf. ll. 100, 2280, 2774. On this meaning of *an*, see also Bugge, Beitr. XII, 371; W. Braune, Beitr. XII (1887), 393, note.   **2415 ceap]** This word is usually translated "bargain, purchase," but Mackie, MLRev. XXXVI, 95f., would take it as meaning "goods, merchandise" and referring to the treasure. He compares Maxims I, 81f., *mid ceape . . . , bunum ond beagum.*   **2421 se]** Grein, Grundtvig, Heyne (1 ed.), Ettmüller, Wülker, Holder (1 ed.), Trautmann, and Holthausen emend to *seo* or *sio* because of the feminine antecedent *wyrd.* But see l. 1260, note.   **2423 no þon lange]** Kock, Anglia XLIII, 304f., taking *þon* as the equivalent of *(to) þæs, to þon*, translates, "however long the royal spirit had been wrapped in flesh." Cf. Kock's similar interpretations in ll. 968, 1508. The usual translation of *no þon lange*, with a semicolon after l. 2423*a*, is "not long then" (Earle, tr.), "not long from that time" (Chambers, note). Holthausen, Anglia Beibl. XLIV, 226, suggests that *þon* is an error for *þa.* But in the absence of a comparative, Kock's explanation of the passage seems more probable. Cosijn, Aant., p. 35, would emend the MS. *lange* to *længe*, a variant form of the comparative *leng.* Cf. the form *lenge* in Guthlac 20, 138, Juliana 375, and possibly in Beow. 83. Klaeber, note, suggests that *no þon lange* is the result of a contamination of *no þon leng* (the normal comparative construction with *þon*) and *no . . . lange.*   **2428 sinca]** On the reading of transcript B, see Malone, PMLA LXIV, 1214, who suggests that the final *-a* was derived from transcript A rather than from the MS.   **2430 Hreðel cyning]** This half-line is metrically shorter than normal. Trautmann, omitting *cyning*, puts *geaf me* at the end of l. 2430*b* rather than at the beginning of the next line. Holthausen (1, 7, 8 ed.) and Sedgefield transpose *geaf me* to the beginning of l. 2430*b*, putting the semicolon after l. 2430*a* rather than after l. 2429*b*. Holthausen (2–6 ed.) puts *geaf* at the end of l. 2430*b* and *me* at the beginning of l. 2431*a*. None of these proposed rearrangements is convincing.   **2432 to life]** "During [his] life." Cf. Judith 322.   **laðra owihte]** "At all the more hateful." For metrical reasons, Holthausen (1–5 ed.) and Schücking emend the MS. *owihte* to *wihte*, following Sievers, Beitr. X, 256; Holthausen (6 ed.) emends to *ohte.* Trautmann and Holthausen (8 ed.) emend to *owiht*, which does not provide the required meaning.   **2435 ungedefelice]** For metrical reasons, Holthausen (1, 2 ed.) and Schücking (8 ed.) emend to *ungedofe*, a form not elsewhere recorded; Schücking (9–14 ed.), Holthausen (3–8 ed.), Klaeber (1 ed.), and Sedgefield (3 ed.) emend to *ungedefe.* Both these emendations were originally proposed by Sievers, Beitr. X, 234, and *ungedefe* also by Klaeber, Eng. Stud. XXXIX, 432. Chambers retains *-lice* in his text but suggests that it was added in error by a scribe, and so also Hoops, Bwst., p. 10.   **2436 stred]** Past participle of *stregdan*, "to strew, spread." Grein, Bib., and Holder (1 ed.) emend to *styred*, "arranged," and Rieger, ZfdPh. III, 409f., accepting this emendation, cites *hildbedd styred*, Andreas 1092. The Andreas passage is, however, our only evidence for either *stýran (stíeran)* or *styrian* with such a meaning.   **2438 freawine]** This word, which ordinarily means "friendly lord" (cf. ll. 2357, 2429), does not seem appropriate when applied to the relationship between brothers, and here it may be a variant form of *freowine*, "dear (or noble) friend." Bugge, Beitr. XII, 103, proposed the emendation to *freowine*, and so Trautmann and Holthausen (7, 8 ed.). Bugge compares *freomæg*, "brother," Genesis 983, and *freobroðor*, Exodus 338. **2441-2442a**] D. Whitelock, Medium Ævum VIII, 198, translates, "That was an encounter unatoned for by money (though) grievously committed, weighing heavily on the spirit." This is undoubtedly the general meaning of the passage, though "an encounter which could not be atoned for by money" would perhaps be closer to the poet's intention. Bugge, ZfdPh. IV, 215, doubting that the shot by which Hæthcyn killed his brother could be called a *gefeoht*, suggested emending to *gewyrht*. But without *gefeoht* the implication of *feohleas* would be lost.   **2442** hreðre hygemeðe] Grein, Bib., unnecessarily emended the MS. *hreðre* to *Hreðle*, and so Trautmann, Holthausen (1-5 ed.), and Sedgefield (1, 2 ed.). Since the meaning of *hygemeðe* should be "wearied in mind" rather than the "wearying the mind" which the context demands, Scheinert, Beitr. XXX, 387, suggested emending to a noun *hygemeðu*, not elsewhere recorded in Anglo-Saxon. Trautmann reads *hygemeððo*, Holthausen (1-5 ed.) *hygemeðo*. Holthausen (6, 8 ed.) and Sedgefield (3 ed.) also emend to *hygemeðo* but retain the MS. *hreðre*.   **2444ff.**] The somewhat obscure comparison between Hrethel, mourning his dead son, and a man who sees his son on the gallows has been cleared up by D. Whitelock, Medium Ævum VIII, 198ff., who points out that vengeance could not be taken for a slaying within the kindred, just as one could not take vengeance for an executed criminal. See *feohleas gefeoht*, l. 2441, and note; also ll. 2464b-2465, below. Thus Hrethel, unable to exact retribution for the slaying of Herebeald, is reminded of the other circumstance under which no vengeance is possible. Sedgefield's suggestion, that these lines refer to the sorrow which Hrethel would feel if Hæthcyn expiated on the gallows the killing of Herebeald, is less likely.   **2446** wrece] Grein, Heyne (1-3 ed.), Ettmüller, Holder (1 ed.), Trautmann, Holthausen, and Sedgefield emend to the indicative *wreceð*. But as Bugge, Tidskrift VIII, 56, pointed out, the MS. *wrece* is to be connected with the preceding subjunctive *ride*. Line 2446b is, in fact, the equivalent of *þæt he þonne gyd wrece*, continuing the *þæt*-clause which begins in l. 2445b. A comma, then, is the proper punctuation before *þonne*.   **2448** helpe] So Kemble (2 ed.) and most later edd., for *helpan*, which was apparently the reading of the MS. Grein, Spr. II, 33, Heyne, Socin, and Wyatt assume a weak feminine noun *helpe*, not recorded elsewhere, beside the strong feminine *help*; so also Chambers, doubtfully. Schücking construes the MS. *helpan* as infinitive, parallel to *gefremman*, with an object "him" for *gefremman* to be supplied in sense. But this interpretation leaves *ænige* unexplained, unless we take it as an instrumental, the equivalent of *ænige þinga*. Kock, Anglia XXVII, 220f., defends *helpan* as an infinitive, but in Arkiv för nordisk Filologi XXXIX, 188, he accepts the emended reading *helpe*. Sievers, ZfdPh. XXI, 357, suggests that the scribe, through misunderstanding of the passage, intended an infinitive here and later forgot to correct his error. See also Klaeber, Mod. Phil. III, 463; Hoops, p. 261.

2451–2500

2453 yrfeweardas] A gen. sing. in *-as*, like *Heaðoscilfingas*, l. 63, and *Merewioingas*, l. 2921. **2454** þurh deaðes nyd dæda gefondad] Grundtvig suggested the transposition of *deaðes* and *dæda*, so as to read þurh dæda nyd deaðes gefondad; in his note, however, he suggested the further emendation of the MS. *nyd* to *nið*, and this reading was approved by Bugge, ZfdPh. IV, 215. Müllenhoff, ZfdA. XIV, 232f., apparently independently of Grundtvig, also proposed the reading þurh dæda nyd deaðes gefondad. But as Klaeber remarks, Archiv CXV, 181, the MS. reading seems less doubtful than these proposed emendations. Klaeber explains *dæda gefondad* as meaning "(has) made the acquaintance of [evil] deeds." Chambers, p. 189, translates, "has experienced deeds (of violence)." Hoops, p. 262, suggests that the phrase is the equivalent of such a modern expression as "has become acquainted with (the seamy side of) life." **2456** windge reste] "The resting-place beat by the winds" (Kock, Anglia XLVI, 178f.). Most of the early edd., together with Heyne, Socin, Wyatt, Schücking, Sedgefield (1, 2 ed.), and Chambers read *windgereste* as a compound, with a similar meaning. **2457** reote berofene] A noun *rēot* is not elsewhere recorded, but Bugge, ZfdPh. IV, 215f., suggests the meaning "rest." Holder emends to *rote berofene*, "deprived of joy," assuming a noun with the same form as the adjective *rōt*, "cheerful." Trautmann emends to *rince berofene*, Sedgefield (3 ed.) to *reorde berofene*, "deprived of speech" (see also Sedgefield's note in MLRev. XXVIII, 229). Kock, Anglia XLVI, 178f., would read *rote berofene*, assuming a noun *rōt* cognate with Old Icelandic *rōt*, "the inner part of the roof of a house"; he translates, "bared of its upper timber." This reading is, however, unlikely; as Hoops points out, Bwst., pp. 124f., Old Icelandic *rōt* belongs with Old Icelandic *hrōt*, Gothic *hrōt*, "roof," and would alliterate in *hr-*. Chambers, Klaeber, Hoops, and von Schaubert accept Holthausen's suggestion, in his edition, that the MS. *reote* reflects an early *rǣte*, later *rēte*, dat. sing. of a noun *rētu*, "joy," a derivative of the adjective *rōt*. Except for the form assumed for the noun, this interpretation is the same as Holder's. **Ridend swefað]** Grein, Bib., suggested emending to *swefeð*, assuming that *Ridend* is singular, and so Grein, ed., Wülker, and Holthausen (2–5 ed.). Klaeber, Anglia XXVIII, 446f., accepting *swefeð*, explains *Ridend* as "the rider on the gallows," that is, the one who has been hanged; in support of this meaning he cites ll. 2445b–2446a. But in his edition Klaeber follows the older interpretation, by which *Ridend* is plural and means "riders, horsemen." As Kock says, Anglia XLVI, 179, the lines describe general desolation. **2458** in hoðman] "In concealment, in the grave"? The noun *hoðma* (or *hoðme*?) is elsewhere found only in Christ 45, þe ær under hoðman biholen lægon. For the etymology, see Holthausen, AEW., p. 171, who takes the word to be masculine. **2460** on sealman] "To his bed." See Hoops, Bwst., pp. 125f. **2460–2461** sorhleoð . . . anum] "He sings a song of lament, one man in sorrow for the other." See Klaeber, Eng. Stud. LXVII, 402, and Hoops, p. 263. Cf. *æfter sincgyfan*, l. 1342; *an æfter eallum*, l. 2268; *æfter Herebealde*, l. 2463, etc. **2464** weallende] In spite of the reading *weal linde* in both the Thorkelin transcripts, the form *weallende*, reported by Conybeare, p. 150, was probably the reading of the MS. In the hand of the second scribe, the heavy vertical stroke of *e* may easily be mistaken for an *i* if the letter is at all obscure. Cf. l. 3160, where both the Thorkelin transcripts report *-rofis*, although the MS. seems to have *-rofes*; l. 2714, where the reading *-niði* in transcript B undoubtedly reflects a *-niðe* in the MS.; and l. 3150, where the letters *-iat-* reported by A. H. Snith probably reflect an *-eat-* in the MS., part of the *e* being illegible even under ultraviolet light. A present participle in *-inde* would be surprising in Beowulf.		**2466** heaðorinc] Malone, Anglia LXIII, 103f., JEGPh. L, 19ff., would accept the uncorrected reading *heaðoric*, translating it as "war-ruler," and would regard this word as an epithet of Hæthcyn. In PMLA XL (1925), 784, 799f., and Widsith, pp. 158ff., he suggests that the Beowulfian Hæthcyn was the prototype of Heithrek in the Old Icelandic Hervararsaga, whom he identifies with Heathoric in Widsith 116. See also his earlier discussion in The Literary History of Hamlet I, 155ff. There can be no doubt that the form *heaðori(n)c* in the present passage refers to Hæthcyn, but in spite of Malone's arguments, the assumption of a common noun *-ríc* in West Germanic is still hazardous. See l. 1176, note.		**2468** swa sar] Since *sār*, "grief, affliction," is regularly neuter, the MS. *sio sar* is open to suspicion. Grein, ed., Ettmüller, Wülker, Holthausen (1, 2 ed.), and Sedgefield (1, 2 ed.) emend the MS. *sio* to *swa*, following Rieger, Lesebuch; with this reading *sar* is best taken as the adjective. Holthausen (3–5 ed.) emends *sio* to *gio*, "formerly"; Klaeber emends *sio sar* to *to sar*, with *sar* taken as nom. sing. feminine of the adjective, and so Holthausen (6 ed.). Schücking omits *sio* entirely. Sedgefield (3 ed.) transposes (with emendation of *sar* to *sare*) to read *sio þe him sare belamp*, citing l. 2222b; see his note in MLRev. XXVIII, 229. The antecedent of *sio* is then *sorhge*. Holthausen (7, 8 ed.) accepts this transposition but retains the MS. *sar*. Chambers and von Schaubert, retaining the MS. *sio sar*, assume that the noun *sar* is feminine here and in l. 2295. In the present text Rieger's *swa sar* is accepted. This reading is supported by *þolian þa þrage, þa hio swa þearl becom*, Meters 1, 77, which Klaeber, Eng. Stud. XLII, 325, note 1, believes may have been influenced by the passage in Beowulf.		**2473** wid] So all edd., following Grundtvig, tr., p. 303. On the form *rid* in transcript A, see l. 702, note.		**2475** oððe] Bugge, Tidskrift VIII, 57, would explain this word as the equivalent of *ond*, here and in l. 649. Ettmüller reads *and* in his text. Sedgefield (1 ed.) emends *oððe* to *seoððe* (a "weak form" of *seoððan*), putting a colon after l. 2474b; Sedgefield (2 ed.) emends to *oð ðæt*. Andrew, pp. 83f., would also interpret *oððe*, here and in l. 3006, as the equivalent of *oððæt*; here he translates, "till O.'s sons were bold in warfare."		him] Explained by Bugge, Tidskrift VIII, 57, as a reflexive dative; such a pronoun is usually found only after verbs of motion, but cf. *wesan him on wynne*, Genesis 367.		**2477** Hreosnabeorh] Holder (1 ed.), Holthausen (1 ed.), and Sedgefield (1, 2 ed.) emend to *Hreofna-, Hrefna-*, following a suggestion by Bugge, ZfdPh. IV, 216, withdrawn by him in Beitr. XII, 11. Conybeare, p. 150, had previously read *Hreofna*, but whether as an emendation or as the reading of the MS., is not certain. There is no doubt that the MS. has *hreosna beorh*. The evidence of the Swedish place names in *Hrefna-*, *Hrefnes-*, ll. 2925, 2935, is of no value, since *Hreosnabeorh* is in the land of the Geats, not of the Swedes. **2481 þeah ðe . . . gebohte]** We need an object for *gebohte*, and Grein, Bib., Heyne (1 ed.), and Arnold supplied *hit* before *his*. Heyne (2–4 ed.), Socin, Schücking, and Sedgefield emend the MS. *his* to *hit*. But perhaps here, as elsewhere, we may supply an object in sense, without emending the text. The *oðer* ("one of the two," as in ll. 1874, 2198, etc.) is, of course, Hæthcyn. Klaeber, note, and Pope, p. 234, suggest putting *his* in the second half-line, since logically it belongs with *ealdre*. The same problem appears in Finnsburh 47, *hu ða wigend hyra wunda genæson*. The arrangement in the text is supported by *on galgan his gast onsende*, Elene 480, where the pronoun must be put in the first half-line for metrical reasons. See Klaeber, Beitr. LXXII, 124, who also cites Genesis 2705. **2484–2485]** "I have heard that then in the morning one kinsman [Hygelac] avenged the other [Hæthcyn] upon the slayer [Ongentheow] with the edges of swords." Kock, Anglia XLVI, 180f., would explain *þa* (= *guðe*) as a pronoun, object of *stælan*, pointing out that in every other case the object of *stælan* is an abstract noun (*fæhðe*, *firene*, *synne*, etc.). But *þa* is more naturally taken as an adverb, as in ll. 74, 2694, 2752, etc., and as Kock himself had previously explained it, Anglia XXVII, 229ff. This interpretation, as reflected in the translation above, was originally suggested by Cosijn, Aant., p. 23 (note on l. 1340); see also Klaeber, Mod. Phil. III, 261, Anglia L, 215f. **2486 niosað]** Grein, Heyne, Ettmüller, Wülker, and Holder (1 ed.) emended to *niosade*, Holthausen (1, 2 ed.) to *niosde*. But for the change of tense here, see l. 1923, note. **2488 hildeblac]** Nothing is lost from the MS. at this point, but the two syllables *hreas blac* do not make a half-line. Grein, Heyne, Ettmüller, Wülker, Holder, Socin (5, 6 ed.), Wyatt, and Klaeber (3 ed.) emend to *hreas heoroblac*, "fell, battle-pale (i.e., mortally wounded)." Even this reading gives an abnormally short half-line, and *hreas hildeblac*, proposed by Holthausen, Anglia XXI, 366, is adopted by Socin (7 ed.), Holthausen, Schücking, Sedgefield, Chambers, Klaeber (1 ed.), and von Schaubert. Cf. *wigblac*, Exodus 204, where, however, *-blac* means "shining, resplendent," rather than "pale," the meaning usually assumed in the present passage. Von Schaubert, note, defends *hildeblac* as meaning "battle-resplendent," that is, resplendent in his armor. Bugge, Tidskrift VIII, 297, suggested *hreas hreablac* ("corpse-pale"?). Pope, p. 305, suggests *hreawblac gehreas*. Hoops, p. 265, defends *heoroblac* in spite of the metrical difficulty, assuming an intensive meaning in *heoro-*. See also Klaeber, Anglia Beibl. LIV/LV, 278. **hond]** That is, Eofor's hand. **2489 feorhsweng]** Holthausen (1–5 ed.) and Sedgefield (1 ed.) emend to *feorhswenge*; see also Holthausen, ZfdPh. XXXVII, 121. But see the note on l. 1520, where the converse emendation (*swenge* to *sweng*) has been made. **2490 him]** That is, to Hygelac. **2493 eðelwyn]** Elsewhere in the poem the acc. sing. of (-)*wyn* is (-)*wynne*. Ettmüller and Holder therefore emended here to *eðelwynne*; this emendation was also proposed, apparently independently, by Sievers, Beitr. IX, 141. For the meaning of *eðelwyn*, see l. 692, note. **2495 þurfe]** Bugge, ZfdPh. IV, 216, would emend to *þorfte*, and so Holthausen

(1, 2 ed.). But for the change in tense here, see l. 1923, note. Andrew, pp. 136f., suggests *scolde*, to avoid the repetition *þearf* . . . *þurfe*.

2501–2550

2501 Syððan] Most edd. put only a comma after l. 2500, apparently assuming that ll. 2501ff. explain Beowulf's possession of the sword mentioned in l. 2499. That is, Beowulf killed Dæghrefn as he had killed Grendel, without the use of a sword (ll. 2506b–2508a), and then took Dæghrefn's sword as his own. See Rieger, ZfdPh. III, 414; Klaeber, Archiv CXV, 181; Chambers, note. But surely this interpretation reads too much into the text. We can hardly doubt that Beowulf owned a sword of his own when he started on the expedition against the Franks and that he had his own reasons for not using it against Dæghrefn. The punctuation adopted in this edition, with a new sentence in l. 2501a, follows Grein, Ettmüller, Arnold, Schücking, and Sedgefield; see also Schücking, Svk., p. 119. There is no reason for connecting ll. 2501ff. with what precedes.   for dugeðum] Either "before the hosts" (cf. l. 2020) or "on account of [my] valor"; the latter explanation is given by Sievers, ZfdPh. XXI, 365, Lawrence, JEGPh. XXIII, 298, and Hoops, p. 267. The interpretation suggested by von Schaubert, note, "wegen meiner Kräfte, meiner Stärke," is less probable.   **2503 ða frætwe**] The gold collar given by Wealhtheow to Beowulf and by him in turn to Hygd (ll. 1195ff., 2172ff.). With the variation *breostweorðunge* in the next line, cf. *hyre syððan wæs . . . breost geweorðod*, ll. 2175f. The meaning of this passage is that Dæghrefn, who had captured the collar, presumably by killing Hygelac, was unable to present it in person to the Frisian king because he was himself killed by Beowulf.   Frescyninge] So all edd., following Grundtvig, tr., p. 304.   **2505 in compe**] Kemble (2 ed.) reads *in compe* for the MS. *in cempan*, and later edd. emend to either *in compe* or *in campe*. Grienberger's defence of *in cempan* as meaning "among the warriors," Zeitschrift für die österreichischen Gymnasien LVI, 750, and Beitr. XXXVI, 84, was rightly rejected by Sievers, Beitr. XXXVI, 409f.   **2508 banhus**] Probably plural, as in l. 3147. See l. 1116, note, and Hoops, Bwst., p. 126.   **2511 niehstan siðe**] See l. 1203, note.   **2514 mærðu**] Kemble II emended the MS. *mærðu* (= *mærðum*) to *mærðo*; Bugge, Beitr. XII, 103f., proposed *mærðu*, and so the later edd., except Holder, Wyatt, and Chambers. Malone, Eng. Studies XV, 151, would retain *mærðum* as a dative of accompaniment, translating, "I will seek battle and glorious deeds, I will do battle and glorious deeds." Mackie, MLRev. XXXVI, 96, also retaining *mærðum*, would translate, "prevail by means of glorious deeds." Cf. the examples of intransitive *fremman* cited by Bos.-Tol., Supp., p. 264, from prose texts. The MS. *fremman* in Seafarer 75, also apparently intransitive, cited by Mackie, is surely a scribal error (since an infinitive is out of place there) and has been emended to a noun form in the present edition. In *fremme se þe wille*, Beow. 1003, an object is understood. All other examples of intransitive *fremman* in the poetry (Genesis 1314, 1493, 2370, 2736, Daniel 185) are followed either by adverbial *swa* or by a *swa*-clause which takes the place of an object.

In view of the parallels in Beow. 2134, 2645, the emendation to *mærðu* here seems justified. A similar scribal error, also by the second scribe, is the MS. *magū þegne*, l. 2079. 2520 ðam aglæcean] Sievers, Beitr. IX, 141, would emend to *þæs aglæcean*, gen. sing., dependent on *gylpe*, "(to grapple with) the boasting of the monster." This emendation is adopted by Holthausen. But *gylpe* is more probably instrumental, "with glory" (Bos.-Tol., Supp., p. 467). 2521 gylpe] Schröer, Anglia XIII, 345f., would emend to *guþe*, "in battle." Trautmann emends to *gyste*, parallel to *ðam aglæcean*. But the MS. *gylpe* gives good sense; see the preceding note. wiðgripan] This verb does not occur elsewhere, but, as Schröer, Anglia XIII, 345f., pointed out, *wiðgripan wið* is the equivalent of *fon wið*, l. 439, *gripan togeanes*, l. 1501, *fon togeanes*, l. 1542. The use of the preposition *wið* (ll. 2520a, 2521b) after a verb compounded with *wið-* is at least a little strange, if we may judge by other verbs such as *wiðfon*, *wiðhabban*, *wiðsacan*, *wiðstondan*, which regularly take a dative of the thing resisted, without preposition. 2523 oreðes ond attres] The emendation of the MS. *reðes* to *oreðes* was first made by Grein, Bib., that of *hattres* to *attres* by Kemble II, following Grundtvig, tr., p. 304. All recent edd. adopt these readings, which are required by sense and alliteration. 2525 forfleon] The MS. reads *oferfleon*, but this improbable verb is found nowhere else in Anglo-Saxon. The form *ic oferfleo*, in Ælfric's Grammar (ed. J. Zupitza, 276, 10), translates the Latin *supervolo* and is undoubtedly a form of *oferflēogan*. Here in Beow. 2525 Sedgefield and Holthausen (7, 8 ed.) omit *ofer-*, following a suggestion by Bugge, Beitr. XII, 104. Cf. *fleon fotes trym*, Battle of Maldon 247. Trautmann and Holthausen (1 ed.) emend to *forfleon*; Holthausen (3–6 ed.) reads *ferfleon*, with a weakened form of the prefix. All the regular meanings of *ofer-* as a verbal prefix seem inconsistent with the meaning of *flēon*, unless we are to translate *oferfleon* as "surpass in fleeing," in which case *fotes trem* would be meaningless. A parallel to *oferfleon* may be sought in the phrase *to oferbuganne*, "to be avoided" (corresponding to *declinandi* in the Latin text), in the Hatton MS. of the Pastoral Care (ed. H. Sweet, 295, 21). But the Cotton MSS. of the same text have *to ferbugonne*, and Sweet in his note is of the opinion that the original text had *to ferbuganne*. All things considered, an emendation seems unavoidable here. From the point of view of meaning, Bugge's *fleon* is as good as Trautmann's *forfleon*, but it does not explain the MS. *ofer-*. furður] Nothing is lost from the MS. here. To provide the missing alliteration, Socin (7 ed.), Schücking (8–10 ed.), and Holthausen (1 ed.) supply *feohte*, following Bugge, Beitr. XII, 104. Trautmann supplies *fæhðo*, following H. Schubert, De Anglo-Saxonum arte metrica (Berlin, 1870), p. 46. Klaeber, Archiv CXV, 181, suggested *furðor*, and so Holthausen (2–8 ed.), Sedgefield, and Schücking (11–14 ed.); Chambers, Klaeber, and von Schaubert supply *furður*. Cf. Battle of Maldon 247a. 2528 þæt] Sievers, Beitr. IX, 141, rejecting the clause of result in l. 2528, would emend the MS. *þæt* to *þæs*. But Klaeber, Mod. Phil. III, 463f., defends *þæt* as a loose connective, citing ll. 1434, 1664, 2577, 2830, etc. 2533 gemet] "Power." Cf. l. 2879, Christ and Satan 489, Order of the World 27. nefne] Restored by all edd., following Grundtvig, tr., p. 304. On the reading of transcript B, see Malone, PMLA

LXIV, 1215. **2534** þæt] So Kemble (2 ed.) and all later edd., following Grundtvig, tr., p. 304. eofoðo dæle] "Dispense [his] strength," that is, fight. Cf. *þon we swa hearde hilde dælon*, Battle of Maldon 33. Kock's explanation of *eofoðo dælan*, "try one's strength," Anglia XLII, 121, is less likely. **2545** stondan] So Thorpe, Grein, Wülker, and later edd., for the *stodan* of the two Thorkelin transcripts, which was probably the reading of the MS. The infinitive is required after *Geseah* and also because of the following infinitive *brecan.*   stanbogan] This word, here and in l. 2718, is usually explained as a reference to stone arches forming the vault of the chamber within the dragon's barrow. See especially Lawrence, PMLA XXXIII, 569ff. Schücking, Bedeutungslehre, pp. 71ff., suggests that the dragon's lair is not within an artificial barrow but is a natural cave in a hill; this conclusion is, however, made very questionable by the adjectives *eallgearo* and *niwe* in ll. 2241ff. Henel's attempt, Anglia LV, 273ff., to explain *stanboga*, here and in l. 2718, as a synonym of *hringboga*, l. 2561, referring to the dragon, is hardly acceptable.   stream] Both the *stream* and the *burnan wælm* in the next line are to be identified with the *dracan leg* of l. 2549. See Hoops, Bwst., pp. 126f. But Schücking, Bedeutungslehre, pp. 74f., identifies the *stream* as a hot spring and uses it as evidence for his conclusion (see the preceding note) that the dragon's cave was a natural one.   **2549** deop] "The depths (of the cave)." Grundtvig, tr., p. 305, suggested emending to *deor*, "animal," and so in his edition. Bugge, Tidskrift VIII, 297, suggested reading *deor* as an adjective, "brave, bold," referring to Beowulf, and so Trautmann and Sedgefield (1, 2 ed.). Sedgefield (3 ed.) emends to *deaþ gedygan*, "to escape death." But emendation is unnecessary. Elsewhere *deop*, "depths," refers to the depths of the sea, as in Exodus 281, Psalms 68, 14, 3; 68, 15, 1; but there is no reason why it may not also be applied to the depths of the dragon's cave.

2551–2600

2552] Holthausen punctuates this line as a parenthesis, following Heinzel, Anz.fdA. XV, 191. With this construction *hlynnan*, l. 2553, is parallel to *faran*, l. 2551.   **2556** freode] Sedgefield emends to *freoðo*, acc. sing., "protection." **2558–2559**] Sedgefield puts a comma after l. 2558*b*, emends the MS. *biorn* to *born*, and puts a semicolon after l. 2559*a*; see his note in MLRev. V, 288, where he translates, "the earth resounded and burned under the hill." Carleton Brown, PMLA LIII, 916, would also take *biorn* as a verb but with *hat hildeswat* as the subject, l. 2558*b* then being a parenthesis. But *hat hildeswat* is apparently a variation of *oruð aglæcean*, l. 2557. All edd. except Sedgefield read *Biorn* as a noun, the subject of *onswaf*.   **2561** hringbogan] This word undoubtedly refers to the dragon and perhaps means "the one coiled in an arc." Cf. *gebeah*, l. 2567, *gebogen*, l. 2569, and *wohbogen*, l. 2827, as well as Old Icelandic *hringlæginn*, "coiled up," and *hringa sik*, "to coil into rings." Sarrazin, Eng. Stud. XXVIII, 409f., would emend to *hringboran*, "armor-bearer," referring to Beowulf.   **2564** unslaw] The MS. has *un gl aw* with a letter erased between *l* and *a*; it is probable that the erased letter was *e* but, according to Zupitza, "not quite certain." The word *unglāw, ungléaw*, however, does not seem applicable to a sword. Klaeber, Anglia XXIX, 380f., suggests that *gléaw*, "sharp-witted," may also mean "sharp," and that *un-* is an intensifying prefix. See also his note in Eng. Stud. XXXIX, 466, where he gives other examples of *glaw* as a variant spelling of *gleaw*. Klaeber (1 ed.) emends to *anglaw*, "very sharp." Grienberger, Zeitschrift für die österreichischen Gymnasien LVI, 751, would explain *-gléaw* as "bright" and *ungléaw* as "dull (in color)"; he compares ll. 2681f., where Beowulf's sword is described as *grægmæl*. Both these attempts to preserve the MS. reading impose an excessive strain on the meaning of *-gléaw*. Thorpe emended to *unsleaw*; Bugge, Beitr. XII, 104, proposed the more normal form *unslaw*, which he translated as "sharp," and so Socin, Wyatt, Holder (2 ed.), Holthausen, Schücking, Sedgefield, Chambers, Klaeber (3 ed.), and von Schaubert. This emendation is also favored by Hoops, Bwst., pp. 127f., who gives examples from Middle English and Modern English to justify *slāw* in the sense of "blunt" and points out further that the Old Germanic cognates (Old Icelandic *slær, sljór*; O.H.G. *slēwo, sléo*, etc.) may also mean "blunt." Bugge's emendation has been adopted in the text.   2567 winia] Grundtvig, tr., p. 305, and in his edition, suggested *wigena*, and so Trautmann. But see l. 1418, note.   2570 to gescipe] This phrase apparently means "to his fate," *gescipe* being a neuter *i*-stem noun related to *gesceap*. This explanation of the word, first proposed by Grein, ed., is adopted by most later edd. Heyne (4 ed.), Socin, Holthausen (1–6 ed.), and Sedgefield emend to *gesc fe* (related to *scūfan*) or to *gescife* (related to *scyfe*, "precipitation"), with various interpretations, all of them unconvincing. Sedgefield glosses *to gescife* as "headlong." Holthausen (8 ed.) emends to *gescire*, apparently a derivative of *-scear*, which is found as the second element of *guðsceare*, l. 1213, and *inwitscear*, l. 2478. 2573–2575a] These lines are extremely perplexing, and all of the proposed interpretations (including the one given here) put at least some strain on Anglo-Saxon syntax. Klaeber, Mod. Phil. III, 464, is unquestionably right in translating *ðær*, l. 2573, as "if"; but his rendering of the entire passage, in Anglia L, 216f., and in his 3d ed., "if he might have controlled events (with particular reference to the length of time his shield would protect him) for the first time (in his life),—but fate (was against him,) decreed otherwise," does not catch the meaning of the *swa*-clause, ll. 2574b–2575a. Nor is Meroney's translation, JEGPh. XLI, 207ff., an improvement: "if, appearing for the first time (*forman dogore*), it could have controlled [i.e., extended] that period (*þy fyrste*); so fate did not assign it glory in battle." Still less attractive is Klaeber's latest interpretation, in his 3d ed., second supplement (1950), p. 469, which puts a semi-colon after *sohte*, l. 2572, and begins a new independent clause with *ðær*: "There he had to spend the (allotted) time (his time) for the first time (*forman dogore*) in such a way that fate did not assign to him glory in battle." It is to be noted that all of these translations take *þy fyrste* as instrumental object of *wealdan*. The interpretations by Kock, Anglia XLVI, 181, Hoops, Bwst., pp. 128f., and Malone, Eng. Studies XV, 96, rightly take the *swa*-clause as the equivalent of a relative construction, but by not translating *ðær* as "if" they 1ail to establish the true relationship between ll. 2573ff. and the preceding lines.

Kock translates, "now that he lived to see the first of days when Fate assigned to him no triumph in his frays"; his translation of *wealdan* as "live to see" is very doubtful. Hoops's version, "da musste er diesmal (*þy fyrste*) den ersten Tag erleben, wo ihm das Schicksal nicht Ruhm im Kampf verlieh," also assumes an improbable meaning of *wealdan*. Malone translates, "now that he had to conquer in the first fight in which fate was not on his side," or, more literally, "when he on this occasion had to rule the first day in which fate had not decreed for him glory in battle." This translation is much more likely than those previously quoted, and the same may be said of von Schaubert's rendering (glossary, p. 211, s.v. *wealdan*), "als er diesmal zum ersten Male walten durfte, ohne dass ihm das Schicksal Ruhm im Kampfe bestimmt hatte." But all commentators have failed to note the connection in thought between the present passage and previous statements (ll. 679–680, 2506*b*–2508*a*) that Beowulf did not use weapons in his fights with Grendel and Dæghrefn. On those occasions he was destined by fate to be victorious, even without weapons. Cf. *Beowulfe wearð guðhreð gyfeþe*, ll. 818f., and note the occurrence of *hreð* in the present passage. (To be sure, Beowulf used a sword against Grendel's mother, but such inconsistencies are not unparalleled.) The point of ll. 2573–2575*a* is that in his fight with the dragon Beowulf did not enjoy the same protective destiny as before and consequently needed the help of his shield if he were to win. Translate (beginning at l. 2570*b*), "The shield protected the life and body of the famous prince a shorter space of time than his mind desired, if he were to be permitted to prevail on that occasion (*þy fyrste*), on the first day (*forman dogore*) on which fate did not decree glory in battle." That is, *forman dogore* is parallel to *þy fyrste* and is the antecedent (if one may call it that) of the relative *swa*. There seems to be no other example of this relative use of *swa* after a superlative, but some support for the construction assumed here may be found in the sentence *se . . . læg fif dagas beforan þæs mynstres geate, swa* ("during which") *he ne æt ne ne dranc, ac he bæd ingonges*, in the life of St. Simeon in the Old English Martyrology (ed. G. Herzfeld, An Old English Martyrology, 128, 27–129, 2). **2577 incgelafe**] For the possibility that *incge-*, never convincingly explained, means the same as *icge* in l. 1107, see the note on that line. Of the explanations and emendations which have been proposed, only a selection will be cited here. Thorpe, Ettmüller, and Sedgefield (1, 2 ed.) read *Incges lafe*, "the heirloom of Ing," and similarly Holthausen (2 ed.) reads *Inges lafe*. Grundtvig suggested *Ingwina lafe*; Holthausen (3 ed.) emends to *Ingwines lafe*. Holthausen (8 ed.) reads *Irincges lafe*, with *Irincges* taken as gen. sing. of the proper name *Iring* (cf. *Iringes weg*, "the Milky Way," Bos.-Tol., Supp., p. 596, and see J. Grimm, Deutsche Mythologie [4th ed., Berlin, 1875], p. 297). Sedgefield (3 ed.) emends to *mid egelafe*, "with a terrible sword." Trautmann, Anglia Beibl. XXIV (1913), 42, proposed to read *irfelafe* (= *yrfe-*), and this suggestion is repeated by Holthausen, Literaturblatt LIX, 166. **þæt**] Hoops, Bwst., p. 129, would expand the MS. *þ* as *þa*, "then," as in l. 3134, and so Holthausen (7, 8 ed.). See l. 15, note. But a clause of result is not inappropriate here, or *þæt* may be explained as a loose connective; see l. 2528, note. **2579 his . . . þearfe**] "Need of it." **2588 grundwong þone**] Most recent edd. explain *grundwong* as "plain," "floor (of the cave)," following Bugge, Tidskrift VIII, 298, and this interpretation has recently been defended by Mackie, MLRev. XXXVI, 96, who takes ll. 2586*b*–2588 as meaning simply that it was unpleasant for Beowulf to retreat. But if so, the following lines have no pertinence at all. It seems better to explain *grundwong* as meaning "earth" and ll. 2589–2591*a* as an amplification of ll. 2586*b*–2588. This interpretation, accepted by Müllenhoff, ZfdA. XIV, 234, and by many of the early edd., was revived by Klaeber, Eng. Stud. XXXIX, 466, MLN. XXIV, 94f., and is approved by Hoops, p. 275. Translate, "That was not an easy course of action, that the famous son of Ecgtheow should be willing to leave the earth (i.e., to die)." Or, in other words, to stay and fight, and perhaps to be killed, rather than to retreat, was a difficult decision for Beowulf to make. Then in ll. 2589–2590*a* it is suggested that he actually did die as a result of the fight. It is important to translate *wolde*, l. 2588, in its literal sense, "should be willing," and not merely as an equivalent of *scolde*. 2589 ofer willan] Nothing is lost from the MS. here, but it is apparent from the lack of sense that something has been omitted by a scribe. All recent edd. supply *ofer*, following Rieger, ZfdPh. III, 410. For *ofer* in this sense, cf. l. 2409. The older readings, *sceolde wyrmes willan*, in Grein, ed., Heyne (2–4 ed.), Wülker, and Socin, and *sceolde wyrme to willan*, suggested by Cosijn, Aant., p. 35, and adopted by Holder (2 ed.), are metrically doubtful and hardly defensible on the ground of meaning. Carleton Brown, PMLA LIII, 916, would supply *wiþer*, but this is no improvement on *ofer*. 2592 þæt ða aglæcean hy] Sedgefield (3 ed.) and Holthausen (7, 8 ed.) read *þæt hy ða aglæcean*; this transposition had previously been suggested by Holthausen, Literaturblatt XXI, 61. 2593*b*] The punctuation in the text, with this half-line taken as a parenthesis, was proposed by Sievers, Beitr. IX, 141, and has been adopted by Holder, Socin, Holthausen, Schücking, and von Schaubert. Other recent edd. put commas after l. 2593*a* and l. 2593*b*. 2594 niwan stefne] See l. 1789, note. 2595 se ðe ær folce weold] "Who had long ruled over his people." So most recent commentators, following Bugge, ZfdPh. IV, 216. Cosijn's interpretation, Aant., p. 36, "he who was then deserted by his people, no longer had them at his command," seems artificial in spite of the following lines. 2599 Hiora in anum] That is, in Wiglaf (ll. 2602ff.). 2600 sibb] For *sibbe*, acc. sing. See l. 338, note. The subject of *mæg* is *wiht*, and the meaning of ll. 2600*b*–2601 is that nothing can alter the loyalty of one whose heart is in the right place. But Klaeber (3 ed.), note, suggests that *sibb* may be subject of the clause, " 'kinship can never change anything,' i.e., 'will always prevent a change (of heart).' "

2601–2650

2606 are] Not "honor, favor," but "property, possessions." See Kluge, Beitr. IX, 192. This meaning is common in the prose texts, particularly in the laws. 2608 swa] This word looks like a relative pronoun, but it probably means "as far as." See l. 93, note. 2612 Ohteres] So Kemble (2 ed.) and later edd., following Grundtvig, tr., p. 305. 2612ff.] For this somewhat obscure allusion to Weohstan's services under the Swedish king Onela, see Introd., p. xli. Like *þam* in l. 2612, the pronoun *his* in l. 2614 probably refers to Eanmund, though Holthausen and Sedgefield apply it to Weohstan. In l. 2616, *him* is Weohstan, and in ll. 2617, 2619, *his* refers to Onela.   **2613** wræccan] The final -*n* of this word is here treated as a restoration rather than as an emendation, though it is possible that the MS. originally had *wræcca*, as in transcript A. Ettmüller, Sc., and Thorpe read *wreccan*; Grein, ed., first read *wræscan*, and so Wülker, Holder, Socin, and later edd. except Sedgefield, who reads *wreccan*. Weohstan] So Kemble (2 ed.) and later edd., except Heyne, following Grundtvig, tr., p. 306. It is necessary to provide a subject for *wear ð.*   **2615** hringde byrnan] Holthausen and Sedgefield (3 ed.) emend to *brynan hringde* for metrical reasons, following Rieger, ZfdPh. VII, 21. Pope, p. 238, also accepts this reading. Trautmann emends *brunfagne*, l. 2615a, to *hasufagne.* Cf. Riddle 11, 1.   **2616]** The punctuation in the text, with a semicolon rather than a comma after *etonisc*, follows Klaeber, Holthausen (7, 8 ed.), and von Schaubert. See Cosijn, Aant., p. 36, and Hoops, pp. 277f., who point out that *þæt* refers logically not merely to the *ealdsweord* but to all the three weapons which are mentioned in ll. 2615-2616a.   **2617** his gædelinges] The word *gædeling* is usually translated "kinsman." Brett, MLRev. XIV, 5, would, however, recognize here the more specific meaning "nephew." He cites the Corpus Glossary, in which the Latin *frat(r)uelis* is glossed by *geaduling* as well as by *suhterga* and *broðorsunu* (Sweet, Oldest English Texts, 65, 914ff.); elsewhere in the same glossary, on the other hand (Sweet, 85, 1496), *geaduling* glosses the Latin *patruelis*, which would suggest the meaning "cousin."   **2620** He frætwe geheold] Grundtvig suggested supplying *ða* after *He*, and so Ettmüller, Holder (1 ed.), Holthausen, and Klaeber. This emendation was also approved by Sievers, Beitr. IX, 141. Either the demonstrative pronoun or the temporal adverb is possible here, but neither is necessary.   **2622** ærfæder] See l. 373, note.   **2623** guðgewæda] Probably acc. plur., parallel to *æghwæs unrim* in the next line. Klaeber, Mod. Phil. III, 464, compares *wunden gold* . . . , *æghwæs unrim*, ll. 3134f.   **2624** he] That is, Weohstan. But *him*, l. 2623, is Wiglaf.   **2626** guðe ræs] See l. 2356, note.   **2628** mæges] So Ettmüller, Sc., and later edd. except Grundtvig. The same scribal error, *mægenes* for *mæges*, appears in l. 2698.   **2629** þæt] So Thorpe and later edd.   **2631** wordrihta] "Instructions, commands," rather than "appropriate words," as it is usually translated. See Hoops, Bwst., pp. 129f., who points out that in Exodus 3 *wordriht* appears as a synonym of (*Moyses*) *domas.* The translation of ll. 2631b-2632a by Bos.-Tol., p. 1266, "told them much of what they ought to do," undoubtedly reflects the poet's intention.   **2636** guðgetawa] See l. 368, note.   **2638** Ðe] For *Ðy*, "For this reason," and correlative with *þe*, l. 2641. See Rieger, ZfdPh. III, 410.   **2640** onmunde usic mærða] "Thought us fit for great deeds." See Bos.-Tol., p. 756; Moore, JEGPh. XVIII, 211. This is an extension of the common meaning of *onmunan*, "consider worthy (of)," found, for example, in Andreas 895. Kock's translation of *unmunde usic mærða*, "remembered us with honors," Anglia XLVI, 70, is less likely.   **2642** us] Thorpe, Ettmüller, and Arnold emended

to *user*, and this emendation was approved by Bugge, ZfdPh. IV, 216. Grundtvig, tr., p. 306, had previously proposed *ure*. But all later edd. retain the MS.
us, "for us." The *þeah*-clause beginning with this half-line is rather awkward,
but the poet's intention is clear: Beowulf considered Wiglaf and his companions
to be worthy of such an enterprise, even though he intended to undertake alone
the fight with the dragon. 2646 dollicra] Trautmann emends to *domlicra*,
Holthausen (1 ed.) to *deorlicra*. But if *dollic* is taken as meaning "audacious,
daring," rather than in its usual sense of "foolish, rash," there is no reason to
object to it as a characterization of Beowulf. 2649 hyt] This word, which
apparently means "heat" (since it is parallel to *gledegesa*), is not elsewhere recorded in Anglo-Saxon. Kemble II suggested emending either to *ðenden hat sy*
or to *ðenden hit hat sy*. The former of these readings has been adopted by
Thorpe and Sedgefield and has recently been advocated by Andrew, p. 136;
the latter was approved by Bugge, Beitr. XII, 105, but has not found the favor
of any editor. Grein, Bib., was the first to assume a noun *hit*, "heat"; all later
edd. except Sedgefield accept this explanation of the MS. reading. See Holthausen, AEW., p. 161, s.v. *hitt* f.

2651–2700

2652] Holthausen assumes the loss of one line after l. 2652, following Sievers,
Beitr. IX, 141. Müllenhoff, ZfdA. XIV, 235, had previously pointed out that
the comparison initiated by *me is micle leofre* is incomplete. For the MS.
fæðmie, see l. 1981, note. 2657 ealdgewyrht] Klaeber glosses as "desert
for former deeds," Sedgefield as "traditional fairness or justice." Chambers,
who reads *eald gewyrht* as two words, in his note translates *gewyrht* as "ties
through deeds done." Cf. *Adomes ealdgewyrhtum*, Dream of the Rood 100,
where, however, the word refers to Adam's sin rather than to any merit on his
part. Heyne, glossary, translates l. 2657*a*, "das hat er von Alters her nicht
verdient," which is probably close to the intended meaning. 2659 urum]
Thorpe, Grein, Bib., Arnold, and Trautmann emend to *unc*. Sedgefield (1, 2 ed.)
emends to *huru*; see his note in MLRev. V, 288. Grein, ed., emended more
extensively to *sceal unc nu þæt sweord and helm*. But Cosijn, Beitr. VIII, 573,
defends *urum bam* as the equivalent of *unc*. He cites *urne hwelcne*, Pastoral
Care (ed. H. Sweet), 63, 1f.; *ures nanes*, ibid., 211, 14; *urra selfra*, ibid., 220,
5 (see also Sweet's note, p. 478). For the confusion of dual and plural, cf. also
Genesis 746, where *us* is parallel to *unc* in the preceding line. 2660 byrne
ond beaduscrud] Bos.-Tol., p. 138, glosses the MS. *byrduscrud* as "the covering of a shield, a shield," taking *byrdu-* as a derivative of *bord*. Most of the
early edd. retain *byrdu-*, and so also Holder, Socin, Wyatt, and Schücking (8 ed.).
But such a form is very doubtful, and Thorpe, Ettmüller, Arnold, Holthausen,
Sedgefield, Schücking (9–14 ed.), Chambers, Klaeber, and von Schaubert emend
to *beaduscrud*, following a suggestion by Ettmüller, Sc. See also Klaeber,
JEGPh. VIII, 258. Bugge, Tidskrift VIII, 59, suggested *bywdu scrud*, "splendidly equipped armor," connecting *bywdu* with the verb *bywan*; he also suggested that a full line has been lost after l. 2660*a*. Holthausen (1–5, 8 ed.), be-

sides emending to *beaduscrud*, also emends the MS. *byrne* to *bord*, following Cosijn, Aant., p. 36; in his other editions, however, he retains *byrne*. It is at least
strange that no shield is mentioned here. **2665 alæte**] Klaeber suggests *alete*,
preterite. be ðe lifigendum] "During your lifetime." Cf. Exodus 324 and the
prose examples cited by Bos.-Tol., Supp., p. 63 (s.v. *be* II. 3a). **2671 niosian**]
That this, and not *niosan*, was the MS. reading is indicated by the reading
mosum in transcript A; the five vertical strokes in A's *-um* correspond to five
vertical strokes in *-ian*. On the reading of transcript B, see Malone, PMLA
LXIV, 1216, who suggests that only the letters *nios-* were still preserved when
the finished transcript was collated with the MS. **2673 Born bord wið rond**]
All previous edd. except Holthausen (8 ed.) put *born* at the end of l. 2672*b*,
making a compound verb *forborn*. This reading leaves l. 2673*a* too short, and
Kemble (2 ed.), Heyne (2–4 ed.), and most later edd. emend the MS. *rond* to
ronde. But the arrangement in the text, first suggested by Pope, p. 320, is
undoubtedly correct. It is adopted by Holthausen (8 ed.), who, however, puts
only a comma after *for*, taking the dragon as subject of both *for* and *born*. The
meaning of *rond* seems to be "boss (of a shield)," as also in Maxims II, 37.
A. S. Cook, MLN. XLI (1926), 361f., and Hoops, p. 281, would translate as
"metal edge," following Grein's old translation, "margo clypei," Spr. II, 363.
2675 se maga geonga] Because of *geongum* in the preceding line, Bugge, Beitr.
XII, 371f., suggested *se maga modga*, and so Holthausen (1 ed.). Andrew, p.
137, suggests *se maga mæra*. **2676–2678**] The restorations *wæs* and *mærða*
were first made by Grundtvig, tr., p. 306. **2678 mægenstrengo**] Dat.
(instr.) sing., "with great strength." **2684b**] Holthausen, Schücking, and
Chambers punctuate this half-line as a parenthesis, to avoid taking the feminine *hond* as antecedent of *se*; with this punctuation, *se* ðe refers back to *him*,
l. 2683. Thorpe, Grein, Bib., Heyne (1 ed.), and Trautmann emend *se* to *seo*.
But for this lack of agreement of the relative, see l. 1260, note. **2686 þonne**]
Holthausen (1–6 ed.) emends to *þone*, following Bugge, Beitr. XII, 105. With
this reading, the antecedent of *þone* is *meca gehwane*, l. 2685. **2687 wundrum**]
So Thorpe and most later edd., for the MS. *wundum*. But Socin (6, 7 ed.) and
Schücking retain *wundum*, translating *wæpen wundum heard* as "das durch
Wundenblut gehärtete Schwert." Von Schaubert, also retaining *wundum*,
explains l. 2687*a* as "die durch (vieles) Wunden(-Schlagen besonders) scharfe
Waffe"; see also her note in Literaturblatt LVII, 28f. Malone, Eng. Studies
XV, 96, retaining *wundum*, would take *wundum heard* as a variation of *he*, l.
2686, referring to Beowulf: "hard by virtue of wounds (received in battle)."
This interpretation, however, involves an unusual word order. In view of
wundrum fæger, Phoenix 85, 232, *wundrum heah*, Wanderer 98, *wundrum scyne*,
Panther 19, etc., the emendation to *wundrum* seems probable and is adopted in
the text. Hoops, Bwst., p. 130, also accepts this reading. **2690 þa him rum
ageald**] "When he had the opportunity." Cf. l. 1665, Genesis 2008. **2692
biteran banum**] Sedgefield and Klaeber explain *banum* as referring to the
dragon's tusks, Heyne, Holthausen, and Chambers as referring to his teeth.
Either of these seems more probable than "claws," suggested by Thomas,
MLRev. XXII, 73. Trautmann emends to *biteran bendum*, following a sug-

gestion by Cosijn, Aant., p. 37.   he] That is, Beowulf.   **2694** gefrægn]
Nothing is lost from the MS. here, but it is evident that a scribe has omitted
the main verb of the sentence. Kemble (2 ed.) and all later edd., except Grundtvig, supply *gefrægn*.   **2695** andlongne eorl] Sedgefield and
Klaeber gloss *andlong* as "standing upright"; similarly Chambers translates
andlongne eorl as "the earl upstanding." Kock, Anglia XLII, 123, suggests
"the related yarl," "his noble kinsman." But Girvan, MLRev. XXVIII,
245f., is on safer ground in connecting *andlongne eorl* with such phrases as
andlangne dæg and *andlange niht*, which he explains as meaning "while day
(night) was with them." He translates *andlongne eorl* as "the noble at his
[Beowulf's] side," and cites *andlangcempa* (which glosses the Latin *miles or-
dinarius*), Bos.-Tol., Supp., p. 40. Von Schaubert, note, also citing *andlangcempa*, would explain *andlongne* as "excellent."   **2697** Ne hedde he þæs
heafolan] Klaeber, note, explains, "he did not care for (i.e. aim at) the head
[of the dragon]," and this interpretation, first proposed by Bugge, Beitr. XII,
105, is borne out by l. 2699. Cosijn, Aant., p. 37, on the other hand, would
take *þæs heafolan* as referring to Wiglaf's own head. Cosijn's interpretation is
quite possible but is less likely than the other. The dragon's head has already
been shown to be invulnerable in ll. 2677ff.   **2698** mæges] So Kemble (2
ed.), Thorpe, Heyne (4 ed.), and later edd., except Wülker. The scribal error
mægenes for *mæges* also appears in l. 2628.   **2699–2701** þæt he . . . þæt ðæt
. . . þæt ðæt] The succession of þæt-clauses gives a very awkward impression.
Kemble (2 ed.) and Thorpe emended *þæt*, l. 2699a, to *þa*, beginning a new sentence, and so also Rieger, ZfdPh. III, 406f. In l. 2700b, Holthausen (1–6 ed.)
omits the second ðæt, following Sievers, Beitr. IX, 141. Holthausen (7, 8 ed.)
emends *þæt ðæt* to *þa ðæt*, following Hoops, p. 283, and puts a semicolon after
l. 2700a. In l. 2701b, Holder, Holthausen (1 ed.), and Sedgefield emend *þæt
ðæt* to *þa ðæt*, following Grundtvig and Sievers, Beitr. IX, 141, and put a colon
or semicolon after l. 2701a. But the MS. reading of these lines, though awkward, is not impossible, and there is no reason to emend. See Klaeber, Mod.
Phil. III, 464.

2701–2750

2703 wællseaxe] Heyne (1 ed.), Holder, Trautmann, Holthausen, and Sedgefield emend to *wællseax*, acc. sing., following Ettmüller, Sc., and this emendation is approved by Krüger, Beitr. IX, 572, and Hoops, pp. 283f. Cf. l. 1545,
where a similar emendation is made in the present text. But *gebregdan* may
take an instrumental object, as in *ic ðy wæpne gebræd*, l. 1664. It is true that
the adjectives in l. 2704a favor an accusative rather than an instrumental here,
but uninflected adjectives following the noun are not unknown elsewhere in the
poetry. Cf. *þrydlicost*, l. 2869, *behongen*, l. 3139.   **2706** ferh ellen wræc]
"Courage drove out his life." The punctuation in the text, with l. 2706b taken
as a parenthesis, is adopted by Heyne, Ettmüller, Socin, Schücking, Chambers,
Klaeber, and von Schaubert. For the meaning of *wræc*, cf. Genesis 1384ff.,
and for the word order (with object preceding subject), cf. *sunu deað fornam*,
Beow. 2119. Thorpe, Holder, Trautmann, and Sedgefield, following Ett-

müller, Sc., emend the MS. *gefyldan*, l. 2706a, to *gefylde*, parallel to *forwrat* or to *wræc* or to both, and this emendation was approved by Sievers, Beitr. IX, 141f.   Kluge, Beitr. IX, 192, also accepting *gefylde*, proposed to emend the MS. *ellen* to *ealne*, and so Holder (1 ed.).   Cosijn, Aant., p. 37, would emend *ellen* to *ellor*, either construing *wræc* as intransitive, "his life departed elsewhere," or reading *gefylde* with Thorpe, the subject of *gefylde* then being also the subject of *wræc*.   This emendation to *ellor*, also made independently by Holthausen, Indog. Forsch. IV, 384f., is accepted by Holder (2 ed.), Holthausen (1, 2, 7, 8 ed.), and Hoops, Bwst., pp. 130f.   Malone, Eng. Studies XV, 96, construing *wræc* as intransitive, would explain *ellen* as a variation of *ferh*.   2710 siðast sigehwila] All later edd. except von Schaubert follow Grein, Bib., and Grundtvig in emending the MS. *siðas* to *siðast*.   Hoops, Bwst., p. 131, however, explains the MS. *siðas* as the result of the loss of -*t*- between consonants, as in *herewæsmun*, l. 677.   See also Bülbring, Altenglisches Elementarbuch I, § 533; Klaeber, MLN. XVIII (1903), 243f.   For the MS. *sigehwile*, Grein, Heyne (1–3 ed.), Ettmüller, Wülker, Holder, Schücking (11–14 ed.), Klaeber (1 ed.), and Holthausen (6–8 ed.) read *sigehwila* as gen. plur.; Kemble (2 ed.), Trautmann, Holthausen (1–5 ed.), Schücking (8–10 ed.), Sedgefield, and Chambers emend to *sigehwil*.   Bugge, ZfdPh. IV, 217, and Mackie, MLRev. XXXVI, 96, explain the MS. *sigehwile* as gen. sing.; as Bugge points out, a gen. sing. goes better than a gen. plur. with the parallel word *geweorces*.   Mackie translates, "the last of the long period of victory."   But after *siðast* we should rather expect the partitive gen. plur.   Klaeber (3 ed.) retains *sigehwile* as gen. plur. with weakened ending, following Malone, Anglia LIV, 97f., and Hoops, Bwst., pp. 131f.   Von Schaubert also retains *sigehwile*, explaining it as either gen. plur. or gen. sing.   2714 bealoniðe] Restored by most recent edd., following H. Schubert, De Anglo-Saxonum arte metrica (Berlin, 1870), p. 35, and Sievers, Beitr. X, 269.   The final -*i* in the reading *bealo niði* of transcript B undoubtedly reflects an -*e* in the MS.; see l. 2464, note.   2717 sesse] According to Sedgefield, JEGPh. XXXV, 166, the word *sess*, usually glossed as "seat, bench," refers here and in l. 2756 to a stone slab at the entrance to the dragon's cave. Besides the two occurrences in Beowulf, the word is found only as a gloss of Latin *transtrum*, in the Epinal and Erfurt glossaries, where it is spelled *ses*, and in the Corpus glossary, where it is spelled *saes* (H. Sweet, Oldest English Texts, 102, 1021; 103, 2050).   2718–2719] The *stanbogan* are apparently, as in l. 2545, the arches which form the roof of the treasure chamber, but whether the word is subject or object has been disputed.   The earliest edd. took *eorðreced* as the subject, and Kemble II translated, "how the eternal cavern held within stone arches fast upon pillars."   Among recent commentators, this interpretation is accepted by Chambers, Klaeber, Hoops, Bwst., pp. 132f., and von Schaubert.   But Heyne (4 ed.), Socin, Trautmann, Holthausen (1–4, 7, 8 ed.), and Schücking (8–10 ed.), taking ða *stanbogan* as the subject and *eorðreced* as the object, emend the MS. *healde* to *heoldon*, following Ettmüller, Sc., and Rieger, ZfdPh. III, 411.   Holthausen (2–4 ed.) further emends *ece* to *ecne* (= *ēacne*, "mighty").   Schücking (11–14 ed.), taking the *enta geweorc*, l. 2717b, to be the treasure, as in l. 2774, rather than the stone cave, regards ða *stanbogan* and *eorðreced* as parallel subjects of *healde*, supplying in sense an object "it" (= *enta geweorc*). Similarly Kock, Anglia XLV, 119, who would, however, construe *ða* (= *enta geweorc*) as acc. plur. neuter, object of *healde*; he translates, "he saw the giants' works—how rocky arches resting firm on columns, the ancient earth-house, kept them safe within." Kock's explanation of the passage is tempting, since there is no reason for a demonstrative pronoun before *stanbogan*. But the old interpretation, with *ða stanbogan* object of *healde*, seems equally possible. For the tense of *healde*, see l. 1923, note.   **2723** helm] Restored by Ettmüller, Sc., Grein, Grundtvig, Heyne (4 ed.), and later edd., following a suggestion by Grimm. On the reading of transcript B, see Malone, PMLA LXIV, 1217.   **2724-2728**] Most early edd. and all later edd. except Wyatt and Chambers assume a parenthesis ending with l. 2728*b*. Grein, Grundtvig, Heyne, Ettmüller, Wülker, Holder, Socin, and Schücking begin the parenthesis with *wisse*, l. 2725; Trautmann, Holthausen, Sedgefield, Klaeber, and von Schaubert begin it with *he*, l. 2724, as in the present text.   **2724** ofer benne] "Over his wound," "wounded as he was" (Cosijn, Aant., p. 37; Klaeber, Archiv CIV, 287ff.; Chambers, note).   **2725** wunde wælbleate] "His deathly pitiful wound" (Chambers, p. 245). See Hoops, p. 288, who cites Guthlac 990f., *þone bleatan drync, deopan deaðweges* (= -*wæges*), as well as M.E. *blēt*, "wretched," and the modern dialectal form *bleat*, "cold, bleak" (J. Wright, Eng. Dialect Dict. I, 295). Grein, Spr. I, 128, suggested that -*bleat* is a variant form of *blāt*, "pale, livid" (cf. *blatast benna*, Christ 771), and Holthausen (2–8 ed.) emends to *wælblate*.   **2727** wynne] Restored by all edd. It is either acc. sing. or acc. plur., parallel to *dæghwila*.   **2734** ymbesittendra ænig ðara] This line is parallel to *se folccyning*. E. A. Kock, The English Relative Pronouns (Lund, 1897), p. 22, translates, "there was not the king, [not] any one amongst the neighbours, that dared, etc." See also his note in Anglia XLV, 119ff.   **2735** guðwinum] In l. 1810 *guðwine* means "sword," but here the word apparently means "warrior." Trautmann suggests the emendation -*wigum*.   **2736** ðeon] For *ðywan*, "to oppress," as in l. 1827. **2743** geong] For *gang, gong*, imperative. In ll. 1009, 1295, 1316 we have *gang* as the preterite form instead of *geong*.   **2748** gearo] Ettmüller emended to *gearwe*, and this reading is accepted by Cosijn, Aant., p. 41.   **2749** swegle] This adjective, which means "bright, splendid," is recorded elsewhere only in *swegle dreamas*, Fates of the Apostles 32. But Old Saxon *swigli*, with the same meaning, appears three times in the Heliand, l. 3577 (where it is spelled *suikle* in the Munich MS.) and ll. 5625, 5782. Rieger, ZfdPh. III, 411f., proposed to emend *swegle* to *sigle*, parallel to *searogimmas*; Holthausen (1–6 ed.) and Sedgefield (1 ed.) read *siglu*, following a suggestion by Rieger, Lesebuch. Cf. l. 1157. Holthausen (7, 8 ed.) emends to *swelce*, "likewise," following Sievers's unpublished edition of the poem.

2751–2800

2757 fealo] Kemble (2 ed.), Thorpe, Grein, Heyne, Ettmüller, and Arnold normalized to *fela*; Kemble (1 ed.), Wülker, Socin, Holthausen (1 ed.), and Sedgefield read *feola*.   **2759** wundur on wealle] Bugge, Beitr. XII, 105f., would read *wundur under wealle*, citing ll. 3060, 3103.   Cosijn, Aant., p. 37, suggests *wundur on wonge*.   ond]   Trautmann, Holthausen, and Sedgefield emend to *geond*, which gives somewhat better sense.   The correction in the MS., doubtfully reported by Zupitza, may reflect confusion on the part of the scribe. **2760** stondan]   Parallel to *glitinian*, l. 2758.   Ettmüller emended unnecessarily to *stodun*, Holder (2 ed.) and Holthausen (1–5 ed.) to *stodan*.   This emendation was also suggested by Cosijn, Aant., p. 37.   Ettmüller puts a colon, Holder (2 ed.) a semicolon after l. 2760*a*; Holthausen (1–5 ed.), reading *geond* in l. 2759*b*, puts a semicolon after l. 2759*a*.   **2765** grunde]   So Kemble and all later edd., following Grundtvig, tr., p. 307.   The final *-e* is required by both sense and meter.   But *grund*, reported by both the Thorkelin transcripts, may have been the reading of the MS., in which case *grunde* would be an emendation rather than a restoration.   **2766** oferhigian]   This verb is not recorded elsewhere, and its exact meaning is uncertain.   As Chambers, note, remarks, "The general drift is that gold gets the better of man," but beyond this we can hardly go with confidence.   Several emendations have been proposed: Grundtvig suggested *oferhiwian*, "to delude, deceive," and so Sedgefield (1, 3 ed.); see also Sedgefield's comments, MLRev. V, 288, XXVII, 450.   Sedgefield (2 ed.) emends to *ofer hige hean*, "to raise above his soul, render presumptuous."   Kluge, Beitr. IX, 192, suggested *oferhydgian*, a derivative of the noun *oferhȳd*, *oferhygd* meaning "to make proud or arrogant," and so Schücking; this emendation involves the assumption of a shift of stress from the prefix of the noun to the root syllable of the verb.   Holthausen (1 ed.), note, suggested *oferhefigian*, "to oppress excessively."   But *oferhigian* has all the appearance of genuineness, and most edd. prefer not to emend.   Bos.-Tol., p. 734, translates, "overreach every man (i.e. make the effort at concealment vain)."   Bugge, Tidskrift VIII, 59f., and Klaeber, Eng. Stud. XXXIX, 466, suggest a connection with the adjective *heah*; cf. the Gothic past participle *ufarhauhiþs*, "puffed up with pride," 1 Tim. iii.6.   Kock, Anglia XLVI, 182, translates, "overrun, overwhelm." Klaeber in his edition glosses the word as "overtake, overpower," citing the modern forms *overhie*, *overhye* (N.E.D.; J. Wright, Eng. Dialect Dict. IV, 388). Of all these proposed meanings, "overwhelm" or "overpower," approved by Hoops, Bwst., p. 134, seem the most probable.   In any case, the sentence is to be taken as a general and irrelevant comment of the moral sort, perhaps implying simply that the burying of gold does not end its pernicious influence on mankind.   hyde]   Holthausen, ZfdPh. XXXVII, 122, suggests that this word is a hypercorrection by a Kentish scribe of *hede*, "let him guard himself who will."   Similarly Kock, Anglia XLVI, 182f., "let him heed it who will." Malone, in A Grammatical Miscellany Offered to Otto Jespersen (Copenhagen and London, 1930), pp. 45ff., accepting "heed" as the meaning of *hyde*, cites other examples in Anglo-Saxon manuscripts of *y*, *i*, *ie* for etymological *ē*; see also the comments by Holthausen, Anglia Beibl. XLII (1931), 134; Malone, Anglia Beibl. XLIII (1932), 284ff.; Holthausen, Anglia Beibl. XLIV (1933), 26f.   But since buried treasure is the subject of discussion here, *hyde* may very well mean "hide," and l. 2766*b* is then to be translated, "let him hide it who will."   See Hoops, Bwst., pp. 134f.   **2769** leoðocræftum]   "With bodily skill, with skill of hands." Cf. *leopocræftas*, Gifts of Men 29.   leoma] So Kemble (2 ed.) and later edd. The scribe who wrote *leoman* apparently expected a dative form of the noun after *ðam*. Cf. the MS. *on nacan*, l. 1903.   2771 wræte] So Thorpe, Grein, Heyne, and later edd. The scribal error *wræce* for *wræte* also appears in l. 3060.   2775 hladon] Thorpe, Grein, Heyne, and later edd. emend the MS. *hlodon* either to *hladan*, following Grundtvig, tr., p. 308, or to *hladon*, as infinitive, parallel to *reafian*.   2777 Bill ær gescod] The earlier edd. read *ærgescod* as a compound adjective, "shod with brass." See, for example, Grein, Spr. I, 71. With this interpretation *bill ærgescod*, like *segn*, l. 2776, is an object of *genom*, and only a comma is needed after l. 2777a. Thorpe, Grein, Heyne (1–3 ed.), and Arnold emended the MS. *þā* (= *þam*), l. 2779, to *þe*; Ettmüller emended to *þæs þe*, parallel to *ealdhlafordes*. Brett, MLRev. XIV, 4f., defending this older interpretation but retaining *þam*, translates, "he took also the standard . . . and the brass-shod sword, with iron edge, of the ancient lord, from him who. . . ." But Heyne (4 ed.) and all later edd. except Wülker read *ær gescod* as two words, following Grundtvig, note, Bugge, Tidskrift VIII, 299f., and Rieger, ZfdPh. III, 412. With this reading *gescod* is a verb and *þam* (= *þam þe*) is the dative object: "The sword . . . formerly injured him who was protector of these treasures. . . ." Brett's objection to this interpretation, that the poet's audience would hardly need to be reminded twice of the death of the dragon, in ll. 2771f. and in ll. 2777ff., is hardly tenable in view of similar repetitions elsewhere in the poem.   2778 ealdhlafordes] If the MS. *ealdhlafordes* is retained, as by most edd., it is dependent on *Bill*, "the sword of the old lord," that is, of Beowulf. But Rieger, ZfdPh. III, 412, and Cosijn, Aant., pp. 37f., would emend to *ealdhlaforde*, dative object of *gescod* and parallel to the following *þam*. So Holder (1 ed.) and Sedgefield. With this reading, the *ealdhlaford* is the dragon.   2779 þam] Sedgefield supplies *þe* after *þam*. For other emendations of the MS. reading in this half-line, see l. 2777, note. 2784 frætwum gefyrðred] Cosijn, Aant., p. 38, compares *elne gefyrðred*, Andreas 983, and *mid gifum and mid gestreonum gefyrðrode*, in the Alfredian Boethius (ed. W. J. Sedgefield, 9, 28).   2785 collenferð] This adjective must describe Wiglaf himself. Ettmüller emended to *collenferhðne*, referring to Beowulf.   2790–2791 hine . . . wæteres weorpan] Here *wæteres* is apparently an instrumental genitive, and l. 2791a means "to sprinkle with water." See Bugge, ZfdPh. IV, 218, and Cosijn, Aant., p. 38. Kemble II suggested emending *wæteres* to *wætere*, and so Thorpe, Ettmüller, Holthausen (1 ed.), and Sedgefield (3 ed.). Rieger, ZfdPh. III, 412, suggested *wætere sweorfan*, "to wipe off with water," and so Trautmann.   2792] Nothing is lost from the MS. between *þurhbræc* and *gomel*, but it is evident that a half-line has been omitted by a scribe. In view of the alliteration in *b*, one would naturally expect Beowulf's name in the missing half-line, and most edd. supply *Biowulf* (or *Beowulf*) *maðelode*, following Grundtvig, tr., p. 308. But A. Heusler, ZfdA. XLVI (1902), 261, points out that if this is the proper reading here, it is the only example in Anglo-Saxon poetry of *maðelode* in the second half-line. And in spite of the fact that in Old Saxon we find *Petrus tho gimahalde*, Heliand 3136, in the second half-line, the complete absence of the *maðelode* formula in this position in Anglo-Saxon can hardly be due to coincidence. Trautmann supplies *Biowulf mælde*, but *mælde* (*mældon*), used to introduce a speech, is always accompanied by *wordum* (Genesis 2913, Andreas 300, Elene 351, 537, etc.). Holthausen (2–8 ed.) supplies *Biowulf reordode*, citing Elene 417, and so Chambers. Schücking supplies *þa se beorn gespræc*, suggesting that the repetition of the letters *-ræc* may have been responsible for the omission, and so von Schaubert. See also Schücking, Eng. Stud. XXXIX, 110. But Klaeber, note, points out that in Beowulf *gesprecan* regularly has an object. Klaeber supplies *Biorncyning spræc*, Sedgefield (3 ed.) *Beorn geomre spræc*. Another possibility would be *Byrnwiga spræc*. 2793 giohðe] So Ettmüller, Sc., Thorpe, and later edd., following J. Grimm, Andreas und Elene (Cassel, 1840), p. 97. Holthausen (7, 8 ed.) emends to the equivalent form *gehðe*; in his other editions he reads *giohðe*, with Thorpe. Cf. *gomol on gehðo*, l. 3095, where Wiglaf is reporting Beowulf's speech to his companions. Kemble II suggested reading *gehðo* here in l. 2793. 2799 Nu] "Now that," introducing a subordinate clause. mine] So Grein, ed., Heyne, and later edd., following Ettmüller, Sc. 2800 gena] Thorpe, Grein, Heyne, Ettmüller, Arnold, Wülker, Holder, Socin, Holthausen (1–5 ed.), Schücking, and Sedgefield (1 ed.) emend to *ge nu*, apparently in order to provide an unnecessary pronoun. But *fremmað ge nu* is less likely on metrical grounds, and if an emendation is to be made, *fremmað ge gena*, proposed by Andrew, pp. 141f., is better. There can be no objection to the form *gena*, which appears also in l. 3093.

2801–2850

2801 þearfe] Chambers, p. 241, translates ll. 2800*b*–2801*a*, "fulfil still the people's need"; similarly Klaeber, Mod. Phil. III, 264, and Hoops, p. 294, who explain *þearfe* as "what is needed," "das, was man bedarf." But *þearfe* may perhaps better be explained as meaning "advantage, profit"; cf. the examples given by Bos.-Tol., p. 1040, s.v. *þearf* V. 2803 nosan] See l. 1892, note. 2803–2804 beorhtne . . . se] Holthausen (1, 2 ed.) emended the MS. *beorhtne* to *beorht* and *se* to *þæt*, in both cases following Sievers, Beitr. X, 306, who suggested that *hlæw* was an old neuter. See l. 2297, note. Sedgefield, JEGPh. XXXV, 167, note 40, would translate *beorhtne* as "clearly visible, prominent," rather than "bright." 2814 forsweop] So Kemble II, Thorpe, Grein, Bib., Arnold, Holder, and later edd., for the MS. *for speof*. Cf. l. 477. Kemble in his text read *forsweof*, and so Grundtvig, Grein, ed., Heyne, Ettmüller, Wülker, and Socin, assuming a verb *forswafan*, "to drive away, banish." 2815 to metodsceafte] "At their appointed destiny" (Mackie, MLRev. XXXVI, 96), that is, at the time appointed for their death. See l. 26, note. The idea "to their destiny" would be expressed by *on* and the accusative, as in l. 1074*b*. 2819 hreðre] Kemble and later edd., except Grundtvig, emend the MS. *hwæðre* to either *hreðre* or *hræðre*. There is no advantage in emending to *hræðre* rather than to the usual *hreðre*; if the scribe thought he saw *hweðre* in his original, he would probably have altered -e- to -æ-. 2821 guman] So Heyne and most later edd., for the MS. *gumum*. Cf. ll. 158, 2860, where similar emendations are necessary. 2828 hine] So Holder, Wyatt, Trautmann, Holthausen (1, 2 ed.), Schücking, and Sedgefield, for the MS. *him*, following suggestions by Grein, Bib., and Rieger, ZfdPh. III, 412. The verb *forniman* elsewhere (eleven times in Beowulf alone) invariably takes an accusative object; cf. especially *hyne ecg fornam*, l. 2772. Other edd. retain *him*, and Klaeber, Eng. Stud. XLII, 323, calls attention to the construction of *forgripan* with the dative. But *forgripan* proves nothing for *forniman*. Malone, Eng. Studies XVIII, 257f., would retain *him* as a late accusative form. See l. 963, note. The case for the emendation to *hine* is very well stated by Andrew, p. 134. 2829 heaðoscearde] Thorpe, Grein, Bib., Arnold, Heyne (4 ed.), Socin, Trautmann, Holthausen (1–5, 7, 8 ed.), Klaeber (3 ed.), and von Schaubert emend to *heaðoscearpe*, and this emendation is accepted by Bugge, ZfdPh. IV, 218, and Hoops, Bwst., pp. 135f. Cf. *beaduscearp*, l. 2704. It is quite possible that *-scearpe* is the proper reading here, since (as has often been remarked) the MS. *-scearde* may have been written in error under the influence of the preceding *hearde*. But *heaðoscearde*, "hacked, notched in battle," may be defended, particularly since *sceard* is applied to a sword in the will of Æthelstan Ætheling (Kemble, Codex diplomaticus aevi Saxonici, III, 363, 23 f.), *ic geann Ælfnoðe . . . ðæs sceardan malswurdes.* 2830 wundum] "As a result of wounds." Sedgefield (3 ed.), note, suggests *wundrum.* 2836 lyt manna ðah] Klaeber, Mod. Phil. III, 465, suggests taking *lyt*, "few men," i.e., no one, as subject and *ðeon* as the equivalent of *geðeon*, "to attain, achieve." Cf. Maxims II, 44f., as well as the prose examples of this use of *geþeon* followed by a clause which Klaeber cites in Anglia XXVII (1904), 282. But *ðeon* in the perfective sense of *geðeon* is very doubtful. The alternative and more probable construction, accepted by most edd., is to take *lyt* as dative with impersonal *ðeon*, translating, "that has prospered for few men, that. . . ." Cf. ll. 3058f. 2841 wæccende] Thorpe and Trautmann emend to *wæccendne.* The uninflected participle is rare in attributive use but is found also in Genesis 1081 and Daniel 475. 2842–2843 Biowulfe wearð . . . forgolden] "The great amount of treasure was requited to Beowulf by means of his death," that is, Beowulf paid with his life for the possession of the treasure. The same idea is expressed in ll. 2799f., 3013f. 2844 æghwæðer] So Kemble II and most later edd. Translate: "Each one of the two had reached the end of [his] transitory life." Cf. ll. 3062ff.

2851–2900

2854 wehte hyne] "Tried to arouse him"? So Klaeber, Mod. Phil. III, 261, note 1, and in his edition. See *bræc*, l. 1511, and note. Trautmann and Sedgefield (1, 2 ed.) suggest *wætte*, "sprinkled." 2857 ðæs wealdendes wiht oncirran] Chambers, note, translates, "change aught ordained of God," and this is probably the intended meaning, though the construction is strange, to say the least. Kock, Anglia XLVI, 183, suggests that the gen. sing. *wealdendes* is an example of "a strong tendency" to turn an accusative into a genitive in a negative construction; he cites *ic gen ne conn . . . monnes ower*, etc., Christ 198ff. Thorpe, Grein, Arnold, Wülker, Holder (1 ed.), Trautmann, Holthausen (1–5 ed.), and Schücking emend *wiht* to *willan*; Heyne and Socin supply *willan* before *wiht*. Klaeber, JEGPh. VIII, 258, retaining *wiht*, suggested emending *wealdendes* to *weorldendes*, "he could not turn aside (or, avert) anything of the end of his life (in this world)." But in his edition Klaeber retains the MS. reading. **2858** wolde . . . rædan] "The judgment of God was accustomed to govern the deeds (of every man)." Bugge, Beitr. XII, 106, suggested *deað arædan*, "appoint death," for the MS. *dædum rædan*, and so Holthausen (1 ed.). But no emendation is necessary. For the meaning of *wolde*, see Bos.-Tol., p. 1227, s.v. *willan* VII. For the idea expressed by the whole clause, cf. ll. 1057*b*–1058. **2860** geongan] So Holthausen, Schücking (9–14 ed.), Klaeber, and von Schaubert, following Barnouw, Textkritische Untersuchungen, p. 36. The strong form after the definite article is hardly possible. Similar scribal errors are found in ll. 158, 2821. **2863** sec] Thorkelin, Kemble (2 ed.), Thorpe, and all later edd. emend the MS. *sec* to *secg*. But Mackie, MLRev. XXXVI, 96f., explains *sec* as a variant form (with Anglian "smoothing") of *sēoc*, "sick (at heart)," parallel to *sarigferð*. This interpretation gives excellent sense, and there is no need to emend. **2867–2870**] Chambers and Klaeber punctuate these lines as a parenthesis. The syntax is thereby made somewhat smoother, but the punctuation in the text is perfectly clear. **2869** þrydlicost] Most edd. emend to *þryðlicost*, the more usual form. Cf. *þryðlic* (*ðryðlic*), ll. 400, 1627. But Chambers, note, points out that the form *þrydlice*, "mightily," occurs in Bryhtferth's Manual (ed. S. J. Crawford, 46, 5). Hoops, Bwst., p. 136, cites the MS. *þrydge*, Genesis 1986, which probably need not have been emended in the present edition (Records I, 60). To explain the uninflected *þrydlicost* it is not necessary to assume an unexpressed object "it," as Klaeber does in his note, since the meter favors the form without *-e*. Cf. l. 2704, where the uninflected adjectives *biter* and *beaduscearp* follow a noun which is apparently dat. (instr.) sing. **2873–2874** fyrdgesteallum gylpan] Elsewhere in Beowulf (ll. 586, 2055, 2583) *gylpan*, "to boast (of)," takes a genitive object, but instrumental objects are found in Genesis 2017 and Psalm 93, 3, 2. **2876***b*] See l. 201*b*, note. **2878** ætgifan] This verb is not recorded elsewhere. Klaeber suggests *gifan*, and Andrew, p. 136, *agifan*. **2880–2881**] The subject of *wæs* is apparently the dragon, rather than Beowulf. Holthausen (1–5, 7, 8 ed.), following Sievers, Beitr. IX, 142, emends *þonne* to *þone*, introducing a relative clause, and *ferhðgeniðlan* to the nominative *ferhðgeniðla*, subject of *wæs*. With these emendations, no comma is required after *sæmra*. Cosijn, Aant., p. 38, suggested taking l. 2880*a* as a parenthesis, with *mæg* (i.e., Beowulf) understood as its logical subject. **2882** Wergendra] So all edd., following Grundtvig, tr., p. 309. **2883***b*] Sedgefield (3 ed.) supplies *on* before *hyne*. Cf. l. 192*b*. But *becuman* is transitive in *flodegsa becwom gastas geomre*, Exodus 447f. **2884** Nu] Kemble (2 ed.) and all later edd. except Grundtvig and Chambers emend the MS. *hu* to *Nu*. Chambers, following a suggestion by Holthausen, retains *Hu* as introducing an exclamatory clause ending with l. 2886*a*. For this use parallels may be found in Andreas 63, Christ 130, 216, 1459, Wanderer 95, etc. But in view of the continued prophecy in ll. 2884–2890*a*, the emendation to *Nu* is more probable. **2886** lufen] This noun, a variation of *eðelwyn*, is now usually explained as meaning "joy, comfort." Mackie, MLRev. XXXVI, 97, translates, "domestic affection." But either of these meanings forms a poor parallel to *eðelwyn*, which in l. 2493 is a variation of *eard*. Kock, Anglia XLVI, 88f., convincingly explains *lufen* as "tenancy"; von Schaubert glosses it as "das liebe Heim, die liebe Heimat." See l. 1728, Daniel 73, and notes. J. Grimm, Deutsche Rechtsaltertümer (1st ed., Göttingen, 1828), p. 731, suggested that *lufen* is a form of *leofen*, "sustenance" (cf. Andreas 1123), and Kemble (2 ed.) and Trautmann emend to *leofen*. Sedgefield (3 ed.) emends to the adverb *lungre*, with no comma after *cynne*. **2887** þære mægburge] Dependent on *monna æghwylc*. See Hoops, p. 301. **2893** ecgclif] Kemble II proposed *egclif*, "sea cliff," citing *ægwearde*, l. 241, and so Thorpe and later edd., except Grein, Bib., Grundtvig, Klaeber, Holthausen (7, 8 ed.), and von Schaubert. But the MS. *ecgclif* may be explained, with Bos.-Tol., Supp., p. 178, as "a cliff with an edge or brink," though a cliff without an edge or brink would seem to be a freak of nature. See also Hoops, Bwst., pp. 136f. **2895** bega on wenum] See l. 1873, note.

2901–2950

2904 sexbennum] The MS. *siex bennū* apparently resulted from confusion with the numeral *siex*. Kemble II, Thorpe, Grein, Bib., Grundtvig, Heyne (1 ed.), Ettmüller, and Arnold emended to *seaxbennum*; Holthausen, Sedgefield, Klaeber, and Hoops, pp. 302f., read *sexbennum*, which was probably the original reading. Cf. *-fexa, fexe* (for *-feaxa, feaxe*), ll. 2962, 2967. Cosijn, Beitr. VIII, 573, cites the form *forsieh* (= *forseah*) in the Hatton MS. of the Pastoral Care (ed. H. Sweet, 111, 23), and K. Sisam, Rev. of Eng. Studies XXII (1946), 268, note, points out examples of *ie* for *ea* in the Cambridge Psalter (ed. K. Wildhagen, Hamburg, 1910), but the value of these for the textual criticism of Beowulf is doubtful. sweorde] Andrew, p. 49, suggests emending to *sweord* as subject of *meahte*, citing the similar personification of a weapon in ll. 2673f. **2909** higemæðum] This word has been variously explained, by some as dat. plur. of a noun, by others as dat. plur. of an adjective. Thorpe read *hige meðum* as two words, "with weary spirit"; all other edd. print as a compound. Sievers, Beitr. IX, 142f., suggested emending to *higemeðe*, adjective, "weary of mind," referring to Wiglaf; this emendation was adopted by Holder (1 ed.), Holthausen (1, 2 ed.), and Sedgefield (1 ed.), but was later withdrawn by Sievers in Beitr. XXXVI, 419. Grein, Spr. II, 128, assumed a noun *higemæ̆ð*, which he doubtfully glossed as "reverentia, diligentia"; Grein, ed., identified the second element of the compound with *mæð*, "measure," and translated *higemæð* (p. 139) as "geziemende Gesinnung, aufmerksame Sorgfalt." A noun *higemæð*, "reverence," is accepted by Wyatt (who glosses it as "mind-honour, heart-reverence"), Schücking, and Chambers. Sedgefield (3 ed.), note, translates, " 'with balance of mind,' *i.e.* impartially"; see also his note in MLRev. XXVIII, 229. Rieger, ZfdPh. III, 413, would read *higemeðum*, dat. plur. of the adjective, referring to both the dead Beowulf and the dragon; so Heyne (4 ed.) and Socin. Von Schaubert retains the MS. *higemæðum*, with Rieger's interpretation. Kock, Anglia XLVI, 77f., would make *higemæ ðum* parallel to *leofes ond laðes*, in spite of the difference in case. But as Klaeber remarks, Anglia L, 219f., it is hard to believe that the dead dragon would be described as *higeme ðe*. Also, the meaning assumed by Rieger is not supported by *hygeme ðe*, l. 2442, which seems to mean "wearying the mind" rather than "weary of mind." Holthausen (3-8 ed.), Klaeber, and Hoops, Bwst., pp. 137f., accept the interpretation suggested by Bugge, Beitr. XII, 106, who reads *higeme ðum* as dat. plur. of a feminine noun *higeme ðu*, "weariness of mind," not elsewhere recorded. Lines 2909–2910a then mean, "[Wiglaf] holds with weariness of mind a deathwatch over friend and foe." For the adverbial use of the dat.-instr. plur., see l. 1072, note. Bugge's is the most convincing explanation of *higemæ ðum*. It is unnecessary, however, to emend to *higeme ðum*, since *æ* for *ē* (*i*-mutation of *ō*) also appears in *onsæce*, l. 1942, and *æht*, l. 2957. See l. 1942, note. For a more complete account of the scholarship on this word, see Hoops, Bwst., pp. 137f.　　**2911** underne] So Grein, Heyne, and later edd., for the MS. *under*. **2916** genægdon] The MS. *gehnægdon* gives double alliteration in the second half-line, and Holder, Trautmann, Holthausen, Sedgefield, Chambers, and Klaeber emend to *genægdon*, "assailed, attacked," following suggestions by Grein, Bib., and Bugge, Tidskrift VIII, 64. E. von Schaubert, Literaturblatt LVII, 27, defends the MS. reading in spite of the irregular alliteration; see l. 574*b*, note. In l. 574*b* no simple emendation is at hand, but here and in l. 1151*b* the omission of an *h* is all that is required to make the text metrically regular. From the point of view of meaning, *gehnægdon*, "subdued," is quite satisfactory.　　**2919b–2920a**] "Not at all did the prince give treasure to the host." Bugge, Beitr. XII, 106, explains that Hygelac, because of his death, was unable to distribute treasure to his warriors after this battle, as he would have done after a victory. The punctuation in the text, with a comma after l. 2919*a*, follows Cosijn, Aant., p. 38, who takes *nalles* as an adversative adverb, as in ll. 338, 1493, 1529, etc. Most edd. put a semicolon after l. 2919*a*. **2921** Merewioingas] Gen. sing., "of the Merovingian," that is, of the Frankish king. This interpretation, accepted by most recent edd., was first given by Bugge, Tidskrift VIII, 300. Thorpe, Grundtvig, Grein, Heyne, Ettmüller, Arnold, Wülker, Socin (6, 7 ed.), and Trautmann emend to *Merewioinga*, gen. plur. Schücking, Eng. Stud. LV, 95f., would read *merewicingas*, gen. sing., as referring to Hygelac, and so Holthausen (6, 8 ed.) and von Schaubert. Cf. *sæwicingas*, Exodus 333. Grundtvig, tr., p. 309, and Kemble (2 ed.) had previously suggested *merewicinga*. But if the MS. reading is taken as referring to a king of the Franks, no emendation is necessary. For gen. sing. forms in *-as*, see l. 63, note.　　**2922** to] So Thorpe and later edd., except Grundtvig, Holthausen (2-8 ed.), Chambers, Klaeber, and von Schaubert. The MS. *te* is probably nothing more than a scribal error. For the phrase *to Sweo ðeode . . . wenan*, see l. 158, note.　　**2924–2925**] The name *Ongen ðio* is the subject of *besny ðede*, and *Hæ ðcen* the object.　　**2929** ondslyht] See l. 499, note. Sedgefield retains the MS. *hondslyht* here and in l. 2972 but glosses the word under *andslieht*.　　**2930** abreot] For *abreat*, preterite singular.　　bryd ahredde]

In spite of the MS. *bryda heorde*, there can be no doubt that the *-a* belongs to the following word. Grein, Heyne, Ettmüller, Wülker, Holder, Socin, Wyatt, Schücking, Chambers, and von Schaubert read *bryd aheorde*. Grein, ed., Schücking, and Chambers assume a verb *āheordan* (related to *heorde*, "care, custody"), which would mean "to release from guardianship"; so also Bos.-Tol., p. 31. Heyne, Holder, Socin, and Wyatt explain *aheorde* doubtfully as preterite of a verb *āhēoran*, "to liberate." But there is no evidence for either of these verbs, and an emendation seems called for. Holthausen (1, 2 ed.) and Sedgefield emend to *bryd afeorde*, "took away the bride"; see Holthausen's note in ZfdPh. XXXVII, 122. Bugge, Beitr. XII, 107, suggested *bryd ahredde*, "liberated the bride," and so Holthausen (3–8 ed.) and Klaeber. This emendation, defended by Klaeber, Eng. Stud. XXXIX, 427, and Hoops, p. 306, is the most probable reading. Von Schaubert retains the MS. *aheorde* but glosses it as the preterite of *āhreddan*. **2931 gomela]** As this word stands in the MS., it is a weak nom. sing., referring to Ongentheow. Grein, Bib., suggested *gomelan*, modifying *iomeowlan*, and this emendation was approved by A. Lichtenheld, ZfdA. XVI (1873), 330. Barnouw, Textkritische Untersuchungen, p. 40, would read either *gomel* or *gomelan*. All edd., however, retain the MS. reading. **2939a]** Ettmüller supplied *hi* after *he*, to provide an object for *getan*; Holthausen (4–8 ed.) emends *he* to *hie*. **2940 getan]** The simple verb *gētan* is not elsewhere recorded, but the compound *āgētan* is not infrequent; cf. especially Andreas 32, 1143, Brunanburh 18. The use of *getan* with *meces ecgum* in the present passage, and of *agetan* with *gara ordum* and *garum* in the passages just cited, suggests that the specific meaning of the verb is "to cut, to pierce." But this meaning is impossible for *getan . . . on galgtreowum*, and in the present passage we must therefore content ourselves with the more general meaning "to kill." The emendation to *gretan*, made by Thorpe, Ettmüller, Arnold, and Sedgefield (1, 2 ed.) is unnecessary. **2940b–2941]** The MS. reading *sum on galgtreowu to gamene* is obviously incomplete, and it is possible that more was omitted by the scribe than is indicated in the text. In l. 2940b, most edd. emend the MS. *sum* to *sume*, following Thorpe, and *galgtreowu* to *galgtreowum*, following Kemble (2 ed.). Holthausen (4–7 ed.) emends *sum* to *oððe*; Holthausen (8 ed.) emends it to *swylce*. But *sum* may be retained as the equivalent of *sume*, with the final *-e* elided before the following vowel; see l. 338, note. In l. 2941a, Thorpe, Grein, Heyne, and all later edd. supply *fuglum*. Bugge, Beitr. XII, 107, partly motivated by doubts as to the possibility of *getan . . . on galgtreowum* (see the preceding note), proposed to assume a more extensive gap in the text before *to gamene* and to read:

> getan wolde, sumon galgtreowu
> [aheawan on holte ond hie ahon uppe
> fuglum] to gamene.

Bugge's form *sumon*, l. 2940b, is dat. plur. In Beitr. XII, 372, he suggested replacing *uppe* by *up*, assuming a trisyllabic pronunciation of *ahon*. See also his earlier note, Tidskrift VIII, 60f. Klaeber, note, conjectures that the text originally had *sumon* (dat. plur.) *galgtreowu gifan to gamene, geoc eft gelamp*, etc., and that a scribe disturbed the alliteration by substituting *frofor* for *geoc*. Mackie, MLRev. XXXVI, 97, suggests the following reconstruction (beginning at l. 2939):

> cwæð, he on mergenne   meces ecgum
> [Geata cempan]   getan wolde,
> sum' on galgtreowu   [gæsne fæstnian
> fuglum] to gamene.

He explains *galgtreowu* as acc. plur., governed by *on* in the sense of "on to." But although such longer additions may improve the logic of the passage, it is possible to make satisfactory sense with only the emendation to *galgtreowum* and the addition of *fuglum*.   **2944 gealdor**] This word, which appears most frequently with the meaning "charm, enchantment" (as in l. 3052), is apparently used here to refer to a battle cry.   Cf. the use of *fyrdleoð*, *sigeleoð* with the verbs *galan* (of which *gealdor* is a derivative) and *agalan* in Exodus 578, Elene 27, 124.   **2949 se goda**] Bugge, Beitr. XII, 372, finding it strange that the Swedish king should be referred to as *se goda*, would emend to *se gomela*, and so Holthausen (1 ed.).   But Chambers, note, points out that a Swedish king is praised in ll. 2382f.

2951–3000

2951 eorl Ongenþio] "The warrior Ongentheow."   This use of *eorl* in apposition to a personal name is striking.   It would theoretically be possible to construe *oncirde* as a transitive verb, with *eorl* (= Hygelac) the subject and *Ongenþio* the object; but since Ongentheow is the subject everywhere else from l. 2949a to l. 2957a, it is probable that he is the subject here also.   For the form *Ongenþio* as nom. sing., cf. l. 2924.   **ufor**] "Farther away."   See Bos.-Tol., p. 1087, s.v. *ufor* I (b); Kock, Anglia XXVII, 236; Klaeber, Anglia LXIII, 425.   **2953 wiðres ne truwode**] The noun *wiþre*, "resistance," is found also in Maxims I, 53.   For the genitive after *truwian*, see l. 670, note.   **2954 sæmannum onsacan**] "Resist, contend with, the seamen."   The verb *onsacan* should not be connected with *hord* in the next line, as some edd. have done. See Kock, Anglia XLVI, 94f.   **2957b–2959**] Most edd. take *æht* as meaning "pursuit," and Klaeber, Eng. Stud. XXXIX, 467, Anglia L, 220, explains it as for *ēht*, an analogical formation (beside the usual *ōht*) on the model of the verb *ēhtan*. For the spelling *æht*, see l. 1942, note. Holthausen unnecessarily emends to *oht*. With this interpretation of *æht*, ll. 2957b–2958a mean "Then was pursuit offered to the people of the Swedes."   The emendation *Higelaces* in l. 2958b, first made by Kemble (2 ed.) and Thorpe, has been construed in two ways: Holthausen, Klaeber, and von Schaubert, putting no punctuation after *Higelaces*, connect l. 2958b with the following line: "the banners of Hygelac went forward over the field of refuge."   Similarly Child, MLN. XXI, 200, and Hoops, pp. 307f.   But Bugge, Tidskrift VIII, 61, would connect l. 2958b with what precedes: "Then pursuit [and] Hygelac's banner were offered to the Swedes." Wyatt, p. 215, translates, "then was pursuit offered to the Swedes' people, Hygelac's standard [raised]."   Other edd. retain the MS. *Higelace*, with various interpretations.   In l. 2957b, Schröer, Anglia XIII, 346ff., would explain *æht* not as "pursuit," but as "treasure, property," and would emend *leodum*, l. 2958a, to *leoda*: "Then the treasure of the Swedish people, the banner, was offered to Hygelac." Sedgefield (1, 2 ed.) also takes *æht* as "treasure" but retains the MS. *leodum*; he translates, "then was treasure offered to Hygelac, a standard, by the people of the Swedes." Similarly Green, MLRev. XII, 340ff. Sedgefield (3 ed.) explains *æht* as a variant form of *eaht*, "deliberation, parley," and translates, "then was a parley offered to the Swedes, and a banner presented (by them) to Hygelac." It will be noted that these interpretations of *æht* in another meaning than "pursuit" all involve the retention of the MS. *Higelace* in l. 2958b and the beginning of a new clause with l. 2959a. Heyne, Socin, and Schücking, translating *æht* as "pursuit," retain *Higelace*: "da war Verfolgung entboten dem Volke der Sweonen, (ihr) Banner dem Hygelac." So also Cosijn, Aant., p. 38, and Chambers, who in his note translates, "Pursuit was offered to the Swedes and a captured banner [was] offered to Hygelac." Malone, Anglia LVII, 315, also retaining *Higelace* and explaining *æht* as "pursuit," would construe *Higelace* as a dative of accompaniment with *segn*: "then the Swedes were pursued, the banners and Hygelac went forward over that field of refuge." Of all these interpretations, that by Holthausen, Klaeber, and von Schaubert seems most acceptable and has been adopted in the text. A complete translation of ll. 2957b–2960 is: "Then pursuit was offered to the people of the Swedes, the banners of Hygelac went forward over the field of refuge, after the Hrethlings (that is, the Geats) pressed forward to the entrenchment." For the gender of *segn*, see the following note.   **2958 segn]** This noun is ordinarily masculine, but it is apparently neuter in l. 2767, and here it may be taken as nom. plur. neuter, subject of *ofereodon*. Sievers, Beitr. IX, 143, proposed emending *segn* to *sæcc*, and so Holder (1 ed.).   **2960 hagan]** In l. 2892 *haga* means merely "enclosure" in a general sense, or perhaps even "camping-place"; but here it is a military term, referring either to an entrenchment, the *eorðweall* of l. 2957, or, as Cosijn, Aant., pp. 38f., suggested, to the *bordhaga* or *wighaga*, the "shield wall" of Elene 652 and Maldon 102. Cf. *bordweal*, l. 2980.   **2961 ecgum sweorda]** So Kemble (2 ed.) and all later edd. except Grundtvig, who suggested *eacnum sweordum*.   **2964 Eafores anne dom]** "What Eofor as sole judge decided, Eofor's absolute judgment" (Kock, Anglia XXVII, 235f.). As Klaeber, note, explains, Ongentheow was completely at the mercy of Eofor. See l. 2147 and note. Other parallels to this legal phrase are cited by Klaeber, Anglia L, 220.   **2970 þyder oncirde]** Ongentheow was at first fighting with Eofor (ll. 2963–2964a) but was attacked from another side by Wulf (ll. 2964b–2967a). He then turned to defend himself against the new opponent. Eofor does not come back into the fight until l. 2977.   **2972 ondslyht]** See l. 2929, note.   **2973ff.]** In l. 2973a, *he* is Ongentheow; in ll. 2974a, 2975b, and l. 2976a, *he* is Wulf. The *Higelaces þegn*, l. 2977b, is Eofor.   **2977 Let se hearda]** Holthausen and Sedgefield (2, 3 ed.) supply *þa* after *Let*, following Sievers, Beitr. IX, 143. Trautmann supplies *ða* after *hearda*. Cf. l. 2550.   **2978 bradne]** So Thorpe and most later edd. The words *eald sweord eotonisc*, l. 2979, are a variation of *bradne mece*. **2982 his mæg]** That is, Eofor's brother Wulf, who has been wounded. Ettmüller emends the MS. *his* to *hira*. **2985** rinc] Apparently Eofor. **2989** ðam] Restored by all edd., following Grundtvig, tr., p. 310. feng] The verb *fon*, "to receive," with the dative alone is very uncommon, the usual construction being with the preposition *to* and the dative. Ettmüller and Sedgefield (3 ed.) emend to *onfeng*, which regularly takes a dative object, as in l. 1169a. **2990** leana mid leodum] Three or four letters have probably been lost from the MS. after *leana*, at the end of a page. Most recent edd. restore *mid*, as in the text, following Bugge, Beitr. XII, 108. Cf. l. 2623. Grundtvig had previously suggested the restoration of *mid* but had also proposed to emend *leana* to *leanian*. Heyne (4 ed.) restored *fore*; Holder (1 ed.), Wyatt, and Trautmann restore *for* as the equivalent of *fore*. Kock, Anglia XLV, 121f., doubting that anything is missing from the MS., would read simply *leana, leodum*, construing *leodum* as a variation of *him*, l. 2989. That *him* is plural, referring to both the brothers, is rendered very probable by l. 2993a. But as Klaeber points out, Anglia L, 220f., it would be strange if Eofor and Wulf, the chief actors in this episode, were denoted by the colorless *leodum*. All edd. (except Grundtvig, who suggested *leanian mid leodum*, and Ettmüller, who emended to *leanian leodum*) accept the gen. plur. *leana*, although this seems to be the only place in which *gehatan* takes a genitive object. gelæste] So Kemble (2 ed.) and all later edd. **2994** hund þusenda] See l. 2195, note. But here, because of the large number involved, one is naturally hesitant to assume that *hund þusenda* refers to hides of land. Rieger, ZfdPh. III, 415, suggested that the unit of value here is the *sceatt*, and that each of the brothers received the value of a hundred thousand *sceattas* in land and jewelry together. Cf. Widsith 91f. This explanation is accepted by most later edd. But Mackie, MLRev. XXXVI, 97, suggests that *hund þusenda* may mean merely "a very large amount." See l. 1498, note. **2995-2996**] The punctuation in the text, with ll. 2995b-2996a taken as a parenthesis, follows Bugge, Beitr. XII, 108, Kock, Anglia XLV, 122, Hoops, p. 310, and von Schaubert. Grundtvig, Ettmüller, Wülker, Holder (1 ed.), and Sedgefield include l. 2996b in the parenthesis. In l. 2995b, *him* is dat. sing., referring to the king. **2998** hamweorðunge] Mezger, JEGPh. L, 243ff., would read *ham, weorðunge* as two words, construing *ham* as an adverb with *forgeaf* and translating *weorðunge* as "honor, honoring." But the usual explanation of *hamweorðunge* as "home ornament," i.e., bride, is supported by the similar compound *breostweorðunge*, l. 2504. **3000** wen] Supplied by Kemble, Grein, and later edd. Cf. l. 383b.

3001-3050

3001 leoda] Kemble (2 ed.), Thorpe, Grein, Bib., Heyne, Ettmüller, Arnold, Socin, and Sedgefield emend to *leode* as the regular form of the nom. plur. of masculine *lēod*. But the form *leoda*, noted by Sievers-Brunner, §264, is also found as nom. plur. in Psalm 71, 10, 5, and as acc. plur. in Maldon 37. **3005** Scildingas] This word has caused considerable difficulty to the commentators, most of whom explain the MS. reading of ll. 3003b-3005 as meaning that Beowulf was at one time king of the Danes. Heyne, Grein, ed., Wülker, and Wyatt emend the MS. *scildingas* to *Scilfingas* or *Scylfingas*, "Swedes." So also Ettmül-ler, Holthausen (2–5 ed.), and Sedgefield, who, however, put l. 3005 between l. 3001 and l. 3002, making *hwate Scilfingas* a variation of *Sweona leoda.* Klaeber, JEGPh. VIII, 258f., rejecting both *Scilfingas* and the MS. reading, proposed to emend to *Sæ-Geatas*, and so in his 1st ed. Hoops, in Britannica, Max För-ster zum 60. Geburtstage, pp. 26ff., and in Bwst., pp. 78ff., suggested the com-mon noun *scildwigan*, "shield-warriors," and this emendation is adopted by Klaeber (3 ed.) and Holthausen (7, 8 ed.). Andrew, pp. 151f., suggests *hwata scildwiga*, in apposition to the subject of the clause. Klaeber, note, suggests *hwate Scildinga folcred fremede*, with *hwate* an adverb. The MS. *Scildingas* is defended by Moore, JEGPh. XVIII, 212f., who, however, emends l. 3005*b* to *hwates Scildingas* (i.e., Hrothgar), gen. sing., dependent on *folcred*, and puts a semicolon after l. 3005*a*. All these emendations are unnecessary. The MS. text of the passage does not say that Beowulf was king of the Danes; it says merely that he maintained the Danes *wið hettendum*. Malone, Anglia LIV, 1ff., Medium Ævum II, 59ff., convincingly explains ll. 3003*b*–3005 as a refer-ence to Beowulf's battles in the service of Hrothgar. The poet may here be thinking of Beowulf's struggles with Grendel and his mother, or (as Malone assumes) of later fights against other enemies of the Danes. Malone cites Beowulf's promise to Hrothgar in ll. 1826ff., as well as the phrase *freca Scyldinga*, applied to Beowulf in l. 1563. There is, of course, also the possibility that the MS. *Scildingas* was due to a momentary lapse of memory on the part of the poet; in that case, it is no more appropriate to emend here than to emend Keats's lines about stout Cortez discovering the Pacific.   **3007 Nu]** Kemble (2 ed.) and all later edd. except Grundtvig emend the MS. *me* to *Nu*. Wyatt and Chambers, although they emend, suggest that *Me is* is a possible reading, "As for me, As it seems to me." But on the whole the emendation is more probable.   **3010 on adfære]** See Judith 57, note.   **anes hwæt]** "A part only" (Chambers, p. 182), "one part, or piece, only" (Klaeber). Cosjin, Aant., p. 39, compares *anes hwæt to singanne*, "to sing something," Pastoral Care (ed. H. Sweet), 347, 6, and *forþæmþe seldhwonne bið þætte auht monegum monnum anes hwæt* ("any single thing") *licige*, Boethius (ed. W. J. Sedgefield), 43, 29ff. In Old Saxon we find *manages huat*, "many things," Heliand 3172, 3934.   **3012 geceapod]** Restored by Kemble and all later edd. except Grundtvig.   **3014 gebohte]** Suggested by Grundtvig, and so the later edd. The form may be either preterite indicative, with Beowulf understood as the subject, or (as most edd. construe it) the plural of the past participle, modifying *beagas*.   **3015 þeccean]** Holthausen, Anglia Beibl. X, 273, suggested emending to *þicgean*, "consume," and so Trautmann. Sedgefield, MLRev. XXVIII, 230, and in his 3d ed., emends to *þecgean*, "parch, consume, destroy," citing *aþecgan*, Wulf and Eadwacer 2, and *þurste geþegede*, Christ 1509. But Klaeber, JEGPh. VI, 196, observes that the same function of *þeccan*, "to cover," is found in Phoenix 216, 365, beside *þicgan*, Phoenix 219, 505, and he compares metaphors such as *fyres fæþm*, Beow. 185.   **3027 wið wulf]** Kemble, Thorpe, and most later edd. emend to *wið wulfe*, following Grundtvig, tr., p. 311. This emendation is also advocated by Sievers, Beitr. X, 289, Martin, Eng. Stud. XX, 295, and

Pope, p. 321. But either of the two meanings which may be intended here, "in rivalry with the wolf" or "in company with the wolf," may properly be expressed by *wið* and the accusative. The metrical considerations on which the emendation to *wið wulfe* have been based seem insufficient. The half-line *þenden he wið wulf* is not too short, though it is one of the few examples of a B-type half-line with alliteration on the second stress. See l. 779, note. **3028-3029** secggende . . . laðra spella] G. Shipley, The Genitive Case in Anglo-Saxon Poetry (Baltimore, 1903), pp. 65f., translates these words as "the teller of grievous tales," explaining *secggende* as a participle used substantively, the equivalent of *secgend*. A genitive object of *secgan* would be very unlikely; in Genesis 2675 and Phoenix 313, Shipley construes *þæs* adverbially, "according as." **3030** wyrda ne worda] "With respect to facts or words." **3034** hlimbed] For *hlinbed*, "bed on which to recline." The assimilation of *-n-* before a labial is also found in *gimfæste*, l. 1271. **3038** Ær hi þær gesegan] A number of edd. have taken exception to the statement that the men saw the dragon before they saw Beowulf and have proposed various emendations. Thorpe emended the MS. *ær* to *ac*. Grundtvig suggested emending *ær* to *æc* (= *ēac*), and so Holder (1 ed.); Trautmann emends to *eac*. Holthausen (7, 8 ed.) emends *ær* to *Ða*, following Sievers's unpublished edition of the poem. Heyne (4 ed.) and Socin omit *þær*, following Bugge, ZfdPh. IV, 219, to avoid the repetition in l. 3039b. Sievers, Beitr. IX, 143, suggested *þær hi þa gesegan*, and so Holthausen (1–5 ed.) and Sedgefield (1, 2 ed.). Sedgefield (3 ed.) emends to *Næs hi ær gesegan*, "They had never seen a more wondrous creature"; see also his note in MLRev. XXVIII, 230. But there is nothing objectionable in the MS. reading. As Klaeber observes, Eng. Stud. XXXIX, 427, the men would naturally see the dragon before they saw Beowulf, because the dragon was larger. syllicran wiht] For the absolute use of the comparative here, cf. *syllicre treow*, Dream of the Rood 4, and see Klaeber, Mod. Phil. III, 251f. **3041** gryrefah] Heyne (4 ed.), Socin, Holthausen (1–7 ed.), and Schücking restore *gry[regæst]*; Holder (1 ed.), Trautmann, Sedgefield, Chambers, Klaeber, von Schaubert, and Holthausen (8 ed.) restore *gry[refah]*, following Bugge, Tidskrift VIII, 62. Other edd. restore only *gry[re]*. There seems to have been room in the MS., at the end of a page, for *gryrefah* but not for *gryregæst*. **3043** lyftwynne] See l. 692, note. **3044** nihtes hwilum] "During the hours of night" (Earle, tr.). Cosijn, Aant., p. 39, compares *ær dæges hwile*, l. 2320. Bugge's explanation, "at times by night," Beitr. XII, 373, though defensible, seems on the whole less probable. See also Hoops, Bwst., p. 139. **3046** hæfde eorðscrafa ende genyttod] "He had enjoyed the end of earth-caves," that is, he had made use of his cave for the last time. See Sievers, Beitr. XXXVI, 411. Since *nyttian* regularly takes a genitive object, Sedgefield emends the MS. *ende* to *endes*, following a suggestion by Holthausen (1 ed.), note. **3049** omige, þurhetone] Scheinert, Beitr. XXX, 377, suggests *ome þurhetone*, "eaten through by rust." **3049b–3050**] The commentators have had difficulty in reconciling the *þusend wintra* specified here with the *þreo hund wintra* of l. 2278, and Holthausen, Anglia Beibl. XLIV, 227, suggests that the MS. *þusend* is miswritten for *þreohund*. But the text does not say that these treasures had lain in the earth for a thousand years. Krüger, Beitr. IX, 576f., is undoubtedly right in taking *swa* as meaning "as if"; for this meaning of *swa*, cf. Christ 180, 1377, Wanderer 96, Psalm 105, 9, 4, etc. With this construction, *eardodon* is subjunctive.

3051–3100

3051 Þonne] Best translated "furthermore, moreover," as also in ll. 377, 1455. So Klaeber, note, Hoops, p. 316, and von Schaubert. Other edd., following Bugge, Beitr. XII, 374, and Cosijn, Aant., p. 40, translate as "then" (that is, when the treasure was laid in the earth); but with the interpretation of ll. 3049b–3050 given in the preceding note, this meaning of *þonne* has no relevance. eacencræftig] This adjective modifies both *þæt yrfe* and *iumonna gold*, which are parallel subjects of *wæs . . . bewunden*. The edd., by omitting the comma after *yrfe*, obscure the parallelism. **3056** he is manna gehyld] This is one of the few B-type half-lines with alliteration on the second stress. See l. 779, note. Holder (1 ed.) emends to *he is gehyht manna*, following a suggestion by Kluge. Grundtvig had previously suggested *gehyht*, but with no change in the word order. Bugge, Beitr. XII, 108f., proposed to read *he is hæleða gehyht*, to avoid the repetition of *manna*. B. Q. Morgan, Beitr. XXXIII (1908), 110, suggested *he is hæleþa gehyld*, emending only *manna*, and so Holthausen (2–8 ed.) and Schücking. Sedgefield (2, 3 ed.) reads *he is gehyld manna*, following a suggestion by Holthausen (1 ed.), note, and this transposition is accepted by Pope, p. 285. **3058–3060a**] These lines are usually interpreted, and rightly, as referring to the dragon: "Then it was evident that this course of action was not profitable for him who wrongly kept the treasures hidden inside, under the wall." Bugge, Beitr. XII, 109, following Grundtvig, note, explains the passage as a reference to the thief who took the cup from the hoard; he would therefore emend the MS. *gehydde* to *gehyðde*, "plundered." So also Holthausen (1–6 ed.). But it is hard to see why the thief should be referred to at this point. **3060** wræte] So Thorpe, Grein, Heyne, and later edd., except von Schaubert, who, retaining the MS. *wræce*, construes *gehydde* as a variant form of *gehēgde* (cf. *gehedde*, l. 505) and translates (glossary, s.v. *ge-hȳgan*), "dem [apparently the dragon] . . . der unrechtmässig Rache geübt hatte." The emendation to *wræte* is very likely, since the scribal error *wræce* for *wræte* also appears in l. 2771. **3061** feara sumne] "One of a few," that is, Beowulf. In l. 3060b, the word *weard* refers to the dragon. **3062b–3065**] This difficult sentence is explained by Sievers, Beitr. IX, 143, and Kock, Anglia XXVII, 233, who point out that *hwar* introduces an indirect question dependent on *wundur*: "[It is] uncertain where a brave warrior will reach the end of his life." For the omission of the verb, Cosijn, Aant., p. 40, cites *uncuð hu longe*, Pastoral Care (ed. H. Sweet), 9, 3; *uncuð þeah þe he slæpe*, Ælfric's Lives of Saints (ed. W. W. Skeat), 390, 119. A close parallel to the meaning of the sentence is in Exhortation to Christian Living 60ff. (Records VI, 69). **3065** magum] Restored by Kemble and later edd., except Grundtvig. **3067** searoniðas] The construction here, with *biorges weard* and *searoniðas* parallel objects of *sohte*, is rather surprising.

Sedgefield (2, 3 ed.) emends to *searoniða*, gen. plur., used adverbially.   **3068**
þurh hwæt] Not "by what means," but "because of what." That is, Beowulf
was ignorant of the spell which had been put upon the treasure.   See Klaeber,
Eng. Stud. XXXIX, 432.   **3069** Swa] Most recent edd. begin a new sentence here, but Holthausen takes ll. 3067*b*–3068 as a parenthesis and *swa*, l. 3069,
as correlative with *swa*, l. 3066.   Thorpe, Wülker, Holder (1 ed.), Trautmann,
and von Schaubert put a comma after l. 3068*b*, and von Schaubert cites ll.
1233ff. as a similar construction.   diope] An adverb, "deeply, solemnly."
Holthausen (1 ed.) and Sedgefield (1, 2 ed.) emend to *diore*, adjective; see Holthausen's note in ZfdPh. XXXVII, 122.   **3072** hergum geheaðerod] "Confined in [heathen] temples," that is, shut away from the grace of God.   Brett,
MLRev. XIV, 5f., would translate *geheaðerod* as "fenced out (from)," but this
gives the reverse of the intended meaning. Holthausen (1, 2 ed.) emends *hergum* to *hefgum*, dat. (instr.) plur. of a noun *hefgu*, "difficulty," not elsewhere recorded; see also his note in ZfdPh. XXXVII, 122.   But in view of the following
phrase *hellbendum fæst*, there is no difficulty in taking *hergum geheaðerod* in its
literal sense.   **3073** strude] This emendation, first proposed by Grundtvig,
tr., p. 311, and adopted by him in his edition, is accepted by Socin, Wyatt, Holder
(2 ed.), and later edd.   Bugge, Beitr. XII, 374, approving this reading, cites
l. 3126*b*.   **3074–3075**] In these two obscure lines, four problems present
themselves: (1) Do ll. 3074f. form a new main clause, or are they a continuation
of the sense of ll. 3069–3073? (2) Does *he* refer to Beowulf, or to *se secg*, l. 3071?
(3) What does *goldhwæte* mean? (4) Does *agendes* refer to God, or does it refer
to an earthly possessor of the treasure, either the dragon or the man who buried
it (ll. 2244ff.)?   The answers which have been proposed for these questions are
so numerous and so diverse that a complete record of them is more likely to
bewilder the student of Beowulf than to help him.   The following discussion is
therefore confined to the main lines of inquiry.   If *he*, l. 3074*a*, is Beowulf, as
most edd. explain it, then ll. 3074–3075 are in all probability a new independent
clause.   Bugge, Tidskrift VIII, 62f., taking *he* as referring to Beowulf, considers
agendes to be a reference to God (cf. *se agend*, Exodus 295).   Chambers, note,
translates, in accordance with Bugge's interpretation, "Not before had he
(Beowulf) beheld more fully the gold-abounding grace of the Lord," that is,
God had never given Beowulf a greater treasure than this one. Cosijn, Aant.,
pp. 40f., takes *agendes* as referring to the owner of the treasure (the dragon?)
and interprets *est* as the equivalent of *laf*: "by no means had Beowulf with gold-
greedy eyes beheld more accurately before his death the owner's legacy."
Kock, Anglia XLII, 123f., taking *goldhwæte* as the acc. sing. of an elsewhere
unrecorded noun *goldhwatu*, "readiness about gold," parallel to *est*, translates,
"more fully had he not before beheld the owner's liberality and bounty!"
Similarly Malone, Anglia LIV, 5ff., who takes ll. 3074f. as a continuation of the
thought of ll. 3066ff., and translates, "By no means more readily had he observed the owner's [i.e., the dragon's] liberality, by no means sooner had he
observed the owner's bounty." He explains this as an example of litotes—
Beowulf did not see the dragon's generosity at all. He would then explain
the entire passage, ll. 3066–3075, as meaning that "Beowulf was no more aware

of the fatal spell than he was aware of the dragon's generosity." In Medium
Ævum II, 63f., however, Malone would emend *goldhwæte* to *goldhwæt*, as Heyne
(4 ed.), Socin, and Wyatt had previously done, and would translate, "he [Beo-
wulf] was not avaricious; he would have preferred the favor of the dragon."
Moore, JEGPh. XVIII, 213ff., takes *agendes* as referring to God; otherwise his
interpretation is along the same lines: "He [Beowulf] was not gold-greedy, he
had rather regarded the grace of the Lord." This is very similar to the explanation given by Heyne (4 ed.). Moore explains *goldhwæte* as an adverb used where
we would expect an adjective, but the examples which he cites in support of
such a construction are unconvincing. Schücking emends the MS. *goldhwæte*
to *goldæhte* and translates, "Er hätte den Goldschatz, das Vermächtnis des
Besitzers, lieber nicht geschaut"; for a fuller discussion of this emendation, see
his note in Eng. Stud. XXXIX, 110f. Andrew, Medium Ævum VIII, 206f.,
translates, "In no wise would he (Beowulf) rather have looked upon the treasure
at the first" (that is, when the thief stole the vessel), or, as he alternatively
phrases it, "well might he regret that he had ever set eyes upon the owner's
golden bounty." Andrew would punctuate ll. 3066–3075 as a single sentence,
swa, l. 3069, then being correlative with *Swa*, l. 3066. Sedgefield (1, 2 ed.)
emends *goldhwæte* to *goldfrætwe*, following a suggestion by Holthausen (1 ed.),
note, and translates, "he had never before looked more willingly upon gold
ornaments, their owner's delight." Sedgefield (3 ed.) emends *goldhwæte* to
goldwæge and translates, "he (the actual thief of l. 2219) had not previously
looked closely upon the golden cup, its owner's delight," explaining that the
thief had come upon the treasure by chance and was therefore not accursed.
But it is going rather far afield to bring the thief in at this point. Also, both
of Sedgefield's readings require taking *est* in a very unusual sense. Holthausen
(4, 5, 7, 8 ed.), following Sievers, Beitr. IX, 143f., emends *goldhwæte* to *goldhwætes*,
modifying *agendes*; in his 8th ed. he also emends *est* to *æht*. Furuhjelm, Neuphilologische Mitteilungen XXXII, 107ff., suggests taking l. 3074*a* as an ellip-
tical expression, with the verb carried over from *strude*, l. 3073*b*; this half-line
would then be the equivalent of *næs he* (Beowulf) *goldhwæte* ("avariciously")
stread. Furuhjelm would then begin a new sentence with *gearwor*. Such an
ellipsis as he assumes is, however, improbable. Of all the interpretations
hitherto discussed, it may be said that ll. 3074f., if taken as a new independent
clause, seem excessively abrupt, and that if a way can be found to relate them
syntactically to ll. 3069–3073, it should be preferred. On the other hand, if
these lines are a continuation of what precedes, then *he* must be *se secg*, l. 3071,
and not Beowulf. Holthausen (4 ed.), besides emending the MS. *goldhwæte*
to *goldhwætes* (see above), emends *næs* to *næfne*; he also emends to *næfne* in his
6th ed., but there reads *goldhwætne* (see below). Lawrence, PMLA XXXIII,
561f., likewise emends *næs* to *næfne*, but *goldhwæte* to *goldhwæt*, nom. sing.; he
translates, "unless he, rich in gold, had very zealously given heed in the past
to the grace of the Lord." See also Klaeber, Anglia L, 221f., who points out
that if the reading *næfne* is to be adopted, it should take the place of *næs he*
rather than of *næs*. The emendation to *næfne* had previously been made by
Trautmann, who, however, emended the rest of l. 3074 out of all resemblance

to the MS. reading. Patzig, Anglia XLVII, 103f., reading *næfne*, would explain *goldhwæte* as acc. plur., object of *gesceawod*: "ausser wenn (auf) die Goldbegehrenden lieber vorher die Gnade (Erlaubnis) des Eigners (Gottes) geschaut hätte." So also Klaeber (3 ed.). As an alternative, Patzig suggests *goldhwætne* as acc. sing., and so Holthausen (6 ed.). Klaeber, Beitr. LXXII, 124f., reading *næfne* and *goldhwætne*, suggests the translation, "es sei denn, dass die Güte des Herrn den goldgierigen (Schatz suchenden) vorher entschieden(er) begünstigte," or as an alternative, and with a different meaning assigned to *goldhwætne*, "... den goldreichen (durch den Schatz bereits bereicherten) ... begünstigt hätte." For this meaning of *sceawian*, "to look with favor on," see Klaeber's earlier note in Anglia L, 221f. Imelmann, Eng. Stud. LXVII, 331ff., and Eng. Stud. LXVIII, 1ff., ingeniously makes ll. 3074–3075 a continuation of what precedes without resorting to an emendation; he explains *næs* as a variant form of *ne ealles* (cf. *Næs*, l. 562), and *est* as the equivalent of *laf* (as Cosijn had explained it); then ll. 3074f. mean "nor would he have beheld the owner's gold-abounding· legacy more fully," or, as Imelmann himself rather freely translates, "ehe er noch des Eigentümers reiches Golderbe genauer beschaut hätte." This is the most promising of all the interpretations of this passage, since it relieves us of the necessity of emending to *næfne* (which is undesirable in view of the numerous other possibilities) and at the same time enables us to avoid the abrupt syntax which would result from treating ll. 3074f. as a new independent clause. Imelmann explains the *agend* as either the dragon or the last of the human possessors of the treasure; it is impossible to know which of these is meant, but either is certainly more probable than God. The word *est* in the sense of "legacy, heirloom," is apparently not elsewhere recorded, but in ll. 2157, 2165 *est* means "gift," and "legacy" is not an extraordinary extension of this meaning. With regard to the meaning of *goldhwæt*, Hoops, p. 319, points out that there is no evidence whatever that this word can mean "gold-greedy"; the other compounds with -*hwæt*, in so far as they shed light upon *goldhwæt*, all point to the meaning assumed by Grein, Spr. I, 520, and by Bugge, Tidskrift VIII, 62f., "gold-rich, abounding in gold." Cf. especially the compounds *bledhwæt*, "rich in fruit," Riddle 1, 9, and *modhwæt*, "strong of courage," Exodus 124, Daniel 356; the word *arhwæt*, Brunanburh 73, is ambiguous but probably means "rich in honor" rather than "desirous of honor." The form *goldhwæte* is acc. sing. feminine, modifying *est*. Other important discussions of ll. 3074f., not cited above, are those by Rieger, ZfdPh. III, 415f., Bugge, Beitr. XII, 374f., and Klaeber, Anglia LVI, 424f.   **3077 anes willan**] The usual translation, "for the sake of one (man)," does not fit the context. Mackie, MLRev. XXXVI, 97f., explains *anes willan* as meaning "owing to the will of one man," and this is undoubtedly the proper interpretation. In the following sentence we are told that Beowulf insisted on fighting the dragon in spite of the advice given him by his followers. Mackie compares *sylfes willum*, "of his own free will," ll. 2222, 2639.   **3078 wræc adreogan**] So Grein, Grundtvig, and most later edd. Kemble (2 ed.) and Thorpe had previously read *wræca dreogan*.   **3084 heold on heahgesceap**] "He adhered to his mighty destiny" (Kock, Anglia XLVI, 183). This arrangement of the text, with the MS. *heoldon* taken as two words,

was first made by Wyatt and has been adopted by Chambers, Holthausen
(6, 8 ed.), Klaeber (3 ed.), and von Schaubert. So also Hoops, p. 320. Other
edd. either read *heoldon*, preterite indicative, with "we" understood as the subject (so, for example, Heyne, Socin, and Schücking, following a suggestion by
Grein, Bib.), or emend to the infinitive *healdan* (or *healdon*), parallel to *licgean*
and *wunian*. Wyatt and Chambers read *heah gesceap* as two words; Holthausen (6, 8 ed.), Klaeber (3 ed.), Hoops, and von Schaubert read *heahgesceap*
as a compound. It is difficult to decide whether to take this half-line as the
final clause of the sentence beginning at l. 3079*a*, as Wyatt and Chambers do,
or to begin a new sentence with *heold*, following Klaeber (3 ed.).   gesceawod]
Probably "seen, examined," in accordance with the usual meaning of *gesceawian*,
rather than "presented, bestowed," as Klaeber, Anglia LXIII, 425, would explain it. From ll. 3163ff. we learn that all the treasure was put back into the
earth. Grundtvig suggested emending to *geceapod*, "purchased," and so Trautmann and Holthausen (1 ed.).   3086 þeodcyning] Nothing has been lost
from the MS. here, but a word must be supplied to complete l. 3086*a*. Grein,
ed., supplied *þeodcyning*, and so most later edd. Grundtvig, tr., p. 311, suggested *þeoden*, and so in his edition; this emendation is adopted by Grein, Bib.,
Heyne, Arnold, Wülker, Holder (1 ed.), and Socin. Klaeber (1 ed.) supplies
mannan, giving *þone* strong stress and alliteration.   3094 wis ond gewittig]
"Alert and in his senses." It is possible that *wis* and *gewittig* are synonyms here;
see N.E.D., s.v. *wise* 4 and *witty* 3.b. See also Klaeber, Anglia XXIX, 381f.,
where attention is called to similar uses of *gewittig* in Ælfric's Catholic Homilies
(ed. B. Thorpe), II, 24, 12; II, 142, 19. In Beow. 2703, *gen . . . geweold his
gewitte* seems to mean "still had control of his senses." To take the adjectives
in their customary sense, "the prudent and wise (one)," as Scheinert does in
Beitr. XXX, 381, note, seems less advisable.   3096 æfter wines dædum]
Bugge, Tidskrift VIII, 300, and Sievers, Beitr. IX, 144, proposed to emend to
æfter wine deadum, "in memory of the dead lord," and so Holder (1 ed.) and
Holthausen (1–5 ed.). But Cosijn, Aant., p. 41, defends the reading of the
MS. as meaning "in memory of the deeds of our (royal) friend." The preposition *æfter* meaning "in memory of" is not uncommon in memorial inscriptions;
the words *æft alcfriþu*, "in memory of Alcfrith," appear on the Bewcastle Cross,
as well as similar phrases on the Collingham, Falstone, Dewsbury, and other
stones in northern England. Cf. also Beow. 2461, 2463.   3100 burhwelan]
Mackie, MLRev. XXXVI, 98, would give this word the concrete meaning
"rich fortress," citing *botlwela Bethlem haten*, Genesis 1799. See l. 692, note.
Most edd. assume an abstract meaning, "wealth of a castle or city."

3101–3150

3101–3102] Nothing is lost from the MS. in either l. 3101*b* or l. 3102*b*, but both
half-lines are too short, and in each the sense is incomplete. In l. 3101*b*, Kemble (2 ed.) and later edd., except Thorpe and Arnold, supply *siðe*, following
Grundtvig, tr., p. 312. In l. 3102*b*, Bugge, Beitr. XII, 109, emended *searo*
(taken by the earlier edd. as the first element of a compound *searo-geþræc*) to

searogimma, as in the text. So also Holder (2 ed.), Holthausen, and later edd. Cf. ll. 1157, 2749. Trautmann, also reading *searogimma*, emends *geþræc* to *gestreon*. But for *geþræc* in the sense in which it is used here, cf. *firendeda geðrec*, "the throng of (my) misdeeds," Psalm 50, 44 (Records VI, 90). **3104** þæt] Sievers, Beitr. IX, 144, objecting to the consecutive use of *þæt* here, would emend to *þær* and punctuate l. 3103*b* as a parenthesis. So Holthausen (1–5 ed.); Holthausen (7, 8 ed.) also emends to *þær* but takes ll. 3104–3105*a* as dependent on l. 3103*b*. But the construction *ic eow wisige, þæt* . . . ("I will point out the way to you, so that," etc.) is not unlike that in ll. 312ff., *Him þa hildedeor hof . . . getæhte, þæt* . . . , to which no objection has been raised. neon] For *nēan*, "from nearby." **3115** weaxan] If this is the verb meaning "to wax, grow, increase," then l. 3115*a* must be treated as a parenthesis, and so most of the edd. But various attempts have been made to avoid the parenthesis and to take l. 3115*a* as a variation of *gled fretan*. Grein, Spr. II, 676, suggested the existence of a verb *weaxan*, "to consume, eat up," citing the adjective *waxgeorn*, which glosses the Latin *edax* in Ælfric's Colloquy (ed. G. N. Garmonsway), 46, 290. This suggestion of Grein's has been further developed by Cosijn, Beitr. VIII, 573f., Holthausen, Archiv CXXI (1908), 293f., and Krogmann, Anglia LXIII, 398. A number of emendations have also been proposed. Trautmann emended to *wēstan*, "to lay waste, devastate." Holthausen (6–8 ed.) emends to *weasan* (= **weosan, *wesan*), "to consume"; see his note in Anglia Beibl. XL, 90f., where he cites Gothic *wisan* and O.H.G. *firwesan*, "to consume, use up." The reading *weasan* is also favored by Hoops, p. 321. Sedgefield (1, 2 ed.), note, suggested that the MS. *weaxan* is the equivalent of *wascan*, used here in the sense "to bathe, envelop." In MLRev. XXVIII, 230, and in his 3d ed., Sedgefield emends to *weaxen*, past participle, and translates, "the sooty flame full-grown." Von Schaubert also emends to *weaxen* but interprets l. 3115*a* as an absolute participial construction in the nominative and translates, "wenn die dunkle Lohe mächtig geworden ist." See l. 31, note. Andrew, p. 141, suggests *weaxwonna leg*, "dull or murky yellow flame." But it seems best to retain the infinitive *weaxan*, as meaning either "grow" or "consume"; and in view of the strong possibility that a verb *weaxan*, "to consume," existed in Anglo-Saxon, parentheses have been omitted in the text. **3116** isernscure] The noun *scūr*, "shower," is regularly masculine in Anglo-Saxon, but Gothic *skūra* and O. Icel. *skúr* are both feminine. **3119** flane] The *flan* is here distinguished from the *sceft* in the preceding line. Moore, in Klaeber Misc., p. 212, explains *flan* as "barb, arrowhead"; for this meaning, not recorded in Bos.-Tol. or Bos.-Tol., Supp., he cites the passage *twa flana of þam strælum scuton on þas cyninges eagan*, in the life of St. Christopher in the same MS. (ed. S. Rypins, Three Old English Prose Texts, 72, 7ff.). **3122** tosomne] Kemble (2 ed.) and most later edd. restore [*to*]*somne*, but Grein, ed., Ettmüller, Wyatt, Chambers, Holthausen (7, 8 ed.), and von Schaubert restore [*æt*]*somne*, and so also Hoops, p. 322. With *acigan*, "to summon, call forth," and in clauses involving motion generally (as in l. 2568), *tosomne* is more normal than *ætsomne*, which regularly means "together" merely in the sense of "in a group, at the same time," and translates the Latin *simul, pariter*, etc. For

other examples of *tosomne* as used here, cf. Daniel 468, Andreas 1093.   **3124**
hilderinca]   The earlier edd. retained the MS. *hilderinc*, putting *sum* in the
first half-line. This reading is defended by Cosijn, Aant., p. 41, and Moore,
JEGPh. XVIII, 215f., who cite Whale 12, Riddle 3, 33, Psalm 57, 4, 4, etc.
But of recent edd. only von Schaubert retains the MS. reading. Ettmüller,
Sc., emended to *hilderinca*, without comment, but put no punctuation after
it, apparently making it dependent on *sum*, l. 3124*b*. Sievers, Beitr. IX, 144,
also proposed to emend to *hilderinca*, but with a colon after it, making it dependent on *eahta sum*, l. 3123*a*. Holder, Trautmann, Holthausen, Schücking
(9–14 ed.), Sedgefield, Chambers, and Klaeber also emend to *hilderinca*, following Sievers's interpretation. For the construction assumed here, cf. *feara sum
. . .wisra monna*, ll. 1412f.   **3126** Næs ða on hlytme]   "It was not according
to lot," that is, they did not wait to decide who should be first. For this function of *on*, cf. *on cyninges dome, on his agenan gewealde*, and other phrases cited
from prose texts by Klaeber, Anglia L, 223.   **3127** orwearde]   It is unnecessary to emend to *orweardne* here, or to *lænne* in l. 3129, since the MS. forms can
be neuter, agreeing with "it" (= *hord*) understood. The construction of *ænigne
dæl*, in apposition to "it," is similar to that of *fela*, in apposition to *hie*, in l. 694.
3130 ofostlice]   Restored by Thorpe and later edd., following Ettmüller, Sc.
3134 þa]   For the MS. þ̄, Thorkelin, Kemble (2 ed.), Sedgefield, Chambers,
Klaeber, and Holthausen (7, 8 ed.) read *þa*. Trautmann emends to *þon*
(= *þonne*), other edd. to *þær*, following Kemble II. Of these three possible
emendations, *þa* seems the most probable; cf. l. 15, where many edd. have
emended the MS. þ̄ to *þa*.   **3135** æþeling boren]   So Grein and most later
edd., following Ettmüller, Sc. Kemble (2 ed.), Thorpe, Grundtvig, and Arnold
emended to *æþeling geboren*, apparently taking the final -e of the MS. *æþelinge*
as a scribal error for *ge*-. For metrical reasons, Barnouw, Textkritische Untersuchungen, p. 9, would supply *ond se* before *æþeling*; Trautmann supplied *ond*.
Malone, Anglia LVII, 315, would retain the MS. *æþelinge* and explain it as a
dative of accompaniment serving as a variation of *hilderinc*. Bugge, Beitr.
XII, 109f., suggested that the scribe's copy had *æþelingc*, and Trautmann and
von Schaubert emend to *æþelingc*.   **3136** hilderinc]   Nothing has been lost
from the MS. at this point, but the MS. *hilde* is inadequate for both sense and
meter. All recent edd. read *hilderinc*, as in the text, following Ettmüller, Sc.
The emendation *hildedeor*, suggested by Grundtvig, tr., p. 312, and adopted by
Kemble, Grein, Bib., and Grundtvig, is also possible. Reading *hilderinc*, we
have a variation of *æþeling*; reading *hildedeor*, we have an adjective parallel to
har.   **3139** helmum]   So Grein and later edd. It is impossible to read
helmbehongen as a compound, as the earliest edd. did, because of the following
datives -*bordum* and *byrnum*.   behongen]   Trautmann, Holthausen (1 ed.),
and Sedgefield emend to *behengon*, preterite, to avoid the lack of agreement in
the MS. reading *behongen*. But cf. l. 2704, where the uninflected adjectives
biter and *beaduscearp* follow a noun which is apparently dat. (instr.) sing.
3144 wudurec]   Restored by Kemble and all later edd.   **3145** swioðole]   So
Grein and most later edd., as the equivalent of *swaþule*, l. 782. But the MS.
swic ðole may be a corruption of *swiolo ðe*, as Bouterwek, ZfdA. XI, 84, suggested;

cf. *sweoloðe*, l. 1115, and the other examples of *sweoloþ, swoloþ* cited by Bos.-Tol., p. 948. Trautmann emends to *swioloðe*.   leg] So Thorpe and most later edd., as parallel to *wudurec*. Bugge, Beitr. XII, 110, emends to *lec*, preterite of *lācan*, and so Trautmann, who also emends *swogende* to *sworcende*, "dunkelnd." Cf. *lacende lig*, Daniel 475, Elene 580, 1110, etc. Bugge's interpretation of l. 3146*b* provides a subject for *lec*; see the note on that line. **3146 wope]** Trautmann emends to *wylme*, Sedgefield (3 ed.) to *woþe*, "with a loud noise." But the MS. *wope bewunden*, "(the roaring flame) encircled by the sound of weeping," gives satisfactory sense.   windblond gelæg] Most edd. punctuate this half-line as a parenthesis, "the tumult of winds had subsided." But many commentators have doubted that the flame would be so strong in the absence of a wind, and J. Grimm in 1849 suggested the addition of *ne* after *windblond*; see his Kleinere Schriften II (Berlin, 1865), 263. Bugge, Beitr. XII, 110, proposed to emend to *windblonda leg* as subject of *lec* (his reading for the MS. *let* in l. 3145*b*). But Cosijn, Aant., pp. 41f., and Kock, Anglia XLII, 124, defend the MS. reading, explaining *gelæg* as pluperfect in sense. See also Klaeber, Anglia Beibl. L, 332, who explains that the wind subsided when the lamentation set in, so that the wailing could be clearly heard, and suggests that *windblond gelæg* serves the same purpose in the narrative as *swigedon ealle* in l. 1699.   **3147 ða banhus]** See l. 1116, note.   **3149 cwealm]** Restored by Kemble and later edd.   **3150ff.]** The last word on fol. 201*a* is *giomorgyd*. Fol. 201*b*, the last page of Beowulf, is in very bad condition, and according to Zupitza almost all that is legible to the unaided eye has been freshened up by a later hand. But the new readings of this page, made by A. H. Smith in 1938 with the help of ultraviolet light (London Mediaeval Studies I, 202ff.), represent a great improvement over what had previously been possible by ordinary visual observation. In some places, however, Smith failed to make out as much of the MS. text as his predecessors had done. Although the report of the MS. readings of ll. 3150*b*–3182 given in the text is based primarily on Smith's transcript, I have also used the Thorkelin transcripts, the collation by Kölbing, Archiv LVI, 117, Zupitza's transcript, and the diplomatic text printed by Wülker. The restoration of ll. 3150*b*–3155*a* follows Pope, pp. 232ff.   **3150b]** The letters *-iat-* reported by Smith probably reflect a MS. reading *-eat-*, part of the *e* being illegible even under ultraviolet light. For the ease with which an *e* in the hand of the second scribe may be misread as *i*, see l. 2464, note. Pope's restoration *Geatisc meowle* is therefore more probable than Zupitza's *seo* (or *sio*) *geomeowle*, though it does not explain the letters *an'* (= Latin *anus*, "old woman") written above the line.

3151–3182

3151a] Bugge, Beitr. XII, 110, restored *æfter Beowulfe* for l. 3151*a*, and this may well have been the MS. reading. Cf. the similar use of *æfter* in ll. 2461, 2463. But Pope, after a study of Smith's photographs of this page, reports "*æ* (?) and a very clear *d* shortly after *meowle*" and suggests either *bræd on bearhtme*, "chanted clamorously," or *bræd ond bodode*. For this use of *bregdan* he compares Guthlac 906, Meters 13, 47. Klaeber, Beitr. LXXII, 125f., suggests *bodode biornum*, with l. 3152 to be punctuated as a parenthesis. In view of the various possibilities, it is inadvisable to adopt a definite restoration in the text. 3152 song] First restored by Bugge, Beitr. XII, 110. swiðe] The Thorkelin transcripts have *sælde*, and so also Kölbing and Wülker. Zupitza reported *sælðe*, Smith *s*- and *-lðe*. But according to Pope, all of *swiðe* can be made out in Smith's photographs except the *w*. Since *swiðe* is a very probable reading, it is adopted in the text. Cf. Wanderer 56, Solomon and Saturn 437, A Prayer 62 (Records VI, 96), etc. geneahhe] Kölbing, Wülker, and Zupitza report *-he* as visible; Smith was apparently unable to see it. 3153 heofungdagas] The restoration *heregeongas* (= *heregangas*, "raiding attacks"), made by Mackie, MLRev. XXXVI, 98, is, from the evidence of the spacing of the MS., less probable than Pope's *heofungdagas*. Klaeber (3 ed.), supplement (1941), p. 459, proposed *hefige dagas*, which is also possible. ondrede] First restored by Bugge, Beitr. XII, 110. 3155 hynðo] Smith reports *hȳðo* as the MS. reading; Kölbing, Wülker, and Zupitza report *hyðo*. hæftnyd] First restored by Bugge, Beitr. XII, 110. swealg] The letters *swe*- and *-lg* are reported by Zupitza (the *w* doubtfully), but not by Smith. All recent edd. restore *swe[a]lg*, following Ettmüller, Sc. 3156 Geworhton] The letters *ge*- are reported by the Thorkelin transcripts and by Zupitza, but not by Smith. 3157a] The edd., except von Schaubert, read *hlæw* as the first word in this half-line, and *hlæw* is reported as the MS. reading by Kölbing and Wülker. But Smith reports *hleo*, and Zupitza also believed that the last two letters of the word were *-eo*. Pope, p. 232, accepts *hlæw*, which is supported by ll. 2802, 3169. The third word in the half-line is reported by Smith as *hoe*. There is no objection to this word here, though it is not found elsewhere in the poetry. See the examples of *hōh*, "promontory," in Bos.-Tol., Supp., p. 557, to which may be added the acc. plur. *hos* at fol. 116*b*, l. 9, of this same manuscript (ed. S. Rypins, Three Old English Prose Texts, 36, 9). Transcript B reports *liðe* as the MS. reading; Zupitza reports *lide*, freshened up from an original *liðe*; Kölbing and Wülker report *lide*. Holthausen (8 ed.), p. 126, believes that Smith's photographs show *liðe* rather than *hoe*. Most edd., accepting *liðe* as the MS. reading, emend to *hliðe*. Von Schaubert accepts Smith's reading *hleo on hoe* for l. 3157a, and so the present text. wæs] The *w*- is reported by Kölbing and Wülker, but not by Smith; to Zupitza it was "scarcely legible." 3158 wægliðendum] This word is printed in the text on the authority of Wülker. Zupitza was apparently able to see only the *g* of *wæg*-, Smith only the *g* and the second half of *æ*. The letters *-liðendum* have been clearly visible to all students of the MS. gesyne] The first *e* of this word, not legible to Zupitza and Smith, is printed here on Kölbing's authority. Wülker also reported this *e*, but doubtfully. According to Kölbing, there are two dots in the MS. above *ge*-; no one else has observed these dots. 3160 lafe] All of this word is reported by Zupitza, who says that the letters *-afe* are "very faint"; Smith reports only *l* and *f*. 3162 foresnotre] All of this word is reported by Zupitza, who says that the letters *-re-* (at the end of a line in the MS.) are "very faint" and that *-s-* (at the beginning of the next line) is "very indistinct";

Smith reports only *fo-* and *-notre*.   3163 beg]   We would expect *begas* here, as acc. plur., and Thorpe and Arnold emend to *beagas*, Trautmann and Holthausen to *begas*.   But Klaeber, Mod. Phil. III, 250, explains *beg* as a collective singular form; in Anglia LXIII, 425, he cites *bryd and begas*, Genesis 1876 (where *bryd* seems to stand for the plural *bryde, bryda*; cf. the plurals in Genesis 1972), as a similar case.   3164 eall swylce hyrsta, swylce]   "All such of treasures, as. . . ." For the correlative use of *swylc . . . swylc*, cf. ll. 1249, 1328f.   3166 eorðan]   All of this word is reported by transcript A and by Zupitza, and *-rðan* by Kölbing, but only *-ðan* by Smith.   Wülker reports the *-r-* as only partially preserved.   3168 swa hit æror wæs]   This restoration, made by Kemble (2 ed.) and most later edd., is in all probability right, in spite of the fact that Smith reports the first two letters after *swa* as *he-* rather than *hi-*. Holthausen (8 ed.) restores *swa he[om ær]or wæs*, in accordance with Smith's reading; see also his note in Studia Neophilologica XIV, 160.   This restoration is quite satisfactory so far as sense is concerned, but it is doubtful whether there is room in the MS. for *he[om ær]or*.   Furthermore, the dat. plur. form *heom* does not occur elsewhere in Beowulf.   It is also possible that Smith's reading *he-* is wrong.   The two Thorkelin transcripts and Zupitza report *hi-*.   Under the circumstances, it seems best to accept only the initial *h-* of the pronoun and the *-or* of *æror* as certain in the MS.   3170 æpelinga bearn]   The whole of these two words is reported by Zupitza, but only *æpeling-* and *-rn* by Smith. twelfe]   So most recent edd., following Ettmüller, Sc.   Klaeber, MLN. XVI, 32f., translates *ealra twelfe* as "twelve of the entire body."   3171a ceare] Grein and most later edd. restore *ceare*.   Klaeber restores *care*, and Sedgefield (2, 3 ed.) *hie*, but these words are too short for the space available in the MS., and Sedgefield's *hie* is extremely doubtful on stylistic grounds.   For the phrase *ceare cwiðan*, cf. Wanderer 9.   3171b]   In the MS. the text of this half-line appears to be either *kyning mænan* or else *cyning mænan* closely preceded by a vertical stroke.   Transcript A and Kölbing report *scyning mænan*, apparently interpreting the vertical stroke as a long *s*.   Transcript B, Wülker, Zupitza, and Smith report *kyning mænan*.   Most edd. accept *kyning mænan* as the MS. reading, and Holder (2 ed.), Trautmann, Holthausen (2–7 ed.), Klaeber, and Sedgefield (3 ed.) supply *ond* before *kyning* for metrical reasons, following Bugge, Beitr. XII, 111f.   But Sievers, Beitr. X, 232, and Pope, p. 350, suggest the possibility that the vertical stroke of *k* is the remnant of an abbreviation for *ond* which once stood in the MS.   Holthausen (1, 8 ed.), accepting this suggestion, reads *ond cyning mænan*.   3172 wer]   Restored by Grein and most later edd.   Socin restores *w[el]*, as an adverb, following Bugge, Beitr. XII, 112; Trautmann restores *w[ean]*.   sprecan]   All of this word is reported by the Thorkelin transcripts and by Wülker and Zupitza, but only *s-* and *-an* by Smith. 3174 duguðum]   An adverbial dat. plur. Chambers, p. 191, translates, "doughtily."   Cf. *dugeðum demað*, Genesis 1718.   But Malone, Eng. Studies XV, 151, would explain the word as a dative of accompaniment serving as a variation of *ellenweorc*.   swa]   Holthausen (1–4 ed.), Schücking, and Sedgefield begin a new sentence with this word.   gedefe]   Restored by Kemble (2 ed.) and later edd., except Grundtvig.   Zupitza reports *ḡ-* and "only indistinct traces" of -*de*-; Smith reports *g̃d*-. 3175 herge] The initial *h*- is reported by the Thorkelin transcripts and by Zupitza, but not by Smith. 3177 lichaman] Smith reports the -*i*- as "certain"; Zupitza had read *lachaman*, saying that the first *a* was probably on an original *i*. læded] Restored by Holthausen (2–6 ed.), Chambers, and Klaeber, following a suggestion by Trautmann. Cf. Soul and Body 21 (both texts). Holder (2 ed.), Trautmann, Holthausen (1, 7, 8 ed.), and Sedgefield restore *lysed*, following a suggestion by Kluge. Kemble (2 ed.), Grein, Heyne, Wülker, Holder (1 ed.), Socin, Wyatt, and Schücking (8–10 ed.) restore *læne*, a less probable reading than either of the participles. The restoration *leored*, "passed away," suggested by Kock, Anglia XLV, 117f., is also unlikely, since the verb *lēoran* is intransitive. 3179 hlafordes] The letters -*e*- and part of -*s* are reported by Zupitza but not by Smith. Transcript B reports the entire word. hryre] Restored by Thorpe and later edd., except Grundtvig. 3180 wyruldcyninga] Transcript B and Zupitza report all of -*cyning* as visible in the MS., but the letters -*ng* were not visible to Smith. The emendation to *wyruldcyninga* is made by Kemble and most later edd. 3181 monð̄wærust] Restored by all edd., following Grundtvig, tr., p. 312. No other restoration is possible, in view of the letters -*dr*- (an obvious misreading of -ð̄*w*-) in both the Thorkelin transcripts.

NOTES ON JUDITH

1–50

Judith] For a discussion of the literary problems connected with this poem, see Introd., p. lix. 1 tweode] It is probable that more than two-thirds of the poem has been lost from the MS.; for an estimate of the extent of the missing matter, see Introd., p. lxi. All previous edd. read *tweode gifena* as l. 1*b*. Grein supplied *No tirmetodes* as l. 1*a*, and Körner supplied the metrically impossible *Torhtes tirfruman no*, citing Christ 206. But any attempt to provide a beginning for this sentence is sheer guesswork, beyond the certainty that there was a negative to go with *tweode*. The arrangement in the text, with *gifena* at the beginning of l. 2*a*, follows Kaluza, Eng. Stud. XXI, 384, and Pope, p. 126, note 12. The resulting half-line has three alliterating words, a pattern not elsewhere found, but there are other metrical irregularities in the text of this poem. 4 hyldo] Cook construes this word as gen. sing., dependent on *þearfe*. So also Körner, who translates, "da sie hatte das grösste Bedürfniss nach der (am meisten bedurfte der) Huld des höchsten Richters." But Bright, MLN. IV, 243f., and Holthausen, Literaturblatt X, 448, take *hyldo* as acc. sing., parallel to *mundbyrd*, and put a comma after l. 3*b*. This punctuation is preferable to that of Körner and Cook and is followed in the text. hehstan . . . hehstan] Ettmüller, Sc., suggested emending *hehstan*, l. 4*b*, to either *hæð̄enes* or *hæð̄enan*. But as Rieger, note, pointed out, a similar verbal repetition is to be found in *beorhtra . . . beorhtan*, l. 340. Cf. also *drencte . . . oferdrencte*, ll. 29–31. 5–6 ð̄æs . . . þe] "On this account, that. . . ." 7 Holofernus]

This name, which appears here and in ll. 21, 46, 180, 250, 336, regularly has vocalic alliteration. (For the problem of l. 250*b*, see the note on that line.) But it seems unnecessary to normalize to *Olofernus*, as some edd. have done; see Beow. 499, note. 9] Since we should expect *swæsendo* to alliterate, Holthausen, Eng. Stud. XXXVII, 202, proposed to emend the MS. *gumena* to *secga*; Trautmann (in Schmitz, Anglia XXXIII, 38f.) suggested reading *girwan gilpswæsendo* or *girwan gliwswæsendo* for l. 9*a*. But Judith, like the Battle of Maldon and other late poems, does not always conform strictly to the older alliterative practices. Klaeber, Anglia LIII, 229f., calls attention to the "curiously modern ring" in the expression *girwan up* (cf. the modern "serve up," etc.). 12 ræswan] Probably nom. plur., parallel to *hie* and *rondwiggende*, and it is so construed by Cook and by Grein-Köhler, p. 545. It may, however, be dat. sing., parallel to *þeodne*. dogore] Cook and Kluge (2–4 ed.) emend to *dogor* for metrical reasons, following Luick, Beitr. XI, 491. 16 weagesiðas] This word may mean either "companions in misery" or "companions in crime," but the latter meaning is rendered very probable by the occurrence of *weagesyþ* as a gloss of the Latin word *satelles* in Prudentius' Peristephanon V.13, found in MS. Auct. F.3.6 in the Bodleian Library (A.S. Napier, Old English Glosses [Oxford, 1900], p. 212). The passage in Prudentius is: *Cum te satelles idoli, Praecinctus atris legibus, Litare divis gentium Ferro et catenis cogeret.* . . . The two other occurrences of *weagesið* are in the Wulfstan homilies (ed. A. S. Napier, 145, 4; 225, 33), both times in the plural and referring to the companions of the devil in hell. 20 þeah . . . wende] Referring back to *fæge*, l. 19. That is, Holofernes did not suspect that he and his warriors were doomed to death. 25 gylede] In view of the lateness of this text, *gylede* may be a unique analogical preterite of *giellan*, which is regularly strong. But both Bos.-Tol., p. 494, and Cook take it as preterite of a weak verb *gylian*; cf. the glosses of Latin *garruli*, *garrula* in MS. 154 of St. John's College, Oxford (A. S. Napier, Old English Glosses [Oxford, 1900], p. 225), both of which are apparently to be restored as *gyliende*. 32 agotene] The exact meaning of this word is not at all clear, and it is easy to share the uncertainty expressed by Cosijn, Beitr. XIX, 444. The verb *āgēotan* regularly means "to pour out, to shed," usually with reference to blood, as in Genesis 984, Andreas 1449, Guthlac 522, etc. A meaning which is more helpful in the interpretation of the present passage is to be found in *ageat gylp wera* ("he destroyed the pride of men"?), Exodus 515, and in the passage *þonne bið se(o) glen(c)g agoten and se þrym tobrocen*, which occurs twice in the Wulfstan homilies (ed. A. S. Napier, 148, 22f.; 263, 7 f.). But there is apparently no close parallel to the passive construction with the genitive which we have here. G. Shipley, The Genitive Case in Anglo-Saxon Poetry (Baltimore, 1903), p. 21, translates *agotene* as "deprived (of)." Sweet glosses *āgēotan* as "drain, exhaust (of)", which is closer to the usual meaning, and similarly Cook defines it as "drain, deprive." It is likely that "to drain" is the meaning which was in the poet's mind and that *agotene goda gehwylces* means "drained of every good thing." aldor] The scribe originally wrote *baldor* but later erased the *b*. Sweet, Körner, and Cook, however, accept the uncorrected reading *baldor*. 33 fylgan] Cook emends to *fyllan*, "to fill up, serve with wine," following a suggestion by Körner, note.   But as Cosijn points out, Beitr. XIX, 444, *fylgan*, like *folgian*, may mean "to serve"; see also Grein-Köhler, p. 234, where *fylgan* (*fletsittendum*) is translated, "sie beim Gastmahl bedienen."   **39** bearhtme] Sweet and Cook relate this word to *bearhtm*, "twinkling (of the eye)," and translate, "instantly."   But it is more likely that *bearhtme* here is instr. sing. of *bearhtm, breahtm*, "noise, tumult," as in Exodus 65, Andreas 1202, 1271, etc.   Körner in the translation accompanying his text rendered *bearhtme* as "augenblicklich," but in his note, written later, "unter lautem Klang."   **45** nihtes inne] These words may be taken as two independent adverbs, "inside, by night," but it is better to connect *inne* with *þær*, l. 44a, as Grein, Spr. II, 143, does.   A similar separation of *her* and *inne* is to be found in Genesis 2466, *Her syndon inne unwemme twa dohtor mine.*   **47b**] Sweet and later edd., except Kluge (1, 2 ed.) and Wülker, omit *ond.*

51–100

54 on reste] See l. 57, note.   **55** stercedferhðe] The alliteration of *st-* with *sn-* is unusual.   Ettmüller, Sc., emended to *snelferhðe.*   Grein, note, suggested *swercedferhðe*, "die sinn-umnebelten, betrunkenen."   Rieger emended to *swercendferhðe*, and Sweet to *sweorcendferhðe*, as in l. 269.   This last emendation is approved by Schmitz, Anglia XXXIII, 40f.   But *sweorcendferhðe*, which in l. 269 seems to mean "gloomy, downcast" (cf. also *þæt sweorcende mod*, Meters 3, 2, as well as similar uses of *sweorcan* in Guthlac 1052 and Deor 29), is less appropriate here.   The MS. form *stercedferhðe* also appears in l. 227, where, however, it alliterates regularly with *st-*.   Cf. also Andreas 1233, Elene 38.   **57** gebroht on his burgetelde] This construction, with perfective *gebringan* construed as a verb of rest and therefore followed by *on, in* and the dative, is discussed by H. M. Belden, Eng. Stud. XXXII (1903), 366ff.   Other examples are *gebrohte . . . on ðam fætelse*, ll. 125ff.; *gebrohte . . . on þære mægðe*, Andreas 273ff.; *in þam fæstenne gebroht hafað*, Whale 71f., etc.   In Judith 54 and Beowulf 3009f., the case of the noun is ambiguous but is probably dative.   **60** him þæs ðinges gestyrde] For other examples of this construction, with genitive of the thing and dative of the person, see Bos.-Tol., Supp., pp. 417f., s.v. *gestiran* II.1.d.   **62**] This line is too short, and a number of emendations have been proposed.   Grein and Körner supply *cyning* after *galferhð*.   Garnett, tr., p. 47, note, proposed to supply *guðfreca* after *galferhð*; Foster, pp. 46f., would read *galferhð and grædig* as l. 62a.   Koeppel, Archiv XC, 140f., suggested supplying *gongan* after *galferhð*, and Cook (1904) and Sweet (9–10 ed.) supply *gangan*.   All these readings give excellent sense.   But Schmitz, Anglia XXXIII, 40f., is probably right in taking *galferhð gumena ðreate* as the first half of an expanded (three-stress) line.   The second half of the line, if it ever existed, has been omitted by a scribe.   **65** swylcne . . . worhte] "Such [an end] as he has striven after."   For this use of *æfter*, cf. *þæt he . . . ær æfter spyrede*, Meters 27, 15f.; *ða he . . . luteð æfter*, Solomon and Saturn 404.   According to Sweet, note, *swylcne* stands for the two correlatives *swylcne swylcum*, but it is unnecessary to bring a dative into the picture here, since in the two passages just quoted *æfter* governs the accusative. 73 nehstan siðe] See Beow. 1203, note. **86–87**] The MS. has *ys* twice, in l. 86*b* and in l. 87*a*. Thorpe, Analecta (2 ed.), and all later edd. except Grein, Kluge, and Wülker omit the *ys* in l. 87*a*, and this is stylistically the best emendation. Grein, Kluge (1 ed.), and Wülker follow the MS.; Kluge (2–4 ed.) omits the *ys* in l. 86*b*. **90a**] The alliteration here is unusual, since the first half of an expanded (three-stress) line regularly has double alliteration. Vetter, Zum Muspilli, p. 40, would transpose the words *geheawan* and *mote*, putting *geheawan* at the end of l. 89*b* and *mote* at the beginning of l. 90*a*. So also Schmitz, Anglia XXXIII, 42. **93 torne on mode**] For this adverbial use of the instr. sing. with forms of *wesan*, cf. *rume on mode*, l. 97, *weorce on mode*, Beow. 1418, Genesis 2028, 2792, and the other examples given by Bos.-Tol., p. 1191, s.v. *weorc* VII. Here (if we may judge by the syntax of *weorce* in the passages cited above) *torne* is a noun, modified by *hate* in the next line. **99 wið hyre weard**] "Toward her." No other example is recorded of this word order with *wið*. The separation of *to* and *weard* (as in *to Lundene weard*, "toward London") is, however, not uncommon; cf. the examples cited by Bos.-Tol., p. 1010, s.v. *tō-weard* II.3.

101–150

102–103 eaðost . . . wel] It is impossible to be certain whether or not these adverbs are parallel. Rieger and Sweet (1–8 ed.) take them as parallel and put a comma after *mihte*. Other edd. punctuate as in the text. The translation given by Bos.-Tol., p. 464, though it errs in taking *swa*, l. 102*a*, as the beginning of a new sentence, apparently does justice to the poet's intention with regard to the adverbs: "so she most easily might have complete power over the wretch." **111 leap**] This is the only occurrence of the noun *lēap* in the poetry. Elsewhere the word regularly refers to one of several kinds of wicker baskets (glossing the Latin *corbis, calathus, nassa*, etc.), but here the context requires us to translate as "trunk (of the body)"—probably, as Rieger suggests, a metaphorical extension of the literal meaning. **125–127 gebrohte . . . on ðam fætelse**] "Put . . . into the bag" (Klaeber, Anglia LIII, 230). See l. 57, note. **127 þe**] To be taken with *on*, l. 129, the two words together being the equivalent of *on ðam*, "on which." **foregenga**] For the form in *-a* with feminine meaning, see *healsgebedda*, Beow. 63, and note. The meaning of *foregenga* in this passage seems to be "attendant, maidservant." Elsewhere it regularly means "predecessor"; in Guthlac 533, however, it seems to mean "advance guard" (so Gollancz, The Exeter Book, Part I, p. 137). **134 hie**] Thorpe, Analecta, and all later edd. except Kluge (1 ed.) omit the second *hie*. **139 feðelaste**] Cook construes as acc. plur., but the word is more probably dat. (instr.) sing.; cf. *feþelastum*, Beowulf 1632. **144 Iudith**] So Ettmüller, Sc. (who, however, read *Judið*), and all later edd. except Rieger and Kluge (1 ed.). In writing *iudithe* the scribe may have been confused by the preceding dative, in spite of the difference in gender. **146**] Grein and Körner begin a new sentence with l. 146*a* rather than with l. 146*b*. **149**] To regularize the alliteration, Rieger, Sweet, and Cook transpose the two half-lines, reading *hyre togeanes gan of* ðære ginnan byrig. But double alliteration in the second half-line is also found in l. 279.

151–200

153 þoncwyrðe] "Deserving of thanks," rather than "memorable," as Sweet and Cook gloss it. Cf. the quotations in Bos.-Tol., p. 1037, s.v. þanc-weorþ. **158** þara læðða] Unless these words are dependent on tir (which is at least doubtful), it is difficult to construe them. Grein, note, proposed to supply on last before þara. Rieger indicated a gap in the text after læ ð ða and suggested that to bote or a similar phrase had been lost. Zupitza-Schipper, Übungsbuch, supply to leane after læ ð ða. But Imelmann, Anglia Beibl. XIX, 7, defends the MS. reading, translating, "Euch ist ruhm verliehen für die leiden, die ihr lange ertragen." He points out that mærra madma, l. 329, also lacks a governing noun. Monroe, MLN. XXXI, 375, compares both þara læ ð ða and mærra madma with landes ne locenra beaga, Andreas 303, which he describes as dependent on an implied noun. **165** þeodnes] So Thorpe, Analecta, and all later edd. except Kluge (1 ed.). **179** starian] So all edd. except Kluge (1 ed.). **182** ond þæt swyðor gyt] The Junius transcript omits þæt, and so the early edd., following Thwaites. But Sweet, Körner, and all later edd. read ond þæt swyðor gyt with the MS., providing the necessary object for the transitive ycan. **189** fysan] For fysen, subjunctive. **189–191** Syððan . . . leoman] The verb sende is probably present subjunctive, used in the sense of a future perfect. These lines, which mean "As soon as God shall have sent the bright light (i.e., the sun) from the east," translate the Latin cum exierit sol, Judith xiv.2. **194** fyllan] Ettmüller, Sc., suggested emending to fyllað, parallel to berað, l. 191.

201–250

201 sigeþufas] So Ettmüller, Sc., and all later edd., except Rieger, Kluge (1 ed.), and Wülker, to provide alliteration. Holthausen, Literaturblatt X, 448, suggested emending l. 201b to segnas bæron. **207** Wistan] Sweet emends to wiston, Cook to wistan. The other edd. retain the MS. westan, but Körner, note, explains westan as a variant form of wiston. begen] That is, both the wolf and the raven. **209** ac] There is no antithesis here. Körner, note, compares the similar use of ac, introducing a continuation of the narrative, in Genesis 847. **211** salowigpada] An alliteration in h- would be more regular, and Kluge (2–4 ed.) suggested haswigpada. **223** stedehearde] The adjective stedeheard is not elsewhere recorded, and the noun stede, "place," gives no sense in this connection. Jiriczek, Eng. Stud. LXIV, 212ff., would connect stede- with Old Icelandic steði, "anvil," and would translate strælas stedehearde as "die auf dem Amboss gehärteten Pfeile (Pfeilspitzen)." It is hardly possible that a native Anglo-Saxon form stede, cognate with steði, could have existed (the Anglo-Saxon form in composition would be *stedd-). Jiriczek suggests, however, that steði was borrowed into English during the Anglo-Saxon period as steðe and that the MS. stede- resulted from it through either graphic or phonetic substitution. It should be noted that the Junius transcript is our only authority for the form *stedehearde*.   228 wrehton]   Grein suggested emending to *ehton*, as in l. 237.   But the form *wrehton* also occurs in l. 243, where the meaning "aroused" is certain.   Although "aroused" seems less likely here, this is probably the intended meaning; it should be noted that the adjective *medowerig* ("dead-drunk"?), which is used to describe the *ealdgeniðlan* in the present passage, is also applied to the Assyrians who are awakened in ll. 243ff.   The verb *wreccan*, "to arouse," is sufficiently attested in other texts; see Bos.-Tol., p. 1273, s.v. *wreccan* III.   234 ricne]   So Grein and all later edd. except Kluge (1 ed.).   243 wrehton]   See l. 228, note.   Leo suggested *weahton* here, and Grein emended to *wehton*.   245 morgencollan]   The second element, -*colla*, is not elsewhere found, but it undoubtedly serves here as a variation of both *færspel* and *atolne ecgplegan*.   A. Pogatscher, Anglia XXXI (1908), 258, connects it with *cwelan, cwalu*, and the **cyllan* which was probably the original of Modern English *kill*.   The meaning of *morgencollan* would then be "morning slaughter."   249 werigferhðe]   The MS. reads *weras ferhðe*, but *ferhðe* as an adjective is meaningless.   Ettmüller, Sc., emended to *weras wideferhðe* and, for the sake of the alliteration, suggested *wornum* instead of the MS. *hwearfum* in l. 249b.   Sweet emends to *weras hreowigferhðe*, "the men sad at heart," following Rieger's suggestion.   Körner and Cook read *weras werigferhðe*. But the MS. *weras* can be merely a scribal error for *werig*, and this seems the most probable explanation of it.   Grein emends to *werigferhðe*, without *weras*, as in the text.   It is unnecessary to emend l. 249b, since the alliteration of the noun *hwearf* (or a by-form *wearf*) in *w*- is not unparalleled; see E. Sievers, Altgermanische Metrik (Halle, 1893), p. 37, note.   Cf. also l. 313, where *hræw* apparently alliterates in *r*-.   250 Hogedon aninga]   The alliteration of this line is probably vocalic, since the name *Holofernus* elsewhere in the poem alliterates with a vowel.   See l. 7, note.   Luick, Beitr. XI, 476f., therefore takes l. 250b as a C-type half-line, with *Hogedon* unstressed, and compares Andreas 1141a, 1392a.   It is also possible, but less likely, that the alliteration is irregular here, being placed on the second rather than on the first stress of a second half-line.

251–300

251 hilde]   So Leo, Grein, Rieger, Sweet, Körner, and Cook, for the MS. *hyldo*. The meaning of the passage is that the warriors wished to announce the battle to their lord before the violence of the attack should fall upon him.   The scribe may well have been thinking of *hyldo bodian* in such a sense as "to announce their loyalty, to pay their respects"; cf. *hyldo gebeodan*, Psalm 94, 1, 3.   Malone, Anglia LIV, 97f., would, however, explain the MS. *hyldo* as the result of late phonetic confusion in unstressed syllables.   259–260 hu . . . geworden]   "How the warrior had decided [to act] toward the holy maid."   For this impersonal construction with *geweorðan*, see Beowulf 1598, note.   In the present passage *geweorðan* is used absolutely, with no genitive of the thing, as also in *he deð swa swa hine sylfne gewyrð*, Ælfric's Preface to Genesis (ed. S. J. Crawford, The Old English Version of the Heptateuch, 80, 108f.).   263 hæfte]   Since

the usual meanings of *hæft*, "captive," "bond, fetter," "captivity," and "handle (of a knife or sword)," are not particularly appropriate here, Grein, Spr. II, 20, suggested *hæste*, "fiercely, violently," and so Sweet (4–10 ed.) and Cook. Kern, Taalkundige Bijdragen I, 210ff., would assume an Anglo-Saxon noun *hæft*, related to Old Icelandic *heipt*, "feud, battle." With Kern's interpretation, *hæfte* is parallel to *fagum swyrdum*.   **266** dægeweorce] A more regular form would be *dægweorce*, and Cook (1904) so emends.   **268** gebylde] If *gebylde* here reflects the usual meaning of *bieldan*, *byldan*, "to encourage," it seems to contradict the word *sweorcendferhðe*, "gloomy of mind," in the next line.   Cook's translation (1888), "mightily roused," was apparently an attempt to reconcile this contradiction. Cosijn, Beitr. XIX, 444, suggested emending to *geblygde*, citing *ungeblyged*, "undismayed," Guthlac 941.   **270** cohhetan] This verb (of which *cohhettan* would be a more regular form) is not elsewhere recorded, and there is no evidence for its meaning beyond the fact that the Modern English verb *cough* must derive from an Anglo-Saxon *cohhian*, of which *cohhettan* would be a derivative. Bos.-Tol., p. 164, glosses *cohhetan* as "to bluster," Cook as "lament (?), wail (?)," Sweet as "cough (?)."   **272a**] "Gnashing their teeth in despair" (Bos.-Tol., p. 1003), though a rather free rendering, seems to give the intended meaning.   **272b**] A similar construction is found in *feores bið æt ende anra gehwylcum*, Judgment Day I, 2f., and in *weorþeð foldræste eardes æt ende*, Christ 1028f. (where *foldræste* and *eardes* are parallel genitives). Sweet and Cook (1904) explain the present passage as the result of a confusion of two constructions, *ða wæs hira tires ende* and *ða wæs hira tir æt ende*. But Körner, note, would take it as an impersonal construction with *hit* omitted, as in ll. 286f.   **273b–274a**] The edd. all put *aweccan* at the beginning of l. 274a, and all except Rieger and Sweet read *Hogedon þa eorlas* in l. 273b. Rieger and Sweet, to regularize the alliteration, transpose to read *þa eorlas hogedon*. Holthausen, Anglia Beibl. XIX, 249, would supply *sona* after *eorlas*, without transposition. But Kaluza, Eng. Stud. XXI, 383f., Trautmann (in Schmitz, Anglia XXXIII, 42f.), and Pope, p. 100, put *aweccan* at the end of l. 273b, and this is undoubtedly the proper solution of the difficulty. Line 273a, like the preceding line, is of the expanded (three-stress) type, and we would expect more than *Hogedon þa eorlas* in the second half-line; l. 274b, like the following lines, is of the normal two-stress pattern, into which *aweccan hyra winedryhten* does not fit.   **274** winedryhten] So the MS., not *wina-*, as reported by Sievers, ZfdA. XV, 461, and Cook (1904).   **275** arod] For other examples of *arod*, "strenuous, bold," not elsewhere recorded in the poetry, see Bos.-Tol., Supp., p. 47.   **279**] Ettmüller, Sc., and Grein suggested transposing the two half-lines, for the sake of the alliteration. See l. 149, note.   **280** lifes belidenne] Elsewhere we find the dat. (instr.) sing. with *beliden*, in Elene 877, Guthlac 1338. But the gen. sing. here may be compared with the occasional use of the genitive with *beleosan* (Guthlac 1170, 1327), *benæman* (Christ and Satan 345f.), *beneotan* (Guthlac 900), and other verbs of separation compounded with *be-* which are more frequently construed with the dative.   **287–288a**] The arrangement of the words *mid niðum . . . forweorðan* has caused considerable trouble to the edd. Ettmüller, Sc., supplied *þa git* after *tide* at the end of l.

286*b*, reading *is mid niðum* for l. 287*a*, and supplied *life* after *we*. Grein, Körner, and Cook, putting *ys* at the end of l. 286*b*, supply *nu* at the beginning of l. 287*a* and follow Ettmüller in adding *life* after *we*. Like Ettmüller, these edd. put *somod* in the same half-line with *losian* and thus spread *mid niðum* . . . *forweorðan* over two and a half lines: *þæt þære tide ys* ‖ *nu mid niðum* | *neah geðrungen,* ‖ *þe we life sculon* | *losian somod,* ‖ *æt,* etc. Rieger supplies *life* with Ettmüller, but does no more than indicate a loss at the beginning of l. 287*a*; he suggests, however, the reading *mid niða bearnum.* Sweet (1–8 ed.) supplies *nu*, with Grein, but adds nothing after *we*, thus failing to provide alliteration; Sweet (9–10 ed.) supplies *life.* Foster, pp. 47f., accepts the addition of *life* after *we* but reads *mid nidgedal neah geðrungen* as his l. 287, citing Guthlac 934. On p. 103, Foster notes a conjecture by Dr. H. Frank Heath that l. 287 originally read *mid niþe niwum neah geðrungen.* But Kluge arranges *mid niðum* . . . *forweorðan* as one and a half expanded (three-stress) lines, as in the text, and supplies *nu* after *sculon.* It should be noted that the following lines are also expanded lines. This arrangement by Kluge represented a notable advance over the handling of the text by earlier edd., but the adverb *nu* which he supplied is less probable than *nyde*, "by necessity," proposed by Klaeber, JEGPh. XII, 258. Klaeber calls attention to the frequent use of *nȳde* (*niede*) with the verb *sculan*, as in Genesis 697, 1977, Christ 1405, etc. In l. 287*a*, Grein, Spr. II, 292, glossed *niðum* doubtfully as the equivalent of *niððum*, and this interpretation, "among men," is favored by Klaeber. From this point to the end of the poem, the line numbers in the present edition are less by one than the line numbers in previous editions.   **297 laðra lindwerod]** The Junius transcript reports the MS. reading as *laðra lind*, but there was certainly one letter, perhaps more, after *-d*, at the end of a line in the MS. Sievers, ZfdA. XV, 462, gives *lindeg-* as the MS. reading, Cook (1904) *linde* followed by one illegible letter. Most edd. read *laðra lind*, following Thwaites, but this is meaningless and is too short for a half-line. Ettmüller, Sc., emended to *laðra lindwigendra*, Grein and Cook to *laðra lindwiggendra.* This emendation, however, results in an expanded (three-stress) line, for which there is no occasion here. Wülker and Kluge (3, 4 ed.) read *laðra linde.* The noun *lind*, however, means merely "shield," and there is no parallel for the extended meaning "shield-bearer" which would be appropriate here. A more satisfactory emendation is *laðra lindwerod*, which has been adopted in the text; cf. Elene 142.

301–349

306 þegnas on ða tid] Luick, Beitr. XI, 486, takes this as an E-type half-line without a secondary stress and suggests emending *tid* to *tide.* But the half-line is more probably A-type, with a stress on *ða.* The demonstrative also bears stress and alliteration in *on þæm dæge*, Beow. 197, 790, 806.   **311 Cirdon cynerofe]** That is, the Jews, after pursuing the Assyrians, returned in order to plunder the corpses.   **312 wælscel]** This compound is not elsewhere recorded, but it is evidently a variation of *reocende hræw*, "reeking corpses." The second element *-scel* is perhaps related to *scolu*, "band, troop"; cf. the form *sceale* (MS. *sceal*) in Christ and Satan 267. But it is more probably to be connected with *scelle*, which glosses the Latin *concisium* in MS. Harley 3376 (Wright-Wülker, Anglo-Saxon and Old English Vocabularies I, 214, 7), and with Old Icelandic *skellr*, "smiting, beating." See Holthausen, AEW., p. 277, s.v. *sciell* 3. Cosijn, Tijdschrift voor Nederlandsche Taal- en Letterkunde I, 149, would emend *wælscel* to *wælstel* (= *wælsteall*), a synonym of *wælstow*. But the meaning of the MS. *wælscel* is not the only problem raised by this passage, since if *wælscel* and *reocende hræw* are objects of the compound preposition *on innan*, as they seem to be, they should be in the dative case. It is possible that a more extensive corruption underlies the MS. reading of l. 312*b*. The emendation *wæl feol* for the MS. *wælscel*, proposed by Binz, Eng. Stud. XXXVI, 130, has little to commend it.   **314** laðestan] For the weak dat. plur. ending in *-an*, see Sievers-Brunner, § 304, note 3.   **317** bradswyrd] All edd. print as two words, but in view of the later form *broadsword*, this word is probably a compound, here and in Maldon 15.   **320** ealdhettende] Undoubtedly acc. plur., as it is construed by Cook and by Kock, Anglia XLIV, 110, rather than nom. plur., as Grein-Köhler, p. 144, takes it. Kock translates, "the keepers of the land had in the field with glory overcome the enemies, and killed with swords their old antagonists."   **323** cwicera] The letters *-wicera* are reported by Sievers, ZfdA. XV, 462; none of them is quite clear in the MS. at the present time.   **325** wlanc, wundenlocc] Nom. sing. feminine, modifying *cneoris*. Rieger, note, proposed to emend to *wlanc wigena heap*, suggesting that *wundenlocc*, which elsewhere (ll. 77, 103) is applied to Judith, is an error by a scribe who interpreted the MS. *mægða*, l. 324, as gen. plur. of *mægð*, "maiden," rather than of *mægð*, "tribe, nation."   **329** mærra madma] Rieger suggested supplying *fela* or *worn* after *madma*. But for a possible independent use of the genitive here, see l. 158, note.   **332** on] So Rieger and all later edd., except Kluge. Ettmüller, Sc., had previously emended the MS. 7 to *æt*.   **344ff.**] The six lines missing from the MS. at the end of the poem (from *in swegles* to the end) are here supplied from the Junius transcript rather than from the copy of these lines in an early modern hand at the foot of fol. 209*b*.   **345a**] Grein and Rieger supply *up* before *to*; Sweet and all later edd. supply *a*, as in l. 7*a*, and so also Foster, p. 48. The emendation is tempting, since the lines preceding and following are expanded (three-stress) lines, but it is not necessary for the sense. **347** þe] Ettmüller, Sc., emends to *he*, putting an exclamation point after l. 347*a*.   **349**] Holthausen, Eng. Stud. XXXVII, 202, and Trautmann (in Schmitz, Anglia XXXIII, 44f.) suggest emending *miltse* to *miht*, partly for metrical reasons. Trautmann would also emend to *swegldreamas* in l. 349*a*. These proposed emendations are based on the assumption that l. 349 is an isolated normal line at the end of the poem. Pope, p. 100, takes it as an expanded (three-stress) line like the preceding ones and suggests the emendation *sæs ond swegles dreamas* for l. 349*a*.